MATHEMATICS AND PHYSICS
FOR PROGRAMMERS

MATHEMATICS AND PHYSICS FOR PROGRAMMERS

DANNY KODICEK

CHARLES RIVER MEDIA, INC.
Hingham, Massachusetts

Editor: David Pallai
Cover Design: Tyler Creative

CHARLES RIVER MEDIA, INC.
10 Downer Avenue
Hingham, Massachusetts 02043
781-740-0400
781-740-8816 (FAX)
info@charlesriver.com
www.charlesriver.com

This book is printed on acid-free paper.

Danny Kodicek. *Mathematics and Physics for Programmers.*
ISBN: 1-58450-330-0

Library of Congress Cataloging-in-Publication Data
Kodicek, Danny.
 Mathematics and physics for programmers / Danny Kodicek.
    p. cm.
 Includes index.
 ISBN 1-58450-330-0 (pbk. with cd-rom : alk. paper)
 1. Computer science—Mathematics. 2. Physics. I. Title.
 QA76.9.M35K59 2005
 510'.24'0051—dc22
                              2005004018

Printed in the United States of America
06 7 6 5 4 3 2

For Tony Revell
and David Hepburne-Scott

Two great teachers sadly missed

Contents

Acknowledgments

I stepped blithely into writing this book without the remotest idea how much work it was going to be. I am extremely grateful to my publisher Dave Pallai, and his team including Jennifer Blaney, Ania Wieckowski, Bryan Davidson, and Meg Dunkerley at Charles River Media, for their patience and understanding. Many thanks also to those who gave their valuable comments and helped to shape the book.

I am indebted to Robert Tweed who provided the translations into C++ and Java found on the Web site.

I am hugely grateful to all those many people who have written explanations and tutorials on various subjects and placed them for free on the Internet. The enthusiasm that experts show for their subject and their desire to help others is confirmation of my opinion that people are, on the whole, good and decent. I have had much encouragement and support from the community of Director users that inhabit various mailing lists, particularly the DirGames-L list. The expertise of people like Jim Andrews, Jonas Beckeman, Thomas Higgins, Martin Kloss, Lucas Meijer, Allen Partridge, Ben Pitt (RobotDuck), Simeon Rice (NoiseCrime), Barry Swan, and Alex (Zav) Zavatone, to name but a few not yet mentioned, has been invaluable. Several other people helped with specific questions, and I'd particularly like to thank Walter Pullen for inspiring me to go a little overboard about mazes.

I have been fortunate enough to have many wonderful teachers over the years, both in mathematics and other areas, who gave me a joy in the subject that lasts to this day. Among many others, including Michael Davies, John Field, Jim Cogan, and Jonathan Katz, there are two, both of whom are sadly no longer with us, to whom this book is dedicated:

Tony Revell was my first maths teacher (I use the British spelling here as I feel he would have preferred!) at Dulwich College Preparatory School, a man I feared above all others at age seven, but whom I grew to love. He recognized my joy in games and puzzles, and showed me how this was really a joy in the aesthetic side of mathematics: a yearning to discover the deeper patterns in the world.

David Hepburne-Scott taught me physics at Westminster School, and could make a class laugh like no other teacher I've known. He cared deeply about the development of everyone in his class, quite aside from the subject, and loved nothing better than to make a bizarre comparison between thermodynamics and the making of a crème brulée.

Finally, and of course, I would like to thank my family: my children Anna and Matthew for letting me snooze on the sofa in the morning, my wife Catherine for putting up with this huge endeavor for so long and her unfailing support, and my mother and father for their encouragement and advice. None of them have a mathematical bone in their body (well, time will tell with the children) so it shows amazing strength of character to deal with comments like "I can't get this quartic to factorize correctly" without flinching.

Introduction

WHO IS THIS BOOK FOR?

I was at school when the home computer had just appeared. The tool of choice in our school was the BBC Microcomputer, which boasted 64 K of memory, an optional disk drive, and its own language, BBC BASIC. As with most schools at the time, computing was taught by a math teacher, who was learning it at the same time that we were.

In the past twenty years, things have changed a great deal. Most people use a computer in their daily lives, and they rarely need to do any programming of their own. Computer studies in school are more likely to look at spreadsheets and word-processing software than at programming, and teachers are less likely to be shoe-horned in from the math department.

In the meantime, programming itself has become less like a math class. Software like Director, Flash, WildTangent, and 3D GameStudio allow people to come a long way in creating animation, interactivity, and even games while scarcely writing a line of code.

Between these two developments, increasingly people are coming into programming from backgrounds other than math. Artists and musicians; authors and screenwriters; businesspeople and teachers all find themselves drifting into the "new media" as a useful additional tool to their trade.

As a programmer frequenting various mailing lists, it has become apparent how many people who are working in the industry are lacking in the mathematical background that they need to advance from basic interactivity into complex games, and particularly 3D. Often they suffer from quite serious math phobia, usually brought on by a lack of understanding of basic principles such as numbers or algebra. And even those who do understand the subject seem to reach a "boggle point" on some topics. So this book tries to address these problems directly by going right back to the fundamentals.

WHAT IS IT ABOUT?

The principal areas of math that you will encounter in programming, particularly for games, have to do with geometry and physics: geometry because you want to move things around on the screen, and physics because you want to do so realistically. So the majority of this book is taken up with these two areas. Every effort has been made to make sure that the topics are cumulative—everything you encounter in a later chapter should have been covered in an earlier one. Almost no knowledge on your part is assumed.

The topics covered in the book fall into four broad categories:

Essential topics: those that you are likely to encounter every day. They are the foundational concepts underlying the whole of mathematics. Most of these are covered in Part I of the book dealing with the basic principles of Numbers, Algebra, and Geometry, as well as the first chapters of Parts II, III, and IV, covering the basics of physics and of 3D mathematics. Essential topics are covered in depth, going right back to basic principles, deriving mathematical results and illustrating them with code samples.

Advanced topics: more complex areas of mathematics and physics which, while you are less likely to meet them on a day-to-day basis, are still necessary for a complete understanding of the subject, or in order to understand and solve other problems that you may encounter. These include calculus (Chapter 6), complex physics concepts (Part III), and detailed 3D math, especially the workings of 3D renderers (Part IV). Advanced topics are covered in a more discursive fashion, with explanations of the principles and terminology, a few examples, and some derivations of important results.

Applied topics: where we look at how these essential concepts can be applied to a more complex situation. These include most of Part II, as well as one or two chapters in Parts III and IV. In these chapters we tend to look at a few particular examples of the topic, solving them in depth, with detailed code samples and derivations of mathematical results, but we do not attempt to cover the whole topic. However, the examples given should get you well along the way to being able to tackle similar problems yourself. We try to cover a range of different methods for achieving the same goals.

Extension topics: more advanced or obscure areas of the subject, particularly those that can be used to illustrate some broader principles. These mostly crop up in Part V, although some of Parts III and IV fit into this category too. The aim is to make you comfortable with the essential concepts and terminology of the topic, without worrying too much about the fine detail.

A full explanation of any one of these topics would require another book, but after reading through the chapters, you should at least know what it is you are trying to achieve and where to look for the solution. These chapters have fewer code examples and equations, with more of an emphasis on verbal explanations and images.

Naturally, these categories overlap to some extent, and every chapter has an element of all of them, but this explanation should make the overall philosophy of the book clearer. The principal aim of the whole book is to leave you understanding almost all of the mathematical principles and concepts involved in programming— not to know everything there is to know on any one subject, but to understand them well enough that you *know what to look for* whenever you encounter some new problem. So it is a book of mathematical techniques (Essential topics), physical principles (Advanced topics), examples of the math in action (Applied topics), and general concepts and terminology (Extension topics).

Chapters differ in the balance of text, code, equations, and illustrations.

Text: used by preference throughout. Most people are much more comfortable with a text-based explanation of a concept than wading through pages of equations or code.

Illustrations: used whenever possible and useful to explain a point, particularly in order to clarify notation used in examples. Mostly these are simple diagrams, although there are also some screenshots illustrating the output of various algorithms.

Code samples: used for various reasons. In Essential topics, examples are given of many equations and formulas translated directly into code. This is generally a simple and obvious operation, and we do less of it as the book progresses. In Applied topics, there are quite extensive and detailed code samples, although every attempt is made to keep them to less than a page. These illustrate the process of actually using a mathematical principle in a real-life context. In Advanced and Extension topics, code samples are used sparingly, only when they provide a clearer explanation of a concept than a long and confusing text description, or in order to summarize a long explanation.

Equations (and other algebra):   used when necessary but avoided when possible. As with code samples, they appear more for the Essential topics, after which they are used primarily when their meaning is immediately obvious. We generally avoid deriving results fully, leaving many of the details as an exercise, but Part I will give you a thorough understanding of the tools with which you can do it.

Each chapter ends with one or more programming exercises for you to try yourself, most of which are answered in examples on the CD-ROM, or on the book's Web site. Appendix E gives some additional hints toward solving these. In the other Appendices, you will find a thorough glossary of all the mathematical terminology, lists of useful online and printed resources, especially those that will allow you to build on the knowledge gained in this book, and some notes on programming techniques and the language Lingo used in the examples on the CD-ROM.

ON THE CD

HOW SHOULD I USE IT?

This book is presented in a cumulative sequence. Most chapters make reference to topics covered earlier. So it is definitely worth at least quickly skimming over the whole book. Even if you are fairly confident with basic mathematics and physics, there are likely to be some parts of the early sections that you are unsure about, and while some chapters are quite specific, it's useful to know they are there.

Try the exercises. Mathematics is a practical subject, and unless you have worked through a problem, you are unlikely to really understand it. And don't stop with the task suggested—think about how you might generalize it or incorporate it into a project. Can you think of a game that uses the principles you have learned? Can you think how to improve an earlier game by incorporating these new elements? As a programmer, you are in a much better position to really get to grips with the principles behind what you are learning than you were at school.

Finally, don't get scared. People are unreasonably afraid of some of these subjects, while being perfectly able to tackle far more complex tasks like arguing about international politics down at the pub. If you don't understand something, first read it again. If it still doesn't make sense then think about why—is there some terminology you don't understand? See if the glossary refreshes your memory, or find an earlier chapter where it is explained. Try a practical example, draw a little diagram, or see if you can rephrase it. If all else fails, skim over it and see if a later explanation throws some light on it. But don't do that too often—that is how problems start.

ABOUT PSEUDOCODE

The aim of this book is to introduce you to essential mathematics, not to teach good programming style. We don't need to get bogged down in specifics of languages, implementation, or user interfaces, or except very briefly, in graphics or sound. So you will find few references to variables, objects, arrays, or sprites. Instead, we will look at particular *functions* and *algorithms*, which perform particular tasks. Because they are entirely mathematical, they should be easy to implement in whatever language you are using, and can be treated as "black boxes" that just do what you want. That does not mean to say that the same mathematics could not be implemented better or faster by integrating it with the rest of your code, or by making use of shortcuts in the language you use. In fact, in the vast majority of cases this is very possible.

In order to avoid worrying about programming style, all code examples in this book are presented as *pseudocode*. This is a generic term that means different things to different people, but in this book it means a fairly detailed version of the code, written in a human-readable language. The pseudocode of this book is essentially a programming language written for a human interpreter rather than a computer one.

Occasionally some "book work" parts of the code are left out in order to concentrate on the important points. These bookwork sections are indicated by a double bar: ||. There are also frequent comments, preceded by a double slash: //.

Most of the code examples on the accompanying CD-ROM are written in Lingo, the programming language used in Macromedia Director. This was chosen because it is a fairly flexible, high-level, uncompiled language, which uses untyped variables and can be used in both an object-oriented and a procedural style. Until a few years ago, Lingo read almost like pseudocode itself—you might say "`set the ink of sprite 1 to 8`"—but these days it uses dot syntax like most other languages. However, to retain backward compatibility the old syntax has been retained (known as "verbose" syntax), and for the functions that tie in with the code examples in the book we have used verbose syntax to increase readability. This also means that the book's pseudocode has a slight Lingo flavor.

Whenever it is possible, we avoid specifics about variables, arrays, and so on, but they are sometimes necessary. The book uses the Lingo convention of saying the first element of an array (list) A is A[1], rather than A[0] as most other languages have it, so as to tie in better with the CD-ROM. Generally, you shouldn't have any trouble following the code, but the examples on the CD-ROM, together with Appendix B, should help. There are also a few examples in C++ and Java on the book's Web site.

ON THE CD

If you don't own Director, you can get a free trial version from Macromedia (see Appendix D), or you can view the most important parts of the code in the text files. Even for non-Director users, Lingo is an easy language to follow, with a few oddities that are covered in Appendix B.

ERRORS, OMISSIONS, AND COMMENTS

In a book of this length and scope, it's inevitable that some errors will have missed the eagle eyes of the author, reviewers, and proofreaders. Most of these will hopefully be minor, but it's possible that some will be more dramatic. In either case, I would be glad to hear about them so that they can be corrected for subsequent editions. Similarly, while of course much has been left out owing to space limitations, there are bound to be some techniques that will have been omitted simply because the author isn't aware of them, and any glaring omissions would be gratefully received. In fact, any comments, positive or negative, are welcome. Please send them personally to the author at dragon@well-spring.co.uk, including "[MPFP]" in the subject line.

Any vital updates or errata, along with additional examples and supporting material, will be posted on the book's Web site at *www.charlesriver.com/titles/ mathphysics.html*.

General Techniques

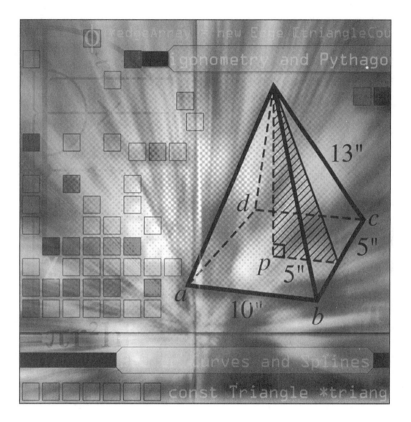

In this first part of the book we will cover the most basic and essential elements of mathematics that you need every day. In all likelihood, much of the material here will already be familiar to you, but we can't deal with the more complex concepts in the later sections without covering this ground first.

1 Numbers

In This Chapter

- Overview
- Writing Numbers
- How Computers Represent Numbers
- Exercises
- Summary
- You Should Now Know

OVERVIEW

Most people would say that numbers are the foundation of mathematics. This is quite a modern view, because for most of the past two thousand years students began with geometry; but numbers are certainly the foundation of computers! A thorough understanding of numbers and how they work is vital to programming.

So we will start our journey by looking at the way numbers are represented on computers, and what you can do with them. We'll be thinking about what a number is, particularly the distinction between the number itself and the way we can write it down or represent it electronically.

ON THE CD
Code samples from this chapter are implemented in *math.cst* in the script *Chapter 1 (numbers, floats and bases)*, apart from `floor` and `ceil` which are in *numerical utilities*. Additional functions related to the exercises can be found in the

3

script *floats*. (If this is not clear, consult Appendix C for details about how to use the CD-ROM.)

WRITING NUMBERS

Our first step is to consider what kinds of numbers you might encounter in the mathematical universe.

Integers, Rationals, and Irrationals

Mathematicians divide the world of numbers into several subsets. The first numbers to be recognized were the *counting numbers* or *natural numbers*, represented by the symbol $\mathbb{N}$. These are the numbers we learn as children—1, 2, 3, 4, ... , as well as the special number 0. Each of these can represent a distinct number of "things." When we add the negative numbers we have the set of *integers* $\mathbb{Z}$. With the integers, we are already getting into difficult territory: what exactly is a negative number?

We can think about negative numbers in terms of a transaction: If you have 5 marbles and Anne has 4, when you give her 2 marbles, we can just as well say she's giving you -2 marbles. Either way, you add 2 marbles to one side and subtract 2 from the other. But it is better to think about negative numbers in terms of an *operation* of "the other way around," because then we can see why two negative numbers multiplied together give a positive number: You give Anne 2 marbles, which is "the other way round" to her giving you 2 marbles (i.e., she gave you -2). If you do this -2 times, it's the other way round from her doing it 2 times, so it's the other way round from -4, giving us $+4$.

If this sounds confusing, that explains why it took centuries for people to accept the idea of negative numbers at all. *Fractions*, the quotients of two integers, came sooner: first the fractions of 1 ($\frac{1}{2}$, $\frac{1}{3}$, etc.)—the *reciprocals* of the natural numbers—then the other *simple fractions* (fractions between 0 and 1, such as $\frac{2}{3}$), then the *vulgar fractions* (fractions greater than 1, such as $\frac{5}{4}$), and finally the complete set of *rational numbers* $\mathbb{Q}$, which includes both positive and negative fractions (as well as the integers, which are a special kind of fraction with denominator 1).

The quotient *of two numbers is what you get when you divide one by another. Similarly, we say the* sum, difference, *and* product *respectively to mean the result of adding, subtracting, and multiplying two numbers. Sometimes,* quotient *means just the integer part of a division, but we'll come to that later. When one integer is divided by another, the result is a fraction, where the first number is called the* numerator *and the second the* denominator.

Beyond the rational numbers, you have the remaining *irrational* numbers: those that cannot be expressed by the quotient of two integers. For a long time it was thought that such numbers didn't exist, but Pythagoras proved, to his discomfort, that at least one number, the square root of 2, was irrational. We now know that there are fundamentally "more" irrational numbers than rational ones, but we won't go into this further here.

The rationals and irrationals together form the set of *real numbers* $\mathbb{R}$. There are other kinds of numbers, especially the *complex numbers*, (numbers that include a multiple of the *imaginary number* i, the square root of -1), but they are beyond the scope of this chapter, although we'll touch on them later when we look at quaternions in Chapter 18.

The square root *of a number* n, *written* $\sqrt{n}$ *or, in programming,* sqrt(n), *is a number* m *such that* m × m = n. *When you multiply a number by itself in this way, this is called the* square *of the number, denoted* n^2, n^2 *or* power(n, 2). *A square is a special case of a* power *or an* exponent. *When you take a number* n *to the power* p, *written* n^p *or* n^p, *this means to multiply the number* n *by itself* p *times (as long as* p *is an integer—later we will look some more at powers). Because two negative numbers multiplied together give a positive number, every positive number has two square roots, one positive and one negative, while negative numbers have no real square root.*

The Number As a String of Digits

It is important to distinguish "numbers" (the "real things" out there in the mathematical universe) from their representation on paper. It is like the difference between the sentence "John met Mary for a drink" and its *meaning* as a piece of "mentalese," which might be just as easily expressed as something like event(meet, John, Mary).purpose(drink).

There are many different ways to represent a number. Let's look at the number 5. We can represent it geometrically as a pentagon or as a set of 5 dots, or physically as 5 beads on an abacus, or use the purpose-made *symbol* "5," which is simply defined to mean what we want it to mean. Each of these representations has its own advantages: if you use beads, you can perform operations such as adding and subtracting simply by counting beads back and forth. On the other hand, once you get to larger numbers, which would need an awful lot of beads, using symbols has a big advantage.

But of course we can't have a new symbol for each number. Instead, we use a limited set of such symbols and combine them typographically to represent any number, no matter how big. We do this by means of a *base* system. We choose a number *b* as a *base*, then to represent a number *n* in that base we perform this recursive algorithm:

```
function NumberToBaseString (Number, Base)
   if Number is less than Base then set Output to String (Number)
   otherwise
      || Find the remainder Rem when you divide Number by Base
      set Output to Rem
      set ReducedNumber to (Number — Rem) / Base
      set RestOfString to NumberToBaseString (ReducedNumber, Base)
      append RestOfString to the front of Output
   end if
   return Output
end function
```

The remainder *when dividing* n *by* m *is the smallest number* r *such that for some integer* a, m × a + r = n. *So the remainder when dividing 7 by 3 is 1, because 7 = 3 × 2 + 1. We will be looking further at the operation of finding the remainder when dividing one number by another in the next chapter.*

Let's quickly look through this algorithm (if you aren't comfortable with recursion, incidentally, there are some notes about it in Appendix B). If we apply it for `Number` = 354 and `Base` = 10, you'll see what happens. First, we find the remainder when we divide 354 by 10, which is 4, the number of "units" in 354. We write down the number 4 into our output. Now we take away this remainder to get 350, and divide this result by 10. The division works exactly by the definition of a remainder, and the answer is 35. Now we feed 35 into the algorithm again to get 5, the number of "tens" in 354, and 3, the number of "hundreds," which, unsurprisingly, gives us the string "354," which is the number we first thought of. It sounds rather unnecessary, really, but this is why you need to bear in mind the difference between the *number* 354 and its *representation* in the base 10.

If you do the operation in reverse, you can find the *value* of the number:

```
function BaseStringToValue (DigitString, Base)
   if DigitString is empty then set Output to 0
   otherwise
      set Output to the last digit of DigitString
      set RemainingString to all but the last digit of DigitString
      set ValueOfRemainingString to BaseStringToValue (RemainingString,
Base))
      add Base * ValueOfRemainingString to Output
```

```
    end if
    return output
end function
```

A number written down in base notation is like an array. Each position in the array represents a value that is `Base` times the next one, and the digit in that position represents the number of times we add that value to the total. So, in *base ten* or *decimal*, the columns, reading from right to left, represent the values 1, 10, 100, ... , and the digits in those columns represent the number of occurrences of that value—e.g., 2631 represents the number given by $2 \times 1000 + 6 \times 100 + 3 \times 10 + 1 \times 1$.

Decimal, Binary, and Hexadecimal

There's nothing special about using ten as a base—in fact, objectively speaking, ten is a poor choice, and we only use it as a historical consequence of the fact that we have ten fingers to count with. Because 10 is a multiple of 2 and of 5, it's fairly easy to determine whether a number written in decimal notation is divisible by these two numbers, but it's much harder to tell if it's divisible by 4 or 7. However, there are some fairly simple tests for divisibility by 3 or 9.

A number is divisible by 3 if and only if the sum of its digits in base ten is divisible by 3. Similarly for 9. You might want to think about this and work out why it is so—it's a consequence of the base system.

So what if we were to use some other base? A good candidate is base 12, which is why the old British currency and Imperial measuring system of feet and inches survived as long as they did: it makes it very easy to divide numbers by 2, 3, 4, or 6. Another is base 60 (used in clocks, along with 12), and another is base 360 (used in measuring angles). However, the last two require a lot of individual symbols to use properly. The Babylonians used them, in fact, but they subdivided them using a base ten system. And base 12, though very logical, never caught on except in limited fields.

Base two, or *binary*, on the other hand, turns out to be useful in quite a different way. In base 2, we represent numbers by powers of two, so the number 11 is written as 1011, or $1 \times 8 + 0 \times 4 + 1 \times 2 + 1 \times 1$. As with base ten, this can be done uniquely (at least when working with integers), and while you need far more digits to represent any one number, you only need two symbols to do it, which you can think of as "Yes and No," or "On and Off."

Base 16 (*hexadecimal*) goes the other way, representing numbers with 16 symbols. We use the standard decimal symbols 0–9, and for convenience use the letters A–F for 10–15. So F1A represents $15 \times 256 + 1 \times 16 + 10 \times 1$, or 3866. Converting between binary and hexadecimal is quite simple, since each hexadecimal symbol can be translated directly into four binary symbols: F1A translates to 1111 0001 1010.

HOW COMPUTERS REPRESENT NUMBERS

The binary system is at the heart of how numbers are represented on a computer. We're now going to look at how this is done, and how the computer processes the numbers.

Representing Integers

Because binary can be conveniently represented by two symbols, On and Off, it's an ideal system for computers to use. Deep inside the machine, everything is represented by numbers, which are in turn represented by sets of "switches" (we're talking conceptually here, of course—the switches are electronic, not physical). Each switch represents one *bit* of information, i.e., one "on" or "off" of a binary number ("bit" is an abbreviation of "binary digit"). With eight such switches, we can represent any number from 0 to 255; and with 32 switches, we can represent any number up to 4294967295. The computer's native environment is designed to perform calculations very fast with any number it can represent in such a way, and this is indicated by the number of bits of the processor—a 64-bit machine can handle far bigger calculations than a 32-bit one. Often, one bit of the number is set aside to represent whether the number is positive or negative, so a 32-bit machine actually handles numbers from −2147483647 to 2147483647.

Binary numbers are particularly fast because performing operations like addition and multiplication is so easy. Here is an algorithm that adds two numbers represented as strings in binary:

```
function AddBinaryStrings (b1, b2)
   || pad out the smaller number with leading zeroes so they are the
same length
   set Output to ""
   set CarryDigit to 0
   repeat with Index = the length of b1 down to 1
      set k1 and k2 to the Index'th characters of b1 and b2
      if  k1 = k2 then
         // the digits are the same, so write the current carry digit
```

```
            set WriteDigit to CarryDigit
            set CarryDigit to k1
            // if k1 and k2 are 1 then we are going to be carrying a digit
            // if they are 0 then we won't.
        otherwise
            // the digits are different, so write the opposite of the
    current carry digit
            set WriteDigit to NOT(CarryDigit)
            // leave the carry digit alone as it will be unchanged
        end if
        append WriteDigit to the front of Output
    end repeat
    if CarryDigit = 1 then append 1 to the front of Output
    return output
end function
```

This may seem confusing, but it's worth examining because these kinds of operations are the key to how computers work. The trick is that in binary we have $01 + 01 = 10$ and $01 + 10 = 11$, so we can add according to whether digits are the same or different, rather than worrying about their actual value. This is easy to implement in the computer's hardware, and means that manipulating integers is a relatively simple operation for a computer. Fundamental to this process are the *logical operators* AND, OR and NOT, which combine binary (or *Boolean*) digits together in different ways.

If a and b are binary digits, then

■ a AND $b = 1$ if and only if both a and b are 1
■ a OR $b = 1$ if either a or b or both are 1
■ NOT $a = 1$ if and only if $a = 0$

Multiplication in binary is similarly straightforward, because it's a combination of two simple operations, multiplying by 2 and adding. Just as we can multiply by 10 in decimal, we can multiply by 2 in binary by shifting the digits of the number by one place: 6 in binary is 110, and 12 is 1100.

Representing Rational and Irrational Numbers

We can use base notation to represent non-integers, too, by counting down from 1 as well as up. We use a marker, the *radix point*, to tell us where to start the count. In decimal, the radix point is called the *decimal point*, and the first column after the decimal point represents tenths, the second is hundredths, and so on. In binary, the first column after the radix point represents halves, the second quarters, and so on. So the number $1\frac{3}{8}$ is represented in binary by 1.011 $(1 + \frac{1}{4} + \frac{1}{8})$.

But there is a problem with this system, which is that not all fractions can be represented in this way. In decimal, we have trouble representing $\frac{1}{3}$, because it can't be expressed as a sum of tenths, hundredths, etc. It turns out to be the limit of the infinite series $\frac{3}{10} + \frac{3}{100} + \frac{3}{1000} + \dots$. We represent this by saying $\frac{1}{3}$ in decimal is 0.333... .

The term "limit of the series" actually has quite a precise and important meaning in mathematics, but we won't go into that here: it should be clear what it means in this case. The key is that the more terms of the series we take, the closer the sum approaches $\frac{1}{3}$, without ever increasing beyond it.

In binary, the situation is even worse—we can't express any fraction whose denominator is divisible by any number other than 2. In decimal, $\frac{1}{5}$ is exactly 0.2. In binary, it is the infinitely repeating number 0.001100110011 ... , so computers have trouble with fractions.

There are two ways to get around this problem. One is to forget radix points and instead to represent the fraction in terms of its constituent integers, the numerator and denominator. Then every rational number can be represented exactly, without any pesky repeating digits. Unfortunately, this makes the situation even worse. If you add $\frac{1}{2}$ and $\frac{1}{3}$ the answer is $\frac{5}{6}$. $\frac{5}{6} + \frac{1}{7} = \frac{41}{42}$. $\frac{41}{42} + \frac{1}{11} = \frac{493}{462}$. Each time we add an incompatible fraction (by "incompatible" we mean that the denominators have no common factor—this will be covered further in the next chapter), we end up increasing the complexity of the denominator. We will quickly find ourselves going above the maximum size for integers, not to mention slowing down all the calculations we are performing. So except in very special cases this is unlikely to be a sensible move.

Another problem with this approach is the existence of the irrational numbers, which can't be expressed exactly as a fraction in any case. We will instead find ourselves forced to find an approximation, in which case we might as well approximate everything! So computers use the base system to represent non-integers, and round the number to the nearest digit.

The most obvious way to do this is simply to say we will represent 8 digits after the radix point. But with only a limited number of bits to play with for each number, this seems wasteful—each bit added to the end means one less bit to use at the top, so we're limiting how large, as well as how small, our numbers can be. So instead of this *fixed-point* representation, most languages now use *floating-point* representation, similar to what is called "scientific notation."

In scientific notation, a number is represented by giving the first "significant" (non-zero) digit, and then as many digits as required after that. Then you give an indication of where to place the radix. For example, the number 201.49 could be represented by (20149; 3). In fact, we represent it as "2.0149 e2"—by convention, we start with the radix after the first digit and count from there. We can count forward or backward—e.g., 2.0149 e-3 is 0.0020149. The index number is called the *exponent*, for reasons we will look at later.

Floating-point numbers use essentially the same system. There are a number of standard formats—the one we will look at here is the IEEE standard. (IEEE is an organization that has created many standard formats that are used commonly by most manufacturers. These standards are very important for creating a common language between different hardware, and there are similar organizations that decide on Web protocols, mobile phone systems, and so on.)

In the IEEE standard, using 32 bits, you use 1 bit for the sign (positive or negative) and 8 bits for the position of the radix point, from -127 (represented by a value of zero) to $+127$ (a value of 255), therefore allowing the value of the actual number to go as high as a little under 2^{128}. The remaining 23 bits represent the *mantissa*, or actual digits of the number. Rather ingeniously, because the first significant digit of a binary number is always 1, there is no need to include this digit in the computer's representation of the number, it is just implicitly there, which gives us one more digit of precision. The actual digits of the floating-point representation are correctly called the *significand*, although often the word mantissa is used for this too.

It's important to keep clear the difference between the size *of the number, which is given by the exponent, and the* precision *of the number, which is determined by the number of bits in the significand. Although we can represent very large numbers indeed, they are no more precise than the small ones. It is impossible to distinguish between 987874651253 and 987874651254 using a 32-bit floating-point number.*

Let's give some examples, to make it clearer.

- To represent the value 10.5 we first **translate it into binary**: 1010.1
- In **scientific notation**, this is 1.0101 e3
- **Translate** the 3 into a binary number and **add** 127 (this value is called the *bias*—it allows us to represent numbers from -127 to 127 rather than 0 to 255), to get 10000010 for our **exponent bits**.
- **Pad** the 1.0101 out with zeroes to give 24 digits of the **mantissa**: 101010000000000000000000
- **Ignore** the first 1, which we can take as read, leaving a 23-bit **significand**: 01010000000000000000000
- And the **final bit** is zero, representing a positive number rather than a negative one.

- To represent the **value** given in decimal by -1 e-35
- In **binary scientific notation**, this is $-1.1010100101011010010110 1 \ldots$ e-117

■ **Translate** the −117 into binary and add 127 to get 1010 for our **exponent**, which we pad out with zeroes to get 8 bits: 00001010
■ The **significand** is the first 23 bits after the decimal point: 10101001010110100101101
■ And the **final bit** is one, representing a negative number.

The only problem with omitting the initial 1 of the mantissa is that it would leave no way to represent a floating-point value of exactly zero. Fortunately, we can add one extra trick, which is to say that when the exponent part of the number is zero, we don't assume a leading 1. This also means we can represent numbers smaller than 2^{127}, as long as we accept that these numbers will be less precise than usual. Using this trick of *denormalization*, we can represent numbers as low as 2^{-149}.

So zero is represented, as you would expect, by the floating point number given by a zero significand, and a zero exponent (the positive/negative bit can be either value). There are also a number of other special cases, which represent overflow and underflow, as well as the value NaN ("Not a Number"), which is sometimes returned when you attempt to do something that has no valid answer, like finding the square root of −1.

We'll illustrate this by one final example: the value given in decimal by 2 e–40

■ In **binary scientific notation**, this is 1.0001011011000010011001 e–132
■ Because −132 is less than −127, we cannot represent this number to the usual precision. But if we **shift the exponent** up by 5 places, we get a value of 0.000010001011011000010011001 e–127
■ We can represent this by an **exponent** part of 00000000 and a **significand** of 00000100010110110000100. This gives us five fewer digits than usual, but it's better than not being able to represent the number at all.

In Exercise 1 you are asked to write a set of functions to work with these floating-point numbers.

Not all languages use 32-bit floats. Even with a 32-bit processor, some languages use *double precision* numbers, which combine two 32-bit numbers into one, to give a 64-bit number. This allows a much wider range of numbers to be represented, and to much greater precision.

abs(), floor(), ceil(), and round()

This seems like a good moment to look at a few important functions that are common, in one form or another, to most computer languages. Many languages do not have all the functions natively, or give them different names, but they are nevertheless processes which are often useful, so worth adding to your personal function library if your language doesn't have them.

The simplest of them is the abs() function, which returns the *absolute value* of a number (float or integer). This is the value of the number, ignoring whether it is positive or negative. We can give the function precisely in just a couple of lines of code:

```
function abs (n)
    if n>=0 then return n
    otherwise return -n
end function
```

Remember that if n is negative then $-n$ is positive, so the absolute value of a number is its value made positive. Of course, natively the computer doesn't need to do anything even this complicated, it simply sets the value of the sign bit in the floating-point or integer representation to 0.

The other three functions are all ways to convert a float to an integer. In a nutshell:

- Floor(n) is the largest integer less than n
- Ceil(n) is the smallest integer greater than n
- Round(n) is the nearest integer to n

See Figure 1.1 for a graphical representation of these three functions. Note that each range has a solid line at one end and a broken line at the other, representing the fact that, for example, floor(n)=3 for n greater than or equal to 3, but less than 4.

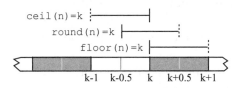

FIGURE 1.1 The ranges of floating point numbers that give the answer k using the floor(), ceil() and round() functions.

Each of these functions is useful in different circumstances. Floor(n) and ceil(n) are fairly simple—and quite easy for the computer to calculate from the floating-point representation too. If the exponent of the number is 5, then we can find the positive integer part (call it p) of the number by taking the first 5 digits of the significand. If it's less than 1, of course, the integer part is zero, and if it is greater than the number of digits in the significand, then we do not know the exact integer part. Now all we need is to check the sign of the number—if it's positive, then floor(n) is equal to p and ceil(n) is $p + 1$. If it's negative then ceil(n) is $-p$ and floor(n) is $-(p + 1)$

In this book we represent the "rounding to the nearest whole number" function you are most likely to have used at school by round(n). Round(n) is the integer such that abs(n-round(n)) < 1. Numbers exactly half-way between two integers, such as 1.5, are ambiguous—we define round(n) to round up in those cases. So assuming we have already defined floor(n) and ceil(n), we can define round(n) as follows:

```
Function round(n)
    Set f to floor(n)
    Set c to ceil(n)
    If n-f > c-n then return c // n is nearer c than f
    If c-n > n-f then return f // n is nearer f than c
    Otherwise return c // n is half-way between c and f
End function
```

However, again there is a slightly simpler way of calculating the value directly from the floating-point representation. We find the integer part p as before. Then to decide whether to round up or down, we just look at the next digit of the significand, which in binary represents the value $\frac{1}{2}$. If that digit is 0, then the fractional part of the number is less than $\frac{1}{2}$, which means we round down. If it's 1, then the fractional part is greater than or equal to $\frac{1}{2}$—either way, we round up. Thus the arbitrary decision to round up halves turns out to be quite handy. If we rounded them down, then if the first digit of the fractional part was a 1, we would still not know whether to round up or down without looking at the rest of the digits.

In Lingo, and thus in the code on the CD-ROM, round(n) *is calculated using the native function* integer(n).

Rounding Errors and Performance

No matter how precise we make our floating-point numbers, they are still not exact except in very special circumstances (such as exact powers of 2). This means that there is a danger of introducing errors into calculations which depend on exact precision. In most circumstances, this is not a major problem, but it is not hard to come up with examples where it is an issue.

For example, let's ask the computer for the result of $(\frac{7}{50}+1) \times 50 - 57$. If you do the calculation on paper, you will see that the answer should be 0, because $\frac{7}{50} \times 50 = 7$, and $1 \times 50 = 50$. But the computer tells us the answer is 7.10542735760100 e-15. Why did it happen? Because when we divided by 50, we ended up with a number with a negative exponent. Adding 1 created a number with an exponent of 0, which meant that a whole lot of bits were dropped off the end of the significand. Multiplying back up by 50 could not restore those lost bits.

Rounding errors are a major source of problems when performing complex and repeated calculations, especially "stretch and fold" calculations such as described above, where small numbers are added to larger ones. In general, there is not a great deal you can do about it, but, in some cases, doing some pre-calculations can alleviate the problem a little.

If you know that you are going to drop and then restore bits, you may be able to make your calculations in a different order to avoid it. In the example above, if we had performed the calculation as $(\frac{7}{50} \times 50) + (1 \times 50) - 57$, dividing by 50 and then multiplying again hardly loses any precision at all, and then simply adding and subtracting a small integer like 50 is not going to change it.

One other issue to notice here is that testing whether two floating-point calculations are equal may prove to be a problem. If we ask whether $(\frac{7}{50}+1) \times 5000 = 5700$, we get the answer no, where it should say yes. In general, it is best when checking for equality of two floats to call them equal when their absolute difference is less than a small value. So, instead of saying `if x = y`, we might say `if abs(x - y) < 0.00001`.

None of these workarounds will solve the rounding error problem completely, so if you are doing calculations that require lots of precision, you may have to use some specialized calculation algorithms that retain as much precision as they can. We will look at some of these in a moment.

Floating-point calculations are also somewhat more expensive in terms of computer time than the same calculations with integers. A quick test in Lingo that calculated 2 × 2 a million times using floats took 1.2 seconds, while integer calculations took under a second. That's a fairly significant difference for such a simple task. So if it is at all possible to use integer calculations to perform the task you are trying, especially in games or other situations where there are a lot of calculations and speed is an issue, then it's worth doing.

You can use integer calculations even if you are working with fractions. Simply multiply all numbers by a sufficiently large number at the start, convert to integers, and do all your calculations before dividing again by the number at the end. Most calculations will work in this way, though you need to be careful.

Having said this, the difference between floating-point calculations and integer calculations is not as big a deal as it once was. In the early days of floats, the difference in speed was much greater, but these days, processors are geared to deal with floats on a hardware level just as they are with integers, and so generally the difference is not so important. You will usually be able to find much more dramatic parts of your code to optimize!

Big Integers

One way to deal with functions requiring a lot of precision is to work with `bigInteger` classes. These are specialized objects which, instead of just using the computer's processor to store and work with numbers, store them as a long array. We did something like this above when we represented a binary number with a long string of digits.

When you do calculations in this way, you are no longer limited by the processor's built-in number storage. Your array can be as long as you like, limited only by the computer's memory—instead of having 32 bits to represent a number, you might have a trillion bits or more! This should be sufficiently precise to deal with any calculation you could conceivably want to perform. Of course, because you must perform the calculations at the level of your language rather than directly within the processor, and because each calculation involves many, many more digits, this is much slower. However, in the kinds of situations where you need this sort of precision (detailed physics simulations of hair, water, or fabric, for example), you generally are thinking in terms of letting the computer do the calculations overnight rather than at lightning speed.

There are `bigInteger` classes available for most languages that are used as standard by scientists—lots of them for C++—and we won't go into how they are used here as it doesn't make a great deal of difference to the actual mathematics.

EXERCISES

Exercise 1.1

Write a function `ConvertBase (NumberString, Base1, Base2)`, which takes a string (or array if you prefer) `NumberString`, representing an integer in the base `Base1` and converts it into the base `Base2`, returning the new string (or array). Make it handle any base from 2 to 16.

You might want to make special cases for binary and hexadecimal translation to speed up the function.

Exercise 1.2

Write a series of functions for calculating addition, subtraction, multiplication, and division using IEEE-style floating-point numbers. Represent the floats as 32-bit strings (or arrays) of 1s and 0s.

Each function should take two floating-point numbers and return another. Don't forget the special case when the exponent is zero. You will probably find division to be the most difficult case.

Remember that there are hints to the solutions of the exercises in Appendix E, and some answers can be found on the CD-ROM as well as the book's Web site.

ON THE CD

SUMMARY

We have covered a lot of ground in this first chapter and it has been quite hard going. There has been a lot of theory and not a lot of practical work, but we've seen how numbers are defined and written, and how they are represented on the computer, and we've seen some of the problems this can create.

In the next chapter, we will start working with these numbers to make some actual calculations.

YOU SHOULD NOW KNOW

- the meaning of the terms *integer, fraction, rational, numerator, denominator, fixed-point number, floating-point number, exponent, mantissa, significand, base, binary, decimal,* and *decimal point,* among others
- the difference between the *value* of a number and its *representation* as a string of digits
- how computers *represent* and calculate with integers and floating-point numbers
- how to *convert* a float to an integer in various ways
- why *rounding errors* are an essential consequence of working with floats and how to avoid them in some circumstances

2 Arithmetic

In This Chapter

- Overview
- Fractions and Remainders
- Proportions, Ratios, and Percentages
- Exponentials
- Logarithms
- Exercises
- Summary
- You Should Now Know

OVERVIEW

For this chapter and the next one, we are going to go right back to basics. We need to cover this ground in order to deal with the more complex topics presented later in the book, though most of it is almost certainly material you have covered in school. Despite this, you should at least skim over it: you would be amazed how many people come up against problems because they didn't understand some simple, basic concepts. They manage for a long time by finding workaround strategies, or using techniques they have learned by rote without really knowing what they are doing.

For the first of our two fundamentals chapters, we will look at some essentials of arithmetic, working with the integers, rationals, and floats, which we saw in Chapter 1. Of course we won't cover the whole of arithmetic, but we'll look at a few particular topics that are often troublesome, and some that are commonly useful in programming.

ON THE CD Code samples from this chapter are implemented in *math.cst* in the script *Chapter 2 (fractions, primes and arithmetic)*. Additional functions related to the exercises can be found in the script *mortgages*.

FRACTIONS AND REMAINDERS

We glossed over the details of working with fractions in the previous chapter, but because so many people seem to have trouble with them, we'll spend a little time looking at them in more detail, starting with some basic arithmetic and then seeing where that takes us.

Calculating Fractions

Remember that a fraction is something like an instruction: it tells you to divide a by b. So the fraction $\frac{2}{5}$ is exactly the same as the value $2 \div 5$. In fact, the division symbol $\div$ is just a representation of this process: the two dots represent the numerator and denominator of a fraction.

In this book, fractions will mostly be represented using a diagonal line, as in $\frac{1}{2}$, rather than a horizontal line as in $\frac{1}{2}$, because it takes up less space, but sometimes we'll use the latter method if it makes things clearer.

NOTE

Multiplying and dividing fractions is fairly straightforward:

- To multiply two fractions, you simply multiply the numerators and multiply the denominators: $\frac{2}{5} \times \frac{3}{7} = \frac{2 \times 3}{5 \times 7} = \frac{6}{35}$.

Multiplication is represented by the English word "of," as in "two fifths of three sevenths," just as with integers you might say "five of these apples" and mean $5 \times$ apple. It's easier to see how it works by breaking the process up into two steps: *dividing* by the denominator ("take *one* fifth of three sevenths"), and then *multiplying* by the numerator ("now we want two of those"). Of course, when multiplying a fraction by an integer, you just remember that an integer is a fraction with denominator 1, which means that you can multiply the fraction's numerator by the integer and leave the denominator alone (multiply it by 1).

- To divide $\frac{2}{5}$ by $\frac{3}{7}$, what we do is to firstly flip $\frac{3}{7}$ over to become $\frac{7}{3}$ (its *reciprocal*). Then we multiply: $\frac{2}{5} \div \frac{3}{7} = \frac{2}{5} \times \frac{7}{3} = \frac{14}{15}$.

Why? Well, let's start with integers. *Dividing* by 2 is *halving* the number, which means taking half *of* the number, which as we just saw is the same as *multiplying* by $\frac{1}{2}$. Similarly, when you divide a number by $\frac{1}{2}$, you want to find out how many halves go into it, which is twice as many as the number of 1s that go into it. And since the number of 1s that go into a number is the number itself (**anything** divided by 1 is unchanged), this means that a number divided by $\frac{1}{2}$ is multiplied by 2. Division is represented by a number of words in English, such as "per"—your speed in miles *per* hour is the number of miles travelled divided by the number of hours taken—as well as "each" and "a."

Addition and subtraction of fractions is a little more complicated. As long as two fractions have the same denominator, we can add and subtract them quite simply. We leave the denominator unchanged, and just perform normal arithmetic with the numerators: $\frac{3}{5}+\frac{1}{5}=\frac{4}{5}$; $\frac{3}{5}-\frac{1}{5}=\frac{2}{5}$. Essentially, we're simply counting, it's just that the objects we are counting happen to be units of $\frac{1}{5}$. But as soon as you want to add fractions with different denominators you hit problems, because the units you are trying to add are different.

Fortunately, every fraction can in fact be represented an infinite number of ways: multiply the numerator and denominator by any number at all and you end up with the same fraction. This is because any number divided by itself is 1, which means that the fractions $\frac{2}{2}$, $\frac{3}{3}$ and so on are all equal to 1, so we can multiply by any of these fractions and leave the number unchanged. This means that we can make calculations easier by choosing the most convenient representation for them. Suppose you want to add $\frac{1}{2}$ to $\frac{1}{4}$. It's much easier to do this by realising that $\frac{1}{2}$ is actually equal to $\frac{2}{4}$ (multiplying top and bottom by 2), and now, because both fractions have the same denominator, we can use the fact that $\frac{1}{4}+\frac{2}{4}=\frac{3}{4}$. This process even works if we are adding fractions which can't be easily converted, such as adding $\frac{2}{3}$ to $\frac{3}{5}$. We simply "cross-multiply," which means that we multiply the numerator and denominator of each fraction by the denominator of the other—in the jargon, we "put them over a common denominator" (see Figure 2.1).

$$\frac{2}{3}+\frac{3}{5} = \frac{2\times5}{3\times5} + \frac{3\times3}{5\times3} = \frac{2\times5 + 3\times3}{3\times5} = \frac{19}{15}$$

FIGURE 2.1 Cross-multiplying.

Let's do this formally as a function. We'll represent each fraction by a 2-element array:

```
function addfractions(f1,f2)
    set num1 to the numerator of f1
    set den1 to the denominator of f1
    set num2 to the numerator of f2
    set den2 to the denominator of f2
    if den1 = den2 then return the fraction(num1+num2, den1)
    otherwise
        set num3 to num1*den2
        set num4 to num2*den1
        return the fraction(num3+num4,den1*den2)
    end if
end function
```

The only problem with this function is that the calculations involved are potentially much more complicated than they need be. Look at the earlier example of $\frac{1}{2}+\frac{1}{4}$. You can see that using this function, it would actually calculate $\frac{4}{8}+\frac{2}{8}$, instead of the simpler $\frac{2}{4}+\frac{1}{4}$. What's more, the final answer would be given as $\frac{6}{8}$ rather than $\frac{3}{4}$, which while technically correct is not what you really need.

Factors and Factorization

Let's look at the latter issue first. Our technique for adding fractions was to switch them to a more complicated representation so they are easier to add. What we need to do is to switch them back to a simpler version at the end. This is called reducing a fraction to its *lowest terms*, and to do it we need to look at factors. A *factor* or *divisor* of an integer is another integer which can be divided into it exactly. So 1, 2, 3 and 6 are all factors of 6. If n is a factor of m then we say that m is a *multiple* of n (or more strictly it's an *exact multiple* or *integer multiple*)

6 is called a "perfect number," because it is the sum of all its factors other than itself: 1 + 2 + 3 = 6. The Pythagoreans were particularly fond of perfect numbers.

If we look at the fraction $\frac{6}{8}$ from the previous section, we can see that it would be much simpler if we divided everything by 2 to make it $\frac{3}{4}$. 2 is a factor of both the numerator and the denominator: it is a *common factor* of 6 and 8. In fact, because 6 and 8 have no common factor greater than 2, it is called the *highest common factor*, or more often, the *greatest common divisor* or GCD. To reduce a fraction to its lowest terms, we need to divide the numerator and denominator by their GCD.

You will sometimes see the GCD of two numbers n and m written as (n, m). We won't use that notation here because it's too easily confused with other notations of the same kind. Instead, we'll write it as gcd(n, m).

In school, you probably found GCDs by finding the *prime factors* of the two numbers. We'll see a simpler method in a moment, but let's look at the prime factors anyway, because they are useful in their own right. To explain prime factors, we first need to define *prime numbers*. A prime number (or just "a prime") is a number whose only factors are itself and 1. Conventionally, we exclude the number 1 from the list of primes, because it's something of a special case and makes for a better pattern. The list of primes goes 2, 3, 5, 7, 11, 13, 17, 19, ... The prime numbers are something like the building blocks of multiplication, and there is a huge body of work about them—looking for patterns in their distribution, and particularly looking for ways to test whether or not a number is in fact prime. They are particularly important in the field of cryptography.

You can generate a list of prime numbers less than some number M quite quickly using a technique known as Eratosthenes' Sieve. To do this, start with a list of all the numbers from 2 to M. Then repeat this process: Take the first number in the list, and delete all the numbers in the list that are divisible by this number (we'll return to the testing of divisibility shortly). Remove the number from the list and add it to your list of primes. You only need to do this until the first number in the list is greater than $\sqrt{M}$. Once you're past that point, all the remaining numbers must be prime, since they're not divisible by any number smaller than the square root (you've crossed those ones off), and any product of two numbers bigger than $\sqrt{M}$ must be bigger than M.

Here's the algorithm in code:

```
function listOfPrimes(M)
   || make an array with all the numbers from 2 to M and call it nlist
   set maxM to floor(sqrt(M)) // the biggest number we need to check
   set index to 1
   repeat while nlist[index] is less than maxM
      set prime to nlist[index]
      repeat for index2 = index+1 to the number of elements in nlist
         if nlist[index2] is divisible by prime then delete it from the
         list
      end repeat
      add 1 to index
   end repeat
   return nlist
end function
```

Now we can come back to prime factors. A *prime factor* of a number n is, much as you might expect, a prime number which is a factor of n. Every number can be represented in a unique way as a product of prime numbers—for example, $12 = 2 \times 2 \times 3$ (this fact goes by the very grand name of the "Fundamental Theorem of Arithmetic"). A number with more than one prime factor is said to be *composite*.

NOTE

The Fundamental Theorem is one of the reasons we say 1 is not prime, because it would be an exception to this rule of uniqueness. We could represent any number as a product of its prime factors and any number of 1s.

To find the prime factors of an arbitrary number *n*, the only absolutely reliable way is simply to keep dividing it by prime numbers until you find one. Of course, this can be a slow process for large numbers, but it's not too bad for small ones, especially if you have already generated a list of primes. Here's a function that will do it.

```
function primeFactors(n)
    // create a list of possible primes
    set plist to listOfPrimes(floor(n/2))
    set rlist to a blank array
    set index to 1
    repeat while index <= the number of elements in plist
        set prime to plist[index]
        if n is divisible by prime then
            set n to n/prime
            add prime to rlist
        otherwise
            add 1 to index
        end if
    end repeat
    return rlist
end function
```

NOTE

When people are searching for extremely large primes (as they often do for cryptographic or other purposes), they don't use this method, as it would take an unfeasibly long time even on a very fast computer. Instead, they generally use various tricks to home in on numbers that are extremely likely to be prime, to within some particular degree of certainty. Depending on the application, this is usually enough.

So let's return to the question of the GCD of two numbers. If we want to find gcd(n, m), we can do it by finding the prime factors of each. So say n is 24 and m is 60, we use our function to find that the prime factors of n are 2, 2, 2, 3 and of m are 2, 2, 3, 5. Then we just take as many elements of each list as we can that match, which is two 2s and one 3. So gcd(n, m) is $2 \times 2 \times 3 = 12$.

On the other hand, we could instead use the phenomenally simple and ingenious method known as *Euclid's Algorithm*, which is approximately a gazillion times faster.

Euclid's Algorithm relies on a simple observation: if you have three numbers *a*, *b*, *c* such that $a = b + c$, and if some number *d* is a factor of both *a* and *b*, then it must be a factor of *c* as well. Armed with this knowledge, we can do the following:

To find gcd(n, m), where $n \geq m$, divide n by m and find the remainder r. Then we know that $n = a \times m + r$, for some a, where $r < m$ (recall that this is the definition of the remainder). If $r = 0$, then m is a factor of n, so gcd(n, m) = m. Otherwise, because the GCD is a factor of both n and m by definition, it must also be a factor of r. So now we repeat the process using the numbers m and r in place of n and m.

```
function gcd(n, m)
    set r to the remainder of n/m
    if r = 0 then return m
    otherwise return gcd(m, r)
end function
```

Eventually we bottom out with a number d that is an exact divisor of the two arguments, and we can then work back to find that it is a common divisor of both of the original numbers. Euclid's Algorithm is one of the most beautiful things in mathematics.

Once we have gcd(n, m), we can also find another useful number, the LCM or *least* (or *lowest*) *common multiple* of n and m. This is the smallest number that has both n and m as factors, and is equal to n*m / gcd(n, m). The LCM brings us finally, in this rather recursive section, back to the sum of two fractions.

When adding two fractions, instead of cross-multiplying, the most efficient system is to "put them over the *lowest common denominator*," i.e., to multiply the top and bottom of each fraction by the smallest possible number such that they have the same denominator. This lowest common denominator is the LCM of the two denominators.

Let's see how this works by calculating $\frac{7}{24} + \frac{7}{30}$. What we do instead of a bare cross-multiplication is to multiply each fraction top and bottom by the denominator of the other, *divided by the GCD of the two denominators.*

- gcd(24, 30) = 6 by Euclid's Algorithm, so we have to multiply the first fraction top and bottom by $\frac{30}{6} = 5$ and the second by $\frac{24}{6} = 4$.
- This gives us $\frac{35}{120} + \frac{28}{120}$, which has a common denominator (the LCM of 24 and 30) of 120.
- Because of the common denominator we can now add simply to get $\frac{63}{120}$.
- Now we just need to reduce this to its lowest terms by finding gcd(63, 120). Using Euclid's Algorithm we see that $120 = 63 + 57$; $63 = 57 + 6$; $57 = 9 \times 6 + 3$; and $6 = 3 \times 2$; so gcd(120, 63) = 3.
- Therefore we can divide our answer top and bottom by 3 to get $\frac{21}{40}$, which is now in its lowest terms.

$\frac{21}{40}$ *is in its lowest terms because* gcd(21, 40) = *1. We say that 21 and 40 are* relatively prime *or* coprime.

Modulo Arithmetic

Euclid's Algorithm, as with several other techniques we've looked at already, relies on a process of finding the remainder when dividing one number by another. This turns out to be such a useful procedure that there is a standard term for it. If you have two numbers n and m, and when you divide n by m you get a remainder r, we say that "n is *congruent* to r modulo m." Congruence is normally expressed with a special symbol " $\equiv$ ", so we write:

$$n \equiv r(\bmod m)$$

Actually, the congruence relation is a little more subtle than that: we say two numbers are congruent mod m whenever they differ by an integer multiple of m. So when working modulo 5, the numbers 4, 9, 14, ... are all equivalent because they are all congruent to 4.

Computers can't really do anything with a congruence relation as it stands. Instead, they have a modulo *function*, which takes two arguments n and m, and returns the remainder r. So we say mod (n, m) = r

If $n \geq 0$, then the mod() function returns a value between 0 and $m-1$. If $n < 0$, it generally returns a value between $-(m-1)$ and 0 (in the most commonly used languages, at least). This is not actually very useful, so we can use a modified modulo function given by:

```
function StrictModulo (n, m)
    set r = mod (n,m)
    if r<0 then return r + m
    otherwise return r
end function
```

StrictModulo() always returns a value between 0 and m $-$ 1, and the congruence relationship

$$n1 \equiv n2(\bmod m)$$

is equivalent to saying

```
StrictModulo (n1, m) = StrictModulo (n2, m).
```

We've already seen a number of situations in which the modulo function is useful. Generally the most common use is to decide whether one number is divisible by another. If n is exactly divisible by m, then StrictModulo(n, m)=0.

The modulo function is not symmetric around zero. In general, StrictModulo (n, m) *is not equal to* StrictModulo (-n, m). *In fact, we generally have* StrictModulo(n, m) = m - StrictModulo(-n, m), *unless* n *is a multiple of* m, *in which case both values are zero.*

You can use another method to calculate the modulo, too. If you find floor(n/m), this gives the largest integer less than $\frac{n}{m}$. Then m*floor(n/m) is the largest multiple of m less than n. This means that for a positive integer, mod(n,m) = n−m*floor(n/m). Obviously, there are minor dangers in switching between floats and integers, though, so it's best to avoid this method as a general rule.

Cycling Through Data

Modulo arithmetic is sometimes known as clock arithmetic, because it is commonly used in situations where something cycles through a small list of options. A clock contains only 12 numbers, so when calculating hours, $8 + 6 = 2$. This is an example of modulo arithmetic in action.

In programming, we can use modulo calculations to deal with circumstances like these. For example, suppose we are creating a clock and we want to be able to add times together, without modulo arithmetic it would look something like this:

```
function naiveClockAdd (oldHours, oldMinutes, addHours, addMinutes)
    set newMinutes = oldMinutes + addMinutes
    repeat while newMinutes>60
        // drop the number of minutes by 60 and add another hour
        subtract 60 from newMinutes
        add 1 to addHours
    end repeat
    set newHours = oldHours + addHours
    repeat while newHours>12
        // drop 12s until we're in the range 1-12
        subtract 12 from newHours
    end repeat
    return array(newHours,newMinutes)
end function
```

Obviously, this isn't a particularly complicated function. But still, using modulo arithmetic we can simplify it substantially:

```
function cleverClockAdd (oldHours, oldMinutes, addHours, addMinutes)
    set newMinutes = strictModulo (oldMinutes + addMinutes, 60)
    add (oldMinutes + addMinutes - newMinutes) / 60 to addHours
    set newHours = 1+ strictModulo (oldHours + addHours - 1, 12)
    return array(newHours, newMinutes)
end function
```

These kinds of calculation take some getting used to, so we'll look at them in more detail. In the first line, we worked out the new minutes. These should be in the range 0–59. So we take the full number of new minutes (oldMinutes + addMinutes), and find their value modulo 60. In the next line, we work out how many hours were taken out in that calculation, and for this we use a trick: remember that strictModulo(n, m) is the remainder when n is divided by m. This means that n = a*m + strictModulo (n, m), for some a. So to find a, we can subtract strictModulo (n, m) from n and divide by m. In this case, a is the number of hours (multiples of 60 minutes). So we increase our addHours by this amount.

Although this method is often useful and so worth seeing, in this case it would be even simpler just to find a *as* floor(n/m).

NOTE

In the third line, we find the newHours. The only complication here is that the newHours need to be in the range 1–12, rather than 0–11 as strictModulo () would give us. To fix this we do something a bit sneaky. We subtract 1 from newHours before taking the modulo, which gives us the number 1 less than the true number of hours, in the range 0–11. Then adding the 1 back on gives us the true answer in the range we need.

Again, these calculations can be a little confusing. But most situations involving the modulo function tend to be variants on the three tricks we saw here.

1. Using mod(n,m) to reduce n to the range 0 to m − 1 (cycling through data)
2. Subtracting mod(n,m) from n to make n exactly divisible by m
3. Pre-subtracting or adding numbers from n before taking mod(n,m), then adding or subtracting them back to bring the value into a different range, especially 1 to m

Another example of this is when initializing large sets of data, especially when creating a grid. Suppose you have an array of $n \times m$ objects which are to represent a grid of squares n wide and m high. Each object knows its number in the array and wants to calculate its position in the grid. We can do this quickly with a modulo function:

```
function positionInGrid (squareNumber, numberOfColumns)
    set positionAcross to 1 + mod(squareNumber-1,numberOfColumns)
    set positionDown to (squareNumber—mod(squareNumber,
numberOfColumns)) / numberOfColumns
    return array(positionAcross, positionDown)
end function
```

PROPORTIONS, RATIOS, AND PERCENTAGES

Let's get back to fractions. One of the most powerful interpretations of a fraction is as a *ratio* between the numerator and denominator, and another is as a *percentage*. We'll look at these two concepts in this section.

Mapping Between Ranges of Values

"Ratio" (or *proportion*) actually means pretty much the same thing as "fraction," but is used in different circumstances, particularly when relating similar objects (*similar* here has a mathematical meaning as well as its normal English one, which we'll encounter in Chapter 5). We write ratios using the colon: the ratio 4:3, for example, is equivalent to the fraction $\frac{4}{3}$. Two objects are in the size ratio 4:3 if one is $\frac{4}{3}$ times the size of the other. We often use ratios to describe how we divide something up, so we might choose to divide a cake in the ratio 1:2, making one piece twice as big as the other. To do this, we use the fact that $\frac{1}{1+2}+\frac{2}{1+2}=\frac{1+2}{1+2} = 1$; that is, we divide the cake into two pieces, one $\frac{1}{3}$ the size, the other $\frac{2}{3}$ the size.

Ratios are most useful when dealing with scales of objects. If a piece of paper is 297 mm wide and 210 mm high (standard A4 size), then when we scale it to double size, its sides remain in the same proportion. This isn't surprising, because as we have seen, multiplying both the numerator and the denominator of a fraction by the same number leaves the fraction unchanged.

This fact is quite useful when scaling an object. If we know the initial ratio of the height to the width, then to calculate the height given the width, all we need to do is to multiply the new width by the same ratio:

```
function newHeight (originalWidth, originalHeight, newWidth)
    return newWidth * originalHeight / originalWidth
end function
```

You can also think about this the other way round: when scaling any object, every linear measure of the object (its diagonal, height, width, perimeter length, etc., but not area or volume) is multiplied by the same amount. So if you know the original value and new value of any one of these, every other dimension must be multiplied by the proportion of the new value to the old. So `newDiagonalLength = originalDiagonalLength * newHeight / originalHeight`, for example.

This fact makes it rather easy to create a mapping function between two rectangles. If you know the coordinates of a point in one rectangle, you can relate them to the equivalent point in the other rectangle by simply multiplying them by the same proportion. As we haven't covered coordinates yet, we won't go into this further here, but you might want to come back to it as an exercise later.

Incidentally, the A classification of paper sizes is chosen specifically so that when you cut a piece of paper in half horizontally (in portrait format), you get the next A-size up (see Figure 2.2). We can represent this algebraically as

$$\frac{aHeight}{aWidth} = \frac{aWidth}{(aHeight / 2)}$$

so $aHeight^2 = 2 \times aWidth^2$

so $\dfrac{aHeight}{aWidth} = \sqrt{2}$

So for each size of paper, the height is $\sqrt{2}$ = 1.414... times the width, or very close to it: $\left(\frac{297}{210}\right)^2 = 2.0002....$

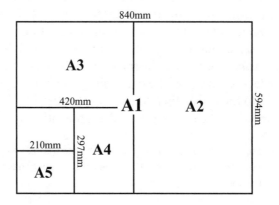

FIGURE 2.2 The A-series of paper sizes.

Another useful proportion is called the *golden ratio*, a favorite of mystical mathematicians and represented by the Greek letter Phi: φ. This is the proportion of a piece of paper such that if you cut a square-sized piece from one end, the remaining piece is in the same proportions as the original (see Figure 2.3). We won't do the algebra here (it's a neat little exercise if you want to practice your quadratic equations later), but it turns out that $\varphi = \frac{1+\sqrt{5}}{2} = 1.618....$

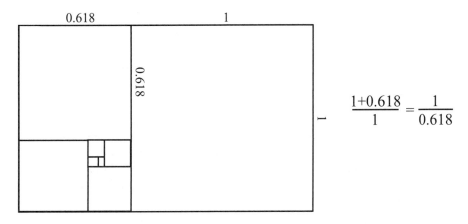

FIGURE 2.3   The Golden Ratio.

The ancient Greeks and other thinkers through the ages have ascribed all kinds of wonderful properties to φ, calling it the Divine Proportion, the Golden Mean and so on, and believing that when objects are placed on the canvas with such proportions they are the most aesthetically pleasing. Actually, recent psychological tests on the subject have shown that this isn't really true, and the proportion 1:sqrt(2), as with the A-series of paper sizes, is much closer to the most popular.

While we are on the subject of the golden ratio, it's appropriate to mention the Fibonacci Sequence. This is the sequence of numbers 1, 1, 2, 3, 5, 8, 13, 21, ... , where each number is the sum of the two previous numbers. This sequence crops up a lot in nature, for reasons that are most likely to do with optimal methods of growth. And as it happens, the ratio between successive terms of this sequence rapidly approaches φ. What is more, this happens with any sequence of numbers generated by the same rule as the Fibonacci sequence.

Making a Slider

Another common area where we use the notion of a proportion is when making a "slider": a graphical representation of a range of numbers. In the standard slider, we have a line representing the range of numbers we are looking at (say from 10 to 100) and a movable pointer representing the current value (see Figure 2.4).

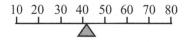

FIGURE 2.4   A standard slider.

To make a slider, we need to know four values: the position of each end of the line, and the maximum and minimum values they represent. For now we won't worry about what we mean by the "position" of the ends of the line (we'll look at coordinates later), just think of it as a number—say 100 for one end and 200 for the other.

On initializing the slider, you can quickly calculate its "intrinsic proportion" (not a standard term). You can think of this as the range of values represented by one unit of the slider, and we calculate it by finding the size of the total range divided by the total length of the slider.

$$intrinsicProportion = \frac{maxValue - minValue}{endPoint2 - endPoint1}$$

Now, to find the value represented by a particular point on the slider, we find how far it is along the slider, multiply that by the intrinsic proportion, and then add on the minimum value:

$$Value = (thisPoint - endPoint1) \times intrinsicProportion + minValue$$

Notice how similar this is to calculating proportions of a scaled piece of paper. Ultimately, it's the same process. You've created a virtual piece of paper whose width is the length of the slider, and whose height is the range of values represented. When we find a new point, we scale down to another rectangle with the new width, but in the same proportions. We just have to remember that our rectangle doesn't necessarily start at zero, so we have to add on our minimum value as well.

We can go the other way too. If we have a particular value we want to represent, we can find its position on the slider by finding its distance from the minimum value and *dividing* by the intrinsic proportion, then adding the endpoint:

$$newPoint = \frac{thisPoint - minValue}{intrinsicProportion} + endPoint1$$

If you have trouble working out which way round to make the calculation—divide or multiply—the easiest way to make sure is to plug in one of the end values and see what happens. Try setting *thisValue* to *minValue* in the first formula. You'll see that you get *newPoint* = 0 + *endPoint1*, which is the first endpoint. If we instead set *thisValue* to *maxValue*, we get

$$newPoint = \frac{maxValue - minValue}{intrinsicProportion} + endPoint1$$

Recall that dividing by a fraction is the same as multiplying by its reciprocal, so we have

$$newPoint = \left(maxValue - minValue\right) \times \frac{endPoint1 - endPoint2}{maxValue - minValue} + endPoint1$$

You can see that in this fraction, the (*maxValue – minValue*) terms cancel out, which gives us:

$$newPoint = endPoint2 - endPoint1 + endPoint1 = endPoint2$$

So this gives us the second endpoint. Try doing the same checks in the second formula.

Scrollbars are a special kind of slider which represent the position of a small image within a large one. The principle is the same as with the standard slider, but it is complicated by the fact that the small image may vary in size. Let's take, for example, the idea of a scrolling piece of text. If you know the height of the text in pixels, and the height of your scrolling window, then your scrollbar is a slider which represents the values between 0 (the topmost position) and *textHeight-windowHeight* (the bottommost position). These values represent the pixel location of the text at the top of your window. When the text is at position *textHeight-windowHeight*, then the bottom of the window, *windowHeight* pixels away, is at *textHeight*, the bottom of the text.

If you look at the scrollbars in standard windows, you see that they also resize the sliding marker within the bar, to represent how much of the image you can see. This proportion is given by *windowHeight / textHeight* (see Exercise 2.1).

Calculating Percentages

Percentages are yet another kind of fraction. The number 20% is nothing more or less than the fraction $\frac{20}{100}$ (the word "percent" means "per cent," or "per hundred"). Calculating with percentages is therefore a fairly straightforward extension of calculating with fractions, with the help of our English-to-Math translation skills.

1. 20% of 1000 is the same as 20/100 multiplied by 1000, which is 200.
2. 20% off 1000 is 1000 − 20% of 1000, which is 1000 − 200 = 800.
3. 20% more than 1000 is 1000 + 20% of 1000, which is 1000 + 200 = 1200.

These last two calculations can be simplified slightly by adding or subtracting the percentage from 100 first:

1. 20% off 1000 is 80% of 1000.
2. 20% more than 1000 is 120% of 1000.

Going the other way is just as simple. If an item is knocked down from $25 to $20, you can calculate the percentage decrease. The item has dropped by $5, which is $\frac{5}{25}$ of its original value. $\frac{5}{25} \times 100 = 20$, so this is a decrease of 20%.

Percentages only become complicated in the world of compound interest, such as when money is added to an account by a fixed percentage each year. If you have a bank account which pays 3% interest, and you put in $1000, how much will you have at the end of 10 years? You might think that it's just a matter of adding 3% of $1000, which is $30, each year, but of course at the end of the second year you don't have $1000 any more, but $1030, so the percentage is wrong; instead, you have to count the increase cumulatively.

The following, and similar lists in this section, are outputs from the mortgage calculating function. See Exercise 2.2 and the *mortgages* script in *math.cst* on the CD-ROM.

ON THE CD

```
At the end of year 1 you have 103% of $1000 = $1030
At the end of year 2 you have 103% of $1030.00 = $1060.90
At the end of year 3 you have 103% of $1060.90 = $1092.73
At the end of year 4 you have 103% of $1092.73 = $1125.51
At the end of year 5 you have 103% of $1125.51 = $1159.27
At the end of year 6 you have 103% of $1159.27 = $1194.05
At the end of year 7 you have 103% of $1194.05 = $1229.87
```

```
At the end of year 8 you have 103% of $1229.87 = $1266.77
At the end of year 9 you have 103% of $1266.77 = $1304.77
At the end of year 10 you have 103% of $1304.77 = $1343.92
```

Notice how quickly compound interest rises compared to just adding $30 each year—after 10 years you have earned $43.92 more than you would have done by adding $30 a year. This is a percentage increase of $\frac{43.92}{300} \times 100 = 14.64\%$—your earnings were nearly 15% higher than they would have been under simple interest. (Could you have done that calculation? If not, look back over the beginning of this section until you understand it.) The interest rises so much faster because it is an *exponential* growth (multiplying by the same amount each year) rather than a *linear* growth (adding the same amount each year). We'll look at this some more in a moment. For now just note that the above calculation can be summed up as:

After n months you have *initialCash* $\times$ *increase^n*, where increase is the percentage increase, given by $\frac{(100 + \text{interest})}{100}$, or $1 + \frac{\text{interest}}{100}$.

Interest on debts is similar, although loans such as mortgages are complicated further by the fact that you are paying off the debt as you go along. You may have seen the "mortgage calculators" you can use to enter the amount of mortgage, interest rate and years of payment. This is probably the most complicated type of percentage calculation, so let's give it a try. (Incidentally, we're describing here a particular kind of capital and repayment mortgage: the precise nature of mortgages varies from country to country and lender to lender.)

Let's start by working the other way round. Suppose you are paying a monthly amount of $1000 on a mortgage of $100000, at an interest rate of 5%. How long would it take to pay off the mortgage?

To start with, we have to convert the interest rate into a monthly form. Let's also make it a fraction so we don't have to worry about percentages. So the annual interest rate is $\frac{5}{100}$ or 0.05, and we divide this by 12 to get the monthly interest rate of 0.00417. Note that this already means that the true interest rate over the year is in fact *more* than 5%, because this is compound interest. The annual interest is $1.00417^{12} - 1 = 0.0511$, or 5.11%. Clever people, those bankers.

So at the end of each month, the debt is increased by 0.00417, that is, it is multiplied by 1.00417. After one month, this would be $100417. Then your payment is taken off the debt, so the current value of the loan is now $99417. Each month, you calculate:

$$newLoan = oldLoan \times 1.00417 - \$1000$$

So let's work it out in a table:

```
At the end of year 1 the loan is $92837.33
At the end of year 2 the loan is $85308.21
```

```
At the end of year 3 the loan is $77393.89
At the end of year 4 the loan is $69074.65
At the end of year 5 the loan is $60329.79
At the end of year 6 the loan is $51137.52
At the end of year 7 the loan is $41474.95
At the end of year 8 the loan is $31318.03
At the end of year 9 the loan is $20641.47
At the end of year 10 the loan is $9418.67
At the end of month 130 the loan is $0
```

So this mortgage took just over 10 years to pay off—and you paid back significantly more than your original loan: your total payment was $129628.96, nearly 30% more.

We can write the above as another formula, although the algebra is a lot more complicated:

$$debtAfterNMonths = initialAmount \times In - monthlyPayment \times (I^{n-1} + I^{n-2} + ... + I + 1)$$

where I is the monthly increase, given by $1 + \frac{annualInterest}{1200}$.

The sequence $I^{n-1} + I^{n-2} + ... + I + 1$ is a special case of what is called a *geometric progression*, and turns out to have a value of $\frac{I^n - 1}{I - 1}$, so the final formula is

$$debtAfterNMonths = initialAmount \times I^n - monthlyPayment \times \frac{I^n - 1}{I - 1}.$$

Suppose, as with a normal mortgage calculator, you want to calculate what monthly payment you will need to pay off the debt in a particular number of years, assuming a fixed interest rate. This means setting the amount of debt to 0 in the above formula, setting n to the correct number of months, and inverting the formula, which is a tricky algebraic exercise which we will not do here (but try it yourself after covering the Simplification section in the next chapter), and leads to:

$$monthlyPayment = initialAmount \times \frac{I - 1}{I^n - 1}, \text{ where } n = numberOfYears \times 12$$

Plug in the values of $100000 at 5% over 10 years, and we get a monthly payment of $1060.66, which is just what the online calculators will tell us.

EXPONENTIALS

We've used the power function several times already, and we said, only half-correctly, that it represents "multiplying a number by itself n times." This is all very well as far as it goes, but the power function is actually more complex than that.

Calculating with Powers

What does it mean to multiply a number by itself –0.3 times? It seems to make no sense, but if you try entering `power(2, -0.3)` the computer will spit the value 0.81 back at you quite happily. The idea of negative and fractional powers actually follows on quite quickly from the original definition. We'll start off slowly by asking some basic questions, then build up:

■ What is n^{p+q}?
   This means: multiply n by itself $(p + q)$ times, which is the same as multiplying it by itself p times and then multiplying the result by it q times. So $n^{p+q} = n^p \times n^q$

■ What is $n^{p \times q}$?
   This means: multiply n by itself $p \times q$ times, which is the same as multiplying it by itself p times, and doing that q times, which means $n^{p \times q} = (n^p)^q = (n^q)^p$

■ What is n^0?
   By the addition formula, we know that for any p, n^{0+p} must be equal to $n^0 \times n^p$. But $n^{0+p} = n^p$, so for any n, $n^0 = 1$

■ What is $(n \times m)^p$?
   This means: multiply $(n \times m)$ by itself p times, which is the same as multiplying n by itself p times and multiplying m by itself p times, then multiplying the results, which means that $(n \times m)^p = n^p \times m^p$

■ What is $(n^m)^p$?
   We saw this the other way round in the first example, but just to confirm, this means: Multiply n^m by itself p times, $n^m \times n^m \times ... \times n^m$, which by the first addition formula we know is equal to $n^{m \times p}$

■ What is n^{-p}?
   By the addition formula, we know that $n^{p-p} = n^p \times n^{-p}$. But $n^{p-p} = n^0 = 1$, so this means that $n^{-p} = \frac{1}{n^p}$

■ What is $n^{1/p}$?
   Take a look at $(n^{1/p})^p$. We know that this is equal to $n^{(1/p) \times p}$, which is equal to n^1, which is n. Therefore $n^{1/p}$ is the number such that when taken to the pth power it is equal to n, otherwise known as the pth *root* of n. So, for example, the square root, or second root, of n is equal to $n^{1/2}$.

So essentially the special definitions for negative or fractional powers follow on quite naturally from just trying to make them consistent with the definition for integer powers. In fact, you can define a power function for all kinds of things, including imaginary numbers, matrices and even functions themselves, but we're getting beyond ourselves.

One warning: Within the realm of real numbers, fractional powers of negative numbers tend to be a bit of a problem. We've already mentioned the fact that there is no square root of –1, but there *is* a cube root (which is also –1). In general, computers and calculators tend to avoid the problem by simply not letting you even try, so even if you were to try to take `power(-1,1/3.0)`, which does have an answer, it won't let you—and given that the computer has no native way to represent the exact fraction $\frac{1}{3}$, it makes sense. If you need to find the cube root (or any other root) of a negative number, find the root of its absolute value and check it:

```
function mthRoot (n, m)
    if n<0 then
        set p to power(-n, 1.0/m)
        if abs(power(-p, m)-n)<0.1 then return —p
        otherwise return "No such value"
    otherwise
        return power(n,1.0/m)
    end if
end function
```

Note that this function uses the trick of checking for closeness rather than equality of floats, to account for likely rounding errors.

The Number *e* and the `exp()` Function

Another word for power is *exponential*, which we encountered earlier. The word is used mostly to describe the behavior of powers in general, rather than any particular power—we speak of an "exponential function," a value "growing exponentially," and so on. When working with exponentials, you're likely to come across the number *e*, which is approximately 2.718. This number has a special property which we will see in a later chapter, but for now just think of it as a number. It happens to be equal to the infinite sum $\frac{1}{0!}+\frac{1}{1!}+\frac{1}{2!}+\frac{1}{3!}+\cdots$, as well as a lot of other rather pretty patterns. The exclamation points indicate the *factorial* function: $n! = 1 \times 2 \times \ldots \times n$, with 0! defined to be 1.

From a programmer's point of view, the number *e* is most likely to be encountered in the `exp()` function, where `exp(x)` equals e^x. To get the number *e* itself, just enter `exp(1)`. It's a kind of "standard" for exponentials.

NOTE

Don't confuse the number e *with the "exponential" notation we saw in Chapter 1, such as 1.53 e6. There "e" is just a label that tells us how many decimal places to shift. Mathematically, it's equivalent to multiplying the mantissa by a power of the current base—in this case, assuming we are in decimal, it is 1.53 × 10⁶.*

Exponential Functions in Real Life and Physics

Mary has a Russian Vine in her back garden, which increases in length by 20% every week. This week it is 1 m long. If it keeps growing at the same rate, how long will it be in a year's time?

You may recognize this problem as very similar to the mortgage calculations we looked at earlier in the chapter. As we saw then, any time that a value is multiplied by a constant increment over time, you will see very rapid changes. This is called *exponential growth*, and it's commonly encountered in real-world problems about growth of populations, organisms or economies.

After one week, Mary's vine is 1.2 m long. After two weeks, it is $1.2 \times 1.2 = 1.44$ m long. After 52 weeks it will be $1.2^{52} = 13104.63$ m long—over 13 km! This explains the reason for the term "population explosion": exponential growth is very, very fast, and even the smallest growth rate can add up to a lot. If it only increased by 5% every week, it would still reach over 12 m in a year.

When something is not growing but shrinking by a constant factor, you have *exponential decay*. This is most familiar from the area of radioactivity, where a radioactive element has a so-called "half-life," which is the length of time it takes for half of any particular sample to decay. Just as exponential growth is very fast, exponential decay is rather slow. In fact, in a sense, it is infinitely slow, because it will never finish altogether. If you keep multiplying a number by $\frac{1}{2}$, it will get smaller and smaller, but it will never reach zero (although it will get as close to it as you like—we say it *tends to a limit* of 0).

Radioactive decay is interesting because people often get the concept rather confused. When they speak of a radioactive element having a half-life of several hundred years, they forget that this means it is *not* very radioactive: it is decaying very slowly. It just means that the element will still be not very radioactive a long time from now. Conversely, very radioactive elements have a short half-life which means they are soon harmless, although they will cause more damage in the short term. The most dangerous elements are those with intermediate half-lives, such as strontium-90 with a half life around 30 years.

LOGARITHMS

The flip-side of the exponential function is the *logarithm*, a useful tool for dealing with very large numbers.

Calculating with Logarithms

A logarithm is the inverse of an exponential. If $a = b^c$ then we say $c = \log_b(a)$, which is said as "the *logarithm to base b* of a," or "log to base b of a." It is the power you have to raise b to in order to get the answer a.

Logarithms are generally available on the computer as one or more of the functions $\log_{10}(\ )$, sometimes referred to simply as `log()`; $\log_2(\ )$, usually `lg()`; and $\log_e(\ )$, often called `ln()` but also sometimes `log()`, which is supposed to stand for "natural logarithm." Your own programming language may vary in its terminology on these—Lingo, for example, has only one logarithm, to base e, which it calls `log()`. We only need one of these, for reasons we'll come to.

Most of the calculations with logarithms are direct counterparts of calculations with powers:

■ **$\log(a) + \log(b) = \log(a \times b)$ [to any base]**
Suppose $n^p = a$ and $n^q = b$, then $n^{p+q} = n^p \times n^q = a \times b$. So $\log(a \times b)$, and since $\log(a) = p$ and $\log(b) = q$, we have $\log(a) + \log(b)$ $p = \log(a \times b)$

■ **$k \times \log(a) = \log(a^k)$ [to any base]**
This follows fairly naturally from the previous result, but we can also derive it directly: suppose $n^p = a =$, then $a^k = (n^p)^k$. So $\log(a^k) = p \times k$, and since $p = \log(a)$, this means that $k \times \log(a) = \log(a^k)$.

■ **$\log^a(a) = 1$**
This is a simple consequence of the definition of a logarithm and the fact that $a^1 = a$.

■ **$\log_b(a) = \frac{1}{\log_a(b)}$**
This neat result follows from the previous two.
$\log_b(a) \times \log_a(b) = \log_a(b^{\log_b(a)})$ (substituting $\log_b(a)$ for k in the above formula). $b^{\log_b(a)}$ is simply a (by the definition of the logarithm), so $\log_b(a) \times \log_a(b) = \log_a(a) = 1$.

■ **$\log_a(n) \times \log_b(a) = \log_b(n)$.**
This is a more general case of the previous result, and comes from the same logic: $\log_a(n) \times \log_b(a) = \log_b(a^{\log_a(n)}) = \log_b(n)$

■ **$\log(1) = 0$ [to any base]**
Any number raised to the power 0 is equal to 1 (apart from zero, which is undefined).

■ **$\log(0) = ?$**
Actually, $\log(0)$ is undefined—you cannot raise a number (other than zero) to any power and get the answer 0. Your computer will probably spit out an error message if you try it.

The warnings that apply to fractional powers of negative numbers also apply here. The log function is not really well-defined over the negative numbers and should be avoided.

Using Logarithms to Simplify Calculations

Before the arrival of pocket calculators and computers, logarithms were one of the most important parts of a mathematician's repertoire. The fundamental tool was the *slide rule*, which showed two sets of numbers drawn in a logarithmic scale (see Figure 2.5).

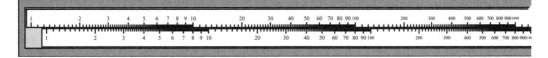

FIGURE 2.5   A slide rule. The lower scale can be slid backward and forward against the upper one to perform calculations.

What exactly is a logarithmic scale? If you look at Figure 2.5 you can see that the numbers are not spread evenly. They are bunched up at one end and more spread apart at the other. It is called a logarithmic scale because if you take the value at each point on the ruler and replace it with its own logarithm to some base, the resulting ruler is linear. Equivalently, a point n centimeters along the rule represents the value p^n, for some base p that depends on the scale.

If you measure the distance on the scale between, say, 1 and 10, it is the same as the distance between 10 and 100. In fact, this is the primary feature of a logarithmic scale: if $a = q \times b$ and $c = q \times d$ for some q, then the distance between a and b on the scale is the same as the distance between c and d. Compare this to the normal linear scale, which has the same property for addition instead of multiplication: if $a = q + b$ and $c = q + d$ then the distance between a and b is the same as the distance between c and d. Basically, a slide rule is to multiplication what a ruler is to addition.

This property is very useful because it means we can multiply two numbers together very quickly using the slide rule. If we want to multiply, say, 12.45 by 37.6, we find the point 12.45 on the top scale and slide the lower scale so that the inner 1 is matched to it (see Figure 2.6).

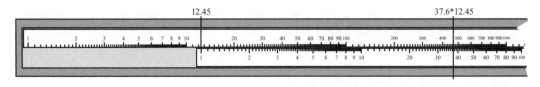

FIGURE 2.6   A slide rule in action.

Now we find the position of 37.6 on the lower scale and find the point which corresponds to it on the upper one (marked in the figure), which is 468.12, the correct product (obviously we can't be this accurate with a physical slide rule, but the concept is the same). This works because of the property we just saw: the distance between 1 and 37.6 on one scale is equal to the distance between 1×12.45 and 37.6×12.45 on the other. Can you see how this follows from the definition of the logarithm? See Exercise 2.3.

Using Logarithms to Deal with Large Numbers

Slide rules are no longer standard issue in classrooms, but the principle behind them remains very important, namely that logarithms are a very handy tool for dealing with large numbers. By applying a logarithm, you can bring enormously large numbers down to a more straightforward scale. As an illustration of this, consider that on a linear scale, the value 5000000 is a thousand times greater than 5000, whereas when working in the logarithmic base of 10, it is only three units greater.

This way of thinking is quite intuitively obvious—we have already used it when describing numbers in scientific notation. In the previous example, these would be represented in base 10 as 5 e6 and 5 e3, showing the linear scale of exponentials quite clearly. In fact, the word "base" for both the logarithmic scale and the base notation we looked at in Chapter 1 is a marker for how similar the two concepts are. As with the slide rule, it is a natural way of thinking when dealing with a multiplicative world instead of an additive one.

NOTE

As we will see in a later chapter, our ears do this too. Both volume and pitch are interpreted by our brains using a logarithmic scale: the C below middle C has a frequency half that of middle C, and the C above that has twice the frequency again, but we hear them as being the same "distance" apart.

In a more prosaic way, logarithms are useful in dealing with problems involving powers. Looking back at Mary's Russian Vine, which if you recall grows by 20% each week (i.e., each week its length is multiplied by 1.2), it's reasonable to ask how many weeks it will be before the vine is, for example, long enough to encircle the world. The Earth has a circumference of approximately 40,000 km, which means that we want to know how many times you have to multiply 1 m by 1.2 to get an answer of 40,000,000 m.

The circumference of the Earth has been known since the Greeks, and was first calculated accurately by Eratosthenes, creator of the Sieve of the same name. His calculation was extremely clever, but beyond the scope of this chapter. You might like to find it online once you have looked at Chapter 5.

This is a simple logarithmic calculation: we know that $1.2p = 40000000$, so $p = \log_{12}(40000000)$. Assuming we have a computer which can calculate logarithms to base e—the $\ln()$ function—we need to convert our base 1.2 calculation to the base of e. We can use our formulae to calculate this:

$$\log_{1.2}\left(40000000\right) = \log_{1.2}\left(e\right) \times \log_{e}\left(40000000\right)$$

$$= \frac{\log_{e}\left(40000000\right)}{\log_{e}\left(1.2\right)}$$

which is approximately 96 weeks: just under two years. To check the answer, find power(1.2,96), and see that the answer is 40000000 (or thereabouts) as desired.

EXERCISES

Exercise 2.1

Make a set of scrollbar functions for scrolling a long piece of text within a window.

Imagine that you have a piece of text and a window in which to display it. Write functions which will use the length of the text and the height of the window to calculate the position of the scrollbar given a location in the text, and vice versa, as well as the size of the scrolling element.

Exercise 2.2

Write a compound interest function.

The function should produce output similar to the examples in the text: You should be able to give it an amount of money and an interest rate, as well as an optional repayment value, and have it tell you the amount owed at the end of various periods of time.

Exercise 2.3

Write a slide rule function for calculating with large numbers.

Follow the description in the text to make a function which uses the same principles as the slide rule to multiply any two numbers. If you are feeling frisky, you could even include a nice graphical slider, too.

SUMMARY

In this chapter we have leaped around various more and less advanced areas of numerical mathematics to play with various techniques which are worth having in your mathematical toolkit. In the next chapter we will look at the second main area of basic mathematics, which is Algebra.

YOU SHOULD NOW KNOW

- how to make calculations with *fractions, ratios,* and *percentages*
- the concept of an *interest rate* and how it can be calculated
- the workings of the mod() function and how to use it to calculate with loops and integer divisions
- the concepts of *factor, prime number, GCD* and *LCM,* and how to use Euclid's Algorithm to calculate the GCD of two integers
- the meanings of *proportion* and *ratio,* and how to use them to map between values and sizes, and create a graphical representation of a range
- how to use *exponentials* and *logarithms* to deal with large numbers and multiplicative functions

3 Algebra

OVERVIEW

For our second chapter on fundamentals, we're going to take a high-speed look at the principles of algebra, which is the branch of mathematics that deals with *variables*. We'll start by looking at the basic principles of the subject, then look at specific techniques, including methods for visualizing equations and functions as graphs.

ON THE CD

Code samples from this chapter are implemented in *math.cst* in the script *Chapter 3 (equations)*. Additional functions related to the exercises can be found in the scripts *algebra* and *graphs*.

BASIC ALGEBRA

We will start the chapter by looking at the meaning of the main terminology. This will give us a solid starting point from which to work.

Variables, Parameters, and Constants

The principal ingredient for algebra is the *variable*. Variables in algebra are essentially the same as in programming: a variable is like a label that represents a quantity. You use it as a token, like a poker chip that represents a certain amount of money.

Variables come in various "flavors." Mathematically and computationally, they are all the same thing, but perceptually they are different.

- A constant is a value that is always the same—we have already encountered the constants e and ϕ, for example—not to mention the symbols "1," "2," and so on, which are also constants. You could define a constant—for example, you might say "define A as $\sqrt{2}+1$"—for ease of reference.
- A *parameter* is a value which is used to define a family of similar mathematical objects. For example, in the linear equation $y = m \times x + c$, which we will encounter later, the values m and c are parameters that define all the possible examples of this equation. Each choice of the parameters defines a particular equation in the two variables x and y.
- An *unknown* is a token which represents a particular value, but you don't know what it is. For example, if we know that x is a particular number, and that $x + 3 = 4$, then we can calculate the value of x.
- Finally, a *variable* proper is a label which represents something that could be any value we choose to give it (within a particular range of values). This is like an argument passed to a function in the computer. For example, we can write a computer function that calculates the cube root of some number n, and n in this function is a variable.

You'll notice that these terms are a little fuzzy. After all, in the equation $x + 3 = 4$, we called x an unknown, but it's also a constant: the value 1. Similarly, the word "constant" is also often used to refer to something which is really a parameter. And as we saw before, in terms of the algebra, they are essentially interchangeable (as long as you are reasonably careful).

The easiest way to think of these terms is as a hierarchy of variability. If you have an expression with a lot of letters, say $u + a \times t$, you can decide that one or more of these are "fixed," and the others are "variable." Those fixed terms might be called parameters. For a particular set of parameters you have a particular behavior for the variable terms. Then you might fix one of the parameters even more strongly and call it a constant. Each choice of a constant gives you a family of families. Finally, you can vary the constant to give you a family of families of families!

Expressions and Terms

When we have a mathematical combination of variables (and constants), we can call it an *expression.* For example, $(a \times x) + (x^2 \times 4) + 3$ is an expression using the variables a and x, and the constants 3 and 4. The constant 2 also appears, as an exponent, but this is only a shorthand for the expression $x \times x$.

NOTE

Mathematical expressions are evaluated in a standard order, which is generally the same as most computer languages: first, any expressions in brackets are evaluated recursively, then the other operators are evaluated in the sequence: divide, multiply, subtract, add. Thus the expression $1 + (2 \times 3 - 4) \times (-5 + 6)$ evaluates to $1 + 2 \times 1$, or 3. Expressions which are used as the numerators or denominators of fractions are considered to be in brackets.

It is convenient to group the expression into *terms.* A term is any sub-expression of the main expression which does not contain any additions or subtractions. In the above expression, if we consider x to be a variable and a to be a constant, then there are three terms, $a \times x$, $x^2 \times 4$, and 3. A term can contain any number of variables multiplied by a constant, which is called the *coefficient.* So in the term $x^2 \times 4$, 4 is the coefficient of x^2.

Terms can be classified according to the exponents of the variables within them. The terms $3 \times x^2$ and $-2 \times x^2$ are considered *like terms* because they both have the same exponent of the variable x, namely 2. $3 \times x^2$ and $3 \times x$ are not like terms, because they contain different powers of x. Two terms are alike if they only differ by their coefficient.

Incidentally, now seems as good a time as any to introduce one piece of notation we have been avoiding up to now for clarity. When two or more values are written next to one another (as in the expressions $2x$ or $p(1 + q)$, this means the product of the two values. As a general rule, a coefficient is always written before the variables ($2x$, not $x2$) and terms outside brackets are generally written first ($p(1 + q)$, not $(1 + q)p$). A term is usually written as a single string without multiplication signs, so the above expression $a \times x + x^2 \times 4 + 3$ would normally be written as $ax + 4x^2 + 3$. This allows us easily to classify the terms visually according to the exponents of their variables ("the x term," "the x^2 term," "the xz term," and so on).

Functions

A *function* in mathematics, as with the word "variable," is much the same as in programming: it is like a machine into which you feed one or more numbers to get an answer. Most functions that you will encounter in math will have a single value as an answer, but this output can be a vector, a variable, or even another function. Formally, a function is a *map*, which takes values from one set called its *domain* (say, the real numbers $\mathbb{R}$) and transforms them into values from the same or another set, called its *range* (say, the integers $\mathbb{Z}$). The `floor()` function, for example, does just that: feed it any real number and it returns an integer. You can also have Boolean functions, which map their input to just two values 0 and 1—for example the `isPrime()` function might return 1 if the input is a prime number and 0 otherwise. In typed computer languages, you generally need to specify in advance both the possible input values of a function ("This function requires an integer argument") and the type of output ("This function returns a floating-point value"). This requirement formalizes the fundamental nature of functions.

Many mathematical functions have their own symbols—for example, we have already seen the $\sqrt{}$ symbol representing the `sqrt()` function. Others are written using the same notation we use for program functions: `sin()`, `cos()`, etc., which we will meet in the next chapter. And still others are written simply as expressions, such as the function $x^2 + 2$. We might define such a function formally like this:

$$squarePlusTwo(x\colon \mathbb{R} \to \mathbb{R}) = x^2 + 2$$

The $\mathbb{R} \to \mathbb{R}$ part of this formulation is required in a formal definition, just as it is in a typed programming language, but we won't include it from now on unless it's particularly necessary. In this case, all it means is that both the input and output of the function will be a real number.

We could, in fact, replace the second $\mathbb{R}$ with an $\mathbb{R}^+$, signifying the set of positive real numbers, since we know that the output of the function is always positive—and even more accurately, we could say that the range of the function is the set [2, ∞], which is a notation for the set of real numbers from 2 to infinity (including 2). In that case, the function maps to the whole of the range.

If we have a function f(x), and there are no two distinct input values a and b in its domain such that f(a) = f(b), then we call the function *one-to-one*, and there is an *inverse* function f' such that for every a in the function's complete domain, f'(f(a)) = a. For example, the cube function $x \to x^3$ is one-to-one, but the square function $x \to x^2$ is only one-to-one when considered over the domain of positive real numbers. A function for which at least some values in the domain map to the same value in the range is called *many-to-one*.

Some functions, such as the mathematical square root function, are *multi-valued*, which means that there is at least one value in the range which can map to more than one value in the domain. So we know that both 1 and −1 are square roots of 1. The multivalued functions we regularly deal with are usually the "inverses" of a many-to-one function, as in this case. Strictly speaking, these are not functions at all, but (as a shorthand) it is useful to refer to them this way. Note that it is impossible for a self-contained *computer* function to be multivalued (assuming it doesn't contain any random numbers or similar oddities)—the computer sqrt() function is a regular one-to-one function from $\mathbb{R}^+$ to $\mathbb{R}^+$, which always returns the positive square root.

A *polynomial* is a particular kind of function of the form $x \rightarrow a_0 + a_1x + a_2x^2 + a_3x^3 + ... + a_nx^n$ where the values a_0, a_1, a_2, etc. are all real numbers. So the function $x \rightarrow 2x + 1$ is a polynomial (it is called a *linear* or *first-degree* polynomial because the highest power of x is 1), as is the function $x \rightarrow 2 - x + 3x^2$ (which is a *quadratic* or *second-degree* polynomial because the highest power of x is 2). It is also possible to have polynomials in more than one variable, such as $x \rightarrow x^2 + 2xy + y^2$.

If we have a function f(x), then we refer to the value f(5) as the result of *substituting* 5 for x in the function. So, for example, the result of substituting 3 for x in the function $x \rightarrow x(x + 2)$ is the value $3 \times (3 + 2) = 3 \times 5 = 15$.

We have been quite formal in using the word "function" here, but from now on we will often refer to an expression such as x² + 1 *as a function, rather than using the mapping notation* x → x² + 1.

NOTE

Equations, Formulas, and Inequalities

An *equation* is like a mathematical sentence. It states that one expression is equal to another. So $1 = 1$ is a simple (and rather obvious) equation, and so is $2 + 2 = 4$. Generally, though, we use the term to refer to a sentence which includes a variable of some sort, such as $x + 2 = 5$. This is a sentence which tells us a fact about the unknown x. Actually, in this case it tells us enough about it that if we know the equation is true, we can deduce what the value of x must be $x = 3$.

This process of deduction is the main focus of elementary algebra, and we'll look at it properly in a moment. The main thing to look at here is the difference between a function, an expression and an equation. A function is like a phrase with blanks in it—something like "the __ with big __ s." An expression fills in the blanks with dummy variables: "the jabberwock with big vorpals." An equation then tells us something about this expression by relating it to another: "the jabberwock with big vorpals is a jubjub."

Of all of these, only an equation can be true or false. In this case, we don't know whether it is true or not, because we don't know what a jabberwock, a vorpal or a jubjub are. But if the sentence was "a jabberwock is a jabberwock," then we know it is true, whatever a jabberwock turns out to be. This kind of equation is called a *tautology*—for example, $x + 2 = x + 3 - 1$ is a tautology because it is true no matter what the value of x is. The equation $x + 1 = 2$ is not a tautology. If $x = 1$, then the equation is true. If x is any other value, then it is false. This is just as in programming: if you are working with a variable x, and you have the line if x + 2 = 3, then the program will execute the next line if and only if x = 1, that is, if the equation is true. Conversely, if we know the equation is true, then we know the value of x must be 1.

A *formula* is an equation with more than one variable, which defines one variable in terms of others. So $v = u + at$ is a formula which defines the value v in terms of the variables u, a and t. This is just a terminological distinction, though—formulas and equations can be treated identically. Formulas are most often used to express relationships between physical values, such as "*distance = speed × time.*"

An *inequality* is like an equation, but tells us something other than that the two equations are equal. It might say that one expression is less than the other ($x + 1 < x + 2$ is a tautological inequality, which is always true no matter what the value of x), or it might say one is greater than the other ($x + 1 > y$ is an inequality which may or may not be true, depending on the values of x and y), or it might simply say they are not the same, for which in computing we may say x != y or x <> y, but which mathematically is usually written $x \neq y$. Other symbols are $\leq$ and $\geq$, representing "less than or equal to" and "greater than or equal to" respectively, and $\approx$, meaning "approximately equal to," as well as $\equiv$, "congruent to," which we encountered in Chapter 2. The latter two are not generally referred to as inequalities, but neutrally as *statements*.

WORKING WITH EQUATIONS

The main reason for using algebra is because it allows you to make deductions about unknown quantities by manipulating them as symbols rather than calculating with them directly. We will now look at the primary techniques involved in this.

Balancing Equations

This is something of a cliché, but an equation is like a set of pan scales. If you know that a pair of scales balances, then you know that if you add or take away the same amount from each pan, the scales will still balance. The same is true of an equation. The two expressions on each side of the equal sign are equal by definition. So if you add the same value to both, they will still be equal. In fact, you can perform any non-multivalued function to both sides of an equation and it will remain true.

Why specify that the function must not be multivalued? Imagine that we have the equation $a^2 = b^2$. It is tempting to take the square root of both sides of the equation, yielding $a = b$, but this is not necessarily true—for example, if $a = 2$ and $b = -2$, then the first equation is true but the second is not. This is because the function $x \rightarrow \sqrt{x}$ is multivalued: two distinct values in its domain can map to the same value in the range. All we can say with safety is that $a = \pm b$, where the $\pm$ symbol means "plus or minus."

The process of *solving* an equation in an unknown involves performing operations on both sides of the equation in order to find the value of the unknown. The most general equation is something like $f(x) = g(x)$ for some functions f and g. If you subtract $g(x)$ from both sides of the equation, you have $f(x) - g(x) = 0$, and we can describe this as a new function $q(x)$, where $q(x) = f(x) - g(x)$. So solving an equation, in its simplest terms, is trying to find the inverse of the function q at 0.

Let's look at an example of solving an equation to make this less theoretical: Suppose the equation is $2x + 3 = 7$.

Here, the left-hand side of the equation has two terms, one containing x, the other a constant. So we can begin by subtracting the constant from both sides:

$$2x + 3 = 7$$
$$2x + 3 - 3 = 7 - 3$$
$$2x = 4$$

Now we have an equation with one term on each side, the left-hand side a multiple 2 of x, and the right-hand side a constant 4. So let's divide both sides by 2 to isolate the value of x:

$$2x = 4$$
$$\frac{2x}{2} = \frac{4}{2}$$
$$x = 2$$

By this process we have found the value of x, which is 2. And if we check it, we find that $2 \times 2 + 3$ is indeed equal to 7.

As we saw above, we could think of this differently in terms of functions. We have a function $x \rightarrow 2x + 3$ which we are trying to invert. The function is a process of multiplying by 2 and then adding 3, so the inverse is a process of subtracting 3 and then dividing by 2 (the reverse steps, in the reverse order). So the inverse function is $x \rightarrow (x - 3)/2$. If we apply this function to both sides of our equation, the left-hand side maps to x (by the construction of the inverse function) and the right-hand side maps to . Of course, we are doing the same thing here as we did above, but the thinking behind it is a little different.

Simplification

It isn't always so easy to solve an equation by this process. If you have an equation like $\frac{x+1}{2(x-1)-3(2-x)-x} = 3x - 8$, you have a bit of work to do before you can isolate the value of x. This process is called *simplification*, and it essentially consists of reorganizing an equation (or function) so that it is in a simpler form. What is "simple" of course may depend on the circumstances, but there are a few processes which tend to be useful.

1. Group "like terms" together (recall our earlier discussion of like terms, essentially, they are terms which contain the same combination of variables, differing only by the coefficient). We can add like terms together, so for example, $2x + 3x = 5x$

2. Use the techniques we covered in the last chapter to simplify fractions, such as cross-multiplication. So for example, $\frac{x}{x+1} + \frac{x+2}{x+3}$ can be simplified to $\frac{x(x+3)+(x+2)(x+1)}{(x+1)(x+3)}$. This may look scary, but it is exactly the same process as in $\frac{4}{5} + \frac{6}{7} = \frac{4 \times 7 + 6 \times 5}{5 \times 7}$, as you will see if you substitute 4 for x in the above equation.

3. If you have a fraction on one side of the equation, multiply both sides of the equation by the denominator in order to remove it. So $\frac{x}{x+1} = 2$ becomes $x = 2(x+1)$

4. Multiply out brackets. If we have a product of one element with an expression in brackets, we can simplify this (in a sense) by turning it into a single expression, multiplying the outside element by each element inside the expression. Here are a few examples of this:

$$2(x+3) = 2 \times x + 2 \times 3$$
$$= 2x + 6$$

$$3x(2 - x + 4x^2) = 3x \times 2 - 3x \times x + 3x \times 4x^2$$
$$= 6x - 3x^2 + 12x^3$$

$$5 - 2(2x + 1) = 5 - 2 \times 2x - 2 \times 1$$
$$= 5 - 4x - 2$$

You might be confused in the third of these examples by the final minus sign. When multiplying a bracket by a negative number, the negativity applies to all values inside the bracket. So in the above case, the whole bracket has been multiplied by the value (–2). If this is still hard to understand, imagine that the original expression had been written as 5 + (–2) × (2x + 1), which means **the** same thing but should make it clearer.

You can also multiply two brackets together. You could do this simply by splitting it into two steps:

$$\begin{aligned}(x-2)(2x+3) &= (x-2)\times 2x + (x-2)\times 3 \\ &= 2x(x-2)+3(x-2) \\ &= 2x\times x - 2x\times 2 + 3\times x - 3\times 2 \\ &= 2x^2 - 4x + 3x - 6 \\ &= 2x^2 - x - 6\end{aligned}$$

Alternatively you can do the whole thing in a single process by taking all possible combinations of one value from each bracket:

$$\begin{aligned}(x-2)(2x+3) &= x\times 2x - 2\times 2x + x\times 3 - 2\times 3 \\ &= 2x^2 - 4x + 3x - 6 \\ &= 2x^2 - x - 6\end{aligned}$$

Of course, this is just the same as before, missing out the first two lines, but it's much quicker, especially when multiplying three or more brackets.

If you spot an expression which crops up a lot, you might be able to transform the equation into another form by defining a new variable. This is quite an obscure technique, but often useful in complicated circumstances.

For example, suppose we want to solve the equation $4x^4 - 9 = 0$, and we don't have a calculator to hand, we might notice that $4x^4 = (2x^2)^2$, so we could define a new variable p by $p = 2x^2$. Then $4x^4 = p^2$, so we have $p^2 - 9 = 0$, or $p^2 = 9$. The square root of 9 is 3, so $p = \pm 3$.

Now to find x, we simply substitute back into our definition: $p = 2x^2$, so $2x^2 = \pm 3$. We know that $2x^2$ must be positive, so we can ignore the negative square root of p, so $2x^2 = 3$, which means that $x = \pm\sqrt{\frac{3}{2}}$. As we said above, this is a difficult technique to use successfully, so don't worry about it too much, but we will encounter it on occasion, as with solving cubics later in this chapter.

Let's finish by looking again at the equation with which we began this section and trying to solve it with these techniques.

$$\frac{x+1}{2(x-1)-3(2-x)-x} = 3x-8$$

We'll start by simplifying the denominator, first by multiplying out the brackets:

$$\frac{x+1}{2x-2-6+3x-x} = 3x-8$$

(Notice that $(-3)\times(-x)=+3x$.) Now we can combine like terms in the denominator:

$$\frac{x+1}{2x+3x-x-2-6} = 3x-8$$

$$\frac{x+1}{4x-8} = 3x-8$$

And then we can clean up that awkward fraction, by multiplying both sides of the equation by the denominator. This gives us:

$$x+1=(3x-8)(4x-8)$$

Now we multiply out the brackets on the right-hand side to get:

$$x+1=(3x-8)(4x-8)$$
$$=12x^2-32x-24x+64$$
$$=12x^2-56x+64$$

And finally we can bring the terms from the left-hand side to the right-hand side and simplify again:

$$x+1=12x^2-56x+64$$
$$0=12x^2-56x+64-x-1$$
$$12x^2-57x+63=0$$

We'll come back to this equation shortly. Incidentally, in the last line you may be wondering why we switched the sides of the equation over. It's traditional, when we have an equation with a constant on one side, to put the constant on the right, for the same reason that we feel more comfortable saying "Patch is a dog" than "a dog is Patch."

Factorization and Solving Quadratic Equations

Another "simplification" technique goes in almost the opposite direction. Rather than multiplying brackets out to get the expression in full, it tries to simplify the expression by finding common factors, rather like we simplified our addition of fractions by finding the gcd() of the denominators. Just as when working with plain numbers, this is called *factorization*.

In general, it's best to leave factorization until you have already gone through the simplification process discussed in the previous section, with all the like terms joined together and no fractions with variables in the denominator. When working with an equation, it is often a good idea to move all the terms over to one side, giving you an equation of the form $f(x) = 0$, for some function f. Factorization, strictly speaking, is an operation to perform on functions (expressions) rather than equations.

Now, what you can do is to look at your function and try to find any *common factors* between the terms. For example, in the expression $6x^2 - 15x + 9$, all the terms have a factor of 3. We can take this factor of 3 out as a separate term, to get $3(2x^2 - 5x + 3)$.

Another example is the expression $x^2 - 4x$. Here, both terms have a factor of x. As before, we factorize the expression on the left-hand side of the equation by turning it into a product of the factor x and an expression in brackets. To do this, we first write down x, and then we write down, in brackets, the value of $x^2 - 4x$ divided by x. This gives us $x(x - 4)$.

NOTE

If this isn't clear, try multiplying the brackets out again to see what you end up with—essentially it is the same process as in the previous case, but with a factor of x instead of the number 3.

We can use the factorized version of our functions to make it easier to solve equations. If we have $3(2x^2 - 5x + 3) = 0$, for example, we can divide both sides by 3 to get a simpler equation $2x^2 - 5x + 3 = 0$. And if we have $x(x - 4) = 0$, then we have two unknown numbers (x and $x - 4$) whose product is zero, and if the product of two numbers is zero, we know that either one number or the other must be zero. This means that we have either $x = 0$ or $x - 4 = 0$, so x is either 0 or 4.

Let's try a few more examples.

■ $12x^3 + 8x^2$ has a common factor of $4x^2$, because 4 is a factor of both 12 and 8, and x^2 is a factor of both itself and x^3. So we take this factor out to the front to get the expression $4x^2(3x + 2)$.

■ $-2x - 3x^2$ has a common factor of $-x$. Remember that a negative number divided by a negative number is positive, so when we factorize we get $-x(2 + 3x)$.

■ $2xy^2z + 4x^2yz$ has a common factor of $2xyz$. Factorizing, we get $2xyz(y + 2x)$.

■ $\frac{x}{2} - \frac{x^2}{4}$ has a common factor of $\frac{x}{4}$. You could think of it as a two-stage process, first of simplification: $\frac{x}{2} - \frac{x^2}{4} = \frac{2x - x^2}{4}$, and then of factorization: $\frac{x(2 - x)}{4}$—alternatively, you might just notice the common factor straightaway. Either way, the end result is the same.

It is not only plain terms which can be factors, whole expressions can also be taken as factors. For example, in the expression $x(x + 1) + 3(x + 1)$, the expression $(x + 1)$ is a common factor, so the expression can be factorized to $(x + 1)(x + 3)$. Of course, if you had followed the earlier advice, you might already have multiplied out the brackets and joined the like terms, to get something like $x^2 + 4x + 3$. Fortunately there are techniques for finding common factors even in these circumstances.

Recall that the expression $x^2 + 4x + 3$ is a *quadratic* in x. A quadratic is any expression of the form $ax^2 + bx + c$. If a quadratic expression can be factorized, it will take the form $(px + n)(qx + m)$, although the numbers a, b, p and q might not be particularly useful.

In fact, we can simplify this a little, since we can always multiply one bracket by any constant (other than 0) and divide the other by the same constant to leave the end product the same, so we can choose to say that $q = 1$, giving $ax^2 + bx + c = (px + n)(x + m)$.

If you multiply out the expression on the right-hand side, you have the following equation:

$$ax^2 + bx + c = px^2 + pmx + nx + nm$$
$$= px^2 + (pm + n)x + nm$$

Now, remember that in this equation, x is a variable, while a, b, and c are parameters. This means that the equation is supposed to be true for *any* possible value of x, given a particular a, b, and c. In order for this to be the case, each of the terms in x must match. So this means that we have:

$ax^2 = px^2$, so $a = p$.

$(pm + n)x = bx$, so $b = am + n$ (since $a = p$)

$nm = c$

Let's look the simplest case, where $a = 1$, so we have $x^2 + bx + c$. In that case, we have $n + m = b$ and $nm = c$, which means that n and m are two numbers whose product is c and whose sum is b.

How can you find these numbers? Well, you can often do it by inspection, as in these examples:

- $x^2 + 4x + 3$. $b = 4; c = 3$, so we need numbers whose product is 3 and whose sum is 4—the answer is 1 and 3. So the expression factorizes to $(x+1)(x+3)$. Note that this is the same as we had above.
- $x^2 + 3x - 4$. $b = 3; c = -4$, so we need numbers whose product is -4 and whose sum is 3, which are 4 and -1. So the expression factorizes to $(x+4)(x-1)$.
- $x^2 - 5x + 6$. $b = -5; c = 6$, so we need numbers whose product is 6 and whose sum is -5, which are -2 and -3. So the expression factorizes to $(x-2)(x-3)$.
- $x^2 - 5x - 6$. $b = -5; c = -6$, so we need numbers whose product is -6 and whose sum is -5, which are -6 and 1. So the expression factorizes to $(x-6)(x+1)$.

Notice that the numbers you are looking for vary according to the sign of the numbers b and c. In the last two examples, the absolute values of b and c are the same, but because the sign of c is different, the answer is changed significantly.

Can we always find numbers n and m satisfying this requirement? Actually, no. For example, if $b = 1$ and $c = 1$, then there is no pair of numbers whose sum and product are both 1. As a general rule, you can only factorize a quadratic expression as long as $b^2 \geq 4ac$. We'll see why shortly.

What if a is not equal to 1? In that case, the equations are slightly different:

$$b = am + n$$

$$nm = c, \text{ so } amn = ac$$

So you are looking for two values am and n, whose sum is b and whose product is ac. The technique remains much the same—but of course, once you have found am, you need to divide it by a to find m.

For example, let's look at the equation we saw at the end of the previous section: $12x^2 - 57x + 63 = 0$. We can start by dividing the whole equation by 3, which is a common factor, to get $4x^2 - 19x + 21 = 0$. For this equation, $b = -19$, and $ac = 4 \times 21 = 84$. So we are looking for two numbers whose product is 84 and whose sum is -19. The numbers are -7 and -12. We can choose either one of these to be n and am, but since $a = 4$, which is a factor of 12, it makes sense to choose $n = -7$, and $m = -3$, so we don't have to use fractions. This gives us finally $4x^2 - 19x + 21 = (4x - 7)(x - 3)$. And since we know this product is zero, we know that either $x - 3 = 0$ or $4x - 7 = 0$, which means that either $x = 3$ or $x = \frac{7}{4}$. Try substituting either of these values into the original equation and see if it evaluates correctly to 0.

It turns out that by using a special technique called *completing the square* you can in fact solve quadratic equations using a single formula, thus making all this effort slightly unnecessary. The formula is $x = \frac{-b \pm \sqrt{b^2 - 4ac}}{2a}$. Notice that if $b^2 < 4ac$ then the value under the square root sign (called the *discriminant*) is negative, which is why there is no real solution for x in these circumstances. Otherwise, this gives you two values for x, one using the positive square root, the other using the negative. If $b^2 = 4ac$ then the quadratic equation is an exact square, and so there is only one solution for x, which occurs twice—as in $x^2 - 6x + 9$, which factorizes to $(x-3)(x-3)$ or $(x-3)^2$.

Incidentally, one special kind of quadratic expression is the *difference of two squares*, such as $x^2 - 25$. This has a rather neat factorization, which is $(x-5)(x+5)$, and gives a useful trick for lightning calculation: If you want to multiply two numbers which differ by a small amount, you can do it by squaring the average of the two numbers and subtracting the square of half the difference. For example, $202 \times 198 = (200 + 2) \times (200 - 2)$.

Solving Cubic Equations

It's possible to solve higher-degree polynomials too, although it involves a little more work. Just as with quadratic equations, we can find a solution to the cubic equation $Ax^3 + Bx^2 + Cx + D = 0$. A cubic function always has at least one *root* (value x such that f(x) = 0), and can have up to three. To find them, the trick is to find a simpler quadratic equation that we can solve using the above method as a half-way stage.

The first stage is to divide the above equation by A to obtain a simpler equation $x^3 + ax^2 + bx + c = 0$. Then we make a *substitution*, replacing the variable x with a new variable t such that $t = x + \frac{a}{3}$. This gives a new cubic equation with no quadratic term:

$$t^3 + 3pt + 2q = 0, \text{ where } p = \frac{b}{3} - \frac{a^2}{9} \text{ and } q = \frac{a^3}{27} - \frac{ab}{6} + \frac{c}{2}.$$

As before, the key to solving this cubic is the *discriminant D*, where $D = p^3 + q^2$.

- If $D > 0$, then the equation has exactly one real root, the value $r + s$, where $r = \sqrt[3]{-q + \sqrt{D}}$ and $s = \sqrt[3]{-q - \sqrt{D}}$.
- If $D = 0$, then the equation has two roots, $2 \times \sqrt[3]{-q}$ and $-\sqrt[3]{-q}$ (a double root).
- If $D < 0$, then we can find the three roots by using a trigonometric function. We won't look at these until the next chapter, but for reference, the roots are given by

$$t = 2\sqrt{-p}\cos\theta, \text{ where } \frac{1}{3}\left(\cos^{-1}\left(\frac{-q}{\sqrt{-p^3}}\right) - 2\pi k\right) \text{ for } k = 0, 1 \text{ or } -1$$

Having found values for t, we can then transform these into values for x by taking $x = t - \frac{a}{3}$ again.

As you can see, this process is much more complicated, but bearable. Here it is as a function:

```
function solveCubic(a,b,c,d)
    // d is the coefficient of the cubic term, the default being 1
    if d is defined then divide a, b and c by d
    set p to b/3 - a*a/9
    set q to a*a*a/27-a*b/6 + c/2
    set disc to p*p*p + q*q
    if disc>=0 then
        set r to cubeRoot(-q+sqrt(disc))
        if disc=0 then set ret to [2*r, -r]
        otherwise
            set s to cubeRoot(-q-sqrt(disc))
            set ret to [r+s]
        end if
    otherwise
        set ang to acos(-q/sqrt(-p*p*p))
        set r to 2*sqrt(-p)
        set ret to an empty array
        repeat for k=-1 to 1
            set theta to (ang-2*pi*k)/3
            append r*cos(theta) to ret
        end repeat
    end if
    subtract a/3 from each element of ret
    return ret
end function
```

This algorithm is adapted from the method described in Mathematics for 3D Game Programming *(Lengyel), which is a particularly elegant formulation. Other methods that may seem to involve fewer miracles can be found on the Web, but tend to require a knowledge of complex numbers.*

A similar process can be used to solve quartic (4th-degree) equations, but we won't worry about that here. If you're not familiar with the trigonometric functions yet, we'll look at them much more in the next chapter and beyond.

Solving Simultaneous Equations by Substitution

If you have more than one unknown in an equation, it is not generally possible to determine them both. For example, if $x + y = 5$ then x could be 1 and y could be 4, or x could be 10 and y could be –5, or an infinite number of other combinations. However, if you have some more information, such as another equation, it may be possible to find both unknowns. In general, if you have n unknowns, then you need n independent equations to find them (where by *independent* we mean that none of the equations can be deduced from the others). Fewer than n equations will not give you enough information, and more than n may give you too much, so that you can't solve the equations consistently.

A set of equations with the same unknowns is called a set of *simultaneous equations*. Let's look at how you might solve a simple pair of simultaneous equations in two unknowns first, then look at more general methods.

Suppose we have these two equations:

1. $x + 3y = 10$
2. $5x - 2y = -1$

There are several ways to solve this, which as usual amount to much the same thing, but are useful in different situations. The first is by *substitution*: we use one equation to find the value of one unknown as a function of the other (essentially a formula), and then substitute that value into the second. In this case, if we rearrange equation 1 we get $x = 10 - 3y$. If we then substitute this value into equation 2, we get

$$5(10 - 3y) - 2y = -1$$
$$50 - 15y - 2y = -1$$
$$-17y = -51$$
$$y = 3$$

This process is called *eliminating x*—we use one equation in order to make a new equation for y that doesn't involve x. Having found the value of y, we can now use our function for x: $x = 10 - 3y = 10 - 9 = 1$. And if we substitute these values for x and y back into equation 2, we get $5x - 2y = 5 - 6 = -1$, just as we needed.

This method is most useful when dealing with *non-linear* equations—those involving terms such as x^2, y^2 or xy. Let's do a difficult example, just to prove that we can (don't worry if you have trouble following this, it's much more advanced than the other examples we've looked at so far). Look at this pair of equations:

1. $3x + 2xy = 7$
2. $2x + 5y - y^2 = 8$

If we look at the first equation, we can factorize the left-hand side to get $x(3+2y) = 7$, which means that $x = \frac{7}{3+2y}$. We can now substitute this value into the second equation:

$$2\left(\frac{7}{3+2y}\right) + 5y - y^2 = 8$$

$$\frac{14 + 5y(3+2y) - y^2(3+2y)}{3+2y} = 8$$

$$14 + 5y(3+2y) - y^2(3+2y) = 8\big(3+2y\big)$$

$$14 + 15y + 10y^2 - 3y^2 - 2y^3 = 24 + 16y$$

$$0 = 2y^3 - 7y^2 + y + 10$$

This is a *cubic* equation, which we know how to solve, but fortunately in this case there is a simple answer which you can see by inspection: if you substitute the value $y = -1$ into the expression on the right, you do in fact get the answer 0. So this means that the expression $(y+1)$ must be a factor. (This is an example of a general theorem which says that if a is a *root* of a function f(x), which is to say a value such that f(a) = 0, then $(x - a)$ is a factor of the function.)

To factorize a polynomial expression when you know one of the factors is quite a simple task. You just take it one step at a time: You know that $2y^3 - 7y^2 + y + 10 = (y+1)(...)$, for some expression inside the brackets. The first term in the brackets must be $2y^2$, so that the first term when expanded will be $2y^3$. This means that the factorization must be $(y+1)(2y^2 + ...)$. If you try expanding this tentative expression, you get $2y^3 + 2y^2 + ...$, but the term in y^2 should actually be $-7y^2$. So we need another term of $-9y^2$ to make up the difference. This means that we now have the tentative factorization $(y+1)(2y^2 - 9y + ...)$. Again, expand this expression to get $2y^3 - 7y^2 - 9y + ...$ Now we need to match the coefficient of y, which should be 1. To get this, we need to add another $10y$ to the answer, which means our final factorization is $(y+1)(2y^2 - 9y + 10)$. When we multiply out these brackets, we get the answer we were looking for.

Now we have a quadratic function, and we can factorize this as before: we need two numbers whose product is 20 and whose sum is –9, which are –5 and –4. This gives us a final factorization of $(y+1)(y-2)(2y-5)$—if you don't follow that step, go back to the section on factorization, as you should be able to factorize a quadratic equation by now.

We are almost there! From the above factorization of the cubic equation, we now know that there are three possible values for y: $y = -1$, $y = 2$ or $y = \frac{5}{2}$. For each of these values, we can now substitute back into equation 1, to get three possible pairs of values x and y: $(7, -1), (1, 2)$, or $(\frac{7}{8}, \frac{5}{2})$. Substituting any of these pairs into equation 2 will give you the answer 8.

Exhausted? That is not surprising, since this was a particularly difficult problem, but it was worth it because it showed you the power of substitution methods. Now let's get back to linear simultaneous equations and look at some shortcuts for solving these.

Solving Simultaneous Equations by Elimination

Here is a new pair of linear simultaneous equations in two variables:

1. $3x + 2y = 2$
2. $2x + 5y = 16$

We could solve this by substitution, but there is another way to eliminate variables, which is by adding multiples of the equations together. If we know that $a = b$, and that $c = d$, then we can add together linear sums of the equations and get a new equation such as $2a + 3c = 2b + 3b$. This process can be used with our simultaneous equations to eliminate a particular variable.

If we multiply the first equation by 2, we get

3. $6x + 4y = 4$,

and if we multiply the second one by 3 we get

4. $6x + 15y = 48$

If we then subtract the first of these new equations from the second, we get an equation in y, which is

$$6x + 15y - 6x - 4y = 48 - 4$$
$$11y = 44$$
$$y = 4$$

We can then substitute this value back into Equation 1, getting

$$3x + 2 \times 4 = 2$$
$$3x = -6$$
$$x = -2$$

How did we choose which values to multiply the two equations by? It's the same process as with finding a common denominator. If we want to eliminate the variable x, then we are essentially trying to put the two equations over the common denominator of the coefficients of x. In this case, the common denominator (or lcm, strictly speaking) of 3 and 2 is 6, and just as with the case of fractions, we multiply each equation by the common denominator divided by the coefficient of x in the equation.

Here is another example, just to make it clearer:

1. $3x + 10y = 2$
2. $5x + 6y = 14$

This time, we'll eliminate y first. The coefficients of y in the equations are 10 and 6 respectively. The lcm of 10 and 6 is 30, so we multiply Equation 1 by $\frac{30}{10} = 3$, and Equation 2 by $\frac{30}{6} = 5$ to get our new equations:

3. $9x + 30y = 6$
4. $25x + 30y = 70$

Subtracting Equation 3 from Equation 4 gives us

$$25x - 9x = 70 - 6$$
$$16x = 64$$
$$x = 4$$

And substituting back in Equation 1 gives us

$$3 \times 4 + 10y = 2$$
$$12 + 10y = 2$$
$$10y = -10$$
$$y = -1$$

As always, check by substituting both values back into the second equation:

$$5 \times 4 + 6 \times (-1) = 20 - 6 = 14$$

This technique is actually very general, and you can use it to solve any system of linear simultaneous equations at all. Since we have been very theoretical for a while, let's look at this process as an algorithm and write a function for it.

Suppose you have n linear equations in n variables. We can write each equation as an $n + 1$-element array, so for example $2x + 3y = 3$ would become [2,3,3]. The complete system of equations is then an array of n such arrays, which we'll call `simul`. Now to solve the system of equations, we perform the following function (which will be explained fully in a moment).

```
function solveSimultaneous(simul)
    set redux to an empty array
    set n to the number of elements of simul
    repeat for i=n down to 1
        repeat for j=i down to 1
            if simul[j][i] is not 0 then
                set row to simul[j] and quit this loop
            end if
        end repeat
        if no row found then return "no unique solution"
        divide row by row[i]
        append row to redux
        delete row from simul
        repeat for j=i-1 down to 1
            if simul[j][i] is not 0 then
                subtract row*simul[j][i] from simul[j]
            end if
        end repeat
    end repeat
    set output to an array with n elements
    repeat for i=n down to 1
        set sum to 0
        repeat for j=i+1 to n
            add redux[i][j]*output[j] to sum
        end repeat
        set output[i] to redux[i][n+1]-sum
    end repeat
    return output
end
```

The function `solveSimultaneous()` is much simpler than it looks. Essentially, it's a formalized version of the process we followed before. The algorithm has two parts. First we go through the equations one by one, at each step picking an equation which has a non-zero coefficient in our next variable. So let's say we are working in three variables x, y, z, and the current variable is x, then we might find an equation such as $2x + 4y + z = 8$. We divide this equation by the coefficient of x to give it a coefficient of 1: $x + 2y + \frac{z}{2} = 4$. We add this equation to our list of reduced equations, which we called `redux`. Then we subtract multiples of this equation from all the remaining equations to eliminate the variable x from each one. Suppose one of the equations is $3x - z = 5$, we subtract 3 times our equation from it in order to eliminate x, getting $-6y - {}^{5z}\!/_{2} = -7$. Notice that while we have eliminated x in this equation, we have brought y into it again! However, at the end of this process, we have an equation in `redux` with a coefficient of 1 in x, and all the remaining equations in `simul` have a zero coefficient in x.

If at any stage we can't find an equation with a non-zero coefficient in the current variable, then we're stuck: the n equations are not independent. In that case, there are two possibilities: either there is no solution to the equations, or there are an infinite number of such solutions. We won't worry about these two cases, however.

When we repeat this process for y and z, we end up with a set of equations in `redux` with the following properties:

- The ith equation has zero coefficients for the first $(i - 1)$ variables
- The ith equation has a 1 coefficient for the ith variable

The second stage of the process is to use this to solve the equations.

We solve the equations by working backwards. Notice that the final equation is simple—it literally tells us the value of the last variable, something like $z = 2$. So we can just write this number into our output. Now we look at the second-to-last equation, which will be something like $y - 2z = 3$. But we know the value of z, so we can substitute it into the equation and quickly find y, which in this case is 7. We keep working backwards through the equations, and at each stage we can find the current unknown by substituting for all the later variables.

We've spent quite a while on this topic because simultaneous equations come up a lot in physics, particularly the collision detection calculations we will be looking at later in the book. But now let's move on to something a little more visual.

FUNCTIONS AND GRAPHS

One useful way to visualize a function is in the form of a *graph*. In this section we will look at graphs and how they can be used.

What Is a Graph?

A graph is a way of representing data visually. The standard form of graph is the two-dimensional *Cartesian* graph, which displays all possible ordered pairs of two numbers in the form of a single point drawn on a flat sheet or *Cartesian plane*. To make a Cartesian plane, you need three things: an *origin*, which is a single point that you define as representing the point (0, 0), and two *axes*, (pronounced "ax-ease," the plural of the word *axis*). An axis is a direction on the plane, and is drawn as a line through the origin, with an arrow to indicate the direction. Figure 3.1 shows an empty Cartesian plane.

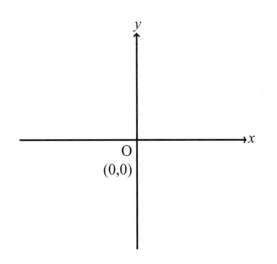

FIGURE 3.1   The Cartesian plane.

For the Cartesian plane to represent pairs of numbers, we need to assign each axis to one number in the pair. The horizontal axis represents the first number, and the vertical axis the second, and they are generally labeled as x and y and drawn at right-angles to one another (see Chapter 4). If we give each axis a scale, then any pair of numbers (a, b) can be represented by measuring a distance a in the direction of the first axis, and a distance b in the direction of the second axis (see Figure 3.2). This process is called *plotting* the point (a, b), and the values a and b are called *co-ordinates*. If the axes are x and y, then a is the *x-coordinate*, and b is the *y-coordinate*.

We can also go through the opposite process, *reading* the value of a point P on the plane. If you draw a line through P, perpendicular to the *x*-axis, it has to meet the *y*-axis at some point Q. If you measure the distance from Q to P in the scale of the *x*-axis, this will give you the *x*-coordinate of P, and if you measure the distance from the origin (often abbreviated to O) to Q in the scale of the *y*-axis, this will give you the *y*-coordinate. (See Figure 3.3, where the point P has been marked—can you see that P is the point (2, 4)?)

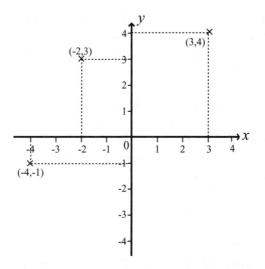

FIGURE 3.2   The points (3, 4), (−2, 3) and (−4, −1) plotted on the Cartesian plane.

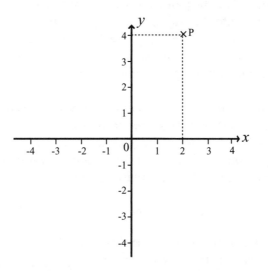

FIGURE 3.3   Reading a point from a graph.

Plotting and Examining Functions on a Graph

Graphs are most useful for representing functions. If you have a function f(x), then you can represent it on a graph by taking every possible value of x, finding the value of f(x), and plotting the point (x, f(x)). Generally, we plot the variable along the horizontal axis, and the output of the function on the vertical axis (called *plotting f(x) against* x). Alternatively, we can label the vertical axis with y and say that we are plotting the graph of $y = f(x)$—so if $f(x) = 2x + 1$ then we would be plotting the graph of $y = 2x + 1$.

For our purposes, we'll just talk here about functions in one variable, although it's perfectly possible to make a graph of a function in more than one variable—you just can't do it on a piece of paper! For example, to draw a function in two variables, you need a three-dimensional graph (a surface), and to draw a function in more variables than that, you need a graph with four or more dimensions, which exists only in the minds of mathematicians. We'll return to functions in more than one variable in Chapter 6.

It's fairly straightforward to make the computer draw a graph—of course, the precise details depend on the mechanism for drawing within your language. Here is a function that will draw a graph on the basis of another function passed to it as a parameter, as well as a range of values for x. The `resolution` parameter is used to determine how accurately the graph is drawn: it represents the number of evenly spaced values of x to be plotted. It will also automatically scale the y-axis to fit the entire function into the graph, whose dimensions are passed in as the last two parameters—the version here always draws the graph to include both axes, although the version on the CD-ROM (in the script *graphs*) has additional possibilities, including drawing multiple graphs and labeling.

Most programming languages draw downwards, representing 0 at the top of the screen and 1 below it. This is the opposite to the way we generally draw graphs. In this function, these details are ignored, it simply says to plot the point or draw the line, but be aware of the issue if implementing the function yourself. Again, the version on the CD-ROM is set to take this into account.

```
function drawGraph (functionToDraw, minX, maxX, resolution, width,
height)
    // calculate values of the function
    set xValues to an empty array
    set yValues to an empty array
    set spacing to (maxX–minX) / (resolution - 1)
    // spacing is the distance between consecutive x values
    repeat for i = 0 to (resolution–1)
        set x to minX + i * spacing
        set y to calculateValue(functionToDraw(x))
        // how this is done depends on how you want to represent
        // the function. In the version on the CD-ROM, you can
```

```
    // pass either a string such as "x*x + 2*x + 3" or the
    // name of any function defined somewhere. The latter is
    // more flexible as it allows you to deal with special
    // cases such as  "undefined" (see later in the function)
    append x to xValues
    append y to yValues
end repeat

// calculate the scale of the graph
set leftX to min(minX, 0)
set rightX to max(maxX, 0)
// leftX and rightX are the x-values at each end of the
// x-axis to be drawn
set xScale to width / (rightX - leftX)
set topY to max(largest(yValues), 0)
set bottomY to min(smallest(yValues) , 0)
// largest() and smallest() should return the largest and
// smallest values in the array respectively
set yScale to height / (topY—bottomY)

// draw axes
set x0 to xScale * (-leftX)
set y0 to yScale * (-bottomY)
// x0 and y0 are the positions within the graph of the axes
draw a line from the point (x0, 0) to the point (x0, height)
// this is the y-axis--you should also add arrows,
// a scale and labels here
draw a line from the point (0, y0) to the point (width, y0)
// this is the x-axis

// draw the function
set currentPoint to 0
repeat for i = 1 to the number of elements in xValues
    set x to xValues[i]
    set y to yValues[i]
    if y = "undefined" then
       set currentPoint to 0
    otherwise
       set thisPoint to ((x—leftX)* xScale, (y-ybottom) * yScale)
       if currentPoint = 0 then
          plot the point thisPoint
       otherwise
          draw a line from currentPoint to thisPoint
       end if
```

```
        set currentPoint to thisPoint
    end if
  end repeat
end
```

In Figure 3.4 you can see some example graphs drawn with this function (or the slightly more complex one on the CD-ROM, which includes labels and scales).

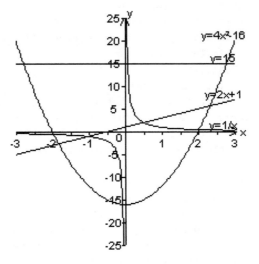

FIGURE 3.4   Graphs of the functions $y = 15$, $y = 2x + 1$, $y = 4x^2 - 16$ and $y = \frac{1}{x}$.

1. The **horizontal** line represents the equation $y = 15$. This equation is based on the constant function $f(x) = 15$, which returns 15, whatever the value of x. You can also draw a vertical line with the equation $x = c$—for example, the y-axis is drawn along the line $x = 0$.
2. The **diagonal** straight line represents the equation $y = 2x + 1$, and now you can see why a function with only a constant term and a term in x is called "linear." All such functions will appear as a straight line graph.
3. The curve, which looks like a big U-shape is called a **parabola**, and represents the equation $y = 4x^2 - 16$. All quadratic functions produce a similar shape (if the term in x^2 is negative then the curve is the other way up).

4. The curve which **hugs the axes** of the graph, disappearing off to infinity near the axes, is the graph of $y = \frac{1}{x}$. As x gets closer and closer to 0, $\frac{1}{x}$ gets very large, and in fact it gets arbitrarily large (we say it *tends to infinity*). Similarly, as x increases to infinity, y gets smaller and smaller, without ever quite reaching 0. When we see this behavior, we say that the lines $x = 0$ and $y = 0$ are *asymptotes* of the function.

It might seem that plotting a graph is a rather useless operation—it doesn't tell you anything new about the function, after all—and this is to some extent true. However, graphs are useful because they allow certain important pieces of data to be seen quickly, such as: where does the line pass through the axes? Does it reach a maximum value or minimum value, or does it go off to infinity? Does it have asymptotes? What's more, you can use this information to deduce other facts about the function.

Let's look at these functions in turn and see what we can determine from the graph.

1. The horizontal line has two main features: First it is horizontal, which means that it is a constant function, independent of x. Second, it crosses the y-axis at $y = 15$. These two facts tell us everything there is to be said about the function.

2. The diagonal line can be described in various ways, but the two most important are the *gradient* and the *intercept*. The gradient of a straight line is defined the same way as the gradient of a hill: if you travel a certain horizontal distance along, you travel a certain distance up. The ratio of these two values, vertical to horizontal, is the gradient. We can measure the gradient by taking any two points on the line, and dividing the vertical distance between them by the horizontal distance. So in this case, we might notice that the line passes through the points $(2, 5)$ and $(-0.5, 0)$, which are 5 units vertically and 2.5 units horizontally apart. If we divide 5 by 2.5 we get a gradient of 2.

The intercept is simply the point at which the line crosses the y-axis, which in this case is $y = 1$. Notice something unusual about these values: if we look at the equation of the line, $y = 2x + 1$, we see that 2 is the gradient and 1 is the intercept. This is a general fact about straight-line graphs: the gradient is the coefficient of the x term, and the intercept is the constant value. The gradient is often represented by the parameter m and the intercept by c, which means that the family of linear equations are often written as $y = mx + c$.

3. Parabolas have rather more information to be found. First, as mentioned above, they can either curve round as a bowl, as here, or as a mountain. This gives you the sign of the term in x^2—a bowl has a positive coefficient of x^2, a mountain has a negative coefficient.

   Second, by observing the points at which the parabola intersects the x-axis, you can determine the *roots* of the function (recall that a root of a function f(x) is a value a such that f(a) is zero). In this case, note that the curve crosses the x-axis at +2 and −2, which means that the roots of the function are +2 and −2. This means that $(x+2)$ and $(x-2)$ are factors of the function. If the parabola only just touches the x-axis, then you would have a function with just one root, which means a square quadratic, and if it doesn't cross the x-axis at all, then it has no real roots and cannot be factorized.

   Third, as with the straight line, you can determine the constant term of the function from the point at which it crosses the y-axis.

   Finally, you can find the *maximum* or *minimum* value of the function from the curve, by finding the point at which the parabola turns back on itself and reading the y-value at that point.

4. Graphs like $y = \frac{1}{x}$ are harder to characterize or read information from in the same way. Still, you can read off the values of the asymptotes directly. Be careful—many functions that seem to have asymptotes are actually just changing very slowly, for example the graph in Figure 3.5, of $y = \log_e(x)$. The logarithm function does not have a maximum value, although it may seem like it from the graph.

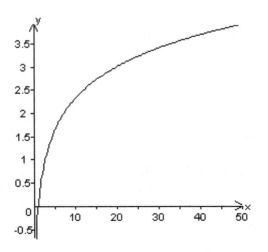

FIGURE 3.5 The graph of $y = \log_e(x)$.

Parametric Curves and Functions

Although simple functions are the most common things to draw on a graph, not all curves can be described in terms of a standard function. The graphs we've seen have all been of single-valued functions, but we can't draw, for example, a circle using this technique because a circle does not have a distinct value of y for each x-coordinate: in terms of functions, a circle is multivalued.

One way to avoid this problem is to use a *parameterization*: instead of using a single function f(x) and plotting $y =$ f(x), we can use two functions x(t) and y(t), and plot the points (x(t), y(t)) for each value of t (t is just a dummy variable here, although because parametric functions are often used to represent motion, t frequently represents time).

For example, suppose our two functions are given by the formulas $x = at^2$ and $y = 2at$. If we plot a graph of the points (x, y) given by allowing t to vary across the real numbers, we get the graph shown in Figure 3.6, which is a parabola lying on its side. In fact, it's the parabola $y^2 = 4ax$, as you can find by substituting for t in the parametric formula.

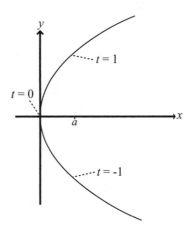

FIGURE 3.6 The parabola formed from the parametric formula $x = at^2$, $y = 2at$.

This curve is one which we couldn't draw using our previous graph-drawing function, because it's multivalued in the y coordinate. As we'll see in some later chapters, parametric formulas allow us to draw far more complex curves than simple functions, including the Bezier curves and splines seen in vector drawing and 3D modeling packages.

EXERCISES

Exercise 3.1

Write a function `substitute (functionString, x)` that will substitute a value for x into a function given in standard notation.

    The function should take two arguments, a string such as `"5x^2+3(4-2x)"` and a value such as 5, and should return the result of substituting the second argument for the variable x in the string (107 in this example). Use the ^ character as above to represent powers, and the / and * characters to represent division and multiplication. Try to make the function as general as possible, particularly dealing with parentheses—here are a few test functions you could try it out on:

```
"5x+3"; "4-2(x-5)"; "(x^3-4)/2"; "(x-4)(2-3x)"; "2^((x-4)/(x-5))"
```

Exercise 3.2

Write a function `simplify (functionString)`, which simplifies a given function as far as it can.

    Simplification is a task requiring intelligence and you won't be able to make the function work as well as a human would, but you should be able to make some headway. Your program should be able to take a function, group like terms together, put fractions over a common denominator, and if you are very ambitious, factorize the result. You could work just with the variable x, or allow multiple variables.

Exercise 3.3

Write a function `solve (equationString)` which solves a given equation.

    As before, this will not be infallible, but it should be able to deal with linear or quadratic equations. Use your previous function `simplify` to help you.

SUMMARY

In the course of this extremely long chapter we have covered several years' worth of basic algebra, which necessarily means we have missed out many details and lots of practice time. On the other hand, applying programming techniques to the concepts will have given you a good head-start in understanding them.

Despite the elementary level of the topics covered, the methods and concepts involved have been presented in quite an advanced way. The key focus to our discussion has been keeping the idea of the *function* at the forefront, its rightful place. As long as you really, truly, understand what a function is, the rest of algebra should fall neatly into place.

In the next chapter we will slow down a little, but only a little, and begin looking at the topics that are directly relevant to programming, which start with the basics of geometry.

YOU SHOULD NOW KNOW

- the meanings of the terms *variable, parameter, constant,* and *unknown;* how they are related and how they are different
- the meaning of the word *function*, the idea of a function as a map between different sets, and the concepts of *one-to-one, many-to-one,* and *multivalued* functions
- what an *equation* is and how to *solve* one for a particular unknown in simple cases, including quadratics, cubics, and simultaneous equations in two or more unknowns
- how to *simplify* and *factorize* functions, and use these skills to help with solving equations
- how to draw a *graph* of a function, and how to use it to read off information about the function
- how to draw a *parametric curve*

4 ▪ Trigonometry and Pythagoras

In This Chapter

- ▪ Overview
- ▪ Angles
- ▪ Triangles
- ▪ Calculations with Triangles
- ▪ Rotations and Reflections
- ▪ Exercises
- ▪ Summary
- ▪ You Should Now Know

OVERVIEW

Geometry is the study of shapes and space, and particularly of *symmetry*. We shall be looking mostly at the practical side of the subject, however, beginning with the measurement of angles and triangles, which is called *trigonometry*. When programming anything involving movement, such as games, you will be using trigonometry constantly, so it is vital that you have a thorough understanding of how it works.

ON THE CD   Code samples from this chapter are implemented in *math.cst* in the script *2D vectors and trigonometry*.

ANGLES

An *angle* is a way of measuring a direction. If two people set off from the same point, after they have both traveled ten meters, they could be anything from zero meters apart (if they set off in the same direction) to twenty meters apart (if they set off in opposite directions). An angle is a measurement of how different the two directions are. In the following section we will look at angles and what they mean.

Angles and Degrees

The most common way of measuring an angle is to consider all the possible directions as radii of a circle. We can then consider the angle between any two radii as a fraction of the circle. For example, in Figure 4.1, the clockwise angle between the lines A and B is a quarter of the circle, and the clockwise angle between the lines B and C is a third of the circle. (What is the clockwise angle between C and A?)

A radius of a circle is a line from its center to its perimeter (or circumference); radii is the plural. A straight line drawn between two points on the circumference which passes through the center is called a diameter of the circle. We will look more at circles in Chapter 8.

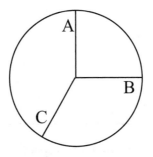

FIGURE 4.1 A circle with various radii marked.

Notice that the phrase "the angle between two lines" is potentially ambiguous, since we can measure the angle in either direction. The counterclockwise angle between A and B, for example, is three quarters of the circle. Generally, when we talk of the angle between two lines, we mean the smallest such angle, and this is the terminology we will use here unless otherwise indicated (later in the book we'll be more interested in measuring the angle in a particular direction).

Angles can be measured in various different units, but the most common is the *degree*. When measuring in degrees, we divide a full circle into 360 equal parts, each of which we call one degree, written 1°. There is nothing special about 360, except that as noted in Chapter 1, it happens to have a large number of divisors, which means that many common fractions of a circle have an integer number of degrees: a quarter-turn is 90° (called a *right angle*), a half-turn is 180° (a straight line), one third is 120°, a sixth is 60°, a fifth is 72° and so on. Figure 4.2 shows some of these angles.

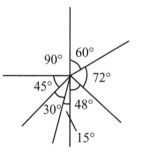

FIGURE 4.2 Some common angles measured in degrees. Measured angles are denoted by a small arc between the lines, and right angles by squares.

Of these values, probably the most important is the right angle. A square has four equal sides, and the angle between each pair of adjacent sides is a right angle. If you draw in the diagonals of the square, they also meet at right angles (two straight lines which meet at right angles are called *perpendicular*). Four right angles (denoted in diagrams by a square drawn inside the angle, as in Figure 4.2) divide the circle into four equal *quadrants*. If the circle is drawn on a graph, as in Figure 4.3, the quadrants can be seen to be in a sense complimentary: for every point (x, y) inside the circle, there are corresponding points $(x, -y)$, $(-x, y)$ and $(-x, -y)$ which are also inside the circle, each in a different one of the four quadrants (except when x or y are zero, of course).

An angle smaller than a right angle is called *acute*, an angle larger than a right angle (but smaller than two right angles) is called *obtuse*, while an angle greater than half a circle is called a *reflex* angle.

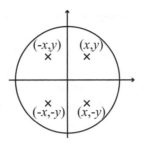

FIGURE 4.3 The quadrants of a graph.

Area and the Number π

If we draw a square around a circle and pick a point at random within it, what is the likelihood that this point lies inside the circle? This question is one way of explaining the concept of the *area* of a shape. If we have two squares, one of which has twice as long sides as the other, and we place them side by side on a table, then repeatedly mark random dots on the table with a pen, four times as many dots will land on the large square as land on the smaller. This makes sense, as you can fit four of the small squares in the larger one. If a square has sides x units long, then the area of the square is x^2 *square units* or units^2 (hence the term *squared*). When $x = 1$, the shape is called a *unit square*.

We can calculate the area of any rectangle easily. A rectangle is a shape which, like a square, has four sides, with each pair of adjacent sides at right angles. Unlike a square, its four sides need not be equal, although each pair of opposite sides must be (which means a square is a special kind of rectangle). The area of a rectangle is the product of the lengths of the pairs of sides: the area of the rectangle in Figure 4.4 is 12 square units: 12 unit squares will fit inside it.

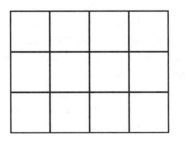

FIGURE 4.4 A 3 × 4 rectangle.

We'll return to areas when we look at triangles, but let's come back to the question which began this section, which we can now rephrase as "what is the area of a circle?" First of all, let's say what we mean by a circle. A circle is the shape drawn when you tie a piece of string to a fixed point, attach a pen to the other end, and draw a curve with the string held taut. The length of the string is called the *radius* of the circle.

The term radius here seems to clash with the same word introduced earlier for a line drawn from the center of a circle to the circumference; however, there is rarely any ambiguity. In fact, we use the same system often, as when we use the phrase "the side of a square" to mean "the length of each side of the square," or "the sides of a rectangle" to mean "the lengths of the two pairs of opposite sides of the rectangle." So "radius" here means "the length of any radius" (and similarly "diameter" can mean "the length of any diameter").

Once we know the radius of the circle, we know almost everything there is to know about it, although we might also need to know the position of the center point. It turns out that the area of a circle is always in a particular proportion to the square of its radius: if a circle has radius r, then it has an area of $3.1415927\ldots \times r^2$. The precise value of this constant $3.1415927\ldots$ is given the symbol π, which is the Greek equivalent of the letter "p," spelled in English "p-i" and pronounced "pie." On the computer, it is usually available either as a pre-defined constant `pi` or a function `pi()`.

π is probably the most ubiquitous irrational number in mathematics, cropping up in all kinds of unexpected places—even more than e, which runs a close second. Mathematicians have proved any number of surprising facts about this number over the centuries, with probably the most elegant provided by the mathematician Leibniz:

$$\frac{\pi}{4} = 1 - \frac{1}{3} + \frac{1}{5} - \frac{1}{7} + \ldots$$

One of the earliest uses of computers on a vast scale was in calculating the digits of π to an enormous precision, using a formula such as the above, although not this one, as it takes rather a lot of terms of the series to get anywhere near to a precise value. Today the digits of π are known to over a trillion decimal places. This is testimony both to the importance of the number and the obsessive nature of computer programmers.

Knowing the formula for the area of the circle, we can answer our original question. A square drawn around a circle has a side equal to the diameter of the circle. If the circle has a radius of 1 unit, then the square has a side of 2 units and so an area of 4 units^2. By the formula for the area of a circle, the circle has an area of π units^2. So the circle has $\pi/4$ times the area of the square, which is a value of approximately 0.7854.

π also turns up in another important element of the circle, the length of its circumference. The circumference is equal to π times the length of the diameter, or π times twice the length of the radius.

Radians

As we said above, there is no particular reason for choosing the degree as a unit of angles, it's simply convenient for some calculations. Another natural unit of measurement is the *radian*, although it may not seem very natural at first. Instead of dividing a circle into 360 equal degrees, we divide it into 2π radians, which is to say, 6-and-a-bit of them. The idea of dividing it into non-integer (and indeed irrational) units is what seems strange at first, but there is nothing wrong with it, and after a while it seems no odder than the fact that there are not an exact number of centimeters in an inch.

It is simple to convert between degrees and radians. One radian is $\frac{1}{2\pi}$ of a circle, so it is $\frac{360}{2\pi}$ degrees; similarly, one degree is $\frac{1}{360}$ of a circle, so it is $\frac{2\pi}{360}$ radians. Thus, an angle of 12° is equal to $\frac{12 \times 2\pi}{360} = \frac{\pi}{15} = 0.209$ radians, and an angle of $\frac{\pi}{2}$ radians is equal to 90°. If you need to convert between the values often (which is quite likely), it is generally simplest just to store the conversion factor as a constant from the beginning.

There is a third unit of angles which is called the *gradian*, but this is not something you are likely to encounter or need, although you can still find it on calculators. It is based on a division of the circle into 400 parts.

TRIANGLES

The *triangle* is the main unit of geometry. A triangle is a figure made up of three *non-collinear* (not lying on a straight line) points called *vertices* (the singular is *vertex*), joined by three straight line segments. In this section, we will look at triangles and their geometry, an area of mathematics called *trigonometry*.

The Types of Triangle

Triangles can be classified into four main types determined by the three angles inside them. We normally label a triangle as in Figure 4.5, using capital letters to label vertices, lower-case letters to label side lengths (with each side labeled to correspond to the opposing vertex), and angles labeled either by Greek letters as in the figure, or with a designation such as $\angle ABC$, listing three points which define the angle. Informally, you may also see the angles denoted simply by the letter of the vertex: angles A, B, C.

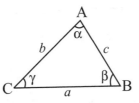

FIGURE 4.5 A triangle with its vertices, sides, and angles labeled.

If you are unfamiliar with the Greek alphabet, it is presented in Appendix A.

If we draw the same triangle three times as in Figure 4.6, you can see that the angles α, β, γ lie on a straight line, which means that the sum of these angles must be half a circle, or 180°. This is true for any triangle.

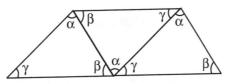

FIGURE 4.6 The angles in a triangle sum to 180°.

In Figure 4.7, you can see the three kinds of triangle.

1. The simplest triangle is the equilateral triangle, which has three equal sides, and also three equal angles, which must therefore each be equal to 60°.
2. An isosceles triangle has two equal sides. If sides a and b are equal, then angles α and β are also equal.
3. A scalene triangle is any other triangle: no equal sides, no equal angles.

FIGURE 4.7   Equilateral, isosceles, and scalene triangles.

One particularly important kind of triangle is also singled out, which is the *right-angled triangle*, which is to say, one which has a right angle within it. A right-angled triangle has two *legs*, which are the sides either side of the right angle, and one *hypotenuse*, which is the side opposite the right angle. The two smaller angles must necessarily sum to 90°, of course. All these pieces of information are to be found in Figure 4.8.

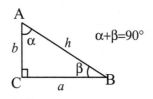

FIGURE 4.8   A right-angled triangle.

One final classification is into *acute* and *obtuse* triangles. An obtuse triangle has one angle greater than 90°, an acute triangle doesn't.

Pythagoras' Theorem

Let's take a closer look at right-angled triangles. There are several reasons why these are important. The first is that they are easy to recognize and crop up in many natural circumstances. For example, when working on a graph, it is often useful to draw the line joining two points and create a right-angled triangle with sides parallel to the *x*- and *y*-axes (see Figure 4.9). We implicitly did this when measuring the gradient of a straight line in the previous chapter.

Secondly, right-angled triangles have a number of useful properties which we will be looking at in this and subsequent sections. And thirdly, any triangle can be easily split into two right-angled triangles by *dropping a perpendicular* from one vertex to the opposing side (see Figure 4.10).

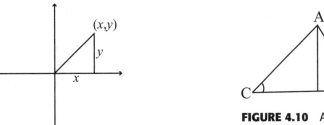

FIGURE 4.9   A right-angled triangle drawn on a graph.

FIGURE 4.10   A triangle split into two right-angled triangles by dropping a perpendicular from vertex A.

In the case of an obtuse triangle, one of the two right-angled triangles may be a kind of negative triangle, but this is a slightly abstract notion which we won't worry about for now.

Right-angled triangles were studied extensively by the ancient Greek mathematician Pythagoras, who gave his name to an important theorem linking the lengths of the three sides. Pythagoras' Theorem states that for a right-angled triangle ABC with the right-angle at vertex C (the usual notation), $a^2 + b^2 = c^2$. There are many ways to prove this fact, but the neatest can be seen in Figure 4.11.

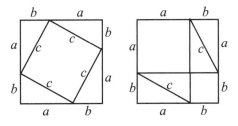

FIGURE 4.11   A geometrical proof of Pythagoras' Theorem.

In the first diagram, we have drawn a square with side $a + b$. Around the outside are arranged four equal right-angled triangles with legs a and b. The hypotenuses of the triangles, with length c, form a smaller square inside the larger, whose area is c^2. In the second diagram, we have an identical square, again with side $a + b$. This time, the four right-angled triangles have been rearranged to fit inside the square as two rectangles meeting at a corner. Each rectangle has sides a and

b, and the remainder of the square is subdivided into two smaller squares, one of which has side a, the other having side b. The total area of these two squares is $a^2 + b^2$. But as these the two large squares and the eight right-angled triangles within them are all the same, the area of the two small squares in the second diagram must be equal to the area of the small square in the first, which gives us $a^2 + b^2 = c^2$ as required.

NOTE

There are an infinite number of right-angled triangles whose sides are all integer lengths. The smallest is the triangle with legs 3 and 4, which has hypotenuse 5. There are a number of ways of generating such triangles, and the sets of three numbers making the sides are called Pythagorean triples. There are no sets of integers for which the same is true in any higher power—there are no sets of positive integers a, b, c, n, with n > 2, such that a^n + b^n = c^n. This fact is called Fermat's Last Theorem and was a famous unsolved problem until very recently.

Using Pythagoras' Theorem, we can quickly determine the third side of any right-angled triangle given the other two sides. For example, if we know that the hypotenuse of a triangle is 13 cm, and one side is 5 cm, then by Pythagoras, the third side's length must be equal to $\sqrt{13^2 - 5^2} = \sqrt{144} = 12$ cm. A right-angled isosceles triangle with sides of unit length (half a square) has a hypotenuse $\sqrt{2} = 1.414...$ units long. Similarly, if you take an equilateral triangle with sides of length 2 and cut it in half, the length of the perpendicular is $\sqrt{3}$ units. See Figure 4.12. Note that the isosceles triangle has interior angles of 45°, and the half-equilateral triangle has angles of 60° and 30°.

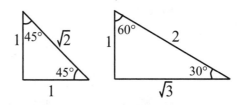

FIGURE 4.12   Two important right-angled triangles.

The Trigonometric Functions

We looked earlier at the concept of a gradient and we saw in Figure 4.9 how this can be represented by drawing a right-angled triangle on a graph. For any right-angled triangle with leg a parallel to the y-axis and leg b parallel to the x-axis, the gradient of the hypotenuse is equal to a/b. It is useful to be able to relate this value to the size of the angles at A and B, and we do this by using the function `tan()` (short for "tangent"). If the angle at A is x, then `tan(x)` gives the gradient of the line AB. Two other functions, `sin(x)` (short for "sine") and `cos(x)` ("cosine") are equal to the ratios a/c and b/c respectively. These three functions are known as the *trigonometric* functions. Notice that `tan(x)=sin(x)/cos(x)`.

NOTE

The trigonometric functions are dependent on the units of measurement of the angles: generally, computer languages assume units of radians, but we will assume degrees in this section for clarity. If you are working in degrees, it is vital to convert your angle measurements to radians (multiply them by $\pi/180$) before applying the trigonometric functions.

By inspecting the triangles in Figure 4.12, we can see that `sin(45)` must be equal to `1/sqrt(2)`, that `sin(30)` is equal to `0.5`, and that `sin(60)` is `sqrt(3)/2`. Calculate the values of `cos` and `tan` for these angles yourself.

If we measure the values of these functions for various right-angled triangles and plot them on a graph, the result is rather interesting, and can be seen in Figure 4.13. On the first diagram can be seen the graphs of y = `sin(x)` and y = `cos(x)` for x = 0° to 360°. Notice that we can measure the lengths of the sides in both directions, as we did when measuring gradients. Both these graphs are the same shape, a continuous wave called a *sine wave*, with the wave for `cos(x)` lagging a little behind the one for `sin(x)` (we say the two waves are 90° *out of phase*). On the second diagram is the graph of y = `tan(x)`, which has a different shape, with asymptotes every 180°.

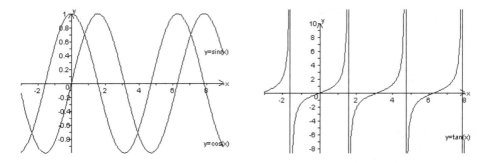

FIGURE 4.13 The graphs of `sin(x)`, `cos(x)` and `tan(x)`.

The functions sin() and cos() are closely related to circular motion, as we shall see in Chapter 16, and it turns out that they are also surprisingly similar to the exp() function. They can be calculated (in radians) by using the following infinite series:

$$\sin(x) = x - \frac{x^3}{3!} + \frac{x^5}{5!} - \ldots$$

$$\cos(x) = 1 - \frac{x^2}{2!} + \frac{x^4}{4!} - \ldots$$

Notice that when x is small, sin(x) is very nearly equal to x. Notice also that sin(0)=0 and cos(0)=1.

There are also a number of formulas (the *trigonometric identities*) involving the trigonometric functions which may prove useful here and there. We will state these here without proof, but you might like to think about how you could prove them, although we will prove the first one a little later.

For any value of x and y:

- $\sin^2(x) + \cos^2(x) = 1$. Here $\sin^2(x)$ is a shorthand for $\left(\sin(x)\right)^2$

- $\sin(x+y) = \sin(x)\cos(y) + \cos(x)\sin(y)$

- $\cos(x+y) = \cos(x)\cos(y) - \sin(x)\sin(y)$

- $\tan(x+y) = \dfrac{\tan(x) + \tan(y)}{1 - \tan(x)\tan(y)}$

- $\sin(2x) = 2\sin(x)\cos(x)$

- $\cos(2x) = \cos^2(x) - \sin^2(x)$

- $\tan(2x) = \dfrac{2\tan(x)}{1 - \tan^2(x)}$

The Inverse Trigonometric Functions

Just as important as calculating gradients from angles is to go the other way and calculate an angle from a gradient. Each of the three trigonometric functions has an inverse function that maps from the domain [−1,1] (for sin and cos) or [−∞, ∞] (for tan) to the range [0,360] This is to say, the function takes a number and maps it to an angle. Strictly speaking, these functions are multivalued, but for each of the functions there is a standard mapping:

- The inverse of the `sin()` function is the `arcsin()` function, also written as `sin`$^{-1}$`()` or `asin()`. This maps positive values between 0 and 1 to values between 0 and 90°, and negative values greater than or equal to −1 to values between 90° and 180°. For all values of x, `arcsin(-x)=180-arcsin(x)`.
- The inverse of the `cos()` function is the `arccos()`, `acos()` or `cos`$^{-1}$`()` function. This maps values in [0,1] to the range [0,90°] and values in [−1,0] to the range [−90°,0]. For all values of x, `arccos(-x)=-arccos(x)`.
- The inverse of the `tan()` function is the `arctan()`, `atan()` or `tan`$^{-1}$`()` function. This maps values in [0, ∞] to the range [0,90°), and negative values in [−∞, 0] to the range (−90°,0]. For all values of x, `arctan(-x)=-arctan(x)`.

NOTE

The notation [a, b] indicates the closed interval *from a to b, which is the set of real numbers between a and b inclusive, and the notation (a, b) in this context means the* open interval, *the set of real numbers between a and b, not including the numbers a and b themselves. Similarly, [a, b) means the set of numbers greater than or equal to a and less than b.*

Although all three functions are useful, because of Pythagoras' Theorem you don't actually need them all and you can manage with just `arctan()`. If you look at Figure 4.14 you should be able to see that

$$\cos^{-1}(x) = \tan^{-1}\left(\frac{\sqrt{1-x^2}}{x} \right)$$

$$\sin^{-1}(x) = \tan^{-1}\left(\frac{x}{\sqrt{1-x^2}} \right)$$

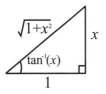

FIGURE 4.14 Calculating `arcsin()` and `arccos()` in terms of `arctan()`.

Because the arctan() function maps infinite quantities to finite ones, it has the unusual ability to cope with fractions with a denominator of zero. Because we can't use these in programming, it can save time to create a special version of arctan() with two arguments instead of one, representing the two legs of a right-angled triangle, one of which may be zero. This function, available natively in many programming languages, is:

```
function atan (y, x)
    set deg=1
    if x=0 and y<0 then deg=90
    if x=0 and y>=0 then deg=-90
    if y=0 and x<0 then deg=0
    if y=0 and x>=0 then deg=-180
    if deg=1 then return arctan(y/x)
    otherwise return deg*pi/180
end function
```

CALCULATIONS WITH TRIANGLES

With the help of the trigonometric functions and Pythagoras' Theorem, we can solve many problems with both triangles and more complex figures. In this section we will see how to do this mathematically and computationally.

The Sine and Cosine Rules

The most common triangle problem is to *solve* the triangle: given an arbitrary triangle ABC and some information about its angles and sides, to deduce all the other facts about the triangle, which is to say, all the values a, b, c, α, β, γ. In general, you need three of these values to solve a triangle, although not all combinations of three will do it. You can solve the triangle given any of the following:

- The lengths of the three sides
- Any two angles and one side
- Any two sides and the angle between them
- In a right-angled triangle, the length of any two sides

Except for a right-angled triangle, you cannot solve a triangle given two sides and a non-included angle, because there may be two possible triangles as in Figure 4.15. You also cannot solve a triangle knowing only the three angles, because there are an infinite number of triangles with the same three angles, as we will see in the next section.

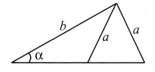

FIGURE 4.15 Two different triangles sharing the same values for *a*, *b* and α.

The two most powerful methods for solving triangles are called the *sine rule* and the *cosine rule*. The sine rule relates angles to the lengths of their opposite sides, the cosine rule relates one angle to the lengths of the three sides.

The sine rule is particularly neat, and says that for any triangle:

$$\frac{a}{\sin(\alpha)} = \frac{b}{\sin(\beta)} = \frac{c}{\sin(\gamma)}$$

To see why, look at the triangle in Figure 4.16. We have dropped a perpendicular from vertex B which meets the line AC at the point P, and we say that it has length *l*. Then we know that

1. $\sin(\alpha) = \dfrac{l}{c}$

2. $\sin(\gamma) = \dfrac{l}{a}$

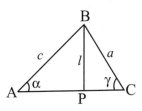

FIGURE 4.16 Proving the sine and cosine rules.

If we rearrange Equation 2 and substitute the value for *l* into Equation 1, we get

$$\sin(\alpha) = \left(\frac{a\sin(\gamma)}{c} \right)$$

$$\frac{a}{\sin(\alpha)} = \frac{c}{\sin(\gamma)}$$

A symmetrical argument applies to b and β.

The cosine rule is a little more complicated, but easy to remember because it is an extension of Pythagoras' Theorem:

$$a^2 = b^2 + c^2 - 2bc\cos(\alpha)$$

Proving this is a little more involved, but again we can use the triangle from Figure 4.16. We've denoted the line PC as k units long, making the line AP $b - k$ units (since the whole line is b units). Now we can see from Pythagoras that

$a^2 = l^2 + k^2$ (using the triangle BCP)
$l^2 = c^2 - (b-k)^2$ (using the triangle ABP)

so eliminating l, we have

$$a^2 = c^2 + k^2 - (b-k)^2$$
$$= c^2 + k^2 - b^2 + 2bk - k^2$$
$$= c^2 - b^2 + 2bk$$

We can now eliminate k by using the angle α, since

$\cos(\alpha) = {b - k}/{c}$ (from triangle ABP)

so $k = b - c\cos(\alpha)$

and therefore substituting this value for k we get

$a^2 = c^2 - b^2 + 2b(b - c\cos(\alpha))$

Using combinations of these two rules, along with Pythagoras' Theorem and the fact that angles in a triangle sum to 180°, we can solve any solvable triangle (see Exercise 4.1).

Similar Triangles

As we saw in the previous section, it is possible to have two triangles with the same three angles but sides of different lengths. Two triangles with the same angles (not necessarily in the same order around the triangle) are called *similar*. Of course, since the sum of angles in a triangle is constant, you only need to show that two angles are the same to know the triangles are similar.

The principal fact about similar triangles is that their sides are in the same proportion. As with the rectangles we looked at in Chapter 2, they are essentially the same triangle, just drawn to a different scale. This means that if we know two triangles are similar then we can use the lengths of a side in one (or indeed any other linear measurement) to deduce the same measure in the other.

In Figure 4.17, you can see a way to measure the height of a building on a sunny day. Place a stick 1m long vertically in the ground and measure the length of its shadow, and also measure the length of the shadow of the building. The triangle formed by the tip of the stick T, the base of the stick S and the end of its shadow U is similar to the triangle formed by the top of the building B, the base of the building A and the end of its shadow C. The angles at S and A are both right-angles, and the angles at U and C are both equal to the angle formed by the sun and the ground. Of course, to get *exactly* the same angle of the sun you need to align the stick so that U and C are in the same place, but the principle is the same.

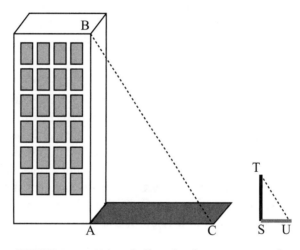

FIGURE 4.17 Using similar triangles to measure the height of a building.

When describing two triangles as similar, you should notate them with the vertices in corresponding order – so if triangles ABC and PQR are similar, this means the angles at A and P, B and Q, and C and R are the same respectively.

Because the triangles are similar, this means that their sides are in the same proportion. This means that the ratio of the height of the building AB to the height of the stick ST is equal to the ratio of the length of the building's shadow AC to the length of the stick's shadow SU. That is to say, in the notation of Figure 4.17:

$$\frac{c}{u} = \frac{b}{t}$$

So we can calculate *c* from the values of the other three lengths, all of which we can measure on the ground.

The notation AB for the length of the line from A to B is useful because it means we need fewer symbols in complicated problems. Notice that in this notation the letters A and B are in normal typeface: when they are written in bold or with an arrow above them as in $\overrightarrow{AB}$, this is not a length but a vector, *which we will see in the next chapter.*

If two triangles have sides of the same lengths and not just angles, then they are said to be *congruent*, which essentially means that they are exactly the same (or at most mirror-images of one another). Congruence is useful in the area of geometrical proofs but not particularly in programming.

The Area of a Triangle

There are various ways to measure the area of a triangle depending on which measurements you know. We can use the triangle in Figure 4.16 again to derive one method. We take a triangle ABC and drop a perpendicular (of length *l*) from the vertex A to the point P on the opposite side BC, dividing the triangle into two right-angled triangles. Then we draw congruent right-angled triangles alongside each of these to create two adjacent rectangles, each of which is twice the area of the corresponding right-angled triangle. The total area of this rectangle is *la*, and you can see that this is twice the area of the triangle ABC, so we say that the area of a triangle is $\frac{1}{2}$ *base* × *height*.

We can also find the area knowing other measurements. For example, if you look at the triangle ACP, you can see that $l = b\sin(\gamma)$, so we can substitute this value into the above formula to get the area as $\frac{1}{2}$ $ab\sin(\gamma)$.

ROTATIONS AND REFLECTIONS

A common use for the trigonometric functions in programming is when working with objects that need to rotate. We will conclude this chapter by looking at the relationship of the trigonometric functions to rotation.

Transformations

An object drawn on the computer screen could be described in terms of the positions of its vertices. For example, triangle T in Figure 4.18 has vertices at (100,150), (125,125) and (150,130). Notice that as this is a figure on a screen, the *y*-axis is measured downward, rather than upward as on a graph. There are a number of different ways we can move this triangle to a new position, which are called *transformations*.

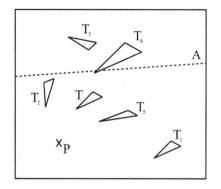

FIGURE 4.18 A triangle and various transformations of it.

- If we move the figure to a new position without rotating it (as with triangle T_1), this is called a *translation*. A translation is described by a *vector*, which we will look at properly in the next chapter. For the moment, just think of it as a value describing how far we are moving the figure in the x and y directions.

- If we turn the figure around by an angle (triangle T_2), this is called a *rotation*. A rotation is described by a single point (the *center of rotation*, or just *center*) and an angle (the *angle of rotation*, generally measured clockwise on a graph or anticlockwise on a computer). We say that triangle T_2 is the result of "rotating triangle T by 45° about the point P."

- If we flip the figure over (triangle T_3), this is a *reflection*. A reflection is defined by a single line (the *axis of reflection*)—we say, for example, that triangle T_3 is the result of "reflecting triangle T in the axis A (the line $y = x$)."

- If we change the size of the figure (triangle T_4), this is a *scale*. Scaling an object can be defined by a single point (the *origin*—not to be confused with the origin of the graph) and a number representing the proportion of the size of the new figure to the old one, called the *scale factor*. So T_4 is the result of "scaling T by a factor of 1.5 from the point P." You can also perform more complex scales by scaling different amounts in particular directions, but we'll ignore that for now.

- If we skew the figure, as if we were to take hold of one point and shift it across relative to the others (Triangle T_5), this is called a *shear*. Shears are defined in terms of a single line (the *line of invariance*) and a number representing the amount of shearing (the *shear factor*).

Each of these transformations can be calculated numerically by performing various operations on the vertices of the object. Many of these calculations involve the trigonometric functions we looked at above.

Rotating an Object by an Angle

In Figure 4.19 we have another triangle T (ABC), which is to be rotated by an angle α around the origin O to make a new triangle T' (A'B'C'). As before, we are measuring y downwards. In the diagram we have drawn the lines from the origin to the points A = (x,y) and A' = (x',y'). We have also drawn in the lines from A and A' to the x- and y-axes, and the points X, X', Y and Y' where these lines meet the axes. Notice that the lines OX and OY have length x and y respectively, and similarly for OX' and OY'. Notice also that the lengths of OA and OA' are both the same (this is a defining feature of a rotation).

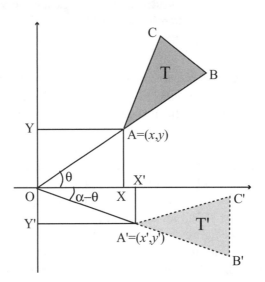

FIGURE 4.19   Rotating around the origin.

What can we deduce from all this information? Well, first we know that since OA = OA', by Pythagoras' Theorem we can say that OA' = $\sqrt{x^2 + y^2}$. Second, we can calculate the value of the angle between OA and the x-axis (called θ in the diagram) as atan(y, x). Because the angle of rotation is α, we know that the angle θ', between OA' and the x-axis, is equal to $\alpha - \theta = \alpha$-atan(y, x). So this means we can calculate the value of x' and y':

$$x' = \text{OA}' \times \cos(\theta') = \sqrt{(x^2 + y^2)} \cos(\alpha - \text{atan}(y,x))$$

$$y' = \mathrm{OA'} \times \sin(\theta') = \sqrt{\left(x^2 + y^2\right)} \sin\left(\alpha - \mathrm{atan}\left(y, x\right)\right)$$

Doing this for each of the vertices of the triangle will rotate the whole triangle about the origin.

You need to be careful about the signs of x and y here. It is best to use the two-argument implementation of `atan()` *in functions like these as it ensures that the correct value of the angle is returned.*

NOTE

What if we wanted to rotate the object around some other point than the origin? In that case, we can do a small trick. First, we *translate* the object so that the center of rotation lies on the origin. Then we rotate it, and then we translate it back. This kind of thinking is based on the idea of a vector, which as we said will be covered in the next chapter, but it should be clear enough from the description.

To rotate a point (x,y) by an angle α around the point $P = (s,t)$: first we translate it by subtracting (s,t) from each point. Then we rotate by α around the origin. Finally we add (s,t) to the resultant points again. This gives a complicated formula for the values of x' and y':

$$x' = \sqrt{\left(\left(x-s\right)^2 + \left(y-t\right)^2\right)} \cos\left(\alpha - \mathrm{atan}\left(\left(y-t\right),\left(x-s\right)\right)\right) + s$$

$$y' = \sqrt{\left(\left(x-s\right)^2 + \left(y-t\right)^2\right)} \sin\left(\alpha - \mathrm{atan}\left(\left(y-t\right),\left(x-s\right)\right)\right) + t$$

You can see the relationship of these formulas to those we saw before: Each one is a result of replacing x and y with $x - s$ and $y - t$, respectively, then adding s or t as appropriate. Combining transformations in this way can be a very powerful tool which we will see much more of in later chapters.

As a quick aside, what we often want to do is to rotate an object around its own center, often called the *center of gravity* or *center of mass*, although these terms are strictly speaking more suitable for a three-dimensional object. For a triangle, this point is called the *centrum*, and is to be found at the intersection of the three lines joining the vertices to the midpoints of the opposite sides (Figure 4.20). Finding the centrum is straightforward: it is the mean of the three vertices. So if the vertices are at $\left(x_1, y_1\right)$, $\left(x_2, y_2\right)$ and $\left(x_3, y_3\right)$, the centrum is at the point $\frac{1}{3}\left(x_1 + x_2 + x_3, y_1 + y_2 + y_3\right)$. You will use this fact in Exercise 4.2.

NOTE

The mean *(or strictly speaking, the* arithmetic mean*) of a number of values* a_1, a_2..., a_n *is the sum of the values divided by the number of values:* $(a_1+a_2+...+a_n)/n$. *This may be written using the notation* $\frac{1}{n}\sum_{i=1}^{n}a_i$, *where the capital Greek letter sigma* (Σ) *denotes a sum of values over the index* i. *The mean is the value colloquially called the* average, *but mathematicians use the word average to denote a number of different functions including, as well as the arithmetic mean, the geometric mean, harmonic mean, median, and mode, each of which is useful in different circumstances.*

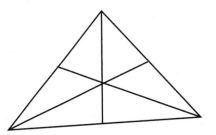

FIGURE 4.20 The centrum of a triangle.

Quick Rotations by Special Angles

While it is obviously useful to be able to rotate an object about any axis, it is also handy to know a few short cuts. Rotating by certain common angles is much simpler.

■ To rotate the point (x,y) by 180° about the origin, simply multiply both coordinates by -1, getting $(-x,-y)$.
■ To rotate (x,y) by 90° about the origin, switch the coordinates around to get $(y,-x)$.
■ To rotate (x,y) by –90° about the origin, switch the coordinates the other way to get $(-y,x)$.

You should by now be able to derive these results from earlier equations.

Reflections

As we saw above, a reflection can be specified completely by giving a single line on the plane, which is called the axis of reflection. The image of a point P reflected in a particular axis A is the point P' such that AP = AP' and such that the line PP' is perpendicular to A (see Figure 4.21).

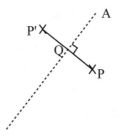

FIGURE 4.21 The image of the point P under reflection in the axis A.

Although we can calculate the position of P' from this information, it is hard to do so without vectors. However, we can also use rotations and translations to reduce this to a simpler problem. Reflecting in the *x*- or *y*-axis is very simple: the point (x,y) reflected in the *x*-axis gives the point $(x,-y)$, and in the *y*-axis gives $(-x,y)$. Therefore, to reflect $P = (x,y)$ in an axis with the equation $y = mx + c$, we can do the following (Figure 4.22):

1. **Translate** P by $-c$ units in the *y* direction to get $P_1 = (x, y - c) = (x_1, y_1)$

2. **Rotate** P_1 by atan(m) about the origin to get $P_2 = (l\cos(\text{atan}(m) - \text{atan}(y_1, x_1)), l\sin(\text{atan}(m) - \text{atan}(y_1, x_1)))$ where $l = \sqrt{(x_1^2 + y_1^2)} = \sqrt{(x^2 + (y - c)^2)}$ is the length of the line OP'

3. **Reflect** P_2 in the *x*-axis to get $P_2 = (x_2, -y_2) = (x_3, y_3)$

4. **Rotate** P_3 by $-\text{atan}(m)$ about the origin to get $P_4 = (l\cos(-\text{atan}(m) - \text{atan}(y_3, x_3)), l\sin(-\text{atan}(m) - \text{atan}(y_3, x_3)))$

5. **Translate** P_4 by c units in the *y* direction to get $P' = (x_4, y_4 + c) = (x', y')$

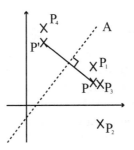

FIGURE 4.22 A series of transformations to find P'.

NOTE

These steps can, of course, be simplified, and by using the trigonometric identities they can be subsumed into a single formula, but it isn't worth going into here—besides, the whole thing gets easier once we start using vectors and matrices. If you want some practice in trigonometric algebra, try simplifying the process yourself.

sin(), cos(), and Circular Motion

The trigonometric functions are not just mathematical abstractions introduced to make calculations easier. They represent a very real and commonplace phenomenon. Imagine that you have a point P at a distance of 1 unit from the origin (see Figure 4.23). As you can see immediately from the definition of sin() and cos(), the coordinates of P must be (cos(a),sin(a)), where a is the angle the line OP makes with the x-axis. If you plot all such points P, you make a circle around the origin.

NOTE

Notice that since the length of the line OP is 1, this proves the identity we saw earlier, which said that $\sin^2 \theta + \cos^2 \theta = 1$.

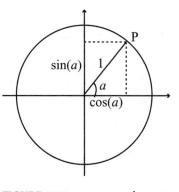

FIGURE 4.23 sin() and cos() on a circle.

This means that the sin() and cos() functions represent the positions of a point moving around a circle at a constant speed. If you were to drive a pin into the side of a wheel, the vertical position of the wheel over time as the wheel spins will be a sin() function (assuming it starts horizontally). We will look into this further in Chapter 16 on oscillations. For now simply note that any point on a circle with radius r centered on the point (x,y) has coordinates $\left(r\sin(\alpha), r\cos(\alpha)\right)$ for some value of α.

EXERCISES

Exercise 4.1

Write a function `solvetriangle(triangle)` which takes an array representing a triangle with incomplete information and returns the array filled in as far as possible.

Your function should accept a 6-element array where the first three elements are the lengths of the sides and the last three are angles (which may be in degrees or radians depending on your preference). Any of these values may be replaced with the string "?" representing an unknown. The function should return 0 if the triangle is impossible, a complete array of six numbers if the triangle can be solved, and an incomplete array if it cannot be solved uniquely.

Exercise 4.2

Write a function `rotatetofollow(triangle,point)` which rotates a particular triangle around its centrum to aim at a given point.

The function should take two arguments, one array representing the three vertices of the triangle (the first of which is taken to be the "front"), another giving the point to aim at. It should return the new vertices of the triangle. If you have trouble with this exercise, you might want to come back to it after reading the next chapter.

SUMMARY

In this chapter we have begun to explore the world of geometry, and you have already learned a number of vital techniques which will be of use in animation and games. In the next chapter we will fill in a lot of the blanks which were touched on in this chapter but left unfinished.

YOU SHOULD NOW KNOW

- the meaning of an *angle* and the different ways of measuring it
- the meaning of the term *area* and how to measure it for an arbitrary rectangle, circle or triangle
- the various types of triangle—*scalene, isosceles, equilateral, right-angled*—and their properties

- how to use the *trigonometric functions* and *Pythagoras' Theorem* to solve problems in right-angled and other triangles
- the meaning of the terms *similar* and *congruent* and what they imply for lengths and angles of shapes
- the meanings of *rotation, reflection, translation, scale* and *shear,* and how to calculate the first three of these for a given point or shape on the plane

5 Vectors

OVERVIEW

In this chapter we will examine the concept of a *vector*, a mathematical object describing relative positions in space. We already used vectors informally in the previous chapter, but now we will look at them in more detail, although a full treatment will wait until later chapters dealing with vectors in three dimensions. We will finish the chapter by looking at some calculations with *matrices* and how to use them to describe changes in space.

 Code samples from this chapter are implemented in *math.cst* in the scripts *Chapter 5 (vectors)*, *2D vectors and trigonometry*, *2D vector algebra* (for the vector intersection code), and *matrices*.

ON THE CD

GETTING FROM HERE TO THERE

We will start by describing vectors more formally and seeing how to perform basic calculations with them.

The Vector As an Instruction

A *vector* is like an instruction that tells something where to move. For example, a pirate's treasure map that says "take four steps north and three steps east, then dig" describes a vector in two dimensions. An instruction in a hotel such as "go to the first floor, go along the corridor then take the first door on the right" describes a vector in three dimensions.

Vectors describe the overall movement, not the journey. In the pirate map, it wouldn't matter if you took one step west, four steps north and three steps east, you would still end up at the treasure—as long as you start in the same place. Vectors don't have an intrinsic position in space, they simply tell you that if you start *here* you will end up *there*.

Vectors are normally denoted by a letter in boldface such as **u** or **v**. When working in Cartesian coordinates, one can write a vector down by giving the distance moved in the *x*-direction and the distance moved in the *y*-direction, normally written in a column array like this: $\begin{pmatrix} x \\ y \end{pmatrix}$. For example, the vector drawn in Figure 5.1 is $\begin{pmatrix} -3 \\ 2 \end{pmatrix}$. Notice that because we are moving in the negative *x*-direction, the value in the *x* position of the vector is negative. These values are called the *components* of the vector in the *x*- and *y*-directions.

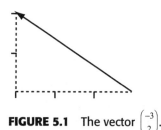

FIGURE 5.1   The vector $\begin{pmatrix} -3 \\ 2 \end{pmatrix}$.

A vector is drawn as a straight line with an arrowhead indicating its direction. Usually the arrowhead is drawn at the end of the vector, although it is sometimes drawn in the middle.

NOTE

A vector can also be thought of as having two properties, a *magnitude* and a *direction*. The magnitude of a vector **v**, written |**v**|, is its length in space, which can be found from Pythagoras' Theorem. So the magnitude of the vector $\begin{pmatrix} x \\ y \end{pmatrix}$ is $\sqrt{x^2 + y^2}$. In two dimensions, we can represent the direction by the angle the vector makes with an axis. A vector with magnitude 1 is called a *unit vector*, and in two dimensions it is equal to $\begin{pmatrix} \sin(\alpha) \\ \cos(\alpha) \end{pmatrix}$ for some angle α.

NOTE

*Some people prefer to write the magnitude of a vector without using boldface, so the magnitude of **v** would be written |v|. We won't use that convention in this book as it can cause confusion.*

If we specify a starting point for a vector ("from the old oak tree, take three steps north"), then it is called a *position vector*. Generally, we choose a standard starting point (the *origin*, as with graphs), then measure all position vectors from the same point. If we draw a position vector on a graph starting from the origin, the coordinates of the end-point are the same as the components of the vector (see Figure 5.2). If we label the endpoints O and P, then we can write the vector as $\overline{\text{OP}}$.

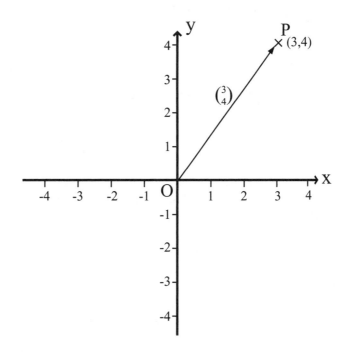

FIGURE 5.2 A position vector.

A common notation is to use subscripts to represent the components of a vector, so for example the vector **v** might have the components (v_1, v_2). This is usefully similar to programming, where the components of the array v might be found by v[1], v[2] and so on (at least in the convention of this book—more commonly it would be v[0], v[1]), so we'll use this notation fairly often.

Vector Arithmetic

Vectors can't be multiplied together in any simple way, although there are two multiplication-like operations we can perform on vectors, one of which we'll see in a moment, the other in Chapter 17, as well as a programmatic trick called *pairwise multiplication* where the components are multiplied in pairs to create a new vector, which is not a standard mathematical tool but often used on "vector-like" objects like colors (see Chapter 20). However, you can perform additions with vectors, and you can also multiply a vector by a *scalar*, which is a fancy word for an ordinary number.

- To multiply a vector by a scalar, multiply each component by the scalar:

$$a \begin{pmatrix} x \\ y \end{pmatrix} = \begin{pmatrix} ax \\ ay \end{pmatrix}$$

- To add two vectors together, add their components in pairs:

$$\begin{pmatrix} a \\ b \end{pmatrix} + \begin{pmatrix} c \\ d \end{pmatrix} = \begin{pmatrix} a+c \\ b+d \end{pmatrix}$$

Multiplying a vector by a scalar changes its length proportionally, while leaving the direction unchanged (see Figure 5.3). If the scalar is negative, then the new vector faces in the opposite direction. In particular, if the vector $\overrightarrow{AB}$ is **v**, then the vector $\overrightarrow{BA}$ is -**v**.

For a non-zero vector **v**, if we divide it by its magnitude |**v**| (equivalently, multiply by the reciprocal of its magnitude $\frac{1}{|v|}$), we get a unit vector, sometimes written $\bar{\mathbf{v}}$ or $\hat{\mathbf{v}}$. This is called the *normalized vector* or *norm* of **v** (not to be confused with its *normal*, which we will look at later).

For the sum of two vectors, look at Figure 5.3, where you can see that the sum of the vectors is equal to the result of following one and then the other—remember that vectors don't care what route you take to the end point, they only care about the final position.

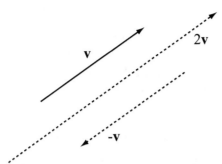 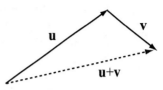 

FIGURE 5.3 Adding two vectors and multiplying by a scalar.

The difference between two vectors is a slightly more subtle concept. If we consider both vectors to be position vectors, one of the point P and the other of the point Q, so $\mathbf{u} = \overrightarrow{OP}$ and $\mathbf{v} = \overrightarrow{OQ}$ then the difference $\mathbf{v} - \mathbf{u}$ is the vector $\overrightarrow{PQ}$ (see Figure 5.4).

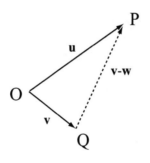

FIGURE 5.4 The difference of two vectors.

The reason this works is that if you start at P, follow the vector $-\mathbf{u}$ and then the vector $\mathbf{v}$, you end up at Q, so $\mathbf{v} - \mathbf{u} = -\mathbf{u} + \mathbf{v} = -\overrightarrow{OP} + \overrightarrow{OQ} = \overrightarrow{PO} + \overrightarrow{OQ} = \overrightarrow{PQ}$.

These calculations are surprisingly powerful. For example, what is the position vector of the mid-point of the line PQ? If you start at O, travel to P, then move halfway along the vector PQ, you reach the mid-point M. So the vector $\overrightarrow{OM}$ is equal to $\overrightarrow{OP} + \frac{1}{2}\overrightarrow{PQ} = \mathbf{u} + \frac{1}{2}(\mathbf{v} - \mathbf{u}) = \frac{(\mathbf{u} + \mathbf{v})}{2}$, which is to say, the mean of the vectors $\mathbf{u}$ and $\mathbf{v}$. Similarly, the position vector of the centrum of a triangle is the mean of the position vectors of its vertices.

Some programming languages have innate support for vector calculations. For example, most languages allow you to add arrays and multiply them by scalars using precisely the rules we used above. 3D engines will usually include functions for calculating the magnitude and norm of a vector. However, to make everything crystal clear, here is the set of functions for the calculations introduced so far.

```
function addVectors (v1, v2)
    // assume v1 and v2 are arrays of the same length
    set newVector to an empty array
    repeat for i=1 to the length of v1
        append v1[i]+v2[i] to newVector
    end repeat
    return newVector
end function

function scaleVector (v, s)
    repeat for i=1 to the length of v
        multiply v[i] by s
    end repeat
    return v
end function

function magnitude (v)
    set s to 0
    repeat with i=1 to the length of v
        add v[i]*v[i] to s
    end repeat
    return sqrt(s)
end function

function norm (v)
    set m to magnitude(v)
    if m=0 then return "error" // you can't normalize a zero vector
    return scaleVector(v,1/m)
end function
```

Let's look at one more important calculation, the angle between two vectors. We'll see an easier way to calculate this later in the chapter, but for the moment, look back at Figure 5.4. Notice that the vectors $\mathbf{u}$, $\mathbf{v}$ and $\mathbf{u} - \mathbf{v}$ form a triangle OPQ. So this means we can use the cosine rule to find any of the angles from the magnitude of these three vectors. In particular we can find the angle θ between $\mathbf{u}$ and $\mathbf{v}$ by:

$$\cos\theta = \frac{\left|\mathbf{u}\right|^2 + \left|\mathbf{v}\right|^2 - \left|\mathbf{u}-\mathbf{v}\right|^2}{2\left|\mathbf{u}\right|\left|\mathbf{v}\right|}$$

```
function angleBetween (vector1, vector2)
    set vector3 to vector2-vector1
    set m1 to magnitude(vector1)
    set m2 to magnitude(vector2)
    set m3 to magnitude(vector3)
    if m1=0 or m2=0 then return "error" // it makes no sense to find an
angle with a zero vector
    if m3=0 then return 0 // the vectors are equal
    return acos((m2*m2+m1*m1-m3*m3)/(2*m1*m2))
end function
```

The Normal Vector

If two vectors are perpendicular, they are also called *normal*. In two dimensions, it is very simple to find the perpendicular to a given vector $\binom{a}{b}$, simply invert the vector and take the negative of one component: $\binom{-b}{a}$. To see why, consider the vector as a position vector and remember our trick for fast rotation by 90°. As any scalar multiple of this vector will still be perpendicular to the original vector, it doesn't matter which component you make negative—multiplying by -1 will give you the same vector in the other direction.

```
function normalVector (vector)
    return vector(-vector[2],vector[1])
end function
```

Two vectors are perpendicular if and only if the sum of the products of their components is zero. In the above example, the product of the x-component of each vector is –ab and the product of the y-components is ab, so their sum is zero as required. We'll look at this further in a moment.

Vectors and Scalars in Real Life

Many day-to-day quantities are best measured with vectors, and it is worth looking at them here as it gives a much clearer indication of what a vector is and why it is important. All these terms are concepts we will be looking at in much more detail later, but they should be familiar enough from normal language to use informally here.

■ **Distance:**   a scalar quantity, measuring the length of the shortest line between two points
  Displacement: the vector between the two points
■ **Speed:**   a scalar, measuring the distance something travels in a certain time
  Velocity: a vector, measuring the displacement traveled in that time
■ **Mass:**   a scalar, measuring how much force is required to move something (in whatever direction)
  Weight: a vector, measuring the force required in a particular direction to keep something in the same place against the pull of gravity

One common factor with these terms is that informally each pair is used interchangeably. We describe an object as having a certain "weight" when really we are describing its mass, or a train traveling with a "velocity" of 100 km/hr when in fact this is its speed. Thinking in terms of vectors does not come naturally to most people.

However, it is an important distinction and worth bearing in mind. When we meet Newton's Laws later, for example, we will talk about forces changing an object's velocity, and it is perfectly possible for an object to change velocity without changing speed: think about a ball on the end of a string moving in a circle. Its direction of travel is changing constantly, but its speed is constant. Describing this in terms of vectors makes things simple: the velocity of an object is a vector, its speed is the magnitude of this vector.

VECTOR MOTION

Let's spend a little time now looking at how we can use vectors to perform some more useful calculations. Pay close attention to this section, we will be using these ideas extensively in later chapters, particularly collision detection and resolution.

Describing Shapes with Vectors

Using vectors is often a very convenient way to describe the relationship between points on the plane. For example, we have already encountered the word *parallel*, where two infinite lines are said to be parallel if either there is no point that lies on both lines, or if all points on one line are on the other (i.e., they are the same line). This works well for infinite lines, but proves to be slightly more complicated for the kinds of lines we deal with most of the time, which have end-points (these are called *line segments*). Using vectors, we can simplify the definition: two lines are parallel if for any distinct points P and Q on one line and P' and Q' on the other, there is some scalar a such that $\overline{PQ} = a\overline{P'Q'}$.

We can also use vectors to provide a "recipe" for creating shapes on the plane. For example, given two points A and B with position vectors **a** and **b**, we can draw a square by first finding the normal of $\overrightarrow{AB}$ (that is to say, of **b** − **a**), which we'll call **n**. We'll assume **n** has the same magnitude as **b** − **a**, which will be true by construction if we use the method described above. If not, we can easily scale it to the right length. Construct the points C and D by **c** = **a** + **n** and **d** = **b** + **n**. Notice that **d** − **c** = **b** − **a** and that $\overrightarrow{AB}$ is perpendicular to $\overrightarrow{AC}$, so the points A,B,D,C form a square (see Figure 5.5).

*Notice that there are two possible squares that can be drawn on the line segment, depending on the direction chosen for the normal vector **n**.*

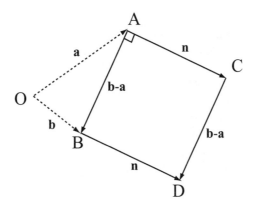

FIGURE 5.5 Constructing a square with vectors.

Constructing an equilateral triangle is just as simple. We start with a little trigonometry: The length of the line from a vertex of an equilateral triangle to the mid-point of the opposite side is $\frac{\sqrt{3}}{2}$ times the length of a side. (This should be simple to prove using Pythagoras' Theorem.) So if we have two vertices A and B, we can construct the third vertex C by $\mathbf{c} = \frac{\mathbf{a}+\mathbf{b}}{2} + \frac{\sqrt{3}\mathbf{n}}{2}$, where again, **n** is the normal vector to **b** − **a**. Remember that $\frac{\mathbf{a}+\mathbf{b}}{2}$ is the position vector of the mid-point of A and B.

We can use similar constructions to create more complex shapes too. In Exercise 5.1 you will be writing a set of functions for creating shapes such as arrowheads and kites. The great advantage of such functions is that they can be very easily parameterized to create a large number of variants on the same theme. For example, here is a function that will create a whole family of letter "A"s:

```
function createA (legLength, angleAtTop, serifProp, crossbarProp,
crossbarHeight, serifAlign, crossbarAlign)
    // serifProp, crossbarHeight, crossbarProp, serifAlign and
crossbarAlign should be values from 0 to 1
    // angleAtTop should be in radians
    set halfAngle to angleAtTop/2
    set leftLeg to legLength*array(-sin(halfAngle), cos(halfAngle))
    set rightLeg to array(-leftLeg[1], leftLeg[2])
    set crossbarStart to leftLeg*crossbarHeight
    set crossbarEnd to rightLeg*crossbarHeight
    set crossbar to crossbarProp*(crossbarEnd-crossbarStart)
    add crossbarAlign*(1-crossbarProp)*(crossbarEnd-crossbarStart) to
crossbarStart
    set serif to serifProp*(rightLeg-leftLeg)
    set serifOffset to serifAlign*serif
    set start to array(0,0)
    drawLine( start, leftLeg)
    drawLine(start, rightLeg)
    drawLine(crossbarStart, crossbarStart+crossbar)
    drawLine(leftLeg-serifOffset, leftLeg-serifOffset+serif)
    drawLine(rightLeg-serifOffset, rightLeg-serifOffset+serif)
    end function
```

You can see some examples of letters drawn by this function in Figure 5.6. One of the most interesting side-effects of this kind of approach is that you can take parameters of this kind and carry them across to related letters, creating a whole font in a similar style.

If you find this kind of thing interesting, you might also want to look at Douglas Hofstadter's Letter Spirit project, which tries to explore the question of what it means for a font to be in a similar "style."

FIGURE 5.6 Letter "A"s drawn with the createA function.

Moving from A to B

All this has been building up to one of the most fundamental questions in programming, especially of games: How do we move *this* from *here* to *there*? In other words, if Jim is at (a,b) and he walks to (c,d), what path does he follow? (See Figure 5.7.)

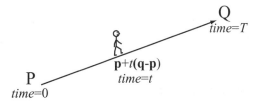

FIGURE 5.7 Jim's path.

Let's break this down into its constituent parts.

- At time 0, Jim is at P $= (a,b)$.
- At time T, Jim is at Q $= (c,d)$.
- We want to know Jim's coordinates at time t, where $0 <= t <= T$

To do this, we need to quickly introduce the concepts of *speed* and *velocity*, mentioned above and to be dealt with in much more detail later. Let's start by looking at the problem in terms of vectors. In the time period of length T, Jim moves straight along the vector $\overrightarrow{PQ}$, which is $\begin{pmatrix} c \\ d \end{pmatrix} - \begin{pmatrix} a \\ b \end{pmatrix} = \begin{pmatrix} c-a \\ d-b \end{pmatrix}$. This is called his *displacement* vector. The length of this vector, $\sqrt{(c-a)^2 + (d-b)^2}$, is the *distance* he travels.

If we divide distance traveled by the time taken, we get the *speed* of the journey, measured in a unit of distance divided by a unit of time, such as a meter *per* second or ms^{-1}. The speed is the distance traveled in each time unit. *Velocity*, similarly, is the displacement vector divided by the time taken (note that time is a scalar quantity), which is the *vector* traveled in each time unit. So in this case, Jim's velocity is $\frac{1}{T}\begin{pmatrix} c-a \\ d-b \end{pmatrix}$.

NOTE

Speed is a little more subtle than this, in fact. If you travel in a long circle, ending up where you started, your displacement is zero, so your total velocity was also zero, and so your mean velocity was: zero! However, your mean speed was not zero, it was equal to the circumference of the circle (the distance traveled) divided by the time taken. So speed is found using the length of the path traveled, not the length of the eventual vector. Of course, when moving in a straight line this is immaterial.

Now we want to know where Jim is to be found at a time t. This is simple: he has gone a proportion $^1\!/_T$ of the way along the vector $\overrightarrow{PQ}$. If we say that this proportion is m (i.e., $t = mT$), his position vector is

$$\overrightarrow{OP} + m\overrightarrow{PQ} = \begin{pmatrix} a \\ b \end{pmatrix} + m\begin{pmatrix} c-a \\ d-b \end{pmatrix} = \begin{pmatrix} mc+(1-m)a \\ md+(1-m)b \end{pmatrix}$$

When programming motion, it is often useful to precalculate many of these values. In object-oriented programming, you will probably be representing something such as a sprite on the screen by an object, which you will send to a new location by some method that takes the new location and time as a parameter. Then you could run a function like this:

```
function calculateTrajectory (oldLocation, newLocation, travelTime)
   if time=0 then
      justGoThere(newLocation)
   otherwise
      set displacement to newLocation-oldLocation
      set velocity to displacement/travelTime
      set startTime to the current time
      set stopPosition to newLocation
      set startPosition to oldLocation
   end if
end function
```

Having done this, whenever you want to update the position of the sprite, you can simply calculate the new position directly:

```
function currentPosition ()
   set time to the current time-startTime
   if time>travelTime then
      set current position to stopPosition
   otherwise
      set current position to startPosition+velocity*time
   end if
end function
```

This method actually uses one variable you can manage without, which is startPosition. *Can you think of how you could do the same thing without remembering your starting position? Hint: try counting down instead of up.*

It is generally more useful to give your object a standard speed and calculate the time to travel from there. You will do this in Exercise 5.2.

More Complicated Vector Paths

Vector motion is not only useful for straight lines. We have already seen that many simple shapes can be described by a sequence of vectors, and in this section we will see a few examples of curved motion created by changing the velocity of a particle as it moves.

The word particle *is mathematical shorthand for an indeterminate moving "thing." Particles are supposed to be infinitely small, although they can have properties like electrical charge or mass, depending on the circumstances. We'll be using it frequently to describe a moving element (sprite) on the screen, as it is conveniently not a word that has an alternative meaning in programming (unlike "object," for example).*

Suppose that instead of approaching Q directly, JimBob wants to skirt round it a little. He can do this by adding a multiple of the normal vector to his trajectory. Take a look at Figure 5.8. Here you see that JimBob does not move directly along the line PQ, instead he travels a short distance along it and a short distance perpendicular to it to the point P'. Then at the next step he does the same thing, moving a little perpendicular to P'Q to P", and so on.

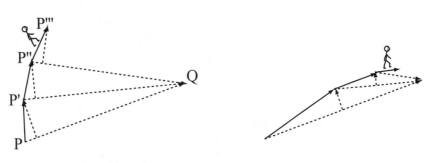

FIGURE 5.8   JimBob's path.

You can see that the path JimBob follows is a spiral, and in the second diagram you can see that the tightness of the spiral depends on how large the normal vector (the *tangential component of the motion*—see later) is when compared to the inward speed (the *radial component*). If the tangential component is zero, then JimBob travels along a straight line. If it is greater than zero but small, he travels along a slightly curved path, if it is large, he spirals in gradually, and if it is infinite (or equivalently, if the radial component is zero), he simply moves in a circle around Q.

Of course, because our time steps are not infinitely small, the path we see the particle traveling on the screen will not be mathematically accurate, but the basic behavior is the same. Here is a function that will move the particle in a curved path of this kind:

```
function curvedPath (endPoint, currentPoint, speed, normalProportion,
timeStep)
    set radius to endPoint-currentPoint
    if magnitude(radius)<speed*timeStep then
      set current position to endPoint
    otherwise
      set radialComponent to norm(radius)
      set tangentialComponent to
normalVector(radialComponent)*normalProportion
      set velocity to speed*norm(radialComponent+tangentialComponent)
      set current position to currentPoint+velocity
    end if
end function
```

You can do some really wacky things by taking vectors out of real life altogether and imagining them as things in their own right. For example, in the curved path function above, the value normalProportion is equivalent to a unit-length vector $\begin{pmatrix} \sin(\alpha) \\ \cos(\alpha) \end{pmatrix}$, where α is equal to atan(normalProportion). What happens if we let *this* vector vary? We can give the vector its own "velocity" by varying α at a constant speed around the circle (this is a taster of angular motion, which we will cover properly much later). Then we get some fantastic paths, like the ones seen in Figure 5.9, generated essentially by this function:

```
function madPath (endPoint, currentPoint, currentAlpha, speed,
alphaSpeed, timeStep)
    set radius to endPoint-currentPoint
    if magnitude(radius)<speed*timeStep then
      set current position to endPoint
    otherwise
      set radialComponent to norm(radius)
      set newAlpha to currentAlpha+alphaSpeed*timeStep
      set tangentialComponent to
normalVector(radialComponent)*tan(newAlpha)
      set velocity to speed*norm(radialComponent+tangentialComponent)
      set current position to currentPoint+velocity
    end if
end function
```

FIGURE 5.9   Paths generated by varying velocity.

Thinking of an abstract quantity in vector terms is a very, very powerful tool, but hard to use to get the results you want and we won't go into it any more here, although you may want to play with the concept yourself. For now, just remember the idea of varying the velocity vector over time, as this will lead us in later chapters to the idea of acceleration.

VECTOR CALCULATIONS

You can use vector algebra to make some quite complex deductions. In this section we'll look at some techniques for creating and solving vector equations.

Separating Vectors into Components

Any two non-parallel vectors, along with a single defined origin, can be used to describe any point on a plane. If **u** and **v** are non-parallel vectors then any vector on the plane can be described uniquely in the form $a\mathbf{u} + b\mathbf{v}$, where a and b are scalars. This is called using **u** and **v** as a *basis*. One example of this is using the vectors $\begin{pmatrix} 1 \\ 0 \end{pmatrix}$ and $\begin{pmatrix} 0 \\ 1 \end{pmatrix}$, often denoted **i** and **j**. The vector $\begin{pmatrix} a \\ b \end{pmatrix}$ is equal to $a\mathbf{i} + b\mathbf{j}$, so the components of the vector translate directly into the basis description. Because the basis vectors are *orthogonal* (perpendicular) and *normalized* (unit length), this is described as an *orthonormal* basis.

Sometimes it is useful to use a different basis. For example, we saw earlier that it is often practical to think in terms of the radial and tangential components of a motion, which is the same as describing the velocity vector in terms of a new orthonormal basis directed toward the goal (see Figure 5.10).

The advantage of doing this is that often the components in these two directions can be considered independently. We'll see in later chapters that when a force is directed along one vector, the velocity perpendicular to that vector is unchanged. Fortunately, converting a vector to a new basis is straightforward.

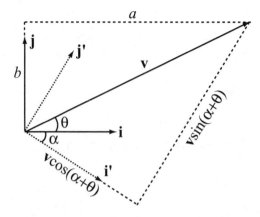

FIGURE 5.10   Converting a vector to a new basis.

NOTE

The word component *has something of a dual meaning. If in some orthonormal basis we have* $v = pa + qb$, *then you can use the term "component of v in the a-direction" to mean either the vector pa or just the number p. It should generally be clear from context which of these is intended, and in code snippets we will use the functions* component(vector1, vector2) *and* componentVector(vector1, vector2) *to distinguish between them.*

In Figure 5.10, the vector v is to be converted from the basis i, j to the basis i', j'. The angle between i and i' is α, and the angle between v and i is θ. We have drawn a right-angled triangle with v as the hypotenuse, and you can see that the magnitude of the component in the direction i' is equal to $|v|\cos(\theta - \alpha)$, and in the direction j' is $|v|\sin(\theta - \alpha)$. What's more, we can calculate the angles θ and α directly from the components of v and i' in the directions of i and j—for example, if v is the vector $\binom{a}{b} = ai + bj$ then $\theta = $ atan(b,a).

Let's summarize this in terms of a function. This function takes two arguments, the vectors v and k, and returns four values: the orthonormal vectors i' and j' (where i' is the normalized version of k), and the components a and b of v in the directions of i' and j'. So at the end, we know that $v = ai' + bj'$.

```
function switchbasis (vector, directionVector)
    set basis1 to norm(directionVector)
    set basis2 to normal(basis1)
    set alpha to atan(basis1[2],basis1[1])
    set theta to atan(vector[2],vector[1])
    set mag to magnitude(vector)
```

```
        set a to mag*cos(theta-alpha)
        set b to mag*sin(theta-alpha)
        return new array(basis1, basis2, a, b)
    end
```

NOTE

Notice that we have used here the two-argument version of the atan() *function introduced in the previous chapter.*

We can also write two simpler functions which find a single component in a new basis. In general, these are more useful:

```
function component (vector, directionVector)
    set alpha to atan(directionVector [2], directionVector [1])
    set theta to atan(vector[2],vector[1])
    set mag to magnitude(vector)
    set a to mag*cos(theta-alpha)
    return a
end function

function componentVector(vector, directionVector)
    set v to norm(directionVector)
    return component(vector, directionVector)*v
end function
```

The Scalar (Dot) Product

Although the methods you've seen in this chapter for finding angles and components of vectors are fairly simple, there is another way which is much more versatile. As we saw earlier, there is no natural way to multiply two vectors, but one common operation which we can do is to take what is called the *scalar product*, which as its name suggests is a function that combines two vectors to get a scalar answer.

The scalar product of the vectors **u** and **v** is written with a dot as **u · v**, and is commonly called the *dot product*. To calculate it, we take the sum of the pairwise products of the vector components:

$$\begin{pmatrix} a \\ b \end{pmatrix} \cdot \begin{pmatrix} c \\ d \end{pmatrix} = ac + bd$$

What is the use of this? Well, let's start by looking at the dot product of a vector with the basis vector **i**, or $\begin{pmatrix} 1 \\ 0 \end{pmatrix}$. You can see that this gives the *x*-component of the vector. Similarly, the dot product with **j** gives the *y*-component. In fact, when you take the dot product of **v** with any unit vector **u**, you end up with the component of **v** in the direction of **u**.

More generally, the dot product of two vectors **v** and **w** is equal to $|\mathbf{v}| \times |\mathbf{w}| \times \cos\alpha$, where α is the angle between the two vectors. This means that we can use the dot product for a number of useful calculations. For example, the dot product of a vector with itself is the square of its magnitude which also follows from Pythagoras' Theorem. Also, we can find the angle between two vectors more simply now by using

$$\alpha = \cos^{-1}\left(\frac{\mathbf{v}\cdot\mathbf{w}}{|\mathbf{v}||\mathbf{w}|}\right)$$

The dot product also has the following useful properties:

- It is *commutative*: $\mathbf{v}\cdot\mathbf{w} = \mathbf{w}\cdot\mathbf{v}$
- It is *distributive* over addition: $\mathbf{v}\cdot(\mathbf{u}+\mathbf{w}) = \mathbf{v}\cdot\mathbf{u} + \mathbf{v}\cdot\mathbf{w}$
- Multiplying by a scalar gives $\mathbf{v}\cdot(a\mathbf{u}) = a(\mathbf{v}\cdot\mathbf{u})$
- If two vectors are perpendicular then their dot product is zero, and vice versa.

The functions for working with dot products are easily created from these definitions, so they are left to you as an exercise, or you can look at the vector functions on the CD-ROM.

ON THE CD

Vector Equations

You can do algebra with vectors just as you can with regular numbers. In fact, we have already done so in a disguised way, when working with simultaneous equations in Chapter 3. A vector equation might be something like this:

$$a\mathbf{u} + b\mathbf{v} = \mathbf{w}$$

Any of the variables in this equation might be unknowns—the scalars a and b, or the vectors **u**, **v**, and **w**, but most common is the situation where we know the vectors but do not know the scalars.

In Figure 5.11, we are trying to find the intersection point of the two lines AB and CD. We know the position vectors **a**, **b**, **c**, **d** of the four points A, B, C, D, and we are looking for the position vector of the point P where the two lines cross.

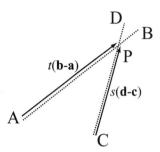

FIGURE 5.11 Finding the intersection of two lines.

The trick here is to try to *parameterize* P, which is to say, to find a way of describing it in terms of the points A, B, C, D. All we know about P is that it lies on both lines AB and CD. So what can we say about a point that lies on a particular line AB? To get to such a point, we can start at the origin O, travel to A, then travel some distance along the vector AB—we don't know how far, so we'll say it's some value t. Therefore we can say

$$\overrightarrow{OP} = \overrightarrow{OA} + t\overrightarrow{AB}$$
$$= \mathbf{a} + t(\mathbf{b} - \mathbf{a})$$

What is more, because P also lies on CD, we can say that

$$\overrightarrow{OP} = \mathbf{c} + s(\mathbf{d} - \mathbf{c})$$

for some scalar s.

This gives us an equation for s and t:

$$\mathbf{a} + t(\mathbf{b} - \mathbf{a}) = \mathbf{c} + s(\mathbf{d} - \mathbf{c})$$
$$t(\mathbf{b} - \mathbf{a}) + s(\mathbf{c} - \mathbf{d}) = \mathbf{c} - \mathbf{a}$$

Now this is a single equation in two variables. However, it is really two equations in disguise, because it must be true separately for both the x- and y-coordinates of the basis. This means that we can separate the vector equation into two linear simultaneous equations:

$$t(b_1 - a_1) + s(c_1 - d_1) = c_1 - a_1$$
$$t(b_2 - a_2) + s(c_2 - d_2) = c_2 - a_2$$

where a_1, b_1, c_1, d_1 are the x-components of the vectors **a**, **b**, **c**, **d**, which is to say they are the x-coordinates of the points A, B, C, D, and similarly for a_2, b_2, c_2, d_2.

It can be confusing to keep these various concepts distinct. Always try to maintain a clear separation between the points, vectors, and components in your particular problem, because it will help you when the problems get more complicated.

NOTE

These simultaneous equations can be solved by the same methods we used before, giving values for t and s, although actually you only need one of the values in order to solve the problem. We've already gone through the process of solving simultaneous equations in detail so there is no need to retread that ground here. Let's just write down the function for solving this vector equation and you can examine it at leisure. This function takes four vectors as arguments and returns the intersection of the lines between them.

```
function intersectionPoint(a, b, c, d)
    set tc1 to b[1]-a[1]
    set tc2 to b[2]-a[2]
    set sc1 to c[1]-d[1]
    set sc2 to c[2]-s[2]
    set con1 to c[1]-a[1]
    set con2 to c[2]-a[2]
    set det to (tc2*sc1-tc1*sc2)
    if det=0 then return "no unique solution"
    set con to tc2*con1-tc1*con2
    set s to con/det
    return c+s*(d-c)
end function
```

You might be wondering why we used the variable name det *for the value* (tc2*sc1-tc1*sc2). *It stands for* determinant, *which is a term we shall be explaining shortly.*

NOTE

We can also do the same thing in a different way starting instead with the position vectors of A and C and the vectors $\overline{AB}$ and $\overline{CD}$:

```
function intersectionTime(p1, v1, p2, v2)
    set tc1 to v1[1]
    set tc2 to v1[2]
    set sc1 to v2[1]
    set sc2 to v2[2]
    set con1 to p2[1]-p1[1]
    set con2 to p2[2]-p1[2]
```

```
      set det to (tc2*sc1-tc1*sc2)
      if det=0 then return "no unique solution"
      set con to sc1*con2-sc2*con1
      set t to con/det
      return t
   end function
```

In this second case, instead of returning the point of intersection, the function returns the value of t. There is a good reason for this: the values t and s are useful for more than determining the position of P. They also tell us the relationship of P to the points A, B, C, D. Suppose the value of t turns out to be 0.5. This means that P is equal to $\mathbf{a} + 0.5(\mathbf{b} - \mathbf{a})$, which is half-way along the line AB. In general, if t is between 0 and 1, then P lies between the points A and B (with a value of 0 representing the point A, and 1 representing B). If it is greater than 1, then P lies somewhere beyond the point B, and if it is less than 0 then P lies behind the point A. Similarly, s determines how far along the line CD P lies. So only if both s and t are in [0,1] does the point P actually lie on the intersection of the line segments AB and CD. In any other case, P lies on the projection of the lines to infinity (see Figure 5.12).

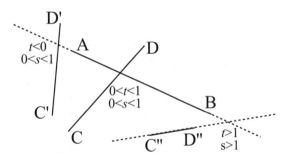

FIGURE 5.12   Various intersections of lines and their vector parameterization.

This means we can create a slightly different function which finds the point where two line segments intersect. This function will be vital when working on collision detection, and again, it's helpful for it to return the value of t.

```
function intersection(a, b, c, d)
   set tc1 to b[1]-a[1]
   set tc2 to b[2]-a[2]
```

```
        set sc1 to c[1]-d[1]
        set sc2 to c[2]-s[2]
        set con1 to c[1]-a[1]
        set con2 to c[2]-a[2]
        set det to (tc2*sc1-tc1*sc2)
        if det=0 then return "no unique solution"
        set con to tc2*con1-tc1*con2
        set s to con/det
        if s<0 or s>1 then return false
        if tc1<>0 then set t to (con1-s*sc1)/tc1
        otherwise set t to (con2-s*sc2)/tc2
        if t<0 or t>1 then return "none"
        return t
    end function
```

What about the case where the value det is zero? In this case the lines AB and CD are parallel, which can have a number of meanings:

- If the segments AB and CD lie along the same line (the points A, B, C, D are *collinear*), then either they intersect for some continuous stretch, or they are separate.
- If they don't lie on the same line, then they do not intersect at all.

Distinguishing these three possibilities isn't particularly difficult: it's another vector equation. If A, B, C, D are collinear then any one of the points can be described in terms of the other two—for example, $c = a + k(b - a)$ for some k. And if the value of k in this equation is between 0 and 1 then C lies somewhere between A and B, with the same holding for the equivalent parameter l for the point D, and as long as either one of C and D lies within the segment AB then the lines intersect. You might want to try making a function which tests for these possibilities as an exercise. However, it's rarely vital, as mostly just knowing the two vectors are parallel is enough.

MATRICES

A *matrix* (plural *matrices*), like a vector, is a mathematical array representing tabular information. In this section we'll examine matrices briefly, and look at the basics of matrix arithmetic.

Multidimensional Arrays

A vector is a one-dimensional array: it is a list of components representing motion in each of a fixed number of directions. Even a vector in three dimensions, such as the vector $\begin{pmatrix} 1 \\ 1 \\ 1 \end{pmatrix}$, is still a one-dimensional object in itself: it has one value for each of the three directions.

A matrix has values in two directions, and is written like a table enclosed in brackets: $\begin{pmatrix} 1 & 3 \\ -2 & 2 \end{pmatrix}$. In this book we will represent all matrices by capital letters in bold-face such as **M**. You can think of a matrix as a table of values relating rows to columns. For example, here is a table of prices of electrical goods:

	Small	Medium	Large
Widgets	$ 1.20	$ 3.00	$ 4.00
Gizmos	$10.00	$15.00	$20.00
Whosits	$ 5.25	$ 8.50	$11.00

Using this table, we can quickly determine the price of, say, a large gizmo, by looking on the *large* column and the *gizmo* row to find the value $20.00. We can write this down as a matrix which we'll call **G**.

$$\mathbf{G} = \begin{pmatrix} 1.2 & 3 & 4 \\ 10 & 15 & 20 \\ 5.25 & 8.5 & 11 \end{pmatrix}$$

G is a 3×3 matrix because it has three rows and three columns. With four columns it would be a 3×4 matrix, and so on. If a matrix has the same number of rows as columns it is said to be *square*. While we're giving definitions, let's also define the *transpose* of a matrix, written with a superscript T, which is the same matrix but with the rows and columns exchanged, so

$$\mathbf{G}^{\mathrm{T}} = \begin{pmatrix} 1.2 & 10 & 5.25 \\ 3 & 15 & 8.5 \\ 4 & 20 & 11 \end{pmatrix}$$

The transpose of an $n \times m$ matrix is $m \times n$ in size. Notice that taking the transpose leaves the numbers on the diagonal from the top-left to the bottom right unchanged: this is called the *leading diagonal* of the matrix.

A vector is an $n \times 1$ matrix. We can use the transpose notation to write vectors in row form as a $1 \times n$ matrix, which saves space so we'll do it from time to time here: instead of writing $\begin{pmatrix} 1 \\ 2 \\ 3 \end{pmatrix}$ we may write $\begin{pmatrix} 1 & 2 & 3 \end{pmatrix}^{\mathrm{T}}$. Another common notation adopted for the same reason uses angled brackets, as in $\langle 1,2,3 \rangle$.

A square matrix has an associated value called the *determinant*, which we mentioned briefly before. The determinant is a fundamental feature of the matrix, and is somewhat equivalent to the length of a vector, which is reflected in the notation: the determinant of $\mathbf{M}$ is written $|\mathbf{M}|$, although it may also be written as $\det(\mathbf{M})$.

For a 2×2 matrix $\begin{pmatrix} a & b \\ c & d \end{pmatrix}$ the determinant is equal to $ad - bc$. For larger matrices the formula is rather more complicated, although we can write it reasonably simply in terms of a recursive function which takes a square matrix $\mathbf{M}$ as an argument. We'll always represent matrices in functions by an array of arrays, with one array for each row, and one element within that array for each column. So the matrix $\mathbf{G}$ would be the array `[[1.2,10,5.25],[3,15,8.4],[4.5,20,11]]`.

```
function determinant(m)
    set size to the number of elements in m
    if size=1 then return m[1][1]
    set mult to 1
    set sum to 0
    repeat for i=1 to size
        set el to m[1][i]
        set newmatrix to an empty array
        repeat for j=2 to size
            append m[j] to newmatrix
            remove the i'th element of this row
        end repeat
        add el*mult*determinant(newmatrix) to sum
        multiply mult by -1
    end repeat
    return sum
end function
```

The determinant of a matrix is the same as the determinant of its transpose.

Matrices, vectors and scalars are all special cases of a general class of mathematical arrays called tensors, *which in a very brief nutshell are ways to describe a variation in values over regions of mathematical space. Working with tensors tends to be more an exercise in number-juggling than anything else, although they are an essential part of any physics of fields, such as general relativity or electromagnetism. They also turn up in rotational physics—we'll encounter the phrase "inertia tensor" later, before moving on swiftly.*

Matrix Arithmetic

Matrices can seem a little abstract at first, but bear with it because, like vectors, they are more useful than they initially appear. We'll now look at the basic operations with matrices.

You can add two matrices of the same size by simply adding their equivalent elements:

$$\begin{pmatrix} 1 & 3 \\ 4 & 5 \end{pmatrix} + \begin{pmatrix} 2 & -1 \\ 0 & 3 \end{pmatrix} = \begin{pmatrix} 3 & 2 \\ 4 & 8 \end{pmatrix}$$

You can also multiply a matrix by a scalar by multiplying each element within it by the scalar:

$$2 \times \begin{pmatrix} 1 & 3 \\ 4 & 5 \end{pmatrix} = \begin{pmatrix} 2 & 6 \\ 8 & 10 \end{pmatrix}$$

All this is just as you might expect. Where matrices come into their own, however, is that you can multiply them together in a particularly special way. You can multiply an $l \times n$ matrix L by an $n \times m$ matrix M by the following process: take the first element in the first row of L and multiply it by the first element in the first column of M. Do the same for each element of the first row and column of the matrices, and put the sum of these values in the top-left column of a new matrix N.

Continue this process for each pair of a row i of L and column j of M to get a value for the ith row and jth column of N. This will eventually give you an $l \times m$ matrix. Notice that this is only possible if the number of columns of L is the same as the number of rows of M.

```
function matrixMultiply (l, m)
    set n to a blank array
    repeat with i=1 to the number of rows of l
        set r to a blank array
        repeat with j=1 to the number of columns of m
            set sum to 0
            repeat with k=1 to the number of columns of l
                add l[i][k]*m[j][k] to sum
            end repeat
            append sum to r
        end repeat
        append r to n
    end repeat
    return n
end function
```

You will see if you try it that multiplication of matrices is not *commutative*—that is to say, $\mathbf{LM} \neq \mathbf{ML}$. In fact, in general it is not even meaningful to multiply matrices in the reverse order. But even for square matrices, the result of multiplying is as a rule different depending on the order. On the other hand, we can say that if $\mathbf{LM} = \mathbf{N}$ then $\mathbf{M}^T\mathbf{L}^T = \mathbf{N}^T$.

NOTE

Notice that the product $\mathbf{u}^T\mathbf{v}$, where $\mathbf{u}$ and $\mathbf{v}$ are column vectors, gives the dot product of $\mathbf{u}$ and $\mathbf{v}$ (or rather, a 1×1 matrix whose sole element is the dot product).

Although matrix multiplication is not commutative, it is *associative*: $\mathbf{L(MN)} = \mathbf{(LM)N}$, and also *distributive* over addition: $\mathbf{L(M + N)} = \mathbf{LM} + \mathbf{LN}$. For square matrices, matrix multiplication also preserves the determinant: $|\mathbf{LM}| = |\mathbf{L}|\,|\mathbf{M}|$.

For each size of square there is a special *identity* matrix $\mathbf{I}$, which leaves other matrices unchanged under multiplication: $\mathbf{IM} = \mathbf{MI} = \mathbf{M}$ (choosing the appropriate-sized identity matrix for each multiplication, of course). The identity matrix has the value 1 in each of the positions on the leading diagonal and 0 elsewhere, so for example the 2×2 identity matrix is $\begin{pmatrix} 1 & 0 \\ 0 & 1 \end{pmatrix}$.

For any square matrix $\mathbf{M}$ whose determinant is not zero, there is a unique *inverse* matrix $\mathbf{M}^{-1}$ such that $\mathbf{MM}^{-1} = \mathbf{M}^{-1}\mathbf{M} = \mathbf{I}$. For a 2×2 matrix $\begin{pmatrix} a & b \\ c & d \end{pmatrix}$, the inverse is equal to $\frac{1}{ad-bc}\begin{pmatrix} d & -b \\ -c & a \end{pmatrix}$. This gives us yet another way to solve simultaneous equations. We start by encoding a set of simultaneous equations as a matrix. Suppose the equations are:

$$ax + by = p$$
$$cx + dy = q$$

This is equivalent to

$$\begin{pmatrix} a & b \\ c & d \end{pmatrix}\begin{pmatrix} x \\ y \end{pmatrix} = \begin{pmatrix} p \\ q \end{pmatrix}$$

where the vector $\begin{pmatrix} x & y \end{pmatrix}^T$ is a single unknown with two dimensions.

Now we left-multiply both sides of the equation by the inverse of the matrix:

$$\frac{1}{ad-bc}\begin{pmatrix} d & -b \\ -c & a \end{pmatrix}\begin{pmatrix} a & b \\ c & d \end{pmatrix}\begin{pmatrix} x \\ y \end{pmatrix} = \frac{1}{ad-bc}\begin{pmatrix} d & -b \\ -c & a \end{pmatrix}\begin{pmatrix} p \\ q \end{pmatrix}$$

$$\begin{pmatrix} 1 & 0 \\ 0 & 1 \end{pmatrix}\begin{pmatrix} x \\ y \end{pmatrix} = \begin{pmatrix} x \\ y \end{pmatrix} = \frac{1}{ad-bc}\begin{pmatrix} d & -b \\ -c & a \end{pmatrix}\begin{pmatrix} p \\ q \end{pmatrix}$$

NOTE

Note the use of the term left-multiply. *Because matrix multiplication is non-commutative, multiplying on the left or on the right are different operations in the matrix world.*

So we now have a single matrix calculation to find the values of x and y, giving us:

$$\begin{pmatrix} x \\ y \end{pmatrix} = \frac{1}{ad - bc} \begin{pmatrix} dp - bq \\ aq - cp \end{pmatrix}$$

ON THE CD

As it happens, we can use a process similar to the one we used to solve simultaneous equations to find the inverse of matrices larger than 2 × 2. A function to do it can be found on the CD-ROM in the script *matrices*. We perform linear operations (multiplying by a scalar and adding linear combinations) on the rows of the matrix in order to turn it into an identity matrix. If we perform the same operations on an original identity matrix, it turns into the inverse of our original matrix.

The Matrix As a Transformation

So what does all this mean? It all seems like a slightly arbitrary exercise, but actually it is quite a natural process. Like a vector, a matrix is best thought of as an instruction. A vector is an instruction to move in a certain direction. If we multiply a matrix and a vector together, we get a new vector, so a matrix is an instruction for how to interpret the vector, like a vector of vectors. In fact, a matrix is a *transformation* of space, just like the transformations we looked at in the previous chapter.

Let's look at some examples in two dimensions:

- If you take the matrix $\begin{pmatrix} n & 0 \\ 0 & n \end{pmatrix} = n\mathbf{I}$ and multiply it with any vector, you get the same vector multiplied by n. This isn't surprising since $(n\mathbf{I})\mathbf{v} = n(\mathbf{I}\mathbf{v}) = n\mathbf{v}$. So this vector represents the scale transformation, and any matrix with a determinant other than 1 (or zero) includes some element of scaling.
- If you left-multiply the matrix $\begin{pmatrix} -1 & 0 \\ 0 & 1 \end{pmatrix}$ with any vector, you get the vector with its x-coordinate reversed, which is to say, the vector reflected in the y-axis. Any matrix with a negative determinant is a reflection of some kind (as well as a possible scale).
- If you left-multiply the matrix $\begin{pmatrix} 0 & 1 \\ -1 & 0 \end{pmatrix}$ with any vector, you get the vector with its x- and y-coordinates switched, and the x-coordinate reversed, which is to say the normal vector, or the vector rotated clockwise by 90° about the origin.
- If you multiply the matrix $\begin{pmatrix} \cos(\theta) & \sin(\theta) \\ -\sin(\theta) & \cos(\theta) \end{pmatrix}$ with any vector, you get the vector rotated clockwise by θ about the origin. Notice that because $\cos^2(\theta) + \sin^2(\theta) = 1$, the determinant of this matrix is 1 and so the vector is not scaled or reflected.

■ If you multiply the matrix $\begin{pmatrix} 1 & 1 \\ 0 & 1 \end{pmatrix}$ by any vector, you get the vector skewed parallel to the x-axis by an amount proportional to the y component, so this matrix represents a shear. Again the matrix has a determinant of 1.

Not all transformations can be represented by a matrix in this way—translations in particular are achieved by adding a constant vector, rather than by a matrix multiplication (we'll look at a special way to represent translations in Chapter 18). But every transformation centered on the origin can be represented by a matrix, and what is more, we can use matrix multiplication rules to calculate the combined results of several such transformations. For example, if we want to rotate a triangle by 75° clockwise about the origin, scale it to twice its size and then reflect it in the x-axis, we can do the following:

1. Multiply the position vector of each vertex of the triangle by the matrix $\mathbf{R} = \begin{pmatrix} \cos(75^\circ) & \sin(75^\circ) \\ -\sin(75^\circ) & \cos(75^\circ) \end{pmatrix}$ to perform the rotation
2. Multiply the resultant vector by the matrix $\mathbf{S} = \begin{pmatrix} 2 & 0 \\ 0 & 2 \end{pmatrix}$
3. Multiply the resultant vector by the matrix $\mathbf{T} = \begin{pmatrix} 1 & 0 \\ 0 & -1 \end{pmatrix}$

This means that the end position of the vertex with position vector $\mathbf{a}$ is $\mathbf{T}(\mathbf{S}(\mathbf{Ra})) = (\mathbf{TSR})\mathbf{a}$. So if we start by calculating the matrix $\mathbf{TSR}$, then we can apply this matrix to all the vertices of the triangle, and any others we happen to need, to transform it in one go.

As before, remember that matrix multiplication, and thus transformation, is not commutative. If you perform the three operations in a different order you will get a different end result. This makes sense, as if you imagine turning left and then looking in a mirror, you will get a different end result than when looking in the mirror and then turning the mirror image left.

Before we finish on this topic, quickly have a look at what happens to the basis vectors $\mathbf{i} = \begin{pmatrix} 1 & 0 \end{pmatrix}^T$ and $\mathbf{j} = \begin{pmatrix} 0 & 1 \end{pmatrix}^T$ under the transformation $\mathbf{M} = \begin{pmatrix} a & b \\ c & d \end{pmatrix}$. You can see that we have $\mathbf{Mi} = \begin{pmatrix} a & b \\ c & d \end{pmatrix}\begin{pmatrix} 1 \\ 0 \end{pmatrix} = \begin{pmatrix} a \\ c \end{pmatrix}$ and $\mathbf{Mj} = \begin{pmatrix} a & b \\ c & d \end{pmatrix}\begin{pmatrix} 0 \\ 1 \end{pmatrix} = \begin{pmatrix} b \\ d \end{pmatrix}$. So the columns of the matrix $\mathbf{M}$ give the results of transforming the basis vectors. This means, firstly, that if we know the result of a transformation on the basis vectors, then we know everything there is to know about it, and secondly that we can use this result to calculate the transformation matrix.

One final useful property of a matrix is its set of *eigenvectors* and associated *eigenvalues*. These are a very handy way to characterize a matrix. In essence, an eigenvector is a vector which maps to a multiple of itself under a particular transformation. The multiple is called the eigenvalue for that vector. So if $\mathbf{p}$ is an eigenvector of $\mathbf{M}$, and λ is the corresponding eigenvalue, we have

$$\mathbf{Mp} = \lambda\mathbf{p}$$

Strictly speaking, we should distinguish between right-eigenvectors and left-eigenvectors—a left-eigenvector is similar to the above, but multiplied on the left of the matrix, however in general we are more interested in the right-eigenvectors. It turns out that while the eigenvectors on left and right are different, the set of eigenvalues on each side is the same for any given matrix.

EXERCISES

Exercise 5.1

Write a set of functions such as `drawArrowhead(linesegment, size, angle)` and `drawKite(linesegment, height, width)`, which create complex shapes from simple initial parameters.

Don't just stick to these two shapes, try making as many as you can think of. Try drawing letterforms as in the chapter—you could create variable fonts based on parameters of widths, heights and angles. Or how about a simple 3D effect which creates a "bevel" for a set of points?

Exercise 5.2

Write a similar function to that shown in the chapter, `calculateTrajectory(oldPosition,newPosition,speed)`, which pre-calculates the velocity vector and other necessary parameters of the journey.

The function should end up with the same set of parameters as the function of the same name presented in the chapter—or even with the slightly simplified version suggested there, which does not remember the initial position.

SUMMARY

In this chapter we have covered the essentials of vector and matrix arithmetic and algebra, giving you what may be a new way to think of space. We've seen how we can use vectors to describe positions and movement, and how to use them to perform complicated calculations like finding intersections of lines. We've also seen how matrices can be used to transform space, and looked at the concept of a basis.

In the final chapter of Part I, we'll return to algebraic manipulation and, with the help of our new geometrical understanding, look at some further ways to analyze functions.

YOU SHOULD NOW KNOW

- what a *vector* is, how to describe it in terms of its *components,* and how to perform basic arithmetic such as adding, subtracting, and scaling vectors
- the meanings of the terms *magnitude, norm* and *normal,* and how to calculate them for a given vector
- how to calculate the *scalar (dot) product* of two vectors, and what it means
- how to use combinations of known vectors to describe a known position in space, and how to *parameterize* a vector description to describe a concept such as "a vector on the line AB"
- how to find the components of a vector in a different direction (putting it into a different *basis*), both geometrically and by using the dot product
- how to solve *vector equations* using linear simultaneous equation techniques, and how to use this to find intersections between lines
- what a *matrix* is and how to perform matrix calculations
- how to solve simultaneous linear equations with matrices
- how to use matrices to create multiple *transformations* of space

6 Calculus

In This Chapter

- Overview
- Differentiation and Integration
- Differential Equations
- Approximation Methods
- Exercises
- Summary
- You Should Now Know

OVERVIEW

We're almost done with the fundamentals of mathematics, we only have one more topic to cover, which is the mathematics of limits, otherwise known as *calculus*. This is the first major topic we are looking at that may not have been part of your mathematical education, and the need for it directly in programming is limited, but it's a necessary part of so much of the mathematical theory that we need to examine it briefly.

ON THE CD

Code samples from this chapter are implemented in *math.cst* in the script *chapter 6 (calculus)*.

133

DIFFERENTIATION AND INTEGRATION

The two principal techniques in calculus are an extension of the work we did in Chapter 3 on graphs, and in Chapter 4 on gradients. Now we'll return to graphs of functions and explore this in more detail.

The Gradient of a Function

We introduced the concept of a gradient already in previous sections, when looking at the slope of a straight line graph such as $y = 2x + 1$. The concept is actually much more general than that. Suppose we have a smooth curve (one which has no corners), and a point P_0 on it. Now imagine taking a series of points on the line, P_1, P_2, ... , each of which is closer to P_0 than the one before (see Figure 6.1). When we draw a straight line joining P_0 to each of these points, it gradually tends toward a particular line, which is called the *tangent* to the curve at P_0. The gradient of the tangent is called the gradient of the curve at P_0.

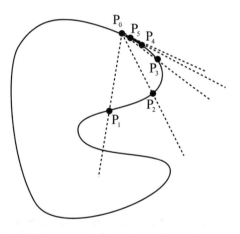

FIGURE 6.1   Finding the gradient of a curve at a particular point.

We can use the same method to find the gradient of a function at a particular value of x, say x_0. If we take a small value δ (this is the Greek letter "delta," often used when dealing with the concept of a limit), and find the value of $f(x_0 + \delta)$, then as δ gets smaller and smaller, this gives us, as required, a series of points on the curve that are successively closer to $(x_0, f(x_0))$ (see Figure 6.2).

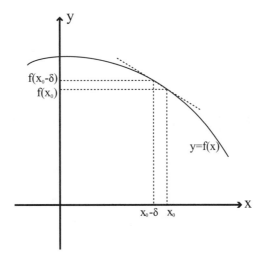

FIGURE 6.2 The gradient of a function.

As before, the gradient of the line joining one of these points to the required point is given by the vertical distance between them divided by the horizontal distance. So it is equal to

$$\frac{f\left(x_0+\delta\right)-f\left(x_0\right)}{\delta}$$

This means that the gradient of the function is equal to the limit of this value as δ approaches zero, which we write as

$$\lim_{\delta\to 0}\frac{f\left(x_0+\delta\right)-f\left(x_0\right)}{\delta}$$

Let's make this a little more concrete. Suppose we perform these operations with a parabola, for example. Let's say our function is ax^2+bx+c, and we want to find the tangent at x_0. Now we have:

$$f\left(x_0+\delta\right)=a\left(x_0+\delta\right)^2+b\left(x_0+\delta\right)+c$$
$$=ax_0^2+2ax_0\delta+a\delta^2+bx_0+b\delta+c$$
$$=\left(2ax_0+b\right)\delta+a\delta^2+ax_0^2+bx_0+c$$

We also know that:

$$f(x_0) = ax_0^2 + bx_0 + c$$

So to find the gradient, we need to find the value of

$$\lim_{\delta \to 0} \frac{f(x_0 + \delta) - f(x_0)}{\delta} = \lim_{\delta \to 0} \frac{\left((2ax_0 + b)\delta + a\delta^2 + ax_0^2 + bx_0 + c\right) - \left(ax_0^2 + bx_0 + c\right)}{\delta}$$

$$= \lim_{\delta \to 0} \frac{(2ax_0 + b)\delta + a\delta^2}{\delta}$$

$$= \lim_{\delta \to 0} 2ax_0 + b + a\delta$$

As the value of δ approaches zero, this approaches $2ax_0 + b$. So the gradient at $x = 1$, for example, is $2a + b$.

Differentiating

The process we just went through is called *differentiating* a function. It takes a function $f(x)$ and produces a new function $g(x)$ which represents the gradient of f at each value of x. We used x_0 above for clarity, but of course x_0 is just a variable and we can call it what we like. We normally write $g(x)$ as either $\frac{df}{dx}$ (said "dee-eff by dee-ex") or $f'(x)$, and we call it the *derivative* of f.

The small d is a kind of shorthand for "very small change in," so the expression $\frac{df}{dx}$ means "the amount of change in f(x) for a small change in x". That is, the derivative represents the *rate of change* of f with respect to the variable x, or how fast the value of f(x) changes as you vary the value of x. We can, if we want, even take the *second derivative* by differentiating the first derivative, to get a new function again, $\frac{d^2f}{dx^2}$ ("dee-two-eff by dee-ex squared") or $f''(x)$, which represents the rate of change of the gradient of f. Similarly, we can find the third derivative, fourth derivative and so on.

One further notation is often used for physical functions whose main variable represents time (or parametric equations with the parameter t, as we'll see in a moment). The derivative with respect to time is represented by a dot, so for a function $y(t)$, the first derivative would be $\dot{y}(t)$ (or just $\dot{y}$), the second derivative $\ddot{y}(t)$ or $\ddot{y}$, etc.

You can differentiate most smooth functions by the process we went through above (called *numeric differentiation* or sometimes "differentiating from first principles"), but there are a number of shortcuts that you can use as well:

1. If a is a constant, then $\frac{d}{dx}\left(a\,f(x)\right) = a\frac{d}{dx}\left(f(x)\right)$.
2. If f and g are functions, then $\frac{d}{dx}\left(f(x)+g(x)\right) = f'(x)+g'(x)$.
3. If f and g are functions, then $\frac{d}{dx}\left(f(x)g(x)\right) = f'(x)g(x)+g'(x)f(x)$.
4. If f and g are functions, then $\frac{d}{dx}\left(f(g(x))\right) = f'(g(x))g'(x)$ (This is called the Chain Rule)
5. The derivative of a constant is zero, and the derivative of x is 1.

The chain rule in particular is an illustration of an important principle about differentiation, which is that in many circumstances the dx's and dy's and so on act like normal variables, so in particular we can cancel them just like a normal fraction. The chain rule tells us that $\frac{df}{dg} \times \frac{dg}{dx} = \frac{df}{dx}$, "canceling out the dg's."

If we apply these rules to a polynomial such as $ax^3 + bx^2 + cx + d$, we can see how powerful they are. By rule 2, we can deal with each of the terms separately. By rule 1, we can ignore the coefficients for now. So we can start by differentiating the function $f(x) = x^n$, for some integer n. If we use rule 3, we can see that $\frac{d}{dx}\left(x^n\right) = \frac{d}{dx}\left(x^{n-1} \times x\right)$.

Since, by rule 5, $\frac{d}{dx}\left(x\right) = 1$, this gives us:

$$\frac{d}{dx}\left(x^n\right) = \frac{d}{dx}\left(x^{n-1}\right) \times x + x^{n-1}$$

$$= \frac{d}{dx}\left(x^{n-2}\right) \times x^2 + x^{n-2} \times x + x^{n-1}$$

$$= \dots$$

$$= \frac{d}{dx}\left(x\right) \times x^{n-1} + x^{n-1} + \dots + x^{n-1}$$

$$= nx^{n-1}$$

If you don't quite follow this, try it with a small value of n, such as 4, and you'll see that you end up with $\frac{d}{dx}\left(x^4\right) = 4x^3$.

If we now use this result, along with rules 1, 2 and 5, we get the result:

$$\frac{d}{dx}\left(ax^3 + bx^2 + cx + d\right) = 3ax^2 + 2bx + c$$

In general, the derivative of a polynomial of degree n is another polynomial of degree $n-1$.

As another example, if we want to differentiate $y = \left(3x+2\right)^2$, we can use the chain rule: suppose we say $g = 3x+2$, so $y = g^2$ then we have

$$\frac{dy}{dx} = \frac{dy}{dg} \times \frac{dg}{dx} = 2g \times 3 = 6\left(3x+2\right)$$

You might want to check this result by multiplying out the brackets in the expression for y and differentiating the polynomial directly.

So what is the point of all this? Well, here are a few things the derivative of a function can tell you:

- If the derivative of a function is **zero** for some value of x, then the function has what is called a *turning point* at x. This means that any maximum or minimum value of a smooth function must occur at a root of the first derivative. (The reverse is not true—not all turning points are maxima or minima, they may also be *points of inflection*.)
- If a function has an **asymptote** at a particular value of x, then its derivative will also have an asymptote at the same value.
- If the derivative of a function is **negative**, this means the function is sloping down from left to right. If it is positive, the function is sloping from right to left.

Look at Figure 6.3 to see examples of all of these. The points marked N, X and I on are minima, maxima and points of inflection of $f(x)$—note that when we say "maximum" or "minimum" here we are referring to what is called a *local* maximum or minimum, as opposed to the *global* minimum or maximum. The function has no global maximum or minimum, and it has an asymptote at A.

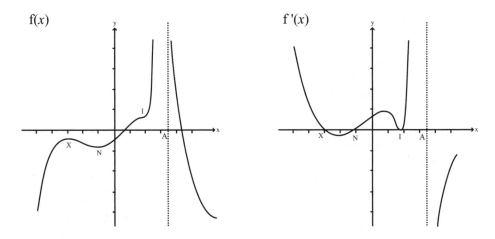

FIGURE 6.3   A function and its first derivative.

If you look at the graph of the first derivative, you will see that for each of the turning points, the first derivative is zero. Maxima and minima are points where the first derivative crosses the x-axis; places where the first derivative touches the

x-axis without crossing it are points of inflection. In fact, we can use the second derivative to work out which kind of turning point we are looking at: a positive second derivative indicates a minimum, a negative one represents a maximum, and a second derivative of zero gives a point of inflection—why this is so is an exercise for you to think about.

 Strictly speaking, a point of inflection does not have to have a zero first derivative, it is any point where the first derivative has a maximum or minimum, that is, a point where the second derivative is zero.

NOTE

Differentiating Logarithms and Exponentials

Polynomials are not the only functions that can be differentiated. Many common functions have simple derivatives, including two we have met before, `exp()` and `log()`.

`exp()` is perhaps the most fundamental function of all in calculus. Recall from Chapter 2 that the value e is equal to $\frac{1}{0!}+\frac{1}{1!}+\frac{1}{2!}+\frac{1}{3!}+\cdots$. It turns out that in general

$$e^x = \frac{1}{0!}+\frac{x}{1!}+\frac{x^2}{2!}+\frac{x^3}{3!}+\dots$$

(if you substitute 1 for x in this expression you get the original value of e). Proving this equation is quite tricky, but you might want to try it for one or two special cases such as $x = 2$.

If we differentiate the above expression, something interesting happens

$$\frac{d}{dx}\left(\frac{1}{0!}+\frac{x}{1!}+\frac{x^2}{2!}+\frac{x^3}{3!}\dots\right)=0+\frac{1}{1!}+\frac{2x}{2!}+\frac{3x^2}{3!}+\dots$$

Each term in this expression is equal to $\frac{nx^{n-1}}{n!}$. From the definition of a factorial, $\frac{n}{n!}=\frac{1}{(n-1)!}$, so the expression becomes

$$0+\frac{1}{0!}+\frac{x}{1!}+\frac{x^2}{2!}+\dots$$

which, of course, is the expression for e^x again. So the derivative of e^x is itself! And in fact, this is uniquely true of the function e^x.

Logarithms are less neat than exponentials, but have a surprising property of their own which we'll present here without proof:

$$\frac{d}{dx}\log_e\left(x\right)=\frac{1}{x}$$

Recall that functions with an asymptote have an asymptote at the same position in their derivative, and this is true here: the logarithm function and the function $\frac{1}{x}$ both have an asymptote at $x = 0$. You might want to see if you can prove this derivative by differentiating the logarithm function from first principles.

Differentiating the Trigonometric Functions

Given the close relationship between e and the trigonometric functions, one would expect these to also have some pleasing properties when it comes to differentiation, and one would be right. Recall the infinite series for $\sin(x)$ and $\cos(x)$:

$$\sin\left(x\right) = x - \frac{x^3}{3!} + \frac{x^5}{5!} - \frac{x^7}{7!} + \dots$$

$$\cos\left(x\right) = 1 - \frac{x^2}{2!} + \frac{x^4}{4!} - \frac{x^6}{6!} + \dots$$

If we differentiate these series, we find that $\frac{d}{dx}\sin\left(x\right) = \cos\left(x\right)$ and $\frac{d}{dx}\cos\left(x\right) = -\sin\left(x\right)$. This also means that both functions are equal to the negative of their own second derivative: $\frac{d^2}{dx^2}\sin\left(x\right) = -\sin\left(x\right)$ and $\frac{d^2}{dx^2}\cos\left(x\right) = -\cos\left(x\right)$.

We can differentiate $\tan(x)$ too, by using the product rule and the chain rule:

$$\frac{d}{dx}\tan\left(x\right) = \frac{d}{dx}\frac{\sin\left(x\right)}{\cos\left(x\right)}$$

$$= \frac{1}{\cos\left(x\right)} \times \frac{d}{dx}\sin\left(x\right) + \sin\left(x\right) \times \frac{d}{dx}\frac{1}{\cos\left(x\right)}$$

Setting $g = \cos\left(x\right)$, we have:

$$\frac{d}{dx}\frac{1}{\cos\left(x\right)} = \frac{d}{dg}\frac{1}{g} \times \frac{dg}{dx}$$

$$= \frac{d}{dg}g^{-1} \times \frac{dg}{dx}$$

$$= \left(-g^{-2}\right) \times \left(-\sin\left(x\right)\right)$$

$$= \frac{\sin\left(x\right)}{\cos^2\left(x\right)}$$

$$= \frac{\tan\left(x\right)}{\cos\left(x\right)}$$

So this gives us:

$$\frac{d}{dx}\tan(x) = \frac{1}{\cos(x)} \times \frac{d}{dx}\sin(x) + \sin(x) \times \frac{\tan(x)}{\cos(x)}$$

$$= \frac{1}{\cos(x)} \times \cos(x) + \sin(x) \times \frac{\tan(x)}{\cos(x)}$$

$$= 1 + \tan^2(x)$$

As with exp(), the inverse trigonometric functions have derivatives which don't include a trigonometric part:

- $\dfrac{d}{dx}\tan^{-1}(x) = \dfrac{1}{1+x^2}$

- $\dfrac{d}{dx}\sin^{-1}(x) = \dfrac{1}{\sqrt{1-x^2}}$

- $\dfrac{d}{dx}\cos^{-1}(x) = -\dfrac{1}{\sqrt{1-x^2}}$

Notice how the square root sign ensures that neither $\sin^{-1}$ nor $\cos^{-1}$ have a well-defined derivative when $|x|>1$.

Partial Differentiation and Parametric Equations

One example of how we can "cancel" the dx terms can be seen when finding the derivative of a function defined parametrically as y(t), x(t). Suppose you are at a particular point with parameter t, and you vary t by a small amount, what will happen? Both the x and y coordinates will change, by an amount $\frac{dx}{dt}$ and $\frac{dy}{dt}$ respectively. So to find the gradient of the curve at that point, we can say, using our dot notation:

$$\frac{dy}{dx}(t) = \frac{\dot{y}}{\dot{x}}$$

It is important to remember that this formula will be a function of t, which is useful as t is usually the value we know. As an example, let's go back to the parabola we looked at in Chapter 3, whose parametric formula was $x = at^2$, $y = 2at$. Taking the derivative of each function with respect to t, we have $\dot{x} = 2at\ (= y)$, $\dot{y} = 2a$, so $\frac{dy}{dx} = \frac{2a}{2at} = \frac{1}{t}$.

Another generalization of the differentiation process comes when we consider functions in more than one variable—for example, we might consider the function

$z = x^2 - 2xy + y^2$, which factorizes to $z = (x - y)^2$. We can plot this function on a surface in three dimensions, taking the x- and y-axes to be the horizontal plane and the z-axis to be vertical.

A surface no longer has a tangent line like a function in one variable; instead it has a tangent *plane*. These kinds of concepts will become clearer in Part IV, but all we need to know at this stage is that a plane can be defined in two ways, either by a (3D) vector describing its normal, or by two (3D) vectors which lie on the plane. We can find two such vectors in this case by using a process called *partial differentiation*. For any point on the surface, what we look at is the two curves through that point in the x- and y-directions. If we find the gradients of these two curves, then we have the two vectors we need.

To find such a gradient, we calculate the *partial derivative* of the surface. This is found exactly the same way as a standard derivative, by differentiating the formula, but *assuming that one variable is constant*. So, for example, the surface $z = x^2 - 2xy + y^2$ gives $\frac{\partial z}{\partial x} = 2x - 2y$, $\frac{\partial z}{\partial y} = 2y - 2x$ (notice the change of notation for a partial derivative).

Integration

As well as differentiating a function, you can also go the other way, taking a function g and finding another function f whose derivative f' is equal to g. This process is called *integration*, and the function f is called the *integral* of g.

You can see immediately that the function f is not unique. Since you can add any constant to a function f and leave its derivative unchanged, the integral of g could be any one of a family of functions f(x)+c, for some value of the parameter c. But the integral is unique apart from variation of this value c.

Integration turns out to have another meaning. The integral of g gives the *area under the curve* g(x), which is to say, the area of the shape drawn between the curve and the x-axis. On the face of it, this doesn't seem to make any sense—how can the value of f(x) represent an area? The area of what? But just as with differentiation, there is a meaning based on the concept of limits. The value of the integral of g at x is equal to the area of an "infinitely thin slice" of the curve area (see Figure 6.4). What's more, this immediately shows how the concept ties in with differentiation, because the steeper the curve at x, the greater the area of a slice under the curve at that point.

Using this concept, we can calculate the area under the curve between two particular x-values, which is called a *definite integral*. An *indefinite integral*, which is what we saw before, is a function, but a definite integral is just a number, a measurement of an area, and it can be found by first finding the indefinite integral f(x), then plugging in the values of x at the two endpoints, so the definite integral between x_1 and x_2 is equal to $f(x_2) - f(x_1)$. Notice that the annoying constant value c which we were forced to introduce for the indefinite integral, cancels out neatly in this calculation, so the definite integral is unambiguous.

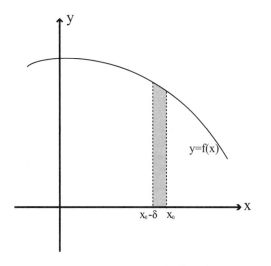

FIGURE 6.4   Integration as finding the area under a curve.

We've got this far without using any actual notation, but here it is now. Integration is represented by the symbol $\int$, and as with differentiation, you must mark the variable over which you are integrating using the letter d, which as before stands for "a very small change in." So the integral of the function $g(x) = 2x - 5$ is written as $\int g(x)dx = \int (2x - 5)dx = x^2 - 5x + c$, meaning that for a very small change in x, g increases by $x^2 - 5x$.

Definite integrals are written the same way, but with the start and end values of the main variable indicated on the integral sign like this:

$$\int_1^3 g(x)dx = \int_1^3 (2x - 5)dx$$
$$= \left[x^2 - 5x \right]_1^3$$
$$= (3^2 - 5 \times 3) - (1^2 - 5 \times 1)$$
$$= -2$$

This calculation gives the area under the line $y = 2x - 5$ between $x = 1$ and $x = 3$.

We've looked at integration quite discursively here, for the very good reason that you are extremely unlikely to need it in programming. It has a certain value when performing particular operations such as finding areas and volumes of complex shapes, but these are quite specialized and rare.

DIFFERENTIAL EQUATIONS

One common situation, particularly in areas of physics, is that we don't know a precise formula for some function $y(x)$, but we do know how something about a relationship between x, y and the derivative(s) of y. This relationship is called a *differential equation* (or strictly an *ordinary differential equation* or ODE, to distinguish it from a *partial* differential equation in more than one variable).

Characteristics of Ordinary Differential Equations

All of these are examples of ordinary differential equations:

- $y' = 2x$
- $\left(y''\right)^2 + 2y = 0$
- $y' - 2xy + y^2 - x = 0$

and so on.

What are we looking for when we see a differential equation? Generally what we are trying to discover is the function $y(x)$, if such a function exists (the *algebraic solution*). If that fails, we can at least try to find one or more particular values of y, or a function which approximates the differential equation (the *numeric solution*).

A very few of these equations are relatively easy to solve: for example, any differential equation of the form $y' = f(x)$ is simply an exercise in integration (which may or may not be possible algebraically, of course). A common example of this kind of problem is the snow-plough: suppose that the speed of a snow plough is inversely proportional to the depth of snow, and that the plough is trying to clear snow which is still falling. We want to find how long it takes for the plough to travel a certain distance x.

Suppose the snow is at an initial depth of s, and is falling at a rate of σ. We know that the speed of the plough is inversely proportional to the amount of snow, so we have

$$\frac{dx}{dt} = \frac{k}{s + \sigma t}$$

We can integrate the right-hand side to get

$$x = \frac{k}{\sigma} \ln(s + \sigma t) + c$$

Supposing that at $t = 0$ we have $x = 0$, we can say that $c = -\frac{k}{\sigma} \ln(s)$, so this becomes

$$x = \frac{k}{\sigma}\left(\ln\left(s+\sigma t\right)-\ln\left(s\right)\right) = \frac{k}{\sigma}\ln\left(1+\frac{\sigma}{s}t\right)$$

Now to find t in terms of x, we invert this equation to get

$$t = \frac{s}{\sigma}\left(\exp\left(\frac{\sigma x}{k}\right)-1\right)$$

Now notice that a part of this calculation involved the unknown constant of integration, c. Before we could solve the problem fully, we needed to know an additional piece of information about the problem, namely the starting position of the plough. This means, as we've seen before, that the differential equation actually has a *family* of solutions, with a valid solution to the equation for any particular choice of c. This is a general feature of differential equations.

This process of setting the integration parameter(s) (or any other unknowns) by means of the *initial conditions* of the system makes sense: a differential equation is like a vector, it tells you nothing about where you are *now*, it only tells you that "if you're currently *here*, doing *this*, then you'll shortly be *there*, doing *that*."

We can illustrate this by a diagram. Suppose our differential equation is the third of the equations above, $y'-2xy+y^2-x=0$. We can draw this on a graph by choosing any particular point (x, y) and calculating the value of y' at that point. Then we draw on our graph a short line at this point with the appropriate gradient. If we do this multiple times we end up with a graph that looks something like Figure 6.5.

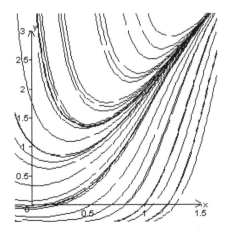

FIGURE 6.5 A numeric plot of the differential equation $y'-2xy+y^2-x=0$.

Each of the lines thus drawn represents a *particular solution* of the ODE, while the *general solution* continues to have one or more unknown parameters introduced by the integration process. Notice that this graph shows certain patterns: Whichever initial conditions we choose, all the functions $y(x)$ converge for high values of x on the line $y = 2x$, which we would expect: for large values of x and y, the linear term in x becomes less significant. Other differential equations can feature *loops, singularities, strange attractors* and many other interesting phenomena.

Solving Linear ODEs

Although as we have said, the majority of ODEs are not solvable algebraically, some are. A particularly tractable set is the set of *linear* ODEs, which is to say, equations of the form

$$f_0(x)y + f_1(x)y' + f_2(x)y'' + ... + f_n(x)y^{(n)} = 0$$

where $y^{(n)}$ is the nth derivative of y and all the f's are functions of x.

Suppose first of all that all the functions in the above formula are just constants. The key to solving an equation like this is the exp function. Remember that this function is its own derivative. Therefore any function of the form $y = e^{rx}$ has a derivative which is a multiple r of itself. For example, suppose our differential equation is $2y - 5y' + 3y'' = 0$. Then we could try the solution $y = e^{rx}$ and see what happens. If we plug this function back into the differential equation, we get

$$2e^{rx} - 5re^{rx} + 3r^2e^{rx} = 0$$

Now, because e^{rx} is always positive, we can factorize it out, giving us $2 - 5r + 3r^2 = 0$, which is just a quadratic equation, whose solution has $r = 2$ or $\frac{1}{3}$.

Now, it's not quite as simple as this, because there are two variants which will also work. If we multiply a valid function by a constant, $y = Ae^{rx}$, this factor A cancels out, so any multiple A will still give a valid solution to the differential equation. Similarly, if we add a constant c to the exponent, $y = Ae^{rx+c}$, this constant disappears when differentiating, so again it doesn't affect the validity of the solution. Therefore, our family of ODEs has two parameters which will be determined by the initial conditions. We'll return to this problem in a more concrete form in Chapter 16.

There is much more to be said about differential equations, but we'll leave it here—in future during the book results of differential equations will usually be presented without proof.

APPROXIMATION METHODS

One important technique for which calculus is very useful is in finding *approximate* solutions to a problem. Even outside the realm of differential equations, many equations cannot be solved by algebraic methods such as the ones we have used in Chapter 3. These are not necessarily complicated equations—even an equation as simple as $\sin(x) = x$ needs a non-algebraic solution.

Any equation in one variable can be reduced to the form f(x) = 0, so our problem becomes one of finding the roots of the function f(x). There are a number of methods that can be used for this. None of them are foolproof, but when dealing with a relatively smooth function f they can work well.

Bracketing Methods

One simple method which can be useful in some circumstances is a system of "homing in" on a solution, of which the simplest is known as the *bisection method*, illustrated in Figure 6.6. Here you can see that we have found two values of x for which f(x) lies on different sides of the x-axis. There is a simple way to check for this, just calculate $f(x_1)f(x_2)$. If this is negative, then one value must be positive and the other must be negative; if it is positive then either they are both positive or both negative (if it is exactly zero, then of course one of the values is an exact root). When we have found two such values, we know that somewhere between them (for a continuous function) there must be a root.

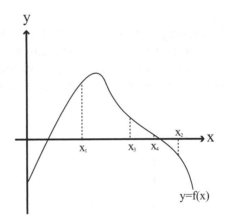

FIGURE 6.6 Homing in on a root.

This gives us a simple algorithm for getting arbitrarily close to (*bracketing*) a root. If $f(x_1)$ and $f(x_2)$ lie on opposite sides of the x-axis then we can look at $x_3 = \frac{1}{2}(x_1 + x_2)$. By checking $f(x_1)f(x_3)$ and $f(x_3)f(x_2)$ we can narrow down the position of the root to one half or the other of the interval $[x_1, x_2]$. Because halving is an exponential process, this method homes in on the root very rapidly—and we can specify from the start exactly how closely we want to find the approximation.

Here's the method as a function. The details of how you calculate the value of f(x) are left vague, since they depend on how the function is specified.

```
function bisectionMethod(func, x1, x2, resolution)
    // check that f(x1)*f(x2)<0 to get the process going
    set f1 to calculateValue(func, x1)
    set f2 to calculateValue (func, x2)
    if f1*f2>0 then return "may be no root in range"
    // if we are already very near to the solution then return one value
    if abs(x1-x2)<=resolution then return x1
    // (in some circumstances you might choose to return
    // the value of x giving a positive value of f,
    // so you'd return x1 if f1>0, x2 otherwise.)

    set x3 to (x1+x2)/2
    set f3 to calculateValue (func, x3)
    if f3=0 then return x3
    if f1*f3<0 then return bisectionMethod (func, x1, x3, resolution)
    return bisectionMethod (func, x3, x2, resolution)
end function
```

A faster bracketing method is called *Regula Falsa* ("false position"). This method takes advantage of the fact that generally, you're more likely to find the root nearer to the bracket with the smallest absolute value. Regula Falsa weights the choice of the new test point by using a method illustrated in Figure 6.7.

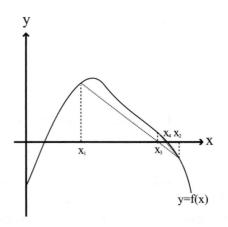

FIGURE 6.7 The Regula Falsa method.

Suppose our current brackets are a and b, we can find the new point c by choosing $c = \frac{af(b) - bf(a)}{f(b) - f(a)}$. Implementing this on the computer is left up to you (it's a simple variant on the `bisectionMethod` function).

Bracketing methods have their limitations: the most obvious being that if the function has two roots close to one another, unless we are extremely lucky in our initial choice of x_1 and x_2 we're going to miss them—and we will never find a double root. The methods also fail if there is a discontinuity, as with the function $y = x^{-1}$ which has no root but a discontinuity at $x = 0$ (in that case, the function returns the discontinuous point). Finding suitable initial values for an arbitrary function can be a rather painstaking job—essentially a matter of trial and error—although a variation of the same technique can be used here too. But in many circumstances, particularly with a function on which you can perform some preliminary analysis, bracketing works just fine. Also, it even works if you don't know the function f(x) that you are using—for example, if all you have is an arbitrary list of heights of the function at particular values of x.

Gradient Methods

For reasonably smooth functions, particularly those which don't have a maximum or minimum near the x-axis, there is a faster algorithm which avoids some of the difficulties associated with bracketing methods, called the *Newton-Raphson Method*. This method takes advantage of a trick illustrated in Figure 6.8.

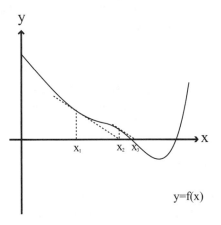

FIGURE 6.8 Using the tangent of a function to move closer to the root.

Here you can see that we have taken the tangent of the function at a particular point and projected it onto the x-axis. The point where the tangent intersects the axis is much closer to the root than the original value of x.

It may not be clear that this trick applies generally: it may seem that it is specific to the kind of function drawn here—and to some extent this is true. If the value of x we choose initially happens to be near a turning point, or there is a turning point between x and the root, then we are going to hit problems as in Figure 6.9. But when your initial value of x is sufficiently close to a root, which for most functions is still quite far away, this method works extremely well. What is more, it is much faster than any other common method.

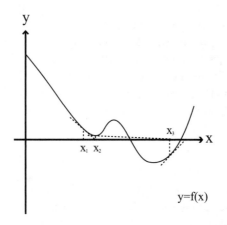

FIGURE 6.9   An example of a situation where the Newton-Raphson method fails to find a nearby root.

Using the method is quite simple and can be calculated using standard graph techniques. The gradient of the tangent at x_1 is given by $f'(x_1)$, so the equation of the line is $y - f(x_1) = f'(x_1)(x - x_1)$. This crosses the x-axis at a point x_2, where $x_2 = x_1 - \frac{f(x_1)}{f'(x_1)}$.

This gives us a simple iteration which we can turn easily into code:

```
function newtonRaphson(func, deriv, x1, resolution)
    set f1 to calculateValue (func, x1)
    if abs(f1)<resolution then return x1
    set g1 to calculateValue (deriv, x1)
    if g1=0 then return newtonRaphson(func, deriv, x1+resolution,
resolution)
    set x2 to x1-f1/g1
    return newtonRaphson(func, deriv, x2, resolution)
end function
```

The only major disadvantage of this method is that unlike the other examples we've seen, it is impossible to apply unless you know the derivative of the function, which if we're dealing with a complicated or random function is not going to be possible. So one last example we can give is the *secant method*, which is illustrated in Figure 6.10.

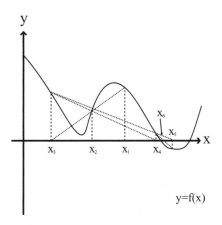

FIGURE 6.10 The secant method.

Essentially, the procedure is identical to Regula Falsa, we simply remove the necessity for having values of $f(x)$ of opposite sign. Instead, we work on the assumption that the gradient of the function is linear near our test points, and extrapolate the line down to the x-axis, just as in Newton-Raphson. See if you can adapt your Regula Falsa function to implement this method (Exercise 6.2).

Again, this method may hit problems for a function with a turning point near the x-axis, and like Newton-Raphson it is quite easy to miss a root near the starting point while catching one further away. Nevertheless, the secant method is probably the most reliable (and fast) method for the computer if all we want to do is find *some* root. If we want a root within a particular region (say within the interval [0,1]), we may be better off using a bracketing method.

If you want to use any approximation method, be sure to include some checks and balances: you don't want to get stuck in an infinite loop looking for a root that doesn't exist!

EXERCISES

Exercise 6.1

Create a function which will draw a diagram of a differential equation, similar to Figure 6.5.

The function used to draw this figure was based on the `drawGraph` function from Chapter 3. See if you can adapt this function to create this kind of graph.

Exercise 6.2

Write a function to implement the secant approximation method.

This should be a reasonably straightforward extension of the `bisection-Method` function which appears in this chapter.

SUMMARY

The main purpose of this chapter was to introduce some key pieces of terminology. You aren't going to need to perform integrals or solve differential equations in everyday programming, but the concepts are an essential part of many of the topics we'll cover later, particularly in Part III. So we've looked at the theory behind differentiation and integration, and seen some applications of the theory in using differential equations to solve a physical problem, and in creating fast approximation methods for solving equations.

This concludes the first, purely theoretical part of the book. In Part II we'll begin to put these ideas into practice by using them to simulate physically realistic motion.

YOU SHOULD NOW KNOW

- the meaning of the terms *integration* and *differentiation,* and of terms like *derivative, partial derivative, indefinite integral,* etc.
- how to differentiate and integrate simple functions such as polynomials
- the derivatives of the *exponential* and *trigonometric* functions
- how to recognize a *differential equation,* and how to solve certain simple examples
- several different methods for finding the *approximate solution* to an equation, and their advantages and disadvantages

Ballistics and Collisions

The second part of the book covers the basic physics of motion: calculating how a particle moves in the real world and translating it onto a computer. At the heart of this material is the understanding of vectors that we looked at in Chapter 5, which allow us to turn one complex problem into a number of simpler ones. At the end of these few chapters we will reach the stage where we can create a complete, if simple, game of pool.

7 Acceleration, Mass, and Energy

In This Chapter

- Overview
- Ballistics
- Mass and Momentum
- Energy
- Exercises
- Summary
- You Should Now Know

OVERVIEW

From here on we are leaving the world of abstract mathematics and entering the world of physical objects, otherwise known as *mechanics*. We began this process in Chapter 5 where we looked at some simple examples of vector motion, and introduced the concepts of velocity, speed, displacement, distance and time. In this chapter we shall add the concept of acceleration, and see how this allows us to simulate the motion of a particle under gravity.

ON THE CD Code samples from this chapter are implemented in *math.cst* in the script *chapter 7 (ballistics)*. The *javelin* demo uses them in context and solves Exercise 7.1

BALLISTICS

The area called *ballistics* is the study of particles moving with a constant acceleration. In most cases, this means particles called *projectiles* flying through the air, falling under gravity. Strictly speaking, bodies moving through the air experience a resistance from the air, but we shall ignore this for now. We will begin the chapter by explaining what we mean by the term *acceleration*, and learning how to calculate the ballistic motion of a particle.

Acceleration and Deceleration

Just as velocity is the rate of change of a particle's position, *acceleration* is the rate of change of velocity. Like velocity, acceleration is thus a vector, whose components are measured in units of velocity divided by units of time. So, for example, if our units of distance are meters and of time are seconds, then distance and displacement are measured in meters (m), speed and velocity in meters per second (ms^{-1}) and acceleration in meters per second per second, or meters per second squared (ms^{-2}).

NOTE

Unlike the pairs of speed / velocity and distance / displacement, there is no equivalent pair for acceleration, the same word being used for both the rates of change of speed (a scalar quantity) and of velocity (a vector). Generally, this is clear from context, but in this book we shall almost always be referring to the vector quantity.

Because acceleration is a vector, it can be measured in any direction, so a particle moving in a straight line whose speed is decreasing at a constant rate is experiencing a constant acceleration in the opposite direction to the motion. This is somewhat different from the common usage of the word "accelerate," which exclusively refers to getting faster. When the speed of a car is decreasing, for example, we usually say it is "decelerating"—we might say that its *deceleration* is the negative of its acceleration. However, this doesn't really tell us a great deal and generally we don't use the term in physics.

The Equations of Motion Under Constant Acceleration

If a particle's acceleration $\mathbf{a}$ is constant, then for each unit of time, the velocity changes by $\mathbf{a}$. So if the particle starts with a velocity $\mathbf{u}$, then after a time t, its velocity $\mathbf{v}$ will equal $\mathbf{u} + \mathbf{a}t$. What will its position be at that time?

We can calculate the position quite simply: take the mean velocity over the time period t. If at time t the velocity is $\mathbf{v}$, then the mean velocity is $(\mathbf{u} + \mathbf{v})/2$, so the displacement $\mathbf{s}$ is $t(\mathbf{u} + \mathbf{v})/2$. Substituting the previous value for $\mathbf{v}$ we get

$$\mathbf{s} = \frac{t\left(\mathbf{u} + \mathbf{v}\right)}{2}$$

$$= \frac{t\left(\mathbf{u} + \mathbf{u} + \mathbf{a}t\right)}{2}$$

$$= \mathbf{u}t + \frac{1}{2}\mathbf{a}t^2$$

If you look back at Chapter 6, you can see that this result makes perfect sense: Differentiate the formula above with respect to time, and you get

$$\frac{d\mathbf{s}}{dt} = \mathbf{u} + \mathbf{a}t = \mathbf{v}$$

$$\frac{d^2\mathbf{s}}{dt^2} = \mathbf{a}$$

This fits our definitions of velocity as the rate of change of displacement, and acceleration as the rate of change of velocity. Notice also that if acceleration is zero, the formulas reduce to the simple version for motion with a constant speed, $\mathbf{s} = \mathbf{u}t$

We now have three formulas relating the values $\mathbf{s}$, $\mathbf{u}$, $\mathbf{v}$, $\mathbf{a}$, and t. Each formula relates four of the five quantities. By artful substitution we can derive a fourth equation relating $\mathbf{v}$, $\mathbf{u}$, $\mathbf{a}$, and $\mathbf{s}$, and another relating $\mathbf{v}$, $\mathbf{a}$, $\mathbf{s}$, and t giving us a complete set of formulas for the five quantities:

1. $\mathbf{v} = \mathbf{u} + \mathbf{a}t$
2. $\mathbf{s} = t(\mathbf{u} + \mathbf{v})/2$
3. $\mathbf{s} = \mathbf{u}t + \dfrac{1}{2}\mathbf{a}t^2$
4. $\mathbf{s} = \mathbf{v}t - \dfrac{1}{2}\mathbf{a}t^2$
5. $v^2 = u^2 + 2as$

The fifth formula doesn't make very much sense in terms of vectors, as there is no simple way to multiply vectors together, so it is presented in terms of scalars, assuming that $\mathbf{s}$, $\mathbf{a}$, $\mathbf{v}$ and $\mathbf{u}$ are all collinear. In any case, it is really just a restatement of the previous formulas, and as we saw, even Equation 3 and Equation 4 can be derived in terms of Equation 1 and Equation 2.

Using these four formulas, we can quickly calculate any of the parameters of the motion in terms of any three of the others. So if we know, say, the current velocity and acceleration of a particle, and we know how long it has been moving, we can calculate both its relative initial position and its initial velocity:

$\mathbf{v} = \mathbf{u} + \mathbf{a}t$

so $\mathbf{u} = \mathbf{v} - \mathbf{a}t$

and then $\mathbf{s} = t(\mathbf{u} + \mathbf{v})/2$

It's unlikely you will need to do this particular calculation often, though. Mostly you know $\mathbf{u}$, $\mathbf{a}$ and t, and it is the velocity or position you will need to find. The formulas allow you to find this directly, such as in the following function

```
function calculatePosition (initialPosition, initialVelocity,
acceleration, time)
    return initialPosition+initialVelocity*time+acceleration*time*time/2
end function
```

Acceleration Due to Gravity

The story goes that Galileo wondered if a heavy ball and a light ball would fall at different speeds, and so climbed to the top of the Leaning Tower of Pisa, dropped two balls off the top and watched. By this experiment, he proved that the speed at which an object falls is independent of its weight.

In fact, he never performed such an experiment. Remarkably, he proved it by pure logic, and it's worth looking at the proof because it's very ingenious. Suppose we have two objects A and B, where A is heavier than B. Now suppose that it were true that heavier objects fall faster than light ones. If we tie A to B and drop them from a height, B will fall more slowly, so it will act as a drag on A, like a parachute. This should mean that A and B tied together will fall more slowly than A. But this makes no sense, because A and B tied together are heavier than A, which should fall faster than A. So something is wrong, and it must be our original hypothesis.

This kind of argument is known as a reductio ad absurdum: *we prove that something is true by assuming the opposite and showing that it leads to a contradiction. It's a very powerful technique, although many people feel it's less elegant than a direct proof.*

Coming back to earth, so to speak, how exactly does a ball fall through the air? What does gravity do? This is actually quite a complicated question (a fundamental one, in fact, to which science does not yet have a final answer), and we will look at it in more depth later, but for now we can give a simple answer: as long as the ball doesn't change height significantly, then while it is flying it experiences a constant downward acceleration, the *acceleration due to gravity* **g**. Ignoring the effects of air resistance, which we will look at in a later chapter, this is the only way the speed and direction of the ball will change. On Earth at sea level, $|\mathbf{g}|$ is approximately 9.8 ms^{-2} —we'll use the value 10 in this chapter to simplify things.

Using this, we can make some simple calculations straight away. For example, we can ask: if we throw a ball straight upwards with a speed of 5 ms^{-1}, how high will it go? There is a small trick here: when the ball reaches the top of its motion, its speed is zero. This means we can use our equation of motion:

$$v^2 = u^2 + 2as$$
$$0 = 5^2 - 2 \times 10 \times s$$
$$s = 25/20 = 1.25\text{m}$$

It's worth looking at exactly what we did here. **s**, **u**, **v** and **a** are all vector quantities, but in this calculation we have treated them as plain numbers, our only concession to their vector nature being that we used the negative value −10 for **g**, since it is in the opposite direction from the other quantities. The reason this is possible is that the whole of the motion takes place in a single vertical line, a one-dimensional space, which means that the vectors have just one component, a single directed number.

In case this seems to be over-stressing the point, think about another question: How fast will the ball be traveling when we catch it again? This time, we are looking for a value of **v** such that **s** = 0. We can use the same formula as before:

$$v^2 = u^2 + 2as = 25 + 0$$

so $v = \pm 5$.

Of course, when $v = 5$, this is the beginning of the motion, when $s = 0$ by definition. At the end of the motion, $v = -5$, which is to say, the speed at which the ball lands is the same as it was when it was thrown, but the direction of motion has been reversed. So the directed nature of the quantities we are measuring is essential to using the formulas correctly.

Just to see how useful these equations are, let's ask one last question: If the ball leaves our hand 1.5 m off the ground and we do not catch it, how long will it be in the air? To phrase it slightly differently, if the ball is launched with a velocity of 5 ms^{-1} upwards, after how long will it have a displacement of −1.5 m?

$$s = ut + \frac{1}{2}at^2$$

$$-1.5 = 5t - 5t^2$$

$$t^2 - t - 0.3 = 0$$

$$t = \frac{1 \pm \sqrt{1 + 1.2}}{2}$$

So t is either 1.2 s or −0.2 s. The negative value we can ignore here (it makes sense if you imagine projecting the motion backwards in time as if the ball had been thrown up from the floor instead of our hand), so the answer is that the ball lands about 1.2 s after being thrown.

The Motion of a Cannonball

What about when the ball is not thrown straight up? In that case, the velocity and acceleration of the ball are no longer collinear, and so we cannot simply make calculations with single numbers. However, we can use the trick we mentioned in Chapter 5, separating the vectors into components. If we take our basis as the horizontal vector $\begin{pmatrix} 1 & 0 \end{pmatrix}^T$ and the vertical vector $\begin{pmatrix} 0 & 1 \end{pmatrix}^T$, then the acceleration due to gravity acts only along one of the basis vectors. This means that the component of motion in the horizontal direction is unaffected by gravity: horizontal velocity is constant. Only the vertical component of motion experiences an acceleration.

Let's look at cannonballs. A cannon, like any gun, is essentially a device for launching a projectile at an exact angle and speed. The barrel of the cannon is a straight tube which forces the cannonball to travel along a particular path, and the velocity can be calibrated, more or less precisely, according to the amount of gunpowder and the weight of the ball (this is an example of conservation of energy, which we will look at in a moment).

If the cannon is aimed at an angle of θ to the ground and the ball emerges with a speed u, then the horizontal component of the ball's initial velocity is $u\cos(\theta)$ and the vertical component is $u\sin(\theta)$ (see Figure 7.1). What is more, if the length of the cannon is l then the height of the ball as it leaves the barrel is $l\sin(\theta)$. How far will the ball travel? Assuming that the ground is flat, the vertical distance traveled by the ball is $-l\sin(\theta)$, so ignoring the horizontal component of the motion, we can use the same technique as before to calculate how long it will be in the air:

$$s = ut + \frac{1}{2}at^2$$

$$-l\sin(\theta) = u\sin(\theta)t - 5t^2$$

$$5t^2 - u\sin(\theta)t - l\sin(\theta) = 0$$

$$t = \frac{u\sin(\theta) + \sqrt{u^2 \sin^2(\theta) + 20l\sin(\theta)}}{10}$$

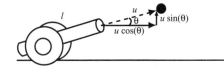

FIGURE 7.1 A cannon firing a projectile at a particular angle.

This is a complicated formula, so we'll put in some numbers to make it clearer. Suppose $\theta = 30°$, so $\sin(\theta) = 0.5$, and suppose the cannon is 2 m long and fires the cannonball at 20 ms⁻¹. Then the time of flight is

$$t = \frac{20 \times 0.5 + \sqrt{20^2 \times 0.5^2 + 20 \times 2 \times 0.5}}{10}$$

$$= 1 + \frac{\sqrt{120}}{10} = 2.1 \text{ s}$$

Now we can use this information along with the (constant) horizontal velocity to calculate the distance traveled:

$$s = ut = u\cos(\theta)t = 20 \times \frac{\sqrt{3}}{2} \times 2.1 = 36.3 \text{ m}$$

Using calculus, it is even possible to calculate at which angle the ball will travel the furthest (you might want to try your luck with this question, it isn't exactly easy but you have all the tools you need. You may want to ignore the height of the cannon for simplicity: assume the vertical displacement when hitting the ground is zero). In Exercise 7.2, you are asked to provide a function which will aim a cannon so as to hit a particular point.

These techniques are quite general, and will work just as well for a person jumping up in a platform game, a slingshot firing pellets in a firing range, or any number of other scenarios. The only tricky part is calculating the initial speed of the projectile, which we will look at now.

MASS AND MOMENTUM

Up to now, the weight of the particles we have been discussing has been irrelevant. Once the projectile is in the air, its flight path is the same no matter how heavy it is. However, we know from experience that it makes a big difference how heavy something is if we want to throw it somewhere. In this section we will look at the concept of *mass*, and why throwing a brick is so much harder than throwing a table tennis ball.

Mass and Inertia

There are two words which we use to describe how heavy something is. The most common in English is *weight*. In physics, this word is used for a force, specifically the downward force on an object due to gravity, which we shall look at in a later chapter. It is this (vector) quantity which is measured by, for example, a weighing scales. The other word is *mass*, or equivalently *inertia*. We need the language of forces to explain the term precisely, but for our purposes, we can think of it as a measurement of "how hard it is to move X." Mass is a scalar quantity, measured in units such as grams, kilograms or pounds, and the reason that these are also the units shown on a set of scales is that it happens to be the case that as long as we remain on the same planet, weight and mass are proportional.

A particle's mass is generally constant (we'll see examples of cases where mass isn't constant in Chapter 15 when we look at rockets), and more importantly, unlike weight it is the same wherever the particle is, whether on a neutron star or in outer space. An object on the moon weighs approximately a sixth of the amount it does on Earth, but its mass is unchanged, and so in either case it will take the same amount of effort to get it to the same speed.

So what *is* mass? It's actually a fundamental property of matter, which goes right down to the level of atoms and below—in its simplest terms, it is a measure of how much "stuff" there is in the object. This means that the mass of an object is distributed over its whole volume, which might potentially cause problems. Up to now we have been thinking about abstract point-sized objects, i.e., particles, so how can we be sure that an object with its mass spread over a wider space will behave the same way? Fortunately, it turns out that we can: to a very good approximation, and apart from rotation, an object moves along exactly the same path as a point particle at a particular point inside the object, known as its *center of mass* or *center of gravity*. The exact position of the center of mass depends on the shape of the object and the distribution of matter within it, but for a symmetrical object like a ball, the center of mass is at the center of the object. We'll cover much more on this in Chapter 13.

Calculating Momentum

Mass tends to be most useful in calculations when combined with other quantities. One particularly important value is the product of a particle's mass and velocity, which is called its *momentum*. As the product of a vector and a scalar, momentum is a vector, parallel to the velocity.

We can think of momentum as a measure of "how hard it is to stop X." It is much more difficult to stop a ten-ton truck traveling at one mile per hour than it is to stop a toy car traveling at 15 miles per hour. This is why in feats of strength people are able to pull a truck along with their teeth: although it requires a huge effort to get the thing moving, once it is under way its own momentum helps to keep it going.

The most important thing to know about momentum is that it is *conserved*. This means that in the absence of any external influences on a particle, or for that matter on a whole system of particles, the total momentum will be unchanged.

When dealing with cannonballs this is not a very useful thing to know. After all, a cannonball *does* have an outside influence: the force of gravity. This means that the momentum of a cannonball changes from moment to moment as it arcs through the air. But again, this only applies to the vertical momentum. Horizontally, perpendicular to gravity, velocity and thus momentum are unchanged. Still, momentum does not really come into its own until we start looking at collisions.

ENERGY

In the final section of this chapter, we shall look at the concept of *energy* and see how it gives us a different way of looking at ballistic motion.

Kinds of Energy

Energy is a measure of how much action an object can do. The more energy a particle has, the more effect it can have on the rest of the world. A cannonball lying on the ground can't do anything to anyone, but one flying through the air can knock down a stone wall. Energy is a scalar quantity, measured in a unit called the *joule* (J), which is equal to 1 kg ms^{-1} (one kilogram-meter per second). Another energy unit, the *calorie*, is mostly restricted these days to the world of food.

Energy can take a number of different forms.

Kinetic energy (k.e.):   Held by any moving object. If a particle of mass m has velocity **v**, then its kinetic energy is equal to $\frac{1}{2}m|\mathbf{v}|^2$. Notice how closely related this is to the formula for momentum.

Gravitational potential energy (g.p.e.):   Held by all objects in the universe, but in a slightly complicated way. It is somewhat meaningless in itself, it is mostly a relative term—you can say that "this object has 5 J more g.p.e. than that one," but it doesn't make much sense to say "this object has a g.p.e. of 100 J." The g.p.e of an object is its potential to fall: going back to our cannonball, if the cannonball is sitting on top of a parapet rather than on the ground, it clearly has the potential to have a much greater influence on a person beneath the parapet. A particle of mass m at height h above another particle has a relative g.p.e of $mh|\mathbf{g}|$, where **g** is the local acceleration due to gravity. To simplify use of g.p.e in problems, it is generally easiest to define a particular height as 0, and measure all g.p.e from that point.

Elastic potential energy: Stored by a stretched rubber band or spring, which when released can fire itself or a projectile some distance. We'll look at springs much more in Chapter 16.

Heat energy: A measure of how badly something can burn you. Generally it's more useful to think in terms of the amount of energy released by a hot object over any particular period of time, a measure of *power* with units of *watts* (W), which are joules per second.

Chemical potential energy: Stored in a reactive substance such as gunpowder. It is a function of the stability of the substance as compared to the stability of the substances it becomes after reacting—for example, iron reacts with air to produce iron oxide or rust. Because rust is more stable than pure iron, the process releases energy.

Electrical energy: Used by objects with an electric current flowing through them. An electric cell (battery) has a certain *voltage*, such as 10 V, which indicates the amount of power used (in watts) for each ampere of current passing across a circuit containing the battery. This rather complicated explanation is not something we need to worry about here.

There are many more! However, they do fall into two clear camps. Kinetic, heat and electrical energy (and others) are actually doing something. In fact, all three of these are actually to do with movement: heat is a large-scale view of the kinetic energy of the atoms and molecules in a substance, and electrical energy is the result of the movement of electrons (or other charged particles) in a conductor. The other forms of energy are potential: they represent the ability of an object to act, given a change of circumstances. Potential energy is usually relative: chemical p.e. depends on the particular chemical reaction involved, g.p.e. on relative heights and so on. Elastic p.e. is a little different, being entirely a property of the particular spring.

Conservation of Energy

Like momentum, energy is conserved within a system, apart from the action of any external force. And in fact, in certain cases we can say energy is conserved even when external forces do act, when these forces are included in our energy calculations. Gravity is an obvious example: the force of gravity does not really count as an "external" force since we take it into account in the form of g.p.e. (All potential energies are associated with some kind of force.)

Conservation of energy is a very useful law, because it allows us to make calculations about parts of a situation that use very different techniques. For example, in the cannonball problem, one of the problems we couldn't solve was the initial speed of the ball as it left the cannon. Using conservation of energy and a number of known facts, we could theoretically calculate this speed. The cannonball is propelled outwards by causing a chemical reaction between the gunpowder and oxygen in the air, which converts some of the chemical potential energy of the gunpowder into heat, which gives kinetic energy to the molecules in the air behind the cannonball, causing it to expand rapidly. This expansion in turn transfers kinetic energy to the cannonball (see Figure 7.2). This means that if we can calculate the energy given off by igniting a quantity of gunpowder, we might be able to use this information to calculate the energy of the cannonball.

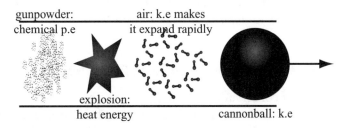

FIGURE 7.2 The energy transfer during the firing of a cannon.

Of course, in real life, energy transfer is never this perfect. A great deal of the heat given off by the gunpowder is absorbed by the surrounding air. This means that the transfer of energy is not 100% *efficient*. We can experiment to find out the particular efficiency, however.

Another important issue is that, as well as the cannonball being energized by the reaction, the cannon itself is propelled backwards, in accordance with the law of conservation of momentum: the explosion within the cannon counts as an "internal force," so if the total horizontal momentum of the cannon and cannonball was zero before the gun fired, it must be zero afterwards (this does not hold for the vertical momentum, because gravity is acting on the ball and the cannon). So if the cannonball has a forward momentum **p** after the explosion, the cannon must have a momentum of −**p** to compensate.

Suppose the cannonball has a mass of 2 kg and the cannon has a mass of 200 kg. Then if after the gun fires the cannonball has a horizontal speed of 30 ms⁻¹, its momentum is 60 kg ms⁻¹. Therefore the cannon must have the same momentum in the opposite direction, which means that its speed must be $^{60}/_{200} = 0.3$ ms⁻¹. This is the classic "recoil" phenomenon. Notice that because the cannon is so much heavier than the ball, its speed is much less than the speed of the ball it is firing.

Now let's look at the energy. The k.e of the cannonball after firing (assuming the cannon is aimed horizontally for simplicity) is $0.5 \times 2 \times 30^2 = 900$ J. The k.e. of the cannon is $0.5 \times 200 \times 0.3^2 = 9$ J. So although the momentum in both directions is equal, the difference in speed makes a major difference to the energy—the energy of the cannon is significantly less than the ball. Nevertheless, it does have some energy, and so if the cannon is braced to prevent it moving backwards the ball will emerge faster! All the energy which previously went into moving the cannon backwards is now available to give extra k.e. to the ball, which means that the ball will have 909 J instead of 900 J (or thereabouts—energy efficiency is not linear, so not all the 9 J may go to the ball). So its speed will be equal to $\sqrt{909} = 30.1$ ms⁻¹.

NOTE

Why does conservation of momentum no longer apply when the cannon is braced? Because the brace is exerting an external force on the cannon to hold it in place. This is an example of Newton's Third Law, which we'll see in Chapter 12.

Using Conservation of Energy to Solve Ballistics Problems

The law of conservation of energy gives us some interesting different ways to approach a ballistics problem. Once a projectile is flying freely, its energy must remain constant (ignoring, as before, air resistance). When it flies up, k.e. is transformed to g.p.e., and when it flies back down, this g.p.e. is converted back into k.e. We can use this to perform many of the same calculations we did before. For example, we can ask how high the ball will reach.

As before, suppose the cannon fires the cannonball at 20 ms⁻¹. Suppose also that the cannonball has a mass of *m*. The ball's initial k.e. is therefore 400 *m*. We'll measure g.p.e. from the muzzle of the cannon, so at the point when the ball leaves the cannon its g.p.e. is 0. Therefore its total energy (the sum of the k.e. and g.p.e.) at all times during the flight must be 400 m.

Suppose firstly that the ball is fired straight up (not a wise move when you consider that the ball lands at the same speed it was fired!). At the highest point of the motion, the ball must have a k.e. of 0, so its g.p.e. will be 400 m. So from the formula for g.p.e. we have $mgh = 400\ m$, so $h = 40$ m: the highest point reached by the ball is 40 m above the muzzle of the cannon. Notice that the mass term cancels out on the two sides of the equation, leaving a height independent of the mass of the ball, which we should expect, since the trajectory of a projectile is independent of mass.

It can be a little confusing that the italic variable m *represents mass, while the letter "m" refers to the units of meters. Remember that only letters in italics are variables. In scribbled calculations it is very easy to let a mass term slip in and out in error, so keep your wits about you: as a general rule, leave units off until the end.*

If the cannon is fired at an angle, again we have to deal with the motion in horizontal and vertical components. Suppose as before that the cannon is at 30° to the horizontal, so its (constant) horizontal velocity is $20 \times \frac{\sqrt{3}}{2} = 17.3$ ms^{-1}. At the top of the motion, vertical velocity is 0, but horizontal velocity is unchanged, so the k.e. is $\frac{1}{2} \times m \times 1.73^2 = 150\ m$ J. Therefore, since the total energy must still be 400 m, we have:

$$150m + mgh = 400m$$
$$gh = 250$$
$$h = 25\text{m}$$

Be aware that both these values need to be adjusted to account for the difference of height above the ground (you can do this as an exercise). Try solving the same problem using the equations of motion and see if you get the same answer.

What conservation of energy or momentum considerations will not tell you is anything about time—they will not tell you how long anything takes to happen. But in many situations they will simplify calculations enormously.

EXERCISES

In all the following exercises assume units of meters, seconds and kilograms, and assume **g** = 10.

Exercise 7.1

Write a function `javelin(throwAngle, throwSpeed, time)` which calculates the position and angle of a javelin over time.

The function should return an array of two values: a vector (array) representing the position of the javelin at time `time` after firing and the angle it makes with the horizontal. During its flight, a javelin is more or less oriented along the tangent to the curve—that is to say, parallel to the velocity vector.

Exercise 7.2

Write a function `aimCannon(cannonLength, muzzleSpeed, aimPoint)` which will return the correct firing angle for a cannon in order to hit a particular point.

Your function should take two scalar arguments, the length of the cannon and firing speed, and one vector (array), the target position relative to the base of the cannon, and calculate the best angle to aim the cannon so as to hit the point, returning this angle in degrees or radians as you prefer. In some cases it may not be possible to hit the target, in which case you should return an error message of some kind, and in others there may be more than one possible firing angle, in which case you can choose any valid angle.

Exercise 7.3

Write a function `fireCannon(massOfBall, massOfCannon, energy)` which returns the speed of the cannonball as it emerges from the barrel.

This function should use the law of conservation of momentum to calculate the speeds of both the cannonball and the cannon after it is fired, assuming that the variable `energy` represents the total k.e. after firing (i.e., it is the chemical energy from the gunpowder that is not lost to heat).

SUMMARY

We have gone through these basics of ballistics very quickly indeed, but this is because the concepts are really very simple—much simpler than the fundamental ideas of vectors and algebra you have already covered! The toolset is small and constant, and most problems are just variations on the same theme.

In the next two chapters we shall make our first forays into the exciting world of collision detection, and then we shall return to the laws of conservation of momentum and energy to learn how to find out what happens when objects collide.

YOU SHOULD NOW KNOW

- the meaning of the word *acceleration* as the rate of change of velocity
- how *gravity* acts on objects near sea level as a constant downward acceleration
- how to use the equations of motion to calculate unknowns in ballistics problems
- the meaning of the words *mass* and *inertia*
- what *momentum* is and how and when it is conserved
- the different forms of *energy* and how they are transformed one into another
- how to use the law of conservation of energy to solve ballistics problems

8 Detecting Collisions Between Simple Shapes

OVERVIEW

We have been building up to this chapter and the next two for some time now. Collision detection and resolution is one of the most fundamental and mathematical parts of game programming, and uses all the tools we have been learning. We'll split the discussion of the two-dimensional case over three chapters here, and return to the topic later in Part III when we look at rotational physics, and in Part IV when we extend it to three dimensions. In this chapter we will look at how you can tell if and when two simple geometrical shapes will collide, and what you can determine about the point of impact. In the following chapters, we'll look at what happens next and then look at some more complex collision situations, before applying the techniques to an actual game in Chapter 11.

This chapter is mostly a set of recipes; it is much more about specific examples than many other parts of the book. For each case we will look at the basic principles first, and then move on to increasingly complex code examples. As always, remember that we are looking at mathematics here, not programming style. All of these recipes can be made "cleverer" to improve performance. But generally the more you shave off the deadwood of a calculation, the harder it is to understand the underlying principles by looking at the code, so understand what it is you are doing first and worry about optimization later. There are a few notes about how to begin the process of optimizing within the chapter.

All the collision detection and resolution methods are illustrated on the most complex demo on the CD-ROM, *collisions.dir*. This allows you to play with collisions among all kinds of different elements. Because it is so complex, you may find that the code requires a certain amount of explanation above and beyond the mathematical concepts discussed in the main part of the book: please look at Appendix C, "About the CD-ROM" for more details. Some functions are also implemented in *math.cst* in the script *2D vectors and trigonometry*.

ON THE CD

GROUND RULES

We'll start by setting up some general principles for the chapter. We're assuming here that you are making some calculation based on one or more moving objects. Generally you know their current position and the vector along which they are moving in the current step of time (their displacement). For example, if the object is moving with a velocity **v** pixels per second, then if it has been 150 milliseconds since the last time you checked, the object should have a displacement of $^{150}\!/_{1000} \times$ **v** pixels.

Even for more complicated motion, where the object is accelerating, you can make the same kinds of calculation based on the current velocity. Assuming that you are checking collisions frequently, it is likely that velocity won't change a great deal in each time step, so you can assume it is constant during that time and won't get too much of an error.

One further principle that will be important throughout the chapter is the *principle of relativity*—the precursor to Einstein's theorem of the same name. The relativity principle is, in essence, that you can add a constant velocity or position to any physical system of particles and all other measurements will remain the same. This is called moving into a different *reference frame*. For example, if Sam and Ella are sitting next to each other in a car and tossing a ball back and forth, they use exactly the same amount of force to throw the ball and it takes exactly the same trajectory through the air relative to them, whether the car is parked or driving at 100 mph. Of course, the ball moves through a different trajectory relative to the ground, but the ground is not part of Sam and Ella's reference frame. The stronger version of the principle is that if the car windows are blacked out, Sam and Ella cannot know by any experiment at all whether they are moving or standing still (and indeed, the two terms "moving" and "standing still" become somewhat meaningless in this context).

Einstein's theory of relativity followed from some discoveries about the nature of light which would violate this principle. Acting on the instinct that the principle of relativity was more fundamental than the assumption, for example, that time runs at the same speed no matter how fast you are moving, Einstein reformulated the equations of motion which would remove the anomalies about light, while overturning most people's notion of what space and time were. His theory has since been proved correct (as far as this is possible for a scientific theory) by countless observations and experiments.

To simplify the code examples in this chapter, we'll adopt a standard programming convention and think of each colliding element as an "object." We can then access its properties by means of a dot notation, as in `circle.radius`. This saves us sending too many arguments to each function. See Appendix B for a brief explanation of object-oriented programming. In the version on the CD-ROM we use various accessor methods instead of accessing properties directly, but we'll ignore this here.

WHEN CIRCLES COLLIDE

We'll begin by looking at the simplest possible collision detection, when the moving objects are circular. Circles are easy because they are completely symmetrical, meaning that there are no points on the circumference that are in any way "special."

Circles

We've looked at circles before: a circle is the set of points that are equidistant from a particular point, the center O. The distance from the circumference is the radius of the circle. The vector from O to any point P on the circumference is $r(\sin\theta \quad \cos\theta)^T$ for some angle θ, and the tangent of a circle at P is perpendicular to the radius $\overrightarrow{OP}$. We'll use the notation $C(\mathbf{o}, r)$ to indicate a circle of radius r centered on the point with position vector $\mathbf{o}$.

It is easy to tell if a point P is inside a circle—all you do is to calculate the distance OP and compare it to the radius. If the distance is less than the radius, the point is inside, if not, outside. If it is equal to the radius, the point is on the circumference.

You can speed up this process by calculating the squared distance OP² and comparing it to the square of the radius. This avoids constantly taking square roots in the Pythagorean Theorem, which is a slow operation.

NOTE

One more fact which is useful: If two circles with centers O and O' are touching at a point P, the points O, P, O' are collinear. This follows directly from the fact that the tangent at P is perpendicular to both $\overrightarrow{OP}$ and $\overrightarrow{O'P}$. This helps us to solve collision problems geometrically.

A Moving Circle and a Wall

Let's start with a circle C($\mathbf{o}$, r) moving at some velocity $\mathbf{v}$ toward a straight line. We're thinking about Pong, of course (see Figure 8.1a).

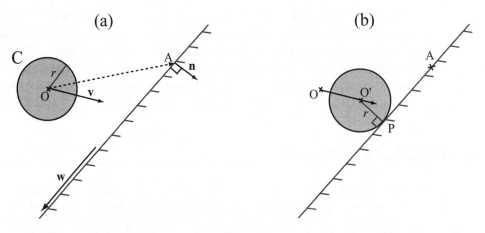

FIGURE 8.1   A circle moving toward a wall a) at its start position, b) touching the wall.

We know the position $\mathbf{o}$ of the center of C at time 0. We also know a point A (with position vector $\mathbf{a}$) on the line and a vector $\mathbf{w}$ along it (we'll assume the wall is infinitely long for now). Given particular values for $\mathbf{v}$, $\mathbf{w}$, $\mathbf{o}$, $\mathbf{a}$ and r, will the circle hit the wall during this time-step, and if so, when?

In Figure 8.1b, you can see the circle C at the point of impact (assuming it does hit the wall). C is touching the wall at a point P, and the center is now at O'. We know that $\overrightarrow{O'P}$ is perpendicular to $\mathbf{w}$ since the wall must be a tangent to C at P. What's more, we know that $\overrightarrow{OO'}$ is some multiple of $\mathbf{v}$, since this is the vector along which C has moved.

So what can we deduce from this wealth of information? Let's start with $\overrightarrow{O'P}$, which we'll call **r**. We know **r** is perpendicular to **w** and its length is r. So all we need to know is which direction it points. We can work this out using the vector $\overrightarrow{OA}$. Take either of the two unit normals to **w** and call it **n**. If the angle between **n** and $\overrightarrow{OA}$ is greater than 90° then **n** is basically pointing toward O, so **r** = r**n**. If it's less than 90° then **n** is pointing away from the circle, and so we want **r** = $-r$**n**. We can distinguish between these possibilities by taking the dot product of **n** and $\overrightarrow{OA}$, that is, the component of $\overrightarrow{OQ}$ in the direction **n**. Notice also that if the absolute value of this component is less than r, then the circle becomes embedded in the wall and our function should return an error.

Once we have **n** we can also make another quick check: if the dot product of **v** and **n** is positive, then the circle is already moving away from the wall, which means that there is definitely no collision. Otherwise, we now have a simple vector equation. We know that P is on AB and it is also a vector **r** away from a point on the trajectory of O. This gives us the equation

$$\mathbf{o} + t\mathbf{v} + \mathbf{r} = \mathbf{a} + s\mathbf{w}$$

for some scalars s and t. We can solve this equation in exactly the way we did before, giving a final grand collision detection function:

```
function circleWallCollision (cir, wal)
   // calculate the normal to the wall
   set n to wal.normal
   set a to wal.startPoint-cir.pos
   set c to dotProduct(a, n)
   if abs(c)<cir.radius then return "embedded"
   if c<0 then set r to n*radius
   otherwise set r to -n*radius

   // check if the circle is approaching the wall
   set v to dotProduct(displacement, n)
   if v>0 then return "none"

   // calculate the vector equation
   set p to cir.pos+r
   set t to intersectionTime(cir.pos, cir.displacement, wal.startPoint,
wal.vector) // see Chapter 5
   if t>1 then return "none"
   return t
end function
```

This function refers back to a number of functions created in Chapter 5. Most are self-explanatory in any case, but in case you have forgotten `intersectionTime()`, this takes the vector arguments `p1, v1, p2, v2` and returns the proportion t of `v1` from `p1` you need to go before you meet the line from `p2` along the vector `v2`. (Confused? Read Chapter 5 again.) As discussed in that chapter, we can draw some helpful conclusions about the intersection point from this value, which are shown in the code. Only if t lies on [0,1] is there an intersection within the time period we are interested in—and t will always be greater than or equal to 0 if the circle is approaching the wall. We will be using this concept extensively throughout this and following chapters.

A Stationary Circle and a Moving Point

Another very simple case is when dealing with a small object, essentially a point particle, moving through space. We want to determine if the point will collide with a circle in the same space.

Determining if a point is *inside* a circle is trivial, as we have already seen. So all we need to do is determine when, if ever, the particle's trajectory enters the radius of the circle. In Figure 8.2 you can see an example of this. In this case we know the position P and vector **v** of the point, and the position O and radius r of the circle.

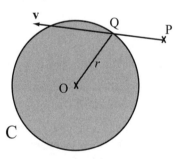

FIGURE 8.2   A stationary circle and a moving point.

To solve this, look at the point Q, marked, which is where the particle would enter the circle. Q lies on the circle C, but also on the trajectory of the particle. So its position vector is **p** + t**v** for some t, and also the magnitude of the vector from this point to O is r. This means we have the following vector equation:

$$\left(\mathbf{p}+t\mathbf{v}-\mathbf{o}\right)\cdot\left(\mathbf{p}+t\mathbf{v}-\mathbf{o}\right)=r^{2}$$

Because we know all of these values except t, this is fairly easy to solve: let's multiply out the brackets and see what we get (we'll give the name w to the vector **p-o**).

$$\mathbf{w}\cdot\mathbf{w}+2t\mathbf{w}\cdot\mathbf{v}+t^{2}\mathbf{v}\cdot\mathbf{v}=r^{2}$$

$$t=\frac{-\mathbf{w}\cdot\mathbf{v}\pm\sqrt{\left(\mathbf{w}\cdot\mathbf{v}\right)^{2}-\left(\mathbf{w}\cdot\mathbf{w}-r^{2}\right)\left(\mathbf{v}\cdot\mathbf{v}\right)}}{\left|\mathbf{v}\cdot\mathbf{v}\right|}$$

This is a scary-looking formula but basically just a matter of simple calculation. What's more, as before we can deduce that if t is less than 0 the point is moving away from C, if it's greater than 1 the point will not hit C in this time-step, and if it is imaginary (that is to say, if the value under the square root is less than zero), then the trajectory doesn't meet the circle at all.

```
function pointCircleCollision(pt, cir)
    set w to pt.pos-cir.pos
    set ww to dotProduct(w,w)
    if ww<cir.radius*cir.radius then return "inside"
    set v to pt.displacement-cir.displacement
    set a to dotProduct(v,v)
    set b to dotProduct(w,v)
    set c to ww-cir.radius*cir.radius
    set root to b*b-a*c
    if root<0 then return "none"
    set t to (-b-sqrt(root))/a
    if t>1 or t<0 then return "none"
    return t
end function
```

If you use the principle of relativity, you will see that this problem and the previous one are in a sense "duals" of one another. Instead of thinking of the circle C in the previous problem approaching the wall with velocity **v**, think of C as stationary and the wall approaching it with velocity –**v**. The point Q on C which will be hit first by the wall is where the tangent at Q is parallel to the wall. Draw a line from Q along the velocity vector and you find the point P. So now this problem looks a lot like the current problem, except that instead of knowing the point P and trying to find Q, we know Q and are trying to find P.

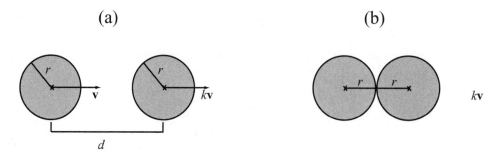

FIGURE 8.3   Two moving circles on a straight line a) before collision, b) during collision.

Two Moving Circles on a Straight Line

Imagine a long track made of two parallel rails, with two balls sitting in it. If we roll one ball along the track toward the other, when will they collide? How about if both balls are moving? In Figure 8.3a you can see this situation. Both balls have radius r, they begin with their centers d units apart and they have velocity $\mathbf{v}$ and $k\mathbf{v}$, respectively. Since the balls are moving along the same straight lines, their velocities are parallel.

Let's answer the second question first. It makes no difference whether one ball or both are moving, because we can apply the principle of relativity. If we subtract the velocity of ball 1 from both balls, then ball 1 is stationary and ball 2 is moving with velocity $(k-1)\mathbf{v}$. So we don't need to worry about this case.

For the first question, look at Figure 8.3b. You can see that the centers of the circles are $2r$ units apart at the moment of contact. This means that all we need to do is use our standard equations of motion to find out at what time the circles are this distance apart:

$$|v|t = d - 2r$$

$$t = \frac{d - 2r}{|v|}$$

This is really quite simple (and extends quickly to the case where the circles are of different sizes, as long as their centers are along the line of collision). We can put it into a function immediately:

```
function circleCircleStraightCollision (cir1, cir2)
   set relspeed to cir1.speed-cir2.speed
   set d to cir1.pos-cir2.pos // linear position
   set r to cir1.radius+cir2.radius
   if d<r then return "embedded"
   set t to (d-r)/relspeed
   if t>1 or t<0 then return "none"
   return t
end function
```

Notice that in this case we haven't specified a velocity and position vector, but a speed and linear position. That is because this function is only of use if you know beforehand that the circles are colliding head-on, in which case we know the velocity must lie on the line joining the two centers. Of course, you will need to calculate the velocity in order to determine the point of contact, but that should be straightforward enough for you to handle by now.

Two Moving Circles at an Angle

In general, life is not so generous as to always give you circles meeting head-on. We need a more general solution which can cope with circles of variable sizes colliding at variable angles. Fortunately, this is possible, and not difficult. In fact, we have already solved it!

If you look at Figure 8.4, you can see the circle $D(a, p)$ is approaching the circle $C(o, r)$ with a relative velocity v. In the Figure, a larger circle of radius $p + r$ has been drawn around O. At the moment of collision between the two circles, the line from A in the direction v enters the larger circle, so we can adjust our pointCircleCollision() function to accommodate it:

```
function circleCircleCollision (cir1, cir2)
   set w to cir1.pos-cir2.pos
   set r to cir1.radius+cir2.radius
   set ww to dotProduct(w,w)
   if ww<r*r then return "embedded"
   set v to cir1.displacement-cir2.displacement
   set a to dotProduct(v,v)
   set b to dotProduct(w,v)
   set c to ww-r*r
   set root to b*b-a*c
   if root<0 then return "none"
   set t to (-b-sqrt(root))/a
   if t>1 or t<0 then return "none"
   return t
end function
```

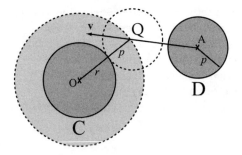

FIGURE 8.4   Two moving circles at an angle.

One Circle Inside Another

In the preceding sections we have considered circular objects colliding on the outside edge, but we can also consider the situation where one circle is bouncing around the inside of a larger circle as in Figure 8.5.

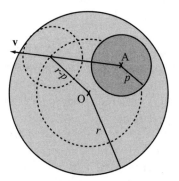

FIGURE 8.5   One circle inside another.

This situation is much like the external collision, except that at the moment of collision the centers of the circles are a distance apart equal to the difference of the radii rather than the sum. To solve this, we can use a function almost identical to the previous one. But notice also that this is no longer a symmetrical function because we are subtracting the radii rather than adding. The function tests whether circle 1 is inside circle 2, not the reverse. Also notice that we now need to look for the larger root: as long as one circle is inside the other, the velocity vector will always collide once in front of the circle and once behind.

```
function circleCircleInnerCollision(cir1, cir2)
    set w to cir1.pos-cir2.pos
    set r to cir2.radius-cir1.radius
    set ww to dotProduct(w,w)
    if ww>r*r then
        set rr to cir2.radius+cir2.radius
        if ww<rr*rr then return "embedded"
        return "outside"
    end if
    set v to cir1.displacement-cir2.displacement
    set a to dotProduct(v,v)
    set b to dotProduct(w,v)
    set c to ww-r*r
    set root to b*b-a*c
    set t to (-b+sqrt(root))/a
    if t>1 then return "none"
    return t
end function
```

The Point of Contact

We can say quite a lot about the point where a circle meets another object. First, we can quickly calculate its position directly from the results of these various functions. Each one returns a variable t which represents the fraction of the time period that passes before the objects collide. So if you know the velocities of the objects (as you always do in these cases), then you can simply calculate shape.pos+shape.displacement*t to get the new position.

Second, we can determine the actual point of contact, although this will vary according to the situation. When a circle hits a wall, the point of contact is along the perpendicular from the center of the circle to the wall (P in Figure 8.1). When two circles collide, it lies along the line joining the centers ($\overline{OQ}$ in Figure 8.4). But whatever the position, the tangent of the circle at that point is perpendicular to the radius, which is going to be very important later.

ON THE CD

The versions of all of the collision functions on the CD-ROM return both the fraction t and the normal vector at the point of contact (as well as information about the collision *moment*, which we'll come back to in Chapter 13). Try adding this facility to your own versions of the functions.

WHEN SQUARES COLLIDE

Having looked at a smooth shape, let's examine what happens with shapes that have corners. The most common such shapes that you will need to deal with are squares and rectangles. Like circles, these have a number of useful properties and symmetries which make them reasonably easy to work with, and rectangular (or *rectilinear*) collision detection is at the basis of many complex collision detection routines.

Squares and Rectangles

We've encountered squares and rectangles before, but let's summarize what we know about them again. A rectangle is a two-dimensional shape with straight sides (a *polygon*), with four vertices (making it a *quadrilateral*), where each of the four angles is a right angle. Both pairs of opposite sides of a rectangle are equal and parallel (making it a *parallelogram*), all of which means that for a rectangle ABCD, where the vertices are labeled clockwise around the shape in the usual convention, $\overrightarrow{AB} = \overrightarrow{DC}$ and $\overrightarrow{BC} = \overrightarrow{AD}$, and $\overrightarrow{AB}$ is perpendicular to $\overrightarrow{BC}$. A square is a special type of rectangle where the lengths AB and BC are equal (and thus all the sides are equal).

To complete the classification of quadrilaterals, a rhombus *is a parallelogram with all sides equal (a diamond shape), a* trapezium *is a quadrilateral with two sides parallel, an* isosceles trapezium *is a trapezium with its non-parallel sides equal in length, and a* kite *is a quadrilateral with two pairs of equal adjacent sides. All of which means that a square is a kind of rectangle and a kind of rhombus, both of which are parallelograms, a rhombus is also a kite, a parallelogram is a trapezium, and all of these are quadrilaterals. These are convex quadrilateral; we'll discuss non-convex shapes later.*

The *diagonals* $\overrightarrow{AC}$ and $\overrightarrow{BD}$ meet at the center of the rectangle ABCD. In a square, these diagonals are perpendicular. The diagonal $\overrightarrow{AC}$ is equal to $\overrightarrow{AB} + \overrightarrow{BC}$ and the diagonal $\overrightarrow{BD}$ is equal to $\overrightarrow{AD} - \overrightarrow{AB}$. In fact, this is true for any parallelogram, which is why the rule for addition of vectors is often called the *parallelogram rule*.

As before, we'll use a simple notation to define a rectangle: we'll say the rectangle R(**u**, **v**, **w**) is the rectangle centered on the point with position vector **u** and whose sides are given by the perpendicular vectors 2**v** and 2**w**, where |**v**| > |**w**| (by analogy with the ellipses we'll meet later on, we could call |**v**| and |**w**| the "semimajor" and "semiminor" axes). Strictly speaking, this description includes more information than we need: we could just as well give only the vector for one side, and the length of the other (any positive scalar), using the fact that the two sides are perpendicular to determine the direction of the second side. This would mean there is no potential for error, with every possible combination of three values yielding a valid rectangle (although possibly a degenerate case where one side is zero, giving a straight line segment rather than a rectangle). But we'll use this notation here because it's simpler and more symmetrical. As a side benefit, if we allow w to take any value, not just a vector perpendicular to v, we get a generic parallelogram, which means that many of the facts we can say about rectangles will generalize to arbitrary parallelograms.

We can determine the vertices of R quickly: they are $\mathbf{u} + (\mathbf{v} + \mathbf{w})$, $\mathbf{u} + (\mathbf{v} - \mathbf{w})$, $\mathbf{u} - (\mathbf{v} + \mathbf{w})$, $\mathbf{u} - (\mathbf{v} - \mathbf{w})$ (we'll use this vertex ordering consistently). We'll also say that a rectangle is *oriented* in the direction of its long side, so R is oriented along the vector v.

It is fairly simple to test if a point P is inside the rectangle R: find the components of the vector $\overrightarrow{UP}$ in the directions v and w. If the component in the direction v is shorter than |v|, and the component in the direction w is shorter than |w|, then P is inside ABCD (see Figure 8.6).

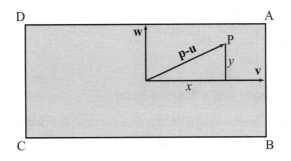

FIGURE 8.6   Determining if a point is inside a rectangle.

Here is the above algorithm in the form of a function:

```
function pointInsideRectangle(pt, rectCenter, side1, side2)
    set vect to pt-rectCenter
    set c1 to abs(component(vect, side1))
    set c2 to abs(component(vect, side2))
    if c1>magnitude(side1) then return false
    if c2>magnitude(side2) then return false
    return true
end function
```

We'll look at another more general method for testing if a point is inside a polygon in the next chapter. Notice that this function counts a point on the perimeter as "inside" the rectangle. If you don't want to allow this, replace the > signs with >= signs.

We can also say that for any point P on the perimeter of R, if we take the vector $\overrightarrow{UP}$ then either its component in the direction **v** has magnitude |**v**| or its component in the direction **w** has magnitude |**w**|. If both of these are true, then P is a vertex of R. Conversely, a point P is on the perimeter if this is true and also the point is "inside" R by the above definition. Again, this is also true of any parallelogram.

```
function pointOnRectangle(pt, rectCenter, side1, side2)
    set vect to pt-rectCenter
    set c1 to abs(component(vect, side1))
    set c2 to abs(component(vect, side2))
    set s1 to magnitude(side1)
    set s2 to magnitude(side2)
    if c1>s1 then return false
    if c2>s2 then return false
    if c1=s1 or c2=s2 then return true
    // NB: for a safer test, use e.g. abs(c1-s1)<0.001
    return false
end function
```

A Stationary Rectangle and a Moving Point

Let's begin with the simplest case of a particle at P with velocity **v** passing through a plane that contains a rectangle R(**u**, **a**, **b**) as in Figure 8.7.

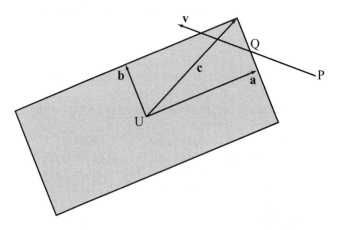

FIGURE 8.7 A stationary rectangle and a moving point.

What we're looking for is a point Q such that Q is on the trajectory of the particle and Q is also on the border of R. We can solve this quickly—we simply test for intersections with each of the four sides. At the first such intersection, the particle collides.

```
function pointRectangleIntersection(pt, rec)
    set c to rec.side1+rec.side2
    set t to 2 // start with a high value of t
    // then repeat over the four sides and look for the first collision
    repeat for v = rec.side1, rec.side2
        repeat for m = 1,-1
            set t1 to intersectionV(pt.pos, pt.displacement, rect.pos-m*c,
m*v*rec.axis*2)
            if t1="none " then next repeat
            set t to min(t,t1[1])
        end repeat
    end repeat
    if t=2 then return "none"
    return t
end
```

*The method for looping through the four sides may seem strange. We create a vector **c** = **a** + **b**, which is the vector from the center of the R to one vertex, which means that −**c** is the vector to the opposite vertex. From the first of these vertices, two sides point in the direction −**a** and −**b**, and from the second, the other two sides point in the direction **a** and **b**.*

This function calls `intersectionV()`, which is a variant on the `intersection()` function used before, taking position-displacement information instead of four endpoints, but in the same way it returns a value of *t* for the intersection time if and only if the two line segments intersect.

As you can see, while the calculations involved here are simple, there are a lot more of them to be done with rectangular collisions. This is inevitable, because there is no smooth mathematical function describing all the points on a rectangle, so you always end up checking several possible options. You also always need to be careful about potential problems at the vertices. For example: look at the above function and think about the question: what happens when P lies somewhere along the line extended from one of the rectangle sides and moves parallel to that side? Does the function catch that case?

In Exercise 8.1 you are asked to find a similar function for parallelograms.

Two Rectangles at the Same Angle

With detection of collisions between particles and rectangles under our belts, collision between two rectangles becomes rather easier than you might expect. Let's start with the simplest case, where the rectangles are aligned along the same axis as in Figure 8.8 .

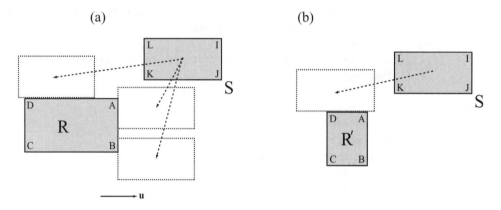

FIGURE 8.8   Two rectangles at the same angle a) similar shapes, b) differing shapes.

Here we have two rectangles R and S, both of which are aligned along the axis u. If you look at Figure 8.8a, you can see that depending on the velocity vector of S, it can collide with R in a number of different ways. However, they all boil down to six possibilities: in this particular example, at the point of collision at least one of the three vertices J, K, L of S must be touching a side of R, and that side is always either the side AB or the side AD of R. What is more, while K can be touching either AB or AD, J must be on AD (or both) and L must be on AB (or both). The other three possibilities come from cases such as the one illustrated in Figure 8.8b. Here the rectangle R' is smaller along the colliding side than S, and so at the point of collision none of the vertices of S are colliding with R'. However, the vertices of R' *are* colliding with S, which means that we can do a similar set of calculations the other way around (and in fact, in the other direction we need only check collisions for vertices B and D).

The following function doesn't take advantage of most of these optimizations, since it uses the original `pointRectangleCollision()` function, which always tests for intersection with all four sides. You might want to see if you can come up with a faster implementation of the same test (you could change the `pointRectangleCollision()` function as well).

```
function  rectangleRectangleCollisionStraight (rec1, rec2)
   set t1 to rrVertexCollisionStraight(rec1, rec2)
   set t2 to rrVertexCollisionStraight(rec2, rec1)
   if t1="none" then return t2
   if t2="none" then return t1
   return min(t1,t2)
end function

function rrVertexCollisionStraight(rec1, rec2)
   set xvector to rec1.axis
   set yvector to normal(rec1)
   set r1 to rec1.side1*xvector
   set r2 to rec1.side2*yvector

   // calculate the points to test
   set points to pointsToCheck(r1.pos, r2.pos, r1.displacement-
r2.displacement)

   // now test each of these for intersection with the second rectangle
   set s1 to rec2.side1*xvector
   set s2 to rec2.side2*yvector
   set t to 2 // we're trying to find a value less than 1 for t
   repeat for each pt in points
      set t2 to pointRectangleIntersection(pt, rec)
      if t2="none" then next repeat
      set t to min(t, t2)
   end repeat
   if t=2 then return "none"
   return t
end function

function pointsToCheck(r1, r2, displacement)
   set points to an empty array
   set c1 to component(displacement, r1)
   set c2 to component(displacement, r2)
   if c1>0 then
      append r1+r2 to points
      append r1-r2 to points
   otherwise
      append -r1+r2 to points
      append -r1-r2 to points
   end if
   if c2>0 then
      if c1>0 then append -r1+r2 to points
```

```
        otherwise append r1+r2 to points
    otherwise
        if c1>0 then append -r1-r2 to points
        otherwise append r1-r2 to points
    end if
end function
```

Although this seems quite long and complicated, it is not as bad as it looks: again, the complication comes of having to check so many different cases. As before, exactly the same calculation can be done with aligned parallelograms, although you need to specify the value of yvector rather than calculating it from the normal of xvector.

A much simpler version of this process can be used when the rectangles are *axis-aligned*: aligned in the direction of the two basis vectors. This case is significantly easier to deal with, and we'll return to it in a couple of chapters.

Two Rectangles at Different Angles

When the rectangles are not aligned along the same axis, you might think the problem gets a lot harder. Actually, it's much the same—in some ways it's conceptually even simpler. This time, the point of contact will always be one of the eight vertices (as opposed to the previous example where, although one of the vertices was always involved in the collision, the "point of contact" was a whole line segment). What's more, you can narrow the number of vertices to check down to six as before, three from each rectangle. See Figure 8.9 for some examples of this.

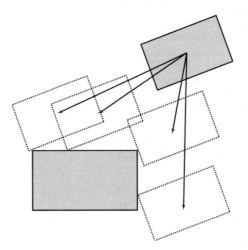

FIGURE 8.9 Two rectangles at different angles.

To work out which vertices to check, you can compare the displacement vector with the diagonals of the rectangles, as in the following function. This time we'll give the values of the sides of the rectangle as vectors, since they are all different. We can take advantage of a great deal of the work we have already done:

```
function  rectangleRectangleAngledCollision (rec1, rec2)
    set t1 to rrVertexCollisionAngled(rec1, rec2)
    set t2 to rrVertexCollisionAngled(rec2, rec1)
    if t1="none" then return t2
    if t2="none" then return t1
    return min(t1,t2)
end function


function rrVertexCollisionAngled(rec1, rec2)

    // calculate the points to test
    set axis to rec1.axis
    set points to pointsToCheck(rec1.side1* axis,
rec1.side2*normalVector(axis), displacement)

    // now test each of these for intersection with the second rectangle
    set t to 2
    repeat for each pt in points
        set t2 to pointRectangleIntersection(pt, rec2)
        if t2="none" then next repeat
        set t to min(t, t2)
    end repeat
    return t
end function
```

So really, there is no very significant difference if the rectangles are not aligned, except with the axis-aligned boxes we'll return to later.

The Point of Contact

A major difference between working with smooth objects like circles and polygons like rectangles is in the point of contact. When two smooth objects collide, there is always a precise normal at the point of contact, which defines the collision precisely. With polygons, this is no longer the case. Either you have a collision between two edges of the polygon, as in Figure 8.8, or between an edge and a vertex, as in Figure 8.9.

It is theoretically possible to get a collision between two vertices as well, but it is so unlikely that we shall ignore it for now—you can use what is called a perturbation to turn it into one of the other two cases.

If the collision is between two edges, then life is simple: the normal is simply the normal of the meeting edge. But a vertex doesn't *have* a normal, which means that when a vertex and edge of a polygon meet you might expect almost anything to happen. Actually, it's not that bad: because the vertex meets an edge, there is always at least one well-defined normal.

Otherwise, things are reasonably straightforward: it is simple to adapt the given functions to return the actual point of contact of the rectangles, and all other useful information.

Incidentally, detecting collisions between a rectangle and a wall is almost identical to this method, as a wall is nothing but a rectangle that is much bigger than the one colliding with it. This means that you do not need to test for collisions between the wall vertices and the rectangle vertices, cutting the problem in half. You can also perform collisions with a line segment, which is essentially a rectangle with one pair of sides having zero length.

WHEN OVALS COLLIDE

This is perhaps a slightly misleading title, as the word *oval* generally means a shape like an egg, with a pointy end and a less pointy end (that's about as precise and mathematical as the definition gets). The correct word for the shapes we are going to look at in this section is an *ellipse*. Ellipses are almost as simple as circles, but because they are not completely symmetrical this introduces complications. A circle has an infinite number of axes of symmetry, an ellipse has only two, and this means that it makes a difference which side you approach an ellipse from.

Ellipses

An ellipse is to a circle what a rectangle is to a square: it is a circle stretched in one direction. One way to imagine drawing an ellipse is to take a length of string and attach it to two drawing pins on a piece of paper at points A and B. Rolling a pencil around the inside of this string draws a shape as in Figure 8.10. This shape is distinguished by the fact that for any point P on the perimeter, the sum of the distances AP and BP is constant (the length of the string).

The perimeter *of a shape is another word for its edge. So the perimeter of a circle, for example, is its circumference.*

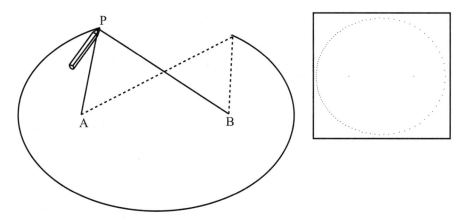

FIGURE 8.10 Drawing an ellipse. (Inset: a computer-generated ellipse.)

The two points A and B are called the *foci* of the ellipse ("foci" is the plural of "focus," and pronounced "foh-sigh") and the length AP + BP could be called the "internal diameter." Notice that if A and B are the same point, then the ellipse becomes a circle, and the internal diameter is equal to the diameter of the circle. ("Internal diameter" is not a standard term.)

Here is one method for drawing an ellipse given the foci and internal diameter:

```
function drawEllipseByFoci(focus1, focus2, diameter)
   set resolution to 100 // increase this number to draw a more
detailed ellipse
   set angle to 2*pi/resolution
   set angleOfAxis to angleBetween(focus2-focus1,array(1,0))
   if angleOfAxis="error" then set angleOfAxis to 0
   set d to magnitude(focus1-focus2)
   set tp to diameter*diameter-d*d
   repeat for i=1 to resolution
      set a to angle*i // the angle made at focus1 with the major axis
      set k to tp/(2*(diameter-d*cos(a)))
      set ha to a+angleOfAxis
      set p to k*array(cos(ha),sin(ha))
      draw point p
   end repeat
end function
```

You might want to see if you can derive this method mathematically (the key is to use the cosine rule on the triangle PAB). The drawback, however, is that it draws more points around one focus than the other (an ellipse drawn by the function can be seen inset in Figure 8.10).

You can also describe an ellipse a different way. Remember that every point on a circle centered on (0,0) with radius r has coordinates $\left(r\cos\theta, r\sin\theta\right)$ for some θ. A similar fact is true of an ellipse: the shape traced by the points with coordinates $\left(a\cos\theta, b\sin\theta\right)$ is an ellipse with internal diameter $\frac{b^2}{2a}$ and foci at $\left(\frac{(b^2-a^2)}{2a}, 0\right)$ and $\left(\frac{(a^2-b^2)}{2a}, 0\right)$. The lengths a and b are called the semimajor and semiminor axes respectively (assuming $a > b$, as is usually true by convention). However, this only draws an ellipse aligned along the x-axis (we say that an ellipse is *aligned* along the vector of its major axis, which is to say the vector between the two foci). Unfortunately, if you want this ellipse to be rotated so that its axes are not aligned with the world axes it gets a little more complicated: you need to adjust each point by rotating it by a constant angle around the center of the ellipse. Here is a function which will draw an ellipse by this method:

```
function drawEllipseByAxes (center, a, b, alpha)
    set resolution to 100 // increase to draw more accurately
    set ang to 2*pi/resolution
    repeat for i=1 to resolution
        set angle to ang*i
        set p to rotateVector(array(a*cos(angle), b*sin(angle), alpha)
        draw point center+p
    end repeat
end function

function rotateVector (v, alpha)
    set x to v[1]
    set y to v[2]
    set l to sqrt(x*x + y*y)
    set x1 to l*cos(alpha-atan(y,x))
    set y1 to l*sin(alpha-atan(y,x))
    return array(x1,y1)
end function
```

We've split off the rotateVector() *function here because we'll be reusing it later.*

Although these two descriptions of an ellipse are equivalent, they are useful in different circumstances. But generally, the most useful is the second, and in fact, the best of all is to return to our original idea of an ellipse as a stretched circle. We can state this precisely: any ellipse centered on the origin can be created from a unit circle by first scaling the space by a factor of a in one direction and b in the other, and then rotating to point in the correct direction. We can describe this with a standard transformation matrix T, made up of a scale followed by a rotation. Once we've done this, we can simply translate the ellipse to the correct position: we'll use the notation $E(c, T)$ to describe such an ellipse.

```
function drawEllipseFromMatrix pos, mat
    set v to mat.column[1]
    set n to mat.column[2]
    drawEllipseByAxes(magnitude(v), magnitude(n), atan(v[2],v[1]))
end function
```

NOTE

All this is a taster for material we'll encounter again in later chapters.

Incidentally, one common term used with ellipses is the value $\sqrt{1-\frac{b^2}{a^2}}$, known as the *eccentricity* of the ellipse. The higher the eccentricity, the more "pointy" an ellipse is, with an eccentricity of 1 giving a circle, and an eccentricity of infinity giving a straight line.

A final useful fact about an ellipse is that the tangent to the curve at P makes the same angle with each of the lines AP and BP. (So if you have an elliptical pool table with a ball at one focus and a pocket at the other, then hitting the ball in any direction will result in it going in the pocket—but more on these concepts later). On an ellipse aligned along the x-axis, at the point $\left(a\cos\theta, b\sin\theta\right)$ the tangent lies along the vector $\left(-a\sin\theta \quad b\cos\theta\right)^{\mathrm{T}}$.

A Stationary Ellipse and a Moving Point

Suppose that the particle at P is moving with velocity **v** in space occupied by the ellipse $E(c, T)$. We want to know if and when the point enters the ellipse.

If we start by translating to the ellipse's frame of reference, by subtracting **c**, then this can be described by the vector equation:

$$\mathbf{Tu} = \mathbf{p} - \mathbf{c} + t\mathbf{v}$$

where **u** is an unknown unit vector and t is an unknow scalar. If we invert the matrix T using the methods of Chapter 5, we end up with the equation

$$\mathbf{u} = \mathbf{T}^{-1}\left(\mathbf{p} - \mathbf{c} + t\mathbf{v}\right) = \mathbf{T}^{-1}\left(\mathbf{p} - \mathbf{c}\right) + t\mathbf{T}^{-1}\left(\mathbf{v}\right)$$

Now notice that since **u** is a unit vector, we know that its dot product with itself must be 1, so we have

$$\left(\mathbf{T}^{-1}\left(\mathbf{p} - \mathbf{c}\right) + t\mathbf{T}^{-1}\left(\mathbf{v}\right)\right) \cdot \left(\mathbf{T}^{-1}\left(\mathbf{p} - \mathbf{c}\right) + t\mathbf{T}^{-1}\left(\mathbf{v}\right)\right) = 1$$

This should seem very familiar: we're looking at the intersection of a particle with a unit circle—a problem we've already solved.

```
function particleEllipseCollision (pt, ell)
    set t to ell.transformationMatrix
    set inv to inverseMatrix(t)
    set p to pt.pos-ell.pos
    set w to matrixMultiply(inv,p)
    set ww to dotProduct(w,w)
    if ww<1 then return "inside"
    set v to matrixMultiply(inv,pt.displacement-ell.displacement)
    set a to dotProduct(v,v)
    set b to dotProduct(w,v)
    set c to ww-1
    set root to b*b-a*c
    if root<0 then return "none"
    set t to (-b-sqrt(root))/a
    if t>1 or t<0 then return "none"
    return t
end function
```

It might help to make this all clearer and more realistic to think about it geometrically. Look at Figure 8.11 and it should convince you: in (a) we have the generalized ellipse. In (b) we have rotated it to a new frame of reference with the axes aligned with the basis. Finally (not shown), we compress the space down to turn the ellipse into a circle. Although everything is moving about, the displacement vector moves along with them, and the relative distances along the lines don't change even if the absolute length does. So here you can really see the power of the relativity principle.

(a) (b)

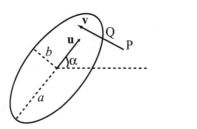
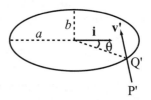

FIGURE 8.11 A stationary ellipse and a moving point a) in the plane, b) rotated to the ellipse's frame of reference.

Two Ellipses

If two ellipses that happen to be aligned in the same direction meet head on, then their collision is an easy analogue of the circular case. Such luxuries are sadly not to be had in the more general case where two ellipses $E(\mathbf{p},S)$ and $F(\mathbf{q},T)$ meet with arbitrary velocities. As before, of course, we can apply the relativity principle to bring the problem down to a simpler case, a stationary unit circle meeting the ellipse F' $(\mathbf{q} - \mathbf{p}, \ S^{-1}T)$. Unfortunately, this time this does not help us as much as it might. Ultimately, you still end up with a highly complicated pair of nonlinear simultaneous equations which are not easily untangled.

There is one additional trick which can help us: we can use the fact that at the point of collision, the normals on the two surfaces are parallel. This is the key to the whole issue, but we don't yet have the tools and vocabulary to deal with it, so we'll return to the question in Chapter 19.

The Point of Contact

Although as with the case of circles, you can determine the point of contact of an ellipse with its partner in collision, you do need to be a little more careful. From the value of *t* in each of the above functions it is trivial to calculate the collision-position of the moving bodies in your simulation. But to work out exactly where on the shapes they collide, as well as additional facts like tangents and normals, we do need to transform back into the correct reference frame, which means that we need to find the point of contact in the transformed frame, then transform this point again with **T**.

WHEN THINGS COLLIDE

For the sake of completeness, we'll finish the chapter with a brief discussion of mixed collisions between different kinds of shapes.

Collisions Between Circles and Rectangles

It's all very well to have these nice neat calculations for objects of the same kind, but what happens when we want to deal with more natural situations? Fortunately, it turns out that these calculations with similar shapes tend to be easy to adapt to such mixed events. In Figure 8.12 you can see a circle $C(\mathbf{p}, r)$ heading toward the rectangle $R(\mathbf{u}, \mathbf{a}, \mathbf{b})$ with velocity **v**. Notice how as **v** varies, the situation falls into three possible forms:

- C hits a vertex of R
- C hits an edge of R
- There is no collision

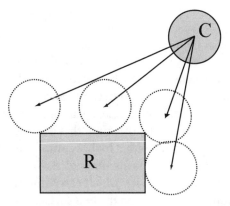

FIGURE 8.12   A collision between a circle and a rectangle.

In the first case, we can calculate the point of contact by considering the vertices of R and checking for intersection with C using our `pointCircleCollision()` function. In the second, we can think of the edge of R as a line segment, that is, a wall, and use the `circleWallCollision()` function to handle it (alternatively, we can expand the rectangle by the circle's radius in all directions, and then use `pointRectangleCollision()`). In both cases, we can work out in advance which of the vertices or edges are potentially involved in the collision just as we did with rectangle-rectangle collision.

Filling in these gaps isn't really worthwhile here, but the *collisions.dir* sample movie on the CD-ROM includes this and many more examples.

The Point of Contact

Circle-rectangle collisions are much the same as rectangle-rectangle collisions in terms of the point of contact. Whether the collision is with an edge or a vertex, the normal is always the normal to the circle at that point; although when colliding with an edge, it's easier to calculate the normal to the edge.

EXERCISES

Exercise 8.1

Write a function `pointParallelogramCollision(pt, displacement, parrPos, side1, side2)` along similar lines to the function `pointRectangleCollision()` in the chapter. It should return either a value between 0 and 1, or the string "no intersection".

To write this function, you can take advantage of the fact that a parallelogram can be transformed into a rectangle by applying a skew transformation to the plane. You could do this within a complete function, or call the `pointRectangleCollision()` function at some stage.

Exercise 8.2

Write functions `rectangleRectangleInnerCollision()`, `circleRectangleInnerCollision()` and `rectangleCircleInnerCollision()` (with appropriate parameters in each case) to test for collisions inside shapes.

As with the circle-circle case, these inner collisions are very similar to the external ones covered in the chapter, but they each have subtle complications of their own. Use the code in the chapter to help you where possible.

SUMMARY

You have probably been waiting for some real programming tips, and now you have completed a long chapter full of them. Our exploration of collisions is only just beginning, however! In the next chapter we will look at what happens after two objects have collided, before going on in the chapter after that to some more general methods for collision detection with more complex shapes.

YOU SHOULD NOW KNOW

- how to describe *circles*, *rectangles*, *ellipses*, and *lines* on the plane in a form useful to collision detection
- how to detect collisions between different combinations of these shapes in various forms, including, for each of them:
  collision with an infinitely small particle
  collision with an infinite wall
  collision with an object of the same kind
- ellipses are more difficult and you do not yet know how to calculate collisions between them in a general case

9 Resolving Collisions

In This Chapter

- Overview
- Resolving a Single Collision
- Multiple Collisions
- Exercises
- Summary
- You Should Now Know

OVERVIEW

Before we look at the more complex collisions possible between irregular shapes, let's see what we can do with the ones we have. In this chapter we will look at how to determine what happens after two objects have collided, which is called *resolving* a collision.

As it turns out, this process is fairly easy. You have done most of the hard work already in the previous chapter. At least until we cover rotational physics in Chapter 13, collisions don't care about the shape of the colliding objects, all that matters is their mass, their velocity, and the normal at the point of collision. This is the reason that in the last chapter we kept returning to the question of how to find the point of contact and the normal or tangent at that point. Now we shall see how to use this information.

Code samples from this chapter are implemented in *math.cst* in the script *chapter 9 (collision resolution)*. The *collisions* demo uses them in context.

RESOLVING A SINGLE COLLISION

The fundamental principles in resolving collisions are conservation of energy and momentum. The easiest collisions to deal with are called *elastic* collisions. These are an abstraction that don't exist in the real world: they are collisions where all kinetic energy before collision is conserved as kinetic energy afterwards.

This isn't true in reality because all objects release energy when they collide: as the molecules in the objects start to move more rapidly, the energy is released in the form of heat, which in turn energizes the surrounding air (part of which is perceptible as the sound of the collision). Even in space, where no one can hear the crash, collisions between astronomical bodies are not totally elastic, although they are close to it. Nevertheless, elasticity is a useful starting point, and in many cases close to the truth.

A Ball Hitting a Wall

In Figure 9.1 you can see a situation where a ball traveling with velocity **v** hits a stationary, fixed wall with normal **n**. This is a particularly simple situation, and we can deal with it directly, without knowing anything more about the ball or the wall.

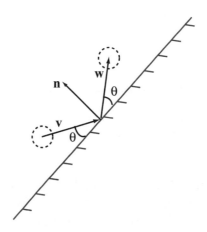

FIGURE 9.1   A ball hitting a wall.

The simplest way to deal with this is to split the vector **v** into two components, one in the direction **n** (the normal component) and the other in the direction of the wall (the tangential component). Because there are no forces acting on the ball in the tangential direction, its velocity in that direction remains unchanged. In the other direction, the velocity is simply reversed. This way, the energy of the ball, the only moving object in the collision, remains unchanged. The end result of this is that you can find the new velocity by simply subtracting twice the normal component, as here:

```
function resolveFixedCollision(obj, n)
    set c to componentVector(obj.velocity, n)
    set obj.velocity to v-2*c
end function
```

This function, as in the previous chapter, uses an object-based model, altering the velocity of the object directly and not returning any value, therefore not being a "function" as such.

This function is wonderfully simple, and what's more, it applies to any collision whatsoever where one of the objects is fixed in place. Once we know the normal at the point of contact (which we have already determined), the colliding object will always follow the same path.

*Try the algebra yourself: remember that if **c** is the component of **v** in one direction, then the component in the perpendicular direction is **v** – **c**.*

A useful geometrical side-effect of this is that the angle between the original velocity vector and the wall (the *angle of incidence*) is equal to the angle between the final velocity vector and the wall (the *angle of reflection*), as in the figure.

All of this discussion centers on the question of the ball's motion before and after the collision. What it doesn't say anything about is what is going on *during* the collision, which is harder to deal with than you might expect, and which we will return to in Chapter 12.

A Ball Hitting a Movable Ball

Things become more complicated when the objects are not fixed in place. If both objects can move, then you need to determine the velocity of both objects after collision.

If you think about it, you will realize that we immediately need more information. A ball bearing hitting a cannonball is going to make a lot less difference than a wrecking ball hitting the same cannonball at the same velocity. We need to know the masses of the two objects to determine the correct solution. More importantly, we need their energy and momentum. When neither of the two objects is fixed, we have a situation where both the conservation laws apply: the total momentum of the two objects after a collision should be the same as the total momentum before, and the same is true for their total energy.

It is easiest to consider the case where the velocity of one object before the collision is zero. Because of the principle of relativity, we can transform any other case to this one by simply subtracting one velocity from the other, as we'll see in a moment. So suppose we have a ball B (the *incident ball*) with velocity $\mathbf{u}$ and mass m hitting a stationary, movable ball C (the *object ball*) with mass p, at a normal of $\mathbf{n}$. After the collision, B has velocity $\mathbf{v}$ and C has velocity $\mathbf{w}$, both of which are unknown. See Figure 9.2 for an illustration of this.

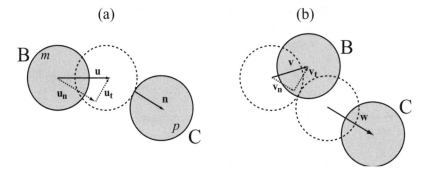

FIGURE 9.2   A collision with a stationary, movable object.

Now, as before, we can split $\mathbf{u}$ into two components with magnitude u_n (normal) and u_t (tangential), and similarly for $\mathbf{v}$ and $\mathbf{w}$. And as before, since there are no forces acting tangentially, the velocity of each ball in the tangential direction remains unchanged, so $v_t = u_t$ and $w_t = 0$. In the other direction, conservation of momentum tells us that

$$mu_n = mv_n + pw_n$$

We'll simplify life for ourselves later by dividing through by p to get a ratio $r = {m}/{p}$, giving $ru_n = rv_n + w_n$.

Meanwhile, conservation of energy tells us:
$\frac{1}{2} mu^2 = \frac{1}{2} mv^2 + \frac{1}{2} pw^2$, which splits up to

$$r\left(u_n^2 + u_t^2\right) = r\left(v_n^2 + v_t^2\right) + \left(w_n^2 + w_t^2\right)$$

Using our knowledge about the tangential direction, this becomes

$$r\left(u_n^2 + u_t^2\right) = r\left(v_n^2 + u_t^2\right) + w_n^2$$

We now have simultaneous equations in the unknowns v_n and w_n which can be solved by substitution. From the momentum equation we have

$$w_n = r\left(u_n - v_n\right)$$

We can substitute this value into the energy equation to get

$$r\left(u_n^2 + u_t^2\right) = r\left(v_n^2 + u_t^2\right) + r^2\left(u_n - v_n\right)^2$$

$$u_n^2 + u_t^2 = v_n^2 + u_t^2 + ru_n^2 - 2ru_n v_n + rv_n^2$$

$$\left(r+1\right)v_n^2 + \left(r-1\right)u_n^2 - 2ru_n v_n = 0$$

So we end up with a quadratic equation in v_r, which factorizes quite neatly:

$$\left(v_n - u_n\right)\left(\left(r+1\right)v_n + \left(r-1\right)u_n\right) = 0$$

This gives us two roots of the equation: $v_n = u_n$ and $v_n = \frac{r-1}{r+1} u_n$. The first of these roots is expected: it is the initial situation. So the other root must represent the situation after the collision. Notice that it depends on the ratio of the masses of the balls, not on their absolute values, which makes sense physically. Also notice that the value of u_t dropped out of the calculation, which is what we would expect: we want the two components to be completely independent.

NOTE

We expected the initial situation to be a valid solution to the equations, because elastic collisions are time-reversible—that is, if you reverse all the velocities after the collision, then run the simulation again, you should get back to your initial position.

We can now determine w_n quickly by substituting back into the momentum equation:

$$w_n = r\left(u_n - \frac{r-1}{r+1}u_n\right)$$

$$= \frac{2ru_n}{r+1}$$

```
function resolveCollisionFree1 (obj1, obj2, n)
    set r to obj1.mass/obj2.mass
    set un to componentVector(obj1.velocity,n)
    set ut to obj1.velocity-un
    set vn to un*(r-1)/(r+1)
    set wn to un*2*r/(r+1)
    set obj1.velocity to ut+vn
    set obj2.velocity to wn
end function
```

Two Moving Balls Colliding

Adding a velocity to the second object is straightforward. You simply subtract the velocity from all objects in order to transform into the previous case. But you do need to remember to add it on again afterwards.

```
function resolveCollisionFree (obj1, obj2, n)
    set r to obj1.mass/obj2.mass
    set u to obj1.velocity-obj2.velocity
    set un to componentVector(u,n)
    set ut to u-un
    set vn to un*(r-1)/(r+1)
    set wn to un*2*r/(r+1)
    set obj1.velocity to ut+vn+u2
    set obj2.velocity to wn+u2
end function
```

And that's all there is to it. The shapes and sizes of the objects don't matter (except when calculating the collision normal). This one function can handle every possible elastic collision.

If $r = 1$, that is, the two masses are equal, then we have $v_n = 0$ and $w_n = u_n$. This is the "Newton's cradle" effect, where the velocity of one ball is transferred entirely to the other, leaving the original ball stationary (at least normal to the collision).

```
function resolveCollisionEqualMass (obj1, obj2, n)
   set u to obj1.velocity-obj2.velocity
   set un to componentVector(u,n)
   set ut to u-un
   set obj1.velocity to ut+obj2.velocity
   set obj2.velocity to un+obj2.velocity
end function
```

As r tends to 0, which is to say that the mass p tends to infinity relative to m, then $v_n \to u_n$ and $w_n \to 0$. This is the same as we encountered previously with a fixed wall, which makes sense: when the mass of the object ball is infinite, it can't move, so this becomes a fixed-wall collision. Conversely, when an object is fixed, it can be considered to have an infinite mass.

Inelastic Collisions

An *inelastic* collision, as you might expect, is one where not all the initial kinetic energy is transferred to kinetic energy after the collision, a certain proportion being lost to heat, sound, etc.

The simplest way to simulate energy loss is to decide a fixed proportion of energy which will be lost at each collision between two objects. This proportion is called the *efficiency* (there is also a related value, the *coefficient of restitution*). If the objects in your simulation are all similar, you can use a global efficiency which applies throughout. If not, you are best off giving one efficiency value to each object and combining them for each collision. So if ball B transfers 95% of its energy at each collision, and ball C transfers 90%, then in a collision between the two, where B has energy E_b and C has energy E_c then the total energy after the collision is $0.95 \times 0.9 \times \left(E_b + E_c \right)$.

Like elastic collisions, this is a simplification, real collisions do not work so linearly. Generally, faster collisions are more efficient than slower ones, and efficiency is affected by factors like the ambient temperature of the surrounding air. Still, the errors are small, especially when working within normal ranges of speed and mass.

With an inelastic collision, the equations get a bit more complicated. Fortunately, we still know that motion tangential to the collision must be unaffected. In the normal direction, conservation of momentum remains as it was before (barring external forces acting, this law is always true), but conservation of energy must be revised to take efficiency into account:

$$\frac{1}{2}emu^2 = \frac{1}{2}mv^2 + \frac{1}{2}pw^2$$

Here, the value e is the product of the efficiencies of the two objects, expressed as a fraction. We can now go through exactly the same process as before: by combining it with our knowledge that tangential motion is unaffected, we have:

$$er\left(u_n^2 + u_t^2\right) = r\left(v_n^2 + u_t^2\right) + w_n^2 \text{ (As before, } r = \frac{m}{p})$$

Substituting for w, $(r+1)v_n^2 + 2ru_n v_n + (r-e)u_n^2 + (1-e)u_t^2$.

Notice that this time, unless $e = 1$, the value of u_t does not drop out of the equation If $e = 1$, perfect efficiency, then the equation reduces to the elastic example. The tangential speed *does* have an effect on the end result, because the more energy the system has, the more it will lose.

This equation again has two roots, which can be calculated from the quadratic formula:

$$v_n = \frac{-ru_n \pm \sqrt{r^2 u_n^2 - (r+1)\left((r-e)u_n^2 + (1-e)u_t^2\right)}}{r+1}$$

The value u_n is no longer a root of the equation (unless $e = 1$). This makes sense, because inelastic collisions are not time-reversible. However, by generalizing from the elastic case, we do know that the particular root we are looking for is the result of taking the negative square root, and substituting back for w, this gives us the following function:

```
function resolveInelasticCollisionFree (obj1, obj2, n)
    set r to obj1.mass/obj2.mass
    set u to obj1.velocity-obj2.velocity
    set e to obj1.efficiency*obj2.efficiency
    set un to component (u,n)
    set ut to mag(u-un*n)
    set sq to r*r*un*un-(r+1)*((r-e)*un*un+(1-e)*ut*ut))
    set vn to n*(sqrt(sq)-r*un)/(r+1)
    set wn to r*(n*un-vn)
    set obj1.velocity to ut+vn+ obj2.velocity
    set obj2.velocity to wn+ obj2.velocity
end function
```

When $e = 1$, this is an elastic collision, and you can see that in this case sq=un*un, which leads to the same final values as before.

Just for completeness, here is the function for dealing with fixed inelastic collisions. This is obtained simply by setting $r = 0$ in the above equations. Compare this to the elastic version to see how similar they are.

```
function resolveInelasticCollisionFixed (obj1, obj2, n)
   set e to obj1.efficiency*obj2.efficiency
   set un to component (obj1.velocity,n)
   set ut to mag(obj1.velocity -un*n)
   set sq to  (e*un*un+(e-1)*ut*ut))
   set vn to n*sqrt(sq)
   set obj1.velocity to ut+vn
end function
```

As before, this function is independent of the mass of either object, which makes it much simpler.

MULTIPLE COLLISIONS

Strictly speaking, this section should be part of collision detection rather than resolution, but it is related to both. How do you deal with the situation where more than one object is moving around on your screen? What happens if more than one object is colliding at a time?

Collision Is a Recursive Function

The key to complex collision detection is to understand the process involved. Let's break the problem down:

1. You have a set of objects $O_1, O_2, ..., O_n$, all of which are moving with some velocity, have some mass, some efficiency etc.
2. Your simulation is divided into time steps (usually variable and dependent on the speed of the user's computer: you calculate the size of each time-step by comparison to the last known time). So at this stage you have a time-step of s time units.
3. In each time step, you need to search through the objects and find the first pair (if any) that collide. The collision detection function returns a value t between 0 and 1, as well as the collision normal.
4. The time taken to reach this collision is ts. So you can move all the objects by a distance ts times their current velocity.
5. Now resolve the collision. Each of the colliding objects now has a new velocity.
6. In this time-step, there are still $(1 - t)s$ time units remaining. So return to step 3 and continue until there are no more collisions.

Here is a function which implements this procedure. It includes a number of calls to other functions which we can assume have already been dealt with. Notice also that we split the list of objects into fixed and movable, which allows us to streamline the algorithm a little.

```
function checkCollision (time, movableObjects,  fixedObjects)
    // check for the earliest collision
    set mn to 2
    set ob1 to 0
    set ob2 to 0
    repeat for i=the number of movableObjects down to 1
       set obj1 to movableObjects[i]
       // find the displacement vector and other
       // relevant facts about this object
       set l to parameters(obj1, t)
       // search for collisions with other movableObjects
       // (don't bother with those already checked)
       repeat for j=i-1 down to 1
          set obj2 to movableObjects[j]
          set l2 to parameters(obj2, t)
          set c to detectCollision(l,l2)
          if c is not a collision array then next repeat
          set tm to c[1] // the time of collision
          set m to min(mn,tm)
          if m<mn then
             set mn to m
             set n to c[2] // the normal vector
             set ob1 to obj1
             set ob2 to obj2
             set lf1 to l
             set lf2 to l2
          end if
       end repeat
       // now search for collisions with fixed objects
       repeat for j=the number of fixedObjects down to 1
          set obj2 to fixedObjects[j]
          set c to detectCollision(l, l2)
          if c is not a collision array then next repeat
          set tm to c[1] // the time of collision
          set m to min(mn,tm)
          if m<mn then
             set mn to m
             set n to c[2] // the normal vector
             set ob1 to obj1
```

```
            set ob2 to obj2
            set lf1 to l
            set lf2 to l2
        end if
    end repeat
end repeat
if mn=2 then set tmove to 1
otherwise set tmove to mn*t
repeat for each obj in movableObjects
    moveObject(obj, tmove)
end repeat
// if there is no collision we are finished
if mn=2 then return
// otherwise, we can resolve the collision here
set res to resolveCollision(lf1, lf2)
setNewVelocity(ob1, res[1])
setNewVelocity(ob2, res[2])
// and now recurse for the rest of the time-step
checkCollision(t*(1-mn), movableObjects, fixedObjects)
end function
```

Many of the details here have been left unfinished, because they depend on the kind of programming environment you prefer. In an object-oriented world, each moving shape would be represented by an object, probably with some kind of sub-classing that tells you which kind of shape it is (some of the more complex example programs include a structure like this for simplicity). In a procedural language, you would use an array of values for each shape. But ultimately the process is the same. We have also have not shown the processes by which the detectCollision() and resolveCollision() functions determine which of the various functions we have looked at so far are relevant. This makes sense, as it allows the process to be far more general.

The function can still be made much more efficient by using processes of *culling* (pre-determining which shapes are likely to collide before making any more calculations), and also by ensuring that calculations which have already been performed once don't need to be performed again. For example, if in the previous time-step calculation, objects A and B did not collide at all (even after the first collision), then they won't collide in the next time-step either, unless struck by one of the objects which has changed its velocity since then. Conversely, two objects that were about to collide probably still are going to, again unless struck by one of the just-collided objects. So unless one of the objects that collided in the last calculation hits anything, all your other calculations will remain valid. We will look into these kinds of optimizations in later chapters.

Simultaneous Collisions

Up to now, we have always considered single collisions between two objects, but what happens when three or more objects collide simultaneously as in Figure 9.3?

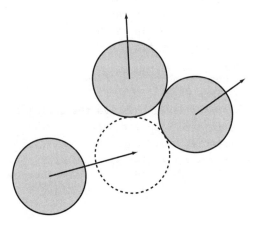

FIGURE 9.3   Three circles colliding simultaneously.

Let's begin by saying that this situation is extremely unlikely. In reality, one of the two objects always touches first, which means that the standard procedure detailed above will apply. But computers are not infinitely precise, and at some stage it might just happen that you get an exact simultaneous collision.

The easiest way to resolve this problem is simply to cheat. By using a *perturbation* (mentioned in the previous chapter), you can alter the parameters of the simulation very slightly to force one of the collisions to happen first. In fact, this is implicitly the case in the existing function: it always chooses the first minimal collision encountered to be the one to resolve.

But you still need to be careful. After resolving the collision, a second will be encountered immediately, with a value of $t = 0$. This means that the collision time will not diminish, creating a potential infinite loop in the function. Fortunately, in almost all situations this will not be an issue. It might occur, for example, when a ball is sliding down a fixed tunnel of its exact width, but this can be easily avoided by not setting up your world this way in the first place.

Another example of a multiple collision is, again, the Newton's Cradle, shown in Figure 9.4. Here, a number of balls are arranged in a row, touching each other, and struck by another ball at one end with velocity **v**. The momentum of the incident ball passes through the group, causing the last ball to move off at the same velocity. It turns out that the same process that deals with simultaneous collisions also covers this case. This time, it is not the incident ball which is struck simultaneously, but the object ball B_1. After the collision, B_1 is moving with velocity **v**, but strikes ball B_2 instantly ($t = 0$). The same process passes down the chain until the final ball experiences just one collision and can move off freely.

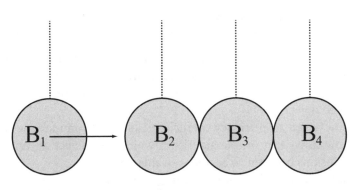

FIGURE 9.4 Newton's Cradle.

EXERCISES

Exercise 9.1

Complete the checkCollision() function by filling in the missing details, particularly the two functions detectCollision() and resolveCollision().

This is mostly a programming exercise rather than a mathematical one: you should try to write these functions in a general way which allows you to create new collision types and resolve them correctly.

Exercise 9.2

Create a simplified Newton's Cradle.

Make a simulation with two fixed walls at either end, a number of touching balls in between, and one or more other balls between the group and the walls, all in a straight line. Any of the balls should be allowed to have an initial velocity along the line. See if you can use the resolution functions to make the simulation behave like a real Newton's Cradle.

SUMMARY

Hopefully, this chapter was much less difficult than you expected, after the hard work of collision detection. You should now be getting a clear idea of the power of the mathematical techniques introduced in the first part of the book, and how they apply to the physical world. In the next chapter we shall go back to the question of collision detection and how to deal with some more complex shapes.

YOU SHOULD NOW KNOW

- the meaning of the terms *elastic, inelastic,* and *efficiency*
- how to use conservation of momentum and energy to *resolve* an arbitrary elastic collision between two moving objects or one moving object and one fixed object
- how to use an efficiency coefficient to simulate an inelastic collision
- how to write a simple algorithm which will detect an unlimited number of collisions between fixed and movable objects
- how to deal with multiple simultaneous collisions

10 Detecting Collisions Between Complex Shapes

In This Chapter

- Overview
- The Problems of a Complex Shape
- Some Reasonable Problems
- Built-In Solutions
- Exercises
- Summary
- You Should Now Know

OVERVIEW

In life, we don't see many perfect circles and rectangles colliding. Most objects have a more irregular shape—and as we have seen, even regular shapes such as ellipses can be very difficult to compute. When a ball bounces on rough terrain or Monty Python's foot comes stomping to the ground, we need more general ways to find the point of contact.

In this chapter we will look at some ways to calculate the solution to the general collision problem, and some shortcuts to make it more tractable. In the process, we will also look at some ways to generate and store details of rough terrain, including how to calculate the normal and tangent.

ON THE CD   Code samples from this chapter are implemented in *math.cst* in the script *chapter 10 (object modeling and collisions)*. In addition to the *collisions* demo, the *collisionMaps*, *splines*, and *inside* demos illustrate specific examples from the chapter (*collisionMaps* includes a solution to Exercise 10.2).

THE PROBLEMS OF A COMPLEX SHAPE

So what is it about complex shapes that makes them so difficult? Well, to start with we can ask: what do we mean by a complex shape? For example, how might you describe the shape of a foot coming down to the ground? In this section we will look at ways to define a complicated shape to help with collision detection.

Bitmaps and Vector Shapes

Computers describe pictures on the screen in two ways. The simplest is called a *bitmap*: literally, it is a precise map of every pixel in the picture, specifying its color to a particular degree of precision. In many cases, this is the only sensible way to store the image—how else might you describe, for example, a painting by Seurat?

The alternative is to use a *vector shape*—such as might be produced by a product like Adobe® Illustrator® or Macromedia® Flash™ (the distinction is between "drawing" and "painting" packages). This stores shapes as pieces of information: a circle as a center and a radius (as well as the fact of its being a circle), a rectangle by four vertices, and so on. This has many advantages over bitmaps for simple drawings: a bitmap of a 500 × 500 pixel square needs 250,000 pieces of information, whereas a vector shape of the same square would only need nine or so: the positions of the four vertices, the fact that there are four straight lines connecting them, and the color. (Of course, what counts as a "piece of information" is blurry.) On the other hand, vector shapes tend to be slower to draw as the computer must reconstruct the bitmap image from the information in order to display it on the screen.

The same principles apply in collision detection. We can store information about a shape either as a vector (as we have been doing in all the examples so far) or as a "bitmap," that is to say, as a precise list of pixels called a *collision map*. As a general principle, the more complex a shape is (in the sense of how much information is required to describe it with vectors), the more likely it is that a plain pixel-by-pixel description will be the best. However, sometimes the best method is to combine the two.

Defining a Complex Shape

For the moment we won't worry about smooth shapes, we'll just deal with *polygons*, that is, sets of vertices connected by a closed loop of straight line segments, as shown in Figure 10.1. This is a random convex octagon (that is, an eight-sided polygon; we'll explain "convex" later), with eight straight line segments connecting the vertices $v_1, v_2, \ldots, v_8$ in order. For the sake of simplicity, we will assume that the origin from which these position vectors are calculated is at the center of mass of the octagon.

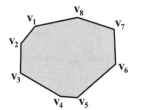

FIGURE 10.2   A collision map for a blob.

FIGURE 10.1   A generic convex polygon.

We'll use the notation $P(v_1, v_2, \ldots, v_n)$ to describe a generic n-gon (polygon with n sides).

The other way to describe a complex shape is using a *collision map*, which is like a 1-bit bitmap of the shape, where black pixels represent the inside of the shape, and white pixels the outside. For example, in Figure 10.2 you can see a collision map for an amoeba-like creature. Although collision maps are expensive to calculate, sometimes they are the best solution, and you can often save on calculations by using a very low-resolution collision map. In the figure, the collision map is only 30 × 30 pixels in size, whereas the amoeba itself is drawn at a much greater precision.

If you are using collision maps, it is generally best to calculate them in advance, either by storing them with your images, or if absolutely necessary calculating them when the program starts (this will save on file size but slow down the start of your program). Here is an example of the kind of function you might use to create the collision map—the fine details depend greatly on the particular language you are using, and on the kind of image it is.

```
function collisionMap(image, resolution, sensitivity)
    // resolution should be an integer representing
    // the number of pixels of the original per pixel
    // of the collision map.
    // sensitivity should be a float between 0 (no
```

```
// fuzzy edges) and 1 (the whole thing is ignored)
set map to an empty 2-dimensional array
set w to ceil((the width of the image)/resolution)
set h to ceil((the height of the image)/resolution)
repeat for x=1 to w
   set xstart to (x-1)*resolution
   repeat for y=1 to h
      set ystart to (y-1)*resolution
      set tot to 0
      repeat for i=1 to resolution
         repeat for j=1 to resolution
            add the color of the pixel at (xstart+i, ystart+j) to tot
         end repeat
      end repeat
      divide tot by resolution*resolution
      if tot<(the color of white)*sensitivity then
         set map[x][y] to 1
      otherwise
         set map[x][y] to 0
      end if
   end repeat
end repeat
return map
end
```

This function deliberately leaves vague the question of how you transform a color to a number, as it depends on the bit depth of your bitmap, which we will worry about later. For now, just think of it as a number from 0 (black) to N (white).

There is one other way to define a shape, which to a certain extent we have already been using, and that is to use a *functional* or *parametric* description. An example of this is when describing a circle: just knowing that it is a circle means that we already know a great many things about it: in particular we know that a point is inside a circle if and only if its distance from the center is less than the radius.

Most objects don't have such a simple functional description, but sometimes they do. For example, the starfish-like shape in Figure 10.3 has a reasonably simple equation describing it:

$$x = r(\sin(5\alpha) + 2)\cos(\alpha)$$
$$y = r(\sin(5\alpha) + 2)\sin(\alpha)$$

FIGURE 10.3   A "starfish" drawn with a
simple formula.

This is a *parametric equation*: both x and y are described in terms of the parameter α (and the constant r). We've encountered several such equations already. Essentially, this shape is like a circle, but with the radius varying as you move around the origin. Functional descriptions are useful for two reasons: first, they allow you to describe a smooth shape accurately and draw it at an arbitrarily high resolution, which also means that you can determine the normal at the point of contact, second, they are often relatively simple to calculate: to determine if a point is on the perimeter, simply plug the values of x and y into the function and see if it fits. For example, in this case we can determine whether a point P is inside the shape by finding the angle α that OP makes with the x-axis, finding the value $x = r(\sin(5\alpha) + 2)$, and comparing this value to the length of OP. However, although being able to determine whether a point is inside a shape is clearly a vital first step toward collision detection, it isn't quite enough if the detection is to be made efficient and fast.

Bezier Curves and Splines

Another common type of parameterized curve is the system used in most drawing packages, called the *Bezier curve*. A Bezier curve is a vector-based description of a curved line that is defined by two sets of information: a list $v_1, v_2, \ldots, v_n$ of *nodes*, or salient points on the line, and a list of *control points* for the nodes, $c_{12}, c_{21}, c_{22}, c_{31}, c_{32}, c_{41}, \ldots, c_{(n-1)2}, c_{n1}$. There are two control points for each node, except the first and last which have one each (unless the curve is closed). Figure 10.4 shows a short Bezier curve, with its nodes and control points marked.

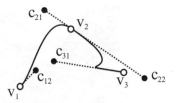

FIGURE 10.4 A three-node Bezier curve.

As you see in the figure, the relationship between the control points and the curve is quite complex. It can be summarized in two ways: the *direction* of the control point from its node gives the tangent to the curve, while the *distance* of the control point tells us the curvature: the further away it is, the closer the curve is to the tangent.

It's simplest to look at curves of just two nodes, since longer curves are just divided into sections, one between each successive pair of nodes. So we'll consider the case where we have $n_1 = (x_1, y_1)$, $n_2 = (x_2, y_2)$, $c_{12} = (p_1, q_1)$, $c_{21} = (p_2, q_2)$.

A Bezier curve is parametric, like the starfish. This means that it is described in terms of a variable t, which varies from 0 to 1. At $t = 0$, the function evaluates to the first node. At $t = 1$, it evaluates to the second node. In between, we get a smooth curve, which follows this cubic parameterization:

$$x(t) = a_x t^3 + b_x t^2 + c_x t + x_1$$

where

$$c_x = 3(p_1 - x_1)$$
$$b_x = 3(p_2 - p_1) - c_x$$
$$a_x = x_2 - x_1 - 3(p_2 - p_1)$$

and similarly for $y(t)$.

If you plug the values 0 and 1 for t into this formula, you'll see that it yields the values x_1 and x_2 as required. Also, if you differentiate once with respect to t and again plug in the value $t = 0$, you'll see that you get the value c_x, so the magnitude of the tangent with respect to x at that point is proportional to the distance between the control point and the node.

A Bezier curve is not the only way to create a parameterized cubic function. Another method is the *Catmull-Rom spline* (a *spline* is just another word for a parameterized curve). Instead of working with control points, the Catmull-Rom curve is a method for interpolating using four points that lie on the curve itself. In Figure 10.5 you can see how this works: the four nodes n_0, n_1, n_2, n_3 define the curve segment between n_1 and n_2 precisely. By creating a chain of $n + 2$ such points, we can define n segments, which have the same tangents at the end points and so give us a smooth curve. (Notice that the first and last control points don't define a segment precisely, so we can't draw in a curve at the ends.)

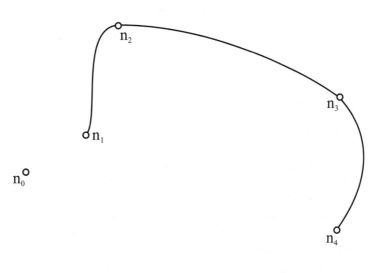

FIGURE 10.5 A Catmull-Rom spline.

As with Beziers, the Catmull-Rom curve is defined parametrically by a value between 0 and 1. The function is:

$$p(t) = \frac{1}{2}(2n_1 + (-n_0 + n_2)t + (2n_0 - 5n_1 + 4n_2 - n_3)t^2 + (-n_0 + 3n_1 - 3n_2 + n_3)t^3)$$

If you plug in the value $t = 0$, you'll see that you get the answer n_1, and if you put in $t = 1$, you get n_2. Catmull-Rom splines are simpler than Bezier curves, but have the disadvantage that they can't be used to define sharp corners at individual nodes.

NOTE

We'll look at a much more complex kind of spline, the NURBS, in Chapter 21.

Because a cubic polynomial is a fairly simple function, it's relatively easy to calculate collisions against these splines. In particular, it's possible to find the intersection of a straight line with a Bezier or Catmull-Rom spline. We're in the usual territory here: we're looking for a point lying on both lines, which means solving the simultaneous equations:

$$u_1 + sv_1 = a_x t^3 + b_x t^2 + c_x t + x_1$$
$$u_2 + sv_2 = a_y t^3 + b_y t^2 + c_y t + y_1$$

Using the notation we used for Bezier curves here, by substituting for s, we find that

$$u_1 + \frac{v_1}{v_2}(a_y t^3 + b_y t^2 + c_y t + y_1 - u_2) = a_x t^3 + b_x t^2 + c_x t + x_1$$

$$(v_1 a_1 - v_2 a_x - v_1 a_y)t^3 + (v_2 b_x - v_1 b_y)t^2 + (v_2 c_x - v_1 c_y)t + (v_2(x_1 - u_1) - v_1(y_1 - u_2)) = 0$$

This is just another cubic equation, all of whose coefficients can be calculated. If we solve this cubic (using the method from Chapter 3), then we can find the values of t and s.

Another solvable problem is dealing with collisions between a moving line and a spline (or vice versa). Solving this requires using a useful property of parametric curves which you will recall from Chapter 6: the gradient of the curve at a particular value of t is given by the quotient of the derivatives with respect to t. That is,

$$\frac{\frac{dy}{dt}}{\frac{dx}{dt}} = \frac{dy}{dx}$$

So finding the gradient of a spline, and hence a collision normal, is fairly simple. It's given by

$$\frac{dy}{dx} = \frac{3a_y t^2 + 2b_y t + c_y}{3a_x t^2 + 2b_x t + c_x}$$

When calculating collisions between a line and a cubic parameterization, we can take advantage of the fact that at the moment of impact, assuming it's not at a vertex or endpoint of the line segment, the two meet along a tangent to the curve. So the gradient of the curve must be equal to the gradient of the line, giving us:

$$\frac{v_2}{v_1} = \frac{3a_y t^2 + 2b_y t + c_y}{3a_x t^2 + 2b_x t + c_x}$$

$$3(v_2 a_x - v_1 a_y)t^2 + 2(v_2 b_x - v_1 b_y)t + (v_2 c_x - v_1 c_y) = 0$$

This is a simple quadratic which is easy to solve, and yields at most two points in a particular section of the curve that could collide with the line, depending on its direction of travel. Now you simply have to find out if either of those points lies within the line segment during its motion, which you can do on your own. Of course, it is also necessary to calculate point-line collisions with the nodes of the curve (for a Bezier curve with sharp corners) and point-spline collisions with the ends of the line segment. Using this method, we can calculate collisions between a cubic spline and any polygon.

Such successes might embolden us to try other collisions, but sadly it is not going to happen: detecting collisions between splines and circles or ellipses, let alone other splines, can't be done anywhere near as easily, producing equations of fifth or even sixth order that cannot be solved algebraically. But for a situation where there is a single object described with a spline, and others described with polygons, these functions can be enough, and in other cases, our approximation methods can help.

Convex and Concave

Shapes can be broadly divided into two kinds: *convex* and *concave*. We've encountered them before, and there is a fairly simple way to define them. A shape is concave if there are three points P_1, P_2, P_3 on the perimeter such that the interior angle $P_1 P_2 P_3$ is greater than 180°; if no such points exist, the shape is convex (see Figure 10.6). The definition works equally for polygons and smooth shapes, as in the figure, and the three points can be any points at all on the perimeter. How we decide which angle is interior is a slightly tricky thing to define precisely but we'll come to it later: for now, we'll consider it obvious.

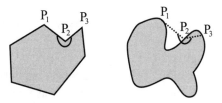

FIGURE 10.6 Two concave shapes.

As a general rule, convex shapes are relatively straightforward. Any line intersects them at most at two points, which means that there aren't too many possibilities to check. If in doubt, you can describe a convex shape arbitrarily accurately with a convex polygon (sometimes called a *polygonal armature*), and then collision detection is just the same as with a rectangle, only with more line segments to check:

```
function pointPolygonCollision(pt, displacement, poly)
   // here poly is an array of vertex points in order
   set t to 2
   set c to the number of points in poly
   repeat for i=1 to c
      set p1 to poly[i]
      set p2 to poly[(i mod c)+1]
      set t1 to intersectionV(pt,displacement,p1,p2-p1)
      if t1="none" then next repeat
      set t to min(t,t1)
   end repeat
   if t=2 then return "none"
   return t
end function
```

This is really much the same as the rectangle case, except that we have defined the sides more generally. However, we can speed things up by finding the leading edges of the shape as we'll see later in the chapter.

Concave shapes are a different matter. A generalized concave shape can be as convoluted as you want to make it—think of a maze of caves, for example. Any line might intersect the shape any number of times, and with the *really* complicated shapes, you can't even approximate them accurately with a polygon. In fact, it's not even trivial to determine if a point is inside a generalized concave shape such as a fractal. However, for the kinds of shapes we are talking about it is often possible to use an approximating polygon.

Determining If a Point Is Inside a Shape

Once we can determine an intersection between a moving point (or a line segment) and a shape, we can use this information to answer one of the most fundamental questions: is a particular point inside the shape?

As we have seen, in many cases, especially when the shape has some functional description, this question can be resolved reasonably simply. In other cases, you need a more general solution. For this we can use *raycasting*, a technique which comes into its own in (and whose name is borrowed from) 3D programming. A *ray* is an infinitely long line from a point in some direction, like a beam of light from a torch. Using our point/shape collision routines, we can determine the intersection of this ray with the shapes we are interested in.

If you have a point P inside a shape S, what happens when you cast a ray from that point to infinity? At some stage it has to intersect with S, since S is a closed line. Of course, if S is concave then the ray may intersect again somewhere else, but after that the ray is inside again, and so we know that somewhere down the line it must intersect yet again. Ultimately, the ray must intersect an odd number of times. Conversely, a ray cast from outside the shape must intersect an even number of times (possibly zero). (See Figure 10.7.)

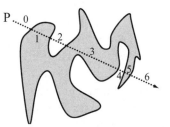

FIGURE 10.7   Casting a ray to determine if a point is inside a shape.

Sharp-eyed readers may have realized that there is a flaw in this reasoning, because the ray might at some stage touch S at a tangent, so that it meets the shape but does not intersect. This is potentially a major problem, but as long as S is a polygon, we can deal with the special case. Otherwise, to be absolutely sure you need to cast two or more rays—generally, if two rays with a small angle between them agree on the disposition of the point, then you can accept their answer with reasonable confidence for a sufficiently simple shape. If they disagree, you can cast a third ray to resolve the answer.

Let's adapt our polygon intersection function to carry out this task. For the moment we won't worry about the special case of tangential rays.

```
function pointInsidePolygonIncomplete(pt, poly)
    // choose an arbitrary point outside the polygon
    set mx to the maximum x-value in poly
    set outpoint to (mx+10,0)
    // now count the intersections along the ray from pt to outpoint
    set intersections to 0
```

```
    set c to the number of points in poly
    repeat for i=1 to c
        set p1 to poly[i]
        set p2 to poly[(i mod c)+1]
        set t to intersection(p1,p2,pt,outpoint)
        if t="none" then next repeat
        add 1 to intersections
    end repeat
    if (intersections mod 2)=1 then return true
    otherwise return false
end function
```

Good. So now what about those rays that touch the perimeter without passing through it? Well, first of all consider the case of a ray that meets the perimeter along one of the sides. If it does not pass through the side, it must be parallel to it. But in that case it also passes through a vertex (two, in fact), so all we really need to consider is the case where the ray meets a vertex. You might have noticed a small change between pointInsidePolygonIncomplete() and the collision detection function: if the ray intersects at a vertex, the routine simply ignores it and doesn't count it. This is clearly wrong, but will be fixed at the same time that we fix the tangent problem. This time, if the ray intersects at a vertex we will simply abandon it and try a slightly different ray. Because this is a polygon and so has a finite number of vertices, this technique is guaranteed to work.

```
function pointInsidePolygon(pt, poly, outpoint)
    if outpoint is not defined then
        // choose an arbitrary point outside the polygon
        set mx to the maximum x-value in poly
        set outpoint to (mx+10,0)
    end if
    // now count the intersections along the ray from pt to outpoint
    set intersections to 0
    set c to the number of points in poly
    repeat for i=1 to c
        set p1 to poly[i]
        set p2 to poly[(i mod c)+1]
        set t to intersection(p1,p2,pt,outpoint)
        if t="none" then next repeat
        if t=0 or t=1 then
            // try a different ray
            return pointInsidePolygon(pt, poly, outpoint+(0,100))
        end if
        add 1 to intersections
```

```
      end repeat
      if (intersections mod 2)=1 then return true
      otherwise return false
   end function
```

There are other ways to determine whether the ray meets the vertex tangentially. The simplest is to check for an intersection with the line segment joining the two neighbors of the vertex and the ray: if there is no intersection within the line segment then the ray met the vertex tangentially as shown in Figure 10.8. However, unless the polygon has a large number of vertices, the method given is fairly simple and unlikely to need more than two runs.

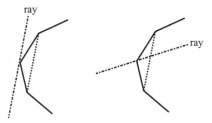

FIGURE 10.8 Determining the type of intersection with a vertex.

SOME REASONABLE PROBLEMS

Although collision detection between arbitrary shapes is always going to be computationally expensive, we can at least make some progress. We'll look now at a few typical problems which, while tough, are not so hard as to be pointless.

When Jelly Hits a Wall: Finding the Leading Edge of a Complex Shape

If a shape S is moving along a constant vector toward a solid wall, you can save a lot of time by pre-calculating its *leading point* relative to the wall, which is to say, the first point on the perimeter of S which will hit the wall (see Figure 10.9). There may be more than one leading point, each of which strikes the wall at the same time, but we only need find one.

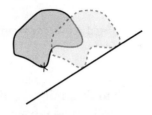

FIGURE 10.9 The leading
point of a complex shape
relative to a wall.

For an image known only by a bitmap description, there is no simple way to calculate the leading point except by just checking all the points and finding the first one in a particular direction. But for a polygon you can do it quite simply, and it is often reasonably simple for a functionally described object, too.

Suppose first that S is a polygon. Using the same technique as we did when working with circles, we can find the distance from each vertex to the wall in the direction of motion. Then the leading point is simply the closest one:

```
function leadingPointOfPolygon(poly, vel, wallPt, wallVect)
    set min to -1
    set minpt to 0
    // calculate the normal to the wall
    set n to norm(normal(wallVect))
    if dotProduct(n,vel)<0 then set n to -n

    repeat for each pt in poly
       set c to component(wallPt-pt, n)
       if c<0 then return "past"
       if min=-1 or c<min then
          set min to c
          set minpt to pt
       end if
    end repeat
    return pt
end function
```

Although this calculation is useful, it may be more generally helpful to find the *leading edge* first. This is the set of points on the perimeter which could strike *any* wall, or for that matter any static object at all. Recall how we did this when calculating collisions between rectangles: there was always at least one point on the rectangle which could never collide with another for a particular direction of motion.

The leading edge is rather more complicated than the leading point. For one thing, it is no longer just vertices we are interested but whole edges—suppose that the shape is going to collide with a particle rather than a wall, then the particle could just as easily collide anywhere along an edge without ever meeting a vertex. So which sides might conceivably hit?

We'll start with a convention. Suppose that all shapes have their vertices listed in an anticlockwise direction as in Figure 10.1. This allows us to conveniently avoid worrying about which side is inside and which one is outside: as long as the vertices are always in anticlockwise order then the inside is always on the anticlockwise side of the edge between two consecutive vertices. We can then always take the clockwise normal of the edge to get a normal pointing outwards (see Figure 10.10).

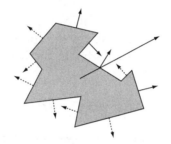

FIGURE 10.10   Finding the leading edge of a polygon.

Suppose that the polygon is traveling along the vector **v** relative to some other object. The edges that could collide are those where the inside is pointing away from the vector **v**, that is, those where the dot product of the normal with **v** is positive (marked with a solid arrow in the figure).

```
function leadingEdgeOfPolygon(poly, vel)
    set edges to an empty array
    set c to the number of points in poly
    repeat with i=1 to c
        set v to poly[(i mod c)+1]-poly[i]
        if dotProduct(clockwiseNormal(v),vel)<0 then
            append array(poly[i],v) to edges
        end if
    end repeat
    return edges
end function
```

We'll return to and define the clockwiseNormal *function in Chapter 13.*

Once you have the set of leading edges, collision detection is simplified a great deal—essentially halved. To detect a collision with S, you merely need to calculate the first collision with any one of these line segments.

Now let's return to leading points, particularly the leading points of functional shapes. As with polygons, the leading point of any shape with respect to a wall is nothing more than the closest point to the wall. Finding this is a matter of calculus, and while in the general case it can be very complicated, in simple cases it is not too bad.

Most shapes described in functional terms can be expressed in terms of a parametric function, so each point on the shape is equal to $(x(t), y(t))$, for some functions x and y and some value of t. For example, in a circle the functions might be $x(t) = r\cos(t)$, $y(t) = r\sin(t)$. To determine the nearest such point to a wall, we need to find the minimum distance to it. As before, we can do this by first determining the normal $(n_1 \ n_2)^T$ to the wall (in the appropriate direction) and then finding the normal component of an arbitrary perimeter point to some reference point $(p_1 \ p_2)^T$ on the wall, which is

$$D(t) = n_1(p_1 - x(t)) + n_2(p_2 - y(t))$$

To find the minimum value of D we differentiate with respect to t, which gives us

$$\dot{D}(t) = -n_1\dot{x}(t) - n_2\dot{y}(t)$$

Notice that the constants representing the reference point disappear, which makes sense—the leading point shouldn't actually be affected by the distance to the wall.

Any minimum value of the function $D(t)$ is to be found at a zero value of $\dot{D}(t)$. Finding such zero values, of course, depends on the functions x and y. Suppose, for example, that x and y are as above for a circle. Then we have

$$\dot{x}(t) = -r\sin(t)$$
$$\dot{y}(t) = -r\cos(t)$$

So $\dot{D}(t) = n_2 r \cos(t) - n_1 r \sin(t)$.

Remember that **n** is a unit vector, so it too is equal to $(\sin(s), \cos(s))$ for some value of s. This means that $\dot{D}(t) = 0$ if and only if $\sin(s)\cos(t) - \cos(s)\sin(t) = 0$ (eliminating the constant factor r). Using our trigonometric identities, this is the same as $\sin(s - t) = 0$, which means that either $s - t = 0$ or $s - t = \pi$ (or other integer multiples of π). So this means that the leading point could either be the point with the same angle as the normal vector, or the one diametrically opposed (which of these is the case depends on the direction of travel and position of the wall). So the method does deliver the expected result.

We won't go into this technique further here as it is quite advanced, but there are hints of it in the sample *collisions.dir* movie on the CD-ROM.

When a Marble Hits a Rock: Using a Collision Map

It can't be denied that in many cases, nothing but a bitmap description of an object will do. Collision maps come in two forms: a full collision map and a *height map*, which is simply a collision map in one dimension. Height maps are most suitable for terrains, which as a general rule are single lines at a varying height, without any "overhangs"—that is to say, they are single-valued functions $y(x)$.

As a general rule, you do not want a simple height map or collision map. These are useful for telling you where the edges of a shape lie (actually, on a full collision map you need to do some initial work even to determine this), but they don't give you the all-important information about the normal at that point. So once you have calculated a collision or height map, you need to create a second one that stores the normal information for each point on the perimeter as well (or more usefully, encode this information for each edge point into a single collision map).

This is a surprisingly tricky problem. Because your information is pixel-by-pixel rather than vector based, it is impossible to know the exact tangent at any point. Look at Figure 10.11, for example, which shows a scaled-up view of a particular collision map (for a smooth object). As you can see, any of the lines marked (and infinitely many more) could be the correct tangent at a particular point of impact: three curves with the appropriate tangents are shown.

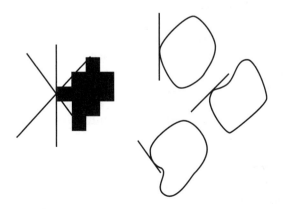

FIGURE 10.11 Problems with finding the tangent to a collision map.

The solution is to make an educated guess. If we find the gradients between adjacent pixels on each side of a point P, we can average them out to guess the correct gradient at P. But this does rather depend on our shape being relatively smooth, with any bumps and curves quite flat in comparison to the size of anything we want to collide with it.

Let's begin with height maps, as these are reasonably simple.

```
function calculateNormals(heightMap)
    set normals to an empty array
    repeat with i=1 to the number of elements of heightMap-1
        set hd to heightMap[i+1]-heightMap[i]
        set v to norm(-hd, 1)
        if i=1 then
            set thisNormal to v
        otherwise
            set thisNormal to (v+lastNormal)/2
        end if
        append thisNormal to normals
        set lastNormal to v
    end repeat
    append lastNormal to normals
    return normals
end function
```

For a more general collision map, this is a little trickier. This time, we'll assume that our collision map is in the form of a black-and-white image. We need to start by tracing the edge of this image. This can be done by allowing each pixel to have three possible values: black for the interior, white for the exterior, and gray for an edge. An edge pixel is a black pixel with a white pixel as an immediate neighbor.

```
function findEdges(bwImage)
    set newImage to a copy of bwImage
    repeat for each point in bwImage
        if the point is black then
            if at least one neighbor of the point is white then
                set the equivalent point in newImage to gray
            end if
        end if
    end repeat
    return newImage
end function
```

This should leave you with an image outlined in gray.

Once you have such a map, the technique for finding the normals is much the same as before. A useful shortcut is to save the normal information in the collision map image itself: instead of using just black, white and gray, allow the amount of gray to vary according to the angle of the normal (we'll see a more complex variant of this when we look at bump maps in Chapter 20). If the image has 8 bits per pixel (a *grayscale* image), you have 254 possible values for each edge pixel, as well as 255 for an empty pixel and 0 for an interior pixel. Thus if the pixel has a value of, say, 200, then this would represent a normal angle of $200 \times \frac{2\pi}{254}$.

```
function calculateNormals(collisionMap)
    set newImage to a copy of collisionMap
    repeat for each point in collisionMap
        if the color of the point is white or black then next repeat
        set clist to an empty array
        set neigh to 0
        repeat for neighbor in (0,1), (1,0), (0,-1),(-1,0)
            if the color of point+neighbor is white then append 0 to clist
            otherwise
                append 1 to clist
                add 1 to neigh
            end if
        end repeat
        if neigh=0 then set v to 0
        if neigh=1 then set v to -(the neighbor vector)
        if neigh=2 then
            if clist[1]=1 and clist[3]=1 then set v to (1,0)
            if clist[2]=1 and clist[4]=1 then set v to (0,1)
            otherwise set v to -(the average of the neighbor vectors)
        if neigh=3 then set v to the non-neighbor vector
        set v to norm(v)
        set the color of the corresponding point of newImage to
writeColor(v)
    end repeat
    return newImage
end function

function writeColor(v)
    set a to atan(v[2],v[1])
    return integer(a*127/pi)
end function

function readColor(c)
    set a to c*pi/127
    return vector(cos(a),sin(a))
end function
```

This function is quite crude: the only possible normal vectors are at multiples of 45°. In Exercise 10.2 you are asked to find a way to smooth the normals out.

On the CD-ROM, you can test these functions out by using the *collision-Maps.dir* movie, where you can draw an arbitrary shape and convert it into a collision map. The answer to Exercise 10.2 is there as well.

Once you have a collision map complete with normals, it is a fairly reasonable problem to find the intersection of the map with a moving particle. Again, height maps are simpler, so we'll start there. Suppose that the particle at P is moving with displacement s near a ground with height map H, which we will assume begins at $x = 1$. The particle travels with its x-coordinate varying from p_1 to $p_1 + s_1$. If at any of these x-positions the y-coordinate is greater than (measuring downwards) is greater than or equal to the height map coordinate, the particle will collide. Let's put that in a function:

```
function particleHmapCollision(p, s, h)
   if s[1]=0 then
      // vertical motion:only one check
      if h[p[1]]<=p[2]+s[2] then
         return (h[p[1]]-p[2])/s[2]
      otherwise
         return "no collision"
      end if
   otherwise
      set grad to s[2]/s[1]
      repeat for i=0 to s[1]
         set x to p[1]+i
         set y to p[2]+grad*i
         if h[x]<=y then
            return s[1]/i
         end if
      end repeat
      return "no collision"
   end if
end function
```

Of course, this function does not return the normal, but to do so is trivial with the help of the accompanying normal map.

An essentially identical process can be used for the general collision map, but instead of simply testing for a height's being greater, it has to check whether the particle at any time is inside the shape. Since we marked the interior points black, this is not difficult. In the following function, we have a shape at position Q with collision map C.

```
function pointCmapIntersection(p, s, q, c)
   set d to magnitude(s)
   if d=0 then return "no intersection"
   set sn to s/d
   set st to p-q
   repeat with i=1 to integer(d)
      set pos to st+i*sn
      set col to the color of the pixel in c at pos
      if col is not black then return d/i
   end repeat
end function
```

Although this function works well, it is quite slow. You also need to fiddle with it a little to find the normal: if the color of the pixel is black then the particle has overshot the edge. However, since we are only checking pixel-length substeps of the motion, the edge pixel is, at most, one pixel away. It would also be sensible here to use integer-only calculations, which means using Bresenham's Algorithm, detailed in Chapter 22. Another optimization would be to not check the full range of motion but just the end-point: only if that is inside the shape do you need to calculate the precise intersection point. This will only be reliable if the particle's displacement is small relative to the size and irregularity of the shape, however.

Another way to speed things up is to use what might be called a "collision halo." Instead of making the outside of the shape plain white, you can use shades of gray to mark the distance to the nearest edge point of the shape. By testing this value, it is possible to calculate whether a collision is possible from any particular position. However, we won't go into that further here.

If the colliding object is not just a point particle but larger, life is much more tedious. For any potentially irregular shape, there is no substitute for testing collision against the entire leading edge of the moving object. Depending on how much you can rely on your colliding objects being reasonably regular, you can take some shortcuts, but for truly complex worlds you just have to bite the bullet.

Finding Bounding Shapes

One technique that can greatly speed up collision detection is to use a *bounding shape* or *armature*. We have been doing this implicitly with the collision maps above: a bounding shape is a simple shape which entirely encloses a colliding object. For example, if you are testing for collision with a person, you might enclose them in a rectangle, while if you are colliding with our starfish shape, this can be enclosed in a circle.

A bounding shape makes it possible to pre-calculate whether there is any chance that two objects collide, before going down to the more detailed level and checking for precise pixel-level collision. But of course it is important to find a shape that is both simple and encloses your object as closely as possible. A bounding circle around a lamp post would stretch a long way beyond its actual collision range.

As a general rule, it is best for you as the programmer to decide in advance what kind of bounding shape is most appropriate—it could be a rectangle or circle, or for that matter a triangle or any other polygon. Once you have made that decision, you need to calculate the dimensions of the bounding shape, which is where the math comes in.

Circles, as always, are fairly easy, especially for polygons. If your polygon has vertices p_1, p_2, . . . p_n, then the center of the circle can be placed at the average (center of mass) of the vertices, $\frac{1}{n}\sum_{i=1}^{n} p_i$ (we'll explain this notation shortly). Then all you need to do is to find the maximum distance of the vertices from the center, which is the radius of the circle:

```
on boundingCircle(poly)
    set c to the number of vertices in poly
    set s to (0,0)
    repeat for each v in poly
        add v to s
    end repeat
    set center to v/c
    set mx to 0
    repeat for each v in poly
        set d to magnitude(v-center)
        if d>mx then set mx to d
    end repeat
    return array(center, mx)
end
```

This won't find the absolutely smallest possible circle, but it works well enough for a reasonably regular shape. There are better algorithms for finding the smallest possible bounding circle, as there are for other shapes.

Bounding boxes are a little more difficult. It's not hard to find a bounding box along a particular axis, but not all axes are as good as one another. Two common options are the *axis-aligned bounding box* (AABB) and the *object-aligned bounding box* (OABB). In the first of these, the box is aligned along the principal axes of your simulation, usually x- and y- (and z- in three dimensions). If all the objects in the simulation have bounding boxes aligned along the same axes in this way, collision detection between the bounding boxes is greatly simplified, which is a good thing. We can test for collisions by just looking at x and y components, and remove many of the dot product calculations in more generalized algorithms. On the other hand, if your objects are not shaped in such a way that an AABB is a close fit, or worse, if they are rotating and so the AABB changes over time, then you lose many of the advantages.

An OABB (sometimes an OOBB or *object-oriented bounding box*) is often a better option, where the axes are chosen to fit as closely as possible to the shape, without worrying about their orientation. Although this complicates collision detection quite a lot, it is much more general, and particularly it means you don't have to recalculate the bounding box whenever the object rotates.

If you look at Figure 10.12 you can see examples of both methods. In the first image, the shape has been enclosed by an AABB oriented along the *x*- and *y*-axes. This rectangle is much too large and does not represent the shape well. But in the second image, we choose a better pair of axes, forming an OABB which encloses the shape snugly.

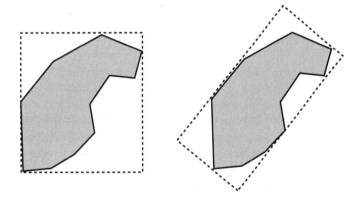

FIGURE 10.12 An AABB and an OABB for the same shape.

Finding the best OABB is a slightly tricky mathematical problem, essentially the same as *factor analysis*. You need to find the axis which *minimizes* the *maximum* distance to the vertices, which is called a *line of best fit*. Generally, we calculate this using the *least-squares method*: we want to find a line such that the squared perpendicular distance of all vertices from the line is minimized. Although minimizing the absolute value would generally be better, it is harder to do analytically. This becomes the long axis of your rectangle. The short axis is perpendicular to it, with half-length equal to that maximum distance. You can use a similar technique in three dimensions, too.

The least-squares method is detailed but straightforward. We first assume that you have a list of points $(x_1, y_1), (x_2, y_2), \ldots, (x_n, y_n)$. First we need to calculate the *mean* of the x- and y- variables, which we will call $\bar{x}$ and $\bar{y}$ respectively. We'll also calculate the *variance* of the variables, which is a measure of how spread out they are from the mean (it's the square of the *standard deviation*). The variance of a set of data is given by

$$v_x = \frac{1}{n} \sum_{i=1}^{n} (x_i^2) - \bar{x}^2$$

Here, we're using sigma notation: the large sigma with "i = 1" at the bottom and n at the top signifies the sum of the subsequent values, where the index i is to be replaced with each of the values from 1 to n—a concept which should be straightforward to a programmer.

Now we'll calculate a quantity we'll call S, which is equal to

$$S = \frac{n(v_x v_y)}{\displaystyle\sum_{i=1}^{n} x_i y_i - n\overline{xy}}$$

The denominator here is a kind of two-dimensional version of the variance, which could be called v_{xy}.

Then the line of best fit is given by the equation $y = ax + b$, where

$$a = -2S \pm \sqrt{4S^2 - 1} \text{ and } b = \bar{y} - a\bar{x}$$

In the form of a (rather inefficient) function:

```
function lineOfBestFit(dataPoints)
    set xlist to arrayOfValues(dataPoints,1)
    set ylist to arrayOfValues(dataPoints,2)
    set n to the number of elements in dataPoints
    set mx to mean(xlist)
    set my to mean(ylist)
    set sx to variance(xlist)
    set sy to variance(ylist)
    set sxy to variance(xlist,ylist)
    if sxy=0 then return "vertical"
    set s to n*(sx-sy)/sxy
```

```
      set a to -2*s+sqrt(4*s*s-1)
      set b to my-a*mx
      return array(a,b)
   end function

   function mean(list)
      set s to 0
      set n to the number of elements in list
      repeat for i=1 to n
         add list[i] to s
      end repeat
      return s/n
   end function

   function variance(list,list2)
      if list2 is undefined then set list2 to list
      set m1 to mean(list)
      set m2 to mean(list2)
      set s to 0
      set n to the number of elements in list
      repeat for i=1 to n
         add list[i]*list2[i] to s
      end repeat
      return s/n-m1*m2
   end function
```

Having found the line of best fit, we can convert it into vector form, giving us the direction and position of the principal axis of the shape, and the perpendicular vector gives us the minor axis. Finally, we calculate the maximum distance of the vertices from each of these axes, giving us the length of the OABB's sides.

Once you have placed your bounding shape, of whatever kind, the technique is the same. As far as the physics is concerned, you simply treat the underlying shape as if it is identical to the bounding shape. When there is a potential collision you can switch to full collision detection, or depending on how closely the shape matches its bounding shape you might even decide to skip the full collision detection altogether: if something is *nearly* a circle, you can just treat it *as* a circle and to the naked eye it will look much the same.

BUILT-IN SOLUTIONS

This section stands on its own because it's not really mathematical. You may find that it is possible to use some built-in function for dealing with arbitrary shapes in your language—Lingo, for example, has the `intersects()` function. Although these functions have drawbacks there are times when using them is just the simplest thing to do.

It's important to remember that at heart, these are the same kinds of functions we have already been looking at. For a bitmap engine like Director they work with essentially the collision map system, while for a vector-based engine like Flash they may work with vector methods like our polygon and spline functions, but either way, they have the same drawbacks: the more complex the shapes, the harder work for the computer.

You can make life easier for the processor by saving it some work. One way to do this is to use a collision proxy—a shape defined by you, which is a simplified (often scaled down) version of the actual colliding objects. We did this when creating collision maps at the start of the chapter and to some extent when creating bounding shapes, and actually it is a useful technique when rolling your own collision detection too. If you *slave* your real colliding objects to the proxies, which is to say that the actual physics happens to the proxy objects somewhere unseen and the real objects just follow them blindly, then all the engine needs to do is calculate collisions for the proxies.

EXERCISES

Exercise 10.1

Write a function `splitPolygon(poly)` which will take an arbitrary polygon with its vertices numbered clockwise and split it into triangles.

This is harder than it sounds. You should use a recursive function which finds three adjacent corners and makes a triangle from them, leaving a polygon with one less vertex. But if it's to work for any polygon at all, you will need to make sure that the triangle you make does not intersect with any other sides.

Exercise 10.2

Write a function `smoothNormals(collisionMap)` which will take a collision map generated by the `calculateNormals()` function and generate a new map with more realistic normals.

The function should use a similar system to that used with height maps, averaging out the normal vectors between neighboring edge points. You might also be interested in trying to implement the "collision halo" suggestion hinted at in the chapter.

SUMMARY

Although we have mostly been talking in general terms in this chapter, you should have a good overall sense of how collision detection techniques can be applied to more generic situations. This is not the last time we shall look at collision detection, we still have some way to go, but we have certainly covered a lot of ground and laid the foundation for what is to come.

In the next chapter we will apply the techniques we have learned to create a complete game.

YOU SHOULD NOW KNOW

- how to describe a general shape using either a *bitmap* or *vector* description
- how to define a curve using a *Bezier* or *Catmull-Rom* spline
- the meaning of the terms *convex* and *concave* and how to recognize a concave polygon
- how to detect collisions with an arbitrary *polygon*
- how to calculate the leading point of any shape when meeting a wall, and the *leading edge* of a polygon
- how to calculate a *collision map* or *height map,* including edge normals, and calculate collisions between a particle and either of these
- how to calculate a *bounding circle* or 2-D object-aligned bounding box (*OABB*)
- how to use *proxies* to speed up collision detection

11 A Simple Pool Game

In This Chapter

- Overview
- The Rules of Engagement
- Taking a Shot
- Exercises
- Summary
- You Should Now Know

OVERVIEW

Congratulations, you have survived a few chapters with a lot of very technical, complicated material. But it is not for nothing. With the techniques you have learned, you have opened the door to a huge variety of simulations and games based on real-life physics. Using the basic collision methods, you can create games like pool, pinball, marbles, pong and breakout. Using the more complex collision methods of the previous chapter, you can even (almost) create games like *Lemmings* or *Worms*.

In this chapter, as a small reward, we shall round off the second part of the book by writing a complete game: a standard pool simulation.

The full game, as well as various more complex variants which we will make over subsequent chapters, can be found in the file *pool.dir* on the CD-ROM.

ON THE CD

Of course, working with a complete game is not like working with individual functions as we have been doing so far. User interface and graphics are very platform- and language-dependent. What's more, they are not particularly in the scope of the book, as their mathematical content is fairly negligible. Similarly, there are a number of details of game logic, such as determining fouls, whether a game has been won and so on, which are not too important here (and the game as programmed is still slightly simpler than true pool). So for the full game, you are best off examining the complete file in the CD-ROM. In this chapter, we will concentrate on the mathematical elements, although we shall touch on the details here and there.

THE RULES OF ENGAGEMENT

As with all programming, we need to start by defining our plan of attack, which means setting up the terms of the simulation. So let's look at what we have to work with.

Defining the Table

A game of pool takes place on a flat horizontal table, which is essentially a rectangle. The balls collide with the walls (and each other) more or less elastically, and because the table is horizontal, gravity is not an issue. Other than friction, there is no acceleration on the balls except when struck by the cue.

There are a number of ways we can define the table. The simplest is probably to split it into six primary elements as in Figure 11.1, each of which is a simple line segment.

FIGURE 11.1   Defining the pool table.

What about the pockets? Well, at the mouth of each pocket, the wall curves around in essentially a quarter-circle. Because once a ball has passed this quarter circle it is known to go in a pocket, we can represent the quarter-circles by actual circles as in Figure 11.2. Notice that most of the circle is inside the table wall, and so is invisible to collision detection.

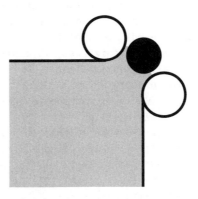

FIGURE 11.2   Detail of the pocket mouth.

So there are 18 possible collisions between a ball and the table: 6 with a wall, and 12 with one of the pocket "jaws."

The dimensions of the table are fairly simple: the rectangle is twice as long as it is wide, so it is essentially two squares. The pockets need to be a little wider than the radius of a ball, but not too much—and don't forget that the circles of the jaws count for that too. These jaws can also be varied in size. In our version, the radius of the jaws is set to half the radius of a ball, and the whole pocket mouth is set to 1.7 times the width of a ball, meaning that the actual gap through which a ball can pass is 1.2 times the width of the ball, which is a little wider than on an actual pool table.

It is convenient to use variables to define all these values, as then if you want to vary the parameters, to make the game more or less difficult, you don't have to go through the whole code and change every value. So let's write a function that will define the table using this system.

In the final version, this function is a little more complicated, as the whole table is offset by a small amount in order to draw the table walls. Here we're defining the top left corner of the table as the point (0,0).

```
function defineTable(ballRadius, tableSize, pocketSize, jawSize)
    set rs to ballRadius*pocketSize
    set rd to ballRadius*sqrt(2.0)*pocketSize // just for convenience
    set walls to an empty array
    append these arrays to walls:
        ((rd,0), (tableSize-rd*2,0)) // top
        ((0,rd), (0,tableSize-rd-rs)) // left top
        ((0,tableSize+rs), (0,tableSize-rd-rs)) // left bottom
        ((rd,tableSize*2), (tableSize-rd*2,0)) // bottom
        ((tableSize,rd), (0,tableSize-rd-rs)) // right top
        ((tableSize,tableSize+rs), (0,tableSize-rd-rs)) // right bottom
    set pw to ballRadius*jawSize
    set jaws to an empty array
    // we now use walls as a guide to draw jaws
    repeat for wall in walls
        if wall[2][1]=0 then // this is a vertical wall
            if wall[1][1]>psize/2 then // it's on the right
                append (wall[1]+(pw,0)) to jaws
                append (wall[1]+wall[2]+(pw,0)) to jaws
            else // it's on the left
                append (wall[1]-(pw,0)) to jaws
                append (wall[1]+wall[2]-(pw,0)) to jaws
            end if
        else // this is a horizontal wall
            if wl[1][2]>psize then // it's on the bottom
                append (wall[1]+(0,pw)) to jaws
                append (wall[1]+wall[2]+(0,pw)) to jaws
            else // it's on the top
                append (wall[1]-(0,pw)) to jaws
                append (wall[1]+wall[2]-(0,pw)) to jaws
            end if
        end if
    end repeat
    return array(walls,jaws)
end function
```

Defining the Balls

Having created our table, the next thing to do is to place the balls on it. Pool has six-teen balls: the cue ball, the black ball, and seven of each of the two colors, which in the version on the CD-ROM are red and yellow (the more complex version of pool has numbered balls, which are generally patterned rather than being a pure color, but this is a nicety we needn't worry about here).

ON THE CD

Initially, the cue ball may be placed anywhere on the baulk line, which is $\frac{1}{5}$ of the way down the table, but we'll say it's always on the same spot for simplicity. The other balls are placed in a triangle in the pattern shown in Figure 11.3, with the front ball placed $\frac{3}{4}$ of the way down the table. The figure has been marked up with distances in order to show how the configuration might be recreated **mathe**matically.

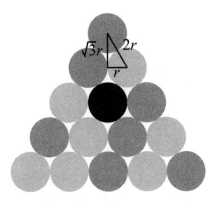

FIGURE 11.3 The initial configuration of balls.

We'll represent the balls with a 16-element array, each element of which has certain information about each ball. For now, we'll just think about the four most important pieces of information: the ball's position, direction and speed, and its color. We'll keep the direction and speed separate, as this is often a useful practice, and we'll represent the direction by a unit vector. Of course, when the speed is zero, the direction is arbitrary. We'll put the cue ball in first, then the other balls in order, black last, and represent their color as "cue," "red," "yellow" or "black."

In Director, there is a useful data type called the "symbol" which is written as a hash (#) followed by a string, as in #red. The final version uses symbols instead of strings as they are more efficient, but the system is equivalent to the one in this chapter.

One important factor is that it is worth setting the balls up marginally separated from one another. If they are exactly touching, then you may find that rounding errors mean the computer thinks they are overlapping. Here is a simple function which will place the balls correctly:

```
function createBalls (tableSize, ballRadius)
    set r to ballRadius*1.02
    set cuestart to (tablesize/2,2*tablesize/5)
    set y to sqrt(3.0)*r
    set tristart to (tablesize/2,tablesize*3/2)
    set balls to an empty array
    repeat for i=1 to 16
        if i=1 then
            set col to "cue"
        else if i=16 then
            set col to "black"
        else if (i mod 2)=0 then
            set col to "red"
        else
            set col to "yellow"
        end if
        if i is
            1: set p to cuestart
            2: set p to tristart
            3: set p to tristart +(-r,y)
            4: set p to tristart +(r,y)
            5: set p to tristart +(2*r,2*y)
            6: set p to tristart +(-2*r,2*y)
            7: set p to tristart +(-3*r,3*y)
            8: set p to tristart +(-r,3*y)
            9: set p to tristart +(r,3*y)
            10: set p to tristart +(3*r,3*y)
            11: set p to tristart +(4*r,4*y)
            12: set p to tristart +(0,4*y)
            13: set p to tristart +(2*r,4*y)
            14: set p to tristart +(-4*r,4*y)
            15: set p to tristart +(-2*r,4*y)
            16: set p to tristart +(0,2*y)
        end if
        append array (p, 0,(1,0), col) to balls
    end repeat
    return balls
end function
```

We'll need a few more properties in the information about each ball eventually, such as whether it has been potted, and particularly a useful "bookkeeping" property defining whether it is currently moving, but we'll look at these later.

It is worth noting that object-oriented programming makes organizing this information much easier. In a real-life version of this game, it would be far more sensible to create an object for each ball, which could then keep track of its own state and respond to queries appropriately, as we do in the more generic collisions.dir. However, as always, this is not a book about programming style but about mathematics, and we shall not deal with these issues further here.

Defining the Physical Parameters

The final aspect of the simulation is to define the physical parameters that remain constant throughout. Many of these need to be determined through a certain amount of trial and error, but you can still make some approximations at the start.

Because the physics of pool is quite simple, it turns out that many parameters can be factored out right from the start. For one thing, all the balls, including the cue ball, have the same mass, and they collide almost entirely elastically, which means that we can use the resolveCollisionEqualMass() function from Chapter 9, ignoring mass and efficiency altogether. Collisions with cushions are somewhat less efficient, and so we need to resolve them inelastically. But as they are fixed in place, this is fairly simple.

Apart from collisions with cushions, the other area where energy is lost is in friction. Dealing with friction realistically is not something we need to do yet, and in fact friction is more complicated here than you might expect—for one thing, without friction, balls wouldn't roll, as we will see in a later chapter. Instead, we will use a simple model of "game friction." There are various ways this can be done, yielding more or less realistic motion:

- We can reduce the energy of the simulation by a constant amount each second.
- We can decrease the energy by a constant factor each second.
- We can decrease the energy by a factor that varies according to the current energy.

You might want to think about which of these is most likely to work. The first will yield a speed that decreases linearly (constant deceleration), the second decreases exponentially (deceleration varying according to speed), and the third is somewhere between the two. You might think that the last is going to be the most realistic, and ultimately it is, but in practice, it's hard to distinguish from the first. The worst is the second option: with exponential decrease, you find that the ball slows down quite fast, but then takes a long time to come to a complete rest, whereas in reality an object moving slowly comes quickly to a halt.

If you do use a variable speed decrease, there is one final parameter that may be useful. It has no physical reality, but is convenient for working with—you can set a parameter for "deactivation": a minimum speed below which a ball is deemed to have stopped. With constant deceleration this is not necessary, however, as all balls are guaranteed to reach zero speed in reasonable time.

So we now have a complete set of parameters which define our game:

- table width
- ball radius
- pocket size
- deceleration due to friction
- efficiency of collision with cushions

The values of these parameters depend on how you want the game to play. Any value for them will yield a game that feels "realistic" to some degree. In reality, the value of the pocket size is determined precisely by the width of the table, but you can change it in order to make the game more or less difficult as we saw above. The physical parameters are more to do with the game "feel" than difficulty or realism. They affect, for example, how long players will have to wait between shots, and how fast the action is. Also, the efficiency of collisions with cushions affects the difficulty of getting out of a snooker (when a player needs to bounce the cue ball off a cushion to make a legal move).

In the version of the game on the CD-ROM, the values of these parameters (as well as one more that determines the maximum speed of the cue ball) can all be adjusted, so try out different versions and see how they feel.

TAKING A SHOT

Now that the game has been set up, we can start things moving. In this section we'll look at how the user can set the ball rolling, as it were, by looking at the user interface of the cue, and how a turn begins, then see how we run the simulation of a single shot.

Creating the Cue

How the user interacts with the game is of course nothing to do with the physics or mathematics. Ultimately, all we are interested in is the initial momentum of the cue ball, everything else is just dressing. But the method used in the version on the CD-ROM is fairly intuitive, and it provides a good example of how a vector-based approach allows for a very flexible system.

At the start of each turn, the cue appears at the position of the cue ball. The cue is seen with its point resting on the outside of the ball, and rotates to follow the mouse, so that it lies along the line from the mouse to the center of the ball. When the mouse button is pressed, the cue begins to pull back, and when it is released, the cue strikes the cue ball, with its initial momentum proportional to the length of time the mouse button was held down. If the mouse button is held longer than a set time, the cue strikes automatically at full power.

Creating this system is rather easy. We know the position of the cue ball and we can read off the mouse position at any particular time, so we can determine the vector between them. Converting this vector into an angle allows us to set the rotation of the cue. Note that the precise details of how the cue is drawn are dependent on platform—in Director, for example, it is simply a matter of setting the rotation property of the cue sprite. Assuming the default rotation of the cue is horizontal, with its point to the right, the rotation at any one moment can be determined by:

```
function cueRotation(ballPos)
    set v to ballPos- (the current mouse position)
    if magnitude(v)>0 then
        set ang to atan(v[2],v[1])
        return ang*180/pi
    otherwise
        return "error"
    end if
end function
```

Notice that we have a potential problem when the mouse is exactly over the ball position. This could be resolved in various ways, such as simply setting the rotation to zero at that moment, but this leads to ugly flickering of the cue as the mouse passes over the ball. Instead, we can remember the last rotation and leave it unchanged at that instant. If there is no previous rotation (i.e., the mouse is over the cue ball at the instant the cue first appears), we can then set the value to zero by default.

When the mouse button is pressed, we can fix the current vector. For simplicity, we normalize it, so that we always have a unit vector for the direction. This direction translates directly to the initial direction of the ball. Now all we need to do is determine the speed.

Pulling the cue back is simple enough: we keep track of the time when the mouse button was pressed and then at each time step we know how long it has been down. This value can then be multiplied by the reverse of the cue vector (along with a constant scale factor), to give the new position of the cue relative to the cue ball. If the time is greater than the maximum time allowed, we strike the ball automatically, otherwise, we go on to the next time step.

When the mouse is released (or the maximum time elapsed), we set the speed of the cue ball proportionally. The simplest way to do this is to fix a maximum initial speed as mentioned previously. Then the speed of the cue ball is simply the proportion of the cueing time to the maximum time, multiplied by the maximum speed. Visually, we could animate the cue moving in to strike the ball, but in practice it works just as well simply to place the cue immediately at the ball position again, and leave it there for a few moments before hiding it and watching the result.

The Main Game Loop

With the cue ball on its way, we now start to run our physics simulation. With all the work we have done already, this is surprisingly simple—just a matter of plugging in the appropriate values to the functions already created in previous chapters. Let's summarize the sequence of calculations for each time step here.

1. Calculate the **time elapsed** since the last time step.
2. For each moving ball, apply **friction** by decreasing its speed by the fixed friction value. If the speed reaches zero, mark the ball as no longer moving.
3. For each still-moving ball, loop through all the other balls, as well as the cushions and pocket corners, to see whether there is a **potential collision** in this time period.
4. If there is **no collision**, then we can simply set all the balls to their new position and finish.
5. Find the **first** such collision. While detecting collisions, we can keep track of the time at which it happens (as a proportion of the total time), as well as the collision normal—these values are returned by the collision detection function.
6. Multiply the time proportion by the total time to get the **collision time**. Set all the balls to their position at this time (by multiplying the collision time by the product of their speed and direction vector and adding it to their current position).
7. **Resolve** the collision, using `resolveInelasticCollisionFixed()` for a collision with a cushion or `resolveCollisionEqualMass()` for a collision between two balls. Set the new velocity of the colliding ball(s) accordingly.
8. Decrease the total time by the collision time to get the remaining time for this time step. **Repeat** from step 3.

Here is a function (one of the longest in this book!) that will perform all the above steps. It is almost identical to the previous `checkCollision()` function, but specifically optimized to deal with this particular domain.

```
function moveBalls (t, table, cushions, pockets, balls, r, f, e)
    // apply friction and deactivate where appropriate
    set mv to 0
    repeat for each b in balls
        if b is moving then
            set the speed of b to max(the speed of b-f,0)
            if the speed of b is 0 then
                set b to not moving
            otherwise
                set mv to 1 // there is some ball moving
            end if
        end if
    end repeat
    if mv is 0 then return "stopped"

    // check for collisions
    repeat while t>0
        set mn to 2 // mn is going to be the minimum time proportion
        set ob1 to 0
        set ob2 to 0
        repeat with i=1 to the number of balls
            set b1 to balls[i]
            set pos1 to the position of b1
            set v to t*the velocity of b1 // ie its speed * its
            direction vector
            // check for collisions between balls
            repeat with j=i+1 to the number of balls
                set b2 to balls[j]
                if b1 or b2 is moving then
                    set pos2 to the position of b2
                    set u to t*the velocity of b2
                    if possiblecollision(pos1, v, pos2, u) then
                        set c to circleCircleCollision(pos1, v, r, pos2,
                                                       u, r)
                        if c is not a collision then next repeat
                        set tm to the time of c
                        set m to min(mn,tm)
                        if m<mn then
                            set mn to m
                            set n to the normal of c
                            set ob1 to b1
                            set ob2 to b2
                            set tp to "ball"
                        end if
```

```
                  end if
              end if
          end repeat
       // check for collisions with cushions
       if b1 is moving then
          repeat for each w in table
              // table is an array of two-element arrays,
              // as defined in defineTable()
              set c to circleLineCollision(r, pos1, v, w[1], w[2])
              if c is not a collision then next repeat
              || check if it is minimal just as before;
              || if so, set n, tm and ob1, and set tp to "wall"

          end repeat
          repeat with p in cushions[1]
              // cushions is a two-element array representing the
              // pocket entrances, the first element being
              // a list of circle centers, the second being
              // the radius of the circles.

              if possiblecollision(pos1, v, p, (0,0)) then
                 set c to circleCircleCollision(pos1, v, r, p, (0,0),
                 cushions[2])
                 if c is not a collision then next repeat
                 || again, check if minimal, and if so
                 || set n, tm and ob1, and tp="wall"
              end if

          end repeat
       end if
   end repeat

   if mn=2 then exit repeat // no collision

   // otherwise there is a collision

   // move balls to collision position
   repeat for each b in balls
       if b is moving set its position to its position+mn*t*its
       velocity
   end repeat
   // resolve collision
   if tp=#wall then
       set u to the direction of ob1
```

```
            set the direction of ob1 to resolveInelasticCollisionFixed(u,
            e, e, n)
        otherwise
            set u1 to the velocity of ob1
            set u2 to the velocity of ob2
            set res to resolveCollisionEqualMass(u1, u2, n)
            set the speed of ob1 to magnitude(res[1])
            if this speed>0 then set the direction of ob1 to norm(res[1])
and set ob1 to be moving
            otherwise set ob1 to be not moving
            || repeat for ob2

        end if

    // decrease time and repeat
    set t to t*(1-mn)
    end repeat

    // move balls for the last section (no collisions)
    repeat for each b in balls
        if b is moving set its position to its position+t*its velocity
    end repeat
end function
```

One element that has been left out of this procedure is determining if a ball has been pocketed. There are a number of ways to achieve this, and you should think a little about it before trying Exercise 11.1.

Basic Culling

Culling is a general term for removing or ignoring elements that are not needed in a particular set of circumstances. For example, we use it to describe the process where, in a 3D model, we determine which parts of the model can be seen and which ones can't, in order to only draw the visible faces and so save time.

In a physics simulation like this, we can use the word to mean the process of pre-checking collisions before actually testing them, in order to cut down the number of collision checks we do. We will look at some of these methods now, but with an initial warning: Culling is not always worth the effort. If your culling checks take longer to perform than the collision detection itself, it's best to ignore them. In this case, we are dealing with colliding circles and straight lines, and these are fairly straightforward to check—especially as there aren't so many of them. For that matter, at the moments that are hardest on the processor, when large numbers of balls are involved, no amount of culling will help.

In the version on the CD-ROM, there is no more culling than we have seen so far, apart from an additional pre-check for distance between balls. But the general techniques are important, and indeed we will look into them in more detail in Chapter 22.

The key culling technique is to *partition* the game world into subspaces. For example, suppose that the current table state in our pool game is as shown in Figure 11.4. Here, the table has been subdivided into eight squares. Ball A is moving toward balls B, C and D, but because A and B are in non-contiguous squares, they cannot possibly collide within a short time period. This means that for ball A, you need only check for collisions with balls C and D. That is: if a ball is in a particular square, it can only collide with balls within its square, and the three squares that its velocity vector could conceivably intersect.

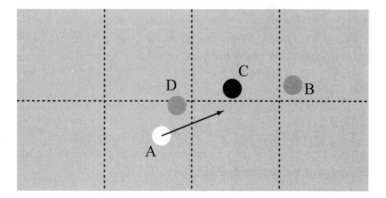

FIGURE 11.4   Partitioning the table into contiguous subspaces.

Another partitioning technique is to use overlapping subspaces as shown in Figure 11.5. In this system, a ball is always within several squares at once, which means that whatever its velocity, you can usually find a subspace such that the ball remains within that subspace for the whole of its motion. Then you need only check for collisions within that space. The two methods are essentially equivalent, simply moving the same calculations to different parts of the process, so it is a matter of personal preference.

It is important in both these cases to ensure that the squares are large enough that no ball will ever pass completely through a square in one turn. This can be done by setting a maximum speed as we have done, but also by setting a minimum

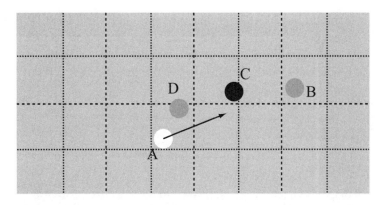

FIGURE 11.5   Partitioning the table into overlapping subspaces.

time step for the simulation. This is necessary because for various reasons, any simulation might be interrupted while playing, leading to an extremely long gap between collision checks. So if you want to have a maximum speed of m pixels/sec and a square size of s pixels, then the maximum time step you can allow is s/m. Actually, even this isn't quite safe, because the balls have a non-zero radius, and so a ball in one square can collide with a ball in a neighboring square. So in fact, you should limit the time steps to $(s-2r)/m$, where r is the radius of a ball.

Game Logic

The final stage of creating the game is to add the game logic: determining fouls, the order of play, and whether a player has won or lost. While most of these are irrelevant to the mathematics, it's worth quickly looking at the two main changes that need to be made to the mathematical system to turn it into a game.

Determining if the correct ball (if any) has been hit in a particular shot. Several foul shots are dependent on the first ball hit during a turn. The moveBalls() function can be simply adapted to return the color of the first ball struck in that time period, which can be used to determine the first ball struck since cueing. If the color is incorrect, or if no ball is struck, this is a foul.

Dealing with potted balls. A potted ball is removed from play. The moveBalls() function can take this into account by ignoring potted balls in collision checks. At the end of each turn, newly potted balls need to be checked for their color, to see if it was a legal pot, resulting in a second shot for the current player, or an illegal one, resulting in a foul. If the black was potted, this is always either a win or a loss for the current player.

It should be pointed out that the version on the CD-ROM does not include all the rules of pool—for example, it does not cause you to lose if you go in off the black, or declare a foul if fewer than two balls hit the back cushion from the break. You might want to implement these rules in your own version.

EXERCISES

Exercise 11.1

Amend the moveBalls() function to include a check for whether a ball has been potted.

There are several ways to make this test, and none particularly stands out as the best. See if your version matches the system on the final game on the CD-ROM.

Exercise 11.2

Add a "preview" function which determines which ball will be struck first and in which direction and displays it while the cue is aiming.

This option is available in the version on the CD-ROM. You should be able to use existing collision detection functions to implement it.

SUMMARY

So there you have it. A complete game of pool in only a few chapters. Hopefully this should show you the power of these general methods we have been discussing. We will return to the game of pool several times during Part III of the book, where we shall be looking at some more complex physics, including friction and spin.

YOU SHOULD NOW KNOW

- how to use the collision detection and resolution routines developed in previous chapters in a real-life game situation
- how to simplify the physics to deal with the specific needs of a game
- the basics of culling, particularly how to partition a space to reduce calculations

Part

III

More Complex Motion

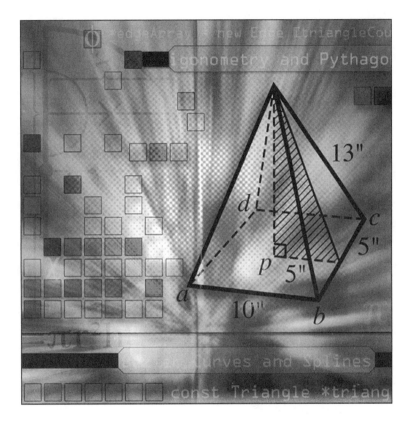

In the third part of the book we will continue with mechanics, looking at more difficult concepts such as angular motion, springs and pendulums, and orbits. We begin by, at long last, formally looking at the concept of force, which we have skirted around up to now. Then we shall move through Newtonian physics, seeing how to apply this idea of force to solve problems that we have kept quiet about up to now, particularly friction.

12 Force and Newton's Laws

In This Chapter

- Overview
- Force
- Gravity
- Rockets and Satellites
- Exercises
- Summary
- You Should Now Know

OVERVIEW

Although we have mentioned the word "force" quite a few times over the preceding pages, we have never really defined it or used it. The study of the laws of motion by Isaac Newton was really the beginning of modern science: his Laws of Motion and Law of Gravitation, which we will look at here, were the first attempt at a truly universal scientific law, and while we now know they are not quite correct, at the scales of space and time that we live in from day to day they are still remarkably accurate.

In some ways, this chapter is something of a recap: we shall spend some time re-examining old results in terms of the new terminology, to see how the two are related, and how one technique can be more useful than another in different circumstances.

ON THE CD

The small amount of code in this chapter is implemented in the *orbits* demo.

FORCE

In everyday speech we use the word "force," as with many scientific words, rather vaguely. It suggests an effort—the words "energy" and "work" are used almost interchangeably with it. But the scientific meaning of the word (and indeed of the others) is a little more formal. Newton defined the concept of force precisely with his three Laws of Motion, and the unit of force is named after him: one newton is one kilogram meter per second per second.

The First Law

Before Newton, it was thought that every moving object required some impetus to keep it moving along its path: that unless something is being pushed, it will slow down. It's not an unreasonable assumption: after all, in our world it is certainly true. But by looking at motion in the vacuum of space where there is no friction (or very little), Newton formulated his first law: *an object continues moving at the same velocity unless acted on by a force.* Of course, this includes a velocity of zero, so an object that is still will remain still unless pushed.

What form this "force" takes is not stated in the First Law, but for the moment we can think of it just as some kind of "influence": a particle will continue to travel in the same way unless influenced by some other particle.

In essence, the First Law is a restatement of the law of conservation of momentum (well, a precursor to it, since it was discovered first), and we have been using it implicitly already, when we assumed that the pool balls in the previous chapter would continue to move with the same velocity unless acted on by some friction, or colliding with another ball.

A body with no forces acting on it (or where the sum of the forces acting on it is zero, as in Figure 12.1) is said to be in *equilibrium.* So we could also state the law as "a body in equilibrium remains at a constant velocity."

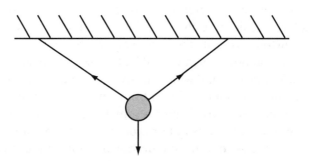

FIGURE 12.1 A body in equilibrium with several forces acting on it (see Chapter 14).

The Second Law

The second law is where we actually start to get technical. Newton stated it in quite a complex way, but stripped to its essentials, it says: *When a body is acted on by a force, it experiences an acceleration which is proportional to the force and inversely proportional to the mass of the body.* More simply still, we can say

$$\text{Force on body} = \text{mass} \times \text{acceleration}$$

An alternative way to look at it is to say that the force on a body is equal to the rate of change of the body's momentum. This is more useful when dealing with forces or masses that change continuously over time, such as centripetal force or the motion of a rocket, both of which we will cover later.

The unit of force is defined according to the Second Law: one newton (1 N) is the force required to accelerate a kilogram mass by 1 ms^{-1} in one second. As we have seen, the acceleration due to gravity at sea level is approximately 10 ms^{-2}. This means that the force of gravity at sea level experienced by a 1 kg mass is approximately 10 N. Each kilogram of our bodies experiences this force constantly, which is the force we feel as our *weight*.

Unlike the equations of motion we saw before, force is intimately tied in with mass. If you want to throw a 10 kg cannonball, it will take twice the force it would take to throw a 5 kg cannonball. This is where the connection comes with momentum, and the concept of mass as *inertia*: how much a body resists the action of any force.

The Third Law

If we're all experiencing a constant force, by the Second Law we should surely all be accelerating downwards the whole time! Why doesn't this happen? Because you are currently in equilibrium: although there is a force acting down on you, there is another force acting upward. If you are sitting down, then this force is acting through the chair you are sitting on. The chair in turn is experiencing a downward force from you, as well as its own weight, but it doesn't move because it is experiencing an upward force from the floor. By the first two laws, we know this must be the case, and it is formalized in the third and most misunderstood law: *If a body is experiencing a force from some other object then it exerts an equal and opposite force on that object.*

This law has to be stated quite carefully, because most people get it wrong. They say "every action has an equal and opposite reaction," but they assume that the two actions are on the same body, which is clearly false. What it says is that force is symmetrical: one object can't exert a force without experiencing a force. The Earth pulls us all toward itself by the force of gravity, but simultaneously we are all pulling the Earth slightly toward us. We don't notice these effects on the Earth because, with the huge discrepancy between our mass and the Earth's, the acceleration of the Earth due to our gravitational pull is infinitesimally small. What is more, there are many of these infinitesimal forces acting on the Earth in all directions, so this tends to cancel their effect. Even the Moon, which is much larger than a person although some distance away, only barely pulls the Earth off its orbit about the Sun, although its gravitational pull on the Earth's water does have a noticeable effect in the tides.

If the First Law is a statement of conservation of momentum for bodies in equilibrium, the third is the equivalent for bodies that are colliding. In fact, aside from conversion of energy into other forms such as heat, it also codifies conservation of energy. So ultimately, Newton's First and Third Laws are just a different way of viewing the methods we have already been using to deal with ballistics and collisions. The Second Law is a little different: it is a mathematical result which allows us to make calculations about motion. While we will be using the First and Third Laws from time to time, it is the Second Law that will concern us most in this and later chapters.

Impulse

If you have been paying particularly close attention, you may have realized that the Second Law is going to encounter problems when dealing with the rigid body collisions we looked at in Part II. In these, we considered the velocities of colliding bodies to change instantaneously at the moment of collision, but of course this implies an infinite acceleration, which means an infinite force. And once you have an infinite force and acceleration, the velocity at the end of it becomes rather uncertain!

To deal with this problem, we introduce the concept of an *impulse*, which is defined as a force acting over a particular time period, equal to *force* × *time*. The Second Law tells us that this impulse is going to be equal to the change in momentum. In a rigid-body collision, an infinitely large force acts over an infinitely short period of time, and these two infinities cancel out to give a finite impulse, which as we saw in Chapter 9, is calculable by conservation of energy and momentum. (If you find this uncomfortable, then just remember that there is not really any such thing as a rigid body, and real collisions always last for some measurable time while the colliding bodies deform and rebound.)

We can use this to rewrite our collision resolution calculations: When two bodies collide, they experience some impulse J in the direction of the collision normal **n**. This causes (or is, depending on your point of view) a change of momentum which is some multiple of **n**, so

$$m\mathbf{v} = m\mathbf{u} + J\mathbf{n}$$

The impulse acts equally and oppositely, so one body experiences J and the other $-J$. Combining these momentum equations with the energy equations, we can calculate the value of J, which turns out to be:

$$J = \frac{-m_1 m_2 \mathbf{u} \cdot \mathbf{n}}{\left(m_1 + m_2\right)}$$

(assuming $\mathbf{n}$ is unit length, and where $\mathbf{u}$ is the relative velocity of the two bodies before collision). You might want to see if you can derive this result and make it match with the results of Chapter 9.

GRAVITY

Newton's other great discovery was the concept of gravity. While other astronomers, particularly Kepler, had observed and recorded the planets, it was Newton who realized that the same principle that causes an apple to fall to the ground could be used to calculate their motion. It was a revolutionary concept: all the planets in the Solar System, including the Earth, are constantly "falling" toward the Sun (and each other). In this section we will look at the force of gravity and how it can be used to explain planetary motion.

The Law of Gravitation

The force of gravity is a universal phenomenon that affects all bodies from the smallest to the largest (although what happens at quantum-mechanical scales is not yet understood). Unlike the other "fundamental forces," gravity is only attractive: every body in the universe attracts every other body in the universe toward itself. Magnetic forces and others can attract or repel, but in the current state of the universe, gravity is one-way only.

Gravity works as an *inverse-square* relationship: the strength of the gravitational attraction between two objects is inversely proportional to the square of the distance between them (where "distance between them" means the distance between their centers of mass). In terms of a formula, the precise relationship is

$$F = \frac{G m_1 m_2}{d^2}$$

Here, m_1 and m_2 are the masses of the two objects, d is the distance between them, and G is a constant, known as the *gravitational constant*, whose value turns out to be approximately $6.67300 \times 10^{-11} \, \mathrm{m^3 kg^{-1} s^{-2}}$.

Given that gravity works at all scales, you might wonder why we don't have to take into account the gravitational attraction between all the various molecules in each body as well, but fortunately it turns out that these effects cancel out for a spherical body, and we can treat most bodies as being particles at the center of mass, as we mentioned earlier.

The Motion of a Planet Under Gravity

So what does it look like? Newton actually deduced the inverse-square relationship by examining the motion of the planets, in particular Kepler's laws of planetary motion. By making painstaking (and astonishingly accurate for the era) observations, Kepler had replaced the previous Copernican view of planets orbiting in circles around the Sun with a new view.

The motion of a planet relative to the Sun is actually an ellipse, with the Sun at one focus. It had been mistaken for a circle for some time because the eccentricity of the ellipse is so small. The speed of the planet as it travels around is also not constant. In fact, the speed varies quite subtly: the *area* of the sector of the ellipse swept out during any time period is constant. In Figure 12.2, you can see how the area of the three regions is the same, so when the planet is nearer the Sun, it moves faster than it does when far away.

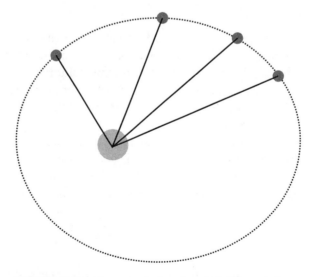

FIGURE 12.2   The speed of a planet at different stages of its orbit.

Figure 12.2 has been drawn quite exaggerated to make the effect clear, but for planets, the deviation from a circle is minimal. However, Kepler's observations don't just apply to planets. They work for all orbiting bodies, such as moons, comets and asteroids. Not only that, but they work for meteorites passing through the Solar System without going into an orbit: rather than moving in an ellipse, they move in a parabola, but the law of equal areas continues to apply.

Newton worked backwards from these observations to realize that they implied an inverse-square law. We're not so interested in the theory here, but we can see it working in practice.

ON THE CD   There is a simple simulation of a solar system, *orbits.dir,* on the CD-ROM. The code is fairly straightforward. At each time step, the gravitational force between each object is calculated and the total of all these forces translated into an acceleration. The whole thing is centered on the Sun, so its velocity is subtracted from each object before it's displayed. (You create your own version of this system in Exercise 12.1.)

If you play with the initial conditions of the simulation, you will see that while it is possible to make each planet travel in an orbit, it is rare to find one that is stable. As a general rule, the orbit tends to be a spiral traveling either inward toward the Sun or outward. This is partly because of inaccuracies in the simulation, (which approximates the curved motion of the planet by small linear sections), but when we try to make a more complex simulation with several planets, or planets and moons, there is also a more fundamental problem of scale. The distance between a moon and a planet is infinitesimal compared to that between the planet and the Sun. This means that they essentially constitute a single body from the point of view of the Sun and orbit as one. Conversely, the distance between planets is very large, so that most of the time they have only a small gravitational effect on one another. In the simulation, we can't get these kinds of scale: if it was drawn to scale, the moons would be so near the planets that we wouldn't even see their orbit, and we wouldn't be able to view more than four or five planets at the same time without losing track of the ones in the middle. A kind of logarithmic scale is possible, but looks strange.

Having said all this, the behavior of the simulation does chime with reality to some extent. All the planets, including our own, are spiraling slowly in toward the Sun. Any less stable orbits would have disappeared many billions of years ago, and certainly would not have been suitable for life, so it is not surprising that the existing planets are in nearly stable orbits, but perfect stability is impossible to achieve. Aside from anything else, the gravitational pull of other planets deflects each one from its orbit slightly, destabilizing it.

The most important aspects of a stable orbit are its *period T*, which is the time taken for one complete orbit, and its semi-major axis *a* (or alternatively its mean radius and its eccentricity). When one body has a significantly greater mass than the other, as with a planet in orbit around the Sun, it turns out that these values are related:

$$T = 2\pi \sqrt{\frac{a^3}{GM}}$$

(where M is the total mass of the two bodies).

The inverse of the period is called the *angular frequency* of the orbit, which is 2π times the angular velocity (see the next chapter), or the number of orbits in a given time. This gives us the equation of Kepler's Third Law:

$$\frac{2\pi}{T} = \sqrt{\frac{GM}{a^3}}$$

The value $\frac{2\pi}{T}$ is also called the *mean motion n*, and the above equation can be rewritten as $n^2 a^3 = GM$, which is a little simpler.

Another important result is that we can calculate the speed v of a particle when at a particular distance r from the center of the ellipse. This can be worked out by conservation of energy, and gives

$$v = \sqrt{GM\left(\frac{2}{r} - \frac{1}{a}\right)} = \sqrt{GM\left(\frac{2a - r}{ar}\right)}$$

Rather surprisingly, despite all these results, the simple question of finding the position of an orbiting body at a particular time t cannot be solved by simple algebra or calculus, although it is possible to find a differential equation which can be solved numerically.

Centrifugal and Centripetal Force

An object rotating in a circle appears to be disobeying Newton's First Law: its velocity is constantly changing, since the direction of motion is changing. In fact, there is no problem, since to achieve the circular motion there must always be a linear force on the object, directed toward the center of the circle. This force is called the *centripetal force* and can be calculated precisely: the centripetal force required to keep a mass m rotating at a constant speed v around a radius r is given by $\frac{mv^2}{r}$. In terms of the *angular velocity ω*, which we will look at in the next chapter, the force is $\omega^2 r$.

Centripetal force should not be confused with *centrifugal force*, which is to some extent a myth. A particle moving in a circle is *only* experiencing a net force inward. However, by Newton's Third Law, the particle exerts a force in turn on whatever is causing it to spin—for example, if we whirl an object around on a string, then there is an outward force on the string equal and opposite to the centripetal force. This force on us is called centrifugal force. Similarly, when we whirl a bucket full of water around, the bucket exerts an inward force on the water, which in turn exerts an outward force on the bucket. It is easy to get confused about this fact, and it's best to ignore centrifugal force altogether and concentrate on the centripetal.

The reason we seem to experience an outward force when moving in a circle is due to Newton's First Law; our tendency is to keep going in a straight line. It is this inertia that feels like a force outward. But if you imagine standing on a "wall-of-death" fairground ride, it is only when on the inside of the wall, with the wall exerting a force toward the center, that you are held in place. If you were on the outside, you would fly off the wheel—and you would fly off tangentially to the wall, not outward.

ROCKETS AND SATELLITES

When working on ballistics problems earlier, we assumed that the effect of gravity was a constant acceleration. Now we see that this is not true, and the force of gravity varies with height. Over small distances relative to the size of the Earth, the difference is negligible, but once we start dealing with objects traveling into space, we have to take variable gravity into account.

Geo-Stationary Orbit

Science fiction had one of its better coups when Arthur C. Clarke realized in 1945 that because the period of a stable orbit varies with distance, at some distance from the Earth the period of an orbiting satellite will be exactly one day. This means that if the satellite orbits parallel to the Equator, it will remain over the same point on the Earth's surface continuously. Clarke envisioned a network of such satellites used for telecommunications and his speculation turned out to be right on the mark. In part inspired by his ideas, *geo-stationary* satellites are at the heart of telecommunications, surveillance, and GPS technology.

We can calculate the correct height of a geo-stationary satellite by noting that, as with any orbiting body, it must experience a centripetal force equal to the gravitational force. This gives us the equation

$$\frac{mv^2}{r} = \frac{mMG}{r^2}$$

If the satellite has a period of T, then we have $v = \frac{2\pi r}{T}$, so

$$\frac{4\pi^2 r}{T^2} = \frac{MG}{r^2}$$

$$r = \sqrt[3]{\frac{MGT^2}{4\pi^2}}$$

If we plug in the correct values for Earth, which has a mass of about 6×10^{24} kg and a *sidereal day* of 86164 seconds (the sidereal day is the time taken for the Earth to complete one rotation relative to a distant star—it's slightly shorter than a *solar day*, which is the time to complete a rotation relative to the Sun, since the Earth is orbiting around the Sun and this adds a little extra relative spin), then we get a value for r of 42168 km.

One current science fiction speculation that seems to be heading toward reality is called a *space elevator*, which is a long fiber connecting a geo-stationary satellite and its corresponding point on the ground. Once in place, such an elevator would vastly reduce the energy needed to get into space, but the technical problems are immense—the weight of the fiber alone is a major issue, as well as the danger to (and from) aircraft, and of course, although the satellite is in geo-stationary orbit, the connecting cable is not, which means that it acts as a drag on the satellite, tending to pull it out of orbit. Having said all this, many research groups are working on overcoming these obstacles and a space elevator does not seem an unlikely possibility some time this century.

A Really *Fast* Cannonball

We don't yet have the tools to deal with rocket travel properly: the key to successful rocket travel is that the mass of the rocket decreases as its fuel is used up, and working with an object whose mass changes over time will have to wait a few chapters. However, we can make a start. We'll consider a very fast cannonball: an object moving at speed into space, but whose mass is constant. How does it behave?

The mass of the cannonball is much less than the Earth, so we can assume that the Earth does not move significantly as a result of the gravitational pull of the cannonball, so we will consider it to be stationary, and we'll assume the ball is fired vertically into space from sea level.

We can solve this problem by means of energy considerations. At a distance x from the center of the Earth, the cannonball has a gravitational potential energy of $\frac{GMm}{x}$. If its initial upward speed was u, then we know that $\frac{1}{2}mu^2 = \frac{1}{2}mv^2 + \frac{GMm}{x}$ at every instant of the motion. As before, this gives us a differential equation:

$$\left(\frac{dx}{dt}\right)^2 = \frac{2GM}{x} - u^2$$

Differential equations are not in general easy to solve exactly in some algebraic form, and this is no exception. However, it does mean that given a particular initial position and speed for the cannonball, we can calculate its motion over time by incremental steps:

```
function moveCannonBall (currentHeight, initialSpeed, timePeriod, G, M)
    set currentSpeed to sqrt(2*G*M / currentHeight - initialSpeed *
initialSpeed)
    return currentSpeed * timePeriod
end function
```

EXERCISES

Exercise 12.1

Write a set of functions which will allow a system of planets to move under gravity.

You can do this a number of different ways technically, but the mathematics are the same: at each time step, calculate the total force on each planet due to the gravitational fields of the others, then convert this to a linear acceleration. Be careful to base all your accelerations on positions at the beginning of the time step: don't use moved positions. See if you can set up a planet to orbit smoothly.

SUMMARY

We haven't seen much code in this short chapter, mostly because for much of it we were simply re-stating earlier results in a new form. But from now on we'll be using the language of forces and Newton's laws much more. In a complex world, linear acceleration will not be enough.

In the next chapter we shall continue the study of orbits by looking at angular motion and particularly angular momentum.

YOU SHOULD NOW KNOW

- *Newton's three laws* and how they relate to earlier results on energy and momentum
- the *Law of Gravitation* and how it can be used to calculate planetary motion
- how to calculate a *geo-stationary orbit*
- how to launch a cannonball into space and calculate its trajectory

13 Angular Motion

In This Chapter

- Overview
- The Physics of a Lever
- Spin
- Spinning Collisions
- Exercises
- Summary
- You Should Now Know

OVERVIEW

So far, we have only looked at the linear motion of objects, but this is not the only way that something can move. A spinning top has no linear momentum, but it is certainly moving. In this chapter we will look at *angular motion*, the physics of spin. We'll also see how it can be incorporated into the pool game developed in Chapter 11.

Code samples from this chapter are implemented in *math.cst* in the script *energy, momentum, and angular calculations*. Angular collisions (mostly using approximate methods) can be seen in action in the *collisions* demo.

THE PHYSICS OF A LEVER

Angular physics begins with the earliest human machine. Levers seem almost magical: somehow it is possible to move a heavy object with the smallest force. Aristotle, who studied them extensively, said "Give me a lever and a strong place to stand and I can move the world."

A lever, in essence, consists of two parts: a *light, strong rod* and a *fulcrum*. The terms "light" and "strong" are used here in an abstract physical sense, to mean an object that has no mass and cannot be bent or broken. Of course, such things don't exist in reality, but it is convenient to pretend that they do (we'll look briefly at how we can deal with real-life materials too). The rod rests on a pivot point which is the fulcrum.

Torque

When a force is exerted on a part of a lever, it causes the lever to rotate. If you look at Figure 13.1, you can see why. The downward force F on the left of the lever tries to cause the lever to accelerate downward, but the fulcrum exerts a reaction force −F upward. Because these two forces are acting on different parts of the lever, the result is that part of the lever moves downward, and part of it moves upward. This rotational force is called *torque*.

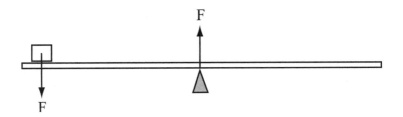

FIGURE 13.1 Torque exerted on a lever.

The reason that the torque is applied is that the force F is offset from the fulcrum. The fulcrum can only exert a force at the point of contact, so any force that acts somewhere other than the fulcrum is going to cause rotation. In fact, the amount of rotation depends on how far the applied force is from the fulcrum. The formula is

Torque = perpendicular force × distance from fulcrum,

or equivalently,

Torque = force × perpendicular distance from fulcrum

(the difference between these two concepts is shown in Figure 13.2; showing that they are equivalent is left to you as an exercise. Hint: use the dot product.)

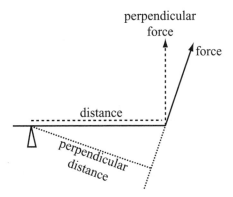

FIGURE 13.2 Calculating torque.

The distance from the fulcrum is really a vector quantity: if the force is applied at the other side of the fulcrum, the torque is reversed. Similarly, you could have a "lever," which is actually a plane balanced on a pinpoint. Then a force could be applied at any point on the plane, with the corresponding torque being a function of the vector from the pinpoint to the position of the applied force. This product of a value with a perpendicular distance is called a *moment*—so we could say that torque is the "moment of force." Similarly we can have a moment of velocity, moment of momentum and so on (although as we'll see with moments of inertia, the term is used a little loosely). We'll return to moments shortly when we look at angular momentum.

If two forces are applied to a lever, then the corresponding torques can be added together. If the sum is zero, then the lever is in equilibrium and therefore balances. This means that we can balance a large force somewhere close to the fulcrum with a smaller force further away. We can use this principle to measure the weight of an object. Suppose we have a lever with an object of unknown weight W resting on it as shown in Figure 13.3. We know the distance x of the object from the fulcrum. If we take a second object of known weight A and move it along the lever until it balances at some distance y, we can calculate:

$$Wx - Ay = 0$$

$$W = \frac{Ay}{x}$$

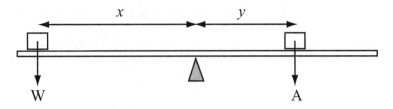

FIGURE 13.3 Two forces acting on a lever.

There is another point worth noticing here. Because neither object on the lever is moving, we can deduce that the forces on the objects are all in equilibrium. This means that there is a force of magnitude W acting upward on the first object. This force is the result of the torque exerted by the other object. We can make this more explicit: any object resting on a lever experiences a force, normal to the lever, with magnitude equal to the sum of torques on the lever caused by all other objects, divided by the object's distance from the fulcrum. This is how we can use a lever as a catapult.

Suppose we have a lever resting on the ground with a particle sitting on it, at a distance x along the lever from the fulcrum. The particle has a weight of W. We place a heavy object of weight A on the other side of the lever at distance y. Immediately, the particle experiences a force due to the other object. The force has magnitude approximately Ay/x (assuming the lever is nearly horizontal) and acts normal to the lever, so the ball accelerates perpendicularly to the lever. Simultaneously, the lever itself rotates, so the force continues to act until the ball is traveling faster than the rotation of the lever, or until the lever stops moving because its other end hits the ground, at which point the particle flies off. The torque gradually decreases as the component of weight tangential to the fulcrum becomes smaller.

How about the other factors we omitted: the weight of the rod, and the possibility of breaking? The first of these is not particularly troublesome: we can simply consider the weight of the rod as one more torque, which can be measured exactly as we did in Figure 13.3. But the second is more difficult. It depends on the strength of the rod's material when subjected to this kind of stress, called *shearing forces* and *bending moments*. We won't look at this further, as it's unlikely to be an issue in your average programming day!

Moments of Inertia

The physics of rotation are much the same as for linear motion. All of Newton's laws, and the equations of motion, momentum and energy, have their counterparts in rotational motion. So, for example, we can calculate an object's *angular velocity*, in units of radians (or degrees) per second, and similarly its angular acceleration. For all rotational quantities, we need to specify the center of rotation, and the axis around which the rotation occurs. There can be only one axis of rotation: if a body is rotating about the axis A and not moving linearly, then its angular velocity about any other axis is zero.

The angular equivalent of mass is called the *moment of inertia*. We've already encountered it to some extent with the lever: the moment of inertia of a light lever is the sum of the products of all masses with their squared distance from the fulcrum. (Notice that in this case, the word "moment" is used differently from the previous section because it includes a square factor of distance.) Thus in Figure 13.4, the moment of inertia of the lever around the fulcrum is $3 \times 4 + 4 \times 1 = 16$ kgm^2.

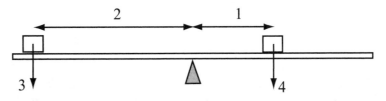

FIGURE 13.4   Calculating a moment of inertia.

When dealing with a solid object rather than a light rod, the calculation is a little more complex: we need to use integration to sum up infinitesimally small pieces. For example, we can calculate the moment of inertia of a uniform rod of a certain mass m and length $2l$ about its center. Because its mass is uniform, any segment of the rod with a length δ has a mass of $m\delta/2l$, so we have the following integral for the moment of inertia:

$$
\begin{aligned}
I &= \int_{-l}^{l} x^2 \left(\frac{m}{2l} \right) dx \\
&= \left(\frac{m}{2l} \right) \left[\frac{x^3}{3} \right]_{-l}^{l} \\
&= \frac{ml^2}{3}
\end{aligned}
$$

For another example, let's look at a circle. We can think of a circle as a succession of infinitely thin concentric rings at a distance x. Because these rings are uniform and every point on the ring is at the same distance from the center, the moment of inertia of each ring about the center (or strictly speaking, about an axis perpendicular to the circle through the center) is just $m_x x^2$, where m_x is the mass of the ring with radius x.

If we take a ring whose width is δ, at a radius x from the origin, from a circle of mass m and radius r, its mass is going to be approximately $\frac{2\pi x \delta m}{\pi r^2} = \frac{2x \delta m}{r^2}$ (assuming δ is infinitesimally small). So if we integrate over all these rings, we end up with

$$I = \int_0^r x^2 \times \frac{xm}{r^2} dx$$

$$= \frac{m}{r^2} \left[\frac{x^4}{4} \right]_0^r$$

$$= \frac{mr^2}{4}$$

Don't worry if these integrals seem confusing or difficult, we haven't really covered integration in much detail. As a general rule, you don't need to worry about how these formulae are derived, you can just use them as they are. But it is still useful to know where they come from.

In general, as in these examples, we are most interested in the moment of inertia about the center of mass of an object. The center of mass is the point at which, however you slice the object, half of its mass is on each side of the line. A similar integration calculation can be used to calculate the center of mass. But you can calculate a moment of inertia about any axis. In fact, it's a simple calculation: if the moment of inertia of an object with mass m about some axis A through the center of mass is I, then the moment of inertia about a parallel axis at a distance p from A is $I + mp^2$.

Another useful trick can be used with *laminar* objects—that is, infinitely thin planar objects like a disc or square. If we have two parallel axes in the plane of the lamina, through the same point O on the object, then the moment of inertia around the axis perpendicular to the laminar plane through O is the sum of the moments of inertia around the other two axes. We can use this trick, for example, to calculate the moment of inertia of a square with side $2d$, around an axis perpendicular to the square through its center (see Figure 13.5). By a similar argument to the calculation with the rod, the moment of inertia of the square around the y-axis (assuming the square is centered on the origin) is $\frac{md^2}{3}$. By symmetry, the same is true of its moment of inertia about the x-axis, so its moment of inertia about the perpendicular axis is $\frac{2md^2}{3}$. Many other simple shapes can be calculated using similar combinations of integration and these two tricks.

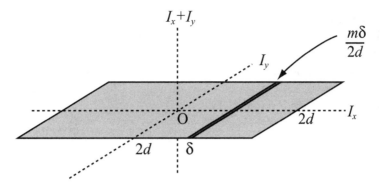

FIGURE 13.5 The moment of inertia of a square lamina.

Just as mass is the measure of how hard it is to push something, the moment of inertia is a measure of how hard it is to spin something. An object with a small moment of inertia, which is to say one whose mass is mostly very near to the axis, is easy to spin, while an object whose mass is far from the axis, with a large moment of inertia, is much more difficult to spin, or for that matter to stop spinning. We can use a variant of Newton's Second Law to say that *torque = moment of inertia ✕ angular acceleration.*

SPIN

Let's look at spin a little more. With the concept of a moment of inertia in place, calculating angular motion is really quite simple.

Ballet Dancers and Spinning Tops

The angular momentum of an object is just what you would expect: its angular velocity multiplied by its moment of inertia. (This is actually only true generally in two dimensions: in three dimensions things get rather more complicated and we need to use the objects called *tensors.*) As with linear momentum, the angular equivalent gives an idea of how difficult it is to stop something. An object with a large moment of inertia has a large *angular momentum,* which means that it takes much more torque to stop it. This is the principle of the flywheel: a large heavy wheel that has a large moment of inertia will spin for a long time. Most of the force opposing its motion comes from friction at the axle, and of course, because this force occurs very near the axis of rotation, the corresponding torque is very small. This makes a flywheel an excellent way to store energy.

You can also calculate a moving object's angular momentum around some axis other than the axis of spin. As in so many other cases, this is as simple as considering the object as a particle. A particle traveling linearly in space still has an angular momentum about any axis, which is the moment of its linear momentum, or $m|\mathbf{v}|d$, where d is the perpendicular distance of the particle's line of motion from the axis, as shown in Figure 13.6.

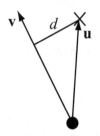

FIGURE 13.6 The angular momentum of a linear particle.

One complication to this is that we need to think about whether it is positive or negative, that is to say, whether the particle is moving clockwise or anticlockwise about the axis. A simple solution is to define the clockwise normal of a vector, then we can use the dot product of this clockwise normal of $\mathbf{v}$ with the vector $\mathbf{u}$ from the particle to the axis, which gives $|\mathbf{v}|d$ as desired, and is positive if and only if the particle is moving clockwise around the axis.

```
function moment (position, vector, axisPosition)
    set n to clockwiseNormal(vector)
    return dotProduct(n, axisPosition-position)
end function
```

Conversely, from the angular velocity, we can calculate the velocity of a point at a vector $\mathbf{r}$ from the center: it is equal to $\omega\mathbf{r}_N$ where $\mathbf{r}_N$ is the clockwise normal of $\mathbf{r}$.

Like linear momentum, angular momentum is conserved, which means that if the moment of inertia of an object changes, its angular velocity must also change to compensate. The classic (and overused) example of this is the ice skater or ballet dancer, who holds her arms horizontally, begins to spin, then raises or lowers them to a vertical position, decreasing her moment of inertia about the vertical axis and increasing the angular velocity of her spin.

Three-dimensional objects generally prefer to spin around the axis with the smallest moment of inertia, which will often be an axis of symmetry. If no other forces oppose them, they will move to orient this axis along the direction of spin. This is called the *gyroscopic* effect, and can be seen most obviously in spinning tops. It can seem quite magical, because the object can be moving quite slowly, then rotates to orient along the axis of symmetry and suddenly is spinning much faster to retain angular momentum. Objects don't spontaneously speed up in linear motion, so when it happens in angular motion it's surprising. The gyroscopic effect is also used in guns: bullets are "rifled" by spinning them through the barrel of the gun, which makes them more stable in flight as they tend to orient along the spin.

Rotational Kinetic Energy

Once again, the energy of a rotating object can be found by the same principle as linear k.e.: rotational k.e. is equal to $\frac{1}{2} \times$ moment of inertia $\times$ angular velocity^2. If you check the units of this you will see that they are the same as those for normal k.e.: kg ms^{-2} (angular velocity should be measured in radians).

Because r.k.e. is just one of the forms of energy, it can be readily converted to linear k.e. or g.p.e. An example of this is the yo-yo, which spins as it falls. By controlling the rate of fall, and thus the momentum, it is possible to perform tricks, as when a yo-yo is made to drop to the ground and then spin in place before returning to the hand. Here, the g.p.e. at the top of the motion converts to both k.e. and r.k.e as the yo-yo falls, then at the bottom, both the k.e. and the original g.p.e. have been converted to r.k.e. A small flick and the r.k.e. is converted back into k.e., allowing the yo-yo to climb the potential well again.

It's interesting to note that this means a yo-yo falls more slowly than a ball. Because some of the g.p.e. is converted to r.k.e., the total k.e. and thus linear speed must be less than it would be if there was no rotation. Similarly, a concrete pipe rolling down a slope accelerates more slowly than a block of ice sliding down it (ignoring the results of friction—see the next chapter), and a solid cylinder of the same size, with a larger moment of inertia, will move more slowly still. This gives another reason why we find it hard to believe Galileo's proof that all objects fall at the same speed: at least when rolling down a slope, larger objects do indeed fall more slowly if they are free to rotate.

SPINNING COLLISIONS

When bodies can rotate, of course there is a potential for more complex collision behavior. There are several factors to take into account: non-rotating bodies that collide at an angle may cause one another to rotate, rotating bodies may collide laterally as well as along the leading edge, and angular momentum affects the results of collisions after the fact.

As with many of the more complicated collision types, and even seemingly simple ones such as between ellipses, angular collisions tend to be difficult to calculate algebraically, and so we often need to use approximation methods. There are far too many possibilities to cover in depth, but hopefully the examples shown here will give enough of a starting point.

ON THE CD

In the *collisions.dir* movie on the CD-ROM, you can experiment with various spinning objects in collision. The code in the program covers more possibilities than we look at in the chapter, and in more detail, so it is worth looking at.

Detecting Collisions Between a Rotating Line and a Circle

Let's start with something simple. In Figure 13.7 we can see a line segment pivoted on the point P, situated at the end of the line. The line is rotating with an angular velocity of ω around P, starting from an initial angle of θ_0 from the vertical. In its path is a circle radius r, centered on the point Q at a distance d from P, and at an angle of α from vertical.

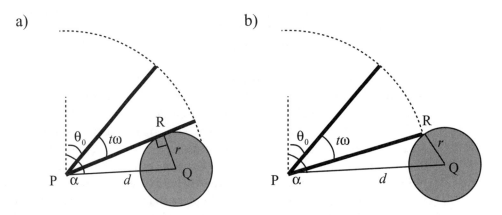

FIGURE 13.7 A rotating line and a circle a) colliding on the flat; b) colliding at the end-point.

For the moment, we'll assume that the circle is far enough within the radius of the line segment that we don't need to consider the end-point as in Figure 13.7a. Now, we know that at any time t, the line has an angle of $\theta = \theta_0 + t\omega$. We also know that when touching the circle at the collision point R as shown in the figure, the line forms a right-angled triangle PRQ, with $QR = r$ and the hypotenuse of length d, and with either $\angle RPQ = \alpha - \theta$ (if the line is rotating clockwise) or $\angle RPQ = \theta - \alpha$ (if it is rotating anticlockwise). This gives us a single equation to determine the point of contact:

$$\alpha - \theta = k \sin^{-1}\left(\frac{r}{d}\right)$$

$$\theta_0 + t\omega = \alpha - k \sin^{-1}\left(\frac{r}{d}\right)$$

$$t = \frac{1}{\omega}\left(\alpha - \theta_0 - k \sin^{-1}\left(\frac{r}{d}\right)\right)$$

where k is 1 for clockwise motion, -1 otherwise.

As we said above, this equation will only work if the circle is close enough to P so that it is struck by the flat of the line, rather than its end-point. If the line segment has a length of l, we can say that it collides on the flat if and only if $d^2 \leq l^2 + r^2$. We also know that if the circle is far enough out, it won't be struck by the line at all—this occurs if $d > l + r$.

What about in the mid-range? This time, we're looking at a slightly different problem as seen in Figure 13.7b. Because the circle is not struck at a tangent, PRQ is no longer a right-angled triangle. However, we do now know the length PR, since it is the length of the line segment l. This means we can use the cosine rule to determine the angle RPQ:

$$\cos(\alpha - \theta) = \frac{l^2 + d^2 - r^2}{2ld}$$

$$\theta = \alpha - k\cos^{-1}\left(\frac{l^2 + d^2 - r^2}{2ld}\right)$$

$$t = \frac{1}{\omega}\left(\alpha - \theta_0 - k\cos^{-1}\left(\frac{l^2 + d^2 - r^2}{2ld}\right)\right)$$

We need to be careful to remember that angular calculations occur in a closed field, where $\alpha + \beta$ is not always greater than α or β. It's simplest to shift calculations around to make sure that no numbers go above 360° or below 0°

So this gives us a simple function to determine all possible collisions of this type:

```
function angularCollisionLineCircle(theto, omega, l, r, d, alph)
    if d>l+r then return "no collision"
    if d<r then return "embedded"
    // move into a calculation within the range [0,2pi]
    subtract theto from alph
```

```
    if omega<0 then
        set omega to -omega
        set alph to -alph
        set k to -1
    otherwise
        set k to 1
    end if
    while alph<0 add 2*pi to alph
    while alph>2*pi subtract 2*pi from alph
    // check if there is a possible collision
    if alph>omega then return "no collision"
    // now perform the appropriate collision check
    if d*d<=l*l+r*r then
        return (alph-k*asin(r/d))/omega
    otherwise
        return (alph-k*acos((l*l+d*d-r*r)/(2*l*d)))/omega
    end if
end function
```

A similar calculation without the option of hitting on the flat will allow you to calculate the collision of a rotating point with a circle, as with a person kicking a soccer ball with the toe of their boot, or the vertex of a rotating polygon.

When the line segment is rotating about some point not on the line, as with an edge of a rectangle, things are not too much more difficult. Take a look at Figure 13.8a, where you can see a line segment rotating around a point P, at a perpendicular distance k from the line. As before, a circle sits at Q, a distance d from P and angle α around it.

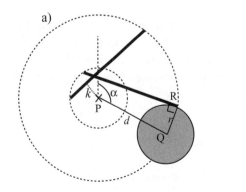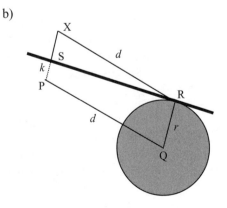

FIGURE 13.8 A line rotating about an offset point a) setup; b) collision detail.

In Figure 13.8b you can see a detail of the moment of collision. We have drawn in the point R where the circle meets the line, and the point S where the perpendicular from P meets the line. We have also drawn in the line PQ. Notice that both PS and QR are perpendicular to the line, so they are parallel. If we draw a new line from R parallel to QP, this meets the extended line SP at a point X, a distance $r - x$ from S, giving us a right-angled triangle XSR, with one side equal to $r - k$ and a hypotenuse of d. From this we can work out the angle RXS ($= \pi - $ QPS) and the distance RS. With a bit of angle juggling, it turns out that there is only the most minor adjustment to the calculation for collision on the flat:

$$ t = \frac{1}{\omega}\left(\alpha - \theta_0 - k\sin^{-1}\left(\frac{r - x}{d} \right) \right) $$

ON THE CD Finishing the code is left to you as an exercise, but see the CD-ROM for some ideas. In particular, you need to take into account again the situation where the circle is struck by the ends of the line rather than the flat. Since the end-points move in a circle around P (at a distance $\sqrt{l^2 + x^2}$ for each length), this is just a re-application of the previous method. This particular collision method is important, as any rotating polygon is just a collection of line segments rotating around some axis.

We'll finish this section with a much more difficult problem: dealing with a circle that is moving when it hits the line. In Figure 13.9, you can see an illustration of this. The circle moves along the path $\mathbf{q} + t\mathbf{v}$, and the line rotates around the point P as before. At some time t, the circle and line touch, and two important construction lines have been drawn in.

This figure is drawn assuming the line begins rotating at the angle 0. In order to calculate other situations, we first need to rotate the frame of reference around P to reduce them to this case. Note also that in these calculations we are assuming that any collision occurs in the first quartile of motion; that is, that the angular displacement of the line in this time step is less than 90°. This simplifies calculations, and assuming your simulation is run reasonably often, shouldn't cause problems. If you need to deal with larger angles, you have to split the calculation into several sub-problems. Finally, we might as well assume that P is the point (0,0).

Once again, the solution hinges around the values α, the angle formed by the line CP at the point of collision, where C is the center of the circle, and β, which is the angle formed at the point of collision between CP and the rotating line. What we can say is that at the moment of collision, either $\alpha - \beta = t\omega$ or $\alpha + \beta = t\omega$ (we can calculate which of these may happen by comparing the initial positions and motions of the two objects). So again, we can say that $\alpha = t\omega + k\beta$, where $k = \pm1$.

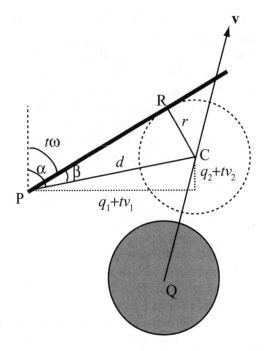

FIGURE 13.9 A moving circle and a rotating line.

With a little work from our trigonometric identities, and making temporary use of the value d, the length of CP (a function of t), we can find an equation for t:

$$\frac{q_1 + tv_1}{d} = \sin\alpha$$

$$= \sin(k\beta + t\omega)$$

$$= \cos\beta\sin(t\omega) + k\sin\beta\cos(t\omega)$$

$$\frac{q_2 + tv_2}{d} = \cos(k\beta + t\omega)$$

$$= \cos\beta\cos(t\omega) - k\sin\beta\sin(t\omega)$$

$$\cos(t\omega)\left(\frac{q_1 + tv_1}{d}\right) - \sin(t\omega)\left(\frac{q_2 + tv_2}{d}\right) = k\sin\beta\left(\cos^2(t\omega) + \sin^2(t\omega)\right)$$

$$= k\sin\beta = \frac{kr}{d}$$

$$\cos(t\omega)(q_1 + tv_1) - \sin(t\omega)(q_2 + tv_2) = kr$$

Sadly, this is as far as we can go algebraically. This equation cannot be solved exactly, so we need to bring out our approximation methods (see Chapter 6). In this case, because the function is fairly smooth and we are looking over just a small range, with clear boundaries (brackets) at 0 and 1, we're safest using the simple bisection or Regula Falsa methods rather than something more sophisticated like Newton-Raphson, which could easily find a root outside the range we're interested in.

To complete the function, we also need to perform a check for collision with the end-point of the line. The basic algebra remains the same, but this time the value of d doesn't drop out of the equation, instead we are stuck with using the cosine rule to discover the value of β: $\cos \beta = \frac{l^2 + d^2 - r^2}{2ld}$. So this leaves us with the slightly more complicated equation:

$$\sin(t\omega)(q_1 + tv_1) + \cos(t\omega)(q_2 + tv_2) = \frac{l^2 + d^2 - r^2}{2l}$$

$$= \frac{(q_1 + tv_1)^2 + (q_2 + tv_2)^2 + l^2 - r^2}{2l}$$

Again, this can't be solved algebraically and an approximation method must be used. A great deal of time can be saved by performing an appropriate initial check to see whether it is possible for the two objects to collide at all: in fact, it is worth performing two, one to see if the circle intersects the complete circle swept out by the line—a cheap, quick test that should be performed before any rotational collision check—and a second to see if the angle swept out by the circle during the time interval overlaps with the angle swept out by the line—this will also give you a value for k. In the version on the CD-ROM, we don't even bother with solving for t, we simply check whether there is any collision during the time period and if so, rebound at the beginning. It's less accurate, but looks all right. We'll cover this more in Chapter 22.

ON THE CD

There isn't space here to cover the case where the rotating line is offset from its rotation point: the algebraic technique is similar, but the calculations are messier.

In all these problems, you need to deal separately with the two ends of the rotating line. When the line is pivoted around one endpoint, this means performing a simple check for a collision between the circle and the stationary pivot. Otherwise, we must perform the calculation twice, adding π to the initial angle for the reverse side of the line.

Detecting Collisions Between Two Rotating Lines

You might have thought this problem would be quite straightforward, but no, again it is quite subtle and requires an approximation method to solve. As before, we'll build up to it gradually. We'll start with the case where a rotating line meets a stationary line segment as in Figure 13.10. As before, there are two separate cases to consider: the first is a collision with the body of the line segment, the second is a collision with one of the endpoints (which for purely artistic reasons are shown in reverse order in the figure).

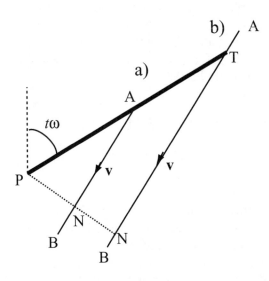

FIGURE 13.10 A rotating line and a line segment a) colliding at an endpoint; b) colliding on the flat.

As usual with these problems, we'll assume that we know the position vector **a** of one endpoint A, and the vector **v** from this point to the other endpoint B. We can also determine the point N where the perpendicular from P (which we'll define as our origin) hits the line segment. Now we'll do what we hinted at earlier in the chapter, and create a useful function clockwise(a,v), which returns either +1 if the vector **v** from **a** is directed clockwise around the origin, or −1 if it is directed anti-clockwise. (In some circumstances it might be useful for the function to return 0 if the vector points directly at or away from the origin, but we won't do that here.)

```
function clockwise (p, v)
    set n to clockwisenormal(p)
    if component(v,n)>0 then return 1
    return -1
end function
```

```
function clockwiseNormal (v)
    return vector(-v[2],v[1])
end function
```

Here, we're specifying a particular direction as clockwise by defining a function clockwiseNormal. This is arbitrary as long as we use it consistently: it depends on whether our *y*-value is measured upward or downward. So for some display purposes what we call "clockwise" could look as if it is running anticlockwise. However, we have to ensure that it ties in correctly with our measure for positive angular displacement, which we can do by creating two more general-purpose functions:

```
function unitVector(ang)
    return vector(sin(ang),cos(ang))
end function

function angleOf(v)
    return atan(v[1],v[2])
end
```

By combining these functions we can ensure that we remain consistent.

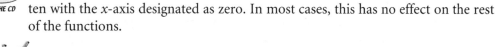

For various reasons, the versions of these functions on the CD-ROM are written with the *x*-axis designated as zero. In most cases, this has no effect on the rest of the functions.

In three dimensions, this process can be dealt with more formally by using the cross product, which will be introduced in Chapter 17.

Now let's return to the problem in hand. We'll deal with the simplest case first: suppose our rotating line strikes the segment at some point T between A and B. In that case, it forms a right-angled triangle PNT, where PT is the length *l* of the line. This gives us immediately a value for the angle at which it lies. What's more, if the line is rotating clockwise, it will strike along the anticlockwise direction of **v**, and vice versa. Then we just need to check that T actually lies on the line, which will be true if $0 \le \overline{AT} \cdot \mathbf{v} \le |\mathbf{v}|^2$.

The endpoints are fairly simple too. If the line is rotating in the same direction as **v**, we only need to look for a collision with A, if it's rotating the other way we need to check for a collision with B. Assuming the former, again the line forms a right-angled triangle PNA, and this time it is the length AN which we can determine in advance, again giving us the correct angle. However, again we do need to be a little careful, as we need to make sure that we measure the angle in the correct direction. We need to check if N lies on AB, that is, if vector $\overrightarrow{AN}$ lies in the same direction as $\overrightarrow{AB}$, in which case we want the anticlockwise angle, or in the opposite direction, in which case we want the clockwise angle (see Figure 13.11).

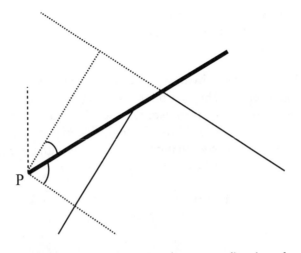

FIGURE 13.11 Determining the correct direction of the collision angle with an endpoint.

This gives us a complete function:

```
function angularcollisionLineStationaryLine (thet0, angvel, length,
linept, linevect, segment)
  // segment=1 if we are checking for endpoints,
  // 0 for a continuous wall
  set n to norm(normal(linevect))
  set d to dotprod(linept,n)
  if d<0 then
    set d to -d
    set n to -n
  end if
  // so n is the normal vector directed towards N
  if d>length then return "none" // too far from wall

  // if checking for endpoints, see if they are relevant
  if segment=1 then
    set pn to n*d  // the vector PN
    set dd to length*length-d*d // the squared length  TD
    if angvel>0 then
      if clockwise(linept, linevect)=-1 then
        set endpt to linept
```

```
      otherwise
        set endpt to linept+linevect
      end if
    otherwise
      if clockwise(linept, linevect)=-1 then
        set endpt to linept+linevect
      otherwise
        set endpt to linept
      end if
    end if

    set d1 to sqmag(endpt-pn) // sqmag is the squared magnitude
    if d1<dd then // there is a potential collision with the endpoint
      set a to acos(d/mag(endpt))*clockwise(endpt,pn-endpt)
      // a is the angle of collision with the endpoint
    otherwise
      set a to acos(d/l)
      if angvel>0 then set a to -a
      // check if this collision occurs outside the line segment
      set ap to pn+abs(a)*sqrt(dd)/a
      // note that abs(a)/a is 1 if a>0, -1 otherwise
      set k to mag(ap-linept)/mag(linevect)
      if k>1 or k<0 then return "none"
    end if

  otherwise
    // check for collision with an infinite wall
    set a to acos(d/l)
    if angvel>0 then set a to -a

  end if

  set tn to angleof(n)
  set t to rangeangle(tn-thet0+a,1)/angvel
  if t<=0 or t>1 then return "none"
  return t
end
```

Dealing with the case where both lines are rotating is too complicated to look at fully here, but the essentials are fairly simple. As you can see in Figure 13.12, the problem is in some ways easier than those we've looked at before, because for all collisions except for the degenerate case where the two endpoints collide exactly, every collision is between the endpoint of one line and the flat of the other.

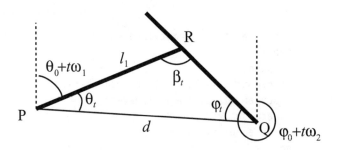

FIGURE 13.12   Collisions between two rotating lines.

We need to do a little initial work here. First we can notice that it is possible to calculate the angle α of the line joining the two pivot points P and Q. Using this angle, we can define two functions giving two angles of the triangle formed by the two lines and the line PQ:

$$\theta_t = \alpha - \theta_0 - t\omega_1$$
$$\varphi_t = \varphi_0 + t\omega_2 - \alpha - \pi$$

Then we know that if the third angle of the triangle PQR can be formed, it will be equal to $\beta_t = \pi - \theta_t - \varphi_t$. So our first check for whether the lines collide is to see whether this value β_t lies between 0 and π. This gives an inequality for t:

$$\pi \leq \varphi_0 - \theta_0 + t(\omega_2 - \omega_1) \leq 2\pi$$

If this inequality holds for any t between 0 and 1 (note that α drops out) then we have a potential collision triangle in this time frame.

If the triangle is formed correctly, then we can use the sine rule to determine whether the triangle is a collision, which occurs if either PR = l_1 and QR l_2, or PR l_1 and QR = l_2. So we have
$\frac{\sin \beta_t}{l_1} = \frac{\sin \varphi_t}{d}$ or $\frac{\sin \beta_t}{l_1} = \frac{\sin \theta_t}{d}$, where d is the length of PQ. However, at this stage we have to return to approximation methods once more. Notice also that we have missed out from this explanation any discussion about the direction of motion of the two lines, which affects exactly which values we should use in the triangle PQR.

If the pivot points are moving relative to one another, this doesn't significantly alter the method, we just need to change d and α into functions of t as well, complicating the calculations but not the theory.

Resolving Angular Collisions

Angular collisions are only mildly more difficult to resolve than linear ones. We'll use the impulses described in the last chapter, and the main trick we'll use is to consider the behavior of the point of impact. Once the two bodies may be rotating, the velocity of a point on the edge may not be equal to the velocity of the body as a whole. Recall that we calculated the velocity of a point spinning about a fixed axis to be $\omega \mathbf{r}_N$, or more generally if the body is moving with velocity $\mathbf{v}$ it is $\mathbf{v} + \omega \mathbf{r}_N$.

At the moment of impact, the impulse J experienced by the two bodies affects both their linear and angular momentum. Suppose their initial velocities are $\mathbf{u}_1$ and $\mathbf{u}_2$, their final velocities are $\mathbf{v}_1$ and $\mathbf{v}_2$, their initial angular velocities are ω_1 and ω_2, and their final angular velocities are φ_1 and φ_2. We'll use m to represent their masses, I for their moments of inertia and $\mathbf{m}_1$ and $\mathbf{m}_2$ for the "moment vectors" (the clockwise normals of the radius vectors: note the boldface). Finally, suppose the collision normal is $\mathbf{n}$. Then we can write the effect of the collision down in four equations:

$$m_1 \mathbf{v}_1 = m_1 \mathbf{u}_1 + J\mathbf{n}$$

$$m_2 \mathbf{v}_2 = m_2 \mathbf{u}_2 - J\mathbf{n}$$

$$I_1 \varphi_1 = I_1 \omega_1 + J\mathbf{m}_1 \cdot \mathbf{n}$$

$$I_2 \varphi_2 = I_2 \omega_2 - J\mathbf{m}_2 \cdot \mathbf{n}$$

Now we're going to make an assumption: The behavior of the points of impact is going to be the same, independently of the angular motion of the objects behind them. Let's break that down a little. The two colliding points are moving with a relative velocity that we can calculate to be $\mathbf{u}_2 - \mathbf{u}_1 + \mathbf{m}_2 \omega_2$. From the point of view of the collision, it doesn't know anything about the rest of the objects, just that they seem to be moving with this relative velocity, and that they have a certain mass. So it's going to make them rebound in exactly the same way as it would otherwise: that is, it "wants" the relative velocity normal to the collision to obey:

$$\left(\mathbf{v}_2 - \mathbf{v}_1 + \mathbf{m}_2 \varphi_2 - \mathbf{m}_1 \varphi_1 \right) \cdot \mathbf{n} = -\left(\mathbf{u}_2 - \mathbf{u}_1 + \mathbf{m}_2 \omega_2 - \mathbf{m}_1 \omega_1 \right) \cdot \mathbf{n}$$

assuming that the collision is elastic.

Although we haven't encountered this equation specifically before, it is actually a restatement of the conservation of energy, and we can see it in the linear collisions we've already encountered. Since collisions can only affect the normal direction, energy can only be conserved if the magnitude of the normal velocity going in to a collision is equal to the magnitude coming out.

Combining these five equations together, we get:

$$\left(\mathbf{u}_2 - \frac{J}{m_2}\mathbf{n} - \left(\mathbf{u}_1 + \frac{J}{m_1}\mathbf{n}\right) + \mathbf{m}_2\left(\omega_2 - \frac{J}{I_2}\mathbf{m}_2 \cdot \mathbf{n}\right) - \mathbf{m}_1\left(\omega_1 + \frac{J}{I_1}\mathbf{m}_1 \cdot \mathbf{n}\right)\right) \cdot \mathbf{n}$$

$$= -\left(\mathbf{u}_2 - \mathbf{u}_1 + \mathbf{m}_2\omega_2 - \mathbf{m}_1\omega_1\right) \cdot \mathbf{n}$$

Combining terms and simplifying, we get

$$2\left(\mathbf{u}_2 - \mathbf{u}_1 + \mathbf{m}_2\omega_2 - \mathbf{m}_1\omega_1\right) \cdot \mathbf{n} - J\left(\frac{1}{m_2}\mathbf{n} - \frac{1}{m_1}\mathbf{n} + \mathbf{m}_2\left(\frac{1}{I_2}\mathbf{m}_2 \cdot \mathbf{n}\right) + \mathbf{m}_1\left(\frac{1}{I_1}\mathbf{m}_1 \cdot \mathbf{n}\right)\right) \cdot \mathbf{n} = 0$$

Assuming **n** is a unit vector, this becomes

$$2\left(\mathbf{u}_2 - \mathbf{u}_1 + \mathbf{m}_2\omega_2 - \mathbf{m}_1\omega_1\right) \cdot \mathbf{n} - J\left(\frac{1}{m_2} + \frac{1}{m_1} + \frac{1}{I_2}\left(\mathbf{m}_2 \cdot \mathbf{n}\right)^2 + \frac{1}{I_1}\left(\mathbf{m}_1 \cdot \mathbf{n}\right)^2\right) = 0$$

which we can rearrange to find J. Finally, we can plug this value for J back into the four momentum equations to find the new velocities.

Notice that this formula yields various different results if you set particular masses or moments of inertia infinitely high, creating an object that is fixed in place either linearly or angularly. For example, if we set both the moments of inertia infinitely high, these terms drop out of the formula, leaving us with the formula for linear collision resolution (notice also that angular velocities are then unaffected by the impulse).

Including inelastic collisions isn't much harder, it just affects that "2" term, replacing it with a $(1 + e)$ term, where e is the *coefficient of restitution*, from 0 (putty) to 1 (atom).

So here's the code, which we're going to combine into one master function:

```
function resolveAngularCollision obj1, obj2, n, mom1, mom2
    set u1 to obj1.getVelocity()
    set u2 to obj2.getVelocity()
    set om1 to obj1.getAngularVelocity()
    set om2 to obj2.getAngularVelocity()

    set J to 2*dotProduct(u2-u1+mom2*om2-mom1*om1,n)
    set denom to 0
    if not obj1.fixedLinear() then
        set m1 to obj1.getMass()
        set denom to denom + (1/m1)
```

```
       end if
       if not obj2.fixedLinear() then
          set m2 to obj2.getMass()
          set denom to denom + (1/m2)
       end if
       if not obj1.fixedAngular() then
          set moi1 to obj1.getMOI()
          set dp1 to dotProduct(mom1,n)
          set denom to denom + (dp1*dp1/moi1)
       end if
       if not obj2.fixedAngular() then
          set moi2 to obj2.getMOI()
           set dp2 to dotProduct(mom2,n)
          set denom to denom + (dp2*dp2/moi2)
       end if
       if denom=0 then exit // coincident axes or other weirdness
       set J to J/denom
       if not obj1.fixedLinear() then obj1.setVelocity(u1+J*n/m1)
       if not obj2.fixedLinear() then obj2.setVelocity(u2-J*n/m2)
       if not obj1.fixedAngular() then
obj1.setAngularVelocity(om1+J*dp1/moi1)
       if not obj2.fixedAngular() then obj2.setAngularVelocity(om2-
J*dp2/moi2)
    end function
```

Note that as before, this assumes that the two bodies are represented by some sort of object whose velocity we can alter directly.

Incorporating Spin into the Pool Game

It should be reasonably simple to see how these ideas might be incorporated into our pool game. As well as defining a vector of motion, we need to decide whether to strike the ball to the left or right of center. This imparts a force that is offset from the center of mass, with the result that an angular momentum is created, which for the sake of the game can be just a linear function of the distance from the center.

This spin is sometimes called "English," but we'll simply call it "side-spin" to spare the feelings of English readers.

Although this angular motion has no effect on collision detection (since the balls are circular), it does affect collision resolution, because one of our assumptions from the previous section does not hold in pool. As a result of friction between the cushions and the balls, and also with the table as we'll see in the next chapter, not all the impulse on colliding objects acts normal to the collision. This means that some of the ball's angular momentum can be transformed into linear momentum, and vice versa.

Figure 13.13 shows an example of this in action. We can imagine the collision to take place in two parts. First of all, the angular velocity decreases by some amount ϕ, but in order to achieve this, there needed to be an impulse J at the point of contact, along the wall. We can calculate J by seeing that $I\phi = Jr$. Now we can apply this impulse to calculate the resulting change in linear velocity:

$$m\mathbf{v} = m\mathbf{u} + J\mathbf{t}$$

$$\mathbf{v} = \mathbf{u} + \frac{I\phi}{m}\mathbf{t}$$

Having calculated this new velocity, we can apply the perpendicular impulse as usual.

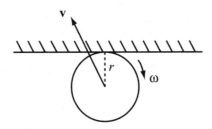

FIGURE 13.13 Collision with a sticky surface.

In our game, we'll assume that ball-ball collisions have no effect on spin (including topspin, which we'll look at in the next chapter), but that ball-cushion collisions do have some effect, which will be somewhere between removing all the angular velocity and leaving it unchanged. The result can be seen by including spin in the pool demo on the CD-ROM.

EXERCISES

Exercise 13.1

Write a function `resolveCushionCollision(obj1, obj2, normal, moment, slow)` which will calculate the result of a collision with a wall that removes some constant amount of angular velocity.

This function should calculate both the angular and linear velocities, given that the proportion `prop` of angular velocity has been lost.

Exercise 13.2

Write a function that will calculate a collision between a moving, rotating square and a wall.

This is a tough one and not for the squeamish.

SUMMARY

Angular motion is very simple in its essence but very complicated in the details and implementation. Easy to understand but hard to deal with, it's no surprise that as a rule, game designers avoid it whenever they possibly can. However, in this chapter you have at least had the beginnings of how to implement a collision system that takes spin into account. At the very least, you now know how to deal with it when working with circles and lines.

In the next chapter, we'll extend this subject a little more by looking at how spin is related to one more force, friction.

YOU SHOULD NOW KNOW

- how a *lever* allows us to move and balance objects
- the meaning of *torque* and its relationship to force
- how *angular momentum* and energy are similar to their linear counterparts
- how to find the point of collision between some simple spinning shapes
- how to resolve a collision between one or more spinning objects

14 Friction

In This Chapter

OVERVIEW

We're not quite done with rotation yet. In the previous chapter we looked at sideways spin in the game of pool, but we glossed over the more common topspin and backspin, otherwise known as rolling. Why does a ball roll? After all, balls moving in a straight line through space wouldn't be expected to roll: in our original calculations of momentum, we ignored spin altogether.

The reason a ball rolls is the same as the reason a block stays still: it's due to the force of *friction*, which is experienced whenever two objects move in opposing directions tangentially to their point of contact. We've already made use of this to explain why pool balls rebound at an angle when they strike a cushion with sidespin applied. Now we'll look at it in more detail.

ON THE CD   Code samples from this chapter are implemented in *math.cst* in the script *chapter 14 (friction)*. The *pool* demo uses them in context.

HOW FRICTION WORKS

Friction is principally caused by irregularities on the surface of an object, so a rough brick will have more friction than a smooth piece of marble. If we imagine looking in close-up at two surfaces moving against each other, pits and ridges on the surfaces will collide with each other, creating a force that essentially acts tangentially to the plane of contact, which in the cases we'll be considering here means along the direction of motion: in the previous chapter we looked at the result of an instantaneous frictional force applied during a collision, here we're looking at the more conventional issue of friction acting continuously on a sliding object.

The Coefficient of Friction

Friction is rather an unusual force because its magnitude varies according to the force perpendicular to it. In fact, friction is proportional to the normal force: for any two objects there is a value μ, the *coefficient of friction*, such that:

Force due to friction $= \mu \times$ *force perpendicular to friction*

In Figure 14.1 you can see an example of friction in action. There is a box with weight W moving on a slope (often called an *inclined plane*) with an angle of θ to the horizontal. The weight of the box acts downward, which means that it is experiencing a force of $W\cos\theta$ perpendicular to the slope. This gives it a frictional force of $\mu W \cos\theta$ along (and opposing) the direction of motion, so the total force experienced tangential to the plane is $W\sin\theta - \mu W \cos\theta = W(\sin\theta - \mu\cos\theta)$.

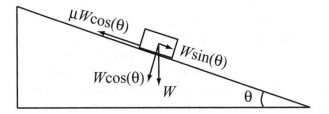

FIGURE 14.1   Friction on an inclined plane.

Remember that because of Newton's Third Law, the box is also experiencing an opposing normal force of W $\cos\theta$, so it is in equilibrium normal to the plane. The friction is created by the opposition of these two forces.

This frictional force applies as long as the box is moving, so for example, if the plane has a slope of exactly the correct angle, friction will cancel the force due to gravity, meaning that the box will move with a constant speed (we use this fact to measure the coefficient of friction). We can calculate this angle: it occurs when

$$W\left(\sin\theta - \mu\cos\theta\right) = 0$$
$$\sin\theta = \mu\cos\theta$$
$$\tan\theta = \mu$$

If θ is smaller than this, then the box will gradually slow to a stop; if greater, then gravity will overcome friction and the box will accelerate.

All the above is somewhat simplified, because in fact there are two different co-efficients of friction. As well as the coefficient of *kinetic friction*, which is what we looked at above, there is also a coefficient of *static friction*, which applies when an object is not moving, but is experiencing a sliding force—that is to say, it's the force that resists getting an object moving. The two coefficients are usually written as μ_K and μ_S. Static friction is slightly harder to grasp than kinetic, because it represents a maximum possible force, rather than the actual value. As long as you push an object with a smaller amount of force than the static friction, it will not move: an equal force will resist you.

In general, μ_S is greater than μ_K, which means that it usually requires more force to make something move than to accelerate it when already moving. In the example of our inclined plane, imagine this time that the box is resting on the plane. The static friction is given by $\mu_s W \cos\theta$, which is the maximum possible frictional force applied while static. As long as the force due to the box's weight is less than this, the box will not move, that is, it remains stationary if $\tan\theta < \mu_S$. This value of θ is sometimes called the *critical angle*.

This means that there is a region of angles for the plane such that if the box is stationary, it will not move, but if it is moving, it will continue to do so: this occurs as long as $\mu_K < \tan\theta < \mu_S$.

We can sum all this up in a function:

```
function resultantForceOnObject (nonFrictionalForce, velocity,
    coefficient)
    set tang to norm(velocity)
    set norm to normalVector(tang)
    set normalForce to component (nonFrictionalForce, norm)
```

```
    set tangentialForce to component (nonFrictionalForce, tang)
    set frictionalForce to coefficient * magnitude(normalForce)
    if frictionalForce>tangentialForce and magnitude(velocity)>0 then
return vector(0,0)
    otherwise return (tangentialForce — frictionalForce) * tang
end function
```

This function works equally well for static and for kinetic friction, you simply need to replace the coefficient with the correct value depending on whether the object is currently moving or stationary. The parameter `nonFrictionalForce` should be the force on the object due to any factors other than its interaction with the plane—the force it would be experiencing if the plane was not there. The return value is then the total force on the object, including both friction and the reaction force due to Newton's Third Law, and is therefore parallel to the plane. You might like to try making a more specialized version of this function to deal with the specific case of an object sliding down an inclined plane.

Friction and Energy

The main problem with introducing friction into a mechanical simulation is that it violates the principle of conservation of energy (momentum, too, but this is not so much of an issue as conservation of momentum isn't useful anyway when dealing with objects that are fixed in place). The energy is mostly lost to heat, to the detriment of both bodies involved, which is why it's so important to keep your car filled with oil!

We can calculate the energy lost due to friction by looking at the *work* done. Work is another word for energy, and means the energy used to perform a task, usually making an object move.

$$\textit{Work done} = \textit{Force} \times \textit{Distance moved}$$

This means the harder you push something, the more energy it takes to travel a particular distance. And notice also that if something doesn't move, no work is done, no matter how hard you are pushing it: work is *useful* energy. This is in contrast to the normal usage of the word "work," which suggests effort. Of course, if you are pushing at a brick wall with all your strength, this will involve energy on your part, but the *wall* does not change, and so it does not use any of the energy, which is mostly spent on chemical reactions in your muscles. So static friction does not have any effect on energy calculations—we'll see how useful this is shortly.

If an object is moving and experiencing kinetic friction, then we can calculate the work done by the friction, which is a constant multiple of the distance traveled:

$$\textit{Work done} = \textit{Frictional force} \times \textit{distance} = \mu \times \textit{Normal force} \times \textit{distance}$$

Of course, this is complicated by the fact that the distance traveled is *also* a function of the force. Suppose our object is sliding on a table, so that friction is the only force acting on it—like a hockey puck, for example. In a particular time *t*, the puck moves by a distance equal to $ut + \frac{1}{2}at^2$. By Newton's Second Law, the acceleration is the force divided by the mass, so we have $d = ut + \frac{Ft^2}{2m}$, so the energy lost is equal to $Fut + \frac{F^2t^2}{2m}$. But of course, the force is dependent on the puck's weight, *mg*, which gives us the following:

$$Energy\ loss = \mu mg\left(ut + \frac{\mu gt^2}{2}\right)$$

On the other hand, it's rather easier to calculate the loss of speed, which is a simple linear decrease:

$$Speed\ loss = \mu gt$$

If we look back at our pool game simulation, you can see that this turns out to be exactly as we calculated it. But hold on to this thought, as we'll look at it again soon. You'll see that things are rather more complicated with balls than boxes.

Air Resistance and Terminal Velocity

There is another kind of friction we haven't looked at yet, which is *air resistance*, or more generally, *fluid resistance* or *drag* (the word *fluid* is used to mean either a liquid or a gas—in general the two have rather similar properties). If you think about it, the previous definition of friction can't really apply to drag, because the force is applied in a different way. A body falling through the air meets resistance due to constant forward collisions with air molecules, rather than a sliding force like a box on the ground.

Calculating drag is rather more complicated than calculating friction. Like friction, the important value is a constant coefficient, the *drag coefficient*, in the equation

$$Drag\ force = \frac{1}{2}C_D\rho v^2 A$$

Here, ρ (the Greek letter rho, not the letter p) is the pressure of the fluid, *A* is the forward area presented to the fluid, and *v* is the speed. We needn't worry about the pressure and area terms: we're dealing with simpler problems where these are going to be constant. For our purposes, all we need to know is that the drag force is proportional to the square of the speed. We'll represent this by our own drag coefficient we'll call μ_D (this is not a standard notation). Then we can say

$$Drag\ force = \mu_D v^2$$

We can see why the other terms should play a part: the pressure of a fluid is a measure of how densely packed its molecules are, so the higher it is, the more collisions the falling body will experience. Similarly, the greater the surface area of the body, the more molecules it will hit on the way down (which is why a parachute falls slower than a pea). We could, in fact, split the coefficient of friction up in much the same way: it too is dependent on the area of contact, for example.

Because drag is dependent on speed, this means that at some stage, a falling object will reach a speed where the drag is equal to the pull of gravity. At this stage, it will stop accelerating. This speed is called *terminal velocity*, and we can calculate it:

$$mg = \mu_D v^2$$

$$v = \sqrt{\frac{mg}{\mu_D}}$$

Since μ_D is proportional to area, terminal velocity will be inversely proportional to the square root of area. Furthermore, the area of a circle or a sphere is proportional to the square of its radius, so terminal velocity is inversely proportional to radius. If you double the radius of your parachute, you will halve your terminal velocity, which has to be a good thing.

FRICTION AND ANGULAR MOTION

Hopefully, the previous section should have been reasonably straightforward. Friction is not too complicated, it's just another small thing to consider, and in practical terms it can mostly be dealt with by simple quick-and-dirty methods such as we used in the pool game. But there are other considerations too.

Wheels

How does a car move? Linear forces in the cylinders are converted to a torque which is applied to the wheel axle (or axles in a four-wheel-drive machine). This causes them to turn, but why does the car then move? Why don't the wheels simply spin, as they do when you're caught in mud? It's all down to friction—which, when we want it to happen, is called *traction* or *grip*.

Grip is basically static friction. When your car's tires are in contact with the road and trying to turn, they meet with resistance from the static friction with the road. This resistance counteracts the torque on the wheels, meeting it with a forward force, which causes them to roll instead of spinning in place. So the force that actually moves your car forward is friction, and it acts in the direction of motion. In fact, the car only moves at all as a consequence of Newton's Third Law—the force that moves it forward is a reaction to the force exerted by the wheels on the road: because the road can't move backward, the car has to move forward instead.

We can calculate the force on the road at the point of contact: if the wheels are experiencing a total torque of T, and they have a radius of r, the force at any point on the surface of the wheel is $T/2r$. What happens if this force is greater than the static friction of the wheel with the road? Then the wheel starts to slip and the car doesn't move, it just sits and literally "burns rubber." So a major part of successful driving is controlling the torque applied to the wheels.

Gearing gives us even more control over the level of torque. When you press the accelerator, it increases the amount of fuel being burned by the engine, which increases the *power*, or amount of energy released per second. But that power can be transferred in different ways. Just as work is force multiplied by distance, we have

$$Power = force \times speed = torque \times angular\ speed$$

So when increasing the power, it can either go to increasing the force / torque, and thus the acceleration, or to increasing the speed. Gearing allows us to make that trade-off: at a low gear, we have high torque and high acceleration, but a low maximum speed. At a higher gear, we have less acceleration but can (perhaps paradoxically) travel faster. This is why we use low gears to get us up to speed, but then switch to a higher gear for efficient cruising. It's also why you're better off shifting down a gear to overtake than shifting up, and conversely why in order to get out of being stuck in the mud or a skid, you should shift into a higher gear, reducing the torque and so making it easier to maintain your grip on the road.

Braking, of course, is much the same process the other way around. When we brake, we apply a reverse torque on the wheels. We don't want to stop them altogether (locking), as this will create a frictional force against the road that is too strong for static friction to overcome, putting us into a skid. Instead we try to bring them to a controlled halt, maintaining traction with the road.

So this brings us back to pool balls. What happens when we strike a pool ball (head-on) is in fact that it tries at first to move without spinning, as if it were on a Newton's Cradle. But it's sliding along the table, and experiencing a kinetic friction. This slows the whole ball down, but it also imparts a spin, since it's a force applied at an angle. Then at a critical speed, when the surface velocity of the spinning ball is equal to the current speed of the ball, it is no longer sliding, but is rolling like a wheel. At this moment, kinetic friction ceases to be an issue, and static friction comes into play. Unlike kinetic friction, static friction doesn't slow the ball down, so its rate of speed decrease changes at this stage, just losing energy due to drag in the air, inelasticity of collisions, and some kinetic friction affecting the speed of rolling (each time the ball moves, it has to squash down fibers of cloth, and this imparts a certain amount of drag in itself).

The result of this is that all balls on a pool table have a tendency to spin forward in the direction of travel, that is to say, to roll. This spin is called *topspin*, and in the reverse direction it is called *backspin* (or in ball games like tennis, *slice*). As with sideways spin, you can impart topspin or backspin when you strike the cue ball by applying the cue impulse off-center. But whatever you do, as soon as the ball starts to move, it begins to try to roll.

There is an additional complication in this situation, though. The topspin or backspin you apply is going to make the ball act a bit like a wheel: for example, if the ball has topspin greater than the natural rolling pace, then the friction is going to act forward instead of backward, accelerating the ball forward at the same time as it slows its spin. Conversely, with backspin the frictional force may be enough to slow the ball and even, if it's spinning fast enough, make it travel in the opposite direction.

All this is particularly noticeable when we deal with collisions: when colliding with another ball (a very low coefficient of friction), topspin is unaffected, so this means that the ball is still trying to roll forward even as it rebounds backward. This spin then acts like a wheel, driving the ball to try to continue in the same direction it was going before. If the ball has backspin at the moment of collision, then this is going to increase its rebound.

You should try these things out when you next encounter a pool table. Remember Newton's Cradle: when one ball strikes another along the line of the velocity vector, the first ball should stop dead while the other moves off at the same speed. But if you hit the cue ball near the top, then when it collides with the object ball it stops briefly, then rolls forward. If you hit it near the bottom it stops, then rolls backward.

We've covered enough of these kinds of calculations in the last chapter, so we won't go into further detail here: Exercise 14.1 gives you a chance to have a go. Making it work correctly is tricky because we have not yet dealt with rotations in three dimensions, but using various tricks you can create motion which is quite realistic, as you can see by looking at the final pool game on the CD-ROM.

ON THE CD

Slipping Over

It's not only wheels that move by using friction. We humans propel ourselves around by the same principle when we can: using our feet to exert a backward force on the ground, to which the ground responds with a frictional force forward that moves us along.

Of course, this relies on us having excellent traction between our feet and the ground: if there is a low coefficient of friction, this technique won't work. Like a wheel spinning, the force we exert backward quickly overcomes the static friction and simply acts as a torque on our bodies, with the result that we too spin, falling over. Various tricks can be used to prevent the risk of this, including swinging the arms to provide a counteracting torque (much as a helicopter uses a second propeller to overcome the rotation induced by the first). If all else fails, we can switch to a different strategy for movement: instead of using friction, we use balance, moving one leg at a time a short distance forward while balancing carefully on the other. Animals with four feet have an advantage here.

Generally, an object will fall over if it experiences a net torque: look at Figure 14.2. Both objects are experiencing an upward force from the ground and a downward force due to their weight, which can be thought of as passing through the center of gravity. In the first case, the weight is directed through a point of contact with the ground at P, which means that the net torque is zero. But in the second case, the weight passes through the ground outside the point of contact, which means that the point Q acts as a fulcrum.

NOTE

You might think in the first case that since the center of gravity is not above the center of the line of contact, there would be a net force to one side of it, giving it a torque. However, just as the weight acts through the center of gravity, the reaction force also balances out and can be thought of as a point force upward at P. The effect is a little like when you use two trestle tables to support a platform: the weight is distributed across the two fulcra. In this case, the trestle is upside down!

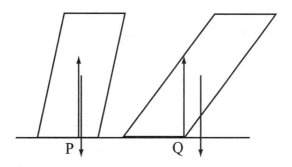

FIGURE 14.2   Falling over.

When we walk, we use our sense of balance to manipulate these forces, rolling our foot to change the point of contact with the ground, shifting our arms and our hips. Eventually, we reach a moment when we begin to fall over, but then our other leg reaches the ground and catches us. But when we're running, we need to take advantage of friction too.

In Figure 14.3, you can see how we make use of the forces in the previous example to maximize the advantage of friction. When running, we get a much stronger torque from the ground, so to stop ourselves from spinning, we lean forward, creating a counter-torque. As a bonus, it also means that the force we can apply to the ground is greater, since a greater proportion of the strength of our legs is directed along the line of the ground.

FIGURE 14.3   Using friction when running.

EXERCISES

Exercise 14.1

Write a function `applyFriction(velocity, topSpin, radius, mass, muK, muS, time)` for calculating the motion of a pool ball taking friction into account.

The function should take the current status of the ball and return its new velocity and spin, taking into account the coefficients of friction with the baize (and assuming friction is applied at a constant level during the short time period).

SUMMARY

This was the first of three chapters dealing with some slightly less common parts of mechanics. These are situations that you're unlikely to encounter in any run-of-the-mill situations, but from time to time you do need to include them, or at the least to understand how they work in order to create your own simplified version. For that reason, they're a little shorter on actual code samples and equations and longer on explanation, which should come as something of a relief.

In this chapter we've seen how friction works and applies in different circumstances, and one example of how to use it in a game context. In the next chapter we'll conclude our exploration of energy and momentum by looking at continuous momentum and tension.

YOU SHOULD NOW KNOW

- why *friction* occurs and how to calculate it
- the meaning of the term *coefficient of friction* and the difference between *static* and *kinetic* friction
- what *drag* is and how it is calculated
- how friction converts between linear and angular momentum
- why moving objects fall over

15 Strings, Pulleys, and Conveyor Belts

OVERVIEW

In this chapter we'll look at some special examples of calculations with energy and momentum, with the slightly tenuous link that they all involve objects that are connected in some way. The first section looks at how we deal with the situation when two objects are tied together with an idealized string, and why using a pulley makes it easier to lift something. In the second part, we look at examples of momentum changes due to continuous changes of mass, such as loading a conveyor belt or burning fuel in a rocket.

ON THE CD Code samples from this chapter are implemented in *math.cst* in the script *chapter 15 (continuous momentum)*.

PULLING THINGS AROUND

When you attach a string to something, you can make it move without touching it, simply by pulling on the string. It doesn't seem very miraculous, but when you think about it, something strange is occurring: somehow the force you exert on the string is being transferred down the string to affect the object at the other end. This is due to a force called *tension*.

The Inextensible String

In this section we're dealing with idealized objects called "light inextensible strings." These are somewhat similar to the idealized levers we encountered a couple of chapters ago: they are supposed to have no mass and to be completely without any elasticity (which we'll look at in the next chapter). They are also supposed to be impossible to tangle.

The only property that our strings have is a length l. If two objects are tied with string then they can't be more than a distance l apart—although they could be nearer than that. When taut, a string experiences a tension. The tension of a string acts in both directions and at all points of the string. In particular, an object tied at either end of the string experiences the same force T from the string (see Figure 15.1).

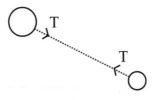

FIGURE 15.1   Two bodies experiencing tension from a taut string.

If you pull on one end of the string, exerting a force on it, then this creates a tension. This is really just an extension of Newton's Third Law: if you exert a force on the string, then it has to exert the same force on you. The end result is that your force is "transmitted" to the other object. Of course, if you tug on the string and stop, rather than pulling continuously, you'll start the other object moving and the string will cease to be taut.

For our ideal strings, length makes no difference to any of this—although it does affect certain other aspects that we'll look at. In the next chapter we'll also look at the way strings swing like pendulums.

Strings on Tables

The basic string is not very interesting from the point of view of physics. But what makes strings useful is that they allow us to change the direction in which a force acts. For example, in Figure 15.2 you can see a string that ties two boxes together, hanging off the edge of a table.

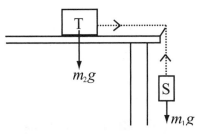

FIGURE 15.2 A string hanging off a table.

Here, the suspended box S is experiencing a force due to its weight. This creates a tension in the string, which is then transmitted through it to exert the same force on box T. Because of this tension, box T accelerates. What's more, because the string is inextensible, we know that both boxes must accelerate at the same rate. This gives us two equations to use with Newton's Second Law:

$$Tension = m_2 a$$

$$m_1 g - Tension = m_1 a$$

Eliminating the tension from these equations, we can see that $\left(m_1 + m_2 \right) a = m_1 g$ —that is, the two objects together accelerate as if they were both experiencing the weight of S.

We can also consider friction: box T will experience friction from the table, and this will depend only on the weight of T. If they are stationary, then the static friction on T is $\mu_s m_2 g$. Also, if they are stationary then we know that box S is in equilibrium, so the tension in the string is equal to its weight. This tells us that $\mu_s m_2 g \geq m_1 g$, so $\mu_s m_2 \geq m_1$. Equivalently, if this inequality is false, then the boxes cannot remain in static equilibrium.

Strings and Circular Motion

Another situation where we encounter strings is illustrated in Figure 15.3. When we hold the end of a string we can use it to make an object fly in a circle, as when you whirl a bullroarer over your head.

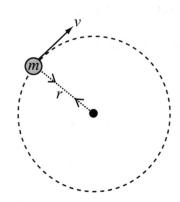

FIGURE 15.3   Using a string to create circular motion.

As we saw in an earlier chapter, to make an object move in a circle, we need to apply a constant centripetal force toward the center of the circle. The string provides this force through its tension, which it exerts in turn on the person holding the string (which they experience as a centrifugal force). We calculated this force to be $\frac{mv^2}{r}$, where v is the speed, r is the radius of the circle (length of the string in this case) and m is the mass of the orbiting body.

Now picture the situation as shown in Figure 15.4. Here, a string is passed through a hole in the table. Suppose the ball T on the table is spun around with a speed v. If we then release the ball S hanging under the hole, this exerts a force of $m_1 g$ downward. Meanwhile, ball T is exerting a force of $\frac{m_2 v^2}{r}$, where r is the length of string from the hole to T.

If the force due to S is greater than the force due to T, then the balls will sink further through the hole. This decreases r, but since angular momentum $m_2 v r$ must be conserved, v must increase proportionally. So we now have a radius $\frac{r}{k}$ and a speed kv for some $k > 1$, giving us a new force of $\frac{k m_2 v^2}{r}$. As the ball sinks further into the hole, the force due to the circular motion increases, while the force due to the weight stays constant. Eventually, they even out at a stable orbit, with $\frac{m_2 v^2}{r} = m_1 g$. There are an infinite number of such orbits, depending on the initial angular momentum of T—of course, in practice friction will slow the spinning ball down too

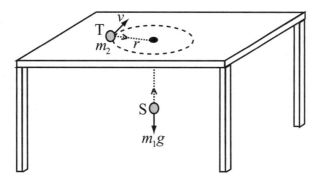

FIGURE 15.4 A string passing through a table.

fast for us to observe this phenomenon clearly. But it is nevertheless a good illustration of the same principle that applies to gravitational orbits. (In fact, mathematically it's rather similar to the interpretation of gravity as seen in general relativity, where an object's gravitational field is represented by a curvature of space due to its mass—like the ball S hanging through the hole.)

Pulleys

In the real world one of the principal uses of "strings"—or rather ropes—is in creating a pulley system such as a block-and-tackle. In Figure 15.5 you can see the simplest kind of pulley. This is really just a variant of the "box on a table" scenario we saw before: it's simply a means of changing the direction in which a force is exerted. To lift an object with this system requires exactly the same amount of effort as to do it without using the string at all (but at least we don't have to climb to the top of the building to do it).

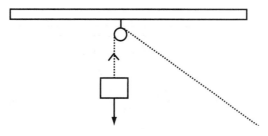

FIGURE 15.5 A simple pulley.

A more useful kind of pulley system is shown in Figure 15.6. In this instance, there are two pulleys. One holds the object to be lifted; the other is attached above it as before. The other end of the rope is also attached above the object. Now the situation is rather different, because *both* ends of the rope are exerting force. You exert a force *F* by pulling, and the ceiling exerts a corresponding reaction force *F*. Together, these combine to give a force of 2*F* on the object, so you double the lifting force.

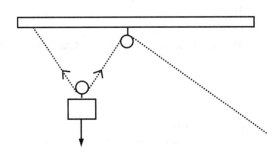

FIGURE 15.6   A two-pulley system.

Now, this should seem fairly magical, and all that force has to come from somewhere—after all, it should take the same amount of energy to lift the object a particular distance however you do it, and this is true. The answer is in the concept of *work* that we looked at before. Although you are lifting the object with twice the force, you move it only half as far—you need twice as much rope to make it lift the same distance. Thus the amount of work done, and hence energy used, is the same.

By adding more pulleys, we can make the force as small as we like (at least until the friction in the pulleys becomes significant). Figure 15.7 shows an example with four pulleys (although in practice this would be very unstable and the pulleys at the bottom would be replaced by a single pulley with the rope wrapped around it in two separate loops).

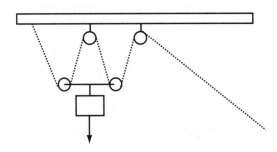

FIGURE 15.7   A four-pulley system.

This is really just another example of the *gearing* concept that we looked at in the previous chapter: trading force for distance or speed.

CONTINUOUS MOMENTUM

We flirted with the question of rockets a few chapters ago, and asked how it might be possible to take into account the fact that their mass changes as they burn up fuel, but deferred this until now—so we'll take a look at how this might be calculated.

Conveyor Belts

Let's start by looking at the opposite problem. Suppose a conveyor belt is being loaded with some fine substance like sand at a rate of k kg per second. We assume that the sand is loaded gently, so that the grains don't roll about. If our conveyor belt is traveling at a constant speed v, how much power does it need?

Apart from friction in the belt, it doesn't actually matter how long the conveyor belt is: once the sand is moving, keeping it moving is not difficult because of Newton's First Law. This means that the only question we're interested in is how much energy is being given to the sand as it is loaded. This is a fairly simple question: each second, k kg of sand is accelerated to a speed of v, so its kinetic energy goes from zero to $\frac{1}{2}kv^2$. This means that the power of the conveyor has to be $\frac{1}{2}kv^2$.

What about the force exerted? With the aid of the power calculation, this is not difficult: since power = force × velocity, the force is $\frac{1}{2}kv$.

We can use the same kinds of calculation to deal with escalators, or with those strange objects called paternosters which are like a vertical escalator. An escalator is just like a conveyor belt, but instead of just moving things horizontally, it also lifts them up. This makes the calculation a little more complicated, as it depends on how long the escalator is.

Figure 15.8 shows an escalator in action with a speed of v, a horizontal length l and a vertical height h. We'll suppose at first that it is fully loaded, and that people walk onto it at a constant rate of k kg per second (of course, this is not realistic and people actually walk on one-by-one, but we'll assume these irregularities average out).

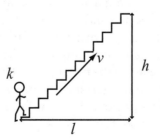

FIGURE 15.8 An escalator.

First of all we'll define the length d of the escalator, which is $\sqrt{l^2 + h^2}$. Using this, we can calculate how heavy the escalator is. It takes a person a time $\frac{d}{v}$ to reach the top of the escalator. During this time $\frac{kd}{v}$ kg will join the escalator, which means that this is always the mass of people on the stairs. Each second, they go up a distance of $\frac{hv}{d}$, so the potential energy they are given is $\frac{kd}{v} \times g \times \frac{hv}{d} = kgh$. (It should be fairly obvious that this could be calculated more simply, but this calculation should make everything clear.) Of course we haven't taken take into account the mass of the escalator itself.

On top of this, we have the kinetic energy calculation, which is the same as before: the kinetic energy added per second is $\frac{1}{2}kv^2$, so the total power is $\frac{1}{2}kv^2 + kgh$, and the force is $\frac{1}{2}kv + \frac{kgh}{v}$. Notice that the horizontal length of the escalator cancels out in the end—it's only the vertical height that is relevant. This makes sense, since a conveyor belt is just a special case of an escalator with height 0.

Subway operators often complain about the additional wear and tear on the machinery due to people walking up the stairs. If people choose to walk up the escalator, then the escalator has to exert the force necessary to propel them faster. This means it needs greater power. On the other hand, increasing the velocity decreases the time during which they are on the escalator, which decreases the total mass being lifted, and this is reflected in the second term of the force equation. So although the power needed is greater, the force may not be: when $v > \sqrt{2gh}$ the force starts to decrease as the velocity increases.

If the passengers walk down a downward escalator, the same kinds of calculations apply. In this case, the power used is less, and up to a certain speed the force will decrease too, after which the force required is higher.

Rocket Fuel

Dealing with rockets is a little like dealing with an escalator when people stop getting on: as they reach the top, they leave and thus decrease the mass being raised. A rocket is much the same: the longer it travels, the lower its mass, because it uses up fuel as it goes.

Suppose a rocket burns fuel at a constant power P, and uses up fuel at a rate of k kg per second. If it starts with a mass of m_0 and travels for a time t, how fast will it be traveling at the end? This is an example of the *rocket equation*, whose derivation is very complicated and involves differential equations so we won't look at it here. The rocket equation makes use of the fact that the force on the rocket results from the ejection of material out of the back. If we know the speed at which it is ejected, and the mass of the fuel, then we know its momentum, and just as with the conveyor belt, we can determine the power and the force. Conversely, if we know the power, then we can calculate how fast it is ejected: each second, we give k kg of fuel an energy of P, so its velocity is $\sqrt{\frac{2P}{k}}$.

The rocket equation is based on this velocity, which we'll call u. Then if the rocket starts with a velocity of v_0, and it moves under constant gravity, its velocity is given by

$$v_0 + u \log \left(\frac{m_0}{m(t)} \right) - gt$$

This applies however the fuel is burned, but in our case we can plug in the values of this particular problem to get

$$v = v_0 + \sqrt{\frac{P}{2k}} \log \left(\frac{m_0}{m_0 - kt} \right) - gt$$

To find how high it will travel in this time, we need to integrate the rocket equation, but we won't do that!

As a general rule, these equations get very complicated very fast, and you're better off using numerical methods—that is, simply calculating the rocket's position from moment to moment. Here's a set of functions that will do this (it's based on a constant gravitational field; you are asked to create one for a varying gravitational field in Exercise 15.1).

```
function getRocketPosition(currentPosition, currentSpeed, currentMass,
massBurnRate, fuelVelocity, gravity, time)
    set MassBurned to massBurnRate * time
    set speed to getRocketSpeed(currentSpeed, currentMass, massBurned,
fuelVelocity, gravity, time)
    return currentPosition + speed * time
end function

function getRocketSpeed(currentSpeed, currentMass, massBurned,
fuelVelocity, gravity, time)
    return currentSpeed + fuelVelocity * log (currentMass/(currentMass-
massBurned)) - gravity * time
end function
```

EXERCISES

Exercise 15.1

Modify the `getRocketSpeed()` and `getRocketPosition()` functions from the chapter to deal with a varying gravitational field.

Your revised functions should calculate the acceleration due to gravity at a particular point and adjust accordingly. If you feel even braver, try adjusting them to deal with velocity in any direction, rather than only vertical.

SUMMARY

This is the shortest chapter in the book, but it was necessary just to tie up a few loose ends, particularly to clarify the concepts of power and work. We've also looked at some examples of more complex calculations involving forces, energy and momentum, and got an inkling of how complicated NASA's job is.

In the next chapter we'll complete our exploration of the more obscure aspects of mechanics by looking at springs, elastics and pendulums. These turn up rather more often than you might think.

YOU SHOULD NOW KNOW

- the meaning of the word *tension* as it applies to a *string*, and how it acts
- how to calculate the motion of objects tied together by a string
- the action of a *pulley* as related to force and energy
- how to calculate motion of objects going on to a *conveyor belt* or escalator
- how to calculate the motion of a *rocket* burning fuel

16 Oscillations

OVERVIEW

In the previous chapter we looked at inextensible strings. Now we're going to see how the behavior of a string changes when it can stretch. In particular, we're going to look at how a particle moves when it is attached to a spring—the bouncing motion we call an *oscillation*. We'll see how the same motion occurs in many circumstances in nature, and then we'll create a function describing a complex spring that has both extensible and inextensible properties. Finally we'll see how these concepts extend to help us deal with waves, and explain some of the properties of light.

Code samples from this chapter are implemented in *math.cst* in the script *chapter 16 (oscillations)*. The *springs* demo uses them in context.

ON THE CD

SPRINGS

When we use the word *spring*, we have in mind a similar kind of idealization as with the inextensible strings in the previous chapter. A spring is a light string with a certain natural length *l*, which can be stretched to a greater length. When stretched, the spring experiences a tension, which acts equally in both directions. These calculations apply to both elastic bands and to actual springs, and we'll use the term spring to refer to both, since the term "elastic" has another meaning in the context of collisions.

The Force in a Stretched Spring

The tension in a spring can be calculated very simply. A spring has a value called the *coefficient of elasticity*, *k*, which describes how stretchy it is. The tension in a stretched spring is then proportional to its *extension*, which is the difference between its current length and its unstretched length. This is *Hooke's Law*:

$$Force = -k \times Extension$$

Why the negative sign? This is conventional because the force is always directed backward, toward the unstretched "equilibrium" length. In particular, if a particle is attached to the end of the spring as in Figure 16.1, it experiences the tension backward along the length of the spring.

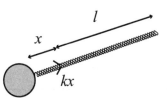

FIGURE 16.1   A particle on the end of a spring.

Some springs are only *extensive*, that is, they only experience a tension when stretched outwards. An elastic band has no tension when unstretched, while an extensive spring becomes something more like a rigid rod. Other springs are *compressive*, which means that they experience a tension outward when their length is less than the standard length—a negative extension leads to a positive tension, in other words.

When a spring is under tension (compressive or extensive), it contains energy, known as *elastic potential energy* or e.p.e. It takes work to stretch a spring, and the energy is released when it is allowed to bounce back. The energy is given by:

$$Energy = \frac{1}{2} \times k \times extension^2$$

From these two equations you can see that the coefficient of elasticity has units of kg s^{-2}.

One more thing about real-life springs. They can't be stretched indefinitely, instead they reach a length called the *elastic limit*. Beyond this point, the coefficient of elasticity increases significantly, making them much harder to stretch; they also won't return to their original length when released. There are further elastic limits beyond that point (until the material is so stretched that the bonds between its constituent molecules start to break and it snaps). For our purposes, though, we can simply say that beyond the elastic limit the spring starts to act like an inextensible string.

Using Springs to Measure Weight

The canonical example of springs in action is illustrated in Figure 16.2. Here we have a particle with mass m attached to an extensive spring (with unstretched length l) whose other end is attached to the ceiling.

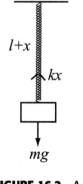

FIGURE 16.2 A particle hanging from a spring.

If the particle is in equilibrium, then we can say that the tension in the spring must be equal to its weight. Therefore we can say:

$$k \times extension = mg$$

$$extension = \frac{mg}{k}$$

Since for a particular spring and in constant gravity the values of g and k are constant, this means that the extension of a spring is directly proportional to the mass of the particle, which is why we can use a spring to measure something's weight.

If the particle is somewhere other than the equilibrium position, with an arbitrary extension x, then the force on it is equal to $mg - kx$ This is equivalent to a different situation: a particle moving horizontally (i.e., without gravity) under the action of a spring that is both compressive and extensive, whose unstretched length is $l + \frac{mg}{k}$, the equilibrium length of the first spring. This is useful, as it allows us to ignore gravity when calculating the motion of the particle.

SIMPLE HARMONIC MOTION

What happens when we pull the particle down from the equilibrium position and release it? It bounces up and down in an oscillation. This oscillation turns out to have a very familiar form, which is called *simple harmonic motion* or *SHM*.

The Equation of SHM

We can calculate the equation for simple harmonic motion by looking at the formula for Hooke's Law. By applying Newton's Second Law, we see that

$$ma = -kx$$

where x is the extension, m is the mass, and a is the acceleration. All of these quantities must be measured in the same direction. This is another example of a differential equation:

$$\frac{d^2x}{dt^2} = -\frac{k}{m}x$$

As we have seen (in Chapter 6 and elsewhere), differential equations can be nasty customers. But in this case it turns out that there is a simple function that solves it. You've already encountered two functions whose second derivative is their own negative: they are sin() and cos(): recall that

$$\frac{d}{dt}\sin t = \cos t; \frac{d}{dt}\cos t = -\sin t$$

so $\frac{d^2}{dt^2}(\sin t) = -\sin t$; $\frac{d}{dt} \frac{d^2}{dt^2}(\cos)t = -\cos t$

It only takes a little tweaking to adapt these functions to create a general formula that solves the differential equation for SHM:

$$x = A\sin(\omega t) + B\cos(\omega t)$$

where A and B, are arbitrary constants and ω is equal to $\sqrt{\frac{k}{m}}$. Another useful way of writing the same thing is as

$$x = C\sin(\omega t + p)$$

where again, C and p are arbitrary constants. We'll be using this form of the equation here, although both forms are common.

It is simple to convert from one form of the equation to the other: recall that sin(ωt + p) = sin(ωt)cos p + cos(ωt) sin p, so we have in the two equations, A = C cos p; B = C sin p.

We can calculate the velocity of the particle at a particular time by differentiating the SHM equation, which gives us

$$\dot{x} = C\omega\cos(\omega t + p)$$

Differentiating again gives us $\ddot{x} = -C\omega^2 \sin(\omega t + p) = -\omega^2 x$ as required.

As usual with a differential equation, we have a family of equations all of which are valid solutions. Any one of these is a possible motion for the object on the spring; we choose which one occurs by setting the *initial conditions*, that is, what the particle is doing at the start. If we pull it down by a certain distance d and then release it, then we will get $C = d$, $p = 0$. If we give it a push from equilibrium so it has an initial velocity v, we get $C = \frac{v}{\omega}$, $p = \frac{\pi}{2}$. We'll look at these calculations more in a moment.

So what does all this actually mean? What does the motion look like? Well, when $t = -\frac{p}{\omega}$, the particle has the position 0 and velocity $C\omega$ (since $\sin(0) = 0$ and $\cos(0) = 1$). If C is positive then the extension gradually increases, until at time $t = \frac{1}{\omega}\left(\frac{\pi}{2} - p\right)$ it reaches a maximum of C. Then it decreases to 0 again and goes back the other way, before returning to zero at $t = \frac{1}{\omega}(2\pi - p)$. This is just the generic sine wave that we saw in Chapter 4 (see Figure 16.3). The time $\frac{2\pi}{\omega} = 2\pi\sqrt{\frac{m}{k}}$ is called the *period* of the motion: the time for one complete oscillation. The value ω itself is called the *frequency* (although really the frequency should be the inverse of the period: the number of oscillations per second). While, we're on the subject, the value p is called the *phase* of the motion—how far the waveform is shifted from zero along the time axis—and *C* is called the *amplitude*, or maximum displacement from equilibrium.

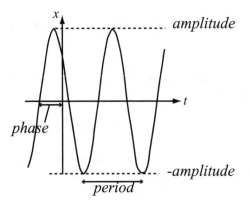

FIGURE 16.3   The position of a particle over time under SHM.

Other Examples of SHM

As you may recall, the position of a particle when moving along a sine wave is equivalent to the *y*-coordinate of a point on the circumference of a turning wheel, so this means that a point on a wheel moves under SHM. In fact, the values *C* and *p* relate to this interpretation: *C* is the radius of the wheel and *p* is a measure of how far round the wheel the particle starts (see Figure 16.4).

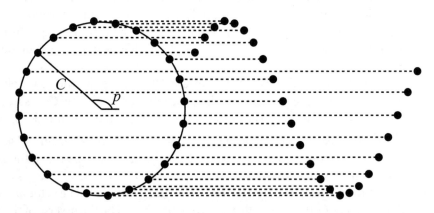

FIGURE 16.4   SHM and circular motion.

We take advantage of this when using circular motion to drive pistons. When we attach a rod to a point on a wheel and allow it to slide up and down as the wheel turns, its tip oscillates under SHM (or close to it: because the angle of the rod changes, the motion is a little different from pure SHM).

SHM also occurs in the motion of a pendulum. Again, it is a slight approximation and only works when the oscillations are quite small. When a particle is attached to a pendulum (a light inextensible string of length l) at an angle θ, it experiences a force W downward due to its weight, and a tension T from the string. In particular, the radial force on the particle (providing the torque) is $-W \sin\theta$ (notice the minus sign: the force is directed in the opposite direction to the angle). As we've noted before, for small values of θ (oscillations of about 5° are usually considered small enough), $\sin\theta$ is very close to θ, so the torque acting on the particle is approximately $-Wl\theta$, which gives us another example of Hooke's Law:

$$Torque \approx -Wl\theta = -mgl\theta$$

$$AngularAcceleration \approx \frac{-mgl\theta}{momentOfInertia} = \frac{-mgl\theta}{ml^2} = -\frac{g\theta}{l}$$

Notice that in this case, the mass of the particle cancels out, so that the frequency depends only on the length of the string: to be precise, the period is proportional to the square root of the length.

Other examples of SHM in action include a buoy floating on wavy water, the vibration of a plucked guitar string, the vibrations of atoms in a crystal, the variation of an alternating current, the variation in a population of animals over time, and many others. Whenever you find a situation where there is an equilibrium position, and a force that is exerted continuously to try to restore that equilibrium, you will find something very like SHM.

It's also worth noting that waves themselves are formed of components moving under SHM. A light wave consists of oscillating electric and magnetic fields, whose field strength at any particular location varies over time in an SHM pattern. Each oscillation induces an oscillation next to it, which lags a little behind, with the result that the situation looks like a sine wave traveling forward over time. We'll look into this a little more, later in the chapter.

Calculating the Parameters

Let's return to the question of those parameters C and p. As we saw above, these represent the "amplitude" and "phase" of the motion respectively. While a particular mass on a particular spring will always oscillate with the same frequency, the amplitude and phase vary from situation to situation, according to how fast the particle is put into motion, and how far away from equilibrium it is released.

The easiest way to calculate these values is to know the velocity v and extension d at time 0. Knowing these, we can use the velocity and position formulae of SHM as simultaneous equations to determine the parameter values:

$$d = C\sin(p)$$
$$v = C\omega\cos(p)$$

so

$$\frac{d}{v} = \frac{\tan(p)}{\omega}$$
$$\omega^2 d^2 + v^2 = C^2\omega^2$$

which is to say:

$$p = \operatorname{atan}\left(\frac{\omega d}{v}\right)$$
$$C = \frac{\sqrt{\omega^2 d^2 + v^2}}{\omega}$$

More generally, we can do the same calculations for any time t: the calculation for C remains unchanged and the calculation for p merely changes to:

$$p = a\tan\left(\frac{\omega d}{v}\right) - \omega t$$

DAMPED HARMONIC MOTION

As always, real life is not as simple as SHM would have us believe. Real oscillations don't go on forever, they lose energy over time. But as it happens it's not too hard to take this factor, called *damping*, into account to create more realistic and varied motion.

The Equation of DHM

Damped harmonic motion or *DHM* is a slight modification to the SHM equation. We add a new *damping factor* to the differential equation, which is proportional to the velocity rather than the acceleration:

$$\ddot{x} = -\omega^2 x - 2D\dot{x}$$

In this book we're using the value 2D to represent the damping factor, because it simplifies later calculations, but it's more conventional to use the letter b to represent this coefficient.

Solving this differential equation is a little more work than before, and involves using a "trial solution," which leads to a particular quadratic equation. Leaving out the details which are not too difficult but outside our scope, the end result is the following:

$$x = Ae^{-rt}$$

where $r = -D \pm \sqrt{D^2 - \omega^2}$.

Now, depending on the values of D and ω, this has different results. If we define the variable α to be $D^2 - \omega^2$ then if $\alpha > 0$ this equation has real solutions, and we end up with a family of equations of the form

$$x = Ae^{\left(-D-\sqrt{\alpha}\right)t} + Be^{\left(-D+\sqrt{\alpha}\right)t}$$

When $\alpha = 0$, so $D = \omega$, the motion is similar to the above except that there is only one value of r. This means that we get a slightly simpler equation:

$$x = \left(A + Bt\right)e^{-Dt} = \left(A + Bt\right)e^{-\omega t}$$

If $\alpha < 0$ then we have a situation where the equation has no real roots. This is not the place to look at complex numbers, but it turns out that you can still solve the differential equation by using the imaginary number i, which is defined as the square root of -1. Using this method, we can derive the formula

$$x = C\sin\left(\varphi t + p\right)e^{-Dt}$$

where $\varphi = \sqrt{-\alpha}$.

This equation, while harder to discover, looks much more like the SHM equation we saw before, but there are two main differences. The first is that it has the additional exponential term, which is negative, so it makes the amplitude of the motion decrease over time. The second is that the frequency is different: the greater the value of D the lower the frequency, until D reaches the *critical damping* value where $D = \omega$. Above that value, we go into the first kind of behavior: now the frequency is essentially zero, that is to say, the particle doesn't oscillate at all. Instead, it follows an exponential curve (or rather, the sum of two exponential curves). So there are three "zones" of behavior:

- *underdamping* (like SHM but decreasing exponentially in amplitude): $\alpha < 0$
- *critical damping* ($\alpha = 0$)
- *overdamping* (exponential decrease with no oscillation): $\alpha > 0$

You can see graphs of these different kinds of behavior in Figure 16.5.

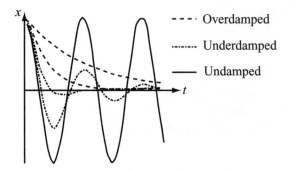

FIGURE 16.5   Possible motions of a particle under different levels of damping. Each starts with the same initial conditions, and all the springs have the same coefficient of elasticity.

Damping in Practice

We can differentiate each of the motion formulas as before to get the velocity function:
Underdamping:

$$\dot{x} = C\varphi\cos\left(\varphi t + p\right)e^{-Dt} - CD\sin\left(\varphi t + p\right)e^{-Dt}$$
$$= C\varphi\cos\left(\varphi t + p\right)e^{-Dx} - Dx$$

Critical damping:

$$\dot{x} = Be^{-\omega t} - \omega\left(A + Bt\right)e^{-\omega t}$$
$$= \left(B - \omega\left(A + Bt\right)\right)e^{-\omega t}$$
$$= Be^{-\omega t} - Dx$$

(remember that for critical damping $D = \omega$).

Overdamping:

$$\dot{x} = A\left(-D - \sqrt{\alpha}\right)e^{\left(-D - \sqrt{\alpha}\right)t} + B\left(-D + \sqrt{\alpha}\right)e^{\left(-D + \sqrt{\alpha}\right)t}$$

or more simply:

$$\dot{x} = Ar_1 e^{r_1 t} + Br_2 e^{r_2 t}$$

Applying damping is really no more than plugging values into these new equations. But calculating the parameters is a little more detailed than before because the velocity function is so much more complicated (incidentally, don't forget that D is a known constant property of the spring, like the coefficient of elasticity, not a parameter like C and p).

If we know the distance and velocity at time t as before, then we can apply them like this:

Underdamping:

$$d = C\sin\left(\omega t + p\right)e^{-Dt}$$
$$v = C\omega\cos\left(\omega t + p\right)e^{-Dt} - Dd$$

so

$$\frac{d}{v + Dd} = \frac{1}{\omega}\tan\left(\omega t + p\right)$$
$$d^2\omega^2 + \left(v + Dd\right)^2 = C^2\omega^2 e^{-2Dt}$$

giving us

$$p = \text{atan}\left(\frac{d\omega}{v + Dd}\right) - \omega t$$

$$C = \frac{\sqrt{d^2\omega^2 + \left(v + Dd\right)^2}}{\omega e^{-Dt}}$$

Critical damping:

$$d = \left(A + Bt\right)e^{-\omega t}$$
$$v = \left(B - \omega\left(A + Bt\right)\right)e^{-\omega t}$$

so

$$\omega d + v = B\left(\omega t + 1\right)e^{-\omega t}$$
$$\left(1 - \omega t\right)d - tv = Ae^{-\omega t}$$

If $t = 0$, then this becomes the simpler:

$$A = d$$
$$B = \omega d + v$$

Overdamping:

$$d = Ae^{r_1 t} + Be^{r_2 t}$$
$$v = Ar_1 e^{r_1 t} + Br_2 e^{r_2 t}$$

so

$$r_1 d - v = B\left(r_1 - r_2\right)e^{r_2 t} = -2B\sqrt{\alpha}e^{r_2 t}$$
$$r_2 d - v = -A\left(r_1 - r_2\right)e^{r_1 t} = 2A\sqrt{\alpha}e^{r_1 t}$$

giving us

$$A = \frac{r_2 d - v}{2\sqrt{\alpha}}e^{-r_1 t}$$

$$B = -\frac{r_1 d - v}{2\sqrt{\alpha}}e^{-r_2 t}$$

Again, if $t = 0$, this is the simpler:

$$A = -\frac{r_2 d - v}{2\alpha}$$

$$B = \frac{r_1 d - v}{2\alpha}$$

So: damping is not difficult, but it does require a bit of thought!

PHENOMENA

Although this is all you need to know about the physics of springs, it's worth looking at a couple of phenomena that are important consequences of the equations. The first in particular is important when trying to build a simulation involving springs, as it can lead to instability.

Resonance: Pushing the Swing

We all know the stories about people who can break glass with their voice. This isn't just a matter of producing particularly high notes which miraculously cause things to break, there is a physical phenomenon behind it which is a major consequence of SHM.

Imagine a simple variation in the situation we saw earlier in Figure 16.2. This time, the top of the spring is attached to a vibrating rod, which moves it up and down at a certain *driving frequency f* with an amplitude of *A*. As you will realize, the driving oscillation will impart a force to the system. Each time the bar moves up it increases the tension in the spring, when it drops it releases it. So what will the particle do?

Well, it's a little messy as you'll see if you try it out. The particle bounces around rather erratically (*chaotically*, in fact). But some patterns do emerge. In particular, you'll see if you change the driving frequency that the amplitude of the motion of the particle (that is to say, the maximum distance from equilibrium during its chaotic path) increases as you get closer to the natural frequency of the spring. When you reach the natural frequency, the particle starts to go crazy: it bounces higher and higher without end—infinitely high, theoretically. Then as you increase the driving frequency further the particle calms down again. Try applying damping too, to see how it affects the motion.

There's a reasonably simple relationship between the amplitude *C* of the motion and the driving frequency:

$$C = \frac{kA}{\sqrt{m^2\left(f^2 - \omega^2\right)^2 + 4D^2\omega^2}}$$

Here the value *kA* represents the maximum force exerted by the driving oscillation, or the *driving force*.

This formula applies when the driving oscillation is sinusoidal (in the shape of a sine wave, i.e., SHM). When the driving oscillation has some other pattern, the formula is different, but only by a constant factor: the basic behavior is the same.

NOTE

When the driving frequency is equal to the natural frequency ω, the first term in the square root drops out. In SHM, with $D = 0$, this means that C becomes infinitely large. Otherwise, C is inversely proportional to the damping factor. So in systems with little or no damping, the oscillation starts to spiral out of control. This is called *resonance*, and the natural frequency is also called the *resonant frequency*.

You use this principle every time you push a child (or yourself) on a swing. At the topmost point of the swing, you apply a force. This force is therefore naturally applied at the same frequency as the oscillation, with the result that the oscillation grows in amplitude and fun. Because a pane of glass also has a natural frequency, if you drive it with a sound wave of the same frequency, it vibrates so hard that it shatters (more on sound in a moment).

All of this shows that when you create a spring system in a simulation, it's important to give it some damping factor, or at least an elastic limit, otherwise you may find things getting out of hand.

Coupling: Linked Motion

When we combine two springs together by means of another they are said to be *coupled*. Coupling means that the motion of each spring is affected by the other: energy is constantly being transferred between them. The result is that you can get some extremely complicated motion. There's no need to look into the mathematics in detail, but it's worth noting one particular result.

If two identical coupled springs are set in motion in the same phase, then they will swing in parallel at the natural frequency. This is true despite the fact that both are experiencing a tension due to the coupling spring. If they are set in motion exactly *out of phase*, meaning that one is lifted up and the other is pulled down and then they are both released at the same time, they will continue to oscillate out of phase, but the frequency will be higher than before. These are called the two *natural modes* of the motion.

In general, any two coupled oscillators yield a system with two natural modes, each with its own frequency, which depends on the frequencies of the two oscillators and of the coupling spring. Any other motion of the system is actually a linear sum of two such oscillations. These concepts are very important in acoustics, for example.

CALCULATING SPRING MOTION

We've managed to get through the whole chapter without any code, but we'll make good on that now. Here we'll create three functions that calculate the motion of a particle attached to an arbitrary spring. We'll give the spring a number of characteristics: coefficient of elasticity, length and so on, and the particle will have a mass. We'll also include an optional force of gravity.

The three functions are useful in different circumstances. The first is a pure mechanical system: it simply returns the force on the particle due to the spring (in this case, you would need to apply gravity separately). This is the only method you can use in general circumstances, such as when neither end-point of the spring is fixed in place.

```
function forceDueToSpring (end1, end2, velocity1, velocity2,
springLength, elasticity, damping, elasticLimit,  compressiveness,
minLength)
   // the particle we're interested in is attached to end2
   set v to end1-end2
   set d to magnitude(v)
   if d=0 then return vector(0,0) // just skip for this timestep if they
coincide

   // loose elastics have no force when compressed
   if d<=springlength then
     if compressiveness="loose " then return vector(0,0)
   end if

   // apply second elastic limit (inextensible behavior)
   if d>=elasticLimit*1.2 or d<=minLength*0.9 or (d<=springLength*0.9
and compressiveness="rigid") then
     return "bounce"
   end if

   // apply first elastic limit (increased force and damping)
   if d>=elasticLimit or d<=minLength or (d<=springLength and
compressiveness=#rigid) then
     multiply elasticity by 20
     set damping to max(damping*10,20)
   end if

   // calculate force by Hooke's law
   set e to d-springlength
   set v to v/d
   if damping>0 then
     set vel to component(velocity1-velocity2,v)
     set f to damping*vel+elasticity*e
   else
     set f to elasticity*e
   end if
   return f*v
end function
```

The only complicated part of this is how we deal with the elastic limit. Simulated springs are a little more complicated than real ones because you can get impossible situations, like a spring that is extended significantly beyond its elastic limit. This happens both by incorrect setting up of the simulation (especially when users are allowed to drag objects around), which is avoidable, and resonance coupled with a gradual accumulation of rounding errors, which isn't. To deal with this, we create a "tiered" elastic limit system. Beyond the set elastic limit of the spring, we increase both the coefficient of elasticity and the damping coefficient. The effect of the former is to create a strong force inward, which is important. But the latter is also necessary because it ensures that the system loses energy rapidly, which means that on the next oscillation it doesn't overcome the elastic limit again.

We also create a second elastic limit, arbitrarily set at 1.2 times the first. If the spring is trying to extend beyond this point, we treat it as a collision with a solid wall perpendicular to the spring. This ensures that the spring can never extend past the second limit.

We're not taking into account the principal aspect of the elastic limit, which is that after it is exceeded, the physical properties of the spring itself would be changed (its natural length may increase, or it may snap, for example).

NOTE

The second method is designed for slightly simpler situations, in particular for undamped, uncoupled springs, that is, a movable particle attached to a fixed point by a spring. The particle can move freely in all directions: for example, this method would be suitable for situations where a user can click and throw the particle, or where it's part of a system with collisions. In these cases, we can take advantage of conservation of energy to avoid the inevitable rounding errors that appear when dealing with forces applied individually at each time step. By knowing that the total energy of the particle is constant, we can calculate its speed at any moment as long as we know its position. The system can even deal with the situation when the "fixed" point is in fact moving under the user's control.

```
function particleOnSpring (end1, end2, speed, direction, mass,
totalEnergy, springLength, elasticity, compressive, timeStep, g)
    // Returns a list of position, speed, direction and total energy.
    // totalEnergy can have the value "unknown", in which case the
    function calculates it and returns it.

    set v to end1-end2
    set d to mag(v)
    set e to d-springLength
```

```
if totalEnergy="unknown" then
  // calculate energy
  set totalEnergy to mass*speed*speed/2
  if e>0 or compressive=TRUE then
    set epe to elasticity*e*e/2
    add epe to totalEnergy
  end if
  if g>0 then
    set gpe to mass*g*end2[2]
    subtract gpe from totalEnergy
  end if
end if

// calculate force
set f to vector(0,mass*g)
if e>0 or compressive=TRUE then
  if d>0 then
    add v*elasticity*e/d to f
  end if

end if

// calculate new position
set a to f/mass
set displacement to direction*speed*timeStep + a*timeStep*timeStep/2
set pos to end2 + displacement

// calculate new elastic energy
set newd to mag(pos-end1)
set newe to newd-springLength
if newe>0 or compressive=TRUE then
  set epe to elasticity*newe*newe/2
otherwise
  set epe to 0
end if

// calculate new kinetic energy and hence speed
set ke to totalEnergy-epe+mass*g*pos[2]
if ke<=0 then // NB: for safety
  set speed to 0
otherwise
  set speed to sqrt(2*ke/mass)
  set velocity to norm(displacement)
end if
```

```
    return Array(pos,speed,velocity,totalEnergy)
end function
```

Our final function is the simplest: it's a pure Damped Harmonic Motion oscillator (or SHM if damping = 0). Feed it an initial position and velocity, and a time *t*, and it will calculate the position and velocity at that time. Actually, we'll separate the functions into three, since it's pointless to calculate the parameters more than once, so it's best to store them. The first function calculates the parameters and the form of the motion, then the other two calculate the actual values when fed with the results of the first.

```
function calculateDHMparameters (initialPos, initialVel, elasticity,
damping)
    set omega to sqrt(elasticity)
    set d to damping/2
    set alpha to elasticity-d*d
    if d=0 then
        set p to atan(omega*initialPos/initialVel)
        set c to  sqrt(elasticity * initialPos * initialPos + initialVel
* initialVel)/omega
        return array("SHM", p, c)
    else if d<omega then
        set v to initialVel + d * initialPos
        set p to atan(initialPos * omega / v)
        set s to initialPos * initialPos * elasticity + v * v
        set c to sqrt(s)/omega
        return array("UnderDamped", p, c, sqrt(-alpha))
    else if d=omega then
        return array("Critical", initialPos, omega * initialPos +
initialVel)
    else
        set sq to sqrt(alpha)
        set r1 to -d-sq
        set r2 to -d+sq
        set a to (r2*initialPos - initialVel)/(2*sq)
        set b to -(r1*initialPos - initialVel)/(2*sq)
        return array("OverDamped", a, b, r1, r2)
    end if
end function

function getOscillatorPosition (elasticity, damping, params, time)
    set omega to sqrt(elasticity)
    set d to damping/2
```

```
    if params[1] is
        "SHM": return params[3] * sin(omega * time + params[2])
        "UnderDamped": return params[3] * sin(params[4] * time +
params[2]) * exp(-d * time)
        "Critical": return (params[2] + time * params[3]) * exp(-d*time)
        "OverDamped": return params[2] * exp(params[4]*time] + params[3]
* exp(params[5]*time)
    end if
end function

function getOscillatorSpeed (elasticity, damping, params, time, pos)
    // determine pos before running this function
    set omega to sqrt(elasticity)
    set d to damping/2

    if params[1] is
        "SHM": return params[3] * omega * cos(omega * time + params[2])
        "UnderDamped": return params[3] * omega * cos(params[4] * time +
params[2]) * exp(-d * time) - d*pos
        "Critical": return params[3] * exp(-d*time) -- d*pos
        "OverDamped": return params[2] * params[4] * exp(params[4]*time]
+ params[3] * params[5] * exp(params[5]*time)
    end if
end function
```

Of course, this set of functions is nothing but the equations of SHM and DHM translated into code.

WAVES

When coupled oscillators are joined together in a row, an interesting phenomenon occurs: an oscillation induced at one end can transfer its energy to the next in line, so the energy is gradually moved through the system, like a Newton's Cradle. The resulting cascade of oscillations is called a *wave*.

Wave Motion

A wave can be thought of in two ways. As you just read, a wave is a set of individual coupled oscillators. Each performs some oscillation and so induces an oscillation further down the line, slightly out of phase with it. So we end up with a picture like Figure 16.6 , which shows the oscillators at a frozen moment in time.

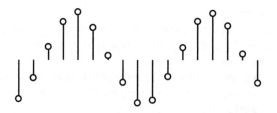

FIGURE 16.6   A series of coupled oscillators.

As you can see, in this case the silhouette of this picture is a sine wave, but it needn't be. However, whatever the motion is, it's a (near) copy of the driving oscillation at one end of the wave. This gives rise to the second picture of the wave, which is as a moving *waveform*: an object moving at a certain velocity. But it isn't an actual object, it's a kind of virtual object: a packet of energy transmitted through some medium. The velocity of the wave is the distance traveled over time by the waveform, and is determined by the physical properties of the medium: for a sine wave we often measure the position of successive *wavefronts* over time, where a wavefront is a peak of the waveform.

Once we know the speed v of the wave and its frequency f, we can calculate the distance between successive wavefronts, which is called the *wavelength*, denoted λ. This gives us a simple equation relating the three quantities: $v = f\lambda$.

Types of Wave

There are two principal kinds of wave, which are called *transverse* and *longitudinal* waves. A transverse wave is the kind pictured in Figure 16.6, where the oscillators are aligned perpendicularly to the direction of travel of the wave. These waves include particularly water waves and electromagnetic waves, otherwise known as light.

Longitudinal waves are a little harder to picture: the simplest example is a coiled spring (or "slinky"). When the string is stretched out and a sudden push is given to one end, this causes a ripple to travel through the coils, where each coil vibrates forward and backward along the direction of motion. Another example is sound waves, which are caused by air molecules vibrating backward and forward, creating small areas of lower and higher pressures (*rarefactions* and *compressions* respectively) which tend to restore equilibrium (see Figure 16.7).

Although they have different physical causes, the two kinds of wave behave in essentially the same way, and we often display longitudinal waves by a graph of, for example, pressure against time, which looks exactly like any other waveform. Longitudinal waves also reflect, refract, and diffuse exactly as transverse waves do.

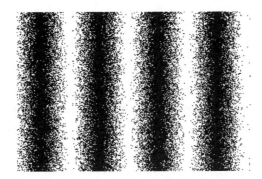

FIGURE 16.7   A longitudinal wave.

Both kinds of waves are often also drawn in a kind of "plan view," where the wave is represented by a series of lines representing particular wavefronts as shown in Figure 16.8.

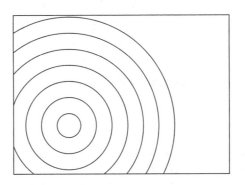

FIGURE 16.8   A wave represented as a succession of wavefronts.

Wave Addition and Subtraction

Because a wave is a virtual object, it's perfectly possible for several waves to be traveling through the same medium—in fact, it happens routinely. The air around you, for example, contains what could be considered to be an infinite number of different waves of light traveling in all directions. However, because waves are virtual, it's only we humans who consider this to be happening. In reality, all that is going on is a constant fluctuation of electromagnetic fields in space. The fact that energy is being transferred in the process is almost accidental.

We can conceive of waves in these two contradictory ways because they have an important property: they can be combined together into a single, more complex wave. For example (and we'll stick to one-dimensional waves here for clarity), we can combine the two waves in Figure 16.9 into a single, more complex waveform just by adding the displacement values at each point.

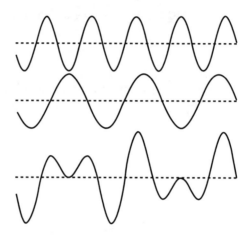

FIGURE 16.9 Adding waves.

This creates some interesting effects: for example, if we add two waves together which are exactly out of phase, they combine to give a straight line: no wave at all. Three waves all mutually out of phase by $2\pi/3$ produce the same result. Electricity is often transmitted in three simultaneous waves out of phase with one another in order to decrease the total current flow.

Of course, this means we can also *decompose* a wave into others by subtracting them. A technique called *Fourier analysis* allows us to decompose any waveform, no matter how complex, into sine waves of varying amplitude and phase. This is essentially what we do when listening to sound: we try to separate out different waveforms that correspond to different sound sources.

The decomposition of a wave into individual sine waves is called its *spectrum*, and it's a kind of "signature" for a particular wave emitter. Spectra are used, for example, to distinguish different kinds of chemical elements, each of which emits a characteristic spectrum of light radiation when burned. This allows us to work out the chemical composition of distant stars, and to find out some other interesting facts too, as we'll see. Particular musical instruments also have a characteristic sound spectrum (*timbre*), consisting of different integer and fraction multiples of the primary note (a sound wave is perceived as a particular note according to the frequency). Our perception of a complex waveform as a single sound at a single frequency is a very impressive bit of mental computation, and is the equivalent to our perception of a complex spectrum of light wavelengths as a single color, which we'll look at again in Chapter 20.

Wave Behavior

Several important behaviors of waves can be seen as a consequence of their physics. We'll start with *reflection*. When a wave strikes a barrier of some kind, depending on the natures of the wave and the barrier it may reflect off the barrier: if the barrier can't absorb the energy it is sent back where it came from. The wave reacts exactly like an elastic collision, bouncing off the wall at the same angle (the *angle of reflection*) as it struck (the *angle of incidence*)—see Figure 16.10.

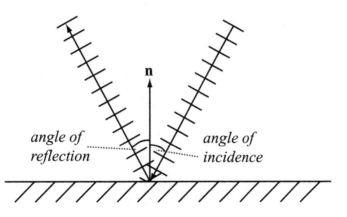

FIGURE 16.10   Reflection.

The next behavior is called *refraction*, and it occurs when the velocity of the wave changes. If you imagine a line of cars traveling at a speed of 60 mph hitting a zone where they have to travel at 30 kph (assuming they pay some attention to the restriction!), you can see that in the slower zone, they will end up bunched closer together. The same thing happens to the wavefronts of a wave: as it hits a new medium where its velocity is lower, the wavelength has to decrease too. This can also be seen directly from the wave equation, of course: since the frequency of the wave is dependent only on the driving oscillation, which is happening somewhere else, this is fixed for any particular wave.

Changing the wavelength has other consequences too, as we can see in Figure 16.11. When a succession of wavefronts hits a new medium at an angle, certain parts of the wavefront hit the start of the new medium (the *interface*) earlier than others. This causes the wave to change its direction, like steering a tank by altering the relative speeds of the two tracks.

You will have already seen this effect any time you looked at a "broken" straw in a drink. It's further complicated by the fact that different wavelengths travel at different speeds in the new material, which means they change directions by different amounts, so a wave made up of several different wavelengths will split into a fan of rays, which is the prism effect that creates rainbows. The amount by which a particular wave is deflected is described by *Snell's Law*, which says that if α is the angle of incidence and β is the angle of refraction, they are related by

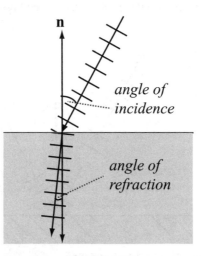

FIGURE 16.11   Refraction.

$$n_1 \sin \alpha = n_2 \sin \beta$$

where the n values are constant properties of the media through which the wave is traveling, called the *index of refraction*. For light, this is equal to the quotient of the speed of light in a vacuum, c, with the speed of this wavelength in the medium.

Another phenomenon is called the *Doppler effect*. Suppose Heathcliff is traveling past Cathy on a train and he calls out to her. The speed of the train means that the wavelength of the sound as she hears it will be shorter, because each wavefront is emitted closer to the previous one as Heathcliff travels forward.

We can calculate the Doppler shift, the amount by which the wavelength is shifted: if the train has a speed s and the sound has a frequency f then the wavelength will be decreased by a value s/f. If this takes the wavelength to a value less than zero, we'll hit a problem—this occurs when s is equal to the speed of sound, approximately 330 m/s. At that point, the wave is overtaken by the wave emitter, and we get a "sonic boom." The calculation works equally well as Heathcliff disappears into the sunset, we simply use a negative speed for s—and if Cathy is somewhere over the hills from the train then we'll need to use the dot product to find the component of the train's velocity that's traveling in her direction.

The Doppler effect is used as one of the principal pieces of evidence for the expansion of the universe. As we saw earlier, the characteristic spectrum of elements is used to determine the composition of stars. When we examine these spectra for particular stars, we find that on average they are all red-shifted, that is to say, their wavelengths have increased because all the stars are moving away from us (not so much the nearest stars, but those further away and in other galaxies). What's more the rate at which they are moving away depends on their distance from us, all of which suggests a picture of the universe as constantly expanding from an explosion.

There's nothing special that puts us at the center of the universe, by the way: All the stars are moving away from all the other stars because space itself is expanding, it's not just the objects expanding in distance to fill the existing space.

NOTE

One final property worth mentioning is diffraction, which occurs when a wave hits a partial barrier, either an obstacle or a wall with a hole in it. In that case, we get a situation like Figure 16.12, where the obstacle starts to act like a new source of the waves.

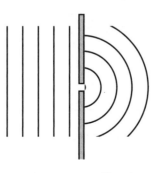

FIGURE 16.12   Diffraction.

When two holes or slits are near one another, the result can be quite interesting, since the two resulting waves, which have the same wavelength, frequency and velocity, combine at each point, creating an interference pattern. As you can see in Figure 16.13 the two waves are at some points out of phase with each other, resulting in no energy transfer, and at other points are exactly in phase, creating a double effect. If we place a bunch of detectors in a line, then we see interference fringes, whose discovery in the case of light was one of the principal pieces of evidence that light was a wave. (Of course, then Planck had to go and confuse things by proving light was a particle as well.)

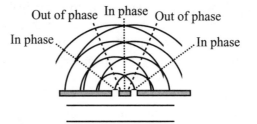

FIGURE 16.13   Interference patterns in double-slit diffraction.

EXERCISES

Exercise 16.1

Incorporate the functions in this chapter into a system that allows you to click, drag and throw an object on a virtual spring.

Try doing this for each of the systems given: you'll find subtle differences between them. The hardest is the `forceDueToSpring()` function, which requires a little work to make it reliable. In the version on the CD-ROM, you'll see that a few "fudging" factors are needed to deal with the problem of resonance.

SUMMARY

In this chapter we've seen a number of ways that an object can move when attached to an elastic band or spring. Springs are very useful in creating physical simulations, as they allow you to connect objects together, making virtual cloth, ropes, chains and similar systems of connected particles. We've also seen how such connected objects can create virtual packets of energy in the form of waves.

This concludes our examination of the more obscure topics of physics, and apart from a few more discussions of collisions in three dimensions we are mostly finished with physics now. We're now going to move back into mathematics and extend what we have already covered into the third dimension.

YOU SHOULD NOW KNOW

- how a *spring* works
- how to calculate the *tension* and *energy* in a stretched or compressed spring
- the meaning of the terms *coefficient of elasticity, damping,* and *elastic limit*
- how to calculate the position and velocity of a particle under *Simple* or *Damped Harmonic Motion*
- how and when the phenomena of *resonance* and *coupling* occur
- what a *wave* is and the meanings of *frequency, wavelength,* and *velocity* as applied to a wave
- how the physics of waves creates *reflection, refraction, diffusion,* and *Doppler shifting*

IV 3D Mathematics

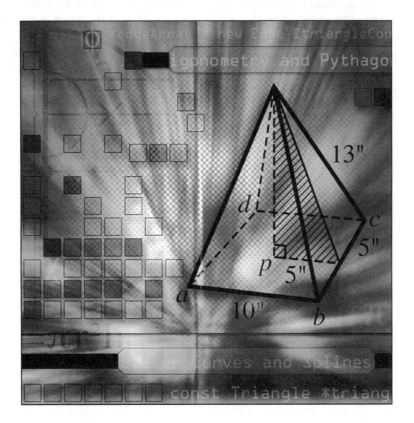

We've already done most of the work to enable us to move from two to three dimensions. The concepts of vectors, forces, energy, and momentum are the same in three dimensions as in two, and collision detection, while more complex, involves all the same techniques as before. In this fourth part of the book, we'll finish our exploration of mathematical and physical theory by taking this final step into 3D.

We'll start by looking at the basics of 3D space, and how it can be represented on a two-dimensional screen. Then we spend another chapter further extending the vector work we have done up to now, and introducing the concept of a transform. Chapter 19 deals with collision detection for 3D shapes, Chapter 20 looks at lighting and shading, and the final chapter covers various 3D modeling techniques for creating complex objects and moving surfaces such as waves on water.

3D is a subject much more widely covered than the more general techniques in this book, and so we won't retread the ground of many other authors. Most of the topics are only dealt with briefly: for a full mathematical treatment, along with much more information on the more obscure topics, you would do well to pick up *Mathematics for 3D Game Programming & Computer Graphics* by Eric Lengyel, also published by Charles River Media.

17 3D Geometry

In This Chapter

- Overview
- 3D Vectors
- Rendering
- Casting a Ray
- Exercises
- Summary
- You Should Now Know

OVERVIEW

Adding a third dimension is mostly just a question of adding another number, but this has a lot of implications. For one thing, your computer screen has two dimensions, not three, and so we have to find some way to "flatten" the extra dimension back to a 2D image. An object has a side that the viewer can't see, and can occlude other objects so that they aren't visible. So we'll start by looking at how 3D space can be represented. In the process, we'll spend a little time getting to know the third dimension a little.

Code samples from this chapter are implemented in *math.cst* in the script *chapter 17 (3D vectors)*. The *simple3D* demo uses them in context to create a basic 3D simulation.

ON THE CD

3D VECTORS

We are used by now to representing a point in 2D space in terms of a pair of Cartesian coordinates measured along a particular basis from a fixed origin, as discussed in Chapters 3, 5, and beyond. Adding the third dimension is not much more than adding a third number to the list.

Adding the Third Dimension

Just as with 2D geometry, we have to start by creating a space. This means defining three orthogonal (mutually perpendicular) axes and an origin. As before, this is arbitrary: we can point our axes in any direction we like. But it's conventional to consider the x-axis as "left to right," the y-axis as "down to up" and the z-axis as "front to back." So if you move down two units, right one unit and forward three units, this would be considered to be the vector $(1 \ -2 \ 3)^T$. This is how we will generally draw 3D diagrams. These are *left-handed* axes, which means that if you imagine grasping the z-axis with your left hand, with the thumb pointing in the positive z direction, your fingers curl round from the positive x to the positive y direction. If you ever have cause to change your coordinate axes, it's sensible to maintain this orientation.

As you can see, the three-dimensional vector is written exactly the same way as before, we just add one more component. Most other aspects of vector geometry stay the same too, with one addition that we'll look at shortly. For example, Pythagoras' Theorem extends simply to give the magnitude of a 3D vector $(x \ y \ z)^T$ as $\sqrt{x^2 + y^2 + z^2}$, and the dot product is given by multiplying all three components pairwise instead of just two:

$$\begin{pmatrix} a \\ b \\ c \end{pmatrix} \cdot \begin{pmatrix} d \\ e \\ f \end{pmatrix} = ad + be + cf$$

Just as in 2D space, we can define a line by taking a point with position vector **p** and a direction vector **v**, so that every point on the line has position **p** + *t***v** for some *t*. We can also define a *plane* in 3D space in much the same way: a point **p** and two non-collinear vectors **v** and **w**, so that each point on the plane is **p** + *t***v** + *s***w** for some *s* and *t*. Actually, there is another way: we can instead choose a point **p** and a normal vector **n**. This vector is perpendicular to all the vectors in the plane. Although this method is more efficient, it's less convenient for some calculations, so we'll occasionally use the first description (see Figure 17.1).

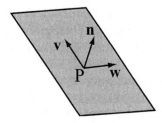

FIGURE 17.1 Defining a plane.

It's worth noting that the normal gives us a useful equation relating points on a plane. If the normal is $n = (abc)^T$ then the points on the plane all conform to the equation $ax + by + cz = d$, where d is the perpendicular distance of the plane from the origin (if $\mathbf{n}$ is a unit vector and $\mathbf{p}$ is on the plane then $d = \mathbf{p} \cdot \mathbf{n}$). This is the 3D equivalent to the line equation $ay + bx = c$.

The Vector (Cross) Product

As well as the dot product which we have already encountered, and which works exactly the same way in 3D, in three dimensions we have a new way to combine two vectors, which is known as the *vector product*, or more commonly the *cross product*, because it is usually notated with a multiplication sign ($\mathbf{v} \times \mathbf{w}$). Unlike the dot product, which returns a scalar value, the cross product returns a vector—specifically, given two vectors it returns a third vector perpendicular to both. It is essentially a three-dimensional equivalent to the `normalVector()` and `clockwiseNormal()` functions we used frequently in previous chapters.

Calculating the vector product is a little more awkward than the dot product. The formula is:

$$\begin{pmatrix} a \\ b \\ c \end{pmatrix} \times \begin{pmatrix} d \\ e \\ f \end{pmatrix} = \begin{pmatrix} bf - ce \\ cd - fa \\ ae - bd \end{pmatrix}$$

If this is hard to remember, one way is to think of it as the determinant of this rather unusual 3×3 matrix:

$$\begin{pmatrix} \mathbf{i} & \mathbf{j} & \mathbf{k} \\ a & b & c \\ d & e & f \end{pmatrix}$$

Here, **i**, **j**, **k** are the basis vectors $(1\ 0\ 0)^T$, $(0\ 1\ 0)^T$, $(0\ 0\ 1)^T$, so essentially each element of the determinant corresponds to one component of the cross product vector. Translating to code is fairly elementary:

```
function crossProduct(v1, v2)
    set x to v1[2]*v2[3]-v2[2]*v1[3]
    set y to v1[3]*v2[1]-v1[1]*v2[3]
    set z to v1[1]*v2[2]-v1[2]*v2[1]
    return vector(x,y,z)
end function
```

Some properties of the cross product include:

- The cross-product is not commutative. In fact, $\mathbf{v} \times \mathbf{w} = -\mathbf{w} \times \mathbf{v}$. Neither is it associative: in general $\mathbf{u} \times (\mathbf{v} \times \mathbf{w}) \neq (\mathbf{u} \times \mathbf{v}) \times \mathbf{w}$.
- The cross product is distributive over addition ($\mathbf{u} \times (\mathbf{v} + \mathbf{w}) = \mathbf{u} \times \mathbf{v} + \mathbf{u} \times \mathbf{w}$).
- The cross product of a vector with itself is the zero vector.
- If you take the scalar product with either of the two original vectors, you get zero (proving that the two are perpendicular).
- If **v** and **w** are orthogonal unit vectors, the cross product is also a unit vector.
- In general, if the angle between **v** and **w** is θ, then $|\mathbf{v} \times \mathbf{w}| = |\mathbf{v}||\mathbf{w}|\sin\theta$.
- The magnitude of the cross product of two vectors is the area of the parallelogram whose sides are defined by the vectors—that is, the area of the shape ABCD where $\overrightarrow{AB} = \overrightarrow{DC} = \mathbf{v}$ and $\overrightarrow{BC} = \overrightarrow{AD} = \mathbf{w}$ is equal to $|\mathbf{v} \times \mathbf{w}|$.
- The direction of the cross product always follows the same handedness as the axes: that is, if you rotate the space so that the input vectors are aligned as closely as possible to the x- and y-axes, the output vector is aligned in the positive z-direction. As long as your basis maintains the same handedness, the cross-product is independent of the basis.

Using the Cross Product

The cross product, like the dot product, is a useful way to "regularize" a situation, removing unnecessary elements. For example, suppose we have a plane for which we know the normal **n** but want to describe it instead by two vectors on the plane. We can use the cross product to do this. First choose an arbitrary vector **w** that is not collinear with **n**. Take the cross product $\mathbf{w} \times \mathbf{n}$. This gives a new vector **v** which is perpendicular to **n** (and also to **w**), and which therefore lies in the plane we are interested in. Now take the cross product again to get $\mathbf{u} = \mathbf{v} \times \mathbf{n}$. This gives a second vector perpendicular to **n**, which also happens to be perpendicular to **v**.

When moving into 3D it becomes a little harder to remember the distinction be-tween position and direction vectors. Remember that a vector "in" a plane simply means one that an ant on the plane could walk along. It does not represent a posi-tion vector for a point on the plane, unless the plane happens to pass through the origin.

Another common use for the cross product is to find an axis of rotation. We'll look at this further later, but for now look at Figure 17.2. An arrow at **p** is pointing along the vector **v**, and we want it instead to point along the vector **w**. By finding the cross product **v** × **w**, we have a vector perpendicular to both. This serves as an axis of rotation: we can rotate the arrow around this vector to turn it in the right di-rection. What's more, by finding the dot product we can calculate the angle of ro-tation too.

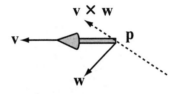

FIGURE 17.2   Using the vector and scalar products to calculate a rotation.

And since we're on the subject of the dot product, it's worth noting one more important calculation: the point of intersection of a line and a plane. Suppose we have a line defined by the point P and a vector **u**, and a plane defined by a point Q and a normal **n**. We want to know a value *t* such that **p** + *t***u** lies on the plane (see Figure 17.3).

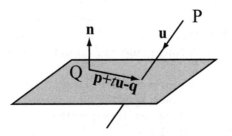

FIGURE 17.3   Finding the point of intersection of a line and a plane.

There are several ways this can be done, but this one is satisfyingly simple: Notice that for any point **a** on the plane, **a** − **q** is perpendicular to **n**. In particular,

$$(\mathbf{p} + t\mathbf{u} - \mathbf{q}) \cdot \mathbf{n} = 0$$

Because the scalar product is associative, this means that $(\mathbf{p} - \mathbf{q}) \cdot \mathbf{n} = t\mathbf{u} \cdot \mathbf{n}$. So

$$t = \frac{(\mathbf{p} - \mathbf{q}) \cdot \mathbf{n}}{\mathbf{u} \cdot \mathbf{n}}$$

As we would expect, this fails when **u** and **n** are perpendicular, since there is no intersection between the line and plane in that case.

We can use a similar technique to find the line of intersection of two planes. If two planes are represented by the points **p** and **q** and the normals **n** and **m** respectively, then we want to find the line that lies on both planes as shown in Figure 17.4.

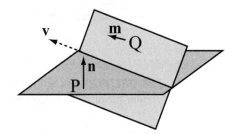

FIGURE 17.4 The line of intersection of two planes.

To do this, we first notice that since this line lies on both planes, it must be perpendicular to both **n** and **m**, which means that we can find its direction vector **v** simply as **n** × **m**. So now all we need is to find a single point on the line. This is simply a matter of applying the previous result: choose an arbitrary vector in the first plane (a good choice would be **n** × **v**) and see where the line through **p** along this vector intersects the second plane. Let's sum this up with two functions:

```
function linePlaneIntersection (linePt, lineVect, planePt, planeNormal)
    set d to dotProduct(lineVect,planeNormal)
    if d=0 then return "no intersection"
    set v to linePt-planePt
    return dotProduct(v,planeNormal)/d
end function
```

```
function planePlaneIntersection (pt1, normal1, pt2, normal2)
    set v to crossProduct(normal1,normal2)
    set u to crossProduct(normal1, v)
    set p to linePlaneIntersection(pt1, u, pt2, normal2)
    if p="no intersection" then return p
    return array(p,v)
end function
```

Homogeneous Coordinates

Although we only need three coordinates to represent 3D space, in practice we often use four, for a number of reasons which we'll see over this and the next chapter. As well as the x, y and z coordinate, we add one more which is called w. This gives us a four-dimensional vector that follows all the same rules as before.

This may seem somewhat arbitrary and just adding complications, but actually the w-component comes in very useful. These are called *homogeneous coordinates*—"homogeneous" means something like "having a similar dimension." For a position vector, w is set to 1, while for a direction vector it is 0, which makes sense since

$$\begin{pmatrix} x \\ y \\ z \\ 1 \end{pmatrix} - \begin{pmatrix} a \\ b \\ c \\ 1 \end{pmatrix} = \begin{pmatrix} x-a \\ y-b \\ z-c \\ 0 \end{pmatrix}$$

So the vector from one position vector to another ought to have a zero w-component. However, this shouldn't be taken too seriously as vector addition with homogeneous coordinates is not quite the same as normal coordinates as we'll see.

To understand the purpose of homogeneous coordinates, it's easiest to nip back into two dimensions again. In Figure 17.5 you can see a two-dimensional plane with axes x' and y'. This is placed in a three-dimensional space with axes x, y, and w, to coincide with the $w = 1$ plane. So any point (x',y') in the plane coincides with a point $(x,y,1)$ in the 3D space.

However, it's not just points on the plane that we can map to the 2D space. We can compress the whole of the 3D space onto the plane by a process of *projection*: for any point P, we draw a line from the 3D origin through P and find its point of intersection with the plane as shown in Figure 17.6.

We can even do this with homogeneous points that have $w = 0$: although the line OP is parallel to the plane, we say that it intersects the plane "at infinity"—infinitely far along the line on the plane parallel to OP. In all other cases, the point on the plane corresponding to (x,y,w) is $\left(\frac{x}{w}, \frac{y}{w} \right)$. In the strictest sense, in fact, there

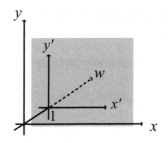

FIGURE 17.5   Homogeneous coordinates in 2D.

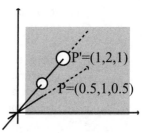

FIGURE 17.6   Projecting 3D homogeneous space to the plane.

is no difference between the homogeneous points (x,y,w) and $\left(\frac{x}{w},\frac{y}{w},1\right)$: they are mathematically considered to be equal. This means that homogeneous coordinates are *scale-invariant*—you can multiply them by a constant factor and they remain the same.

As a simple introduction to the use of homogeneous coordinates, let's look again at the problem of finding the point of intersection of two lines in 2D. The line through (a,b) with a vector $\begin{pmatrix} p \\ q \end{pmatrix}$ can be represented by the equations

$$a + tp = x$$
$$b + tq = y$$

which give

$$\frac{x-a}{p} = \frac{y-b}{q}$$
$$qx - py - aq + bp = 0$$

In general, a line in 2D can be represented as $ax + by + c = 0$, or in homogeneous coordinates by $ax + by + cw = 0$ (a line in 2D corresponds to a plane in homogeneous coordinate space). If we represent two lines in this way, we can find their point of intersection by

$$ax + by + cw = 0$$
$$px + qy + rw = 0$$
$$\frac{x}{w} = \frac{br - cq}{aq - bp}$$
$$\frac{y}{w} = \frac{cp - ar}{aq - bp}$$

giving us homogeneous coordinates $(br - cq, cp - ar, aq - bp)$. Notice that if $aq - bp = 0$ then the two lines are parallel, which means that in standard coordinates there is no solution to the equation, but in homogeneous coordinates they meet at a point at infinity with $w = 0$. Notice also that the position vector of this point is just the cross product

$$\begin{pmatrix} a \\ b \\ c \end{pmatrix} \times \begin{pmatrix} p \\ q \\ r \end{pmatrix}$$

This makes sense when you consider that the two vectors give the normals of the planes in 3D space, so their cross product gives the intersection of the planes as we've seen, which corresponds to the intersection of the 2D lines.

We'll leave homogeneous coordinates for now and return to them in the next chapter where you'll see how all this has a practical application in 3D. But keep them in mind as you read the next section where we discuss the projection plane for 3D rendering, as the two are closely related.

RENDERING

The process of translating a 3D scene into a 2D picture is called *rendering*. This is a complex process which we'll return to at a later stage, but we'll look at the fundamentals here.

The Projection Plane

To draw a 3D scene, we have to think a little about light. When we look at the world, our eyes receive light reflected from the objects around them. Light rays travel in a straight line, so if we draw a line from our eye out into the world, what we see is the first thing it hits. To be precise, we have a *field of view* that encompasses all the lines coming from us within a particular angle from our eye, as shown in Figure 17.7.

 One of the difficulties in describing 3D geometry is drawing clear diagrams on a 2D page. Figure 17.7 shows a 3D cube transformed into a 2D picture on the projection plane.

You can also see in the figure how we can translate this into a 2D image. We imagine that the observer is viewing the 3D world through a rectangular "window" at some distance d. The window is called the *projection plane*. To work out what is to be found at each point of the plane, we can either draw a line from the observer

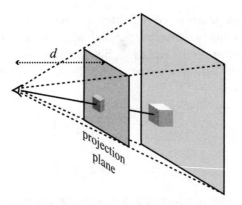

FIGURE 17.7   The field of view and the view frustrum.

and see what it hits (*raytracing*), or more commonly for real-time animation, we can calculate where in the space each object is, draw a line to the observer, and see where this line intersects the plane (seem familiar?). The precise situation is complicated by lights and texturing, but this is the essential principle.

To find the point on the projection plane that corresponds to a particular point in space, we use the intersection method we calculated above. We'll assume that the observer is facing in the direction **n**, and the point we are interested in is at **p**. Finally, we'll suppose the projection plane is at a perpendicular distance d from the observer, who is at the point **o**.

As you can see from Figure 17.8 (drawn in cross-section), we have drawn a line from the point at P to the observer, which passes through the projection plane at some unknown point. This is exactly the same as the previous example. The plane normal is the same as the direction the observer is facing, and we can find a reference point on the plane (which will be drawn at the center of the screen) as **o** + d**n**, assuming **n** is normalized. So the point on the projection plane corresponding to P is given by the intersection of the line starting at P in the direction **o** − **p** with this plane, which as we saw before is the point **p** + t(**o** − **p**), where

$$t = \frac{\left(\mathbf{p} - \left(\mathbf{o} + d\mathbf{n}\right)\right) \cdot \mathbf{n}}{\left(\mathbf{o} - \mathbf{p}\right) \cdot \mathbf{n}} = -d\frac{\mathbf{n} \cdot \mathbf{n}}{\left(\mathbf{o} - \mathbf{p}\right) \cdot \mathbf{n}} - 1 = \frac{d}{\left(\mathbf{p} - \mathbf{o}\right) \cdot \mathbf{n}} - 1$$

(remember that since **n** is normalized, $\mathbf{n} \cdot \mathbf{n} = 1$).

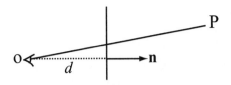

FIGURE 17.8 Projecting a point to the projection plane.

Having calculated what the projection plane looks like, we can now draw its contents at the correct size on the computer screen, called a *viewport*. There are a number of different ways we can do this: for example, we can simply specify the scale, saying that "one unit of the projection plane corresponds to one pixel on the screen." More commonly, we specify it by giving one of the maximum angles in the field of view of the observer, such as the vertical angle θ as shown in Figure 17.9. (Sometimes the whole field of view angle 2θ is specified instead.)

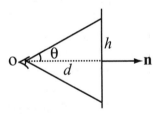

FIGURE 17.9 Specifying the field of view.

Since we know that $\tan\theta = \frac{h}{d}$, this tells us the height of the topmost point on the projection plane. This then becomes a scale for drawing to the screen.

All this is, however, highly overcomplicated, since really we don't need the value of d. All we actually need to know is the size of the picture on the screen and the angle of the field of view. We can then "place" our projection screen at the appropriate place to make the figures come out correctly. Then we simply need to use similar triangles.

We can calculate the distance of the point from the observer along the camera vector to be $(\mathbf{p}-\mathbf{o})\cdot\mathbf{n}$ and its "vertical" displacement as $(\mathbf{p}-\mathbf{o})\cdot\mathbf{u}$, where $\mathbf{u}$ is the "up" vector of the camera. If the projection plane is to have a height of h, then we must also have that $d = h/{\tan\theta}$, so the height of the point as projected onto the screen is given by $h\tan\theta(\mathbf{p}-\mathbf{o})\cdot\mathbf{u}$.

Here's a function that draws everything together, translating a point in space to a point on the screen, given the observer position and normal, the vertical field of view angle, the height of the screen and the "up" vector of the observer as well. We need the latter for completeness, but we'll look into it more in the next chapter.

```
function pos3DToScreenPos (pt, observerPos, observerVect, observerUp,
    fov, h)
    set observerRight to crossProduct(observerUp, observerVect)
    set v to pt-observerPos
    set z to dotProduct(v,observerVect)
    set d to h * tan(fov)
    set x to d*dotProduct(v,observerRight)/z
    set y to d*dotProduct(v,observerUp)/z
    return vector(x,-y)
end function
```

This returns the point's position on the screen relative to the center of the 3D viewport—with y measured downward as usual. Now, of course, in practice you can pre-calculate many of these values, so this could be made more efficient. There are also some complications about points behind the observer. On the other hand, in practice you can let your 3D card handle this part, as we'll see in a moment!

The set of points visible by a particular observer is called the *view frustrum*; a frustrum is the base of a truncated pyramid as shown in Figure 17.7. This is a six-sided shape, whose sides are at an angle determined by the field of view, and whose front and back faces are determined arbitrarily (called the *hither* and *yon* of the camera). In reality we can theoretically see infinitely far and infinitely near, but in practice it is convenient to "clip" the scene at a certain distance, often using fogging to obscure the distant objects before they disappear from view.

Notice that although changing **o** and θ both affect the image on screen, they do so in different ways. Moving the observer while leaving θ constant simply moves the view frustrum: it changes the scale of the image linearly. By changing the field of view, however, the shape of the view frustrum can be changed—this is like altering the angle of a camera lens. Choosing the correct field of view for your scene can take a little fiddling with the parameters to make something that looks right, just as a director or cinematographer may spend a long time choosing the right lens. None is more "correct," but they have different visual effects. The most natural-feeling will be a viewing angle that is the same as the angle the computer user has to the computer screen—but this of course depends on how near they are to the screen and the resolution they are using.

Perspective

There is an alternative way to consider this concept, which was discovered many centuries ago in the Renaissance, although the basic principles had been used before without a complete mathematical backing. This is the technique called *perspective*, which is a simple way to draw a 3D scene on paper.

To draw a scene in perspective, you start by creating a *horizon*, which is supposed to be the height of the observer's eyes. Each point on the horizon is a *vanishing point*, which means that it represents an object infinitely far away along a line drawn from the observer's vertical axis. The classic example of this is a road stretching into the distance as shown in Figure 17.10.

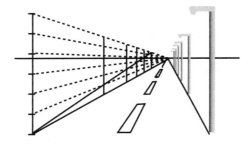

FIGURE 17.10   A perspective drawing.

Notice in the figure that we have also drawn a number of lampposts, which are supposed to be evenly spaced along the road. The way we construct these is to use a trick illustrated on the left-hand side of the picture: we start by placing one post in the foreground and another in the background. Then we divide the vertical line of the front post into several equal parts, joining each one to the vanishing point. Next, we draw in the diagonal from the bottom of one post to the top of the other. Our remaining lamp posts are placed so that they coincide with the points where the diagonal meets the lines into the distance.

Essentially, this process means that the image size of an object decays exponentially with distance:

$$Height\ in\ image = height \times e^{-k(d-d_0)}$$

where k is some constant and d_0 is the distance of an object whose height in the image is equal to its height in reality. There's nothing special about using e in the equation, any base will do if we scale k accordingly.

Perspective is not particularly useful in computer 3D engines because it requires a lot of recalculations if your observer moves, but if you're working with simple scenes and a fixed observer, it can be an easy way to create a quick 3D effect. You might want to try verifying that it is equivalent to the previous method, and to find how the values k and d_0 in perspective drawing relate to d and θ in standard 3D rendering.

Orthographic Projections

Although the standard perspective projection method (sometimes called *central projection*) described in the previous section is the most usual way to draw a 3D scene, there are other methods that are useful in some circumstances, particularly in architectural and technical drawings.

What happens in central projection as we move further and further from the projection plane, decreasing our field of view to compensate? As d increases and θ decreases, we get to something like Figure 17.11. Instead of objects decreasing in size on the screen as they move further away, they always appear the same size. The view frustrum has become a simple box.

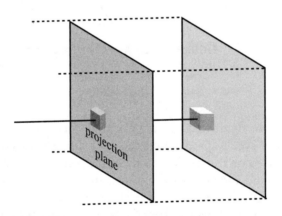

FIGURE 17.11   Orthographic projection.

This view is called *orthographic*. When the object we are looking at is at a different angle, it can also be called *oblique, axonometric,* or *isometric,* but all these are equivalent to the orthographic view, only the orientation of the object has changed. In an orthographic view, the distance of an object from the viewer, or from any other object, has no effect on its size, although it does affect the position on the screen and the drawing order. Otherwise all we need to know is the size of the viewport.

In gaming, the most common of these orthographic views is the isometric view. This is where we look down on an object in an orthographic projection at such an angle that each side of the object is at the same angle to the projection plane, so they are all viewed as the same length. We'll look at isometric games briefly in Part V.

One more projection technique is worth noting. Instead of a projection plane, we use a projection sphere or cylinder around the observer. In some ways, you might imagine this to be more realistic, after all, we aren't actually looking at the world through a window but through two movable eyes. However, this mostly creates some rather strange effects. One example is the Mercator projection of the Earth, which is the most commonly seen map of the planet. In a Mercator projection, we imagine placing the Earth inside a cylinder of paper and shining a light from the center. The shadow cast on the cylinder forms a map, which we can then unroll.

This is a good way to deal with the problem of mapping a spherical object like the Earth onto a planar map, but has some problems: measuring distance is extremely difficult. The further away you move from the Equator, the more spread out the map is, until the North Pole is actually infinitely spread out, and infinitely high up the cylinder. This is why on a flat map, Greenland, is for example, so enormously out of proportion to its actual size. Navigating through a world using this kind of projection would be very weird and confusing.

CASTING A RAY

As we saw before in 2D, it can often be useful to get a list of all objects along a particular one-ended infinite line called a *ray*. We've already seen how to calculate the intersection of a ray with a plane, and in the next couple of chapters we'll calculate ray collisions for both simple shapes and polygonal meshes. But right now we'll look at a few applications of this method, assuming that you can just use your 3D engine to calculate the ray for you.

Raycasting is useful in many circumstances, but two are the most common. The first is in user interaction, for example when someone clicks on the 3D scene and you want to calculate what object is underneath it. The second is in collision detection, where one or more rays cast in front of a shape can be used like a beam of headlamps to determine whether there are any obstacles ahead.

Using the 3D Engine to Find Objects Along a Path

The basic principle of raycasting is quite simple: you send a query to your real-time engine, passing it a starting point and a direction vector, and it returns a list of models with which the ray intersects. Depending on your particular 3D engine it may contain some optimization methods, for example the Director engine allows you to specify a maximum number of models to return, a list of models to check against, a maximum length for the ray, and whether you want a simple list of models returned (for example if you're just using it to pick a model which the user has clicked on), or more detailed results such as the collision point and collision normal (for collision detection) or the texture coordinates clicked on (for painting or higher-resolution picking—we'll look at textures in Chapter 20).

A good example of how this can be useful is in *terrain following*, that is, when an object is moving along a ground of varying height. Suppose your ground is a continuous triangular mesh (generally it's better to split it into smaller meshes corresponding to different regions to speed up the engine, but we'll return to that later), and you are creating a 4×4 vehicle that is driving along the terrain. So how can you make the vehicle move realistically across the various bumps? We want to know how high each wheel needs to be, and orient the vehicle accordingly. One way to do this is to store the information about the ground as a 2D height map, like the 1D height map we used in Chapter 10. This provides rapid information at the cost of high amounts of storage space. But another method (which may be quicker depending on the speed of your 3D engine and card, and the complication of the geometry of the terrain) is to cast a ray downward from each wheel (possibly from the middle of the 4×4 too, if the terrain is very rough) and orient according to the collision points—this also has the advantage of working equally well with a terrain that is changing over time, such as water waves.

A similar simple example is gunfire: in a first-person shooter, each player or enemy has a weapon that generally fires in a straight line (depending on the realism of the physics). At the moment the gun is fired, a quick raycasting collision check determines where it will hit.

The technique is less useful when dealing with objects three or four times bigger than the scale of the mesh against which they are colliding, or colliding with other objects that may be smaller than them. In that case you need rather a lot of rays to determine whether the path is definitely clear. If the objects are significantly different in size, though, it becomes more possible to approximate the collision by using a proxy shape such as a sphere or bounding box.

Picking, Dragging, and Dropping

So let's look at the other principal application, which is user interaction. The simplest example is when your user clicks on the screen to select an object in 3D space. How do you determine which object they have clicked on? (There may be a built-in method for this, too, incidentally.)

By choosing a point on the screen, your user has actually selected an angle for a ray—in fact, we're running in reverse the process of drawing a 3D point to the screen as seen earlier in the chapter. The simplest way to determine this point is to use the projection screen method to find a particular 3D point under the mouse position, and then use this to create your direction vector. To do this, you need the field of view angle θ and the height h of the viewport as before. Then the distance to the projection plane can be found as $d = {}^{h}/_{\tan\theta}$ as before.

Having found this distance, and knowing the camera's forward and up vectors, we can quickly calculate the point under the mouse:

```
function screenPosTo3DPos(viewportPos, observerPos, observerVect,
observerUp, fov, h)
    set observerRight to crossProduct(observerUp, observerVect)
    set d to h / tan(fov)
    return observerVect*d - observerUp*viewportPos[2] +
observerRight*viewportPos[1]
end function
```

We now have all we need to cast a ray: the start point is the camera position, the direction is the vector to the point we found. So this will tell us the model clicked on.

Suppose we need to drag the model to a new position. This gives us a technical problem: there are three dimensions to move it in, but only two dimensions for the mouse. Somehow, the user's movements need to be translated into 3D space. How this is done, of course, depends on the particular circumstances. If the model is part of a plane, for example an object on the ground, a sliding tile, a picture on the wall and so on, then our two directions of motion are sufficient, and we need only find a way to constrain the motion in the particular direction. If it's free to move in space but not rotate, then the best solution may be to combine the mouse movement with a key—perhaps pressing the shift key while moving the mouse will cause the object to move in the camera's xz-plane rather than the xy-plane. Alternatively, you can make the drag occur only in the current xy-plane but allow them to move freely around the object to change which plane that is, or give them multiple views of the same object as in 3D drawing programs. Finally, if the model is supposed to be rotating in place, then mouse movements can correspond to rotations in the direction of two axes.

So let's start with constraining to the plane. This is actually just an extension of what we've already seen and is really quite straightforward: as the mouse moves, we cast a ray from its current position to the plane we're interested in (actually, it doesn't even have to be a plane, it can be rough terrain or even other models— think about the pool game example where we created a "ghost" ball demonstrating where the collision would occur), and use this as the new position for the dragged object, offsetting it by its height or radius as appropriate.

For a more sophisticated variant, you can "fake" the ray position so that the user feels they're dragging the middle of the object instead of its base. In Figure 17.12 you can see how this might work. First we calculate the current offset of the base of the object from its midpoint as they appear on the screen coordinates. Then we apply this offset to the current mouse position to get the ground position we're interested in. Now we drag the object to sit correctly at that position. The user isn't precisely dragging the midpoint of the object, but it feels that way.

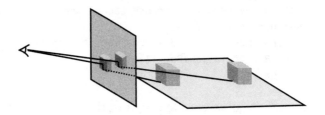

FIGURE 17.12   Dragging an object along the plane.

Dragging the object freely in space is just an extension of this: you'll always have to constrain to a plane, but you can give a freer choice as to what plane that is. Generally, the most natural is to use a plane normal to the camera, but you could also use one normal to the up vector, or any other vector that seems convenient.

A much more difficult problem comes when you want to allow the user to rotate objects with the mouse. Let's start with the simplest of these situations, which is when we want to rotate ourselves, as in a mouse-driven FPS. Here, a mouse movement corresponds to a camera rotation.

This problem is reasonably easy because there's a straightforward mapping from the mouse movement to the desired movement: at each time step, rotate the camera to point along whatever ray is currently underneath the mouse. We'll see in the next chapter how to rotate an object to point in a particular direction, so this is easy to do. Of course, we also need to decide whether to keep rotating if the mouse is held still but off-center, or whether to rotate only when the mouse is moved. In the latter case, we need to reset the cursor position to the center of the screen each time we move (which means it is best to hide the cursor when using this system).

When using the mouse to rotate an object in the camera view, things get a little trickier: there's no hard-and-fast translation from one to the other. We can make a start: the most natural assumption for someone rotating an object is that the point of the object clicked on will remain under the mouse as it rotates. We can do this as long as we know the intersection point of the ray. The difficulty is knowing which way should be up—as we'll see in the next chapter, we can specify an up vector for a point-at operation, and in this case there's no obvious winner. But we'll look at one candidate as an example.

Assume that the object to be rotated has position vector $\mathbf{p}$, and the point on its surface which was clicked has position vector $\mathbf{q}$. Now the mouse is moved so that it defines a ray $\mathbf{o} + t\mathbf{v}$ from the observer. We want to know which direction to point the object so that it points "toward the mouse position"—that is, toward the ray.

To find the correct direction, we need to find the point of intersection of the ray with the sphere centered on $\mathbf{p}$ whose radius is the magnitude of $\mathbf{q} - \mathbf{p}$. If there is such an intersection, then this tells us the new position toward which the object should point. If there is no intersection, then the mouse is outside the range of the object, in which case we can either continue to rotate (equivalent to considering the spherical projection of the mouse position onto the object) or point it as closely as possible toward the mouse—that is to say, along a vector perpendicular to the vector $\mathbf{v}$ through the plane containing $\mathbf{v}$ and $\mathbf{p} - \mathbf{o}$.

So what about the up vector? We could choose several. One option is to use the camera's up vector. This works reasonably well, but leads to problems when you want to rotate the object to align with this vector. Another is to use the axis of rotation, but this causes the object to rotate rather erratically. A good compromise is to use the cross-product of the camera's direction vector and the movement vector of the point.

EXERCISES

Exercise 17.1

Create a function that will draw a three-dimensional cube, culling the back faces.

You can determine which faces of a cube are visible by using the normal of the plane, as we'll see in a later chapter. For the moment, concentrate on the projection, but see if you can work out how to use the cross product to determine if a particular face of the cube is visible. Use the function to make a cube that spins around its center. Look at the effect of using different projection techniques and fields of view.

SUMMARY

In this chapter you've had a brief introduction to three-dimensional space and how it works. As you've seen, the third dimension doesn't change things very much, but it does add some complications, because of all that extra freedom of movement, and because we have to work with an observer who can't see the whole space.

In the next chapter we'll look further into how the space works, and extend the matrix math we met in Chapter 5 to deal with the much more complex motions and transformations available to us.

YOU SHOULD NOW KNOW

- how to extend *vectors* into three dimensions
- the meaning and use of the *cross (vector) product*
- how to find points and lines of intersection between *lines* and *planes*
- the meaning of the term *homogeneous coordinates* and how to use them to calculate intersections
- how to use different kinds of *projection* to create your own 3D engine
- how third-party *3D engines* and graphics cards work
- how to use *raycasting* to create user interaction with 3D space

18 ⫶ Transforms

OVERVIEW

We've already seen how a 2D matrix can be used to describe a sequence of transformations in 2D space. In this chapter we'll look at the 3D equivalent of this, the *transform*. We'll also see how transforms can be used to create objects with a relationship to one another.

 Code samples from this chapter are implemented in *math.cst* in the script *chapter 18 (transforms)*.

DESCRIBING LOCATIONS IN SPACE

The 3D world is populated by objects called *models*, which are essentially sets of vertices joined together in triangles to make a *mesh*. In order to work out where these models are, the 3D engine treats them as a single object called a *node* at a particular location and orientation and works out the positions of the vertices relative to that node. The same method is also used to describe the location of lights, cameras, and other members of 3D space.

Position, Rotation, and Scale

To describe a node, we need to know three things: its position, rotation, and scale (it could also be reflected, skewed, etc., but we generally ignore this). Rotation and scale can be handled by a transformation matrix as before, while position is a simple vector. The simplest way to visualize this combination of transformations is as a single process acting on the "raw" model: first scaling, then rotating about the origin, then translating to the correct point. All these transformations are *affine*, meaning that if two lines are parallel before transformation, then they remain parallel afterwards. Shears and reflections are also affine transformations (in fact, any transformation that can be performed by a matrix is affine). Rotations and translations (and reflections) are slightly stricter: these are *rigid-body* transformations, because as well as affinity, they preserve angles between lines in space: although the relative positions of vertices may change, the angles between them remain the same. This is not true of scales in general as you can see in Figure 18.1.

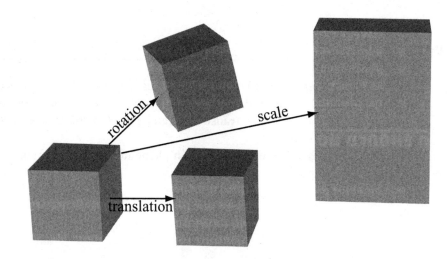

FIGURE 18.1   The three basic transformations.

The simplest transformation to visualize is the scale. Scaling an object by a constant factor is simply a matter of multiplying each position vector by the scale factor, or in matrix terms multiplying by the matrix $n\mathbf{I}$, where $\mathbf{I}$ is the identity matrix. More generally, we can scale by different amounts in each direction: multiply the vectors by the matrix

$$\begin{pmatrix} a & 0 & 0 \\ 0 & b & 0 \\ 0 & 0 & c \end{pmatrix}$$

Any scale transformation can be calculated in this way: for example, a scale factor of 2 in the direction $(1\ \ 1\ \ 0)^{\mathrm{T}}$ is equivalent to the scale

$$\begin{pmatrix} \sqrt{2} & 0 & 0 \\ 0 & \sqrt{2} & 0 \\ 0 & 0 & 1 \end{pmatrix}$$

Rotation is rather more complicated. In two dimensions, rotation about the origin is relatively straightforward: it's described by a single angle. But with a third dimension we also need to specify an axis of rotation: any vector in space can act as an axis. However, as with the pool balls we looked at before, which had both top-spin and side-spin, any rotation can be decomposed into simpler rotations about the basis vectors.

A rotation about one of the basis vectors can be described by a matrix like this one:

$$\mathbf{R}_x = \begin{pmatrix} 1 & 0 & 0 \\ 0 & \cos\theta & \sin\theta \\ 0 & -\sin\theta & \cos\theta \end{pmatrix}$$

Combining all three such matrices gives us a generic rotation:

$$\mathbf{R} \equiv \mathbf{R}_z \mathbf{R}_y \mathbf{R}_x = \begin{pmatrix} \cos\xi & \sin\xi & 0 \\ -\sin\xi & \cos\xi & 0 \\ 0 & 0 & 1 \end{pmatrix} \begin{pmatrix} \cos\phi & 0 & \sin\phi \\ 0 & 1 & 0 \\ -\sin\phi & 0 & \cos\phi \end{pmatrix} \begin{pmatrix} 1 & 0 & 0 \\ 0 & \cos\theta & \sin\theta \\ 0 & -\sin\theta & \cos\theta \end{pmatrix}$$

The symbol $\equiv$ here means "is defined as" or "is identical to." It's like a stronger kind of equal sign.

NOTE

372   Mathematics and Physics for Programmers

Multiplying these out gives a fairly horrific monster matrix, but it's not as bad as it might seem. Suppose we transform the vectors **i**, **j**, and **k** under **R**, we end up with the column vectors **u**, **v**, and **w** of the matrix. One feature of a rotation is that the vector between a point and its image must always be perpendicular to the axis of rotation, so if we now take the cross product $(\mathbf{u}-\mathbf{i})\times(\mathbf{v}-\mathbf{j})$ we find a new vector **a** perpendicular to both. This vector **a** is the overall axis of rotation.

What's more, we can calculate the angle of rotation α by finding the components of **i** and **v** perpendicular to **a** (that is, the result of projecting vectors **i** and **v** to a plane normal to **a**):

$$\mathbf{i}_N = \mathbf{i}-(\mathbf{a}\cdot\mathbf{i})\mathbf{a}$$
$$\mathbf{v}_N = \mathbf{v}-(\mathbf{a}\cdot\mathbf{v})\mathbf{a}$$
$$\mathbf{i}_N\cdot\mathbf{v}_N = (\mathbf{i}-(\mathbf{a}\cdot\mathbf{i})\mathbf{a})\cdot(\mathbf{v}-(\mathbf{a}\cdot\mathbf{v})\mathbf{a})$$
$$= \mathbf{i}\cdot\mathbf{v}-(\mathbf{a}\cdot\mathbf{i})(\mathbf{a}\cdot\mathbf{v})(2-\mathbf{a}\cdot\mathbf{a})$$

*This only works if **i** (and therefore **v**) is not parallel to **a**: otherwise we must use a different basis vector for comparison.*

Assuming **a** is a unit vector (if not, we can normalize it), and noting that the dot product with **i** and **v** must be equal (by the definition of rotation), this means that

$$\cos\alpha = \mathbf{i}\cdot\mathbf{v}-(\mathbf{a}\cdot\mathbf{i})^2$$

This kind of process can always be used to combine transformations into one. Conversely, we can decompose a rotation **R** into primitive rotations about the basis vectors as we'll see later. So a rotation is often described by means of a *rotation vector* giving the angle of rotation about the three axes. We'll be coming back to this issue several times over the course of this section.

All this works fine, but then we hit a snag: how can we represent translations? It would be good to be able to perform a complete transformation in one step, including translations. Otherwise, any combination of transformations would mean first translating back to the origin, then performing rotations and scales, then re-adding the position, then translating again and so on. But of course, position information is additive, not multiplicative, which makes this seemingly impossible.

The Transformation Matrix

The solution to this problem is to use the homogeneous coordinates we introduced in the previous chapter. With the aid of the fourth dimension, we can now perform translations using a 4 × 4 matrix like this:

$$\begin{pmatrix} 1 & 0 & 0 & a \\ 0 & 1 & 0 & b \\ 0 & 0 & 1 & c \\ 0 & 0 & 0 & 1 \end{pmatrix} \begin{pmatrix} x \\ y \\ z \\ 1 \end{pmatrix} = \begin{pmatrix} x+a \\ y+b \\ z+c \\ 1 \end{pmatrix}$$

Notice that the last row of the calculation is almost irrelevant, it's just a piece of "bookkeeping." Also notice that if we perform a translation on a direction vector instead of a position vector, so that the w-coordinate is zero, the vector is unaffected by the transformation.

If we combine this matrix with the scaling and rotation matrices from before, we end up with a generic transform:

$$\mathbf{T} = \mathbf{PR}_z\mathbf{R}_y\mathbf{R}_x\mathbf{S}$$

where $\mathbf{P}$ is a translation, $\mathbf{S}$ is a scale $\begin{pmatrix} a & 0 & 0 & 0 \\ 0 & b & 0 & 0 \\ 0 & 0 & c & 0 \\ 0 & 0 & 0 & 1 \end{pmatrix}$, and $\mathbf{R}_x = \begin{pmatrix} \cos\theta & \sin\theta & 0 & 0 \\ -\sin\theta & \cos\theta & 0 & 0 \\ 0 & 0 & 1 & 0 \\ 0 & 0 & 0 & 1 \end{pmatrix}$ (and similarly

for $\mathbf{R}_y$ and $\mathbf{R}_x$). The non-translation matrices are created simply by replacing the 3×3 matrix at the top-left of the 4×4 matrix with the appropriate 3D matrix as used before.

Because the bottom row of $\mathbf{T}$ is always $(0\ \ 0\ \ 0\ \ 1)$, this matrix has twelve unknown entries. However, not all such matrices are valid transforms: those with a determinant of zero are invalid, and of the rest, exactly half would perform a reflection and most others would create some form of shear. It's easy to see that there are nine degrees of freedom in creating a valid transform: three rotation angles, three scale factors, and three translation values.

Each of the matrices that make up a transform can be inverted fairly easily: for a translation, replace each value with its negation, for a rotation, negate the rotation angle, for a scale, replace the scale factors by their reciprocals. In fact, as it happens, inverting translations and rotations is even easier than that: their inverse is actually their transpose (recall that you take the transpose of a matrix by exchanging its rows and columns). We say the matrices are *orthogonal*, which is equivalent to the rigid-body nature of the transformation. This means that we can invert the whole transform—remembering of course that we need to apply the inverses in the opposite order:

$$\mathbf{T}^{-1} = \mathbf{S}^{-1}\mathbf{R}_x{}^{\mathsf{T}}\mathbf{R}_y{}^{\mathsf{T}}\mathbf{R}_z{}^{\mathsf{T}}\mathbf{P}^{\mathsf{T}}$$

This process is straightforward providing that we keep track of the primitive transformations making up the transform. Otherwise, we have to either decompose the general transform into its component parts or invert it as it stands, which is easier (a simple method for inverting a matrix was sketched out in Chapter 5) but less useful.

The process of decomposing a transform into position, rotation, and scale information is awkward but not impossible. The first part is reasonably simple: we can strip off the translation element immediately from the last column of the matrix. To calculate the scale and rotation, notice first that $\mathbf{S}$ multiplied by the basis vectors just multiplies them by the scale factors a, b, and c, so for example $\mathbf{RSi} = \mathbf{R}(a\mathbf{i}) = a\mathbf{Ri}$. Also, since $\mathbf{R}$ is a rigid rotation, $\mathbf{Ri}$ is a unit vector, and what's more it is the first column of $\mathbf{R}$. So a must be the magnitude of the first column of $\mathbf{RS}$ and the first column of $\mathbf{R}$ is the normalized version of this vector, and similarly for b and c. So this allows us to split the transform into the three underlying transformations.

Decomposing $\mathbf{R}$ further into rotations about the three axes is also possible, although not always necessary (again, we'll look at a neater way to perform rotations shortly). We're looking for θ, ϕ, ζ such that

$$\begin{pmatrix} \cos\zeta & \sin\zeta & 0 \\ -\sin\zeta & \cos\zeta & 0 \\ 0 & 0 & 1 \end{pmatrix} \begin{pmatrix} \cos\phi & 0 & \sin\phi \\ 0 & 1 & 0 \\ -\sin\phi & 0 & \cos\phi \end{pmatrix} \begin{pmatrix} 1 & 0 & 0 \\ 0 & \cos\theta & \sin\theta \\ 0 & -\sin\theta & \cos\theta \end{pmatrix} = \begin{pmatrix} x_1 & x_2 & x_3 \\ y_1 & y_2 & y_3 \\ z_1 & z_2 & z_3 \end{pmatrix}$$

(ignoring the w-coordinate which is not involved in this transformation).

Since the z rotation doesn't affect the z-coordinate and the x rotation doesn't affect the x-coordinate, we can see that $z_1 = -\sin\phi$. This tells us the value of ϕ. Having done that, we can see that $z_2 = -\cos\phi\sin\theta$, which gives us θ, and $x_1 = \cos\phi\cos\zeta$, which gives us ζ. The only problem is that there is more than one set of solutions to this system, so different sets of rotations will combine to give the right answer. This might seem trivial, but it does cause problems, particularly when *interpolating* transforms, as we'll see.

One advantage to working with (or at least retaining a record of) the "raw" transformations underlying a transform is to provide a validation system against rounding errors. Because of the redundancy in the transform matrix, small errors can accumulate to give a transform that is not valid—especially by introducing a small shear factor. We can counteract this by checking a transform against its underlying transformations and ensuring that the two are true to one another. To some extent this decreases the value of combining transforms into a single matrix, but remember that the main value occurs when applying a transform to multiple objects in a scene, where such a validation isn't necessary. One only needs to validate the transform when modifying it in some way.

APPLYING TRANSFORMS

Transforms simplify 3D calculations enormously. We'll take a quick tour through some of their applications.

Creating Motion with Transforms

In practice, it's easiest to work with transforms by ignoring the full transform matrix and concentrating on the underlying raw transformations. In general, you'll have some node with a transform $\mathbf{T}$, and you'll want to move it somewhere else. The only time we need to use the full transform is when calculating the actual position of the vertices of a model. For example, the basic unit cube has eight vertices, at the eight permutations of the homogeneous vector $\begin{pmatrix} \pm 0.5 & \pm 0.5 & \pm 0.5 & 1 \end{pmatrix}^{\mathrm{T}}$. We can use a transform to move this cube to any other position and size in space. Once we have calculated the appropriate transform, we simply multiply it by each of the vertices in turn to determine the new location of the cube.

The same process also incidentally works for direction vectors, so for example the vector along one side of the cube will be unaffected. However, you do need to be a little careful about normal vectors: because the scale transform does not preserve angles between lines, a direction vector that is normal to a line or plane before transforming is unlikely to still be normal afterwards if the transform includes a scaling element.

If we know that $\mathbf{n}$ and $\mathbf{v}$ are perpendicular vectors, then to find a vector normal to the transformed vector $\mathbf{Tv}$ we would like to find some new transform $\mathbf{T}_n$ such that $\mathbf{T}_n \mathbf{n} \cdot \mathbf{Tv} = 0$. Recall from the definition of the dot product that $\mathbf{u} \cdot \mathbf{v} = \mathbf{u}^{\mathrm{T}} \mathbf{v}$, so this means that $\left(\mathbf{T}_n \mathbf{n} \right)^{\mathrm{T}} \left(\mathbf{Tv} \right) = 0$, and so $\mathbf{n}^{\mathrm{T}} \mathbf{T}_n^{\mathrm{T}} \mathbf{Tv} = 0$. Since $\mathbf{n}$ and $\mathbf{v}$ are perpendicular by definition, if $\mathbf{T}_n^{\mathrm{T}} \mathbf{T}$ then the equation is solved, so we can conclude that $\mathbf{T}_n = \left(\mathbf{T}^{-1} \right)^{\mathrm{T}}$, the *inverse transpose* of $\mathbf{T}$.

Yet again, it should be stressed that these kinds of calculations will mostly be handled behind the scenes by a decent real-time 3D program, so that you don't need to worry about them, but it's worth bearing them in mind, and they will become more relevant as we head toward collision detection.

Let's look at some examples of how you could use transforms to perform a common task, such as aligning an arrow to point at a particular position vector (recall that we postponed this problem in the previous chapter). Suppose the arrow is a model whose "root" position (i.e., its appearance under the identity transform) is as shown in Figure 18.2. Notice that it is pointing along the positive z-axis.

Now we imagine that the arrow is located at position $\mathbf{p}$, pointing along the vector $\mathbf{v}$ (if we know the transform of the arrow, we can calculate $\mathbf{v}$ simply: it is the normalized third column of the transform matrix). We want the arrow to point at a point $\mathbf{q}$ instead, and rotate it appropriately. To do this, we can first calculate the

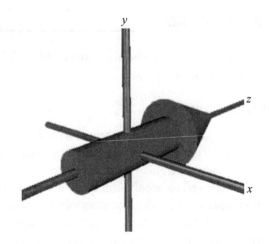

FIGURE 18.2 An arrow model in its untransformed state.

vector $\mathbf{q} - \mathbf{p}$. This is the new direction for the transform's z-axis—normalized, we'll call it $\mathbf{u}$. Taking the cross-product $\mathbf{u} \times \mathbf{v}$, we can find the axis around which we would like the arrow to rotate, and by taking the dot-product $\mathbf{u} \cdot \mathbf{v}$ we can find the cosine of the rotation angle.

Now all we need to do is to perform this rotation. The general matrix for rotating around an arbitrary axis is a little ugly, as you'd expect from the 2D version, but we can calculate it to be:

$$\mathbf{R} = \begin{pmatrix} c_+ + a_1^2 c_- & a_1 a_2 c_- - a_3 s & a_1 a_3 c_- + a_2 s \\ a_1 a_2 c_- + a_3 s & c_+ + a_2^2 c_- & a_2 a_3 c_- - a_1 s \\ a_1 a_3 c_- - a_2 s & a_2 a_3 c_- + a_1 s & c_+ + a_3^2 c_- \end{pmatrix}$$

where the axis is given by the vector $\begin{pmatrix} a_1 & a_2 & a_3 \end{pmatrix}^T$, and if the angle is θ then s, c_+ and c_- are defined as $s = \sin\theta$, $c_+ = \cos\theta$ and $c_- = 1 - c_+$.

If we were working with non-homogeneous coordinates, we'd have to combine this with a translation to the origin, the rotation, and then translating back. In our case we needn't worry because the translation and rotation parts of the homogeneous matrix are essentially independent (since translation is applied last). So we can create a transform $\mathbf{S}$ that has $\mathbf{R}$ in the top-left portion and an identity position element. Then all we need to do is to combine the matrix $\mathbf{S}$ with the original transform $\mathbf{T}$ to apply the rotation. But there is one potential problem: should we right-

or left-multiply the transforms? Since **S** is to be applied *after* **T**, we need to combine it on the left as **ST**, not as **TS**. By contrast, a scale transform is more likely to be applied before **T**, and therefore right-multiplied with it, since it's generally more useful to apply the scale to the object in its unrotated form before applying rotations.

There is one other complication: what happens if the node we are interested in is not symmetrical? For example, if the node is not an arrow model but a camera, then it's not enough to point at a particular location, we also need to specify which way is up, otherwise our camera will spin in strange directions. This means that we don't need just one rotation but two: first we rotate the object as before to point in a particular direction (often along its local *z*-axis as in the above example), then we rotate again around this direction vector to keep the preferred up-vector (usually the local *y*-axis) pointing as close to upward as possible. There's nothing special about the up-direction, we could just as easily align to keep a preferred left-side, but in a gravitational world it's often sensible to single out the vertical direction particularly. Figure 18.3 shows this process.

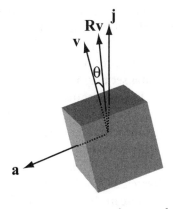

FIGURE 18.3   Keeping a preferred up-vector.

Determining the angle of rotation needs a little calculus: we are looking for an angle that maximizes $\mathbf{Rv} \cdot \mathbf{j}$, where **R** is a rotation matrix around the (normalized) pointing direction $\mathbf{a} = \mathbf{q} - \mathbf{p}$, and **v** is the current direction of the "up" vector. Plugging this into the matrix for **R** as above shows that we are trying to find θ that maximizes

$$\left(a_1a_2v_1 + a_2a_3v_3 + a_2^{\,2}v_2\right)\left(1 - \cos\theta\right) + v_2\cos\theta - \left(a_3v_1 + a_1v_3\right)\sin\theta$$

Differentiating, we see that θ must solve

$$\tan\theta = \frac{\left(a_3v_1 + a_1v_3\right)}{\left(a_1a_2v_1 + a_2a_3v_3 + \left(a_2^{\,2} - 1\right)v_2\right)}$$

This yields two possible values for θ, one gives the angle to point down, the other to point up. And of course when the numerator and denominator are both zero, we are in the situation where the pointing vector **a** is parallel to **j**, so all directions are equally far from pointing upward.

Interpolation

One of the most powerful features of transforms is the ability to create smooth motion by *interpolating* between two matrices. For example, we might want to create a camera which automatically follows a race car, but if we simply place it at a constant distance relative to the car it feels like it's tied on the back. Instead, we want it to feel like a helicopter that follows the car smoothly.

To do this, we can calculate two transforms. The first is the current transform **C** of the camera (which we presumably know already), the second is the "target" transform **T**, which is at a set position relative to the moving car. Then instead of moving the camera to the new transform, we move it part-way along: to some transform $t\mathbf{C} + (1 - t)\mathbf{T}$. This makes the camera "ease" into position, and works particularly well when following an object that is moving continually, like a car. A similar process can be used for following a third-person perspective character in a game like *Super Mario World* or *Tomb Raider*, but calculating the target transform is rather more complicated as you have to deal with the possibility of there being some other objects or landscape in the way (we'll return to this issue in Chapter 24). Generally, camera controls are one of the most difficult aspects of game design, and can often make or break the game in terms of playability.

Quaternions

Now it's time to make good on the promise to find a simpler way to handle rotations. Admittedly it's not *that* much simpler, but it is an improvement. The key concept is called a *quaternion*, which is a special kind of 4D vector. A quaternion **q** can be written as $\begin{pmatrix} w & x & y & z \end{pmatrix}^{\mathrm{T}}$, or alternatively as $w + xi + yj + zk$, where the numbers i, j, and k are related to the "imaginary number" i we have touched on before, which is defined to be the square root of -1. In this case, i, j, and k are "orthogonal" imaginary numbers, in the sense that squaring any of them gives -1, and they satisfy the following equations: $ij = -ji = k; jk = -kj = i; ki = -ik = j$. Of course, no real numbers satisfy these equations, but that's fine—these aren't numbers in that sense, they're just mathematical abstractions that do what we want them to do. So we basically have a kind of "imaginary vector," and in fact the quaternion $\mathbf{q}$ may also be written in the form $w + \mathbf{v}$, where $\mathbf{v}$ is the vector $\begin{pmatrix} x & y & z \end{pmatrix}^T$. We also define the *conjugate* of $\mathbf{q}$ to be the quaternion $w - \mathbf{v}$.

Having defined our strange imaginary basis, we can calculate the product of two quaternions:

$$\left(w_1 + x_1 i + y_1 j + z_1 k \right)\left(w_2 + x_2 i + y_2 j + z_2 k \right) = w_1 \left(w_2 + x_2 i + y_2 j + z_2 k \right) +$$
$$x_1 i \left(w_2 + x_2 i + y_2 j + z_2 k \right) + y_1 j \left(w_2 + x_2 i + y_2 j + z_2 k \right) + z_1 k \left(w_2 + x_2 i + y_2 j + z_2 k \right)$$
$$= \left(w_1 w_2 + w_1 x_2 i + w_1 y_2 j + w_1 z_2 k \right) + \left(x_1 w_2 i - x_1 x_2 + x_1 y_2 k + x_1 z_2 j \right)$$
$$+ \left(y_1 w_2 j - y_1 x_2 k - y_1 y_2 + y_1 z_2 i \right) + \left(z_1 w_2 k - z_1 x_2 j - z_1 y_2 i - z_1 z_2 \right)$$
$$= \left(w_1 w_2 - x_1 x_2 - y_1 y_2 - z_1 z_2 \right) + \left(w_1 x_2 + x_1 w_2 + y_1 z_2 - z_1 y_2 \right) i$$
$$+ \left(w_1 y_2 + y_1 w_2 - z_1 x_2 + x_1 z_2 \right) j + \left(w_1 z_2 + z_1 w_2 + x_1 y_2 - y_1 x_2 \right) k$$

This is rather unpleasant-looking, but can be simplified if we use the vector form: if we say $\mathbf{q}_1 = w_1 + \mathbf{v}_1$ and $\mathbf{q}_2 = w_2 + \mathbf{v}_2$, then the product is given by

$$\mathbf{q}_1 \mathbf{q}_2 = w_1 w_2 + \mathbf{v}_1 \cdot \mathbf{v}_2 + w_1 \mathbf{v}_2 + w_2 \mathbf{v}_1 + \mathbf{v}_1 \times \mathbf{v}_2$$

Notice that because of the cross-product component, the product of quaternions is not commutative.

Armed with this result, let's take the product of a quaternion with its conjugate:

$$\mathbf{q}\bar{\mathbf{q}} = w^2 - \mathbf{v} \cdot \mathbf{v} - \mathbf{v} \times \mathbf{v}$$

Since for any vector, $\mathbf{v} \times \mathbf{v} = \mathbf{0}$, this tells us that

$$\mathbf{q}\bar{\mathbf{q}} = w^2 - \mathbf{v} \cdot \mathbf{v}$$

And because $i^2 = j^2 = k^2 = -1$, this means that $\mathbf{q}\bar{\mathbf{q}} = \mathbf{q} \cdot \mathbf{q} = |\mathbf{q}|^2$. So the inverse (both left and right) of a quaternion can be given by $\mathbf{q}^{-1} = \frac{\bar{\mathbf{q}}}{|\mathbf{q}|^2}$, or in particular for a unit quaternion, $\mathbf{q}^{-1} = \bar{\mathbf{q}}$. The product of a quaternion with its inverse is the quaternion $(1 \ 0 \ 0 \ 0)^T$, which is equal to the scalar 1.

So what does all this mathematical sleight of hand have to do with rotations? It turns out that if we consider the vector $\mathbf{u}$ to be a quaternion with zero scalar part, then if we calculate the product $\mathbf{q}\mathbf{u}\mathbf{q}^{-1}$ for some quaternion $\mathbf{q}$, this represents a rotation of $\mathbf{v}$ about a particular axis.

Notice first that the product $\mathbf{quq}^{-1}$ is the same for any scalar multiple of $\mathbf{q}$, so we can consider $\mathbf{q}$ to be a unit quaternion $s + \mathbf{v}$, whose inverse is $\bar{\mathbf{q}} = s - \mathbf{v}$. This gives the product as:

$$
\begin{aligned}
\mathbf{quq}^{-1} &= \left(-\mathbf{v}\cdot\mathbf{u}+s\mathbf{u}+\mathbf{v}\times\mathbf{u}\right)\bar{\mathbf{q}} \\
&= -s\mathbf{v}\cdot\mathbf{u}+\left(s\mathbf{u}+\mathbf{v}\times\mathbf{u}\right)\cdot\mathbf{v}+s\left(s\mathbf{u}+\mathbf{v}\times\mathbf{u}\right)+\left(\mathbf{v}\cdot\mathbf{u}\right)\mathbf{v}-\left(s\mathbf{u}+\mathbf{v}\times\mathbf{u}\right)\times\mathbf{v} \\
&= \mathbf{v}\cdot\left(\mathbf{v}\times\mathbf{u}\right)+s^{2}\mathbf{u}+2s\left(\mathbf{v}\times\mathbf{u}\right)+\left(\mathbf{v}\cdot\mathbf{u}\right)\mathbf{v}-\left(\mathbf{v}\times\mathbf{u}\right)\times\mathbf{v}
\end{aligned}
$$

By the identities of the dot and cross products, the first term is zero and the last term is $|\mathbf{v}|^{2}\mathbf{u}-\left(\mathbf{v}\cdot\mathbf{u}\right)\mathbf{v}$, so we have

$$
\mathbf{quq}^{-1} = \left(s^{2}-|\mathbf{v}|^{2}\right)\mathbf{u}+2s\left(\mathbf{v}\times\mathbf{u}\right)+2\left(\mathbf{v}\cdot\mathbf{u}\right)\mathbf{v}
$$

If we say $t = |\mathbf{v}|$ and set $\mathbf{a}$ to the normalized vector $\mathbf{v}/t$, then we can rewrite this as

$$
\mathbf{quq}^{-1} = \left(s^{2}-t^{2}\right)\mathbf{u}+2st\left(\mathbf{a}\times\mathbf{u}\right)+2t^{2}\left(\mathbf{a}\cdot\mathbf{u}\right)\mathbf{a}
$$

This represents a rotation about the axis $\mathbf{a}$, with an angle θ given by $\cos\theta = s^{2}-t^{2}$, $\sin\theta = 2st$ and $1-\cos\theta = 2t^{2}$. Of these, we only really need the last, since the first two together only confirm that $s^{2}+t^{2} = 1$, which we knew because $\mathbf{q}$ is of unit length. The last is equivalent to saying that $t = \sin\left(\frac{\theta}{2}\right)$, which implies that $s = \cos\left(\frac{\theta}{2}\right)$. So we can sum all this up by saying that a rotation around an axis $\mathbf{a}$ with angle θ can be calculated using the quaternion

$$
\mathbf{q} = \cos\left(\frac{\theta}{2}\right)+\sin\left(\frac{\theta}{2}\right)\mathbf{a}
$$

This is a fairly significant improvement on the matrix form, first because far fewer calculations are involved in the transformation, and second because it's much easier to see the relationship between the rotation and the quaternion than it is with the matrix. Also, just as with matrices, we can interpolate between two quaternions by taking a linear combination of them (although the rate at which the interpolation occurs is not the same as the rate at which the angle varies).

Parents and Children

As well as combining transforms in order to move an object from one place to another, we can use them to define relationships between different nodes. This allows us to move whole groups of nodes together by varying a single transform, just as varying a node's transform can affect all the vertices of its model mesh.

We arrange all the nodes of the 3D world in the form of a tree, where each node has exactly one *parent* and any number of *children*. The topmost node is the world itself, and each of the world node's children has its own transform relative to the world. But the transform of a child node is applied relative to its parent: that is to say, if the child's relative transform is **C** and the parent's transform is **P** then the child's transform relative to the world's coordinate system (reference frame, basis) is **CP**.

For example, suppose one model is sitting in the world with a world transform consisting of a rotation about the x-axis and a uniform scale. Now any child of this model will be rotated and scaled before its own transform is applied. So the model and its children act as a group: if the parent model is translated, rotated or scaled, its children, grandchildren, and so on will move along with it.

This means that there is a potential ambiguity when transforming an object: if you want to, for example, move it 5 units along the z-axis, which z-axis does that mean? It could be the node's "local" z-axis, or its z-axis relative to its parent, or the actual z-axis of the world. Figure 18.4 illustrates this issue.

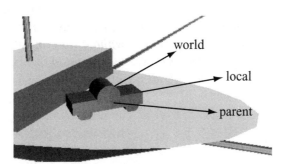

FIGURE 18.4 Relative motion in 3D space.

In the figure, we have a model of a car, whose parent is the ship on which it is sitting. The car was modeled with its z-axis pointing along the body of the car. So, if we want to translate it by 5 units "along the z-axis," this could mean any of the directions indicated. The first is the car's own z-axis, which is pointing along the world vector $(1 \ 0 \ 1)^{\mathrm{T}}$. The second is the ship's z-axis, which is pointing along the world's x-axis. The third is the world's z-axis. And in fact, we might want to use the z-axis of any other node in the scene.

Fortunately, each of these is easy to calculate. The z-axis of the node is given by the last column of its complete world transform matrix—and in general, any direction vector can be found simply by transforming it with the node's world transform. Similarly, we can work out the direction of the parent's z-axis, or any other model's, and of course the world's z-axis is trivial.

More commonly, we want to go the other way round: we need to know how to change the node's personal transform in order to make it move along a particular vector (or scale or rotation). In this case, the simplest situation is transforming the object in its local reference frame—this is just a matter of altering its own transform, which we have already looked at. To change it relative to its parent's transform is a little harder: suppose we want to move it 5 pixels relative to the parent's z-axis, we first need to calculate that vector in the child's reference frame. That is, we need a vector $\mathbf{v}$ such that $\mathbf{Cv} = \mathbf{k}$, which is given by $\mathbf{v} = \mathbf{C}^{-1}\mathbf{k}$. In English, this means that the vector $\mathbf{v}$, when "untransformed" into parent-space, is equal to the z-vector $\mathbf{k}$. Notice that this is the same independent of the parent's own transform. Similarly, to translate (rotate, scale) relative to a world-vector, we have to invert the complete world transform of the child node.

The vector $\mathbf{v}$ does not need to be of unit length, since any of the transforms involved may include a scaling element. Actually, this is convenient, as it means we can perform our translation of 5 units without worrying about scale, simply multiplying by the already scaled vector $\mathbf{v}$. But for rotations we need to remember to normalize the axis vector before performing the rotation.

EXERCISES

Exercise 18.1

Create functions that will apply a translation, scale, or rotation for a particular node relative to the world, the node's parent, or the node itself.

You should think about which method of storing transform information is most useful: as a single matrix or as three transformation vectors? Using quaternions for rotations?

SUMMARY

In this chapter we have seen how homogeneous coordinates and mathematical gizmos like quaternions can be used to create a simple representation of a node's disposition in 3D space. In the process, we've also learned how to create smooth motion incorporating simultaneous rotation, translation, and scale transformations by interpolating between transforms.

In the next chapter we'll take one final look at collision detection by extending our previous work into the third dimension.

YOU SHOULD NOW KNOW

- the meaning of the term *transform* and how it is represented in various forms: as a single matrix, as a combination of separate matrices, and as three vectors
- how *quaternions* can be used to create a simpler representation of rotations
- how transforms can be combined to move objects from place to place, and to create groups of objects with a fixed position relative to one another

19 Collision Detection in Three Dimensions

OVERVIEW

As you might expect, while there is nothing fundamentally different about the techniques of collision detection in 3D, adding another dimension does make things more complicated. For one thing, the range of shapes in 3D is much more complex, in particular the addition of the cylinder and the cone. Also, there are more ways for two objects *not* to collide: two non-parallel straight paths in 2D will always intersect, whereas in 3D they will generally miss each other.

Most of the techniques we'll look at will be fairly familiar, and we won't use as many code examples as in previous chapters on the subject—you should be able to apply the mathematics for yourself by now. Our main goal is to create a toolset for dealing with these kinds of problems, and we'll look at a few different examples of techniques that are useful in different circumstances.

WHEN WORLDS COLLIDE

The simplest collisions in 3D are between balls or *spheres*, the 3D analog of the circle. Most of the techniques for detecting collisions with spheres are direct translations of the 2D equivalents.

Spheres

A sphere is defined as the set of points at a constant distance r from the center—in fact, in a mathematical sense a circle is just a specific kind of sphere. You can have a sphere in any number of dimensions (in more than three dimensions it's often called a *hypersphere*), but we'll reserve the term for 3D. We'll use the terminology $S(\mathbf{c}, r)$ to refer to such a sphere.

The general term for a point on a sphere is a little more complex than a circle. In vector terms, it's the point $\mathbf{c} + r\mathbf{v}$, where $\mathbf{v}$ is any vector of unit length. Unfortunately, there is no neat trigonometric way to characterize $\mathbf{v}$. The easiest way is to think of a particular unit vector, such as $\mathbf{i}$, and imagine rotating it by a certain amount in two directions. This gives us a general expression for these vectors:

$$\mathbf{v} = \mathbf{R}_y \mathbf{R}_z \mathbf{i}$$

$$= \begin{pmatrix} \cos\phi & 0 & -\sin\phi \\ 0 & 1 & 0 \\ \sin\phi & 0 & \cos\phi \end{pmatrix} \begin{pmatrix} \cos\theta & -\sin\theta & 0 \\ \sin\theta & \cos\theta & 0 \\ 0 & 0 & 1 \end{pmatrix} \begin{pmatrix} 1 \\ 0 \\ 0 \end{pmatrix}$$

$$= \begin{pmatrix} \cos\phi & 0 & -\sin\phi \\ 0 & 1 & 0 \\ \sin\phi & 0 & \cos\phi \end{pmatrix} \begin{pmatrix} \cos\theta \\ \sin\theta \\ 0 \end{pmatrix}$$

$$= \begin{pmatrix} \cos\phi\cos\theta \\ \sin\theta \\ \sin\phi\cos\theta \end{pmatrix}$$

For a one-to-one mapping between values of θ and ϕ and points on the sphere, θ should take values between 0 and 2π, and ϕ should take values between 0 and π. Think of them as longitude and latitude. Of course, there are lots of variations on this theme which will serve just as well.

A Moving Sphere and a Wall

We want to find, as in Figure 19.1, the intersection of a sphere $S(\mathbf{c}, r)$, moving along a vector $\mathbf{v}$, with an infinite plane defined by the point $\mathbf{p}$ and the normal vector $\mathbf{n}$ (from here on, we'll call this the plane $P(\mathbf{p}, \mathbf{n})$).

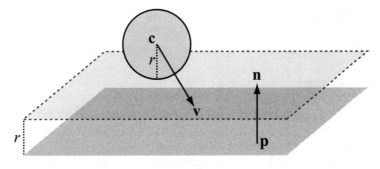

FIGURE 19.1 A moving sphere and a plane.

The technique is almost identical to the problem of a circle and a line, which we have seen before. First of all, we find the value $\mathbf{n} \cdot (\mathbf{c} - \mathbf{p})$: if this value is positive then the sphere lies on the positive normal side of the plane, otherwise it lies on the negative normal side, in which case we replace $\mathbf{n}$ by $-\mathbf{n}$. Now we can reduce the problem to the simpler one, solved in Chapter 17, of finding the intersection of a point with a plane. We simply offset the plane by the vector $r\mathbf{n}$, and find the intersection of the line $\mathbf{c} + t\mathbf{v}$ with the new plane $P(\mathbf{p} + r\mathbf{n}, \mathbf{n})$.

Often we're only looking for a one-way collision with a plane: in particular, when calculating collisions between solid objects we assume that the normal to each face is pointing outward. This is also used in visibility determination, as we've seen. That means we can simplify the above problem: we needn't calculate which side of the plane the sphere is on; it will only collide with the plane if the dot product $\mathbf{v} \cdot \mathbf{n}$ is negative.

A Sphere and a Moving Point or Two Spheres

This time we'll think of the sphere as stationary at the origin, and consider a particle at $\mathbf{p}$ moving along the vector $\mathbf{v}$. We now need to solve the equation $|\mathbf{p} + t\mathbf{v}| = r$, which is equivalent to

$$(\mathbf{p} + t\mathbf{v}) \cdot (\mathbf{p} + t\mathbf{v}) = r^2$$
$$\mathbf{p} \cdot \mathbf{p} + 2t\mathbf{p} \cdot \mathbf{v} + t^2 \mathbf{v} \cdot \mathbf{v} = r^2$$

This is simply a quadratic equation in t, which can be solved with the quadratic formula as usual, giving us two possible collision points, of which we're interested in the smallest positive value (if one value is negative then our particle was inside the sphere to start with).

Having solved this problem, it's simple to extend it to two general spheres colliding. As with the case of two circles, the problem of two spheres of radius r and s colliding is equivalent to a particle colliding with a single sphere of radius $r + s$.

The Point of Contact

With the extra dimension, two objects no longer collide along a line, instead they meet along a collision plane. As before, the collision normal is the most useful to know: when resolving the collision, only the component of motion normal to the collision is affected, while the tangential component is unchanged.

Finding the collision normal with a sphere is straightforward, since as with the circle, the normal is simply along the line from the point of contact to the center. When two spheres collide, this line is directly along the vector between the two centers. Of course, when the sphere collides with a plane, then the plane's normal is the collision normal.

WHEN FOOTBALLS COLLIDE

All right, so this was pretty easy. But as you'll have suspected, life gets a lot harder once we consider shapes that are more complex than spheres.

Ellipsoids

An *ellipsoid* is the 3D equivalent of the ellipse: as with the 2D case, the easiest way to think of it is a sphere that has been transformed by a general scale in three dimensions. So a point on an ellipsoid centered on the origin has the general form $\mathbf{v} = \mathbf{RSi}$. In fact, a general ellipsoid including position, orientation, and scale is described exactly by a general transform $\mathbf{T}$, applied to the unit sphere described by $\left(\cos\phi\cos\theta, \quad \sin\theta, \quad \sin\phi\cos\theta\right)^{\mathrm{T}}$.

NOTE

An ellipsoid with a circular cross-section along one axis (i.e., with two of the scale factors of S equal) is called a spheroid, *which can be either* oblate *(flattened like a UFO) or* prolate *(extended like a football) but never* latte *(shaped like a coffee-cup).*

Incidentally, for the purposes of this chapter we'll be using the word "transform" somewhat loosely, sometimes to describe just the rotation and scale parts of the transform proper, in the form of a 3×3 matrix, and we'll keep the position part of the transform separate for clarity—we'll use the notation E($\mathbf{p}$, $\mathbf{T}$). In practice it's more efficient to use the full 4×4 transform. As with the 2D ellipse, we can also describe the ellipsoid by means of a list of its principal axes and the values a, b, c. The two descriptions are, of course, equivalent—translating from one to the other is left to you as an exercise.

An Ellipsoid and a Moving Point or Plane

Calculating a collision between an ellipsoid $E(\mathbf{p}, \mathbf{T})$ moving along a vector $\mathbf{v}$ and a point or plane, as with the 2D case, is best accomplished by transforming space so that the ellipsoid becomes a sphere. Given the above description of the ellipsoid, this is a fairly simple process—we simply need to invert the transform $\mathbf{T}$. Then we're looking for the collision between the unit sphere starting on $\mathbf{T}^{-1}\mathbf{p}$ with a displacement of $\mathbf{T}^{-1}\mathbf{v}$ and the transformed plane.

We're also now in a position to deal with the problem left dangling at the end of Chapter 8: calculating the normal at the ellipsoid (or ellipse) surface. Remember the discussion from the previous chapter about normals: in the case of the plane, the transformed normal $\mathbf{T}^{-1}\mathbf{n}$ would not be normal to the transformed plane. Instead, we have to use the inverse transpose matrix, which is just the transpose of $\mathbf{T}$. Similarly, after performing the calculation we would need to apply the inverse transpose $\left(\mathbf{T}^{-1}\right)^{T}$ to any collision normals to determine the collision normal in world space again.

Here's an example of this method in code:

```
function ellipsoidPlaneCollision(ell, pl)
    set inverseTransform to inverseMatrix(ell.matrix)
    set inverseTranspose to transpose(ell.matrix)
    set planePoint to matrixMultiply(inverseTransform, pl.refPoint-
ell.pos)
    set circleVel to matrixMultiply(inverseTransform, ell.displacement-
pl.displacement)
    set normal to matrixMultiply(inverseTranspose, plane.normal)
    set t to circlePlaneCollision(circlePos, 1, circleVel, planePoint,
normal)
    return t
end function
```

Two Ellipsoids

So how can we find the intersection of two ellipsoids? You should be able to guess, based on the difficulty of the 2D case that this will not be possible to solve algebraically. But we can make a good start. Let's see how we might describe this problem in terms of matrix algebra: suppose our ellipsoids are $E_1\left(\mathbf{0}, \mathbf{T}_1\right)$ and $E_2\left(\mathbf{p}, \mathbf{T}_2\right)$, and the relative velocity is $\mathbf{v}$. We're looking for two unit vectors $\mathbf{u}_1$ and $\mathbf{u}_2$ which satisfy.

$T_1 u_1 = T_2 u_2 + p + tv$, Taking T_1 to the other side, we have $u_1 = T_1^{-1} T_2 u_2 + T_1^{-1} p + t T_1^{-1} v$.

Here, there are five unknowns: the unit vectors u_1 and u_2, with two degrees of freedom each, and the scalar t. However, we can add one more condition to narrow down the solution: the two ellipsoids must meet at a point, which means that at the point of contact the normals must be parallel. The normal of an ellipsoid at the point Tu is the point $\left(T^{-1} \right)^T u$, so we have:

$$\left(T_1^{-1} \right)^T u_1 = \left(T_2^{-1} \right)^T u_2$$

Inverting the first transform, this becomes

$$u_1 = T_1^T \left(T_2^{-1} \right)^T u_2, \text{ which we can write as } u_1 = M u_2.$$

This means that we can now eliminate u_1 from the first equation, which tells us that $M u_2 = T_1^{-1} T_2 u_2 + T_1^{-1} p + t T_1^{-1} v$.

Between them, these two results form a system of three independent equations in three unknowns (since u_2 is known to be a unit vector). These equations, containing a mixture of trigonometric and linear terms, are not possible to solve algebraically, so a numerical approximation method must be used. However, we can simplify things somewhat if the ellipsoids are the same size (have the same transform T), or a scalar multiple of one another (transforms T and aT). Then we can invert the transform matrix to turn the problem into a collision of two spheres, which we've already solved:

$$u_1 - a u_2 = T^{-1} p + t T^{-1} v$$
$$\left(T^{-1} \right)^T \left(u_1 \pm u_2 \right) = 0$$

From the second equation (saying that the normals are parallel) we know that either $u_1 = u_2$ or $u_1 = -u_2$ (since a transform can't have a zero determinant). The first case corresponds to when one ellipsoid is inside the other—we're likely to be more interested in the second case. Then by substitution in the first equation we find that

$$(1 + a) u_1 = T^{-1} p + t T^{-1} v$$
$$\left| T^{-1} p + t T^{-1} v \right| = 1 - a$$

(This follows since u_1 is a unit vector.) The remainder of the method follows as for the collision of two spheres.

WHEN BOXES COLLIDE

Our next 3D analog is the box or *cuboid*. However, as with the generalization of rectangles to other convex polygons, the techniques for detecting collisions with a cuboid generalize to other convex *polyhedra*, that is to say, shapes with any number of flat faces connected by edges, such as cubes, pyramids, cut diamonds, or soccer balls.

Boxes

A cuboid has eight vertices joined together by twelve edges, making six faces in all—like a brick. As with ellipsoids, we can consider a general cuboid to be a transform **T** applied to a standard unit cube centered on the origin: its eight vertices being the eight different combinations of $(\pm0.5 \quad \pm0.5 \quad \pm0.5)^T$. Knowing this transform, it is simple to test whether a particular point **p** is inside the cuboid: find $\mathbf{T}^{-1}\mathbf{p}$ and determine whether each of its coordinates has absolute value less than 0.5.

A Box and a Moving Point

This gives us one method for finding the point of intersection of a line **p** + *t***v** with the box whose transform is **T**. We're searching for the smallest value of *t* such that $\mathbf{T}^{-1}(\mathbf{p}+t\mathbf{v}) = \mathbf{T}^{-1}\mathbf{p}+t\mathbf{T}^{-1}\mathbf{v} = \mathbf{q}+t\mathbf{w}$ lies within the cube. This amounts to six inequalities:

$$-0.5 < q_1 + tw_1 < 0.5$$
$$-0.5 < q_2 + tw_2 < 0.5$$
$$-0.5 < q_3 + tw_3 < 0.5$$

There is a very efficient algorithm for solving systems of linear inequalities such as this, called the *simplex algorithm*, but we'll leave that for now since for the purposes of this problem it's a little specific to cuboids. The more general method is to check for intersection with each of the faces of the cuboid, or other polyhedron, in turn. In fact, as with the rectangle, we can immediately discount all faces on the other side of the cube from the particle (using the dot product of the face normal with the collision vector as mentioned above).

We've already seen how to calculate the point of intersection of a particle with a plane. This means we can quickly calculate the three possible collision points with the infinite planes through each face. We can then check just these points to find which, if any, of them lies within the rectangle of the face by a method which will work for any planar convex polygon: test whether the point lies on the correct side of each of the edges of the rectangle as illustrated in Figure 19.2.

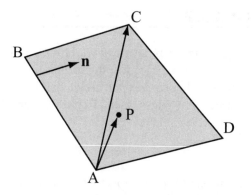

FIGURE 19.2   Testing whether a point lies inside a polygon.

As in the figure, you can test if the point P lies on the correct side of AB by finding the dot products $\overrightarrow{AP} \cdot \mathbf{n}$ and $\overrightarrow{AC} \cdot \mathbf{n}$. If these have the same sign (i.e., their product is positive), then P and C must lie on the same side of AB. Perform this test for each of the sides of ABCD and you have shown that P is inside the rectangle.

The same basic method will work for any polyhedron, although if its faces are not convex then you need to use a more general technique for testing whether P lies on the face, such as the raycasting technique discussed in Chapter 10.

Two Boxes

With two colliding boxes, there's not really much of an alternative to face-by-face checking, or more specifically face-by-vertex checking as in 2D. There are rather a lot of possible face-to-vertex collisions when dealing with boxes at any possible size and angle, but in each of them one of the vertices of one box is in contact with one of the faces of the other. We don't need to check all possible vertices, only those at the leading edge of the cuboid, and in fact for each face there is only one vertex that can collide with it (unless the cuboids are aligned). This is the vertex nearest to the face in the direction of the face normal, as shown in Figure 19.3.

We can calculate this for each face by calculating the distance of each vertex $\mathbf{v}$ of one cube to each face $(\mathbf{p}, \mathbf{n})$ of the other (the minimum value of $(\mathbf{v} - \mathbf{p}) \cdot \mathbf{n}$). If any distance is negative then there is no possible collision on this face, and the same goes for any convex polyhedron. If two vertices are the same distance from the face then either of them could collide. Nevertheless, this still leaves quite a few possible collisions to check.

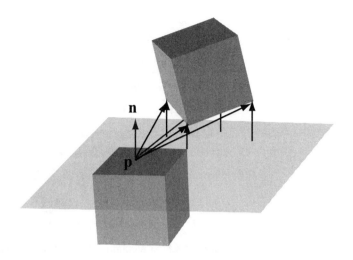

FIGURE 19.3   The colliding vertex.

We've also missed out another possible collision, as illustrated in Figure 19.4, where two boxes collide at the edges (this also includes the case where an edge of one box collides with the face of another). In this case, there is no vertex-to-face collision at all, so we have to perform a completely different calculation.

FIGURE 19.4   Edge-to-edge box collision.

To solve this, we can consider the parallelogram swept out by the first edge as it travels along the vector $\mathbf{v}$ (see Figure 19.5). If this parallelogram intersects with the second edge, then there is a collision at point $\mathbf{c}$ as shown.

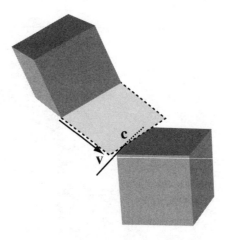

FIGURE 19.5   Calculating the collision of two lines.

This is just a line-polygon collision of the kind we've already seen. A collision like this is only possible if the normals of all four of the faces involved have the correct dot product with the velocity vector (positive for the moving box, negative for the static one). And as with the vertex-face collisions, we're only interested in the closest edges, which we can calculate in much the same way.

We won't write the whole function explicitly here (it's somewhat long) but we'll return to it in Chapter 23 where we'll write a specialized function to test for collisions between an axis-aligned box and a quadrilateral whose edges are aligned to the x-z plane, for use in tile-based 3D games.

A Box and a Sphere

When a sphere might collide with a box there are, again, several possibilities: the sphere might, in particular, collide with a face, edge or vertex. Collisions with a vertex are straightforward point-sphere calculations, which we have already covered. Collisions with a face are also simple enough, as we can adapt the same technique as before. First we calculate if the sphere might collide with the infinite plane containing the face, then we check if the collision point is inside the face just as we did in the above example.

Collisions with an edge are slightly more problematic. This is essentially the problem of calculating a collision between a sphere and a line, as shown in Figure 19.6. That is, given a sphere $S(\mathbf{p}, r)$ moving along the vector $\mathbf{v}$, and a line $(\mathbf{q}, \mathbf{u})$, where do they meet?

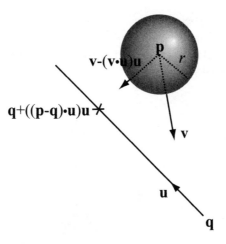

FIGURE 19.6 A sphere and a line.

One way to simplify this is to realize that we're only interested in the component of motion perpendicular to the line's vector. If we subtract from the velocity vector the component $(v \cdot u)u$, and add the vector $((p - q) \cdot u)u$ to q, then we end up with a projection of the problem into 2D space. Now we're looking for the intersection of a circle of radius r centered on p with the point $q + ((p - q) \cdot u)u$. You should be able to solve this simplified problem for yourself.

As before, we can cull several of the sphere-box collisions as impossible *a priori*. A face-sphere collision is only possible if the face normal is pointing in the opposite direction from the velocity, edge-sphere, and vertex-sphere collisions are only possible if at least one associated face normal is doing so.

WHEN CANS COLLIDE

The preceding discussion leads us nicely into one last shape which has no 2D equivalent, the *cylinder*.

Cylinders

A cylinder is the set of points at a distance r from some line (its *axis*). It can either be infinitely long or have two circular "caps" whose normals are parallel to the axis (the cylinder's length is defined as the distance between the two caps). The intersection of an infinite cylinder with any plane perpendicular to the axis is a circle, and with any other non-parallel plane is an ellipse. We'll use the notation $C(p, v, r, l)$ to represent a cylinder of radius r centered on p, with axis vector v and length l.

A cylinder is a specific case of a more general shape called a *cone*, which is like a cylinder except that the radius of the two end-caps is different: that is to say, the radius of any circular cross-section is proportional to the distance along the axis, as shown in Figure 19.7.

FIGURE 19.7   A cone.

If you take an infinite mathematical cone (which looks like two identical paper cones joined at the tips), and find its intersection with a plane, you'll get one of three shapes: an ellipse, a parabola, or an asymptotic shape called a hyperbola, *such as the graph of* $y^2 = 1 + x^2$. *These three curves are collectively known as* conic sections *and have rather similar properties.*

Cylinders and cones are examples of what is called a *surface of rotation*, which is to say a 3D shape formed by taking a 2D profile and spinning it around an axis, like a pot forming on a potter's wheel. Most 3D modeling software includes the facility for creating a surface of rotation (sometimes called a *lathe* tool). We'll return to these shapes in the next chapter.

A Cylinder and a Point or Sphere

We've already done most of the work for this question: the collision of a point with the body of a cylinder is equivalent to a sphere colliding with a line, which we dealt with in the previous section. And in general, a sphere with radius *r* colliding with the body of a cylinder of radius *s* is equivalent to a sphere of radius *r* + *s* colliding with the cylinder's axis.

The only complication is introduced by the end caps, which entails finding the collision point with a flat circle or disc of radius s, center **c** as shown in Figure 19.8.

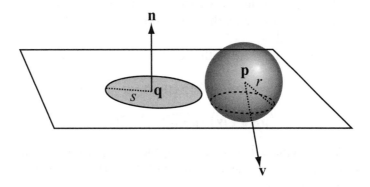

FIGURE 19.8   A sphere and a flat disc.

There are various ways to solve this, which are of course all equivalent. Here's one approach that gives a different perspective on the problem and is often useful for collisions with flat (*laminar*) objects (it's related to the method we used for circle-line collisions). At any moment, we can calculate the intersection of the sphere with the infinite plane containing the circle (or other lamina). The intersection of a sphere with a plane (if there is one) is a circle whose radius depends on the distance of the sphere from the plane.

To be concrete, a sphere S(**p**, r) moving along **v** intersects a plane P(**q**, **n**) as follows: We define the distance of the sphere from the plane at time t to be $d = (\mathbf{p} - \mathbf{q} + t\mathbf{v}) \cdot \mathbf{n}$ (the value can be positive or negative). Then if $|d| > r$ there is no intersection, otherwise the intersection is a circle, whose radius is $r_c = \sqrt{r^2 - d^2}$ and whose center is $\mathbf{p}_c = \mathbf{p} + t\mathbf{v} - d\mathbf{n}$.

Now, this should give a clear idea of how we could find the collision between a sphere and a disc. There are two possible collisions: in the first, the sphere collides somewhere inside the disc, so $d = r$ and $|\mathbf{p}_c - \mathbf{q}| \le s$. This tells us that

$$\left(\mathbf{p} - \mathbf{q} + t\mathbf{v} - r\mathbf{n}\right) \cdot \left(\mathbf{p} - \mathbf{q} + t\mathbf{v} - r\mathbf{n}\right) \le s^2$$
$$\left(\mathbf{p} - \mathbf{q} + t\mathbf{v}\right) \cdot \left(\mathbf{p} - \mathbf{q} + t\mathbf{v}\right) - 2r\left(\mathbf{p} - \mathbf{q} + t\mathbf{v}\right) \cdot \mathbf{n} + r^2 \mathbf{n} \cdot \mathbf{n} \le s^2$$
$$\left(\mathbf{p} - \mathbf{q} + t\mathbf{v}\right) \cdot \left(\mathbf{p} - \mathbf{q} + t\mathbf{v}\right) \le s^2 + r^2$$

So if we find the point of collision of the sphere with the laminar plane, we can use the above test to check whether it lies within the circle (of course, the same result could be found much more simply with Pythagoras' Theorem, but bear with it).

Now let's look at the other possibility that the sphere collides with the circumference of the disc. In that case, we know that the circle of intersection of the sphere and the laminar plane must be touching—that is, $|\mathbf{p}_c - \mathbf{q}| = r_c + s$. Since in our case we're looking at a cylinder, we know that the sphere can collide only on one side of the disc, so we also know that d is positive (this would not be the case for a literal flat disc like a CD).

So to find a collision with the circumference, we are looking for t such that

$$\left(\mathbf{p} - \mathbf{q} + t\mathbf{v} - r\mathbf{n}\right) \cdot \left(\mathbf{p} - \mathbf{q} + t\mathbf{v} - r\mathbf{n}\right) = \left(\sqrt{r^2 - d^2} + s\right)^2$$

$$\left(\mathbf{p} - \mathbf{q} + t\mathbf{v}\right) \cdot \left(\mathbf{p} - \mathbf{q} + t\mathbf{v}\right) - 2rd = -d^2 + s^2 + 2s\sqrt{r^2 - d^2}$$

We can replace d by its full dot-product expansion here to yield an equation in t which can't be solved algebraically but is nevertheless a fairly smooth function (essentially quadratic). It shouldn't come as a surprise to find no algebraic solution here: the cross-sectional circle is rather similar to a moving ellipse, when viewed from the perspective of the disc.

If we're dealing only with a particle of zero radius, then we can ignore the possibility of a collision along the circumference. So there is an algebraic solution in this case.

A Cone and a Sphere or Particle

To calculate the collision of a sphere with a cone, we need to take into account the angle of slope of the sides. As before, we can expand the cone by r to reduce the case of a colliding sphere to one of a colliding particle, but we have to be a little careful with this method when calculating the point of impact.

For simplicity, we'll assume that the cone's *apex*, the point at which its radius is zero (which may not be part of the physical cone if it is not infinitely long) is at the origin. From there, its sides come out at an angle α. If the particle is at $\mathbf{p} + t\mathbf{v}$ and the cone's normalized axis vector is $\mathbf{u}$, then we can calculate the particle's distance from the axis to be

$$d = \sqrt{\left(\mathbf{p} + t\mathbf{v}\right) \cdot \left(\mathbf{p} + t\mathbf{v}\right) - \left(\left(\mathbf{p} + t\mathbf{v}\right) \cdot \mathbf{u}\right)^2}$$

The radius of the cone on the plane containing the particle at that time is

$$r = \left(\mathbf{p} + t\mathbf{v}\right) \cdot \mathbf{u} \tan \alpha$$

When the particle collides, these two values must be equal, giving us an equation for t:

$$\sqrt{(\mathbf{p}+t\mathbf{v})\cdot(\mathbf{p}+t\mathbf{v})-\left((\mathbf{p}+t\mathbf{v})\cdot\mathbf{u}\right)^2}=(\mathbf{p}+t\mathbf{v})\cdot\mathbf{u}\tan\alpha$$

$$(\mathbf{p}+t\mathbf{v})\cdot(\mathbf{p}+t\mathbf{v})=\left((\mathbf{p}+t\mathbf{v})\cdot\mathbf{u}\right)^2\left(\tan^2\alpha+1\right)$$

$$=\left((\mathbf{p}+t\mathbf{v})\cdot\mathbf{u}\right)^2\Big/\cos^2\alpha$$

As you can see, this is a fairly minor change to the equation for the cylinder. To transform to the case of a sphere is simple, except that in collisions with the end-caps we can no longer be sure that the distance from the sphere to the cap plane is positive at the moment of collision.

Two Cylinders

When we're looking at the collision of two cylinders, the most sensible thing is to consider them as ellipses moving through a plane (this is for collisions along the body of the cylinder rather than the end-caps). Simply choose a plane in space—perpendicular to one axis is sensible—and project both cylinders onto this plane.

If the cylinders are aligned along the same axis, this is simple to solve, as it's equivalent to two moving circles. But if they are not aligned on the same axis, this becomes an elliptical collision and so requires numerical methods to solve.

To calculate the projected ellipse onto a plane through a cylinder (see Figure 19.9), we first calculate the center of the ellipse, which is the point at which the plane intersects with the axis. The halfminor axis of the ellipse is always the radius of the cylinder, and directed along the cross-product of the plane normal and the

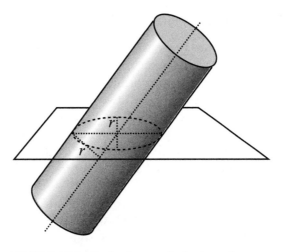

FIGURE 19.9 Projecting a cylinder to a plane.

axis. By finding the cross-product of this with the plane normal, we can find the vector of the major axis, and by finding the angle between this vector and the axis, we can find the length by trigonometry.

WHEN STUFF COLLIDES

As you can see, even these simple shapes can involve complicated calculations, often with no algebraic solution. For more complex shapes you need a strategy to perform the calculations necessary in a realistic time scale.

Bounding Spheres, Ellipsoids, and Boxes

As in 2D, the most useful technique for calculating collisions of more complex shapes is to create a *bounding volume*: a shape that is known to contain the whole of your object. When the object is very nearly the right shape already, you can use the bounding volume as a proxy for collision calculations. If not, then the bounding shape can at least be used to perform an initial, simpler collision check before performing a full triangle-by-triangle calculation.

The process of calculating a bounding volume in 3D is very similar to the process in 2D. To create a bounding sphere, for example, we can average all the vertices of our model to get the center and then calculate the radius as the maximum distance of one point from the center (as in 2D this won't usually yield the smallest possible sphere but it's a quick and cheap method). Bounding ellipsoids can be found by a process of factor analysis as before, and we can create both axis-aligned and object-aligned bounding boxes.

Collisions with an Arbitrary Mesh

For a more complex shape there is generally no better method than to check collisions with an arbitrary mesh, which consists of a number of vertices joined together in triangles, with the normal of each triangle known and pointing "out" of the shape (a two-sided mesh has two sets of triangles, one pointing inward, the other outward; the direction of the normal is calculated according to the order of the vertices, so that when you are looking at the triangle, with its normal pointing toward you, the vertices are ordered in a clockwise direction). Usually it is still possible to create a simplified shape as a proxy, however, with fewer triangles to calculate.

The technique for calculating collisions with a triangular mesh is essentially the same as for a box, using the trick illustrated in Figure 19.2 to determine whether a point is inside a triangle: assuming the point is in the plane of the triangle, it is inside it if it's on the correct, interior side of each of the three edges. This means it has to be on the same side as the other vertex of the triangle: thus, its dot-product with the cross-product of the edge and the normal must be positive. That is, if we set $\mathbf{n}_1 = \mathbf{n} \times (\mathbf{v}_2 - \mathbf{v}_3)$, then $(\mathbf{n}_1 \cdot (\mathbf{v}_1 - \mathbf{v}_2)) \cdot (\mathbf{n}_1 \cdot (\mathbf{p} - \mathbf{v}_2)) \geq 0$.

RESOLVING COLLISIONS IN THREE DIMENSIONS

The laws of physics, unsurprisingly, don't change a great deal by adding another dimension. Things bounce and collide just the same way as before. This means that all the techniques we used in 2D carry across almost unchanged although we now have a tangential plane rather than just a tangential line, as mentioned earlier.

The one exception (and isn't it always so) is rotation. As we've already seen, spin can take place in several directions—or rather, a spin in one direction can be conceived of as three spins in perpendicular directions. This makes it a little hard to handle, and we don't have space to look into it here. Actually, the underlying concepts don't really change here either, but the calculations do get a little messy. In any case, calculating collisions between 3D spinning objects is definitely beyond our scope.

EXERCISES

Exercise 19.1

Translate one or more of the examples in the chapter into a concrete function, and include a function to resolve the collision.

Most of the examples were given without code, but with the experience of 2D collisions you shouldn't find this too hard for spheres and boxes at least.

SUMMARY

With luck, you'll have reached the end of this chapter thinking that linear collision detection in 3D doesn't look too bad—not much harder than you've already tackled. If so, you can feel pleased with yourself, as it means you understood the techniques already covered. If not, you should go back to earlier chapters and see what you've missed. We've looked now at a large number of different shapes and seen how we can make some calculations to detect collisions between them, as well as more general techniques which will work on any mesh. There is still plenty of work to do in order to fill in the gaps, though!

For the next chapter in this high-speed tour of 3D, we'll look at how surfaces are given shape by light.

YOU SHOULD NOW KNOW

- the meaning of *sphere, ellipsoid, spheroid, cuboid, cylinder, cone,* and *mesh*
- how to calculate the intersection of each of these with a ray, or collision with a small particle
- how to calculate collisions between spheres and each of the others, and between pairs of similar objects
- how bounding volumes can be used as an extension of 2D bounding shapes

20   Lighting and Textures

In This Chapter

- Overview
- Light
- Materials
- Shading
- Exercises
- Summary
- You Should Now Know

OVERVIEW

In this chapter we're going to look at how an object is made to come to life instead of being a wireframe drawing. To create the illusion of solidity, we need to understand the nature of light and how it can be simulated in real time.

ON THE CD

Code samples from this chapter are implemented in *math.cst* in the script *chapter 20 (color)*. The *textures* demo demonstrates texture projection.

LIGHT

Before a 3D scene can be drawn to the screen, as well as knowing the position of each polygon, we need to know what colors to draw. This involves *lighting* the scene. We'll take a quick look at how lights work and how they are used to create complex color effects.

Real Lights

When atoms gain and then lose energy, they emit it in the form of a wave of oscillating electric and magnetic fields we call *electromagnetism*, which, depending on the amount of energy, has varying frequencies and wavelengths (but the same velocity in a vacuum). Our bodies include detectors that respond to a certain range of these frequencies, which we call *light* (or more accurately, *visible light*). One of these detectors, the *rod*, is sensitive to levels of brightness (the amplitude of the wave), while the other, the *cone*, is sensitive to the frequency. Actually, we humans have three different kinds of cone, sensitive to three different ranges of light that we experience as red, green, and blue. Most mammals have two kinds of cone, and some animals can see ranges of light that we consider invisible—for example bees see into the ultra-violet (higher-frequency light than we can see), while snakes can see into the infra-red (lower-frequency), although not through their eyes.

We don't only see three colors, however. Most light contains several overlapping waves with a broad range of frequencies, so generally all three kinds of cone are activated to different levels, as are the rods, and this mixture of frequencies is discriminated / experienced as a single color. Even a single-wavelength beam that doesn't trigger one cone precisely can be discriminated by the amount to which it activates the neighboring cones. So a wavelength half-way between "pure" red and "pure" green is experienced as yellow, and half-way between green and blue is experienced as a sky-blue color called "cyan," while a mixture of blue and red is experienced as a purplish color called "magenta." In fact, our visual system considers the colors to go in a cycle red-yellow-green-cyan-blue-magenta-red, although this bears no relationship to the underlying wavelengths of light. A mixture of lots of different wavelengths is experienced as white, while no light at all is experienced as black.

Computers take advantage of this peculiarity of our visual system by mimicking it in the way they display colors: each pixel of the screen is actually made up of three separate emitters of red, green, and blue, which can take any value between off and on—for a high-resolution display, each one can have a value between 0 and 255. When all three are fully lit, this creates a white dot, when none are lit, this makes a black dot, and we can create 16777216 different colors this way. We can represent each color by a 3D *RGB* vector, representing the size of each color by a real number between 0 and 1, so the color $\langle 0 \quad 0.5 \quad 0.5 \rangle$ would be a mid-intensity cyan. The advantage of this is that it allows us to perform arithmetic with colors, as we'll see shortly.

It's worth going into all this detail because many people think color is just "the wavelength of light," which misses an important issue that color is actually a micro judgment by the brain based on all the wavelengths the eye receives, and is also affected by global issues, so that if we are in an environment with an "ambient" light that has a blue tinge, or with strong shadows, our perception of the scene soon learns to subtract these global values off to see the underlying color. There are a number of optical illusions that make use of this phenomenon.

We see objects in the world because light, from the sun or elsewhere, bounces off their surfaces and reflects into our eyes. Each surface reacts to light differently: a mirror reflects all light exactly as it comes in, like an elastic collision (*specular* reflection); a white ball absorbs the light and then emits it all again in all directions, in the process losing any detail (*diffuse* or *Lambertian* reflection), and a black piece of charcoal absorbs nearly all of the light but doesn't emit it again (at least, not as radiation: it heats up and loses it to the air). A red surface is part-way between the two: it absorbs most of the light, but releases some of it back, in a mixture of wavelengths we experience as red. And a red pool ball has two surfaces, a specular glaze, which reflects some of the light unchanged, and beneath it a diffuse surface that absorbs and emits it, creating a surface with some mirrored qualities and some red.

To model all these factors in a real-time engine would take enormous computing power (although we're getting constantly closer to it). But we can use certain tricks in order to fake it. So let's start by considering ideal lights.

Fake Lights

The light striking any given point on a 3D object is a combination of three factors. The first is *ambient* light. This simulates the light that "surrounds" us: for example light that has come in from a window and bounced around the room several times until it has no real direction—it just illuminates everything in the scene. Ambient light is easy to calculate because it acts equally on all polygons in all directions (although more complex models allow the ambient light color and brightness to vary through space).

The second is *directional* light. As the name suggests, this light comes from a particular direction, like the light of the sun, but it is not affected by position: all objects in the scene are illuminated by it equally. A scene can have any number of directional lights, which for convenience are placed in the scene as if they were ordinary nodes, but only their rotation vector is relevant to their effect.

Finally, there is what might be called *attenuated* light, which has two forms, spot lights, and point lights. These are objects that can be placed in a scene and illuminate the objects around them with a particular color. Objects nearer to the light and, for spot lights, objects closer to the main beam of the light, are illuminated more than those further away. How much this happens depends on three *attenuation constants* that modify the brightness of the beam by a factor b: for a point light we have

$$b = \frac{1}{k_1 + k_2 d + k_3 d^2}$$

while for a spot light pointing in the direction **u** and at a unit vector **v** and distance d from the surface, we have

$$b = \frac{\max(-(\mathbf{u} \cdot \mathbf{v}), 0)^p}{k_1 + k_2 d + k_3 d^2}$$

where p is a special constant which measures the spread or focus of the light: a high value of p means that the light mostly illuminates a very narrow beam, while a low value makes it spread out more widely. An alternative method is to specify an actual angle for the beam. We use the $\max(-(\mathbf{u} \cdot \mathbf{v}), 0)$ term to ensure that only surfaces whose normal is pointing toward the light are illuminated.

Figure 20.1 shows an object illuminated by different kinds of lights.

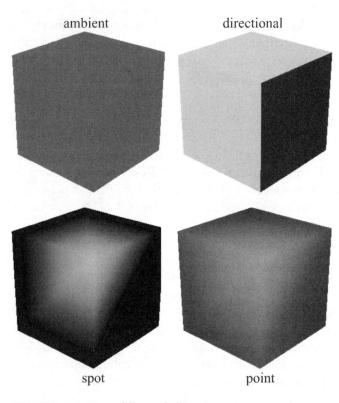

FIGURE 20.1 Four different lights.

MATERIALS

Each of these lights strikes the surface of objects in the scene and reflects off them to make them visible. How they do this is determined by the quality of the surface, which is achieved by means of an object called a *material*, which you can think of as a "coating" applied to the object.

We're using the word "material" to cover a number of different concepts here— much as, for example, Director's 3D engine uses the word "shader" which unfortunately has a number of different meanings in 3D engines and so we're avoiding it here. Different 3D modeling programs and APIs use different terminology for the same idea.

The Color Elements of a Surface

A material describes all the different qualities of the surface, and includes a number of different color components, which can either be single values or *image maps*. We'll look at image maps in the next section, for now we'll simply think of these as single values applied across the whole surface. Let's look at some of these components now.

The simplest element is called the *emissive* color: this is a color actually given off by the object, like a glowing lamp. Emissive light is a cheat: unlike real light it has no effect on any other object, just changes the color of the object emitting it, in all directions. But this makes it computationally cheap and a simple way to create objects of different colors. We'll call this color c_{em}.

The next component is the diffuse color, which tells us the color of light that would be Lambertian reflected if the surface was illuminated with full-spectrum white light (in other words, it's the best candidate for "the color of the surface"). The diffuse color is not dependent on the position of the observer, but it does vary according to the angle of the light falling on the surface. The closer the light angle is to the surface normal, the more of it is reflected, since the surface is illuminated by more of the beam as shown in Figure 20.2.

This gives us a formula for the diffuse color component from a surface with normal $\mathbf{n}$, due to a particular light. If the diffuse color of the material is $\mathbf{d}$, and it's illuminated by a light of color $\mathbf{c}$ from the (unit) direction $\mathbf{v}$, then the Lambertian reflection c_{diff} is given by $\mathbf{c}\mathbf{d}\max(\mathbf{n}\cdot\mathbf{v},0)$, where the multiplication of the colors is performed pairwise. Remember that color vectors are not the same as linear vectors in space—pairwise multiplication is said to *modulate* one color with another, so making a blue vector redder, for example. It's the correct method to use when dealing with a surface which absorbs some frequencies and reflects others. Note that

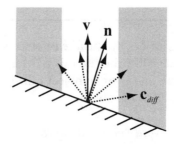

FIGURE 20.2 Calculating the diffuse component.

ambient light is normal to all surfaces, so the diffuse component of an ambient light is just **cd**.

The specular component has two elements, a color **s** and an exponent m. These combine to create a light of a single color, called a *specular highlight*. What they don't create is a mirror-reflection. This is because to create a mirror-reflection we'd need to model not just the direct light on the object due to the various lights in the scene, but the light reflected off all the other objects as well, which brings us into extremely computationally expensive ray-tracing territory. The illumination of an object in a real-time 3D scene is only affected by the lights themselves, not by light emitted, absorbed or reflected by other objects, which affects not only the possibility of mirror-images but of real-time shadows as well. Both of these have to be modeled in a different (not entirely satisfactory) way: we won't be looking at shadows here, but we'll look at mirror reflections later.

As we saw above, a specular reflection is the light-equivalent of an elastic collision, which means that the light bouncing off the surface is emitted preferentially at the same angle as it strikes, as shown in Figure 20.3. This means that the nearer the viewing vector is to this (unit) reflection vector **r**, the brighter the specular light is. We modify how near the vector needs to be by means of the exponent m, which "focuses" the reflection in much the same way as the exponent p did for spot lights.

So, again, we can calculate the specular reflection due to a particular (non-ambient) light as before. There are different formulations, but this one works pretty well: assuming that $\mathbf{n} \cdot \mathbf{v} > 0$ and the observer is at a vector **w** from the point on the surface, we have $\mathbf{c}_{spec} = \mathbf{sc}\left(\max\left(\mathbf{r} \cdot \mathbf{w}, 0\right)\right)^m$. A specular color of white is usually the most appropriate. The exponent m can take any value: a value of 0 essentially gives you a diffuse color, while an infinitely high value gives what would in theory be a mirrored surface—only a viewing angle exactly along **r** will detect the light.

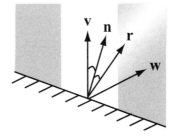

FIGURE 20.3 Calculating the specular component.

Each of these values needs to be calculated for each non-ambient light applied to each surface. The sum of the values due to all the lights in the scene is the color seen by the viewer. Notice that in this case we add the colors (with a maximum of 1 for each primary color), because this time we are combining the effects of several light sources, not using one color to modulate another.

We can sum all this up with the following functions:

```
function surfaceColor (normal, position, material, lights,
observerPosition)
    set color to emissiveColor of material
    set observerVector to observerPosition - position

    repeat for each light in lights
        set lightColor to illumination(position, light)
        if light is not ambient then
            set v to the direction of light
            set diffuseAngle to max(-dotProd(normal, v),0)
            if diffuseAngle>0 then
                set diffuseComponent to modulate(diffuseColor of material,
                lightColor)
                add diffuseComponent*diffuseAngle to color

                set specularReflection to v + 2* dotProd(v, normal)
                set specularAngle to max(dotProd(observerVector,
                specularReflection), 0)
                set brightness to power(specularAngle, specularFocus of
                material)

                set specularComponent to modulate(specularColor of
                material, lightColor)
                add specularComponent*brightness to color
```

```
            end if
        otherwise
            add lightColor*diffuseColor of material to color
        end if
    end repeat
end function

function modulate (color1, color 2)
    return rgb(color1[1]*color2[1], color1[2]*color2[2],
color1[3]*color2[3])
end function

function illumination (position, light)
    set color to the color of light
    if light is spot then
        set v to the position of light − position
        set brightnessAngle to max(-dotProd(v, direction of light), 0)
        if brightnessAngle=0 then return rgb(0,0,0)
        set brightness to power(brightnessAngle, angle factor of light)
        multiply color by brightness
    end if

    if light is spot or point then
        set d to mag(v)
        set denominator to the constant factor of light
        add the linear factor of light * d to denominator
        add the quadratic factor of light * d * d to denominator
        divide color by denominator
    end if
    return color
end function
```

There are additional components to materials, all of which are described by some kind of image map, which we'll look at next.

Image Maps and Textures

Of course, not all objects are a solid color. Most have some kind of detail, which gives them a pattern or *texture*. In order to create these details, we use an image called a *map*, which gives information to the 3D API about the surface of the shape at a higher resolution than just polygon-by-polygon. How these maps are created and projected onto the surface we'll see shortly, but for now we only need to know that they allow you to specify values for the various parameters of the surface at a pixel-by-pixel level. That is to say, it is a *texel-by-texel* level, because the pixels of the image map are converted to "texels" when they are applied to the surface, and can apply to different surface areas depending on how they are projected. But we're getting ahead of ourselves.

Some examples of image maps are:

Texture maps: (or just textures) modify the diffuse component of the surface

Gloss maps: modify the specular component

Emission maps: modify the emission component

Light maps: modify the texture map and thus the diffuse component

Reflection maps: create a reflected image over the top of the main texture

Bump maps and **normal maps:**   create the illusion of more convoluted surfaces

All of these are supported by most modern graphics cards, and as things get faster, new methods are added. You can also get 3D ambient light maps which are applied to whole volumes rather than individual materials.

Reflection maps are actually the same as texture maps, they are just applied differently to the surface, as we'll see.

Texture, gloss, and emission maps are fairly simple to understand. Each of them is simply an image which gives the value of the appropriate color of a material at particular points. By specifying how this image is mapped to the surface, like clothing a paper doll, we can alter the end result. None of these really affect the calculations we performed above. All the equations remain the same, we simply have to add an additional color component drawn from the image map. (This is in addition to global diffuse, specular, and emissive components applied to the whole surface.) Textures can be combined to create more complex effects, in essentially the same way that they can be combined to create a complex 2D image in a program like Adobe Photoshop, using color techniques like adding, cycling, or blending.

The most important example of this is the *light map*. It may seem strange that we have two different images for modifying the diffuse component. We don't really need them, but they provide a useful method for saving memory. Textures are the most memory-hungry part of the 3D scene, and most 3D games and other real-time applications try to re-use them as much as possible to avoid filling up the memory space. But on the other hand, calculating all the lights in a scene is the most processor-hungry part of the operation, and most of the time you're recalculating exactly the same values every time, when the lights in a scene are basically static. So we'd like to pre-calculate the lighting in the scene and save it into the texture file (known as *baking*), allowing us to decrease the number of real-time lights, but doing so would be a huge increase in the amount of texture information.

To get around this catch-22, we create a second map, a light map. This defines the lighting levels for each part of the scene, generally in a much lower resolution than the texture map. By using the light map to modulate the texture map, we can reuse textures across an entire room, while still gaining most of the processing advantage of an image map. In Figure 20.4 you can see how this works: the texture map in the first picture has been combined with the lower resolution light map in the second picture to create an image with a shadow. Most 3D modeling software includes the option to create baked textures, both as light maps and as new complete texture maps.

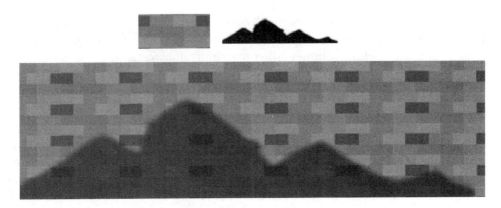

FIGURE 20.4 Using a light map to modulate a texture map.

A *bump map* is a way to model variations in height at a level of detail smaller than the polygon, such as pockmarks, blisters, and embossed text, by creating shadows and highlights. It's a cheat of sorts, because the bumps are faked—like drawing a *trompe l'oeil* 3D image on a piece of paper. When the surface is viewed head-on it's very convincing, but you can see it's not really 3D when your eye is almost level with the paper.

Bump maps are essentially height maps, where each point on the map represents a distance from the surface, usually as an 8-bit grayscale image. An alternative is the *normal map*, in which each texel encodes a normal direction as a color, by mapping the x, y and z coordinates of the (unit) vector to red, green, and blue values. Ultimately, the two maps are equivalent, with normal maps trading off an increased amount of memory used against a gain in performance. These normals are then used to *perturb* the normal of the surface, thus changing the results of the directional and specular components of any lights as shown in Figure 20.5.

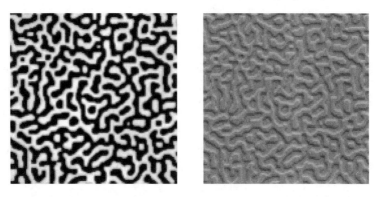

FIGURE 20.5   A bump map and its effect on the lighting of a surface.

A normal map can be derived from a bump map in the way we read the height maps in Chapter 10, by comparing the heights of pixels in small neighborhoods of the bump map.

Fitting a Map to a Shape

In order to use our image maps correctly, we need to tell the engine which part of the image corresponds to which part of the surface. To do this, we have to create a *mapping* from the image to the surface: that is to say, for each point on the surface we have to match it to a texel in the image map (which for the sake of argument we'll say is a texture).

We start by labeling our texels using standard coordinates. Textures are usually 2D images, although for materials such as grainy wood, many people prefer to use 3D texels, which map to the whole volume of an object, creating more interesting effects. However, 3D textures are generally too costly to calculate in real-time and are not supported by all graphics cards. We label the texels using a separate coordinate system for clarity, such as s and t or u and v.

To map the texels to the surface, we can use a transform again, but in a limited way—essentially restricting it to 2D, although with homogeneous coordinates intact in order to perform scaling operations. This allows us to rotate, translate, and scale the map before attaching it to each polygon. But we still need to work out what mapping to use. Some standard maps are:

Planar: the texture is applied as if it passes the whole way through the object and emerges on the other side

Cylindrical: the texture is wrapped around the object like a roll of paper

Spherical: the texture is scrunched onto the object like a sphere

Cubical: six textures are combined to form a cube which is mapped to the outside

Bespoke: for some complex meshes like characters, we need to specify the texture coordinates for each triangle in the mesh individually

Each of these options, apart from the last, consists of a way to translate the 3D information about the points on the surface of the object into 2D form. Let's use the first three as simple examples: in a planar map, we just project the 3D coordinates of each vertex to a plane, whose xy- coordinates are used to map to the st- coordinates of the texture map. In the simplest example, the x and y coordinates of the object are mapped directly to the s and t coordinates of the image as shown in Figure 20.6.

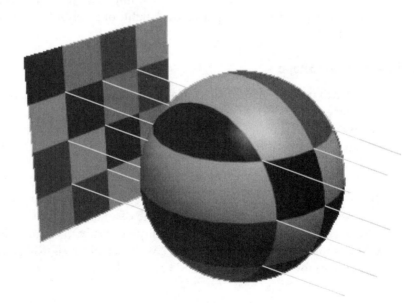

FIGURE 20.6 Planar mapping.

In a cylindrical map, we start by choosing an axis for the object, then we calculate the distance of each vertex along that axis, which scales to our t-coordinate. For the s-coordinate we use the angle the vertex makes around the axis, as shown in Figure 20.7.

FIGURE 20.7   Cylindrical mapping.

In a spherical map, we might use the latitude and longitude of each point as projected to a sphere (discarding the distance from the center), as shown in Figure 20.8. There are alternative methods for spherical mapping, none of which is perfect.

Notice that in all these cases, the positions of the vertices are directly related to the texture coordinates. Of course, there are different values for these positions: we could use the object's local geometry, or we could use its position in the world. This is going to create different effects. If we use the local geometry, then the texture will remain the same no matter how the model is transformed. We can rotate it, scale it, and so on, but the texture always looks the same. But if we use the world basis, the texture changes depending on how the object is placed. In particular, if we spin the object on its axis, the texture remains where it is, which simulates the effect of a reflective surface: we can make a texture that represents the reflection, and it will always be oriented the same way.

FIGURE 20.8 Spherical mapping.

Reflection maps don't always have to be used for reflections. A light map applied the same way allows your object to simulate the effect of constant shadows, like an apple turning under the dappled sunlight of a tree. You could even apply it to stranger objects like bump maps, although it would be an odd effect—lumps moving around under the surface, like the flesh-eating scarabs from the movie *The Mummy*.

Mip-Maps

One problem with image maps is that the image to which they are applied may be near to or far from the camera. If it's far away, then we're using much more information than we need about the surface: if each pixel on the screen covers a hundred different texels then we don't really need to know the color of each one (in fact, having more information than we need can do more harm than good). Conversely, if it's close then a single texel may cover a large amount of screen space, leading to *aliasing*, or jagged edges between texels.

Let's deal with the latter issue first. When working with an object that is close to the camera, we don't normally want to draw each texel as a solid plane of color, we want to interpolate smoothly from one to another, which we can do using *bilinear filtering*, illustrated in Figure 20.9. Here, for each pixel, we determine the four nearest texels to a particular screen pixel and create a weighted average of all the colors at that point. In the figure, the two faces of the cube have the same 4×4 pixel texture, but the one on the left has bilinear filtering turned on.

FIGURE 20.9   Bilinear filtering.

As you can see, bilinear filtering is not without its problems—it can be a little overenthusiastic, blurring the texture too much. One alternative (or complementary) technique is *oversampling*. Here, instead of finding a single texel point under a pixel and then blurring with nearby texels, we find the texel points under a number of nearby pixels and blur them. The result is that near to the camera, we don't see serious blurring, instead we see strongly delineated areas of color, but with nicely antialiased lines between them. Technically, oversampling is a ray-tracing technique rather than a real-time rendering technique, although the principle can be applied to both.

For textures at a distance, one solution is to use a *mip-map*, which is a set of pre-calculated textures at different levels of detail ("mip" is an unusually intellectual piece of technical terminology, standing for the Latin phrase "multim in parvo," or "many in a small space"). So we might have a texture that is 256×256 texels in size, but also store lower-resolution versions at 128×128, 64×64, and so on down to 1×1 (the last being the equivalent of the average color of the whole texture). The 3D engine can then choose which of these maps to use depending on the amount of screen space a particular polygon takes up. The amount of memory used by the mip-mapped texture is higher than before, but not much higher (less than 50% more), and the gains in both processing speed and image quality more than make up for it.

Having created our mip-maps, we still have a number of issues to deal with. For example, what happens at the transition point between different maps? If a large plane is being viewed, the nearest edge of it will be seen with the highest-quality texture map, while the further edge will be using the lowest quality. In between, there will be places where the engine switches from one map to the other, which will be noticeable as a sudden increase in image quality. To avoid this, we can interpolate from one map to the other using *trilinear filtering*, combining the effects of different resolutions at the boundaries. In trilinear filtering (which really is something of a misnomer), we calculate the (bilinearly filtered) color due to both nearby mip-maps, then use a weighted average of the two to determine the appropriate color, so smoothing the transition (see Figure 20.10).

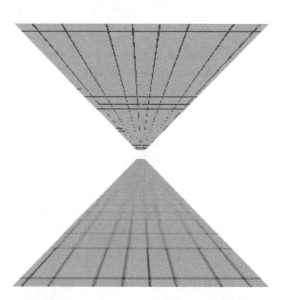

FIGURE 20.10 Using a mip-map, with and without trilinear filtering.

Some cards use a more intelligent "cheat" dubbed "brilinear" filtering, which only applies trilinear filtering near the transition points to save time. More modern cards also use a more advanced technique called *anisotropic* filtering, which instead of merging square combinations of pixels, combines regions of pixels that are related to the angle of view, so that if the surface being viewed is heavily slanted away from the viewer, a more elongated section of it is used to create the combined pixel color. This is much heavier on the processor, but produces a very realistic effect.

SHADING

Another way to create more detailed sub-polygon contours on a model is to use *shading*, which is a way to interpolate the surface color according to the surrounding faces to create a smooth object (rather than a faceted one such as one gets when using plain surface normals).

Gouraud and Phong Shading

The simplest shading method is called *Gouraud shading*, which works by calculating the correct color at each of the three vertices of a triangle, and then interpolating them across the triangle. Gouraud shading affects only the constant components of a material—that is, it is not affected by image maps.

The interpolation is done using *barycentric coordinates*, which are rather like homogeneous coordinates. The barycentric coordinates $\left(w_1, w_2, w_3\right)$ of a point P in a triangle can be defined as a set of weights that could be placed at the vertices of the triangle to put the center of gravity at P, or equivalently to balance the triangle on a pin placed at P, as shown in Figure 20.11.

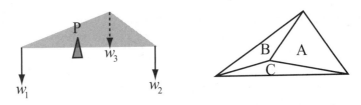

FIGURE 20.11 Barycentric coordinates.

If this seems somewhat obscure, it is—perhaps a slightly less strange way to describe it is in terms of the three areas A, B, and C in the second diagram. We find that choosing $w_1 = A$, $w_2 = B$, and $w_3 = C$, gives a solution to the problem (only one possible solution since, like homogeneous coordinates, barycentric coordinates are invariant under scaling). Since the area of a triangle is half the magnitude of the cross product of two of its sides (Chapter 17), this gives us a simple function to calculate the barycentric coordinates of a point:

```
function barycentric p, v1, v2, v3
    set t1 to v1-p
    set t2 to v2-p
    set t3 to v3-p
    set a1 to t1[1]*t2[2]-t1[2]*t2[1]
    set a2 to t2[1]*t3[2]-t2[2]*t3[1]
    set a3 to t3[1]*t1[2]-t3[2]*t1[1]
    return norm(vector(a1, a2, a3))
end
```

We can use these coordinates (scaled to unit length) to interpolate the colors: for each point of the triangle we multiply each vertex color by its appropriate weight and add them together.

```
function colorAtPoint (pos, vertex1, vertex2, vertex3, color1, color2,
color3)
    set coords to barycentric(pos, vertex1, vertex2, vertex3)
    return color1*coords[1] + color2*coords[2] + color3*coords[3]
end function
```

In reality, this process is made much more efficient by using a number of optimizations, allowing integer calculations to be used. And incidentally, once we know the barycentric coordinates of a point, we can tell if it's inside the triangle if all three coordinates are between 0 and 1.

With a faster graphics card, we can do additional work and create a kind of global bump map for the triangle: instead of calculating the colors and interpolating them, we interpolate the normals of the triangle (by the same method as before) and use these for pixel-by-pixel lighting calculations. This is called *Phong shading*, and obviously is a great deal more difficult for the processor. To save time, the 3D engine does do some interpolation, calculating the light intensity due to each light on a vertex-by-vertex basis and interpolating this across the triangle when calculating the contribution of each light.

The Normal at a Vertex

Both these shading methods rely on calculating the normal of the smoothed surface at each vertex. This is a problem we've encountered before, and we can solve it similarly here. The normal at each vertex can be calculated in two ways. The simplest is just to calculate the mean of the normals of all triangles that share that vertex. This works well for fairly regular shapes.

A more advanced method is to weight the normal according to the size of each triangle, so that more prominent triangles have a greater influence. We can do this fairly simply by using the cross product as we did in calculating barycentric coordinates.

As we've seen before, we find the normal to a triangle whose vertices are ordered conventionally (anticlockwise as you look down on the triangle) as v_1, v_2, v_3, by finding the normalized cross product of $v_2 - v_1$, and $v_3 - v_1$. If instead we take the *un*normalized cross product, we end up with a normal whose length is twice the area of the triangle. Averaging out these vectors before normalizing gives a weighted sum as required.

If the model is not smooth, then there is no single answer to "what is the normal at this vertex?": there can be three or more of them.

EXERCISES

Exercise 20.1

Create a function that will apply a cylindrical, spherical or planar texture map to a surface.

If you have a 3D engine, you can try the results of this function "in the field," but even without a 3D engine, you should be able to calculate the *st*-coordinates for any vertex in the mesh. You'll find the most difficult part is dealing with the "singularities" where the texture meets itself, for example the top of the sphere.

SUMMARY

We've taken a fairly detailed look at lighting, textures, and shading in this chapter. We've learned how lighting in a 3D simulation relates to real-world light, and how surfaces can react in different ways to the light that falls on them. We've also seen how to use materials, how to make image maps, and how to project them to a surface. Finally we've examined shading and how it can be used to create the illusion of a smooth shape.

In Chapter 21, the last in Part IV, we're going to take a look at some 3D modeling techniques, including how to create surfaces from level maps and how to model water waves.

YOU SHOULD NOW KNOW

- how we use the *visible light* spectrum to see objects
- the different ways that objects can react to light
- how light is modeled in the computer
- the meanings of *ambient, diffuse, directional,* and *attenuated* as they apply to lights
- the meanings of *diffuse, specular,* and *emissive* as they apply to surfaces
- how to create an *image map*
- how to *project* an image map to create textured surfaces, shadows, and reflections
- how to use a *mip-map, bilinear,* and *trilinear filtering* and *oversampling* to remove aliasing effects
- how colors are *interpolated* across a triangle to create a smooth surface

21 Modeling Techniques

OVERVIEW

For the final chapter on 3D, we're going to look at some techniques for creating more complex objects at the mesh level. So far, we've been looking at how to move objects from place to place without considering how they were made—we've assumed that the objects are either primitives like spheres or boxes, or pre-existing polygonal meshes—but now we'll examine the underlying surfaces and how they can be defined. We're also going to look at how surfaces can be created which will animate in real time, particularly water and cloth simulations, and finish with a very brief look at creating animated characters, including the knotty problem of inverse kinematics.

Most of the topics in this chapter are quite advanced. Whole books have been written on the subject of each of them.

NURBS code samples from this chapter are implemented in *math.cst* in the script *splines*. The *splines* demo uses them in context.

MATHEMATICAL 3D MODELING

So we'll start by looking at static modeling techniques: how to build a realistic-looking surface from simple parts.

Surfaces of Rotation

As we've already seen a couple of times, one simple way to create a surface is by using a "lathe" technique, or more technically, by creating a *surface of rotation*. To create a surface of rotation, we begin by defining a function f in one variable, usually one that does not have any roots in a particular interval. We then define our surface as the set of 3D points whose distance from the *x*-axis at a particular value of *x* is f(*x*), over some range of *x*-values, as in Figure 21.1. In the figure, the function is a cubic, and the resulting surface is a kind of vase shape.

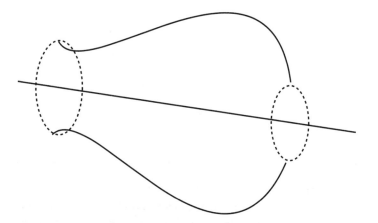

FIGURE 21.1 Creating a vase as a surface of revolution.

A surprising number of useful shapes can be created as surfaces of revolution—anything with complete rotational symmetry along one axis, or more physically, anything that could be modeled on a potter's wheel. The big advantage of this approach is that many physical elements become reasonably easy to deal with—for example, the moment of inertia of a surface of revolution about its axis of symmetry is proportional to $\int f(x)^2 dx$.

Similarly, collision detection with a surface of revolution, while not simple, is somewhat simplified. We can consider the surface to be a succession of frustra of cones, and we're only interested in collisions along the main surface, not with the top or bottom, the cause of most complications.

Splines in 3D

In order to create more complex surfaces, our best bet is to extend the concept of a spline into three dimensions, creating a spline surface. We're going to build up to this a little, as the spline surface of choice in 3D, the B-spline or NURBS, is a fairly complex mathematical beast and takes some work to master. However, we can think a little about how we might extend the concept of a Bezier or Catmull-Rom spline into 3D.

The simplest application would be to create a single curve in space, but to give it some depth by defining a normal at each control point. The result is something like a 3D track curving and twisting through space as shown in Figure 21.2. Here, the main curve follows a standard Catmull-Rom spline, where each control point is a 3D vector. However, a second "virtual" Catmull-Rom spline in one dimension defines a "curve" of angles from the vertical—we associate an angle with each control point, then create a normal vector at each point which is both perpendicular to the curve and at the correct angle to the vertical. The result is a smooth track in 3D.

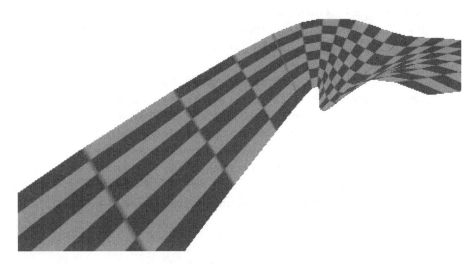

FIGURE 21.2 Using a spline to create a curved track.

We'll return to this example in Chapter 23 when we look at tiled 3D splines.

The problem with this method is that it doesn't enable us to create a complete surface, just one that follows a specific line. We can adapt it by creating a grid of curves instead: define $n \times m$ control points, then use splines to interpolate a grid of n splines in one direction and m in the other. But the result is quite a lot of calculation and no real integration of the two directions into one (although it works just fine).

NURBS

All right, we've had two very brief sections to break us in gently, but there is no sense in putting it off any longer. The most common utility for drawing surfaces in 3D packages is the *NURBS*, which stands for *Non-Uniform Rational B-Spline*. B-splines are an extremely versatile form of spline, which encompass both Bezier and Catmull-Rom, as well as being able to represent accurate circles, ellipses, spheres, and toruses, among other familiar shapes.

A torus is a "doughnut-shape;" the plural should be "tori" but it isn't widely used.

Unlike the splines we've looked at up to now, B-splines are not defined segment-by-segment as individual cubic curves, instead they are created by a single *knot vector*, which is a set of values $\{t_0, t_1, ..., t_m\}$ such that for each $i < m$, $0 \le t_i \le t_{i+1} \le 1$ (actually, it's not necessary to scale the values between 0 and 1, but it's more familiar for our purposes). This creates a set of points on the curve called *knots*, each of which is the result of setting the parameter t to one of the knot vector values.

The knot vector is the principal way we classify B-spline curves, because different kinds of knot vectors create curves with particular kinds of behavior. In particular, when the knots are evenly spaced, the curve is called *uniform* (hence "non-uniform" in the NURBS acronym). However, as well as the knots, the physical shape of the curve is created, as always, by a number of *control points*, $\{P_0, P_1, ..., P_n\}$, where $n \le m$. We define the *degree* of our spline to be equal to $k = m - n - 1$.

Now we need one more element, which is a set of functions called the *basis functions* or *blending functions*, defined by a recursive process:

$$N_{i,j}(t) = \frac{t - t_i}{t_{i+j} - t_i} N_{i,j-1}(t) + \frac{t_{i+j+1} - t}{t_{i+j+1} - t_{i+1}} N_{i+1,j-1}(t), \text{ for } 0 < j \le k, \text{ with } \frac{0}{0} \text{ defined as } 0.$$

$$N_{i,0}(t) = 1 \text{ for } t_i \le t < t_{i+1}, 0 \text{ otherwise.}$$

Recall the definition of a basis from the world of vectors: as it happens, it's possible to extend the concept of a vector space into more abstract realms, particularly that of functions. Just as with more conventional vectors, a basis in an abstract vector space is a set of elements such that any element of the space can be written uniquely as a linear sum of multiples of the basis elements, so for example a basis for the infinite-demensional space of polynomial functions might be the functions 1, x, x^2, x^3 and so on.

These functions are a little hard to visualize, so it may help to have a simple example: suppose that we have just five knots, at 0, 0.2, 0.5, 0.8 and 1, and a curve of degree 2 (so it has two control points) for which we want to find $N_{1,2}$. By the recursive definition, we have $N_{1,2}(t) = \frac{t-t_1}{t_3-t_1} N_{1,1}(t) + \frac{t_4-t}{t_4-t_2} N_{2,1}(t)$.

Applying the definition again, we get

$$N_{1,2}(t) = \frac{t-t_1}{t_3-t_1}\left(\frac{t-t_1}{t_2-t_1} N_{1,0}(t) + \frac{t_3-t}{t_3-t_2} N_{2,0}(t)\right) + \frac{t_4-t}{t_4-t_2}\left(\frac{t-t_2}{t_3-t_2} N_{2,0}(t) + \frac{t_4-t}{t_4-t_3} N_{3,0}(t)\right)$$

Now we have reduced all the functions to $j = 0$, which means we can now apply the elementary definition, giving us several different behaviors:

- If $t < 0.2$, then all of the functions evaluate to 0, so $N_{1,2}(t) = \frac{(t-t_1)^2}{(t_3-t_1)(t_2-t_1)}\left(=\frac{(t-0.2)^2}{0.6\times 0.3}\right)$

- If $0.2 \le t < 0.5$, then we have $N_{1,0}(t) = 1$, so $N_{1,2}(t) = \frac{(t-t_1)^2}{(t_3-t_1)(t_2-t_1)}\left(=\frac{(t-0.2)^2}{0.6\times 0.3}\right)$

- If $0.5 \le t < 0.8$, then we have $N_{2,0}(t) = 1$, so $N_{1,2}(t) = \frac{(t-t_1)(t_3-t)}{(t_3-t_1)(t_3-t_2)} + \frac{(t_4-t)(t-t_2)}{(t_4-t_2)(t_3-t_2)}$

- If $0.8 \le t < 1$, then we have $N_{3,0}(t) = 1$, so $N_{1,2}(t) = \frac{(t_4-t)^2}{(t_4-t_2)(t_4-t_3)}$

Notice that if $j = k$, then the function contains a reference to $k + 1$ of the functions $N_{i,0}$. Notice also that the functions are entirely independent of the values of the control points, hence the reason that the knot vector has such a profound impact on the behavior of the curve. And although the definition of the basis functions seems a little horrific, computationally it is quite simple (in the code below remember that by the convention of this book, arrays begin with element 1):

```
function NURBSbasisFunction i, j, t, knotvector
    if j=0 then // bottom out recursion
        if t<knotvector[i+1] then return 0
        if t>=knotvector[i+2] then return 0
        return 1
```

```
      end if
      // otherwise recurse
      if (knotvector[i+j+1]-knotvector[i+1])=0 then set a to 0
      otherwise set a to (t-knotvector[i+1]) / (knotvector[i+j+1]-
knotvector[i+1])
      if (knotvector[i+j+2]-knotvector[i+2])=0 then set b to 0
      otherwise set b to (knotvector[i+j+2]-t)/(knotvector[i+j+2]-
knotvector[i+2])
      return a*NURBSbasisFunction(i,j-1,t,knotvector) +
b*NURBSbasisFunction(i+1,j-1,t,knotvector)
   end function
```

All right, so having defined the basis functions, we can at last give the equation of the B-spline curve, which is:

$$C(t) = \sum_{i=0}^{n} P_i N_{i,k}(t)$$

The function is easy to compute, but notice that it is rather more abstract than the splines we've seen before. However, we still have a local behavior, where each curve segment is affected only by the nearby control points. In this case, as we have seen, each basis function, and thus each control point, contributes to exactly $k + 1$ of the curve segments.

So what about the "rational" part of the NURBS acronym? If we use homogeneous coordinates to define our control points, we can think of them as a 3D vector and a scalar w_i, which is the *weight* of the control point. This can be done for all B-splines (simply setting w_i to 1 for each control point), but allowing w to vary gives us a little more control. Curves in which w is always 1 are called *non-rational*, while curves in which w is allowed to vary are called *rational*, and this, finally, leaves us with the general formula for a NURBS curve:

$$C(t) = \frac{\sum_{i=0}^{n} P_i w_i N_{i,k}(t)}{\sum_{i=0}^{n} w_i N_{i,k}(t)}$$

NOTE

Although NURBS is a singular noun, strictly speaking, and we can speak of "a NURBS," this sounds awkward, so we usually think of the acronym as a plural or an adjective, as in "a NURBS surface" or "a NURBS curve."

Rational B-splines have one major advantage over NURBS, which is that they are invariant under all transformations: if you transform space then objects on one side of the NURBS surface may not end up on the same side afterward, but they always will for a rational spline. However, NURBS are invariant under affine transformations, and all transforms.

One great advantage of the NURBS over other splines is the ease with which this concept can be transferred to a surface instead of a line, simply by adding a second sum:

$$S(s,t) = \frac{\sum_{i=0}^{p}\sum_{j=0}^{q}P_{i,j}w_{i,j}N_{i,k}(s)N_{j,l}(t)}{\sum_{i=0}^{p}\sum_{j=0}^{q}w_{i,j}N_{i,k}(s)N_{j,l}(t)}$$

Here, the control points are now arranged in a grid, with p in one direction and q in the other, with two knot vectors of degree k and l respectively.

In Exercise 21.1 you are asked to translate this description into an explicit algorithm, which should help to make everything clearer.

Surfaces Generated with `sin()` and `cos()`

NURBS surfaces are an excellent way to create generic solid objects, but in some circumstances there are effective alternatives. One particular example is when creating an infinite "ground"—that is, a height map. A height map in 3D is basically a function in two variables: for each value of x and z, it gives a single value y. It is useful to have a method for creating such a function simply, so we can specify an entire ground surface with just a few bits of information.

We've seen one method for this already, which is to use combinations of trigonometric functions. As we saw in Chapter 16, when several waves are combined, they produce a complex pattern. If we combine these in two directions, we end up with a random-seeming mountainous landscape as in Figure 21.3.

A useful side-effect of using this method for generating a random landscape is that we can guarantee the maximum and minimum height of any mountain or valley. If we combine a number of waves, the maximum possible height for any mountain is just the sum of their amplitudes (this maximum height may not be reached, of course). Another advantage is that we don't need to remember the height map for the whole landscape—the function is fixed in advance, so we can forget about distant areas and draw them at a later stage, without having to store them explicitly.

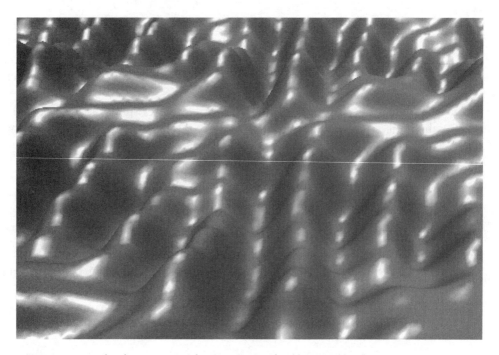

FIGURE 21.3 A landscape created using sine and cosine.

Tessellation

The main reason for specifying a surface algorithmically is that it enables us to describe a richly contoured and, above all, smooth surface without using an infinite number of points. Of course, in practice our 3D engine can't display these surfaces like this. It needs to translate the surface into a set of polygons to display in the usual way. But if we've stored our surface as a precise, infinitely smooth curve, this enables us to create the polygonal mesh at runtime, a process called *tessellation*.

To tessellate a surface, we begin by calculating the coordinates of a number of points on the mesh, usually uniformly spaced out along the *s* and *t* values for a NURBS surface, or along the *x* and *z* values for a ground surface such as the trigonometric surfaces described above. These values are then converted to a mesh by joining them into triangles, and depending on the 3D API we can either send them as individual triangles or as a set of vertices and a set of values defining which vertices are to be connected with triangles. For example, DirectX allows you to define triangles as lists of three points, or as a "strip" of triangles, each of which extends the strip by one point, or as a "fan" of triangles emanating from a single point.

So given that we're going to convert our surfaces to a mesh anyway, why not just store them as a mesh and be done with it? There are three principal reasons.

The most obvious advantage is storage. Just as with the distinction between vector graphics and bitmaps, it generally requires less memory to store a shape as a description than as a pre-defined set of points, especially when the shape is quite simple. Of course, if the shape is *very* simple then using NURBS is overkill and we may be better off using an even simpler description ("this is a sphere of radius 2"). Conversely, if the shape is very complex, like a character, or if it is naturally composed of polygons, like a jewel, then a polygon-by-polygon description may be more appropriate (although there are still alternatives which may improve things). But in the middle-ground, a NURBS or similar system is likely to save on memory, although it does increase the load-time at the start while the engine builds the model by calculating the formula.

Another advantage is scaling: it is possible to choose how detailed your mesh will be, otherwise known as the *level of detail* or *LOD*. If your end-user has a fast machine, then you can create a highly detailed mesh with lots of polygons. On the other hand, if they have a slower machine, you can create a simpler mesh with fewer polygons. Either way, the polygons are still calculated by means of the same underlying curves, and this means that they will always be good approximations to the "true" surface. You can even choose to vary the level of detail of the mesh according to how far away it is from the camera—like a mip-map for the model, if you like, and indeed we use the term LOD to describe the different levels of mip-maps too.

Many 3D engines can calculate LOD meshes automatically, and may even perform the switch between them according to distance. You can sometimes tell in a game the moment at which a model in the distance changes its mesh to the simpler form.

There is a third advantage too, which is that we can calculate the normal at a particular point on a surface generated algorithmically by using the partial derivatives (see Chapter 6). This gives us two vectors tangential to the surface, and taking the cross product of these vectors gives us the normal as shown in Figure 21.4.

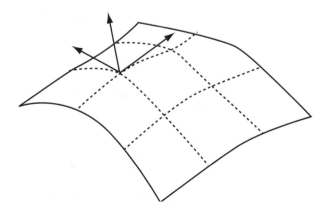

FIGURE 21.4 Finding the normal to a surface.

In the case of a NURBS surface, for example, the partial derivative of the basis functions in each direction can be described by a single polynomial of degree $k - 1$ (or $l - 1$), which is constant for each knot span, and we can combine these partial derivatives into a partial derivative for the whole surface function. So for each vertex of our mesh, as well as calculating its position, we can calculate its normal. Similarly, we can calculate the normal for our trigonometric surface.

As with Bezier curves, there are also mild advantages for these surfaces in collision detection too, but the complications are fairly large and generally a polygon-by-polygon collision detection turns out to be simpler.

ANIMATED SURFACES

Given that it's reasonably simple to create a complex surface in real time, why not go the whole way and generate it from moment to moment, making a surface that can change over time?

Cloth and Hair

Sex is not the only reason that female characters in games tend to be clothed in figure-hugging bodysuits. Realistic movement of hanging clothes is a very computationally intensive task, and for many years it has been simpler just to avoid the problem. However, as computers get faster, it becomes more feasible to simulate such surfaces, even in real time.

The basic trick in a cloth simulation, as well as related models like hair and skin, is to create a system of coupled oscillators, as discussed in Chapter 16. A piece of cloth is essentially a grid of particles mutually connected by springs, as shown in Figure 21.5.

FIGURE 21.5   A cloth simulation.

We've already seen how to calculate the motion of a particle attached to a system of springs, so we'll take it as read that this can be done (any good physics API will allow you to create virtual springs). However, we still need to consider how best to set up the system. Real-life cloth is usually woven from a set of interlocking fibers, giving it different behavior when stretched in different directions. When a force is applied along the direction of the fibers, either along the "warp" or the "weft," the cloth scarcely stretches at all, while when stretched along the "bias" or "cross," diagonally to the fibers, it stretches easily, like a garden trellis, as shown in Figure 21.6.

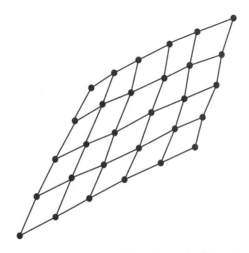

FIGURE 21.6   Stretching along the bias of a piece of cloth.

So in actuality, cloth is not stretchy at all, instead it is like a set of short inextensible strings arranged in a lattice. But as we've seen, these are actually rather harder to simulate than ordinary springs. An inextensible string is essentially the same as an extensive spring with an infinite coefficient of elasticity, but on the computer, setting up such a thing, especially in a coupled lattice, leads almost instantly to major feedback problems as small errors accumulate and the whole simulation spirals out of control. Adding damping doesn't help, it rather tends to make the situation worse.

Instead, we create a cloth simulation which is more like rubber, that is, it is equally stretchy in all directions. Here, we make a lattice as before, using springs with a fairly high coefficient of elasticity, and we also add cross-braces, as shown in

Figure 21.7. The whole simulation is set up so that the natural length of the springs is the same as their length when the whole thing is flat (or if we want it to be more rubbery, we can set it up so that all the springs are naturally a little shorter than that, so the whole thing is under tension. In that case, we need to brace some of the vertices so they can't move, or the cloth will spring back when the simulation starts).

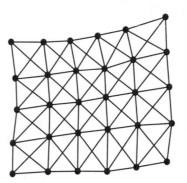

FIGURE 21.7 A rubber cloth with cross-bracing.

To make the simulation more like skin rather than cloth, so it is essentially held in place, we can add an additional set of springs attaching each vertex to the underlying surface—these zero-length springs are sometimes called *dashpots*. We can also simulate hair, or a piece of rope, by a set of springs joined in a chain instead of a surface.

With this method, we can create quite realistic cloth which will hang, flap, and even drape (if we include collision detection with the particles at the vertices). The only complication is user interaction, because as we've seen before in spring calculations, the mouse has no physical constraints in the simulated world, which means that a user can easily set up situations which are physically impossible, such as dragging a particle on a spring a long way past its elastic limit. One way to avoid this problem is that if you're allowing the user to drag parts of the cloth around, instead of directly dragging a particle, apply a force no greater than some set maximum on the particle, in a direction determined by the cursor. This will limit the amount by which it can move away from equilibrium.

Water

There isn't really a vast difference between water and cloth: just like cloth, we can create a realistic water surface as a series of coupled oscillators. The actual forces underlying the coupling of the oscillations of nearby points on a water surface are quite complicated, involving a combination of gravitation, pressure, and surface tension, but the end result is reasonably simple, at least until we want to start surfing.

An alternative method, though, is to model the waves on the surface directly. As with the trigonometric surfaces we looked at before, a wavy surface can be defined by a series of wave functions, which can be calculated independently: the height at a particular point on the surface is just the sum of all the waves at that point.

Depending on how accurately you want to model the waves, you could use various different systems for this. The simplest is just to set up each vertex of the surface as an independent oscillator under SHM. With this model, the various vertices should all move with the same frequency, but can vary in amplitude and phase. The variation might be specified by a function, for example, or perhaps a texture map of some kind. This is the most common form of waving surface used in games (at least based on observation—of course we can't generally know for sure what system is being used). This system is simple to use and reasonably fast to calculate, but is not flexible, and particularly is not interactive—it isn't affected by anything else that happens in the simulation.

To make more realistic waves, we can actually model them directly. The advantage of this is that the waves can then have different frequencies, and can change over time—so for example we could make the waves increase in strength over time, to simulate different weather conditions. Waves on the surface can be of two kinds, either simple parallel wavefronts moving in a straight line, or circular wavefronts emanating from a point source, such as a pebble dropped in the water. This allows us to create interactive waves that respond to player actions.

All these methods create "fake" waves, which for example don't have crests or breakers. These are caused by a wave moving from deep water to shallow water, where the wave can no longer move symmetrically (because it can't drop to its lowest negative amplitude) and so its energy is transferred to the top of the wave, making it move forward instead of just up and down. The effect is further complicated by reflected waves experiencing the same thing in the opposite direction. Obviously to model such things is much more complicated than we need or want to waste valuable processing power for in a real-time game, although it can be done by means of the equations of fluid dynamics, and is in fact done routinely for CGI graphics in films such as *Titanic* or *The Incredibles*.

Calculating reflections and refractions on a water surface to create a realistic texture mapping is also possible, but not something we'll do here.

BONES ANIMATION

We'll finish this chapter, and the 3D section in general, by looking at how to create an animated character, and the problems this entails.

Working with Bones

A standard method has been used for some time for animating characters, called a *bones* system. A character is defined by a series of lines representing bones, arranged in a parent-child relationship as shown in Figure 21.8. These bones are fleshed out to create a single model, which can vary over time as each bone is rotated relative to its parent (often, in fact, modelers sculpt the whole character first, then add bones later, but the principle is the same).

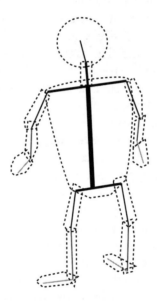

FIGURE 21.8   A bones system.

The details of how this model is created are quite subtle, since the surface has to be modeled in such a way that the skin doesn't distort at the joints when a bone is flexed particularly far. Modern modeling software includes many systems to do this kind of thing automatically, as well as adding automatic muscle bulges and other clever gizmos. But for our purposes, all we need to think about are the bones themselves. Animation is then created either by using a pre-set series of motions such as "run," "jump," "fall over," and so on, often recorded by means of a motion capture system with a live model, or else by directly animating each bone in real-time. The former, being much easier, is the most common system, with the latter being used mostly for *ragdoll* animations, where the body is simply moving as a set of connected rods under gravity, without any muscle actions. (For this, read "they've just been shot"—the *Half-Life* engine, for example, can switch to ragdoll physics when a character is hit, so that they collapse according to the point of impact.)

Even creating a realistic ragdoll figure is very difficult, because our joints are constrained in various ways: the human body includes "ball-and-socket" joints such as the shoulder, which can swivel freely in two dimensions, with limited motion in the third, and simple hinges like the elbow, which can rotate only in one dimension (the twisting motion of the forearm is achieved by using two separate bones rather than by motion in the elbow joint). These constraints, again, can be programmed in with standard modeling packages, but require significant computational effort to achieve in real time. However, these niceties aren't generally too noticeable in a game context—especially when the character in question is flying under the impact of a high-velocity bullet.

Making a ragdoll character is essentially an exercise in *kinematics*—the ballistic motion of series of bones. The calculations involved are fairly extensive (a combination of rigid-body motion and 3D collisions) but solvable numerically—at each time-frame we can calculate all the various momentum and energy values and move the bones accordingly, just like any other physical simulation.

As an example, consider the simplest possible situation, illustrated by the 2D diagram in Figure 21.9. The system consists of two bones, connected by a single "pin." Let's suppose that for each of the two bones, we know the current linear and angular velocity $\mathbf{u}_i$, ω_i, and the mass and moment of inertia m_i, I_i (in 3D we'd need to know the moment of inertia about all three principal axes). For each bone, we'll suppose the pin is currently at a vector $\mathbf{x}_i$ from the center of the limb. All the motion occurs in two dimensions, but without any collisions—the various limbs can be supposed to pass over or under one another.

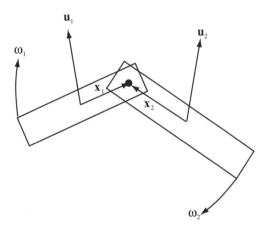

FIGURE 21.9   A simple ragdoll problem.

It's convenient to think in terms of the values $r_i = |\mathbf{x}_i|$ and $\mathbf{t}_i = {(-x_{i2} \;\; x_{i1})^\mathrm{T}}/{r_i}$, respectively the distance of the pin from the center and the clockwise vector tangential to the center, through the pin. The pinning of the various limbs implies that at all times, the local velocity of these points of contact must be equal. We can calculate the local velocity of a particular point as a function of the motion of the limb:

$$\mathbf{w}_i = \mathbf{u}_i + d_i \omega_i \mathbf{t}_i$$

So, at any time this value must be equal for all pairs of bones at a particular pin. This gives us a set of equations for the new linear and angular velocities $\mathbf{v}_i$, φ_i:

- From conservation of energy, $m_1 |\mathbf{u}_1|^2 + I_1 \omega_1^2 + m_2 |\mathbf{u}_2|^2 + I_2 \omega_2^2 = m_1 |\mathbf{v}_1|^2 + I_1 \varphi_1^2 + m_2 |\mathbf{v}_2|^2 + I_2 \varphi_2^2$.
- From conservation of linear and angular momentum, as long as there are no external collisions, we have $m_1 \mathbf{u}_1 + m_2 \mathbf{u}_2 = m_1 \mathbf{v}_1 + m_2 \mathbf{v}_2$ and $m_1 r_1 \mathbf{u}_1 \cdot \mathbf{t}_1 + m_2 r_2 \mathbf{u}_2 \cdot \mathbf{t}_2 = m_1 r_1 \mathbf{v}_1 \cdot \mathbf{t}_1 + m_2 r_2 \mathbf{v}_2 \cdot \mathbf{t}_2$.
- From the pinning, $\mathbf{v}_1 + d_1 \varphi_1 \mathbf{t}_1 = \mathbf{v}_2 + d_2 \varphi_2 \mathbf{t}_2$.

Between them, these give us four equations in four unknowns (two of which are vectors), which can be solved, although it isn't easy since there is no neat division into "radial and tangential" parts, for example.

One disadvantage to this formulation is that there is a tendency for numerical errors to creep in, making the various bones drift apart. An alternative formulation takes advantage of the parent-child relationship of the bones, and considers one bone to be the root, with the other bone(s) slaved to it, so all we need to know is their angular velocity about the pivot point with their parent. This is actually a simpler, and more appropriate, formulation in many ways, but is slightly harder to set up so we won't explore it further here.

Inverse Kinematics

A far more difficult task is the one which our brains accomplish every second of the day, which is to control each bone of the animation directly in order to achieve a task. This immediately leads to a major and still mostly unsolved problem called *inverse kinematics* or *IK*, which can be broadly thought of as "which bones should I move in order to pick up that cup?"

As you can imagine, this is a vital practical problem in the field of robotics, not just simulations, and a wide variety of approaches have been made to it (the most promising being in the fields of AI, particularly genetic algorithms, which we'll look at in Chapter 26). We'll look at a couple of simple examples in this section, just to get a small feel for the scale of the task.

Let's start with an example similar to the one in the previous section: a pair of bones with a single joint. We'll suppose that the first bone is fixed in place at one end, and the second bone is joined to the other end, as shown in Figure 21.10. Suppose we want to reach the point P—that is, to touch it with the end-point of bone 2.

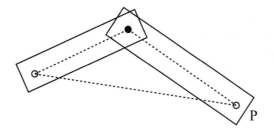

FIGURE 21.10 A simple IK problem.

As you can see, in this case, finding the correct final configuration to meet P is reasonably easy: it's a simple application of the cosine rule, since we know the lengths of all three sides of the appropriate triangle. Having said that, even in this case there are some complications, because as well as finding the end-point, we need to work out the best route to reach it. Ideally, we want to minimize the amount of movement required to get from our initial configuration to the end—we don't want to do something like the motions in Figure 21.11.

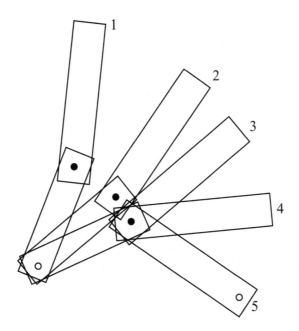

FIGURE 21.11 A poor solution to the IK problem.

One way to deal with this question is to create the complete motion path, by attempting to move smoothly so that the end of bone 2 follows a simple line from its starting point to P, as shown in Figure 21.12. The advantage to this approach is that each movement is small and gets us progressively nearer to the goal, which means that some kind of iterative method might well be successful. If the end-point is reachable then this approach will always give a possible solution in the two-bone problem, but it may not be physically plausible when dealing with real characters with limited movement in the joints.

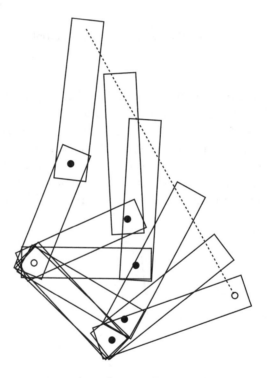

FIGURE 21.12 A better solution to the IK problem.

In case this seems to be overstressing the difficulty, remember that when there are more than two bones involved, typically there are an infinite number of possible configurations which solve the IK problem. Choosing the appropriate path for the bones is non-trivial. To repeat: the best solution tends to be some kind of iterative approach, where the bones try to orient themselves toward the target a small amount at a time. One simple method, for example, is at each time step to just rotate each bone a little more toward the target, in proportion to how far away from the target it currently is (see Exercise 21.2).

The same approach works well in three dimensions too, although it's harder to make it work realistically because there are more degrees of freedom. However, it's less successful when dealing with a system of bones that is not just a simple chain, or when you need to worry about collision avoidance.

EXERCISES

Exercise 21.1

Create a program that will draw a 2D NURBS.

Your program should allow you to experiment with moving the control points around, changing the knot vector, etc. If you're feeling brave, try extending to a 3D NURBS surface.

Exercise 21.2

Create an iterative function `IKapproach(chain, target)` that will adjust a simple IK chain to hit a specified target.

Your function should take a chain of bones (specified in whichever way you prefer) in a particular configuration and move it toward a particular target by some small amount. When applied successively, it should adjust the chain to hit the target.

SUMMARY

We've concluded the section on 3D techniques to look briefly at a few methods dealing with surfaces, mostly in fairly broad terms. You have seen how we can use mathematical techniques to define a complex surface using various methods, especially B-Splines, and how to use this to make a surface with an adjustable level of detail. We've also looked at animated surfaces and bones systems.

We now leave the subject of 3D to spend the rest of the book looking at some algorithmic techniques, especially in the context of games.

YOU SHOULD NOW KNOW

- how to define an object in 3D in terms of a *surface of revolution*, *NURBS* or trigonometric function
- how to use these mathematical descriptions to draw the object at different *levels of detail*
- how to *animate* a surface to simulate water or cloth
- how to create a *bones* system and use it to make a *ragdoll* simulation
- how to solve a simple *IK* problem in two dimensions

Part

V

Game Algorithms

Most of the mathematics we have looked at up to now have been quite general—they relate to real-world physics and geometry, and how to simulate it on the computer. But for the final part of the book, we will look at some mathematical ideas specific to computing, and games in particular. As before, we're only going to cover these concepts briefly, since each is a huge topic; but this introduction should help you to know where to look when you encounter these issues in your work.

We'll begin by looking at some techniques for optimization and simplification of physics calculations, particularly collisions. Then we'll spend two chapters on game level design, looking at tile-based games and mazes. This leads us into discussion of pathfinding algorithms, which in turn takes us to the topic of artificial intelligence. Finally, we'll look at some techniques for using the computer as a problem-solving tool, for searching through data and creating puzzles.

22 Speeding Things Up

In This Chapter

- Overview
- Cheap and Expensive
- Pseudo-Physics
- Culling
- Exercises
- Summary
- You Should Now Know

OVERVIEW

Throughout this book, the emphasis has been on the mathematics and physics behind the code, and we've been stressing the fact that all our code examples could be made to run faster by sensible optimizations. This chapter is the only one where we'll be breaking that rule: we're going to look at some techniques for speeding up your code by the use of pre-calculated values and segregation of space.

 Code samples from this chapter are implemented in *math.cst* in the script
ON THE CD *Chapter 22 (optimization)*.

CHEAP AND EXPENSIVE

The principal key to speedy code is an understanding of which kinds of calculations are computationally "cheap" and which are more "expensive." We'll start by discussing how this can be measured, and looking at some ways to replace the expensive algorithms with cheaper look-up tables.

Computational Complexity

The length of time an algorithm takes is called its computational *complexity*, expressed in terms of the size of the function arguments. For example, the process of incrementing a number stored on the computer by 1 is essentially independent of the size of the number, but it would be pointless to use this method to add two numbers together:

```
function sillyAdd (n1, n2)
    repeat for i=1 to n1
        add 1 to n2
    end repeat
    return n2
end function
```

The length of time this algorithm takes is roughly proportional to the size of n1: as this value becomes very large, the length of time for simple operations like storing the value n2, returning the answer and so on becomes increasingly irrelevant. So the algorithm is linear, having an *order* of 1, which we write as O(n), which will make more sense as we go along.

A much more efficient algorithm for adding two numbers is the method we use in school—specifically the binary form we looked at in Chapter 1. Here, if we assume that n2 is fixed, the time taken by the algorithm is mostly dependent on the number of digits in the binary representation of n1, which is roughly proportional to the logarithm of the number, so we say the algorithm is O($\log(n)$). The larger our numbers get, the faster this algorithm is in comparison to the sillyAdd() function.

Notice that we don't care about the base of the logarithm, because this only multiplies the length of time by a constant: this may be important for small values in the function, but is irrelevant when dealing with very large numbers. While this makes sense mathematically, it's a little misleading when dealing with practical computations, which are just as likely to involve small numbers as large ones: if your function is proportional to $1000000n$ and you are comparing it to another that is proportional to n^2 then for large numbers, the former is far more efficient, but for smaller ones you're better off using the "less efficient" algorithm. So take complexity calculations with a pinch of salt.

The same warnings apply to "benchmark tests," where a particular calculation is calculated a large number of times with different methods in order to evaluate their speeds. These benchmarks need to be considered carefully in order to put them into context—after all, how often do you need to perform the same calculation a million times in succession? Usually, a calculation is a part of a larger process, and this may affect the value of the different algorithms. For example, one process may be significantly faster but involve higher memory usage—a common occurrence since one of the principal ways to speed calculations up is to use look-up tables as we'll see. Another process may take slightly longer but produce a number of other intermediate values which are useful later and reduce the time taken by another process. Having said all this, complexity calculations and benchmark tests are an important tool and shouldn't be discounted.

The most common kinds of algorithm are:

- *Polynomial time* calculations. These have a time which is some power of n. We've already seen linear and quadratic calculations, but generally all kinds of polynomial time algorithms are similar, and worth aiming for. It's often the case that the rate of a polynomial calculation depends slightly on the "grain size" of the problem: a problem that's ostensibly quadratic may turn out to be cubic if one takes into account machine-level operations.
- *Exponential time* calculations. These take a time proportional to e^n, and are to be avoided at all costs since they get slow very rapidly as n increases. An example is a recursive algorithm which tries to fill in a crossword from a list of words by placing one word, then filling the remaining crossword (the final chapter of this book looks further at algorithms of this kind).
- *Logarithmic time* calculations, such as we saw above. There are also combinations of logarithmic and polynomial time, such as the "long-multiplication" algorithm, which has an order of $n\log(n)$. Logarithmic time is much faster than polynomial time and generally worth striving for.
- *Constant-time* calculations: the Holy Grail of algorithm creators. These are few and far between, but one example is the concatenation of two "linked lists," which are chains of data implemented by each member of the chain knowing its own information and a pointer to the next link. To join the lists together, we simply link the last link of the first chain to the first link of the second, which is theoretically independent of the lengths of the chain (in practice this isn't quite achieved, but close to it).

Using Look-Up Tables

When dealing with computationally expensive calculations, one solution is to use a *look-up table*, which is simply a list of values of the function pre-calculated over a given range of inputs. A common example is the trigonometric functions: instead of calculating sin(x) directly, we can look it up from the table by finding the nearest entries to *x* in the table and interpolating between their respective answers. Of course, for the trigonometric functions we can use some optimizations to limit the number of entries, since we only need the values of sin(x) from 0 to $\pi/2$ to calculate the complete list of entries for sin, cos and tan. We can also use the table in reverse to find the inverse functions.

How many entries a table needs to contain depends on how accurate the look-up needs to be, and also on the interpolation method: a linear interpolation is quicker but requires more memory, while a cubic interpolation, such as one based on the same principle as the Catmull-Rom splines we looked at in Chapter 10, uses fewer points but requires a little more processing. The difference is fairly significant: using no more than 15 control points, we can use cubic interpolation to calculate the values of sin(x) to an accuracy of 4 decimal places (to save on calculation, you could store $15 \times 4 = 60$ cubic coefficients). Using linear interpolation, we would need well over 200 points to get the same degree of accuracy; 200 points with cubic interpolation is accurate to 7 decimal places.

Although look-up tables can save some time, it's worth realizing that the engine powering your programming language almost certainly uses a look-up table of its own to calculate these kinds of values. If you want to calculate the trigonometric (or logarithm, exponential, etc.) functions to a high degree of accuracy, it's almost certainly going to be quicker just to use the inbuilt calculations. Look-up tables are only useful if you're willing to drop quite a lot of information. Of course, if you're willing to drop even more information, you can ignore the interpolation step altogether, and simply find the nearest point in your table.

As well as calculating standard values, you can use a "bespoke" look-up table for your own special purposes. A common example is for a character using some kind of jump function, such as in a platform game. Instead of calculating the motion through the air using ballistic physics each time, you can pre-calculate the list of heights over time. In addition to the speed advantages, this also helps to standardize the motion across different times and machines.

Integer Calculations

As we saw in Chapter 1, it's significantly faster to use integers for calculations than floating-point values. Although we've mostly ignored this issue for simplicity, it's often possible to improve the speed of an algorithm by replacing floats with integers. In the simplest example, instead of finding some value as a float between 0 and 1, we just find it as an integer between, say, 1 and 1000, and scale all other calculations accordingly.

However, there is a problem with this approach, which is, of course, rounding errors. The errors that accumulate when performing multiple calculations with floats are even more prevalent when you are restricted to integers. This means that we have to be quite clever in order to ensure accuracy is maintained, which generally means trying to find algorithms which rely only on the initial data, and do not build calculations on intermediate values (we've already discussed this briefly when looking at ballistic motion calculations).

It's easiest to explain this by means of a concrete example, so we'll look at a common problem: suppose that you want to move from A to B along a grid of squares as in Figure 22.1. We want to find the set of squares which most closely approximates a straight line. This is the problem that painting software faces every time it draws a line as a sequence of pixels with no gaps.

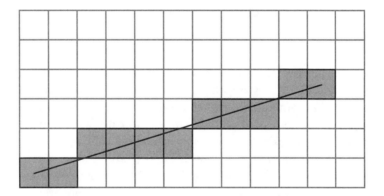

FIGURE 22.1 Approximating a straight line on a square grid.

The best method known for this problem is called the *Bresenham Algorithm*, which is illustrated in Figure 22.2. Suppose we are drawing a line between two points $P_1 = (x_1, y_1)$ and $P_2 = (x_2, y_2)$, where we say for the sake of argument that $x_2 > x_1$, all the values are integers, and the gradient m of the line, measuring y downward, is between 0 and −1 (we'll fix these assumptions at the end).

In the figure, we have focused on the start of the line. The pixel at point A is filled in, and because of our assumptions about the gradient of the line, we know that the next point we're interested in is either the next pixel to the right (R), or the pixel diagonally upward (D). Which one we want to fill in depends on the slope of the line: in particular, if the point marked P_1, above the point $x_1 + 1$, lies above or below the line between R and D.

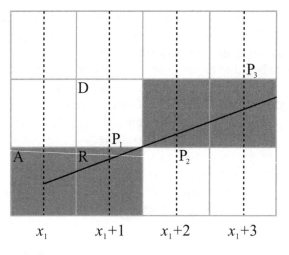

FIGURE 22.2 Bresenham's algorithm.

We can continue this process step by step, moving either right or diagonally at each point depending on whether our line at the midpoint is above or below the half-way line: you can see that all the squares we will fill in are lightly shaded in the figure. So all we need is an efficient way to calculate whether the line is above or below our test position at each step, such that only integer values are involved.

Let's rewrite m as $\frac{a}{b}$, where $a = y_2 - y_1$ and $b = x_2 - x_1$ (note that a and b are both integers). Then our line equation $y = mx + c$ becomes $by - ax - bc = 0$, with bc found by substituting the coordinates of A into this equation, so $bc = by_1 - ax_1$. So we can define a function $L(x, y) = by - ax - bc$. For any point (x, y) above the line, $L(x, y) < 0$, and for any point below the line, $L(x, y) > 0$.

What we're going to do is create an *iterative* method of solution, which is the opposite of a recursive algorithm. An iterative algorithm works by defining two elements: what we do on the first step, and how we get from any particular step to a subsequent step (for example, an iterative algorithm for climbing a flight of stairs might be "go to the bottom of the first step; then for each step, walk onto the next step until you reach the top"). In this case, we're going to create a series of midpoints given by P_1, P_2, p_1, ..., each of which is determined based on the previous one. For each one, we calculate the value of $L(P_{i+1})$ based on the value of $L(P_i)$.

So now consider the first step, where we are moving from (x_1, y_1). In this case, the midpoint we're interested in is $P_1 = \left(x_1 + 1, y_1 - \frac{1}{2}\right)$, and we want to know if $L(P_1) = by_1 - \frac{b}{2} - ax_1 - a - bc < 0$. Substituting in the value of bc, we get $L(P_1) = -\frac{b}{2} - a$. To keep everything in integers, we can multiply the inequality by 2 (which does not affect the result). If the inequality is true, then we move diagonally, otherwise (almost always) we move right.

Now that we know this, we can think of what we do at each further step. The situation breaks down into two cases (refer to Figure 22.2). If at the previous step we moved right, then the midpoint we're interested in has the same y-coordinate as before but an x-coordinate that is one greater. If we moved diagonally, then the y-coordinate has to decrease by 1.

So in the first case, if the last midpoint P_i we checked had coordinates (x_i, y_i) and we moved right, then we know that $P_{i+1} = (x_i + 1, y_i)$, so we move right again if $L(x_i + 1, y_i) < 0$, diagonally otherwise. This gives the inequality $by_i - ax_i - a - bc < 0$. Notice that this is the same as $L(x_i, y_i) - a < 0$. In the second case, having moved diagonally, $P_{i+1} = (x_i + 1, y_i - 1)$, so we have $by_i - b - ax_i - a - bc < 0$, or $L(x_i, y_i) - a - b < 0$. Again, we multiply everything by 2 to ensure that we are still in integer territory.

So the code for the algorithm is fairly simple:

```
function drawBresenham(startCoords, endCoords)
    drawPixel(startCoords)
    set x to startCoords[1]
    set y to startCoords[2]
    set a to endCoords[1]-x
    set b to endCoords[2]-y
    set d to 2*(a+b)
    set e to 2*a
    // calculate 2L(P1)
    set linefn to -2*a-b
    // perform iteration
    repeat for x=x+1 to endcoords[1]
        if linefn<0 then // move diagonally
            subtract 1 from y
            subtract d from linefn
        otherwise // move right
            add e to linefn
        end if
        drawPixel(x,y)
    end repeat
end function
```

Of course, we need to adapt this code slightly to deal with the other cases, where the absolute value of the gradient is greater than 1 (in which case you need to switch x and y in the algorithm) or where it is positive (this means adding 1 to y at each stage instead of subtracting, and switching the sign of a), or where the x-coordinate of the start point is greater than that of the end point (in which case you can just switch them round). You are asked to do this in Exercise 22.1.

We've gone into this in some detail simply because it is a good illustration of the principles of integer calculations, in particular, approximating to integers efficiently without losing the original detail. Having said that, Bresenham's algorithm is very useful in its own right, not just for simple drawing, but also in pathfinding, motion, and collision detection (particularly at a pixel level). It allows you to "digitalize" a world with complex lines and angles into a more tractable and faster form—and of course by adapting the line function L, it is possible to extend it to other types of curve to some extent. A related algorithm in two dimensions can be used to draw a triangle or other polygon, for example when creating a 3D texture.

PSEUDO-PHYSICS

Having looked at simplifying motion and creating faster paths, it is natural to pursue this further by looking at what might be called "pseudo-physics": motion that looks realistic but is actually simplified or faked.

Simplifying Collisions

As we've already seen, collisions can get fairly unpleasant fairly quickly. Even a simple problem like finding the point of collision between two ellipses, or a circle and a rotating line, leads to situations that require a numerical solution, which is computationally expensive.

If our time slices are small enough, we can fake these collisions to a reasonable degree of accuracy by a simple process: find out whether a collision has (or has probably) occurred during the particular time slice, and make a guess as to when it happened. This two-step process is not too hard to implement in most cases and produces a fairly believable effect. There are a few potential pitfalls, but we can mostly get around them.

We won't look at all these possibilities, but let's look at a simple example, the collision of two ellipses. As before, we can reduce the collision of two ellipses to the collision of one ellipse aligned along the x-axis with a unit circle, so suppose we have an ellipse $E(\mathbf{p}, (1\ 0)^T, a, b)$, moving along a displacement vector $\mathbf{v}$, and we want to see if it collides with the circle $C(\mathbf{0}, 1)$.

If our time slice is small enough, then for the ellipse to collide during this time period, it must intersect the circle at the end of that time. If it doesn't, then the only way it can collide is if it glances off the circle at a very shallow angle, which we'll ignore (such collisions don't have much effect on motion anyway).

So deciding if there is a (pseudo-)collision is essentially the same as calculating if the ellipse $E'(\mathbf{p} + \mathbf{v}, (1\ 0)^T, a, b)$ intersects with C: that is, we're looking for a point on E' at a distance less than 1 from the origin:

$$\left(a\sin\theta+q_1\right)^2+\left(b\cos\theta+q_2\right)^2<1$$

where $\mathbf{q}=\mathbf{p}+\mathbf{v}$. We can do this by searching for the minimum value of this expression, which we can find by differentiating and setting the derivative to 0:

$$2a\left(a\sin\theta+q_1\right)\cos\theta-2b\left(b\cos\theta+q_2\right)\sin\theta=0$$

$$a\sin\theta+q_1=\frac{b}{a}\left(b\cos\theta+q_2\right)\tan\theta$$

Substituting this back into the inequality, we are looking for

$$\left(\frac{b}{a}\left(b\cos\theta+q_2\right)\tan\theta\right)^2+\left(b\cos\theta+q_2\right)^2<1$$

$$\left(\frac{b^2}{a^2}\tan^2\theta+1\right)\left(b\cos\theta+q_2\right)^2<1$$

Then by noticing that $\tan^2\theta=\frac{1-\cos^2\theta}{\cos^2\theta}$, and with a little algebraic manipulation, we end up with the following quartic inequality:

$$b^2d^2c^4+2bd^2q_2c^3+\left(b^4+q_2d^2-a^2\right)c^2+2b^3q_2c+b^2q_2^2<0$$

where $c=\cos\theta$. We can solve this inequality algebraically (we won't go into details of how that is done here as it's a little complicated), and if it yields a value of c between −1 and 1, we know there is a collision. Yes, it's not exactly simple, but at least it's solvable!

We can make similar simplifications when dealing with rotational motion. For example, collisions between two moving objects that are spinning can be calculated by ignoring the spin: at each stage, calculate a linear collision between the objects in their current orientation (obviously, this won't work when neither object is moving linearly, but then the angular collision becomes more tractable). Again, this will miss some collisions, but only on the fringes where they are less noticeable.

Simplifying Motion

Several other aspects of motion can be cheated too. Consider friction, for example: in our Pool game, we implemented a simple system of pseudo-friction, where the balls slowed down at a constant rate. As a general rule, you can simplify things roughly in proportion to how attuned people are to them—we have a very accurate intuition about objects in flight, for example, so ballistics have to be implemented accurately. Our innate understanding of oscillations is much less strong, so we can cope with a fairly rough simulation of objects on springs. An example would be applying a uniform backward acceleration whenever a spring is extended, perhaps combined with a uniform frictional deceleration applied at all times.

Similarly, we have a natural understanding of linear momentum and energy (even very young infants seem surprised when these laws are violated), but not much of angular motion, which is why some consequences of spin seem strange or magical. This means that we can simplify angular motion significantly—an example would be in resolving a spinning collision, where we can simply apply an additional "kick" in the direction of spin, instead of accurately resolving the angular and linear components.

Funnily enough, in game contexts we are almost more comfortable with the pseudo-physics than with accuracy. Games that use realistic physics for, for example, driving a racing car or 4 × 4 are much harder to control than those which use simplified, discrete motion (forward, backward, left, and right, perhaps the occasional skid—see Exercise 22.2), and game designers have as a rule found it difficult to make real-time physics a genuine part of the game rather than just a gimmick that allows them to make someone collapse authentically when shot in the head.

CULLING

We've mentioned culling before in a couple of contexts, as part of both collision and visibility calculations. Culling is the process of quickly eliminating obvious non-candidates in a particular problem, such as the objects behind the camera when determining what parts of a scene are visible. There are a number of useful techniques which can be used to improve culling, most of which fall under the category of *partitioning trees*.

Segregating Space

You may recall from Chapter 11 that we talked a little about techniques for partitioning or segregating the game world into smaller chunks. This technique can be generalized in two ways. One is to make the chunks smaller and tie them in to the actual game world design, which leads us to the tile-based games we'll examine in the next chapter. The other is to create a recursive process that organizes the world into regions within regions, called a partitioning tree. We're going to look at a number of different types in this section. All of these methods work equally well in two or three dimensions, but we're going to concentrate on the 2D case because it's easier to draw! Less facetiously, it's rare that you really need a 3D implementation, as even 3D games tend to take place on a ground of some kind, making them essentially 2D (or 2.5D). Only a few games, such as space battles, really use all three dimensions fully.

A partitioning tree is a data structure which stores information about the world in some form of hierarchy. The form of the tree is essentially the same as the system we used in Chapter 18 to deal with relative parent-child transforms: it consists of a number of *nodes*, each of which (except one) has a single *parent* and zero or more *children*. A childless node is called a *leaf*, and the topmost, parentless node is called the *root* (so trees are generally drawn upside down!). A tree contains no loops: no node can be its own parent, grandparent, etc. Associated with each node will be some information which is used to make calculations: we're in OOP territory here.

A tree is a special case of a graph, *which we'll look at much more in Chapter 24.*

NOTE

In a partitioning tree, the root node represents the whole world, which is then split into smaller (generally non-overlapping) parts based on some criterion. These parts are then split again, and again, and so on, until some pre-set condition is reached (such as a minimum size). Hopefully, the partition is performed in such a way that calculations such as raycasting or collision detection are simplified. In particular, if something is not true (visibility, proximity, etc.) of a parent node, then it is not true of any of that parent's children, which means that we need not bother checking any further along that branch of the tree.

As was pointed out in Chapter 11, these trees can't solve all ills and shouldn't be expected to: one issue, for example, is that checking each parent node in itself adds an additional calculation. If we happen to be looking toward every object in the world, then we're going to be performing all our visibility culling calculations for nothing. Similarly, if we're performing a break in a game of pool, we can't avoid the fact that every ball on the table is involved and has to be checked. Nevertheless, in many circumstances partitioning space is helpful, and in some cases such as working on a vast outdoor terrain it is essential.

There is a second form of partitioning, that is relevant to collision detection, which is at the level of individual objects. Both collision maps and polygonal meshes can be stored in the form of a partitioning tree: we can subdivide the bounding box or bounding sphere repeated times in order to make a closer and closer approximation to the object.

Quadtrees and Octrees

Probably the simplest, and certainly the commonest, form of partitioning tree is the *quadtree*, or its 3D equivalent, the *octree*. A quadtree is the most natural extension of the system we looked at in our pool game, where the world is broken up into square regions. Suppose that we start with one large square which encompasses the whole 2D plane—the root node. We can break that up into four equal squares, which are its children, and each of those into four smaller squares, and so on, until our squares are a pre-set minimum size (the strange tartan in Figure 22.3 gives a graphical representation of a quadtree).

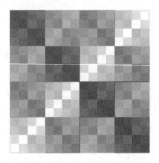

FIGURE 22.3   A 2D plane broken into a quadtree.

Associated with each leaf node is the set of objects contained in the node's area, which might be either complete geometrical objects (such as balls) or individual line segments of a polygon (or polygons of a mesh in 3D). Objects in more than one square are associated with all these leaves. Associated with each parent node is its set of vertices on the plane (in fact, all we need is its center and its size, and actually we can determine its size by its level in the tree hierarchy), as well, possibly, as a duplicate list of all the objects contained within it (depending on the application of the quadtree this may be more or less useful).

It should be fairly easy to see how this organization can be used to solve the kinds of problems we've been discussing. There are various different algorithms for searching the tree, but here's one example which can be used for collision detection. For each object, we cull out any parent nodes whose partition does not contain any part of the object's trajectory during a given time slice. So in Figure 22.4, we would begin by removing the partitions shaded with the darkest gray, then the children shaded with the next darkest, and so on. We end up with a set of leaves which intersect the motion, and can quickly check for collisions with any objects in those leaves.

Despite the simplicity of this algorithm, it is not significantly quicker than just partitioning the space into a flat grid as we did before, and in some circumstances it can be slower. We can speed things up by precomputing sets of nodes that can be culled automatically for an object in a given leaf—if the amount of motion is quite small relative to the size of the grid, we can assume that an object in the middle of a first-level partition can't ever get to one of the other first-level nodes. Of course, this won't work for nodes on the edges of a particular parent.

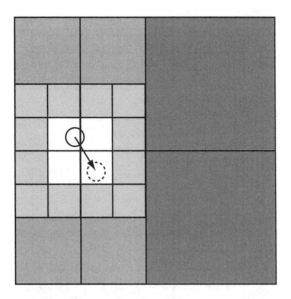

FIGURE 22.4 Culling for collision detection with a quadtree.

Nevertheless, quadtrees are not the most useful partition for collision detection at the world level. They are very useful for visibility determination, though—certainly they are better than a flat grid, because they allow us to reduce the number of leaves we need to consider in our calculations. They also can be useful for raycasting—again, we can determine the set of parent nodes intersecting with a ray. If a parent node is known to be empty, then we can ignore it, otherwise we recurse over its children. You might want to see if you can adapt Bresenham's Algorithm to make a fast integer-only version of this.

At the object level, quadtrees are most useful for storing a collision map. In Figure 22.5 you can see a collision map which has been divided into a quadtree by the following algorithm: If a particular partition is either completely empty or completely full (partitions A and B, for example), we stop subdividing the tree at that stage, otherwise we recurse over its children. We could even optimize further and stop whenever a particular node contains a flat edge. When detecting collisions between such shapes, we work down through the nodes of the trees until either a collision is detected (a black leaf from each shape intersects) or all nodes at that level in one or other shape are empty.

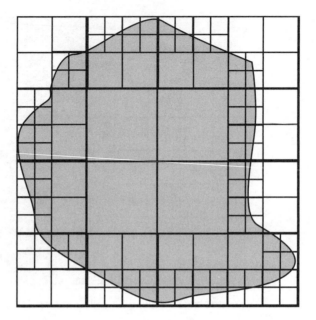

FIGURE 22.5 A collision map organized as a quadtree.

Binary-Space Partitioning

A second type of partition is the *BSP tree* or *binary space partitioning tree*. Unlike quadtrees, BSP trees use two children for each non-leaf node, so each partition is divided into two parts at each stage, either by a line in 2D or a plane in 3D. We can choose how to make the partition in various ways: one method is to do it in such a way that each leaf node contains exactly one object, as in Figure 22.6, or exactly one line segment / polygon (one common method is to use a split line oriented along a particular line segment / polygon of the region). However, it's worth noting that a method such as this means that your BSP tree has to be recalculated every time an object moves out of its current partition, so this kind of tree is best suited for a scene that is mostly static.

Each node of the BSP keeps a record of all objects that are entirely contained within it.

One useful feature of a BSP is that all the regions are convex—it provides one neat way to divide a concave object into convex parts. As with quadtrees, BSP trees are best suited at the world level to working with visibility and raycasting (the *Doom* engine used BSP trees for visibility, and it's also a major part of the *Quake* and *Unreal* engines), but at the object level they can be very helpful for object-to-object collisions too.

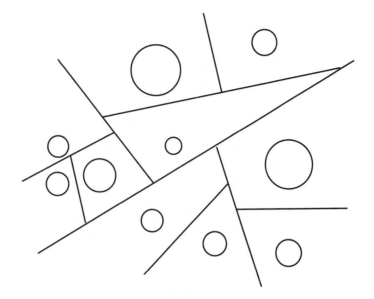

FIGURE 22.6   A binary partition of a plane.

Bounding Volume Hierarchies

A *bounding volume hierarchy* or *BVH* is in some ways the opposite of the space partitions we've looked at so far. Instead of concentrating on space, a BVH focuses on the objects, and organizes them according to bounding shapes (it's most commonly used in complex 3D worlds, hence the word "volume," but it is equally applicable to 2D). The bounding shapes might be spheres, AABBs, OABBs, or any other useful armature. The crucial difference between this scheme and the previous ones is that the BVH does not in general cover the whole game world, since any large regions of empty space are likely to be outside the bounding volumes, and conversely that its various volumes / areas can overlap if appropriate. Figure 22.7 shows an example of a 2D bounding area hierarchy where the bounding shapes are circles.

BVHs are an extremely useful tool for culling, and have a number of advantages over the other systems, particularly in a game world made up of lots of potentially moving objects (quadtrees have the advantage slightly when dealing with large terrains). They can also be combined with space partitioning systems in various ways.

The most difficult part of working with a BVH is constructing the tree in the first place—we want it to be as efficient as possible, so that at each level of the tree, the bounding volumes are as small as we can make them. Depending on the way your game is constructed, you could choose a number of different systems. In particular,

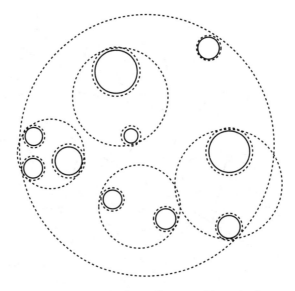

FIGURE 22.7 A 2D bounding area hierarchy for segregating a space.

objects that generally appear together should obviously be grouped together, while objects that are moving relative to one another should not. Within an object, you can also create a hierarchy of bounding volumes that gradually approaches the shape of the object—Figure 22.8 shows an object surrounded by a hierarchy of smaller bounding OABBs.

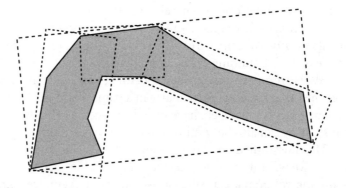

FIGURE 22.8 Using a BVH to whittle down the geometry of a shape.

When objects are moving significantly relative to one another, then you need to create a more dynamic BVH, which means you have to be able to quickly split, merge, and insert new nodes in the tree. This is obviously a very complex process, but there has been a lot of work done on the subject and it is worth looking into if you want to explore these partitioning tree systems further, particularly if you are dealing with a large, complex world. There are also other systems of culling, such as a visibility graph that stores details of which areas are visible from which other areas. But hopefully this taster should have given you some insight into the tricks of this very interesting trade. There are plenty of further references to be found in Appendix D.

EXERCISES

Exercise 22.1

Complete the `drawBresenham()` function by extending it to deal with all possible gradients.

Some hints as to how to complete this Exercise were given after the function.

Exercise 22.2

Write a function that will control a "car" with the cursor keys using simplified physics.

The standard car-control system used in most games uses the up and down arrows to accelerate and brake, and left and right to turn (oriented in the forward direction so that a left turn makes you point right if you're moving backward). If you have the urge, you might want to extend this with a skid option: if the momentum perpendicular to the forward direction is above some threshold, then the turn function ceases to be effective.

SUMMARY

It's unfortunate that we have to devote so little space to such a major part of modern game programming, but it's very much on the fringes of what this book is about, so if (or more likely, when) you need to make use of these techniques, you will need to explore elsewhere before you can really make the most of them. But at the very least these few pages should have given you some insight. You've seen how particular calculations can be simplified and optimized, and we've looked briefly at some of the techniques for culling and optimizing the game world data. In the next chapter we'll explore the other side of the partitioning coin by creating the partition first and making the game to fit it.

YOU SHOULD NOW KNOW

- how we measure *complexity* using O() notation
- how to use *Bresenham's Algorithm* to calculate a path
- how to use *approximate solutions* to create faked motion and collisions
- how to use a *quadtree, BSP tree,* or *BVH* to speed up visibility and collision determination

23 Tile-Based Games

OVERVIEW

One of the most common game genres (in the broadest sense) is the "platform" game, where a character has to negotiate their way around some kind of world made up of common ingredients. This genre encompasses both the obvious 2D platformers such as *Super Mario World* and some possibly less obvious examples such as 3D adventures like *Tomb Raider* and games based on long curved lines like *Sonic* or *Crash Bandicoot*, as well as "God games" such as the *Sim* series, puzzle games like *Sokoban,* and many, many others. All of these games are based on the same basic principle: a game world made of *tiles* or small identical pieces. This system has many advantages: particularly the ease of designing levels, the lower memory cost due to reuse of graphics, the possibility of creating a generic interaction and navigation system, and the major simplification of collision detection. Most of these are outside the interest of this book, but the last two issues are relevant and worth looking at briefly.

ON THE CD Some code samples from this chapter are implemented in the demo *tileScroller.*

GENERATING A GAME FROM BITS

So let's start by looking at the essentials of the system and how it can be used to generate, store, display, and run games.

Creating a Tile-Based World

A tile-based game (TBG) generally begins life in a simple program called a *level editor*, where individual tiles from some graphics gallery (for a standard 2D platformer usually 16 × 16 pixels in size) can be dragged into a grid of squares. Here, the level designer can create the level, designing the various puzzles. The level editor varies in complexity according to the details of the game, but the end result is much the same: each square is assigned to a particular tile. This grid data is then transferred into memory when the level is loaded, in the form of an array.

Each tile can have several properties—for example, a piece of ground can be able to melt, have a low friction value, be deadly to the touch, or be animated in some way (water waves, for instance). These details are not so important to us, however, as the fact that we can store data about collisions in the tiles.

On top of the game world, we create a number of moving characters or enemies, as well as perhaps moving scenery such as floating platforms. These might interact with the game environment, and we can also place discrete objects such as obstacles or tokens, which do not need to correspond to tiles. We also might create some kind of background image, also made from tiles, which we'll look at in the section on camera control.

So in general, the game engine has four main ingredients to think about: the tile data, the fixed objects, the moving environment objects, and the characters, including the player. As the game is played, the engine has to composite these various images into a single picture on the screen.

Basic Movement and Camera Control

Movement in the game world takes place in its own coordinate system, which is usually called *game space*. Each moving object has some position relative to the origin of game space (usually the top-left of the grid), and all calculations of collisions and so on take place in this coordinate system. Then our screen can be imagined as a "viewport" onto this scene, just as we did with 3D geometry. So in exactly the same way as before, we can consider a semi-independent camera object that follows the player characters as they move about the game world (or are under direct control of the player in games with no protagonist, such as God games). In a simple 2D view, we can consider the camera to be at a particular distance from the main plane of the game such that one pixel of the game world corresponds to one pixel on the screen.

Given a particular camera position (which for the sake of argument we'll assume is the game-world coordinates of the pixel at the middle of the screen), it's simple to draw the correct portion of the game world in the viewport:

```
function drawWorld (tileList, cameraX, cameraY, w, h)
    set x to cameraX-w/2
    set y to cameraY-h/2
    set hoffset to (x mod 16) // assuming 16-pixel tiles
    set voffset to (y mod 16)
    set leftmost to 1+(x-hoffset)/16
    set topmost to 1+(y-voffset)/16
    || add error checks to ensure we aren't out of range
    set largeImage to an empty buffer
    repeat for i=0 to w/16
        repeat for j=0 to h/16
            draw tileList[i+leftmost, j+topmost] to
square(i*16,j*16,(i+1)*16,(j+1)*16) of largeImage
        end repeat
    end repeat
    copy rectangle(hoffset,voffset,hoffset+w,voffset+h) of largeImage to
screen
end function
```

Of course, this is far too inefficient to be useful in reality. In practice, there are two strategies to speed this up. For a game that scrolls in only one direction (a *side-scroller* or *top-scroller*), it makes sense to draw the world column by column or row-by-row, adding a new chunk to the image each time another chunk goes out of range. This saves time on compositing, but is still a little slow when dealing with an image that can scroll in any direction, as well as being marginally inefficient since the same chunks of image have to be calculated again if the player chooses to go backward. Depending on the size of the level, an alternative is to draw the whole level at the start into a single image held in memory, of which we copy some portion to the screen.

We can add some additional interest to the image (at the expense of some processing speed, as always) by adding further image layers to create *parallax scrolling*. This is where we have a background and/or foreground image, which is placed at some other distance from the camera, with the result that it scrolls at a different speed. For example, we might create a background image for which one pixel of the image represents two pixels of world-space, that is, one that is conceptually twice as far away as the focal plane.

Having drawn our tiled planes, we then have to draw all the movable objects on top, which is simply a matter of translating their position from world coordinates to screen coordinates. Given that they are generally based on the focal plane, this just means that we can subtract the position of the top-left of the viewport from their position to work out where they are placed (if they are onscreen at all).

So the final question is: where do we place the camera? As in the 3D world, it's generally advisable not to have the camera linked directly to the character position. For one thing, when the character is at the edges of the game world, this produces images with a lot of blank space at the sides. So at the very least, we want to offset the camera whenever the character approaches an edge.

More generally, we want to have a camera that acts like a real one, following the character around by interpolation. For example, when they move in one direction, we can lag behind a little bit. We can also choose to focus a little to one side of the character to take into account which direction they are looking: in a side-scroller, for example, we're usually much more interested in what's in front of us than what's behind. So when they've stopped, we don't really want them to be in the center of the screen, but if they're looking right, we want them somewhere to the left of center.

Basic Collisions

The biggest advantage of using tiles apart from memory and speed is that it simplifies collision detection dramatically. In the simplest case, each tile in the landscape can be defined either to be solid or permeable—or some combination of the two, such as a tile that is only solid from the top, a common convention for platform games. Then when a character is moving, we only need to check for collisions when some part of it is entering a new tile:

```
on detectCollisionWithWorld c, w, h, displacement, tiles
    // w and h are the width and height of the box
    // c is the top-left corner

    // determine the colliding edges
    if displacement[1]=0 then set edge1 to "none"
    else if displacement[1]>0 then set edge1 to c[1]+w
    else set edge1 to c[1]
```

```
if displacement[2]=0 then set edge2 to "none"
else if displacement[2]>0 then set edge2 to c[2]+h
else set edge2 to c[2]

// calculate first collision
set t1 to 2 // time to collision along vertical edge
if edge1<>"none" then
   set currTileX to ceil(edge1/16.0)
   set newTileX to ceil((edge1+displacement[1])/16.0)
   if currTileX>newTileX then
      set t1 to ((currTileX-1)*16.0-edge1)/displacement[1]
   otherwise if currTileX<newTileX then
      set t1 to (currTileX*16.0-edge1)/displacement[1]
   end if
end if

set t2 to 2 // time to collision along horizontal edge
if edge2<>"none" then
   set currTileY to ceil(edge2/16.0)
   set newTileY to ceil((edge2+displacement[2])/16.0)
   if currTileY>newTileY then
      set t2 to ((currTileY-1)*16.0-edge2)/displacement[2]
   otherwise if currTileY<newTileY then
      set t2 to (currTileY*16.0-edge2)/displacement[2]
   end if
end if

if min(t1,t2)=2 then return "none" // no change of tile

if t2<t1 then // first collision is along horizontal
   set newTile to newTileY
   set currTile to currTileY
   set checktile to [ceil(c[1]/16.0), ceil((c[1]+w)/16.0)]
   set mx to the number of columns of tiles
   if displacement[2]>0 then set dir to "bottom"
   otherwise set dir to "top"
otherwise
   set newTile to newTileX
   set currTile to currTileX
   set checktile to [ceil(c[2]/16.0), ceil((c[2]+h)/16.0)]
   set mx to the number of rows of tiles
   if displacement[1]>0 then set dir to "right"
   otherwise set dir to "left"
```

```
   end if
   // at the end of the above process, newtile and currtile give the
   // changed row or column, checktile gives the start and finish
   // of the tiles containing the player

   set t to min(t1, t2)


   if newTile<1 or newTile>mx then
      // edge of map
      return [c+t*displacement, (0,0),dir]
   end if

   // check whether any new tiles entered are solid
   repeat with i=checktile[1] to checktile[2]
      if dir="bottom" or dir="top" then set tile to ptiles[newTile][i]
      otherwise set tile to ptiles[i][newTile]

      if tile is not empty then
         // potential collision
         if tile.solidity="solid" or (tile.solidity="top" and
         dir="bottom") then
            // tile collision (there could be more options here)
            // move to collision point

            return [c+t*displacement, (0,0),dir]
         end if
      end if
   end repeat

   // no collision: recurse
   if t=0 then set t to 0.001
   return detectCollisionWithWorld(c+t*displacement, w, h,
   (1-t)*displacement)

end function
```

It's conventional and convenient to consider the moving character to be an axis-aligned box, although similar techniques could be applied to other shapes, of course.

We can take advantage of all the time-saving methods introduced in the previous chapter—in particular, we can pre-calculate the heights of a jumping character over time and store them in a table. We can also save time using various tricks: for example, a character who is known to be currently walking on the ground is necessarily at the junction between two tiles in the vertical direction (in a "profile" game like *Mario*). This means that the first thing to check is always whether they are still standing on solid ground, since this is always the immediate collision. Only then do we need to worry about collisions in the horizontal direction.

Physics in platformers is not realistic—conventionally, for example, it's possible to change direction in mid-air while jumping, and objects do not as a rule bounce when they hit the ground.

Complex Tiles

Although most TBGs use solid tiles as described above, this isn't necessary. It's perfectly possible to subdivide a tile into smaller pieces with a collision map. Instead of calculating collisions according to whether the tile is solid or empty, we can define them to be solid only in places, as with Figure 23.1.

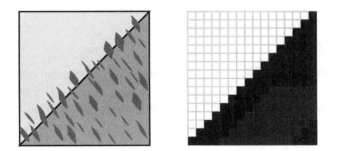

FIGURE 23.1   A tile with its associated collision map.

As usual, we store the normal details along with the collision information. Of course, this approach does make collision detection more complicated, so it's sensible to limit the number of complex tiles in use. You can also consider, instead of a collision map bitmap, using a vector approach, so the tile in Figure 23.1 might instead simply be thought of as "a wall from top-right to bottom-left." While less versatile, this does make things quicker.

Another extension of the tile concept is tiles that change over time, either continuously (conveyor belts, for example) or when triggered by some action (such as a "melting" tile that gradually disappears when stood on, or a tile that reveals some bonus). These aren't complicated in principle, but are marginally more awkward to deal with in the compositing process. To save time, you don't want to be redrawing the whole level each time a particular tile changes, so you need to only change those tiles that are currently in view. These can then be drawn over the existing level image.

Tiles that move from place to place, such as moving platforms, can be dealt with as characters rather than level tiles, and drawn on top of the level image after the fixed world has been copied across. It's a judgment call regarding other examples, such as growing trees, exploding barrels, or whatever else your imagination comes up with, whether you want to see them as discrete objects drawn on top of the world, or tiles in their own right. In general, if something can be a tile, it's better to keep it that way for speed.

ADVANCED TILING

We've concentrated on 2D TBGs up to now, but actually the approach applies just as well in a 3D world, especially a "2.5D" world, where most of the action takes place on a flat plane. And it can even be used for games where the action takes place on a spline surface.

The Isometric View

The most traditional form of tile-based 3D game is the isometric world. Isometric games are actually not too different from a 2D TBG: the only difference is that the tiles, which represent areas of ground, are drawn as rhombuses instead of squares, as shown in Figure 23.2. However, this is not the whole story, since as we're in 3D now, tiles can have height as well as length and width. Generally, the height of a tile is stored along with it, and we simply draw the tile at the appropriate position, just offset by its stored height.

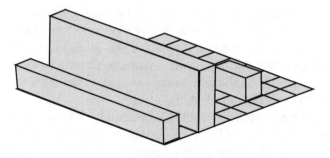

FIGURE 23.2   An isometric game.

Many games today take advantage of 3D acceleration to display these kinds of worlds (for that matter, they often use 3D acceleration even for normal side-scrollers or top-scrollers). But the original games of this type (*Zalaga* is credited as the first) drew them in real time in the same way as the flat games we just looked at.

One of the hardest parts of creating a good isometric game is dealing with control of the character. The principal problem is that movements corresponding to "left/right" and "up/down" on the grid don't correspond to equivalent movements on the screen. There are various solutions to this. One is to use a point-and-click interface, where you instruct a character to move to a particular spot by clicking there. Another is to use diagonal keys, as in the classic *Qbert*.

A more fundamental problem affects games like *Zalaga* where the player is flying over an isometric landscape. Being in 3D, we have no way to distinguish between an object near the camera but high up and an object further away but low down—and because it's isometric, we can't even use relative size to help us out. *Zalaga* solved this by means of a shadow, which showed the plane's position relative to the tile plane, and many other games have followed its example.

Platform Games in 3D

There's no reason you have to use isometric 3D—mostly it's just tradition. The same tile-based technique works just as well for any 3D world. The original *Tomb Raider*, for example, clearly shows its origin in tiles: most of the world is made up of square-based blocks of various sizes and shapes. In fact, there's little essential difference between *Tomb Raider* and *Super Mario World*: at heart, each is a simple game where you have to find your way to a goal in a tile-based environment, dodging or defeating enemies and collecting items along the way.

Not all 3D games are tile-based, however it may seem from this chapter. The Doom *and* Quake *engines, for example, are based on an extrusion system, where walls are drawn to follow lines on a 2D map.*

Most of the issues in these games come down to camera control, which we'll look at in the next chapter. Otherwise, the same techniques apply, we just have the option for more interesting tile shapes since they no longer have to conform to the isometric grid, so they can have slanted tops. We can also apply textures and lights to the surface independently of the tile shape, which gives us much more leeway for design: the collision and visual elements of the tile are separated.

From a collision point of view, as with the complex tiles we looked at earlier, we have two options for our tiles. We can either define them with a height map, or we can use a vector description such as "sloping down from left to right at an angle of

30° from a height of 50." If our tiles are reasonably small, the latter is almost certainly a better choice, as it still leaves us plenty of leeway to create rich surfaces, especially with the addition of textures and bump maps.

Here's a long function that works in the second way, testing for collision between a 3D AABB and the top of a single tile (calculating collisions with the other faces is your task in Exercise 23.1). We assume the tile has a flat top whose normal is known, as well as the height of the center point, and that the tile has a size of 16 and its other faces are all aligned to the coordinate axes.

```
function box3DTileTopCollision (center, width, length, height,
displacement, tileCenter, tileHeight, tileNormal)
    // width, length and height are the half-lengths of the sides of the
box
    // calculate tile top edges
    set edge1 to crossProduct(tileNormal, (1,0,0)) // edge vector
parallel to z-axis
    set edge2 to crossProduct(tileNormal, (0,0,1)) // edge vector
parallel to x-axis
    multiply edge1 by 16/edge1[3]
    multiply edge2 by 16/edge2[1]
    // find vertices
    set c to tileCenter+(0,tileHeight,0)
    set v1 to c-edge1/2-edge2/2
    set v2 to v1+edge1
    set v3 to v2+edge2
    set v4 to v1+edge2

    set t to 2

    // find collision time with base of box
    if displacement[2]<0 then // box is going down
        set planec to center+(0,-height,0) // start height of base
        set vtop to the one of v1, v2, v3, v4 with the highest y-
coordinate
        set t1 to (vtop[2]-planec[2])/displacement[2]
        if t1<1 and t1>=0 then // possible collision during time period
            // check for intersection within box base
            set p to vtop[2]-t1*displacement-planec // vector from box
center to intersection point
            if abs(p[1])<width and abs(p[3])<length then
                set t to t1 // top vertex collides
            end if
        end if
    end if
```

```
            // NB: if there is a collision with this vertex, it has to be the
               first collision
end if

if t=2 then // try other collisions with base
    if dotProduct(displacement, tileNormal)<0 then
        // find the vertex of the box which would collide with the
           tile face
        set basevertex to planec
        if tileNormal[1]<0 then add (width,0,0) to basevertex
        otherwise add (-width,0,0) to basevertex
        if tileNormal[3]<0 then add (0,0,length) to basevertex
        otherwise add (0,0,-length) to basevertex
        // basevertex is the leading vertex on the box with respect to
           the tile top

        set t2 to dotProduct(basevertex-c, tileNormal) /
        dotProduct(displacement, tileNormal)
        if t2<1 and t2>=0 then // leading vertex intersects tile plane
            // check for intersection within tile
            set p to basevertex +t2*displacement-c
            if abs(p[1])<8 and abs(p[3])<8 then
                set t to t2 // leading vertex collides
            end if
        end if
    end if
    // NB: again, this collision will always come before any other
       potential collision
end if

if t=2 then // try edge-to-edge collision
    set n1 to crossProduct((1,0,0), norm(displacement))
    // n1 is the normal of the plane swept out by x-aligned edge of
       box
    set s1 to dotProduct(basevertex-vtop,n1)
    if s1>0 then
        set s1 to -s1
        set n1 to -n1
    end if
    // check for intersection with z-aligned axis of tile
    divide s1 by dotProduct(edge1,n1)
    if dotProduct(c-vtop,edge1)<0 then set s to -s1
    otherwise set s to s1
```

```
    if s>=0 and s<1 then
        set p1 to vtop+s1*edge1 // intersection point with edge
        set t3 to magnitude(p1-basevertex)/ magnitude(displacement)
        if t3<1 and t3>=0 then set t to t3
    end if
    || repeat for other edge pair
  end if
  if t<1 and t>=0 then return t
end function
```

This function takes advantage of rather a lot of optimizations due to the alignment of the boxes. For example, since the edges of both boxes are aligned with the axes, there are only two possible edge-edge collisions, as shown in Figure 23.3. (Note that the vertices marked vt and bv correspond to the variables vtop and basevertex in the previous code.)

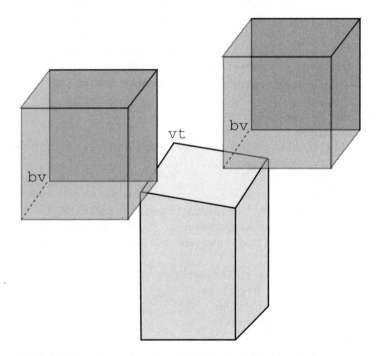

FIGURE 23.3 Possible edge-edge collisions with a 3D tile.

Spline-Based Tiles

One final example of a TBG, which we won't look into in detail as it's quite complicated, is a game set on one or more curving paths, one obvious example being *Crash Bandicoot*. Although nominally in 3D, this game is mostly limited to a single path that curves through the game world, with a small range of movement in either the *x* or *y* directions.

Of course, we can't be sure how a particular game is programmed, but it's interesting to speculate how such a game might be created. One way would be to describe the main path in terms of a 3D spline, which is then mapped to a simple 2D tiled map (recall Figure 21.2).

When the game is loaded, we translate the 2D map into 3D just as with a normal platform game, but we also curve it to fit onto the spline. Similar methods can be used to create racing games: we can transform a straight line into a curved track, either on a plane or curving through space as in more space-age racing games like *Wipeout*.

The most useful aspect of working this way is that we can perform all our collision detection routines in the simple tile space, and only use the actual 3D space for display purposes. Working this way requires more than a little fiddling to make it robust and natural-feeling (especially dealing with speeds along different curves of the track), but does pay off in the end.

EXERCISES

Exercise 23.1

Complete the `box3DTileTopCollision()` function and extend it to take into account collisions with the other faces of the tile.

The version given in the chapter leaves some of the working unfinished, so see if you can complete it, then finish it off by doing some of the easier work of detecting collisions with the other faces. Note that there are only two other possible face-face collisions, which should be reasonably straightforward—but don't forget that the top edge is not parallel to the ground.

SUMMARY

This chapter focuses more on programming techniques as opposed to mathematics. Much of the programming is broadly discussed, but the topic is so important in gaming that it couldn't be left out altogether. This material also provides us with a nice introduction to the next chapter, where we'll be looking at the quintessential TBG, the grid-based maze.

YOU SHOULD NOW KNOW

- how to create and draw a 2D tile-based game
- how to scroll through it either by copying from a pre-rendered image or drawing on the fly
- how to control the camera to create natural movement
- how to calculate collisions in a 2D game, or a 3D game with vector-based tiles
- how to create a game based on a spline by mapping from a simpler 2D description

24 Mazes

OVERVIEW

A particularly common type of game world could loosely be described as the "maze." The variety of games that fits into this category in one way or another is quite large: everything from obvious mazes like *Pac Man* to driving games based on a city grid, and even to some extent the tile-based games and exploratory 3D platformers we looked at in the previous chapter. In this chapter we'll look at how to create, work with, and navigate through a maze, and also how to create simple AI routines that will search through the maze for a quarry.

ON THE CD   Code samples from this chapter are implemented in *math.cst* in the script *Chapter 24 (mazes)*. The *mazes* demo uses them in context.

CLASSIFYING MAZES

Before we can look at how to work with mazes, it's worth understanding what the term *maze* formally means. Then we'll discuss some ways to classify mazes. There are two different ways to think of a maze. One is to think of its physical properties, which include the shape of the underlying grid (rectangular, triangular, circular, and so on), how convoluted the paths are, the dimensionality, and so on. The other is to consider its *topology*, which is to say the mathematical form stripped of these physical factors: essentially, to think of it as a set of branching points joined by paths.

Graphs and Connectivity

Mathematically, a maze is a kind of *graph*. This word is used in a different sense here than we have used it previously: a graph is basically a diagram consisting of a number of points (conventionally called *vertices* but in this chapter we'll use the computing term *nodes*) joined by lines or *edges*, as shown in Figure 24.1. Here you can see that the simple maze on the left has been converted to a graph on the right, where each node represents a fork, crossroads, or dead end in the maze, and each edge represents a path that can be taken from one to the other. There are also two special points, the start and finish, which for neatness are given their own nodes, although they could just as easily be placed at the nearest branching point or dead end. A maze doesn't have to have a start and finish, but it usually does.

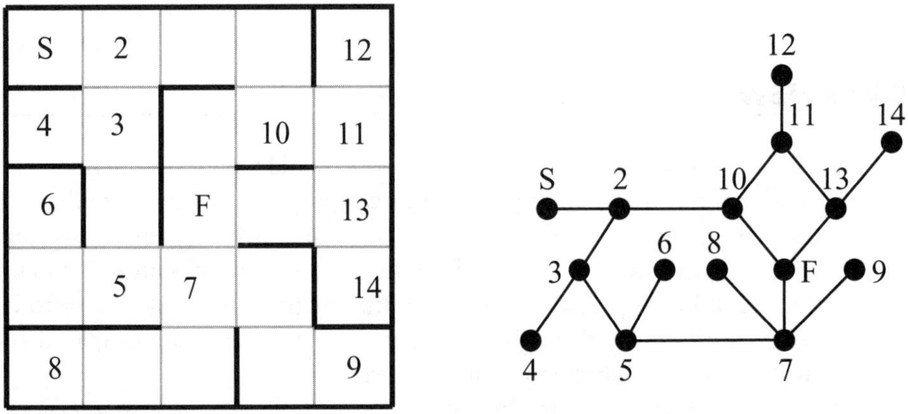

FIGURE 24.1 A maze and its associated graph.

A graph is in most cases considered independently of how it's drawn on the page, we are only interested in its topological properties: that is, which points are connected to which. However, it is possible to *label* the edges of a graph with some number, which often represents the length of the edge. We can also label the vertices, often representing some kind of cost or distance. A graph labeled in this way is known as a *network*. Alternatively, the edge or vertex labeling can simply be a way to index the graph for reference. Finally, we can assign a direction to any edge, restricting movement in one direction or another, creating a *directed* graph.

Conventional mathematical graphs may have at most one edge between any pair of vertices, and no vertex may be joined to itself, but these strictures don't apply to mazes, so we need to consider what are sometimes called *pseudo-graphs*. It's possible to convert any pseudo-graph to a true graph simply by removing the offending edges, with no effect on the main properties of the maze (particularly finding a path from one point to another). However, a directed graph or network is affected by the different choices of edge, so it's important to allow these multiple connections when searching for optimal paths. So we can instead convert a pseudo-graph to a normal graph by inserting additional vertices, which in a network are connected by edges of length zero.

There are a number of other ways to classify graphs that apply naturally to mazes:

- A graph is said to be *connected* if there is a path from each node to every other node. (Figure 24.2a is connected, while Figure 24.2b is disconnected.)
- If there is exactly *one* path from any node to any other node, the graph is called a *tree*. Any connected graph with n nodes and $n - 1$ edges is a tree, and vice versa. (Figure 24.2c is a tree.)
- A graph is called *planar* if there is some way to draw it on paper so that no two edges cross over. (Figure 24.2d shows how the graph in Figure 24.2a can be drawn in this way, proving that it is planar.) All trees are planar.

A maze whose graph is a tree is called *simply connected*, and has exactly one correct solution (unless you count backtracking). If the graph is connected but not a tree, then the maze is *multiply connected*, and contains some loops. Of course, if the graph is not connected, then there is some set of nodes that can't be reached from some other set: that is, it can be divided into a number of connected subgraphs, which are not connected to one another. For a maze, this means either that it has no solution (if the start and end nodes are in different regions) or that there is some part of the maze which is irrelevant, as it can't be reached.

Graph theory is a very large and complex mathematical topic and we won't explore it any further here, but it helps to have some of the terminology in place. We'll discuss some graph theory issues in the next two chapters when we look at search strategies.

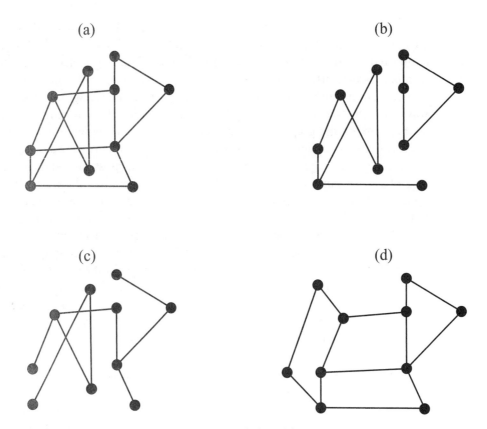

FIGURE 24.2   Examples of connectivity and planarity.

Twists and Turns

Although the topology of the maze is the only thing that should affect finding a path through it, in reality the physical properties have a big effect too. After all, real-life labyrinths and traditional hedge mazes are not in general based on particularly complicated graphs—the classical labyrinth, such as the labyrinth of the minotaur, did not have any branching points at all, but was simply a convoluted path to the center, like the decorative labyrinths used in many ancient mosaics. (This is generally considered to be the technical distinction between a "maze" and a "labyrinth.")

What makes a maze complicated are the psychological factors: for a labyrinth that you are looking down on in a plan view, optical effects based on the player's tendency to want to aim toward the goal; and for a first-person maze, the difficulty of remembering sequences of twists and turns.

The main physical properties of a maze are:

dimensionality: is it 2D, 3D, or even 4D and beyond? We're most used to 2D mazes, but it's perfectly possible to create a maze in a cube, or a sequence of cubes with portals between them. We can also create a kind of "2.5D" maze by allowing bridges and tunnels, or teleports, connecting different parts of a 2D maze. More complicated mazes can also be created by allowing the maze itself to mutate over time, as in the movie *Cube*.

geometry: for example, a 2D maze can be based on a plane, but it can also be allowed to "wrap" in various directions, as with the *Pac-Man* maze, which wraps from left to right as if it's drawn on a cylindrical surface. This could also be considered a teleport, as in the 2.5D mazes mentioned previously: in fact, any 2.5D maze can be considered to be a 2D maze that "curves" through 3D space.

underlying grid: a maze can be based on a grid of squares, as in Figure 24.1 and other examples in this chapter, or on triangles, hexagons, or concentric circles, and can also be distorted in various ways such as perspective transforms. A maze can also have no underlying grid at all, just a bunch of walls in various directions.

"texture":   for example, how far one normally travels before encountering a branching point, how far one travels before encountering a (non-branching) turn in a corridor, and the proportion of dead ends (or equivalently, the average length of a dead-end passage). Different maze-generation methods tend to produce mazes of different textures, even if they are all simply connected.

Of these, the maze texture is the most subtle, and worth looking at in more detail. We can classify texture further by using some useful terminology, which along with a number of other terms in this chapter, originated with Walter Pullen (the creator of the Freeware maze software *Daedalus*). Figure 24.3 shows two mazes with different degrees of what he calls *river*. The first consists essentially of one long passageway with a few very short dead-end passageways leading off it. This is described as having a low river, whereas the second has a much higher river: there are fewer dead-ends but they are longer and more convoluted. Notice, however, that the longest path is much the same length in both mazes. High-river mazes are easier to solve because there are fewer choices. We can assign a numerical value to the river by calculating the percentage of dead ends in the maze.

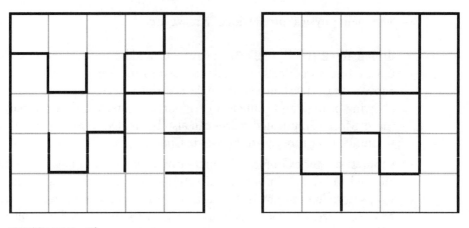

FIGURE 24.3   River.

A related concept might be called the *convolution* of the maze, which might be measured by the *standard deviation* of the length of a path from any end-node to any other end-node of the underlying tree. Standard deviation is a common statistical tool, which essentially measures the average distance from the mean: if the mean of a set of numbers $x_1, x_2, \ldots, x_n$ is μ, then the standard deviation σ is the square root of the mean squared difference of each number from μ (that is, the square root of the *variance*, which we introduced in Chapter 10). We write:

$$\sigma = \sqrt{\frac{1}{n}\sum_{i=1}^{n}\left(x_i - \mu\right)^2}$$

We don't have space to look at statistics in this book, so we won't look at this further. However, the higher this standard deviation is, the lower the value of the convolution. The highest convolution would be obtained by a maze that looks like a spider, with a number of equal-length paths radiating from a central branch point. In this case, the standard deviation of the path length would be zero. An alternative measure would be simply the mean distance from one node to another in the graph. A maze with higher convolution tends to be easier to solve, although the path to the goal is usually longer.

Figure 24.4 shows the difference between mazes with different degrees of *run*, both of which have the same degree of river. Run is a measure of the twistiness of the maze: how far you can generally travel in a straight line. The run can also be biased in particular directions, giving a maze which has a long run in one direction but short in another. A maze based on concentric squares, for example, will have differently biased run values at different points in the maze.

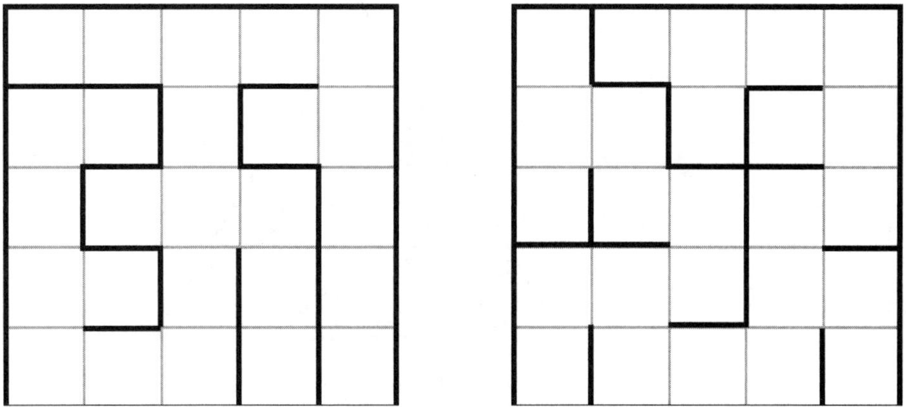

FIGURE 24.4 Run.

CREATING MAZES

Now that we know how mazes work, we can take a look at how a maze might be handled on the computer, and also at some techniques for generating a maze at random. We'll deal only with mazes based on a grid in this chapter, as these are the most tractable—really, these are an extension of the tile-based games we just looked at. Non-grid-based mazes are common (for example, most first-person shooters can be considered mazes of this kind), but rarely generated automatically, instead they are created by hand using level editors and navigated using the collision detection techniques we've discussed in previous chapters.

Handling Maze Data

A tile-based maze can be considered as a list of cells with walls between them. For example, a square grid consists of an $n \times m$ array of cells each of which can have a wall to the north and/or to the east. To determine if there is a wall to the west of cell (i, j), we just look if there is an east wall in $(i - 1, j)$, and similarly for the south. If you have a particularly good memory, you might recall that in Chapter 2, we set up a function for initializing a grid of this kind using the modulo function.

NOTE

An alternative formulation is to consider the list of all the walls, storing the coordinates of the cells on each side. The two are equivalent, but as we usually know where we are in the maze, it's more useful to know where we can go from there instead of having to search each time through all the walls to find where we can't go.

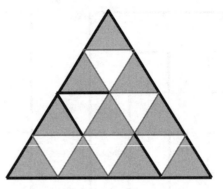

FIGURE 24.5 Storing maze data in a triangular grid.

The same kind of principle can be applied to other grids. Triangular grids such as Figure 24.5 are best considered as two interlocking sets of cells with different properties, or one set of rhombuses (equivalent to squares), which may or may not be split in half.

Generating a Maze Automatically

There are quite a few standard maze generation algorithms, but we'll only look at a few here. In general, generating a maze can be done either by "growing" the walls out from the border, or by starting from a (tile-based) maze with all the walls in place and removing walls until the maze is complete. In graph theory, when creating a simply connected maze, this is equivalent to trying to find a *minimal spanning tree* for a particular multiply-connected graph (although when removing walls, this is what might be called the "dual" maze graph where each edge represents a wall rather than a passageway). Most algorithms can be performed either way, but we'll only consider the first kind here, since it's more convenient when the maze is set up as suggested above.

ON THE CD

All of these algorithms can be tested using the *mazes.dir* file on the CD-ROM. The simplest method for generating a maze is called the *recursive backtracker*, which is essentially what is known as a *depth-first search* (see Chapter 26). In this algorithm, we maintain a memory of the path we have taken, and at each stage we look at a neighboring cell to the current one (choosing one at random, or biasing in particular directions to create a maze with a higher run factor) to see if it has yet been visited. If it has, we try another cell, if not, we remove the wall and move into that cell. If all cells have been visited, we backtrack along our path until we find another cell with an unvisited neighbor. If we get back to the first cell with no more neighbors to reach, then the maze is complete. Here's the code:

```
function recursiveBacktrack maze, startcell, endcell, path
    if path is empty then add startcell to path
    set currentcell to the last cell in path
    set neighborList to the neighbors of currentcell in maze
    randomize neighborList
    repeat for each cell in neighborList
        if cell is not in path then
            set found to 1
            add cell to path
            remove wall between cell and currentCell in maze
            recursiveBacktrack(maze, startcell, endcell, path)
        end if
    end repeat
end function
```

A slight variation on this method is *Prim's Algorithm,* which instead of backtracking, picks a random unvisited neighbor of any cell on the path. This takes a little more computational effort, as you need to maintain a complete list of all unvisited neighbors (the "frontier" of the maze), but runs somewhat faster and produces a maze with more dead ends. Either of these methods could also be used as a paint program's "floodfill" command, as they will explore any space completely. They are therefore rather convenient methods for creating a maze of an irregular shape, and work well with any underlying grid. Figure 24.6 shows two mazes created using these two algorithms.

FIGURE 24.6 Mazes created using recursive backtracking (left) and Prim's Algorithm (right).

A second algorithm is included here as a matter of interest, although it's less useful in practice as it's slightly slower. This is called *Kruskal's Algorithm,* and works rather differently. Instead of working with a path, we start by numbering each cell in the maze. Then we pick walls at random, and if the cells on each side have different numbers, we remove the wall and renumber all the walls on each side with the same number. This gradually builds connected regions in the maze, until all cells have been numbered the same, at which point the maze is complete. (Prim's and Kruskal's algorithms are examples of what is called a *greedy algorithm.*)

```
function kruskal (maze)
    set wallList to a list of all walls in maze
    randomize wallList
    set idList to an empty array
    repeat for i=1 to the number of cells in maze
        id maze[i] with i
        add [i] to idList
    end repeat
    repeat for wall in wallList
        set cell1 and cell2 to the neighbors of wall
        set id1 to cell1's id
        set id2 to cell2's id
        if id1 <> id2 then
            remove wall from maze
            repeat for each cell in idList[id2]
                add cell to idList[id1]
                id cell with id1
            end repeat
            set idList[id2] to an empty array
        end if
    end repeat
end function
```

Of course, this could be optimized somewhat, but it's still clearly harder work for the computer than the other method. But it is quite a pretty method to watch in action, and again is suitable for a grid of any type or shape.

The final method we'll look at is the fastest, called *Eller's Algorithm.* It has a few minor disadvantages over the others, particularly that it only really works for rectangular mazes and tends to have a bias in one direction, but it's very quick and also memory-efficient. In this method, we work through the whole maze a row at a time, using a similar method to Kruskal's Algorithm. Each cell in a particular row is given an ID number according to how it is connected to other cells in previous rows. There has to be at least one path from the previous row to the current one for each remaining ID number, and we can have at most one path with the same ID from the previous row to any connected set in the new row (to avoid creating a loop). It sounds complicated, but the algorithm itself is reasonably simple, although more complicated than the others we've looked at. Notice that this time we start with a maze whose walls are all down:

```
function Eller (maze, hfactor)
    set w to the length of a maze row
    set h to the number of rows

    // create first row
    set currentRow to ellerRow(maze, w, 1, 1, hfactor)

    // create body of maze
    repeat for j=2 to h
        set newRow to ellerRow(maze, w, j, w*(j-1)+1, hfactor)
        set testList to a list of elements from 1 to w
        randomize testList
        repeat for each i in testList
            set id1 to newRow[i]
            set id2 to currentRow[i]
            if id1 <> id2 then
                repeat for each element in newRow
                    if element=id1 then set element to id2
                end repeat

                repeat for each element in currentRow
                    if element=id1 then set element to id2
                end repeat
            otherwise
                add a wall between cell (i, j) and (i, j-1) in maze
            end if
        end repeat
        set currentRow to newRow
    end repeat

    // adjust final row to ensure span
    set idlist to an empty array
    repeat for i=1 to w
        if currentRow[i] is not in idList then
            add currentRow[i] to idList
            remove the wall between cell(i, h) and (i-1, h) in maze
        end if
    end repeat
end function
```

```
function ellerRow (maze, w, row, id, hfactor)
    set r to an empty array
    repeat for i=1 to w-1
      add id to r
      if random(1000)<hfactor then
        add 1 to id
        add a wall between cell (i, row) and (i+1, row) in maze
      end if
    end repeat
    add id to r
    return r
end function
```

Figure 24.7 shows two mazes generated by this algorithm using different values of hfactor, which should be a number from 1 to 1000, representing a probability. As you can see, this value affects the run factor in each direction and needs to be approximately 50% to create a successful maze.

FIGURE 24.7   Adjusting the random factor for horizontal walls in Eller's Algorithm (left: 20%, right: 80%).

The greatest advantage of Eller's Algorithm is that it can be used for a maze of any size at all (at least in a particular direction): you don't need to worry about memory requirements because only one row of the maze at a time needs to be held in memory. It can also be very easily adapted to create a 3D maze, working one layer at a time instead of one row at a time.

Multiply-Connected Mazes

Strange as it may seem, a maze does not become easier by removing dead ends. In fact, it generally becomes significantly harder to solve, not so much computationally as psychologically. Computationally, the faster algorithms work much the same way whether the maze has loops or not, although the simpler algorithms such as wall-following may fail, and any algorithm based on storing the whole path is going to have memory problems in a sufficiently large maze. But psychologically, the existence of loops means that it is much easier to get lost. However, it's this psychological factor which makes creating a random multiply-connected maze a difficult proposition, since it's hard to have a random algorithm which will also generate a psychologically interesting maze.

The simplest way to generate a multiply-connected maze is to create a variant of the recursive backtracker algorithm, where at the end of each pathway you open up a wall back into the existing path. This works fairly well, but does tend to create mazes with primitive loops—four cells in a square, for example, or a 3×2 group with a single wall in the center.

An alternative method, which is much more computationally expensive but more effective, is to start with a simply-connected maze and then remove walls in this way: first choose a few walls at random and for each one, calculate the length of the shortest path from one side of the wall to the other (for example, using the A* algorithm described later in the chapter). To create a maze with long loops, you could remove the wall with the longest path; for shorter loops, choose the median path (the one in the middle of the sample). Of course, this won't lead to a complete multiply-connected maze with no dead ends (a *braid* maze), but it does produce mazes which are generally interesting. To create a braid maze by this method, we could remove a wall from all dead ends, but it would be unlikely to look very good.

```
function multiplyConnected (maze, connections)
   // assume maze is already created and simply connected
   repeat with i=1 to connections
      set wallList to an empty array
      repeat for 11 walls in maze
         set s1, s2 to squares on either side of the wall
         set dist to path distance from s1 to s2
         add wall to wallList, sorted by dist
      end repeat
      remove the last wall in wallList

   end repeat
   return maze
end function
```

It can't be denied, though, that for multiply-connected even more than simply-connected mazes, human-generated patterns tend to be better than anything produced by a random algorithm. Random processes are best used for filling the gaps around the principal areas of the maze with additional convolutions and blind alleys.

More Complex Mazes

Although the grid-based maze is the most common, other maze types can also be used. Topologically, there is no difference between a maze based on a grid and one based on another substructure, or no structure at all, but it does make a difference both psychologically and in terms of computation.

One common maze type that is not grid-based is the circular maze, such as Figure 24.8. Topologically, this maze is essentially identical to the maze in Figure 24.1, but of course its substructure is very different.

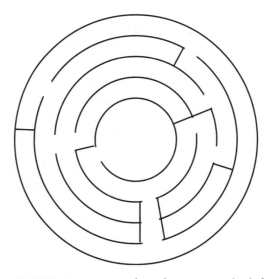

FIGURE 24.8   A maze based on concentric circles.

Creating a maze of this form can be done in a number of ways, but a particularly effective method is to use a simple variant on Eller's Algorithm, where instead of working row by row, you work circle by circle from the inside out. Working in circles instead of rows is simple, the only change being that regions now wrap from one side of the row to the other—equivalent to creating a maze on a cylinder.

Having created this cylindrical maze, we simply give it an exit at the top and another at the bottom, then map the whole thing to a circle, where the exit at the bottom actually leads to the center of the maze, and the exit at the top leads to the outside, as shown in Figure 24.9.

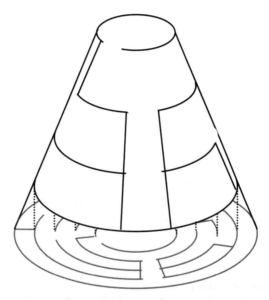

FIGURE 24.9   Converting a cylindrical maze to a circular one.

Of course, a maze created like this won't be entirely regular, in the sense that the walls on inner circles are more closely packed than walls on the outer circles, since there are more grid cells in a smaller space. We can offset this problem by varying the horizontal wall density factor we called hfactor, making more walls the further out we travel.

One further consideration when creating these mazes is how to draw them on the computer, which is much harder to do effectively than with a grid of straight lines. In general, making these mazes look good is quite hard work and requires a little tweaking by hand—having said that, the maze in Figure 24.10, created using the program on the CD-ROM, looks quite reasonable.

ON THE CD

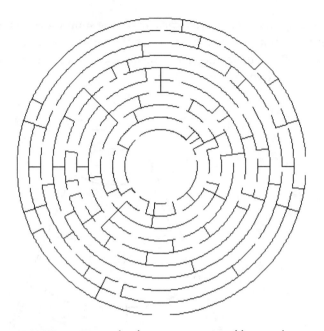

FIGURE 24.10   A circular maze generated by a variant of Eller's Algorithm.

NAVIGATING WITHIN MAZES

Having generated our maze, we need to move through it. The main thing that distinguishes a maze game from other tile-based games such as we looked at in the previous chapter is that in general, the size of your character is smaller than the size of the maze cells, whereas characters in TBGs tend to cover two or more cells.

The simplest kind of maze movement is just to step from one cell to another, but for most applications, this is not enough, and we would like to be able to move smoothly and navigate around. And of course there's the reason we created a maze in the first place: how do we find our way from A to B?

Collision Detection and Camera Control

The main trick to maze navigation is to consider each square as a different "room"—really, it's no different from working with quadtrees, except that we have the added advantage that the trees aren't arbitrary but an essential part of the landscape. As long as a character is moving within a room, we know that there is no collision. Then all we need to do when they are leaving the room is to find which room they are trying to enter and check if there is a wall in the way. It couldn't be simpler.

We've already done all the work you need for this, so the details can safely be left to you as an exercise. One issue that is worth mentioning here, though, is the rather unrealistic navigation convention that has become standard in gaming, which is wall-sliding. When following a path that would naturally take you into a wall, rather than either stopping dead or rebounding, the convention is that we remove the normal component of motion but retain the tangential component, with the result that you appear to approach the wall and then slide along it. It's a very strange concept, but it feels quite natural and is computationally simple.

In a first-person 3D view, you need to keep the camera a little away from the wall (otherwise you'll get part-views of the room next door), so it's best to treat the observer as a sphere rather than a point. In a third-person 3D view, things get a little more complicated, as you have two sets of collisions to consider: once you have worked out where the character is, you still need to determine where the camera will go. Generally, we consider the camera to have a "natural" resting point, usually somewhere behind and a little above the character. If possible, when the character moves, we want the camera to follow, but often this isn't possible, as shown in Figure 24.11, where the character at A has turned, so the camera that was previously at B would now like to be at C, which is unfortunately inside a wall.

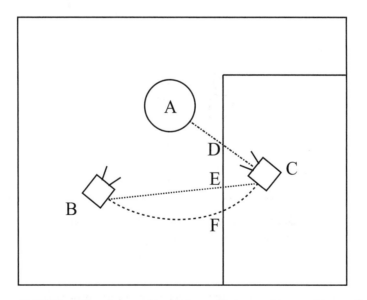

FIGURE 24.11 A camera movement hitting problems with a wall.

We can treat the camera essentially as another observer following its own path, and deal with its collisions exactly as we do the first observer. But we still have to decide what happens when the collision occurs. For example, in Figure 24.11 the best solution might be for the camera to stop at the point D, the nearest available point along the line AC. This might be a little too close to the observer, and one would need to lift the camera up into the air, looking down at the observer slightly. Two alternative positions are the point E, where it first hits the wall on a straight-line path from B to C, and F, the same on a curved path, however both of these suffer from the problem that we cannot now see everything the character sees. Meanwhile, for a situation like Figure 24.12, it would be foolish to take any of these options when there is a perfectly good camera position at C, and in this case we might be better off, instead of interpolating the camera from B to C and passing through the wall, just cutting to C in a jump.

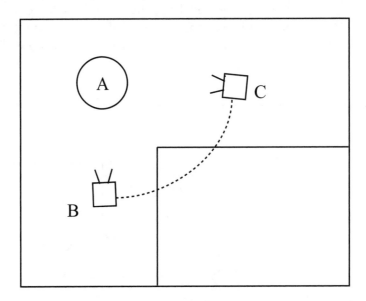

FIGURE 24.12 A perfectly reasonable camera movement running into problems on the way.

As we've seen before, these decisions about camera control are very much a matter of preference and always require very careful handling. If in doubt, always make sure your user can override whatever stupid thing your particular system chooses to do in some unanticipated situation—it *will* happen.

Line of Sight

Another aspect of (grid-based) mazes that makes them quite convenient to work with is that it's relatively easy to calculate which areas are visible from any particular point. This is useful both for visibility culling in a 3D FPS, and when calculating enemy AI behavior, for example with a *Pac-Man*-style ghost, or a sentry in a stealth game like *Thief*. As always, we're going to concentrate our attention on square-based mazes, although similar methods work just as well for other grids.

The simplest way to demonstrate the line of sight algorithm is to take a look at a diagram such as Figure 24.13. Here, a character is situated at the point marked with a cross. All the places the character can see are shaded: notice that as well as the cells along the principal rows, a number of neighboring cells are also partially visible.

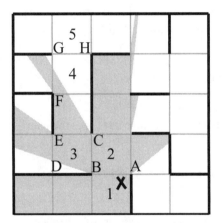

FIGURE 24.13 Visibility determination from a particular point.

It should be immediately clear that even in a grid, this is not by any means a simple calculation. However, there are some useful shortcuts that we can take, particularly in a simply-connected maze. Once again, the trick is to make use of recursion: each time we pass through a "doorway," we're entering a new simply-connected area, "illuminated" by a beam of light defined by the doorway and the beam of light we began with. That is to say, we're splitting the 360° sweep around the observer into smaller and smaller pieces each time a doorway is passed.

Look at Figure 24.13 again. From the point X, there are four possible "doorways" through which our imaginary light can shine. Two of them are closed and two are open, of which the line AB subtends the largest angle at X (recall that two points A and B are said to "subtend" the angle AXB at X). So we now look at the neighbors of the cell marked 2, and we see that all three of the doorways are open, so we recurse over each of these—let's go through the door BC into cell 3, splitting the beam further into the angle BXC. Now, notice that the vertex D is outside the illuminated angle, so we can ignore it. However, since vertex E is illuminated, some light still gets through the doorway DE—specifically, the beam BXE. We also know already that C is illuminated, which means that the whole beam EXC passes through CE.

We continue recursing in this way until we reach either a blank wall or a doorway such as GH. Cell 4 is partially visible, illuminated by the beam FXC, but both G and H lie outside this beam. This means that none of the light from X passes through GH. What's more, since the maze is simply connected, we can be sure that none of the light will reach any cell beyond that point.

Here's a very rough version of this visibility algorithm (it could be very much faster, as we're calculating lots of the values several times over):

```
function visibleSquares (observerPoint, beamStartAngle, beamEndAngle,
fromSquare, thisSquare)
    if beamStartAngle is not defined, then set beamStartAngle to -pi;
beamEndAngle to pi;
    if thisSquare is not define, then set thisSquare to observerPoint's
    square

    set ret to an empty array
    append thisSquare to ret

    repeat for each neighbor of thisSquare except fromSquare
        if there is a doorway from thisSquare to neighbor then
            set v1 to the first vertex of the doorway clockwise from the
            observer
            set v2 to the other vertex of the doorway
            // find angles of these vertices (in the range -pi, pi)
            set a1 to the angle of v1 with observerPoint
            set a2 to the angle of v2 with observerPoint
            if both a1 and a2 are between beamStartAngle and beamEndAngle
            then
            if a1<a2 then // vertices are on the same side of the angle
            range
            set start to max(a1, beamStartAngle)+0.02 // the increment is
            added to rule out 'just visible' squares
            set finish to min(a2, beamEndAngle)-0.02
            // recurse over all visible squares
```

```
        set s to visibleSquares(maze, observerPoint, start, finish,
        thisSquare, n)
        append all elements of s to ret
    otherwise
        // the doorway 'straddles' the angle range
        set start to min(a1, beamEndAngle)+0.02
        set finish to max(a2, beamStartAngle)-0.02
        // split the angle range into two parts
        // and recurse along both paths
        set s1 to visibleSquares(maze, observerPoint, finish, pi,
        thisSquare, n)
        set s2 to visibleSquares(maze, observerPoint, -pi, start,
        thisSquare, n)
        append each element of s1 and s2 to ret

    end if
  end repeat
  return ret
end function
```

You might want to think about alternative methods for dealing with the situation where the doorway straddles the start and end angles, as in this version it does mean some re-calculation. In general there are a number of ways to speed up this algorithm by storing doorway vertex values—maybe Bresenham's Algorithm (Chapter 22) could also be used to avoid the need for floats and trigonometry.

As it happens, the same algorithm works just as well for multiply-connected mazes, however you sometimes find that you may be investigating the same square twice from different directions—in fact, it's more than likely that two parts of the same square may be visible from different sides. This means that the recursion will often be checking illumination of particular vertices under several different beams. For a simply-connected maze, the greatest advantage is that as soon as we have determined a particular cell is out of sight, all passages beyond that cell can be culled from a 3D scene. This possibility is much less applicable in a multiply-connected maze.

Maze-Threading

When trying to "solve" a maze, there are two different situations. The first is when you are placed inside the maze at a particular point and need to find your way to the goal (or exit) without knowing anything about the maze. The second is when you are looking down at the maze on paper, or you are a computer with the complete maze in memory, and trying to find a path from one point to another, often the shortest such path. We'll look at the second situation in the next section, but here we'll be looking at some methods to solve the first, which is sometimes called "threading" a maze. Implementing the algorithms is left to you (see Exercise 24.1): the methods are very similar to those we have already encountered when generating mazes.

The classic method for solving a maze is so ridiculous that you would think it never works: Turn in the same direction every time you reach a junction—or equivalently, walk along keeping one hand on the same wall throughout. For any simply-connected maze this is guaranteed to work, and for a multiply-connected maze it will also always work if you are trying to get from an "entrance" to an "exit" on the outer walls. It won't enable you to find a way to the center of a multiply-connected maze if there is a loop surrounding the center, however, and it certainly won't find the shortest path, nevertheless it is computationally simple, requiring no memory of the path traveled.

Another method that is faster in general and also guarantees a solution in even a multiply-connected maze is a simple recursive search: the equivalent of the recursive backtracker maze generator, this algorithm will follow every path as far as it will go, backtracking and trying alternative paths each time you reach a dead-end, or a cell you have already visited. This algorithm can even be used "blind," walking in particular directions and banging into walls—a kind of dead end of length 0.

If you know where your goal is (you just don't know how to find a path to it), then it's possible to improve on the recursive backtracker by preferentially trying to form a path that divides the maze into smaller regions. If you can, for example, make a path that splits the maze in half, then you know (for a planar maze) that there is no need to try any path on the wrong side of it. This can massively reduce your search time. Interestingly, this can sometimes mean that specifically searching for paths that *don't* lead to the goal can be more useful in the long term.

Another method that has the advantage of being easy to apply even by hand, because it does not involve a potentially huge memory stack, is to use a system of marking—imagine walking through an actual maze, making marks on the walls to indicate passages that you have explored. In computational terms, it does mean that you need to maintain the whole maze grid in working memory, since you have to be able to "annotate" the cell data in some way. In all other respects, the algorithm is identical to the recursive backtracker.

To run it, you make a mark at each junction along the paths you enter by and leave. A single mark behind you means that you are moving forward. When you turn around, you'll be leaving a second mark, meaning that the current path has been completely explored and was unsuccessful. To ensure that each path is explored, you always preferentially enter a passage with no marks. As with the recursive method, we also treat all loops as dead ends: if when moving forward you encounter a junction that you have already visited (as indicated by a marked path) then you turn around. When moving backward, of course, you expect to encounter marks, but there should only ever be one passageway with a single mark, which is the last one you will leave by. As an added bonus, when you reach the goal, you also have a marked path back to the entrance: take the passageways marked once. You could think of this algorithm as literally "threading": the marked paths are like a thread, which forms loops that indicate dead ends. When you reach the goal, pulling the end would draw all the loops of thread in, leaving a single path back to the start.

Pathfinding and the A* Algorithm

The flip-side of the maze-threading problem is the pathfinding problem, where you know the maze in advance, but want to find a path, usually the optimal (shortest) path from A to B. There isn't a very sharp cutoff between the two problems, and indeed in the computer they are somewhat equivalent, since the computer almost always does know the complete maze (the only exception being "mouse" problems, where a computer-controlled robot has to explore a physical maze).

One example finds a path in the same average time as the recursive backtracker, but by the opposite method: instead of searching an individual path to the full before abandoning it (a "depth-first search" in the terminology of Chapter 26), it searches all paths simultaneously (a "breadth-first search"). This strategy is somewhat equivalent to Prim's Algorithm, spreading along a frontier to fill the maze. At each step, we travel one step further in all possible directions, creating a frontier consisting of all squares at the same distance from the start point. Each cell remembers the neighbor which spread to it, which means that when we find the solution, we can follow the path back to the start, which is by definition the (or perhaps "a") shortest possible path.

However, the most interesting algorithm is one that combines the best of both depth-first and breadth-first searches, which has the name A* ("A-star"). It's easiest to explain this algorithm by presenting the code first, and for once, we're going to write it pretty much optimally. In the following code, "maze" could be anything, really, as long as we have some way of describing a "distance" between two nodes. In the version on the CD-ROM, the squared linear distance between two points is used.

ON THE CD

```
function aStar (maze, start, goal)
    set pathList to an empty array
    set d to distance from start to goal in maze
    append [d, 0, start] to pathList
    sort pathList on element 1 of paths // by estimated distance to goal
    repeat until break
        set path to pathList[1]
        // extend each path to all possible neighbors
```

```
            delete pathList[1]
            set currentSquare to the last square of path
            set previousSquare to the second-to-last square of path if any
            repeat for each neighbor of currentSquare except previousSquare
                set p to a copy of path
                // no loops
                if neighbor is not an element of p then
                    append neighbor to p
                    add 1 to p[2] // length of path
                    set p[1] to p[2]+distance(neighbor, goal) // distance
                    underestimate
                    append p to pathList // retaining the sort on element 1
                end if
            end repeat
            if pathList is empty then return "No path to goal"
            if pathList[1] ends with goal then return pathList[1]
        end repeat
    end function
```

The main trick here is that the algorithm sorts the found paths according to the *underestimate* of the distance from the goal, that is, the length of the path added to the linear distance from the last square to the goal, and gives precedence to searches approaching the goal. This is a somewhat similar idea to the "collision halo" approach to collision detection we considered in Chapter 10. It should be fairly clear that although A* is the optimal maze-search algorithm known to date, it is still not going to give the solution very fast in a well-designed maze where paths are specifically designed to lead away from the goal. However, on a random maze it is by far the fastest, and it is particularly good at finding optimal *local* paths, that is, paths to a nearby target, as with an AI "enemy" in a maze who is trying to follow a moving target.

So let's look at it in a little more detail now. We start with the goal square, and at each stage we take the current best path and extend it to all possible neighbors. If we've made a loop, we ignore that path, otherwise we calculate the underestimate for the new path and add it back to the list of paths, sorting on the underestimate.

What does this sorting on the underestimate entail? Look at Figure 24.14. In this maze, the path marked by a dotted line is found first by A*, since it begins in a good line for the goal. However, along the way it encounters a few twists and turns, and so its length increases while the distance from the goal also increases. At the moment pictured, its underestimate has now for the last time increased above that of the initially less promising-looking path marked with a jagged line, with the result that the algorithm's attention now switches entirely to the new path, which eventually achieves the goal faster, even though there is a perfectly reasonable route to the goal along the original path.

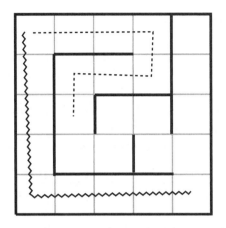

FIGURE 24.14   The A* algorithm in action.

It's actually perfectly possible for a path to even get to the goal with this algorithm, but be placed somewhere else in the list because another path of maximal underestimate has only just come into the sights of the algorithm—although you do have to work quite hard to contrive such a maze.

EXERCISES

Exercise 24.1

Create a program that will navigate through a maze by either wall-following or recursive backtracking
    The algorithms are in the chapter—go to it!

SUMMARY

We've indulged ourselves in this chapter by going into a little more detail than usual for a relatively obscure subject. This is because, while knowing how to generate and navigate mazes is not the most vital thing for you to know, it provides a very good introduction to the more general concepts of searches, AI and game theory, which we will be finishing up with in the final two chapters. In particular, we'll be making fairly common use of the language of graph theory which we introduced in this chapter.

YOU SHOULD NOW KNOW

■ how to classify a maze according to its physical or topological properties

■ the meaning of certain fundamental graph theory terms such as *node, edge, tree, network,* and *connected*

■ how to store the details of a grid-based maze on the computer and use it to walk through and control a camera

■ how to generate a maze using a variety of different methods, including *Prim, Kruskal,* and *Eller's* algorithms.

■ how to navigate through a maze either blind or with the whole maze in front of you, especially using the *A* Algorithm.*

25 Game Theory and AI

OVERVIEW

For the final two chapters, we're going to have a very rapid look at an important and growing field of interest: *Artificial Intelligence* or *AI*. This term is commonly misused, and can be seen in all kinds of different contexts. The field is almost as old as computing itself: the computer pioneer Alan Turing wrote a seminal paper on the concept at a time when state-of-the-art computers were using waves in tubes of mercury to store memory (8 bits per mercury tube). Today AI is an important part of cognitive science, with researchers trying to create models of different parts of thinking to try to gain an insight into how the mind works.

But AI has always been a fundamental part of game design too. We've already seen how pathfinding algorithms are used to create "intelligent" opponents, and most games today feature an AI engine to create realistic flexible behavior for their various "bots." The aims of such AI researchers are different from the aims of the cognitive scientists: they are not generally trying to create programs that "really" think (sometimes called *strong AI*), but ones that behave in a way that seems sufficiently realistic to the player (*weak AI*). This goes equally for AI opponents in a 3D shooter and for opponents in a board game. Nevertheless, the ultimate aim is the same: to try to create a set of simple rules that nevertheless produce flexible behavior, perhaps even learning.

In this chapter we'll look at the principal theories of AI. We'll focus on board games rather than bots, but the principles apply to both, and we'll discuss the differences too.

Code samples from this chapter are implemented in *math.cst* in the script *Chapter 25 (Game theory)*. The *ticTacToe* and *headsOrTails* demos use them in context.

INTRODUCTION TO GAME THEORY

The other great pioneer of computing, as well as Turing, was John Von Neumann, whose design of computer architecture still underlies to this day every computer we use. As well as computing (and many other contributions to the field of mathematical logic), Von Neumann also laid the foundations for another field, which turned out to be much more important than its name suggests, *game theory*. This is the study of how we can create a strategy for solving puzzles where two or more people are competing in a limited domain. As such, it forms the basis not just of game AI, but of military strategy, and is also a vital part of evolutionary theory.

Zero-Sum Games

The basic kind of game that Von Neumann considered was the *zero-sum game*. In this game, two or more players compete by making a choice of some kind, at the end of which the "losing" player(s) gives a certain sum of money to the "winning" player(s), and the aim is to try to maximize the winnings (or minimize the losses). The term "zero-sum" means that the total amount of money in the game is constant: whatever one player gains, the others must lose. For simplicity, we'll only look at two-person games from now on, although the same analysis applies to more complicated games too.

Figure 25.1 shows a simple example of a two-person zero-sum game, which is the game "rock, paper, scissors." Andy and Beth both reveal their hands at the same time, and have a choice of three options, R, P, or S. If they match, then no money passes hands, otherwise the winner is determined by the system R > S > P > R (where > is used to stand for "beats"). We represent this by a matrix: Andy's choices are listed on the left and Beth's on the top, with the elements of the matrix representing the amount of money Andy pays to Beth (negative if the payment is the other way) for a particular pair of choices.

Another example is shown in Figure 25.2, a game called *Undercut* (see Douglas Hofstadter, *Metamagical Themas*). Here, Andy and Beth have to choose a number from 1 to 5, and the player who chooses the higher number wins the difference of the two numbers unless the numbers differ by one, in which case the other player wins the sum.

		Andy		
		R	P	S
Beth	R	0	−1	1
	P	1	0	−1
	S	−1	1	0

FIGURE 25.1 A two-person zero-sum game.

		Andy				
		1	2	3	4	5
Beth	1	0	3	−2	−3	−4
	2	−3	0	5	−2	−3
	3	2	−5	0	7	−2
	4	3	2	−7	0	9
	5	4	3	2	−9	0

FIGURE 25.2 *Undercut.*

Not all games are zero-sum. Figure 25.3 shows the so-called *Prisoner's Dilemma* matrix, in which players don't compete with each other but try to maximize the amount of money received from a third party (or in the usual formulation, try to minimize the amount of time they have to spend in jail). Here, the payout is listed as a payout vector, with both Andy's and Beth's payouts.

		Andy	
		C	D
Beth	C	(3,3)	(5,0)
	D	(0,5)	(1,1)

FIGURE 25.3 The *Prisoner's Dilemma.*

Solving a Game

Any game that is zero-sum can theoretically be "solved," in the sense that each player has an ideal strategy for play that will maximize their winnings. For example, let's look at the simple game shown in Figure 25.4, which we'll call Rube, since you would have to be a fool to play.

		Andy			
		J	**Q**	**K**	***Min***
Beth	**J**	−100	2	−100	*−100*
	Q	−50	−100	2	*−100*
	K	1	2	5	*1*
	Max	*1*	*2*	*8*	

FIGURE 25.4   Rube.

In the game of Rube, Andy and Beth choose one of the cards J, Q, or K, and the payout matrix is as shown (we can imagine Beth to be a carnival shyster offering a "maximum payout" of $100). It should be immediately obvious that Beth's best strategy is to always choose the King, and Andy's is to choose the Jack, meaning that Andy will be paying Beth $1 each time. But why is this the best?

If you look at the matrix, we have added some figures on the edges. These represent, for Andy, the maximum amount he would pay to Beth given a particular choice of card, and for Beth, the minimum amount Andy would pay to her (or equivalently the maximum she would pay to him). So in both cases they represent the "worst-case scenario" for a particular card.

Each player's preferred option, then, is to choose the card which *minimizes* the *maximum* payout to the other player—otherwise known as the *minimax* strategy. So Andy will choose J and Beth will choose K. Notice that in the payoff matrix, the value $1 is minimax for both Andy and Beth (remembering, of course, that Beth is minimaxing the negative value of the table entries), which means that this is a *stable* strategy for each player: if Andy chooses J, then Beth's best choice of card is K—any other card will produce a worse outcome for her. Conversely, if Beth chooses K then Andy can't do better than to choose J. So as long as either player is using this strategy, the other player must also do so—the strategy pair is called the *Nash Equilibrium*, and there is a theorem which states that every finite, two-person zero-sum game must have either one or infinitely many pairs of strategies with this property. In fact, other games have it too: the Prisoner's Dilemma has a Nash Equilibrium where each player chooses D.

In this case, the Nash Equilibrium strategy is to choose a single move every time. The payoff $1 is called the *value* of the game, and the game is strictly determined because the minimax for each player is the same—that is to say, the value $1 in the payoff matrix is both the minimum value in its column and the maximum value in its row—it is called a *saddle point* of the matrix. Rock-paper-scissors is not determined in the same way. If you look at the payoff matrix you will see that there is no saddle point (in fact, there is not even a single minimax for either player), which means that there is no single strategy that will work: for any choice Andy makes, there is a choice that Beth can make which will beat it. Instead, both players must use a *mixed* strategy: specifically, they need to choose each option precisely one third of the time, and at random. It is the fact that human beings are not very good at picking numbers at random that makes the game interesting, because we can try to notice patterns in the other player's actions and anticipate them, but more on that later.

When dealing with games with no saddle point, we need a way to determine the appropriate mixed strategy. This requires a little bit of probability theory which we haven't looked at in this book: a *probability* is a number between 0 and 1 representing the likelihood of one event occurring out of a set of possible events. So, for example, the probability of throwing heads with a fair coin is 0.5, and of rolling a 6 on a die is 0.167. In general, the probability of a discrete event occurring is given by

$$P\left(event\right) = \frac{\text{Number of ways event can occur}}{\text{Total number of possible events}}$$

So the chance of throwing a number less than 3 on a single die is $\frac{2}{6}$ ($= \frac{1}{3}$), since there are two ways to throw a number less than 3, and six possible events altogether.

Suppose Mary offers that if you pay her $3 per throw, she'll pay you $1 for each pip that shows on a die. We can calculate the *expected* amount of money you will receive when throwing the die. This is the average amount you will win per game if you were to play it for a long time, and it's essentially a weighted average:

$$\text{Expected payout} = \sum_{events} P\left(event\right) \times \text{event payout}$$

In this case, the expected payout is the sum $\frac{1}{6} \times 1 + \frac{1}{6} \times 2 + \frac{1}{6} \times 3 + \frac{1}{6} \times 4 + \frac{1}{6} \times 5 + \frac{1}{6} \times 6 = \frac{21}{6} = \$3.5$

Taking off your initial payment of $3, your expected profit is $0.50, so the game is worth playing.

Just for the sake of comparison, the British National Lottery, which at the time of this writing is using the slogan "you have a much better chance of winning if you actually play," actually has an expected loss of around 50p per £1 ticket. So like most gambles, your expected profit is much higher by not playing. The best odds in pure luck gambling are to be found in Blackjack, with the average payout for a perfectly played game coming out nearly even.

So an optimal strategy for a game is a set of probabilities of choosing each of the options such that the expected payout is the same whatever choice the other player makes. For a matrix with a saddle point, the strategy is simple: choose one option with probability 1. For others, we have to determine the probabilities algebraically. Consider the game Undercut, for example. Since the matrix is symmetrical, we know that the expected payout must be zero. This gives us five equations for Andy's expected winnings based on a particular strategy where he picks the number i with a probability p_i:

$$\begin{pmatrix} 0 & -3 & 2 & 3 & 4 \\ 3 & 0 & -5 & 2 & 3 \\ -2 & 5 & 0 & -7 & 2 \\ -3 & -2 & 7 & 0 & -9 \\ -4 & -3 & -2 & 9 & 0 \end{pmatrix} \begin{pmatrix} p_1 \\ p_2 \\ p_3 \\ p_4 \\ p_5 \end{pmatrix} = \begin{pmatrix} 0 \\ 0 \\ 0 \\ 0 \\ 0 \end{pmatrix}$$

Because the determinant of the matrix is zero, there are infinitely many solutions to this set of equations, but we also have an additional piece of information: we know that the sum of the probabilities is 1. This gives us a strategy for Andy that always has an expected payout of 0, no matter what Beth does (solving this is left as an exercise—recall the method for solving a set of linear simultaneous equations from Chapter 3). The same strategy also works for Beth. If we didn't have a symmetrical matrix and therefore didn't know the value of the expected payout, we'd need to solve separately for Beth and include one more unknown, the value of the payout.

This kind of approach can be used to analyze any zero-sum game where all the information is known to both players. For non-zero-sum games or games with incomplete information such as poker, things get more complicated, although there is plenty of game-theoretical work on such problems if you are interested.

The kind of games we are interested in are complex in a different way. Instead of being simultaneous, as in the examples we've seen, they're sequential: players take turns choosing an option until one wins. A full analysis of games like this involves some complicated work with strings of matrices called *Markov Chains*, but from a computational point of view we can use a different approach.

A Game Theory Approach to Tic-Tac-Toe

We're going to use as an example the game tic-tac-toe, which happens to be a very nice "toy game" to practice all our AI theories. In the very unlikely event that you are not familiar with this game, it is illustrated in Figure 25.5. Andy plays crosses, Beth plays noughts, and they alternate placing a symbol in a square of the grid until either the grid is full or one player has three symbols in a row, including main diagonals of the square.

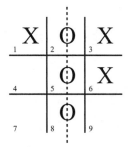

FIGURE 25.5   Tic-tac-toe.

In the figure, the squares have been labeled for ease of reference. So what is the game theory approach to playing this game? We can adapt the minimax concept (which mutates to the *min-max algorithm*) to deal with a longer game by creating a *search tree*, rather like the octrees and quadtrees we created in previous chapters, or the maze networks of the previous chapter. Each possible game position is represented by a node on the tree and they are connected by the moves that lead from one to another: the top of the search tree is illustrated in Figure 25.6. Each layer, or level, of the tree represents a move by a particular player.

The term "search tree" is actually something of a misnomer because the graph is not a tree: two or more different positions at one level can lead to the same position at the next.

NOTE

Notice that we have already begun to make some optimizations in this representation: because the game is symmetrical, many of the game positions are equivalent. So there are only three distinct first moves for Andy: corner, edge or center.

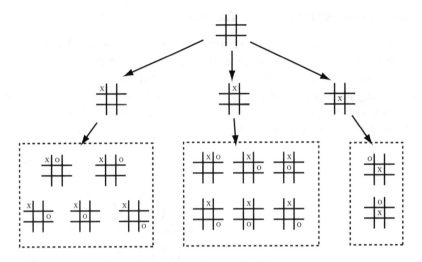

FIGURE 25.6   The start of the search tree for Tic-tac-toe.

To apply the min-max algorithm, we do the following: We first go through the tree and find all ending positions, that is, all positions with three symbols in a row or a full board. Positions with a win for player 1 are given a score of 1, wins for player 2 are given a score of −1, and drawn positions get a score of 0. Now we follow all the links up the tree from these ending positions (we can erase any downward links from the positions, as these will never be passed). This will tell us the possible positions which could lead to our ending. If these occur on Beth's layer, then we label each node with the minimum value of the nodes beneath: this tells us if Beth can win from this position. If they occur on Andy's layer, then we label it with the maximum value of the nodes. Figure 25.7 shows a portion of the search tree with these values calculated.

Now we simply repeat this process, working up the tree until we reach the root node. This will tell us, for each player, the best possible move(s) for any given position. In the case of tic-tac-toe, both Andy and Beth can force a draw from any of the start positions, so all the early nodes have a value of 0.

Here is a group of functions (one of the longer examples in this book!) that will find a perfect strategy for playing the game. The first two functions create the search tree, the other two calculate the winning strategy. Because this is only theoretical and we're not worrying about speed or memory usage, we'll save work by not eliminating symmetrical game positions.

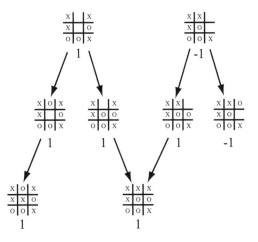

FIGURE 25.7   Labeling the search tree nodes.

```
function makeTTTlist()
    // creates a list of all possible game boards
    set blist to an empty array
    repeat for i=0 to 5
        set blank to an array of 9 0's
        if i=0 then add blank to boardlist
        otherwise
            set bl to boardlist(blank, 1, i, 1) // list of all boards with
i 1's
            repeat for j=i-1 to i
                if j=0 then next repeat
                repeat for each b in bl
                    set bl2 to boardlist(b, 2, j, 1) // i 1's and j 2's
                    add all of bl2 to bl
                end repeat
            end repeat
        end if
    end repeat
    return blist
end function



function makeTTTtree(blist)
    // creates a tree of all possible moves in blist:
    // for each node, creates a list of all possible parents and
children
```

```
      set tree to an empty array
      set e to array(empty array, empty array)
      add as many copies of e to tree as the elements of blist
      repeat for i=1 to the number of elements of blist
         set b to blist[i]
         // find all parents of b
         if b has no '1's then next repeat
         if b has an odd number of '0's then set s to 1
         otherwise set s to 2
         repeat for j=1 to 9
            if b[j]=s then
               set p to a copy of b, replacing the s with 0
               set k to the position of p in blist
               append i to tree[k][2] // children of i
               append k to tree[i][1] // parents of k
            end if
         end repeat
      end repeat
      return tree
   end function

   function boardlist (board, symbol, n, start)
      // fills a board with n copies of the symbol
      // in all possible ways (recursive)
      if n=0 then return array(board)
      set bl to an empty array
      set c to the number of 0's between board[start] and board[9]
      repeat for i=1 to c-n+1
         set b to a copy of board
         set k to the position of the next 0
         set b[k] to symbol
         set bls to boardlist(b, symbol, n-1, i+1)
         append all elements of bls to bl
      end repeat
      return bl
   end function

   on makeMinimaxStrategy (tree, bl)
      // 'prunes' tree by removing all unnecessary children,
      // and returns an initial strategy and minimax tree
      set strategy and minimaxtree to arrays of the same length as bl
      set each element of strategy and minimaxtree to "unknown"
      repeat for i=1 to the number of elements of bl
         set b to bl[i]
```

```
        if b is a win for 1 then
            set strategy[i] to "WinX"
            set minimaxtree[i] to 1
            deletechildren(tree,i)
        if b is a win for 2 then
            set strategy[i] to "WinO"
            set minimaxtree[i] to -1
            deletechildren(tree,i)
        if b is full then
            set strategy[i] to "draw"
            set minimaxtree[i] to 0
        end if
    end repeat
    return [strategy, minimaxtree, tree]
end function


on minimaxIteration(strategy, minimaxtree, tree, bl)
    repeat with i=the number of elements of bl down to 1
        // ignore nodes with no parent
        if tree[i][1] is empty and i>1 then next repeat
        // ignore nodes that have already been calculated
        if minimaxtree[i] is not "unknown" then next repeat
        set c to the number of O's in bl[i]
        set ply to mod (c,2)
        if ply=0 then set ply to -1

        if there is any j in tree[i][2] such that minimaxtree[j]=ply then
            set minimax to ply
            set mv to j
        otherwise
            // find best non-winning move
            set minimax to "unknown"
            repeat for j in tree[i][2]
                set m to minimaxtree[j]
                if minimax="unknown" then set minimax to m
                if ply=1 then set minimax to max(m, minimax)
                otherwise set minimax to min(m, minimax)
                if minimax=m then set mv to j
            end repeat
        end if
        set strategy[i] to mv
        set minimaxtree[i] to minimax
    end repeat
    return strategy
end function
```

A few minor problems like figuring out whether a position is a winner, deleting the children of a node, and using the strategy created to play a game, are left for you to complete: the full code is on the CD-ROM in the movie *ticTacToe.dir*.

It's a good system (creating a complete winning strategy for tic-tac-toe in only about half an hour on an ordinary PC), so why can't we use it all the time? Well, it's pretty inefficient. For even a game as simple as tic-tac-toe there are over six thousand possible positions, more than a thousand even if we eliminate reflections and rotations, and the number of games that can be played with these boards is several times higher. For a game like chess there are many, many more positions, with thirty or more possible moves from each position, so the number of possible games is vast—significantly more than there are particles in the universe, for example. To calculate the search tree for chess would take billions of years, and to use it in a game afterward would still take years, even if you could find the storage space!

There are a number of ways to optimize the search tree, of which the most important is the *Alpha-Beta search*. Here, when searching through moves at a particular depth, you keep track of two values: Alpha, the best score you know you can achieve, and Beta, the worst score that your opponent can force on you.

For example, in tic-tac-toe, suppose Andy has played squares 3 and 8, and Beth has played square 6. It's now Beth's turn, and she has six squares to choose from. Suppose she moves into 5, the center: it's theoretically possible that Andy will not notice the threat and will play somewhere other than 4, but it's not likely to happen. Instead he's going to play the correct move and block her. Because we assume that each player will always play the best move they can, it's no good thinking in terms of the best-case scenario, we must always think about the worst case. Alpha-Beta searching means that we focus on the best moves the players can be sure of playing.

If in the course of a search you encounter a node whose value is less than the current alpha-value, you know you can ignore it, since you've already discovered a better one. Similarly, if you find a node whose value is higher than beta, you can ignore this too, since you know you'll never get to play it. (It's notable that this assumption of a perfect opponent is rather unrealistic when dealing with a human game, and it's one of the major problems with "rational" models of game theory, and thus of models which use it, such as economics.)

But our main goal in creating an intelligent player is to give them the tools to play without such brute-force methods: to analyze a board and choose a move appropriately. In particular, we're looking for a way to reduce or simplify the *search space*, by performing some kind of pre-analysis to "sniff out" promising paths through the tree. We'll look at such tools now. But always bear in mind the search tree: underlying most board game architectures you'll find this structure somewhere.

TACTICAL AI

When we play a game ourselves, we don't generally think in terms that have much in common with game theory (although most chess players do perform some degree of looking ahead). Instead, we think in broader terms: gaining territory, gambits, threats, and maneuvers. This is what might be dubbed *tactical* thinking, as opposed to the strategic thinking we'll look at later. Strategy is the planning of a long-range goal, but tactics are the execution—or abandonment—of that goal in the context of the other player's moves: the moment-to-moment play.

How Chess Programs Work

In 1997 one more item had to be struck off the list of "things computers can't do" when the program Deep Blue beat World Champion Gary Kasparov at chess. This was a climactic moment that fulfilled half a century of work in designing AI programs that could play chess.

Chess is one of the most complicated and intractable games played on this planet, especially given that, just like tic-tac-toe, it has complete information available to both players at all times, and no randomness at all. Only Go has proved harder to analyze. The number of valid games of chess is more than astronomical, it's virtually inconceivable, so it didn't take long for programmers to realize that creating a search tree for chess was impossible. Instead, they focused on trying to understand how a human being plays the game and how to formalize this into rules that a chess program could follow.

The key insight was in realizing that chess is primarily about *territory*. When Grand Masters are given a chessboard position to memorize, they can do so very quickly, and can reconstruct the board much more accurately than novices. What's more, this only works for genuine game positions. When the pieces are scattered randomly on the board, the Grand Masters and amateurs perform much the same. Also interesting to note is that when the Grand Masters make an error, it is often a highly global one, with lots of pieces in positions that are far from where they should be, but leaving the board tactically much the same: the same squares under threat, the same pieces in danger.

This led naturally to the idea that, instead of analyzing a position in terms of how likely it is to lead to a win, we could analyze it in terms of its current tactical advantage to one player or another—what is known as an *estimation function*. This allows us to assign a number to any particular position. By combining this with our search tree, we can limit the depth of our search: we simply replace the win/lose/draw value with the result of our estimation function for a particular node, then continue with the alpha-beta algorithm. (The estimation function is basically an equivalent of the underestimate function in the A* Algorithm.)

This can be combined with more sophisticated methods: for example, a quick estimation can be made of all the first layer moves, then most of these can be discarded to create a smaller set to be evaluated to a second layer (or *ply*), which can be culled again, so that only the most promising paths are explored by more than one or two steps. This is also in keeping with real players: experts tend not to analyze many possible moves, and bad moves are not just ignored, they aren't even perceived (just as even an amateur player won't consider the impossible option of a pawn moving backward or a castle moving diagonally).

The down-side of using an estimation approach to limit the search depth, and it is unavoidable, is that some winning paths might never be discovered because they look bad at the start. For example, programs that rely on estimation functions find it difficult to discover a winning plan involving a major sacrifice: the immediate loss is much more perceptible than the long-term gain. But again, human players have the same failing.

Training a Program

Obviously we've missed out the most difficult part of the process, which is calculating the estimation function. This is something that involves a lot of guesswork, plenty of trial-and-error, and some mathematical analysis, but in essence it boils down to this: You need to find a set of measurable parameters that describe the current position succinctly and which might affect your chance of success. For a chess program, for example, the total number of pieces (in pawn value) for each player is an obvious factor, as is the number of pieces under threat. More subtle concepts include "control of the center," "exposure of king," "pieces in play," "strength of pawn line" and so on.

You'll notice that this kind of description has another advantage, which is that it can be used just as effectively when dealing with games with a random element, such as backgammon. Even when you can't determine the moves you'll be able to make next time, you can still classify the strength of your current position: how full is your home? How spread out are your pieces? How many are exposed to capture? And so on.

Once you have determined your parameters, you then need to create a *weighted sum* of these numbers, which is to say a value $a_1 p_1 + a_2 p_2 + ... + a_n p_n$, where the *weights* $a_1, a_2, ...$ have been predetermined.

Coming up with the parameterization is something you have to do as the designer of the program. But there is no way you could calculate the correct value of the weights theoretically, you need to find some way to calculate them by trial and error. The most effective method is to use an algorithm based on natural selection, which we'll look at in the next chapter. But another is to use a *training* system. In this method, the program modifies the weights it uses by analyzing the success or failure of particular moves.

In a simple example of such a method (related to the *bucket-brigade algorithm*), the program, under a certain system of weights, enumerates the value of the current position. Then, looking ahead by a certain number of moves, it chooses the move which maximizes its expected value. Now the opponent (usually another copy of the program) makes its move, and the program starts again. If its estimation function for the current position gives a current value equal to or higher than the program expected to be the case, the move was deemed successful, and the weight of the parameter which was most involved in the decision is increased slightly. If it is lower than expected, the move is deemed a failure, and the weight of the parameter responsible is decreased. Finding which parameter is "responsible" is mildly tricky.

This kind of "learning" algorithm is related to the concept of "operant conditioning" as seen in behavioral psychology: a behavior is reinforced according to its past success. It's also similar to the system of training a neural network, which we'll look at later.

A Tactical AI Approach to Tic-Tac-Toe

So how might this approach work with tic-tac-toe? Although the domain is very simple, it's easy to suggest a few plausible candidates for measurable parameters of potential success:

1. The number of empty rows (or columns or diagonals)
2. The number of rows containing only your symbol
3. The number of rows containing only your opponent's symbol
4. The number of potential "forks" (intersecting rows containing only your symbol)
5. The number of potential opponent forks
6. The number of "threats" (rows with two of your symbol and an empty square)
7. The number of opponent threats

You can see immediately that some of these conflict. For example, if Andy plays the top center and Beth plays the bottom center, she blocks one of his potential rows, thus improving her score by criterion 3. On the other hand, by playing a bottom corner she improves her score by criterion 2. Which of these is the better option? This is by no means an obvious question, and we could use a training process to find out which criterion should be assigned a higher weight (it's more than possible that one or more criteria might be assigned a weight of zero, meaning that it has no effect on the eventual outcome). We might also find that there are different sets of weights which each produce a different, but equally effective, style of tactical play.

TOP-DOWN AI

Instead of applying a tactical approach, another way to approach the AI problem is to use *strategy*. In other words, we can use a system which works by setting itself some kind of *goal* and trying to achieve it. This is what is sometimes called a *top-down* approach: decisions at a high level of reasoning about the situation are used to make decisions at a lower level of reasoning. It's also sometimes called GOFAI, which stands for "Good Old-Fashioned AI," because for many years it was the primary route for mental modeling: researchers worked by creating a "symbolic architecture" to represent the world and a reasoning module which would try to deduce facts and make decisions. The slightly patronizing title reflects the fact that these days the approach is mostly out of favor by cognitive researchers and the bottom-up method is more popular; but this doesn't in any way invalidate the top-down approach for dealing with limited domains and "expert problems" like games.

Goals and Subgoals

The goal-based approach to AI is very similar to the process of programming. You start with a difficult task ("I want to make a first-person shooter"), then you break it up into smaller subtasks ("I need a character, an environment, and some enemies"), then you break these up into still smaller subtasks until eventually the tasks are "primitive," in the sense that they can be programmed directly.

The toughest part of the process is how to determine the subgoals. After all, it's not always obvious what steps you need to take to get to a particular destination. In a game of chess, the goal is "checkmate my opponent's king," but breaking that down into smaller subgoals is a complex task. What the program needs is a *knowledge base*: a representation of the world (or its own limited domain) that it can use to make deductions and judgments. A chess program, for example, might be equipped with advice (*heuristics*) such as "avoid getting your king trapped," "try to castle early" or "if you are ahead then exchange like pieces for like" (these are very simplistic examples, of course). It would have some mechanism for deduction, and in particular for speculation: "if I had a castle on that side, it would protect the queen when she checkmates the king."

Armed with this knowledge, the program formulates its strategy. Given a particular situation, it forms a representation of it, assesses its goal ("checkmate the king with my queen on e8"), notices potential pitfalls to the goal ("the bishop on g7 could move in to block it"), creates a subgoal ("eliminate the bishop"), searches for a solution to the subgoal ("capture it with my knight") and so on. Finally, it homes in on a single move which will advance the most immediate subgoal.

This process should sound much more like a human being playing chess than the method we called "tactical," and of course this is why AI researchers held so much hope for the top-down approach in the early days. The method has had many successes, especially in expert domains, but is very hard to scale up into more lifelike areas such as natural language because of the sheer scale of the knowledge base required.

When to Change the Goal

Strategy has to go hand-in-hand with tactics for the obvious reason that every plan has some potential flaw. No one can anticipate everything, and constrains on computing time mean that every strategy must necessarily contain some blanks. In fact, that's the essence of strategic thinking: we don't worry about calculating every last move, we simply try to advance our position toward some final, quite nebulous goal. We don't care if the queen is protected by the knight or the bishop, we only know that if the master plan is to succeed, the queen has to be protected *somehow*. But this leaves the way open for any plan to be blocked by an unexpected move.

One useful way to combine the two is to think of a strategy as a particular set of weights in the estimation function of a tactical program. This wouldn't work so well in a game like chess, but we can see how it would work in a simpler game like backgammon. In backgammon, there are two primary strategies. The first, the most usual game, is to try to protect your playing pieces from being captured, while building up a strong base to trap opposing pieces. But when bad luck strikes, it is sometimes appropriate to switch to a different strategy called a back-game. Here, you try to get as many of your pieces captured as possible. While this worsens your position in some senses, it also gives you a strong chance of capturing your opponent and perhaps preventing them from reaching the goal, so reversing the fortunes of the game dramatically. The back-game is a risky strategy and not one to attempt lightly, but it can lead to very exciting play.

We could model this in terms of an estimation function with variable weights. At each stage, the function yields a best possible score under the current strategy. But if this score drops below a particular threshold, the program starts to try out alternative sets of weights. If any of them yield a higher result for some move, or for several moves, then the program might "decide" to switch to this alternative strategy.

When playing against a strategic program, it becomes advantageous to try to induce its strategy from the moves it plays—just as one does when playing a human opponent. So another important part of strategic play is *pattern analysis:* trying to determine an underlying principle to the past few moves of a player.

There are a number of examples on the web of programs that will play you at rock-paper-scissors and will most likely beat you, because as we saw before, humans are poor random-number generators. These programs search for patterns in your previous moves and extrapolate to guess what your next move will be. The simplest such system just keeps track of each triple move you have made: so in the sequence RPRSSRP, the program finds RPR, PRS, RSS, SSR, SRP. The program then predicts that if you have just played RP, you will probably play R. As you play more and more rounds, the program determines that, for example, having just played RP you are twice as likely to play P as S, so it guesses that this pattern will continue. In general, the longer you play these games the less well you will do. A more subtle system might also take note of different play according to whether you won or lost the previous round, for example. In Exercise 25.1 you are asked to create such a program for yourself.

For a more complex game, pattern analysis will have to rely on the program's own strategy module—in particular, the ability for it to ask "what would I do in that situation?" The advantage of this is that it gives a much more powerful way to estimate the likelihood of different moves from your opponent—even the ability to class them as "aggressive" or "defensive" could enable invaluable culling of the search tree.

One final example of goal-changing under pressure is the system of "scripts," where a person follows a pre-determined strategy unless an unexpected event occurs. An example of this is a bot in a stealth game, which moves in a standard pattern (or even a random pattern with certain parameters) until it hears a noise or discovers a dead body. Then its script changes and it switches to a different "alarm" or "search" strategy, with goals of "warn the others" or "find the intruder" respectively.

A Top-Down AI Approach to Tic-Tac-Toe

There isn't much scope for goals and subgoals in tic-tac-toe, but the principal subgoal is the "fork." This is effectively the only way to win a game. Below that, there is a subgoal of gaining control of empty pairs of rows. Notice immediately how these goals coincide with the parameters we used above to create our estimation function. This is not surprising: the situations which are useful tactically tend also to be useful strategically. However, this is also to some extent an artifact of the simplicity of the game. In a more complex domain, there are levels of description which are beyond the scope of the estimation function—consider, for example, "can the queen reach square b5?" This is a question whose usefulness depends on your current goal—for most strategies, it will be a completely irrelevant question, so it would be a useless addition to the estimation parameters.

Even tic-tac-toe is not immune to these issues. Your primary goal may be "create a fork," but a subgoal would be "create a fork between the left and top lines," which leads to the question "is the top row empty?" Again, this is too specific to be useful in an estimation function: it's only relevant once you have created a strategy.

Let's examine this in more detail. Figure 25.8 shows a complete game of tic-tac-toe with the moves numbered (the square numbers are omitted for clarity).

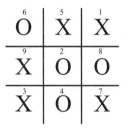

FIGURE 25.8   A strategic game of tic-tac-toe.

Andy begins with a blank slate. His goal generator immediately starts looking for a possible fork, and he decides to play the corner square 3 (this would be a probabilistic decision). From his knowledge base, he knows that a good route to a fork using a corner square is to get the corner 7, forcing Beth to move in the center and leaving him open to move in one of the other corners, making a fork on two edge rows. This is his current strategy. Notice the difference between this and the tactical approach: when thinking strategically you are mostly thinking in terms of best-case scenarios: what you would like to happen if your opponent doesn't guess what you're up to. In the game theory approach you think in terms of the worst-case and assume your opponent will do the worst thing possible from your point of view. Of course, you do need to think about your opponent's reaction when deciding which strategy is best, though: there's no point choosing a strategy that is bound to fail.

Beth, too, knows the three-cornered fork trick, so she knows that she can't let Andy force her into that situation. The easiest way to foil it is to block the diagonal, so she considers placing her next move in the center. She realizes that this move would also be a useful step toward creating her own fork, with three pieces in some corner.

Andy's original strategy is now partially damaged: he can't force the fork on Beth any more, so he now has to find some other way to take advantage of his original move. However, all is not lost because he still currently has partial control over the top and right rows, and there are only two other rows not controlled by Beth. This leaves him with two possible forks, and one move, in the corner 7, which leaves both of them possible (this is the move he was aiming toward before, of course, but he's taking it for a different reason now).

Beth's strategy is incidentally also damaged here. One of the rows she wanted to use, on the bottom, is now unavailable. So is an alternative on the left. Now her only possible rows are the two in the center and the remaining diagonal—and what is more, there is no way to create a fork without forcing Andy to stop her. Her only option is to force him to a draw, so this becomes her new primary strategy. A quick prediction shows that if she plays a corner, he will fork her, so she has to play one of the edge pieces. From here on, play is predetermined: each player is forced to play the only move which blocks the other.

Of course, in this domain such an analysis is overkill, but it should be clear that it is more interesting and truer to how it feels to be a human playing the game. Whether it is true to what is actually happening in your brain is another story.

BOTTOM-UP AI

In the opposite camp from the top-down goal-led AI programmers are the *connectionists*, who advocate a *bottom-up* approach. The connectionist approach is to try to create intelligent behavior by the interaction of large numbers of simple, stupid elements, in much the same way that your brain works through the interaction of its nerve cells, or an ant hill creates purpose-like behavior through the interaction of many mindless ants. In this view, purposes, goals and decisions arise as *epiphenomena* or higher-level interpretations of mechanical events.

While the bottom-up approach is rarely used in gaming, it is very interesting in itself and worth examining.

Neural Networks

Perhaps the "purest" example of connectionism is the *neural network* (or just neural net). A neural net is like a simulated massively parallel processing computer made up of lots of extremely simple smaller computers modeled on the nerve cells in the brain, called *neurons*. These artificial or simulated neurons are joined together in a simple network with some input and output, and trained to produce appropriate results by a simple learning process.

To understand how neural nets work it is worth looking briefly at the real neurons in your brain (see Figure 25.9). A neuron is basically a simple calculation device. Each one has a main cell body or *soma*, with about a thousand filaments called *dendrites* leading into it, which form the "input." From one end comes an *axon*, which gives the "output." The axon in turn splits into various filaments called *terminals*, again about a thousand, each of which ends in a small nodule called a *terminal button*. These are connected to the dendrites of other neurons via a connection called a *synapse*.

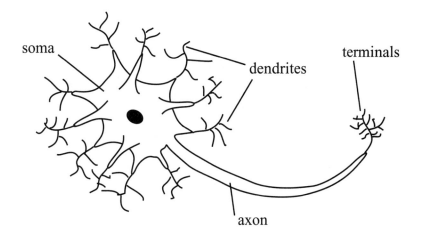

FIGURE 25.9   A neuron in the brain.

The neuron works by electrical signals. At any time it can *fire*, or send a signal of a certain strength down the axon. The signal strength is always the same for a particular neuron, although the frequency at which the signals are sent can vary. Whether a neuron fires at a particular moment depends on the signals coming into the dendrites. At any moment, the neuron will fire if the total signal coming into the dendrites is above a certain threshold. The sum is weighted according to the dendrite: some dendrites are *excitatory*, meaning that a signal received will be added to the total sum, while others are *inhibitory*, meaning that the signal is subtracted. There is also some additional processing which will interpret rapid weak signals as a single stronger one.

Once the logic of the neuron was understood, it was an obvious step to try to use it in computing. To create a neural network we need to model an artificial neuron. This strips out most of the complication of a real neuron and replaces it with a simple function as shown in Figure 25.10.

The artificial neuron has a certain number of inputs each of which has an associated weight. It may be given a stimulation threshold which determines whether it will fire (although in the examples we'll be using here, we won't do this). Finally it has an output, which can be connected to any number of other neurons. At each time step in the program, we determine the output strength of each neuron by calculating the weighted sum of the inputs and seeing if they exceed the threshold (if there is one). The output can either be a discrete 1 or 0, as in the brain, or it can vary according to the size of the input; we can avoid worrying about it by assuming the

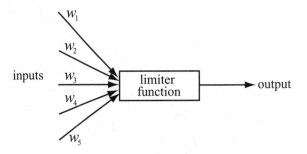

FIGURE 25.10   An artificial neuron.

total sum of inputs is passed through a *limiter function,* which constrains the output into a value between 0 and 1. For a discrete output using a threshold, this would be the *step function* which outputs 1 if the input is greater than a certain value, 0 otherwise. For variable output we'd usually use the *sigmoid function* $\frac{1}{(1+e^{-x})}$. There are many variations on this general theme. Here is a simple function which will do this:

```
function neuralNetStep (netArray)
    set nextArray to a copy of netArray
    repeat for each neuron in netArray
        set sum to 0
        repeat for each input of neuron
            set n to the source neuron of input
            add (weight of input)*(strength of n) to sum
        end repeat
        set strength of neuron in nextArray to limiterFunction(sum,
threshold of neuron)
    end repeat
end function
```

Now all we need to do is to give the network some kind of connection to the problem. To do this we create an *input layer* of neurons, which are connected to the source, such as a visual display or the values of a problem, and an *output layer,* which might give another picture, some text, a number and so on. Between them, we place one or more *hidden layers,* to create a *multi-layer perceptron* (MLP) network like Figure 25.11.

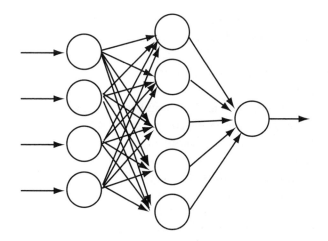

FIGURE 25.11   A multi-layer perceptron.

For example, in the figure the network might be calculating the emotional state of a photographed face, which it classifies as "smiling" or "frowning." The input nodes are given a strength according to the greyscale color of the pixels in the bitmap, and the answer is determined by the output strength of the single output neuron, from 1 (smiling) to 0 (frowning). A more complex network could have more output nodes.

Each neuron in a layer is connected to every neuron in the neighboring layers, so information from one layer is "available" in some sense to every neuron in the next. In this kind of model, there is no *feedback*—no neuron can pass information back from one layer to an earlier one. This makes training the network easier, as we'll see, but is rather unrealistic when compared to the brain. Other kinds of networks include feedback, but are much more difficult to handle.

Training a Neural Network

Given a particular problem, we need to train the network to solve it. The interesting thing about the neural net approach is that the "program," such as it is, knows nothing about the task it is to solve. There are no explicit procedures or rules, all the answers emerge from the interaction of all the neurons. So training the network amounts to creating a computer program "by magic"—or more sensibly, by an evolutionary process.

The key trick in training a MLP network (and most other simple networks) is called *back-propagation*. Rather like the training method we saw earlier for the alpha-beta search, this works by a kind of behavioral conditioning: we give the network an input and "reward" it for an output close to the one desired, or "punish" it for an output that is incorrect. The rewards and punishments consist of alterations to the weights of the network that will improve the result in a particular instance.

Let's look again at the smiling-frowning detector and try to train it on a particular image. Suppose we feed the image in to the input layer as a set of color values, and the output neuron has given us a value of 0.62 when we wanted a value of 1. So the error value was 0.38. We now feed this value backwards through the network.

The idea is to adjust the weights of each layer so that they would produce a better result in the next. We start by altering the weights of the output layer so that *if* it were to receive exactly the input it does, it would produce a result closer to the expected value of 1. Next, we trickle this effect back to the hidden layer(s), altering their weights to produce a value closer to the desired value on their own layer, and so on. The process is very similar to the training process we saw before, and indeed a neural network is one useful way to create the estimation function for an alpha-beta search.

It's also possible to train a neural network differently by using an evolutionary mechanism, "mating" different networks to produce child networks, then selecting the best ones. This is a variant of the genetic algorithms we'll look at in the next chapter.

Actors and Emergence

At a level up from neural networks is another brand of connectionism, which is based on the idea of small interacting subprograms, which are given various different names but often *actors* or *agents*. This approach is popular with those working in object-oriented languages because it fits in well with the OOP approach: an actor, like an object, is a self-contained "entity" in the software space that can be treated as autonomous. It has a very simple "behavior," but because it can interact with the other actors in various ways the overall effect can be to produce complex higher-level behavior.

An example of the use of actors is the *bulletin board* model, where actors interact by posting "messages" on a bulletin board, which other actors may pick up. The messages are marked with an urgency and contain goals that need to be achieved or useful information, which different actors may be more or less able to do or use. Another example has a *blackboard* with messages written on it for all actors to see. Actors may erase or alter existing messages in light of their own knowledge.

The common feature of all these connectionist approaches is *emergence*: higher degrees of organization "bubbling up" from the interaction of simple elements. Emergence is a very exciting phenomenon but of interest mostly to the strong AI camp. Nevertheless, understanding it is worthwhile when looking at any situations where lots of individuals interact, for example traffic, crowds, and economics.

One example is the modeling of *flocking* behavior: the motion of flocks of birds, schools of fish, or herds of animals. An early and extremely influential model was Craig Reynolds' *Boids* program, which featured a number of simple "organisms" following just three rules (see Exercise 25.2):

1. move toward the center of mass of all the other boids (or all the boids in the local neighborhood)
2. try to match velocity with the average velocity of the other (local) boids
3. never move closer than a certain distance to any boid (or other obstacle)

A number of other rules can be added, such as avoiding predators or searching for food, but even with these three rules we see surprisingly realistic flocklike behavior, suggesting that such rules might well be behind the motion of real flocks. The boid principle has been used for computer graphics and games, and most notably in films such as *Jurassic Park* and *Finding Nemo*. More complex actor-based systems are used for battle simulations such as were seen in the *Lord of the Rings* trilogy.

A final method that is less mainstream is also worth mentioning, simply because it is a personal favorite. Douglas Hosftadter's research group's work on a process he calls "high-level perception": the building up of a representation of a situation under various top-down "pressures." So it is a kind of half-way house between the bottom-up and top-down approaches. The system uses a number of code objects called *codelets* which search for patterns in data, using criteria in a shifting network of associations called the *slipnet*. This contains all the concepts the model understands, such as "sameness," "difference," "opposite," "group," and so on, and it uses them to build up a picture of the particular situation. The interesting aspect of the model is that it can "perceive" a situation differently according to circumstances—in particular, in making analogies between different situations (for example, "abc" might be seen in one context as a "successor-group" of letters, but in another as a "length-3 group"). This intertwining of perception and cognition seems intuitively very lifelike.

A Bottom-Up AI Approach to Tic-Tac-Toe

It can't be denied that tic-tac-toe does not lend itself well to the bottom-up approach. A neural network could of course be used in place of the estimation function for the alpha-beta search, but would be unlikely to be an improvement, and there is very little analysis of the board position for the actors to share between them. This isn't to say that a bottom-up approach wouldn't be interesting, but it wouldn't be useful as a way to create an intelligent program, as compared to the other approaches.

One method that could be successful would be to create a neural net that takes any board position and returns the next. It would involve a slightly unusual training regime: instead of presenting it with a single stimulus and evaluating the response, it would have to play a complete game and be evaluated according to whether it won or lost. Whether this could be done with a standard neural net is hard to say.

EXERCISES

Exercise 25.1

Create a pattern-matching program which will play a good game of "heads or tails" against a human opponent.

You could use any of the approaches we've looked at in this chapter, but the easiest is the method mentioned in the top-down AI section.

Exercise 25.2

Create a simulation of flocking boids.

The three rules described in the chapter are fairly easy to implement and produce very satisfyingly lifelike behavior, especially in 3D. You might like to play with adding predator avoidance rules as well.

SUMMARY

In this chapter we've presented a rapid overview of a vast topic, which should have given you a good understanding of the general approaches to AI and how they are applied to different problems. You don't have enough information here to create your own AI implementation, but you should at least know what you are looking for.

In the final chapter we will follow up with a look at genetic algorithms and other methods for searching through large problem spaces.

YOU SHOULD NOW KNOW

- how to analyze a simple game using *game theory*
- how to create a complete strategy for a short game
- how to simplify a strategy using *alpha-beta* searching
- what an *estimation function* is and how to train it
- the difference between *top-down* and *bottom-up* approaches, and between strong and weak AI
- how a program can break a problem up into *goals* and *subgoals*
- how a *neural network* is built and how it can be used to solve problems

26 Search Techniques

In This Chapter

- Overview
- Problem-Solving
- Case Study
- Genetic Algorithms
- Exercises
- Summary
- You Should Now Know

OVERVIEW

So we arrive at long last at the final chapter, which follows on naturally from the previous one by looking at some methods for using the computer to solve problems. We're interested particularly in how the computer can be used to search through lots of possibilities in order to find an answer to a problem, or for that matter a problem with a particular answer. As we saw in Chapter 22, finding the optimum solution to a difficult problem can be a very big task, with no computationally efficient algorithm that can solve it. However, as we saw in Chapter 24, we can take advantage of some clever tricks in order to arrive at better answers. While we're looking at such tricks, we'll also have some things to say about how to organize the computer's resources during a long search (which could quite easily take days or even months).

Many of the techniques in this chapter are exact analogs of ideas in the previous two chapters—there isn't really a strict dividing line between AI problems and complex search problems. However, the domain in which they are being applied is different, and it should be instructive to see how similar methods can be adapted to different situations.

ON THE CD Code samples from this chapter are implemented in *math.cst* in the script *chapter 26 (genetic algorithms)*. The *geneticAlgorithm* demo uses them in the context of Exercise 26.1.

PROBLEM-SOLVING

The computer is a wonderful tool for problem-solving. It works very fast and doesn't get bored. We'll start by looking at some general ways in which a problem can be broken down into a form that the computer can be set to solve.

Representing a Problem

There are two main areas in which you might want to use the computer to solve problems, especially in a game context. The most obvious is as a game-player, when you want to solve a difficult puzzle and don't know how—an example might be an anagram generator that you would use to find an elusive answer in a crossword or jumble. Less obvious is as a game creator, who wants to use the computer to create a puzzle with a particular answer—an example would be filling a crossword grid with words, or creating a chess problem.

The two situations are fairly similar, but the latter is arguably more interesting, and that's what we will concentrate on in this chapter, although the methods mostly carry across straightforwardly.

Whatever problem you are looking at, the first step is always to try to classify your *search space*, that is, the set of possible answers to your problem. If you're filling the crossword grid in Figure 26.1, for example, your search space is the set of all possible combinations of one letter in each blank square or *cell*: a total of 26^{25} possible crosswords. You can represent this as a 25-element array.

However, this may not be the best way to represent the grid: after all, only a tiny proportion of these arrays represent *valid* solutions to the problem. Perhaps a more useful method would be to represent the *words* instead of the cells. This would yield an 8-element array, with each entry containing a single word. This is going to be much more amenable to searching. But of course, you need to take into account the links between words as well as the words themselves. You could do this by creating a *template,* which sits alongside the solution in progress, where each word is named and represented by a smaller array, something like this:

```
2dn: [1ac/3; blank; 6ac/3; blank; 7ac/3]
```

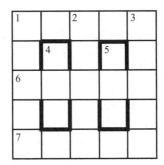

FIGURE 26.1 An empty crossword grid.

Now any time your algorithm fills in a potential solution to a word, it can check the template for cross-references, and fill these in simultaneously.

These kinds of initial considerations can be crucial to creating a representation of your problem which is useable by the computer to execute a search strategy.

Searching for Answers

We'll be looking at some specific examples of search strategies shortly, but let's consider some general concepts first. The main feature that distinguishes the kinds of problems that we would like our computer to solve is that they have a very large search space, but simple solutions. For example, the crossword above had over 10^{35} possible combinations of letters, a figure far too vast to search through exhaustively, but given any particular combination of letters, it's easy to check if it's a valid solution, simply by checking whether each word appears in your dictionary.

This is a rather informal way of describing the class of problems known as *NP-hard*. In a slightly more formal (although still not entirely accurate) description, an NP-hard problem is one for which there is no (known) algorithm that can find the solution in polynomial time, but for which, once you have found the solution, it is possible to prove in polynomial time that it *is* a solution. NP-hard problems are rather common, and there is an interesting sub-species known as the *NP-complete* problems, which are equivalent to one another: if we were to find a polynomial-time algorithm that could solve any one of them, then the same algorithm could be adapted to solve all the others in polynomial time too. It's an unsolved problem whether the class of NP-complete problems are actually solvable in polynomial time, although most mathematicians would probably think not. (There are some interesting developments in quantum computing which may change things, however.)

So given that we know these problems are impossible to solve quickly (for certain values of "impossible" and "quickly"), why do we bother? The answer is that although there is no general algorithm guaranteed to find an answer to any given problem, we can find algorithms that will improve our chances—speed up the journey through the search space. Recall the discussion of the A* Algorithm from Chapter 24: although in a worst-case scenario this is no faster than an exhaustive search, in the vast majority of cases it will be much faster than that.

The principal tool in these searches is to look for "bottlenecks." This is basically the equivalent of the alpha-beta search we looked at in the previous chapter. A useful starting point is to try to solve a simple example by hand and see where you naturally focus your attention. In the crossword grid above, you might start by filling in 1ac at random, let's say with the word SPACE. Now it's natural to focus on the three long down words (or "lights," as they are known by crossword aficionados). In particular, the most obvious word to look at is 2dn, which begins with the letter A, since there are fewer words starting with A than there are with S or E. Now you might choose the word ANVIL, which would lead you naturally to focus on the V in the center. Alternatively, you might decide against ANVIL and choose ALTER, since this gives a greater number of options for the crossing words.

This process can be semi-formalized as follows: choose a word that *maximizes* the *minimum* number of options for the crossing words (this should seem rather familiar). Then search on the light which has the *smallest* number of options remaining. If you find that a particular light is blocked—there are no possible words which fit—backtrack one step and choose another word.

We won't look further at the question of how to search through a dictionary for entries that fit a particular pattern as this is a less difficult task. A number of programs will perform it for you, and the Perl programming language, among others, includes the extremely useful Regular Expression syntax to make such searches even easier.

The strategy, which as mentioned in Chapter 24 is an example of what is called a *depth-first search*, is applicable in lots of circumstances, generally in any case where several co-dependent options have to be chosen in parallel. Another example is searching for a solution to the polyominoes problem: finding how to fit a certain set of shapes into a particular space as shown in Figure 26.2. In the partially complete example shown, one might perhaps try focusing on the square marked with an X, which can only be covered by one of the remaining pieces, or on the piece shaped like a cross, which can only fit in three spots on the board. Either of these approaches is equivalent to the method we used above.

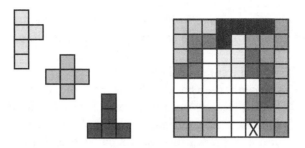

FIGURE 26.2   A pentominoes problem.

The alternative to a depth-first search is a *breadth-first search*, which is where all the possible alternatives at each stage are considered in parallel. Generally breadth-first searches are less efficient than a well-informed depth-first search, because of the large number of possibilities to be considered. The only circumstances where you might consider a breadth-first search would be where there is a good chance that the search depth is likely to be quite shallow—the kind of problem where you know there is a simple solution but you don't know what it is, and where there is no particular reason to try one solution rather than another.

As you can imagine, such situations are quite rare, as it's almost always possible to think of some heuristic that can be used to prefer some solution paths over others. Having said that, it is often possible as with the A* Algorithm to combine depth-first and breadth-first strategies into a more complex method that uses the best features of both—a shallow analysis of all possible paths that informs the choice of paths for a more thorough exploration. This provides a more complex heuristic for choosing the paths for the depth-first search: it's reminiscent of the look-ahead strategy we discussed in the previous chapter.

Interaction

An important point to consider is how you can get an indication of progress with the problem, and also how you can influence it if necessary. If a problem is going to involve several hours or days of computer time, you don't want to set it going and have no idea whether it is working correctly, and more importantly, if the computer crashes during the run you don't want to have to start the whole thing over again.

One result of this issue is that, despite the obvious benefits in terms of problem solving, as a general rule you can't use direct recursion in your search algorithm.

This is a pity, because many of these problems lend themselves obviously to a recursive structure—consider the crossword problem again, which can be considered as

1. Try to fill in the next light.
2. If you can't, then backtrack and try another possible word for the previous light (if there are no other words for that light and it was the first word, then there is no solution).
3. If you can, then if this was the last word you're done, otherwise find the next word to try and repeat.

This recursive structure seems quite natural in a depth-first search, and it's relatively simple to construct an algorithm that implements it. Unfortunately, it quickly leads to a call stack that is very large and memory-hungry. What's more, if the computer crashes, the whole stack is lost. So you need to *unroll* the recursion—keep the recursive structure, but fake it by creating your own call stack. This allows the search to be broken into discrete steps, instead of running as a single function call.

Having done this, you can take advantage of the discrete steps of the function to intersperse them with visual displays of the current state of the search: a partially completed crossword, for example. You can also take periodic "snapshots" in the form of text files that represent the best result so far—best in the sense that it combines a large number of steps through the search with a large number of alternative options at each step.

CASE STUDY

It's quite interesting to examine how these concepts can be used to deal with a complex problem, so we'll spend a little time examining the process of creating a program that finds chess problems: that is, given a particular checkmate position, it searches for a starting position that leads to this checkmate, of the form "white to move and mate in *n*." Although this problem is very specific, the problems it highlights serve as a useful illustration of the issues involved.

In the following discussion, we assume that you know a little about how chess works, but you don't really need to know more than the fact that players take turns to move a single piece, which may or may not capture (remove from the board) one of their opponent's pieces, and if one player maneuvers the other into a position where his or her king piece can be captured (*checkmate*), then this player wins the game.

Preparing the Ground

As before, we need to start by defining the search space and how it can be represented. This is fairly straightforward in this instance, as a chessboard is simply an 8 × 8 array whose elements can either be empty or contain one of 12 different pieces: a pawn (P), knight (N), bishop (B), castle (R for rook), and king (K) or queen (Q) of either color (W or B). For convenience, we label the squares of the board with letters for each column and numbers for each row, so a 1 is in the bottom-left corner and so on (see Figure 26.3). We also need one more piece of information: i.e., which player is due to play next.

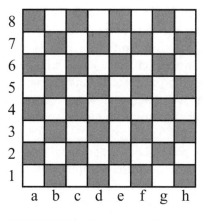

FIGURE 26.3   A chessboard.

For a completely free chess problem, the only other constraint on the search space is that each color must have exactly one king on the board, but we can define a few other constraints that apply to any position that occurs as the result of an actual game (actually, most of these constraints could be violated in extreme circumstances due to special rules such as promotion of pawns, but we'll ignore that in this case).

- There can be at most 8 pawns, 2 knights, bishops and castles, and one queen and one king of each color on the board at any one time.
- If there are two bishops of any one color, they must be on different colored squares of the chessboard.

- No pawn can be on rows 1 or 8 (after a move is completed—a white pawn can move to row 8 but is immediately promoted to some other piece).
- The player who last moved cannot currently be in *check*—that is, their king cannot be under threat from any opponent's piece.

Of these, all but the last are what might be called "syntactic" constraints: that is, you don't need to know anything about the rules of chess to determine if they have been violated, you just need to be able to count pieces, look at the board, and so on. The last one is a "semantic" constraint: to determine if it is true, you have to know how each piece can move.

These kinds of considerations quickly lead us to create some initial functions for working with this search. The most fundamental is one we might call `possibleMoves(board)`. This function takes as input a board position (including the current player) and returns a list of all possible moves in some useful format, such as "a1b1". This function in turn calls a function `possibleMovesForPiece (board, square)`, which returns a list of all possible moves for a particular piece. Now we can use this to create a function `underThreat(board, square)`, which looks through the list of all possible moves and determines whether any of them end on a particular square, in which case the square is considered to be under threat.

To create the `possibleMovesForPiece()` function requires implementing the rules of chess, and it's not entirely simple, especially if you want to take into account special moves such as castling or pawn capture *en passant*. In general, however, such special moves are not used in chess problems. The only issue that really needs to be considered is pawn promotion, but we'll leave this detail out here.

With these functions in place, we can create a function `validBoard(board)`, which returns TRUE if the board is a possible position and FALSE otherwise. This function will take into account all the considerations we mentioned above, using the `underThreat()` function to determine if the opponent's piece is in check. We can use this to improve the `possibleMoves()` function, making a `validMoves()` function that not only checks whether a move is possible, but also whether the resulting position is valid: in particular, whether after the move has been played, the player's king is under threat. With this function, we can quickly determine if a player is in checkmate: this is equivalent to saying that their king is under threat and there are no valid moves (if there are no valid moves and the king is not under threat, this is called a *stalemate*, which also occurs in a number of other special cases).

We now need just one more function, which might be called `validMovesInto (board)`. This function calculates all valid moves, which could *lead* to a particular position. Fortunately, because most chess moves are reversible, this is fairly similar to the `validMoves()` function, but there is an added complication, which is that for most moves, the moving piece could have performed a capture. This means that when undoing the move we might "reveal" a new piece that wasn't on the board before, so there are many more possible moves that lead *to* a particular position than there are moves that lead *from* that position.

So, with all these functions created, we are now in a much better position to define exactly what it is our search function is to do. We want it to take a board position, usually a checkmate by white, and to find a position preceding it by *n* moves such that

- No sequence of moves from this position leads to any other checkmate in *n* moves or fewer, as long as black plays perfectly.
- No sequence of moves from this position leads to black avoiding checkmate after *n* moves, as long as white plays perfectly.

Creating the Search Function

The simplest case is a "mate in one": we give the computer a checkmate position, it finds all possible board positions that lead to this position, using validMovesInto(). For each of these positions, it then finds the list of validMoves(). If any of these leads to a checkmate that is not the final game position we're looking for, then this is not a satisfactory chess problem (chess problems should have exactly one correct answer). But if we've found one that has no other checkmating move, our search is complete.

Notice the back-and-forth nature of this search. We first take a step backward to find a possible pre-position, and then we *play a game of chess* from that position (in this case just one move), to see whether this position is suitable for our purposes. Each step involves a search process: one search through all the possible pre-positions looking for the most likely to be suitable, and the other through all the possible post-positions looking for one that invalidates the step. So we need a suitable heuristic in both cases to find the best order to search.

As before, the key is to minimize our alternatives. So when searching through the pre-positions, we want to preferentially choose those that have the fewest valid moves from that position. This makes the eventual puzzle easier to solve, but more likely to have a unique correct answer. Of course, in the forward search, we have to check every move, although recall that there are fewer forward moves than backward ones, but again we want to look for those most likely to invalidate the puzzle first, which means using normal chess heuristics to find the best moves from that position.

The search becomes more complicated when finding a mate in more than one move because we now have to take black's moves into account as well. Having found a mate in one, we then have to consider a black move which could lead to that position. Again, this is going to involve a backward search followed by a forward one, but this time, the black move has to be forced, in the sense that the particular move we're interested in has to be the best possible move black can make. In this case, when the next move by white is to be the checkmate, black's move has to be the only valid move available—any other move, even if it leads to checkmate, will not lead to the same checkmate as we want. Further down the line, black may have other moves available, but they must all lead to checkmate sooner than the target path.

Having established black's move, we now have another position to aim for with white, which means another back-and-forward check, and so on. No matter how good our heuristics are, there is a lot of ground to search. But this process is still going to find a suitable position faster than a simple examination of all possibilities. What's more, it seems intellectually plausible because if you try to create a chess problem for yourself, you'll find yourself working through exactly the same process.

GENETIC ALGORITHMS

One further example of a search method is worth examining because it shows a different approach, essentially being to connectionist AI what standard search methods are to top-down AI. The *genetic algorithm* simulates the force of natural selection acting on a population of computer programs.

Natural Selection

To understand the workings of the genetic algorithm, it helps to understand a little about real-life genetics, so as we did with neural networks, we'll take a break from mathematics and physics to look at biology—although this is such an often-told tale that we'll look at it very briefly. An organism's physical structure (and slightly more contentiously, its behavior) is principally determined by a molecule called DNA, which is a long chain-like structure made up of copies of four different molecular units called *bases*, denoted by the symbols A, C, G, and T (we needn't worry about the details of the chemistry involved, and of course the actual mechanism of the cell is significantly more complicated than we're going to look at here). So a typical strand of DNA might consist of the bases AGCCATAGTTACGT. Each cell in a particular organism (with a few exceptions) contains a copy of the DNA molecule, with the same sequence of bases, but the exact sequence varies from organism to organism: your DNA is different from the DNA of every other human being, unless you happen to be an identical twin, or a clone.

For our purposes, the most useful way to think of a DNA strand is as a program, containing instructions on how to build the organism. For convenience, we often consider a DNA strand to be made up of individual sub-sequences called *genes*. The word is used rather loosely to refer to various different structures, from sequences that code for particular proteins (the most "realistic" definition), to abstract components of the DNA that happen to determine a particular trait of the organism (a more dangerous definition, although it's also useful), but from a programming point of view we could consider them to be like functions or objects. A particular complete set of genes is referred to as the *genotype*, and the organism built by the genes is called the *phenotype*.

The simplest way for an organism to reproduce is just to create a new organism with an exact copy of its DNA. This is called *asexual reproduction*, and most bacteria, fungi and plants, as well as many animals, can reproduce in this way. Asexual reproduction is very rapid, although it has one problem: when all organisms come from copies of the same genotype, they tend to be highly susceptible to diseases, predators, and parasites, since if a particular disease comes along that can harm one organism, that disease can most likely harm the whole population. This description is dangerously close to the doctrine of "species selection," which is contrary to the standard view of evolutionary biology, but it's sufficient for our purposes.

The alternative to asexual reproduction is, of course, *sexual reproduction*. Here, two different individuals, with different genotypes, join together, mingling their DNA to create a new unique individual. This, of course, requires that their DNA structure must be compatible, in particular, they need to have a similar set of genes (*genome*), distributed in similar places along the DNA strand. So if Romeo and Juliet are to create a child, the gene determining Romeo's eye color must be in the same position on his DNA as Juliet's eye color gene on her DNA. These different versions of the same gene are called *alleles*. Continuing the programming analogy, they are like different instances of the same object class, with different properties, or perhaps different classes implementing the same interface.

In fact, for the vast majority of genes, we inherit not one but two alleles, one from each parent. So Romeo and Juliet's child will have two genes for her eye color. Of these alleles, one is *dominant*, and determines the color of her eyes. However, either of them might be passed on to her own children. Two organisms whose genomes are organized in the same way are said to belong to the same *species* (again, this is a non-technical definition).

The process of creating a child by sexual reproduction is quite simple. First of all, each parent produces a number of sex cells or *gametes* (for animals, usually sperm and eggs). These are like normal cells, except that they contain only one copy of each gene. The key step is called *mitosis*, which is where the two versions of the genes line up in the cell and split in half to create two gametes, with half of the alleles going into one gamete, and the rest into the other. The distribution of alleles is random: it makes no difference whether a particular allele came from the father or the mother, they each have the same chance of ending up in either gamete. These gametes are then sent out to see if they can find a gamete of the other sex, in which case they combine their half-set of genes (or rather, complete set of unpaired genes) with those of the other gamete to create a new cell which now has a complete, and entirely new, combination of genes. In the process, there will also be occasional copying errors called *mutations* which means that the alleles received by the new organism are not exactly the same as those of its parents (although the DNA-copying process is generally very accurate indeed).

What is the advantage of all this effort? The answer is easiest to see if we move back to the level of the organism. In a population of similar organisms, only some can survive to reproduce. Many will die of diseases, or be eaten by predators, before they can mate. Others (especially males, in species where females devote more time and effort to bringing up offspring) will fail to reproduce because they will not be deemed attractive by potential mates. The result is that only those alleles that are carried by successful organisms will be carried forward to the next generation, and generally they will be carried forward in proportion to the success of those organisms carrying them. This creates a process called *natural selection*, first described by Charles Darwin and named to suggest a similarity with the process of *artificial selection*, or *selective breeding*, which had been used for centuries by farmers, both wittingly and unwittingly, to improve the yield of their crops and livestock. Natural selection will occur in any situation where you find *heredity* (reproducing organisms passing on their characteristics to their offspring), *variation* between different organisms in the population, and *competition* for resources. And sexual reproduction is an excellent way for genes to improve their chances of spreading through a population.

Under natural selection, successive generations of organisms *evolve* to adapt to changing environments (especially competition from other members of the same species). Natural selection, unlike artificial selection, is a blind process: evolution is not directed toward a particular goal but simply proceeds by incremental steps depending on the reproductive success of one generation after another. Random events like meteor strikes or ice ages can mean that whole species that were well adapted to existing environments are suddenly obsolete and die off before they can evolve new mechanisms to cope. However, it's possible after the fact to see the existence of particular *evolutionary pressures* that happened to direct evolution in one direction rather than another for a particular species—so we humans evolved under evolutionary pressures (a whole host of influences from the environment, random chance, sexual selection, and especially competition with other humans) toward an upright stance, larger brains and tool use, among other things.

Evolutionary pressures are emergent phenomena, in the sense that they are the result of any number of smaller "micro-evolutionary" events. One way to conceive of them is to imagine organisms as exploring a "search space" of possible strategies for existence. There are vast numbers of ways to create an organism, most of which are doomed to fail. A particular species consists of small variations on a theme, all exploring the same region of the search space, otherwise known as an *evolutionary niche*. But if some of these strategies happen upon a previously unexplored corner of the niche, then they may find themselves doing a little better than the rest of their species. Their success means that this new area of the search space can be opened up for further exploration, and if it proves better than the area they inhabited before, the whole species may start to migrate toward it (or alternatively, the pioneers may break away and eventually form a new species of their own, inhabiting the new niche). You can think of it like prospectors digging in a hillside and occasionally coming upon a new seam of gems, which they then explore fully, excavating a new cave (and becoming very rich) in the process.

Evolution by natural selection may seem a hopelessly inefficient way to develop new strategies. After all, artificial selection is hugely faster and more reliable. But in fact it's a remarkably good way to find hidden solutions to a problem. With sufficient environmental pressures, organisms can evolve dramatically in just a few generations, especially if they reproduce sexually.

The Genetic Algorithm

As you will have gathered, genetic algorithms apply the evolutionary approach to search through complex spaces. They follow the biological model fairly closely, although of course they are an idealization, just as neural networks are an idealization of biological neurons.

It's easiest to consider an actual problem, so let's return to the realm of chess and imagine that we're searching for a solution to the puzzle presented in Exercise 26.1, of finding a way to place eight queens on the board so that none of them are threatening any of the others. To create a genetic algorithm, we have to characterize our search in terms of a genome: a list of values that represent the search space. So in this case, we could use a 48-element list in which each element is either 1 or 0 (this binary nature isn't a necessary condition for the list, but it's convenient). Each set of eight bits represents the position of one of the eight queens; if there is a duplicate, then the list is invalid, but we can deal with this by simply ignoring invalid genotypes, which might be considered as "miscarriages": phenotypes that are not viable organisms.

The other factor that we need in order to create the algorithm is a *utility function*, which tells us how close we are to a correct solution. In this case, we could calculate the number of ways in which each queen is under threat, for example, in Figure 26.4 the function would evaluate to 8. Our aim is to minimize the value of the utility function. The value of the function for each possible organism gives what is called a *fitness landscape:* a mountainous region representing the success of different answers. Valleys are areas that are successful, and we are searching for the lowest such valley (or in a case like this, for any valley with a minimum of zero).

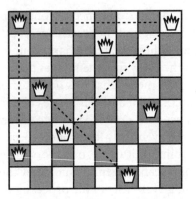

FIGURE 26.4   A set of eight queens
which does not solve the problem.
Its genotype is 000000 000111
001100 011001 100101 101011
110000 111101

The utility function is the weakest link in the genetic algorithm approach, because if our problem is an "all-or-nothing" deal, then there is no advantage to being close to the correct solution, which means that our algorithm has nothing to get hold of (the valleys in the fitness landscape have very steep sides, so it can't find them). This is the classic objection to evolution suggested by creationists, the problem of intermediate forms ("what is the advantage of having half an eye?"), and it's an important one. Advocates of natural selection are generally glad to admit that if anyone could find a biological structure that had no immediate advantage at each stage of its evolution for the organisms carrying it, then it would be a serious problem for evolutionary theory. Fortunately no such structures have been found to date (half an eye is actually quite a big improvement on no eye at all). In computation, it's similarly almost always possible to find some utility function that allows you to evaluate the success of a particular proposed solution. What's more, the function can often be quite coarse-grained, with lots of different phenotypes having equal fitness—in fact, this can be positively advantageous to the algorithm.

The basic principle of the genetic algorithm is very simple. We take a small population of "organisms" and evaluate them with the utility function. The ones that do best (in our case, the ones with the lowest score) are allowed to "mate," producing a new generation of organisms. The mating process is based on mitosis: we take the DNA strand of each organism, and splice them together:

```
function mateOrganisms (strand1, strand2)
    set child to an empty array
    set currentStrand to strand1
```

```
     set length to the number of elements of strand1
     repeat for i=1 to length
       // randomly switch strands
       if random(length)<5 then switch currentStrand
       set element to currentStrand[i]
       // randomly mutate the occasional element
       if random(length)=1 then set element to not(element)
       add element to child
     end repeat
     return child
  end function
```

The figures are set fairly arbitrarily, but from experience, approximately one mutation per strand and five switches per strand seems to work quite well. It seems like magic, but the algorithm tends to approach an optimal solution. What's more, it deals well with *local minima* in the fitness landscape—that is, answers that are close to optimal but are dead ends: the lowest point in the particular valley is not an actual minimum. Local minima are the biggest problem for all search strategies, but the random element of genetic algorithms gives them a means of exploring far-flung areas of the search space at the same time as they focus on the current primary route.

Tweaking

Despite the simplicity of the system, there are rather a lot of ways to vary the genetic algorithm methodology in order to improve the rate of searching. Which of them is more effective depends very much on the situation, particularly the number of local minima. One of the principal problems with genetic algorithms is that they have a tendency to get stuck in a rut, with the gene pool losing a lot of variation and one basic pattern taking over. Conversely, too much mutation can mean that the algorithm never gets a chance to approach a solution before it gets distracted by some alternative. So here are a few variations on the theme.

1. In the standard method, there is no distinction between the winners of the evolutionary race. At each stage, the field is simply divided in two: suppose there are 15 organisms, we choose the 6 best, and mate each one with each of the others, which produces a new set of 15 organisms. An alternative is to weight the results, by awarding more children to the most successful organisms. For example, in this case the overall winner might get to mate twice with each of the others, while the worst does not get to mate with anyone except the winner. This speeds up the process of finding a solution in a landscape with few or no local minima.

2. We can use a *radiation* variable, which affects the rate of mutation and possibly also the rate of crossover. By raising and lowering the radiation periodically, we can give the algorithm periods of stability in order to focus on the current path, interspersed with periods of instability in which more far-flung ideas may get tried out. An example of this can be seen in the *geneticAlgorithm* demo. This helps to break free of ruts—although it may be worth "cryogenically freezing" some of the more successful genotypes in case they get lost.

3. We can alter the population size, allowing for a more varied gene pool to be maintained (this tends to make less of a difference than one might think, and a population of around 50–100 organisms seems to be fairly optimal from personal experience).

4. Generally, the new generation completely supplants the previous one. Instead, we can allow parents to compete with their children, so that the previous best solution is never completely lost.

5. We can introduce "mass extinctions" by occasionally killing off a larger number of the population—possibly even the more successful ones. This would be equivalent to an epidemic that attacks the most prevalent genotype in a population, allowing the underdogs to come through.

6. We can allow a kind of "speciation" by splitting off separate populations and allowing them to evolve separately, and then put them together again to compete and interbreed.

7. We can introduce a system of paired genes, as in biology, where each organism inherits two alleles instead of just one. This does, however, mean coming up with some reasonable method for determining which allele is dominant.

As you can see, most of these ideas are designed with a view to simulating conditions in biology, particularly the process of artificial selection where we give natural selection a helping hand in order to speed it up. The danger, however, as in all search strategies, is that we might push the algorithm too hard and lose track of all its advantages.

The alternative method is to tweak the utility function, for example by changing its "grain size"—as we saw above, coarser-grained utility functions can help to smooth out local minima, while finer-grained ones can make it easier to approach a solution once it's in sight.

Another interesting option is to create a second utility function that uses an alternative means of evaluating the success of an organism. For example, when searching for an algebraic solution to a differential equation, we might have one measure for "simplicity" and another for "accuracy." An ideal organism would minimize both, but in general there is a tradeoff between the two. When comparing two organisms, one is considered better than the other if it does better on both measurements: otherwise they are considered equally good.

It's also worth remembering that the utility function is generally the most computationally costly part of the algorithm, as it needs to be evaluated at every stage for each member of the population. Simply speeding up the execution of the function allows more generations to be completed in a particular time.

EXERCISES

Exercise 26.1

Following the suggestions in this chapter, create a genetic algorithm process to solve the eight queens problem: place eight queens on a chessboard so that none of them is threatening any other.

The chapter contains a number of suggestions for creating the genome and utility function for this problem: combine them with the genetic algorithm process and see if you can use it to find an answer. See the file *geneticAlgorithm.dir* ON THE CD on the CD-ROM.

SUMMARY

In this chapter we explored a few methods for searching through large numbers of possibilities in order to solve difficult problems, focusing specifically on extensions of the AI approaches from the previous chapter, and also introducing the genetic algorithm method. This concludes our exploration of the more algorithmic elements of computational mathematics, and brings the book to a close.

It has been a long and hopefully enjoyable journey from the simple principles of numbers and elementary algebra we saw in Part I. From the foundational elements of mathematics and physics, we've seen how you can build some extremely complex and subtle techniques and apply them to programming, particularly in games. Although some of the more difficult topics have been only sketched out, you've had a chance to think about the issues involved and get to know some of the key terminology, and see the principles in action, so that you are in a much better position to deal with the more technical coverage to be found in specialized resources on the subject. And perhaps along the way you've found some tidbits that have inspired you to try something new: perhaps an AI bot or a game of 3D bowling.

You'll find some further resources in the Appendices to help you move on and apply these ideas in more detail.

YOU SHOULD NOW KNOW

- how to classify a problem in terms of a *search space*
- how to explore a search space using *depth-first* or *breadth-first* strategies
- the relationship between *genetic algorithms* and evolutionary biology
- how to create a genome to represent a search space
- the meaning of the terms *utility function* and *fitness landscape* and how a genetic algorithm uses them
- some strategies for optimizing the speed of a genetic algorithm

Appendix
A
Glossary of Mathematical Terms

This glossary can't cover all the mathematical terms introduced in this book, but it aims to be quite comprehensive with the most fundamental terms that appear frequently. Rarer words will generally appear close to their definitions in the main text. Some terms whose strict mathematical definition is a little complicated are left undefined, since their vernacular meaning is clear enough (for example, words like *point*, *shape*, etc.). A few other terms that don't appear in the book are introduced here to help make other explanations briefer and more rigorous (such as *locus*), although many of the definitions still fall short of a strict mathematical formulation.

absolute value   For a **real number** n, if $n < 0$ then its absolute value is $-n$, otherwise it is n. In other words, the absolute value of a number other than zero is always positive.

acceleration   The **rate of change** of **velocity** or **speed**

acute angle   An **angle** smaller than a **right angle**

affine transformation   A **transformation** that preserves **parallel** lines

air resistance   The **force** experienced by an object moving through the air, resisting the motion; also called fluid resistance or **drag**

algebraic solution   The result of finding the values of the **unknowns** in an **equation** in general terms of the other **variables** in the equation; cf **numeric solution**

algorithm   A computational process, consisting of a number of pre-defined calculations that take on particular **arguments** (essentially a program with inputs)

aliasing   The process by which a line vector is converted to hard-edged pixels; cf **antialiasing**

alpha-beta search   A method for searching through a **search tree** (usually of a game) by pruning each branch as we go, ignoring branches which will never be taken by a rational player

ambient light   The general illumination of a region as a result of light **reflected** in all directions (the amount of illumination in areas of shadow); see also **directional light**, **attenuated light**

amplitude   The maximum distance from **equilibrium** achieved by an oscillator during any **oscillation**

angle   A measure of **rotation**, defined as a **fraction** of a **circle** and measured usually in **degrees** or **radians**

angle of incidence   The **angle** at which an object or **wave** strikes a **surface**

angle of reflection   The **angle** at which an object or **wave** bounces off a **surface** after colliding with it

angular frequency   The number of **rotations** completed by a rotating object in a particular time period (see **frequency**)

angular velocity   The **angle** turned through by a rotating object in a particular time period

antialiasing   The process by which a line vector is converted to smooth-colored pixels by gradually **interpolating** its color with the background

area   The amount of flat surface of an object in two or more dimensions, measured in **squared** units of length**base.** The value on which some calculation is rooted, for example the 'radix' of a number system (as with base ten or **decimal**) or the base of a **logarithm**

argument   A **variable** provided as an input to a mathematical or programming **function**

armature   A **polygon** or **polyhedron** used to create a simplified description of an object for the purposes of collision detection; cf **collision map**

associative   Of some **operator** #, says that for each a, b, c in the **domain**, $a \# (b \# c) = (a \# b) \# c$ (e.g.: $a + (b + c) = (a + b) + c$); cf **commutative**, **distributive**

asymptote   A line or plane such that the **graph** of some **function** approaches it infinitely closely

attenuated light   Light emitted from a particular point which diminishes with distance as a result of spreading out; see also **ambient light**, **directional light**

average   A generic word for various kinds of "middle" value of a set of values; most commonly the **mean**

axis   Of a **Cartesian space**, a line through the **origin**, **parallel** to one **vector** of the **basis**

axis of rotation   The line around which an object is **rotating**

baked texture   A **texture map** in which lighting calculations have been made in advance

ballistics   The study of objects in motion when acted on only by the **force** of gravity

barycentric coordinates   A **homogeneous coordinate** system where the coordinates of a point P are given by the (**signed**) areas of the three triangles made between P and three pre-defined points A, B, C

base   The value on which some calculation is rooted, for example the 'radix' of a number system (as with **base** ten or decimal) or the base of a **logarithm**

basis   A set of **vectors**, together with a defined **origin**, used to define a **Cartesian space** (or any other **vector** space)

Bezier curve   A **spline** defined by a **cubic** function between successive **control points**, with a defined **tangent** at each control point; cf **Catmull-Rom spline**

binary   The number system using a **base** of 2. Numbers written in binary have several useful properties which make them ideal for calculations, in particular their suitability for use in **Boolean algebra**

Boolean algebra   A system for working with "Boolean numbers": numbers which can take only two possible values, TRUE and FALSE, using operators such as AND, OR, and NOT

bottom-up   An artificial intelligence methodology where programs act by the emergent behavior of many sub-programs or agents whose individual behavior is simple and deterministic; cf **top-down**

bounding volume   For some shape in 3D space, a volume of space entirely enclosing the shape; similarly "bounding area"

bounding volume hierarchy   A **partitioning tree** in 3D space (similarly, "bounding area hierarchy" in 2D) in which objects are divided into successively smaller regions that enclose smaller sets

bracketing method   A method for finding the approximate **numeric solution** to an **equation** by narrowing down an **interval** within which the solution is to be found

breadth-first search   A method for searching through a **search tree** by examining each possible branch at a particular level; cf **depth-first search**

bump map   A **texture map** describing the height of a surface at particular points

calculus   The study of infinitesimally small values, particularly **integration** and **differentiation**

Cartesian coordinates   The set of numbers that define the position of a point in **Cartesian space** under some **basis**

Cartesian plane   A two-dimensional **Cartesian space**

Cartesian space   (also called **Euclidean space**): a set of points defined by a **vector** of n **real numbers** such that every triangle of points has three **angles** summing to 180° (very briefly!)

Catmull-Rom spline   A **spline** defined by a **cubic** function between successive **control points**, such that each curve segment is determined by four control points, creating a smooth transition; cf **Bezier curve**

center of mass   For any object, the point such that for any line or plane through the point, half the object's **mass** is on each side of the line

centrifugal force   The **force** exerted by a rotating object moving in a **circle;** cf **centripetal force**

centripetal force   The **force** required to keep an object moving in a **circle;** cf **centrifugal force**

centrum   The **center of mass** of a triangle

child node   In a **tree**, a **node** x is a child of node y **if and only if** y is the **parent node** of x

circle   A shape defined as the **locus** of a point at a constant **distance** r from another point in a given plane

circumference   The **perimeter** of a **circle**

coefficient   The **constant** part of a **term** in an **expression**—so the coefficient of the term $4x$ is 4

coefficient of elasticity   The **constant of proportionality** relating the **extension** of a stretched **spring** to the **tension**

coefficient of friction   The **constant of proportionality** μ relating the force **perpendicular** to the interface between two surfaces to the **frictional** force that resists their motion

coefficient of restitution   The **constant of proportionality** ε relating the relative speeds of two objects before and after a collision. In an **elastic** collision $\varepsilon = 1$; for an **inelastic** collision $\varepsilon < 1$

collinear   Of three or more points, means that they lie in a straight line

collision map   An **image map** describing an object's shape in simplified form for the purposes of collision detection; cf **armature**

common factor   For two values a and b, a number (or **expression**) that is a **factor** of both a and b

commutative   Of some **operator** #, says that for each a and b in the **domain**, $a \# b = b \# a$ (e.g.: $a + b = b + a$); cf **associative, distributive**

complex numbers   The set of numbers that can be represented as the sum of a **real number** and an **imaginary number**, denoted by the symbol $\mathbb{C}$

component   The length of a **vector** when **projected** in a particular direction. If the direction is defined by some **unit vector u**, then the component of the vector **v** in that direction is found by the **scalar product** $\mathbf{v} \cdot \mathbf{u}$; sometimes as "the components of a vector" means its components in the directions of the underlying **basis**

composite number   A **natural number** that is not **prime**

computational complexity   A measure of the time taken for an **algorithm** to run, as a **function** of the size of its **arguments**

concave   Of a shape, means that it is not **convex**

cone The **surface of rotation** of a line rotated about a non-**parallel** line in space; cf **cylinder**

congruent Two **integers** a and b are congruent **modulo** a particular base m **if and only if** $a = b + nm$ for some integer n

conjugate Of a **complex number** or **quaternion**, the result of taking the number and changing the sign of the **imaginary** part

conservation of energy The **law** stating that for any set of objects with no net **force** acting on them (other than those included in **potential energy** calculations), the total **energy** of the system is constant

conservation of momentum The **law** stating that for a system of **particles** moving with no external **force**, the total **momentum** of the system is constant

constant An element in a **function** that is considered to be fixed when evaluating the function

constant of proportionality See **proportional**

control point Of a **spline**, a point defining the shape of the **curve** in some way, usually a point on the curve

convex Of a shape, means that any line drawn between two points on the **perimeter** does not pass outside the shape; cf **concave**

coordinates See **Cartesian coordinates**

coprime Two **natural numbers** a and b are said to be coprime **if and only if** their **greatest common divisor** is 1

countable set A **set** whose elements can be listed in some order, even though the list may continue forever (they can be put in a **one-to-one** correspondence with the **natural numbers**)

counting numbers See **natural numbers**

coupled oscillators Two or more **oscillators** that are connected, so that each exerts a **force** on the other

critical Of some value, the point at which the behavior of a system changes qualitatively: for example, the critical **angle** at which light cannot escape from a particular medium due to refraction

cross product See **vector product**

cubic A **polynomial** of **degree** 3

curve A **set** of connected points in space definable by a single continuously varying **parameter**

cylinder The **surface of rotation** of a line rotated about a **parallel** line in space; cf **cone**

damped harmonic motion The motion of an oscillator that would normally undergo **simple harmonic motion** but is also experiencing a **damping** factor

damping   A factor opposing the motion of an **oscillation**, **proportional** to the **speed**

decimal   The number system using a **base** of ten: our usual counting system, based on tens, hundreds, thousands and so on.

degree   Of a **polynomial function** f(x), the largest **exponent** of x—so the function $x^3 + 2x$ has degree 3

degrees   A unit of **angle**, defined as 1/360 of a **circle**

denominator   In a **fraction**, the number on the bottom (also called the "divisor")

depth-first search   A method for searching through a **search tree** by examining a particular branch until it succeeds or fails, then backtracking; cf **breadth-first search**

derivative   The **function** g that gives the **gradient** of some other function f for each value of its **arguments;** cf **integral** and see **rate of change**

determinant   The "magnitude" of a **matrix**: the amount by which the matrix **scales** a cube when used as a **transformation**

diagonal   A line connecting two **vertices** of some shape; more specifically, the longest possible such line

difference   The result of subtracting two values

differential equation   An **equation** relating a **function** to its various **derivatives**

differentiation   The process of finding the **gradient** of some **function** (the derivative)

diffraction   A phenomenon where a **wave** changes shape as a result of passing through a small gap, acting as if the gap were a new emitter for the wave

diffuse reflection   (also **Lambertian reflection**) Light emitted from a **surface** as a result of light incident on the surface, with no preferred direction; cf **specular reflection**

dimension   Of a **vector** or **Cartesian space**, the number of **components** or **basis** vectors required to define it

directional light   Light emitted in a particular direction, with no presumed diminution over distance (e.g., sunlight); see also **ambient light, attenuated light**)

discriminant   A number derived from the **parameters** of a **function** whose value can be used to classify the behavior of the function in some way, e.g. to find the number of its **roots**

displacement   The **vector** from one point to another

distance   The length of a line from one point to another, defined as the **magnitude** of the **vector** between them

distributive   Of some **operators** # and @, says that for each a, b, c in the **domain**, $a \# (b @ c) = (a \# b) @ (a \# c)$ (e.g.: $a \times (b + c) = (a \times b) + (b \times c)$); cf **commutative, associative**

divisor See **factor**

domain The **set** of values for which a **function** is defined

Doppler shift A phenomenon where a **wave** has a different **frequency** in a different **reference frame**

dot product See **scalar product**

drag See **air resistance**

e The number 2.718… such that the **function** $x \rightarrow e^x$ has a **derivative** equal to itself

eccentricity The amount by which an **ellipse** deviates from a **circle**, defined by $\sqrt{1 - b^2/a^2}$, where a and b are the **halfmajor** and **halfminor axes** respectively

efficiency The proportion of **energy** used in some system which is converted to useful **work**

elastic Of a collision, says that no **kinetic energy** is lost; cf **inelastic**

elastic limit The maximum **extension** of a stretched **spring** for which the **coefficient of elasticity** remains valid

elastic potential energy The **potential energy** of an object under the influence of a stretched spring or elastic

ellipse The **locus** of a point in a plane whose total **distance** from two defined points is constant

ellipsoid The result of an **affine transformation** applied to a **sphere**

emergent phenomenon The collective behavior of a group of simple interactive processes

energy A measurement of the amount something is moving, or could move given an opportunity; see **kinetic**, **potential**, **gravitational potential** and **elastic potential energy**, and also **conservation of energy**

equation A **statement** that two values are equal to one another, usually with one or more **unknowns**

equilateral triangle A 2D shape with three sides of equal length

equilibrium A state of a system of objects where there is no net **force**

estimation function A **function** evaluating how likely a particular solution to a problem is to be near to the correct answer

Euclidean space See **Cartesian space**

exponent The **power** to which a number has been raised—so in the **term** x^5, x has an exponent of 5

exponential Of a **function**, says that it behaves similarly to the **power** function mapping $x \rightarrow e^x$; cf **logarithm**

expression A **function** consisting of a combination of **terms**, such as $3y^2 + 10xz - 5\left(x^3 - 2\right)$

extension The amount a **spring** or other elastic material is stretched from its natural length (see **elastic limit**)

factor   For two values a and b, a is a factor of b **if and only if** b is an **integer multiple** of a

factorization   The process of separating a **function** or number into a multiple of two or more **factors**

field of view   The area visible at a particular distance from a camera; alternatively the **angle subtended** by the **viewport** at the camera

finite set   A **set** with a limited number of elements

fixed-point number   A value stored on a computer as its **integer** part and a certain fixed number of digits after the **radix point**; cf **floating-point number**

floating-point number   A value stored on a computer as a certain fixed number of significant digits, along with an indication of its overall size (e.g. 5.25 e3 = 5250); cf **fixed-point number**

focus   Of an **ellipse**, one of the two points which define it (pl. foci)

force   An action which causes an object to change its **momentum**, with a value equal to the **rate of change** of momentum

formula   An **equation** containing more than one **variable**, which relates these quantities to one another (usually defining one variable as a **function** of the others). Formulas do not have **unknowns**, they are supposed true for all possible (true) values of their variables.

fraction   The result of dividing one number by another (when both numbers are **integers**, this is a **rational number**)

frequency   The number of complete **oscillations** completed by an oscillator in a particular time; cf **period**

friction   The **force** experienced between two surfaces **parallel** to their direction of motion, resisting the motion, **proportional** to the force between them **perpendicular** to their surfaces; see **coefficient of friction**

frustrum   A 3D shape formed by taking any kind of pyramid or cone and cutting off the top

fulcrum   The point or line around which a lever or other object rotates; its **axis of rotation**

function   A mapping from one **set** of values (the **domain**) to another (the **range**). A function can be represented algebraically ("$f : x \mapsto x^3$," or more succinctly "$f(x) = x^3$") or simply by a description ("f(n) = 1 if n is odd, –1 otherwise").

general solution   A **function** defining all possible solutions to a **differential equation** in terms of **parameters** remaining to be defined by the **initial conditions**; cf **particular solution**

genetic algorithm   A method for searching through a **search space** by "evolving" solutions using an analogue of natural selection

global maximum   The highest value of some **function** for any value of its **arguments** (similarly "global minimum"); cf **local maximum**

gradient   The slope of a line in some **Cartesian space**, defined by the vertical distance moved divided by the horizontal distance for some infinitesimal movement

graph   Either: A picture of a **function** created by plotting its values against its arguments; or: the **Cartesian plane** on which this happens; or: a set of **nodes** connected together by edges

gravitational potential energy   The **potential energy** of an object under the influence of gravity

greatest common divisor   For two **natural numbers** a and b, the largest number which is a **common factor** of both

greedy algorithm   An **algorithm** that searches preferentially for a **local** solution to a problem

halfmajor axis/halfminor axis   Of an **ellipse**, the halfmajor axis is half of the **distance** between the two most extreme points on the **perimeter** (along the line through the two **foci**). The halfminor axis is then the longest distance from this line to the perimeter.

homogeneous coordinates   A method of representing a point in a space of n **dimensions** by a **projection** of a line in $n + 1$ dimensions

hypotenuse   In a **right-angled triangle**, the side opposite the **right angle**

identity   A value which leaves all other values unchanged under some **operator**. For example, the identity **function** $f(x) = x$, the identity **matrix** which has 1s in the **leading diagonal** and 0s elsewhere, the number 0 under addition or 1 under multiplication.

if and only if   To say one statement is true "if and only if" the other is true means that either both are true or both are false (sometimes written "iff")

image map   An image (usually in 2D) that is **projected** to a **surface** by some mapping, or vice versa, to represent some property of the surface; see **collision map, texture map, bump map**

imaginary number   Any multiple of the value i, defined as the **square root** of -1. The set of imaginary numbers is in a sense **perpendicular** to the set of **real numbers**.

independent equations   Two or more **simultaneous equations**, none of which can be derived from the others

inelastic   Of a collision, says that the total **kinetic energy** after the collision is less than it was before; cf **elastic**

inequality   A **statement** that two values are related to one another in some way (for example that one is greater than the other); cf **equation**

inertia   See **mass**

initial conditions   Facts about the initial state of a system that allow us to deduce its later behavior, particularly when using a **differential equation**

integer multiple   For two values (numbers or **expressions**) a and b, b is an integer multiple of a **if and only if** there is some **integer** n such that $b = an$; cf **factor**

integers   The set of **natural numbers** combined with the set of negative natural numbers: $\ldots, -2, -1, 0, 1, 2, \ldots$, and denoted by the symbol $\mathbb{Z}$

integral   The **function** f that gives the (**signed**) area of an infinitesimally thin slice between some other function g and the **axis** (indefinite integral), or by **substituting** two values for its **arguments**, the area under the curve between those two points (definite integral). The **inverse** of the **derivative**.

integration   The process of finding the area between a **graph** of some **function** and the horizontal **axis** (the **integral**)

intercept   For a **function** f(x), the value f(0)

interpolation   The process of finding an intermediate value between two other values by **parameterizing** the line between them

interval   A **set** of **real numbers**, which may be "open" (not containing its end points, as in the set $-1 < x < 0$) or "closed" (containing the end points, as in the set $-1 \leq x \leq 0$), or a mixture of the two

inverse function   The inverse of a **one-to-one function** f, denoted f^{-1}, is defined over the **range** of f such that if f$(x) = y$, then $f^{-1}(y) = x$. Equivalently, $f^{-1}(f(x)) = x$ for all x in the **domain** of f. A **many-to-one function** can also be loosely defined to have an inverse by restricting the domain or accepting a **multivalued function**.

inverse kinematics (IK)   The process of calculating the motion required by a series of connected rigid bodies to achieve a particular goal

inverse matrix   Of a **square matrix** $\mathbf{M}$, with non-zero **determinant**, the matrix $\mathbf{M}^{-1}$ such that $\mathbf{M}^{-1}\mathbf{M} = \mathbf{M}\mathbf{M}^{-1} = \mathbf{I}$, where $\mathbf{I}$ is the appropriate-sized **identity** matrix

inversely proportional   Two values x and y are inversely proportional if there is some **constant** k such that $x = \frac{k}{y}$ for all valid values of x and y; cf **proportional**

inverse-square law   A **formula** relating two quantities x and y, saying that x is **inversely proportional** to the **square** of y

irrational numbers   The **set** of **real numbers**, such as π and the **square root** of 2, which are not **rational**

isosceles triangle   A triangle with two of its sides having equal length

iterative function   An **algorithm** that works by successively using the results of each step in the next; cf **recursive function**

kinetic energy   The **energy** of a moving object, defined as half the **square** of its **speed** multiplied by its **mass**, with similar calculations for **angular velocity**

kinetic friction   The **friction** between two surfaces moving relatively to each other; cf **static friction**

Lambertian reflection   See **diffuse reflection**

lamina   An idealized object in three-**dimensional** space with a thickness of 0

law   Also called a "physical law," a **formula** that states some kind of supposedly fundamental truth about the physical world, usually false

leading diagonal   Of a **matrix** $\left(m_{ij} \right)$, the values along the diagonal from top left to bottom right, with values m_{ii}

leaf node   Of a **tree**, a **node** with no **children**

line segment   A **curve** of points with **position vectors** $\mathbf{a} + t\mathbf{v}$ for some vectors $\mathbf{a}$ and $\mathbf{v}$ and some value $0 \le t \le 1$

linear function   A **polynomial** of **degree** 1

local maximum/local minimum   A local maximum is a value of some **function** f for some values of its **arguments** such that all values of f for nearby arguments are less (similarly "local minimum"); cf **global maximum**

locus   The **set** of points with a particular property (for example, a straight line is the locus of a point in a plane at an equal **distance** from two other points)

logarithm   The **inverse** of the **power** function: for two numbers a and b, a number x such that $b^x = a$. b is called the "base."

lowest common multiple   For two **natural numbers** a and b, the smallest number that is an **integer multiple** of both a and b

lowest terms   Of a **fraction**, means that the **numerator** and **denominator** are **coprime**

magnitude   The length of a **vector** defined by the Pythagorean formula as the **square root** of the **sum** of its **components**

many-to-one function   Of a **function**, states that several elements in the **domain** can map to the same element in the **range**; cf **one-to-one** and **multivalued function**

map   See **function**

mass   The property of matter that defines how much **force** is required to make it **accelerate**; also called **inertia**

matrix   A two-dimensional array of **real numbers**

maximum   A point on the **graph** of some **function** where it is at its highest. For a smooth curve, the **gradient** is zero; see also **local maximum**, **global maximum**

mean   For n values, the **sum** of the values divided by n; cf **average**

mechanics   The study of objects in motion or **equilibrium**

mesh   A shape in a computer-generated 3D world, consisting of a number of **vertices** connected by **polygons**

minimax   In a game, the move for any player that minimizes their maximum possible loss (equivalently, maximizes their minimum possible gain). Hence an **algorithm** making use of this concept to find the best strategy for playing a game.

minimum   A point on the **graph** of some **function** where it is at its lowest. For a smooth curve, the **gradient** is zero; see also **local maximum**, **global maximum**

mip-map   A **texture map** in several variants of different sizes used to create smooth shading over distance

model   A shape created in a computer-generated 3D world, made from a **mesh**

modulo   A **function** mapping the **set** of **integers** to the **finite set** $\{0, 1, \ldots, m-1\}$ for some **natural number** m, by mapping each number to its **remainder** when divided by m; also called a "congruence relation"

moment of inertia   The angular equivalent of **mass**, which for a **particle** is equal to the **product** of its mass and the **square** of its **distance** from the **axis of rotation**

momentum   The **product** of an object's **mass** and **velocity**; see **conservation of momentum**

multivalued function   Of a **function**, states that some elements in the **domain** can be mapped to more than one element in the **range** (this is not a function in a strict definition of the word); cf **one-to-one** and **many-to-one function**

natural numbers   The set of "counting numbers" including zero: 0, 1, 2, …, denoted by the symbol $\mathbb{N}$

neural network   An idealized model of a simple brain made of artificial 'neurons' or nerve cells

network   A **graph** in which the edges have been assigned a value, usually representing a "cost" of some kind

node   A virtual object, such as a **vertex** of a **graph** or element of 3D space

normal   Of two **vectors**, means that they are **perpendicular**. Of a **surface**, means a vector perpendicular to the surface.

normalized   Of a **vector**, the result of dividing it by its **magnitude** to get a **unit vector**

NURBS   Non-Uniform Rational B-**Spline**: a **curve** or **surface** defined by a number of points in space (**nodes**), a set of **weights** defining the importance

numerator   In a **fraction**, the number on the top (also called the "dividend")

numeric solution   The result of finding the values of the **unknowns** in an **equation** by searching for the specific numbers which make the equation true (as opposed to an **algebraic solution**)

obtuse angle   An **angle** greater than a **right angle** but less than a straight line

octree   See **quadtree**

one-to-one function   Of a **function**, states that each element in the **domain** is mapped to exactly one element in the **range**, and vice versa; cf **many-to-one** and **multivalued function**

operator   A **function** that maps one or more **arguments** from a particular **set** to a single result in the same set. We usually think of the binary operators such as $+, -, \times, \div$.

origin   A point defined as the starting point of some **basis**

orthogonal   Of two or more **vectors**, means that they are mutually at **right angles**

orthonormal basis   A **basis** where the basis **vectors** are **orthogonal** and have a **magnitude** of 1

oscillation   A motion that repeats over time, such as a bouncing **spring** or an object bobbing on water; see **frequency, period, amplitude**

out of phase   Of two **oscillations**, means that they have the same **frequency** but their **phase** is different, or specifically is half the **period**

pairwise multiplication   Of two **vectors**, the **operator** that creates a vector from the **products** of each **component** of the **arguments**: for example, the pairwise product of the vectors $\begin{pmatrix} 2 & 3 \end{pmatrix}$ and $\begin{pmatrix} 1 & -2 \end{pmatrix}$ is the vector $\begin{pmatrix} 2 & -6 \end{pmatrix}$

parabola   A **curve** in two dimensions, the **graph** of a **quadratic function**

parallel   Of two **vectors**, means that one is a **scalar** multiple of the other. Of two lines, means that any vector on one is parallel to any vector on the other.

parallelogram   A **quadrilateral** with two pairs of **parallel** sides

parameter   An element in a **function** that can be varied to create a family of different functions with similar properties

parameterization   Defining some **curve** or **surface** in terms of a **parametric equation**

parametric equation/parametric function   A set of **formulas** relating one or more **variables** to one or more **real**-valued **parameters**. Similarly, parametric function

parent node   In a **tree**, the **node** next in line from any particular node toward the **root node**; cf **child node**

partial derivative   The **derivative** of a **curve** drawn on a **surface**

particle   An idealized object in space, with a size of zero but some **mass**, as well as perhaps other properties

particular solution   A **function** for which a **differential equation** holds true, given particular **initial conditions**; cf **general solution**

partitioning tree   A **tree** representing a group of objects in space according to their relative positions

perimeter   The **curve** or **surface** defining the outer border of some shape

period   The time taken for some oscillator to complete a single **oscillation**; cf **frequency**

perpendicular   Of two vectors, means that they are at **right angles**; cf **orthogonal**

perturbation   Altering a value by some small amount

phase   Of two **waves** with the same **waveform**, the distance by which their **wavefronts** are separated at a particular time

plane   The **locus** of a point in space at the same **distance** from two defined points. Equivalently, it has **position vector** $\mathbf{a} + t\mathbf{v} + s\mathbf{w}$, where $\mathbf{a}$, $\mathbf{v}$, and $\mathbf{w}$ are defined **vectors** and t and s are **parameters**.

ply   In a game, a move by one player

point of inflection   A point on the **graph** of some **function** where its second **derivative** is zero

polygon   A closed shape made up of a number of straight **line segments** connecting the same number of **vertices**

polyhedron   A closed 3D shape whose **perimeter** is a number of **polygons** joined by straight edges

polynomial   A **function** in one **variable**, consisting entirely of **terms** of the form ax^n, such as $2x^3 + 3x^2 - 4$

position vector   A **vector** from the **origin** to a particular point

potential energy   The **energy** held by an object under the influence of an external **force**, particularly gravity, a stretched spring, magnetic fields, etc. Generally, the amount of **work** a system is capable of doing.

power   1. A number obtained by multiplying a value by itself a certain number of times, so 8 is the third power of 2, denoted 2^3. More generally, it can be defined as the power **function** mapping pairs of numbers to either a **real** or a **complex number**. 2. The amount of **work** done (**energy** released or used) by a system or machine over time

prime factors   For two **natural numbers** a and b, a **prime number** that is a **factor** of both a and b

prime number   A **natural number** greater than 1 with no **factors** other than itself or 1

principle of relativity   The principle that all physical calculations should be independent of the **reference frame** within which they are calculated

product   The result of multiplying two values

projectile   An object moving under gravity

projection   A **map** that reduces the number of **dimensions** of a space, such as mapping a sphere to a circle

projection plane   The virtual **plane** in space representing the position of the image we are looking at through a particular camera

proportional   Two values x and y are proportional, or "in proportion," if there is some **constant of proportionality** k such that $x = ky$ for all valid values of x and y; cf **inversely proportional**

quadrant   An area of the **Cartesian plane** such that all the points are of the same sign in each of their **coordinates**

quadratic function   A polynomial of degree 2

quadrilateral   A 4-sided **polygon**

quadtree   A **partitioning tree** in 2D space, in which objects are divided according to their position within successively smaller squares (in 3D, an **octree**)

quaternion   A special kind of 4D **vector**, the vector equivalent of a **complex number**

quotient   Either the result of dividing one number by another (see **fraction**) or the **integer** part of this division (see **modulo**)

radians   A unit of **angle**, defined as $1/2\pi$ of a **circle**

radius   The **distance** of a point on the **circumference** of a **circle** from its center

radians   A unit of **angle**, defined as $1/2\pi$ of a **circle radius** The **distance** of a point on the **circumference** of a **circle** from its center **radix point** In column number notation, the dot which signifies the end of the **integer** part of the number (also called the 'decimal point') **range**. The **set** of values returned by a **function**.

radix point   In column number notation, the dot that signifies the end of the **integer** part of the number

range   The **set** of values returned by a **function**

rate of change   The amount by which a value changes over time—equivalent to the **derivative** with respect to time

rational numbers   The set of numbers that can be represented as a **fraction** of two **integers**, denoted by the symbol $\mathbb{Q}$

ray   A line in 3D space from a given point to infinity

real numbers   The set of numbers that can be represented on an infinitely precise number line, denoted by the symbol $\mathbb{R}$

reciprocal   For any number n, the **fraction** $\frac{1}{n}$

rectilinear   Of a system of lines, means that any two are either **parallel** or **perpendicular**

recursive function   An **algorithm** that works by calculating each step in terms of the same algorithm applied to a simpler case, until it finds a case simple enough to solve directly; cf **iterative function**

reductio ad absurdum   A process of deduction where we prove something to be true by assuming it is false and deducing a contradiction: "if x were true then y would be true, but we know y is false therefore x must be false"

reference frame   In a physical situation, the **basis** of the physical space along with a reference **velocity** used to define all other calculations; see **principle of relativity**

reflection   A **transformation** that moves each point to another point opposite it in some mirror line or plane

reflex angle   An angle greater than two **right angles**

refraction   A phenomenon where a **wave** changes its direction of travel as a result of changing its **speed**

remainder   When dividing one **natural number** n by another, m, the value r such that $0 \leq r < m$ and $n = am + r$ for some natural number a

resonance   A phenomenon where an **oscillation** gradually increases in **amplitude**, as a result of an oscillating **force** of the same **frequency**

rhombus   A **parallelogram** whose sides are all of equal length

right angle   An **angle** of 90 **degrees** or $\pi/2$ **radians**

right-angled triangle   A triangle with one of its **angles** being a **right angle**

rigid-body transformation   A **transformation** which preserves **angles** between lines

root   Of a **function** f, a value x such that $f(x) = 0$

root node   Of a **tree**, the **node** with no **parent**

rotation   A **transformation** that moves each point by some **angle** around a particular center

saddle point   Of a **surface**, a point which is a **local maximum** in one direction and a **local minimum** in another

scalar   A value that is not a **vector**, that is, it has no direction; alternatively, a vector of **dimension** 1

scalar product   The **sum** of the pairwise **products** of the **components** of two **vectors**, written with a dot as $\mathbf{u} \cdot \mathbf{v}$: for example, the scalar product of the vectors $\begin{pmatrix} 2 & 3 \end{pmatrix}$ and $\begin{pmatrix} 1 & -2 \end{pmatrix}$ is the sum $2 \times 1 + 3 \times (-2)$ (also called the **dot product**)

scale   A **transformation** that moves each point to some multiple of its **vector** relative to some reference point

search space   The **set** of all potential solutions to a problem

search tree   A **tree** representing all the possible moves in a game, or equivalent for similar problems, which some **algorithm** is sought to solve

set   An unordered collection of objects ("elements"), which may be **finite** (the set {1,3,5,7}), **countable** (the set of all odd numbers), or **uncountable** (the set of all numbers between 0 and 1)

shear   A **transformation** that moves each point by a multiple of a **vector, parallel** to some reference line or plane, proportionally to its distance from this line or plane

signed   Of a value, indicates that it may be positive or negative (e.g., the signed distance of a point from a line is positive in one direction, negative in the other)

similar   Of two shapes, says that they are identical except for a **scale transformation**

simple harmonic motion   A **sinusoidal oscillation**, generally associated with the motion of a stretched **spring**; cf **damped harmonic motion**

simplification   The process of manipulating a **function** or **statement** algebraically to put it into a more tractable form

simultaneous equations   Two or more **equations** in the same **unknowns,** which are all considered to hold true for the same set of solutions

sinusoidal   Having the form of the function $A\sin(\omega x + c)$, where A is the **amplitude**, ω is the **frequency** and c is the **phase**

specular reflection   Light **reflected** from a **surface** directly, such that the **angle of incidence** equals the **angle of reflection** (mirror reflection); cf **diffuse reflection**

speed   The **distance** traveled by a moving object over time

sphere   The **locus** of a point in (usually 3D) space at a constant distance from a particular center

spline   A **curve** defined by some **parametric function**

spring   An object that can extend, experiencing a **tension** as a result, and may also be compressed; see **extension**, **coefficient of elasticity**

square   Either: a planar shape with four sides of equal length and four **right angles**; or: the result of multiplying a number by itself

square matrix   A **matrix** that has the same number of rows as columns

square root   The **inverse** of the square function x^2: the square root of x is a number that when multiplied by itself gives the answer x

stable strategy   In a game, a set of strategies for the players such that if any single player changes strategy, they do worse than before

standard deviation   A measure of the spread of a set of values, defined as the **square root** of the **mean** squared distance of the values from their own **mean**

statement   A numerical "sentence" relating some values to one another

static friction   The **friction** between two surfaces exerting a force on one another but not moving relatively to each other; cf **kinetic friction**

substitution   The process of evaluating a **function** for a particular set of values of its **arguments**

subtend   If you draw a triangle from some point P to two points on the **perimeter** of an object, the **angle** at P for the largest possible such triangle is said to be the angle subtended by the object at P (P is often an observer of the object)

sum   The result of adding two values

surface   A **set** of connected points in space definable by a pair of continuous **parameters**

surface of rotation   For some **function** f(x), the **locus** of a point in 3D space whose **perpendicular** distance from the x-**axis** is equal to f(x) at any x-**coordinate**

tangent   A straight line (or plane) that touches some **curve** or **surface** at a particular point without passing through it (i.e., it has the same **gradient** as the curve at that point)

tends to a limit   Of a sequence of values $a_1, a_2, \ldots$, this says that there is some value x such that for any small number d we can find a number N such that for every $n > N$, $|a_n - x| < d$

tension   The **force** in an object being pulled from each end, such as a string or **spring**

tensor   A generalization of the concepts of **vector, matrix,** and **scalar**: an array of values in one or more **dimensions**

term   An element of an **expression** consisting only of a constant value multiplied by some combination of **variables,** such as $5xy^2$

terminal velocity   The maximum downward **speed** of a falling object as a result of the **air resistance,** or generally of any object experiencing **drag** or **friction**

texel   A point of a **texture map**

texture map   An **image map** describing the reaction of a **surface** to light at particular points

topology   The study of the shapes of objects without reference to **distance,** using only notions of connectedness, holes, twists, etc. Hence, these properties of an object.

top-down   An artificial intelligence methodology where programs act on the basis of explicit rules or goals; cf **bottom-up**

torque   The angular equivalent of **force,** defined as force $\times$ **perpendicular distance** from the **axis of rotation**

torus   A 3D shape, the **locus** of a point whose **perpendicular distance** from a particular **circle** is **constant**

transform   A special kind of 4×4 **matrix** representing an **affine transformation** of **homogeneous coordinates**

transformation   A **map** from one set of points to another in some space

translation   A **transformation** that adds a constant **vector** to each point in the space

transpose   Of a **matrix M,** describes the matrix whose rows are the columns of **M** and vice versa

trapezium   A **quadrilateral** with a pair of **parallel** sides

tree   A **graph** in which each **node** has exactly one **parent** (except the **root node**) and zero or more **children,** and with no loops

trigonometric functions   The **functions** relating the **angles** in a **right-angled triangle** to the lengths of its sides

trigonometric identities   **Formulas** relating the various **trigonometric functions** to one another

trigonometry   The study of the properties of triangles

turning point   A point on the **graph** of some **function** where its **derivative** (and all **partial derivatives** for a **surface**) is zero. May be a **maximum, minimum, point of inflection,** or **saddle point.**

uncountable set   A **set** with an infinite number of elements that cannot be listed even in infinite time

unit vector   A **vector** with a **magnitude** of 1

unknown   An element in an **equation** or other statement whose value is to be found by presuming the statement to be true

utility function A method for evaluating a particular solution to a search problem when using e.g., a **genetic algorithm**

variable An element in a **function** that can be replaced throughout by some value from the **domain** in order to return some other value (also called an argument); also a generic term used to cover constants, parameters, and unknowns

vector An ordered set of two or more **real numbers** (or other values more generally) that can be added together by adding their **components**, and can be multiplied by a **scalar**

vector product The 3D **vector** formed by combining two other such **vectors** such that its **magnitude** is equal to the **product** of their magnitudes with the sine of the angle between them, and its direction is **perpendicular** to both (also called the **cross product**)

velocity The **vector** traveled by a moving object over time; the vector equivalent of **speed**

vertex A corner of a shape. In a **graph**, equivalent to a **node**. (pl. vertices).

view frustrum The volume of space visible from a particular camera

viewport The area of the **projection plane** visible on the screen

visible light Light whose **wavelength** lies within the range detectable by the human eye (approximately 10^{-7}m)

wave A phenomenon where a group of **coupled oscillators** transfer **energy** from one place to another

waveform The shape of the **graph** of a particular **wave** measuring **distance** from **equilibrium** through space

wavefront The **surface** in space representing equivalent points in the **oscillation** of a **wave** as it travels

wavelength The **distance** between successive **wavefronts** of a **wave**

weight The force acting on an object as a result of gravity, proportional to its mass; also a value representing the relative importance of a value in a sum (see weighted sum)

weighted sum Of a set of values $x_1, x_2, ...$, the result of adding together the values multiplied by some pre-defined values $w_1, w_2, ...$, i.e., the **sum** $\sum_i w_i x_i$

work The **energy** given up by an object to induce movement in some other object

zero-sum game A game in which players compete for "money," where at each stage, the total amount of "money" is **constant**

THE GREEK ALPHABET

Greek letters are often used in mathematics, and it's useful to know how to read them out loud. Many of them tend to appear in standard contexts, some of which are listed here (some are rarely used because they look too much like Roman letters).

Greek Letter	English Name	Mathematical Usage
α	Alpha	Often symbolizes an angle
β	Beta	Often symbolizes an angle
γ	Gamma	Often symbolizes an angle
δ	Delta	An infinitesimally small number, especially in calculus
ϵ	Epsilon	An infinitesimally small number, especially in functional analysis
ζ	Zeta	Occasionally symbolizes an angle
η	Eta	Occasionally symbolizes an angle
θ	Theta	Usually symbolizes an angle
ι	Iota	Rarely used
κ	Kappa	Rarely used
λ	Lambda	The symbol for wavelength, also used to symbolize a ratio or proportion, especially eigenvalues
μ	Mu	The symbol for "micro," or a one-millionth-part; also the symbol for various material constants such as the coefficient of friction
ν	Nu	Rarely used
ξ	Xi	Sometimes symbolizes an angle
o	Omicron	Rarely used
π	Pi	The constant value 3.14159..., the ratio of the circumference of a circle to its diameter
ρ	Rho	The symbol for pressure, and used for some material constants
σ	Sigma	Used for some material constants
τ	Tau	Rarely used
υ	Upsilon	Rarely used
ϕ	Phi	Often symbolizes an angle or frequency, also the constant 1.618..., the golden ratio
χ	Chi	Sometimes symbolizes an angle
ψ	Psi	Sometimes symbolizes an angle or frequency
ω	Omega	Often used for the frequency of an oscillation or rotation, and a number of other physical properties

B Language References and Pseudocode

The "pseudocode" used in this book is actually rather more complete than the term usually implies. Pseudocode in general means a stripped-down algorithm with lots of English sentences such as set p to the nearest point to q, or even just find the nearest point to q. Although the code samples in this book do include some examples of this kind of shorthand, in general they are far closer to an actual working algorithm, just presented in a human-readable form.

As stated in the Introduction, the main inspiration for the pseudocode used here is the "old-style" or "verbose" syntax of the language Lingo, first because this allows a reasonably easy translation to and from the examples on the CD-ROM, and second because this language is extremely readable. Because the examples on the CD-ROM are in actual Lingo, and because this language is likely to be unfamiliar with many readers working in C++, Java, ActionScript, or many other languages, it is sensible to have a quick explanation of the terminology and how it translates to other languages.

ON THE CD

The following is only the briefest of introductions, designed for those who are already familiar with some kind of programming language—although any nonprogrammers who have reached this far will probably be able to cope! It should also be noted that for the majority of functions illustrated on the CD-ROM, very little of this is necessary to know: you only really need it if you want to dig deeper into the more complex examples such as *collisions.dir* where the functions are put into use in a real context. Further details of the organization of the CD-ROM can be found in Appendix C.

Objects

Lingo is an *object-oriented* language, with some quirks that make it different from more conventional compiled languages such as C++. An *object* is a piece of code that has its own identity in memory and can be treated as an autonomous program. Each object is an *instance* of a *class*: a class is like a template from which any number of copies can be struck, each of which then becomes an individual in its own right. Lingo allows us to control both pre-defined objects that come as part of the Director engine (the sprite, cast member and member type objects, for example) and user-defined objects created as *parent scripts*. (A "script" is a piece of code.)

Lingo can also be placed in *movie scripts*, which have a global scope and can be accessed by any other Lingo function. The great majority of functions from this book are held in movie scripts for clarity, although this is not what one would probably do with most of them in a real-life context.

Data Types

Lingo is a *loosely typed* language, meaning that we don't need to specify what kind of data is held in a particular variable, or returned by a particular function. It's quite easy to switch between most of the following data types:

Boolean: (TRUE or FALSE); essentially identical to the numbers 1 and 0

Integer: a standard 32-bit integer

Float: a single-precision floating-point number

String: a string of ASCII characters (double-byte characters can be used if specified)

Symbol: A data type peculiar to Lingo—in a sense, the symbol is to a string what a float is to an integer. Symbols are represented by the hash sign and are used for "labels" like #positive. They're just like strings but can have no spaces or non-alphanumeric characters and are not case-sensitive

List: Lists are the equivalent of "linked lists" in other languages: an array with no defined length. Lists are actually objects and have a number of methods for setting, deleting, or searching for values

Point / Vector: Specialized lists of two and three floating-point values. The vector object has methods such as getNormalized() and dot(). Similarly there are other specialized list objects such as rect, transform, rgb, time, etc.

Object: This covers everything else. As we said above, most things in Lingo are objects.

The loosely typed nature of Lingo allows us to do things like this:

```
set number to 7
if number then
    return "yes"
else
    return "no"
end if
```

This returns "yes" so Lingo is quite happy to treat a number as a Boolean for the sake of `if` statements, and operators and so on.

Variables

There are three kinds of *variables* in Lingo:

Local variables: exist only during the running of a particular function (method; handler). These include function arguments, as well as any variable specified during the course of the function. Because they are local, there is no need to worry about naming conflicts. In this book we try to use only local variables unless it makes things harder to read

Property variables: are held by a particular object. Each instance of an object can have its own values for these variables: for example, the standard Sprite object has the properties `loc`, `width`, `height` and so on. Some of these properties can be set directly, others can't. One of the drawbacks of Lingo is that it is not possible to create either Private or Read-only properties in a user-defined object. In a script object, we create a property variable by declaring it, usually at the beginning of the script, by saying something like `property pSize`. An object property is accessed using dot syntax (`object.propertyName`) or verbose syntax (`the propertyName of object`). In the example movies, the prefix letter `p` is used to name property variables, as in `pName`, `pMember`.

Global variables: have the scope of the whole movie, and can be accessed at any time. Although there's nothing wrong with using global variables, many see it as a sign of poor program organization, and they are only very rarely used on the CD-ROM.

Lingo has only quite basic operators: `+ - * / =`. It does not have equivalents to common features of other languages such as the increment operator `++`, or the distinction between "equals" (`==`) and "set to" (`=`). So the equivalent of `a+=b` could be any of the following (from most verbose to most succinct):

```
set a to a+b
set a = a+b
a = a+b
```

Notice that in the pseudocode of this book we do use increment operators, written as, for example, `add b to a`

Functions, Methods, and Handlers

As well as properties, each object has various *methods*, which are functions that can be addressed to the object. Here is an example of a complete Lingo parent script, which is assigned to the cast member "name object". A cast member is an object that contains information Director can use; see the next section.

```
property pName

on new me, nm
    pName=nm
    return me
end

on getName me
    return pName
end

on setName me, nm
    pName=nm
    return true
end
```

We start with the property declaration, setting pName as a property variable. Now we have Lingo's *constructor* method new(). This allows us to create a new object as follows:

```
nameObj=script("name object").new("Bobby")
put nameObj.getName()
  -- "Bobby"
nameObj.setName("Sue-Ellen")
put nameObj.getName()
  -- "Sue-Ellen"
```

The first line of code creates a new instance of the object, and assigns it to the variable nameObj. In the next line, we access the object's getName() method and the put command is used to print it to Director's Message window, a panel for text output (shown indented). Finally we invoke the setName() method to change the name of the object, and output this new name to the Message window to ensure it is correct.

The Message window can also be used to input commands, usually for testing purposes.

Sprites, Cast Members, and Score

Director itself is essentially an engine for compositing graphics (and sound) using Lingo to add interactivity. All graphics, and indeed everything in Director, is stored in an area called a *cast library* or just *cast*, with each item held as a *cast member*, a special object with a name, number, and indicator of the data type held. Each member type has its own properties and methods.

Graphic cast members can be placed onscreen (the *stage*) as *sprites*: each cast member is assigned to a particular *sprite channel*. It's possible to change which cast member is assigned to a channel while the program is running by changing the member property of the sprite (sprite(10).member=member("happy face")). Other important sprite properties include

.loc: The sprite's position on screen relative to the top-left corner (a point object)

.rect: The bounding rectangle of the sprite (a rect object)

.width, .height: The width and height of the bounding rectangle (integers)

.ink: the method used to composite the sprite with its background (an integer or symbol)

A sprite can have one or more scripts attached to it, called *behaviors*. These are also cast members, and each behavior is simply an instance of the script object, just like the plain script objects we saw before. The behaviors allow us to add interactivity to a particular sprite. Each behavior can receive various *events*, such as whether the mouse has been clicked on the sprite. These are treated just like any other method: simply create a handler in the behavior to accept them like this:

```
property pMouseDown
property pSprite
property pNormal, pDown, pRoll

on beginSprite me
    pMouseDown=0
    pSprite=sprite(me.spritenum)
    pNormal=pSprite.member
    pDown=member(pNormal.name&&"down")
    pRoll=member(pNormal.name&&"roll")
end

on mouseEnter me
    if pMouseDown then pSprite.member=pDown
    else pSprite.member=pRoll
end
```

```
on mouseLeave me
    pSprite.member=pNormal
end

on mouseDown me
    pSprite.member=pDown
    pMouseDown=1
end

on mouseUp me
    pSprite.member=pRoll
    pMouseDown=0
end

on mouseUpOutside me
    pMouseDown=0
end
```

This is an example of a complete "button" behavior in Director. When the engine first encounters a sprite with this behavior on it, the beginSprite event occurs, which causes the behavior to initialize the various properties. Notice that it works out which cast members represent the up, down, and roll states of the button by looking at the name of the cast member initially assigned to the sprite. The other events are all received whenever the user interacts with the sprite, either by rolling over it with the mouse or clicking (mouseUpOutside is received when the user releases the mouse, having previously clicked the sprite).

Notice that all these events include an argument which is usually assigned the parameter me. This allows the behavior to reference itself during the running of the movie.

Behaviors can be given a special method, getPropertyDescriptionList, which allow us to set the initial values of the properties of a behavior instance.

Ancestry

Director allows a form of inheritance, where objects can extend their methods and properties by including a special ancestor property. If an object has an ancestor, then any function calls sent to that object, if not picked up by the object itself, are passed to the ancestor. So a generic "colliding shape" script can have an ancestor which says it's a "circular colliding shape," which in turn has an ancestor saying that it's a "bounding circle" for another "colliding shape" and so on. Alternatively, the ancestor chain can go the other way, so that a behavior could have a standard "button" ancestor which gives its sprite the features of a button. There are all kinds of arguments about different inheritance models, but we steamroller blithely over them in this book.

Just to reiterate: you don't need to know much of this to understand most of the code in the CD-ROM. Objects, behaviors, sprites, and so on are only relevant to the demo movies, not to most of the code examples from the book. If you do want to learn more about Lingo, there are many books out there—see Appendix D.

NOTE

ON THE CD

RECURSION

Although this is not a Director-specific issue, recursion is such a fundamental part of programming style that it's worth giving it a little space of its own, especially because we use it extensively in this book. The essence of recursion is to define a function in terms of a simpler version of itself. It's often the most elegant way to define an algorithm. For example, let's consider the factorial function $n!$, defined as $1 \times 2 \times \ldots \times n$, and as 1 for $n = 0$. To calculate it, we could use a loop, like this (we'll use Lingo here rather than pseudocode, since we're in that mode for this Appendix):

```
on factorial n
   c=1
   repeat with i=1 to n
      c=c*i
   end repeat
   return c
end
```

Alternatively, we could use the shorter, and in many ways neater, formulation:

```
on factorial n
   if n=0 then return 1
   return n*factorial(n-1)
end
```

A *recursive function* has two parts: one or more *bottoming-out conditions*, stating what to do in a simple case, and a *recursive step* where the argument is broken into simpler parts and the function is called again. It's vital that any recursive function always reaches its bottoming out case, or it'll get into an endless loop. The opposite is an *iterative function* which gives a first step and then a means of getting to each successive step (as well as an *upper bound* for the loop).

Appendix

C

About the CD-ROM

The CD-ROM accompanying *Mathematics and Physics for Programmers* includes a large number of sample files that demonstrate techniques from the chapters, as well as solutions to a few of the exercises. The CD-ROM also contains a full set of all of the figures from the book.

FOLDERS

Demos: Contains the support files for the MPFP demo program, in a protected format.

Docs: Contains the text files, in html format, of the code samples.

Figures: Contains all of the figures from the book, organized in folders by chapter.

Source: Contains the original Macromedia Director movies used to create the demos.

ABOUT THE CODE SAMPLES

There are three ways to view these code samples.

1. Through the executable file *MPFP.exe*. Using this you can view the various demos by means of the File menu, and also read and try out most of the code samples through the Code Reader utility. The executable should work on most computers, with very few demos requiring a particularly fast machine. A 3D graphics card would be appropriate for some of the 3D elements, but is not essential (for full specifications, see the book cover).

2. As Macromedia Director movies in the folder *Source*. For this you will need a copy of Macromedia Director 8.5 or later (see Appendix D for details of how to obtain a trial version). The Director files do not include all the user-interface elements of the executable (such as the code viewer and navigation elements), since some of these use proprietary Xtras which mean you would not be able to make changes to the code; however, when running in Director you shouldn't need to use these additional elements. These files should work equally well on both Windows and MacOS. Full details of how these files are organised will be explained below.

3. As text files in HTML format, contained in the *Docs* folder. These files (mostly taken from the file *math.cst*) are simple transcriptions of the key finctions derived from the book, but in general do not include any user-interface or display code. The HTML files are cross-referenced by hyperlinks, so you can move between different functions (it is recommended that you start from the file *Documentation Index.html* on the root of the CD-ROM and navigate from there to the code you are interested in). The only different file is *collisionsFull.rtf*, which contains a full listing of all the code from the *collisions* demo.

Additional files, including more answers to Exercises, updates, and samples in other programming languages, can be found on the book's Web site at *http://www.charlesriver.com/titles/mathphysics.html*.

To install the Director files onto your own computer to work with them, simply copy the folder *Source* to your machine. You can run the executable directly from the CD-ROM or copy it to your machine along with the *Demos* folder. Any additional files or updates from the Web site should be placed into the *Demos* folder, except for updates to the executable itself (full details will be included alongside any files on the site). The files in this folder are protected to ensure that they work correctly, but they are simply copies of the files in *Source*.

Most of the functions included in this book are to be found in the external cast library *math.cst*, which has to be in the same folder as the other demos. A few others which are relevant or particularly important have also been documented. Very few of them are exact replicas of the pseudocode in the book; most of them have refinements, or have been adapted slightly to fit in with the needs of the accompanying demos, just as they would be in a real-life situation. However, no attempt has been made to make them optimally fast: comprehensibility takes first place to speed. Similarly, few of them include extensive error checking, so it is up to you to ensure you pass the appropriate arguments to each function (particularly when using the Code Reader utility).

The more complex or interesting functions are accompanied by demos to show them in action (the simpler functions tend to be used in every movie). The most difficult demo of all is *collisions.dir*, which is a generic 2D physics simulation. This is significantly more sophisticated than the other demos, and deserves a little explanation (you need to be reasonably comfortable with OOP to work successfully with this movie).

collisions.dir

Each shape is a sprite, with a *moving object* behavior attached. This behavior, which handles the drawing of the shape on the screen and includes information about its position, mass, velocity and orientation, inherits one of a number of script objects specific to its shape, such as *shape circle*. These mostly handle collision detection.

Some shapes have other shapes slaved to them, such as the rectangle, which includes four line segment objects and four vertices. These are "virtual" — they're invisible to the *moving object* behavior, but they can detect collisions in their own right. Each of them is an instance of the *child shape* script, which is equivalent to the *moving object* behavior, and calculates its position, velocity and so on with reference to the parent shape.

It's possible to specify a bounding shape for any object (and any rotating object automatically has a bounding circle attached). These are inserted into the chain at the topmost level. So a rotating rectangle is going to have the structure shown in Figure C.1, where a vertical line indicates inheritance, and a horizontal line indicates a reference to another object slaved to its parent. The name of the script containing the code is shown in italics at the bottom of each box.

When detecting collisions between shapes, their bounding box is checked first (to all intents and purposes, they *are* the bounding shape until it is intersected). Only if there is an overlap with this bounding shape is the underlying object checked.

Each object handles its own collision detection, with each collision pair held in one or other of the objects involved. Most of these are divided into spinning and non-spinning versions. Each collision function returns either #none or a list such as [#t:0.5, #normal:point(1,0), #moment1:point(10,5.2), #moment2:point(-5,10.4), #ref1:..., #ref2:...], where the two 'ref' properties are references to the underlying colliding objects. In any time period, the collision with the lowest time value is executed first, with the result being handled by one of the resolution functions (depending on whether each of the objects is free to rotate or move linearly, or both).

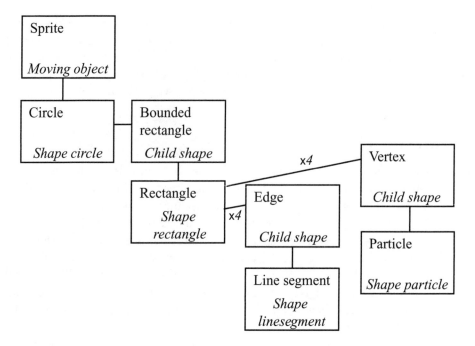

FIGURE C.1   An object diagram of a rotating rectangle in collisions.dir.

Naturally, this is fairly hard to follow, but it's difficult to find a better way to handle the generality of the problem without a complex structure of this kind (although OOP purists would probably be horrified). However, this at least means that you can see an example of these functions being used in a more sophisticated context. The engine is definitely a work in progress, and new elements will probably be added from time to time and posted on the book website.

Other Demos

The other included demos, in chapter order, are:

Each of these includes some notes on its workings and suggestions for further development. Any bug reports or further suggestions would be welcome.

File name	Related chapter	Content
javelin.dir	7	Click and drag the javelin to throw it
inside.dir	10	Draw a polygon and then check whether a point is inside or outside it (using raycasting)
splines.dir	10 and 21	Draw Bezier curves, Catmull-Rom splines, and NURBS
collisionMaps.dir	10	Draw a bitmap, then convert it to a collision map with calculated normals
pool.dir	11, 13, 14	The complete pool game, with and without spin
orbits.dir	12	A virtual solar system (see notes in the chapter about its limitations)
springs.dir	16	Various examples of springs using different calculation methods
simple3D.dir	17	A very basic 3D wireframe world, with backface culling but no *z*-ordering
collisions3D.dir	19	A simple 3D walkthrough world, using ellipsoidal collision detection for the player
textures.dir	20	An example of different texture mappings applied to a simple 3D shape
tileScroller.dir	22	A scrolling tile-based 2D world, navigable with the cursor keys
mazes.dir	23	Various maze generation, search and lighting examples
tictactoe.dir	24	A program to generate a perfect tic-tac-toe strategy, and play it against you
headsOrTails.dir	24	A program that tries to outguess you at heads or tails
geneticAlgorithms.dir	25	A genetic algorithm to solve the eight queens problem

SYSTEM REQUIREMENTS

To run the executable file:

- Windows 95, 98, ME, NT4, 2000, XP
- 266 MHz processor with a current hardware accelerated 3D graphics card or 300 MHz Intel Pentium II processor without a current hardware accelerated 3D graphics card.
- 32 MB or more of available RAM
- 256-color monitor capable of 800 x 600 resolution
- DirectX 5.0 or greater (recommended)

To view the Director demos (folder Source):

- A Windows computer with Macromedia Director 8.5.1 or later installed. (Any computer capable of running Director can view the demos: see Macromedia's Web site for their minimum specifications)

To view the HTML files and figures:

- Any computer with a Web browser installed.

Further Reading and Resources

As a good general rule, if the material in a book like this is original, this is probably because it's wrong. Mathematics doesn't change much (it grows, but what was true yesterday remains true today), and most of the facts and methods described in this book are well-known and standard. This means that if there is anything you are having trouble understanding, there are a great many other resources you could use to help you out. In this Appendix, we'll list a number of resources which were helpful in compiling this book, although there were many others which aren't included, and as mentioned in the Acknowledgments, thanks are due to all those who created these sites.

Unlike the rest of the book, this section is necessarily short-lived. We can't guarantee that any of the recommended books or Web sites will still be available when you look for them, or that the Web sites will continue to have the content they had when the book was written. For the same reason, books are listed below without a publication date, since in many cases new editions come out so it's best to search for the most current one.

Fortunately, where research is concerned, the Internet is your friend, and so the first resource to mention is Google (*http://www.google.com*), justly the search engine of choice for most people. Other more specialized search engines include Cite-Seer (*http://citeseer.ist.psu.edu/*), which allows you to search through scientific literature (although to see full texts you need to pay), as well as retailers such as the online bookshop Amazon (*http://www.amazon.com*).

On the subject of search resources, many thanks to the members of the DirGames-L community (see below) for recommendations for this section.

DIRECTOR AND LINGO

If you want to experiment in more depth with the code examples on the CD-ROM, you'll need to look into Macromedia Director. A trial version (30 days) is available

ON THE CD

from Macromedia's Web site at *http://www.macromedia.com*. It's well worth the money to buy.

There are several books on the market for learning Director and Lingo. *Using Director MX* (Gary Rosenzweig, QUE) is a very good high-speed introduction at the basic level, while more confident programmers might prefer the *Director MX 2004 Bible* (B Underdahl et al., Wiley). 3D is covered well in *Director's Third Dimension* (Paul Cantanese, Sams).

Online Director resources include Director Online (*http://www.director-online.com*), a good resource for mathematical tricks and algorithms, and a number of sites created by users, particularly NoiseCrime (*http://www.noisecrime.com*), Gary Rosenzweig's Developer Dispatch (*http://developerdispatch.com*), and many others. Most of these include links to others, so search around. There are also several excellent and friendly Director mailing lists, particularly DirGames-L, a very lively and well-informed bunch of people devoted particularly to games, which you can sign up for or search at *http://nuttybar.drama.uga.edu/mailman/listinfo/dirgames-l*. A similar list devoted to 3D Director development is Dir3D-L, which you can subscribe to at *http://nuttybar.drama.uga.edu/mailman/listinfo/dir3d-l*. Both lists are hosted by Allen Partridge, himself the author of the very interesting *Real-Time Interactive 3D Games* (Sams). Other useful groups include Direct-L, Lingo-L, and Shockwave-L, all of which can be found by following links from Macromedia at *http://www.macromedia.com/cfusion/knowledgebase/index.cfm?id= tn_3101*.

GENERAL MATHEMATICS

There is a wealth of mathematical resources on the Internet, far too many to list and mostly free. We'll look at some specialized sites below, but firstly a few more general resources. The first and most useful is MathWorld (*http://mathworld.wolfram.com*), and the related ScienceWorld (*http://scienceworld.wolfram.com*), both hosted by Wolfram, the creator of the excellent mathematical program *Mathematica*. For a more descriptive approach to physics problems, Wikipedia (*http://en.wikipedia.org/ wiki/Main_Page*) is a good source of information on almost anything, and How-StuffWorks (*http://www.howstuffworks.com*) is much better than its title suggests. A good place to go if you want to ask math-related questions is Math Forum (*http://mathforum.org*), the home of "Ask Dr Math."

Many sites are devoted to games computing, particularly GameDev.net (*http:// www.gamedev.net*) and GamaSutra (*http://www.gamasutra.com*), both of which tend to focus on 3D techniques, mostly for the more advanced programmers. A moderated and very focused mailing list for hardcore game enthusiasts is GD Algorithms-List (*http://lists.sourceforge.net/lists/listinfo/gdalgorithms-list*). Also for more advanced math, MIT has rather wonderfully released many lectures and course notes in their MIT Open Courseware project: a list of math topics can be found at *http://ocw.mit.edu/OcwWeb/Mathematics.*

More elementary math is covered in a variety of sites, mostly aimed at children but as a result usually easy to follow! One large resource is the BBC Education Web site, including an area devoted to the 16+ age group, which is well written and thorough: *http://www.bbc.co.uk/schools/16/maths.shtml.*

Similar comments apply to books: again, there are huge numbers on the market. Having said that, surprisingly few cover the same kind of ground as we have here. One that does have a similar remit is *Beginning Math and Physics for Game Programmers* (Wendy Stahler et al., New Riders). It doesn't go quite as far as this volume, but covers much of the same early ground. A more advanced book that also covers a broad range of topics is *Tricks of the Windows Game Programming Gurus* (Andre LaMothe, Sams). Between the two of them, if this book doesn't work for you, they probably will. For physics, there's *Physics for Game Developers* (David Bourg, O'Reilly), with a very thorough treatment of how to model physical simulations in terms of forces. For general hints, tricks, and algorithms, the *Game Programming Gems* series (various authors, Charles River Media) are a must-have (as one correspondent put it, "They're not on my shelves, because they're on my desk all the time").

In a more general mathematical vein, Martin Gardner's many books culled from his *Scientific American* column are an excellent source of mathematical inspiration, featuring many interesting puzzles and tidbits. Also an essential book for anyone interested in problem-solving is *How to Solve It* (G. Polya, various editions), which despite being over fifty years old does the best job anywhere in explaining the process of mathematical intuition.

SPECIALIZED RESOURCES

Collision Detection

There are surprisingly few sites and books devoted to collision detection specifically, although naturally the topic crops up a great deal on game-related sites and forums. The best book is *Collision Detection in Interactive 3D Environments* (Gino Van Den Bergen, Morgan Kauffman), which is very thorough indeed and includes a working 3D collision engine on the CD-ROM. *3D Game Engine Design* (David Eberly, Morgan Kauffman) also includes a large section on the topic. Chris Hecker has also written a very readable and accessible series of tutorials on rigid body dynamics, including source code, which is available at Definition Six *http://www.d6. com/users/checker/dynamics.htm#articles.*

3D Engines and Geometry

In contrast to the above, the number of resources on 3D topics is enormous, which is one of the reasons that the subject is dealt with relatively briefly here. Most of them have a large focus on graphics issues, but an excellent mathematical treatment is to be found in *Mathematics for 3D Game Programming and Computer Graphics, Second Edition* (Eric Lengyel, Charles River Media).

Game Physics

There's a very good tutorial on car physics at Monstrous Software (*http://home. planet.nl/~monstrous/tutcar.html*). Many places deal with pool, although rather fewer try to cover spin! One book that does is *The Illustrated Principles of Pool and Billiards* (David Alciatore, Sterling), which has an excellent supporting Web site of technical information at *http://www.engr.colostate.edu/~dga/pool/technical_proofs/ index.html.*

Mazes, Searches, and AI

Several Web sites are devoted to AI topics, particularly GameAI (*http://www. gameai.com*). There are also many books on the subject, from general titles such as the *AI Game Programming Wisdom* series (S. Rabin, editor, Charles River Media) to more specialized titles, of which a particular favorite is *Fluid Concepts and Creative Analogies* (Douglas Hofstadter, Penguin). Dealing with "cognitive AI," it was something we couldn't cover properly in this book but it is highly recommended. A Web site on mazes, which was extremely helpful for this book (and made Chapter 24 one of the more fun to write) was Think Labyrinth (*http://www.astrolog.org/ labyrnth/algrithm.htm*).

This really is the barest sampling of the resources available in a very rich field. Further links will be added to the Web site devoted to this book at Charles River Media (*http://www.charlesriver.com/titles/mathphysics.html*) as they come to my attention.

Answers to Exercises

There isn't space in this book to give even brief code listings for all 26 chapters' worth of exercises. Also, no one wants to read page upon page of code in a book anyway. So these "answers" are really more like hints and suggestions, with some brief code snippets, and a guide to where to find the answers. Most of the actual answers are on the CD-ROM in some form, but many others are on the book's Web site at *www.charlesriver.com/titles/mathphysics.html*. References in italics without a ".*dir*" are to script cast members in the *math.cst* cast library on the CD-ROM (also the equivalent HTML page in the documentation), while those with the extension refer to demo movies—see Appendix C.

ON THE CD

■ **Exercise 1.1** `ConvertBase (NumberString, Base1, Base2)`
The easiest way to do this (although not the most efficient) is to create one function that converts the string from `Base1` to a number, and then another which converts it from a number into `Base2`. You can pretty much use the functions in the text for this, but look at `base()` and `fromBase()` in *floats*.

■ **Exercise 1.2** Floating-point numbers
This is fairly easy until you try to deal with division. The trick is to implement a binary version of the long division algorithm: at each stage you have a current "remainder," to which you append digits of the dividend (the number being divided) until it is greater than or equal to the divisor, at which point you subtract off the divisor, calculate the new remainder and continue until you reach the end of the dividend. In *floats* you'll find the `mantissaExponent()` function which converts a number into an IEEE-style float.

■ **Exercise 2.1** Text scrollbar
The wording of the exercise was left deliberately vague about whether your scrollbar should be calculated according to the size of the text image, or according to the number of characters in it: that is, whether the scrollbar ratio should be "pixels/ character" or "pixels/ pixel." The second is more standard

(and much easier): try working on the first and see how it looks. You need to calculate how many characters are visible on the screen at any one time, in order to work out the furthest extent of your scrollbar.

■ **Exercise 2.2** `compoundinterest(amount, percentage, years)`
As mentioned in the chapter, this function, and all the mortgage calculator functions, are on the CD-ROM in *mortgages*. This one should be easy enough: you just multiply the amount by `(100+percentage)/100` for each year.

■ **Exercise 2.3** Slide rule function
This was a rather fancy way of saying "write a function that multiplies two numbers by summing their logarithms." So you're just going to use

```
return exp(ln(a)+ln(b))
```

Of course, the graphical element is just padding, but is still more complicated than this part.

■ **Exercise 3.1, 3.2, 3.3** Solving equations
These functions are part of the same overall concept. The CD-ROM, in *algebra*, contains a rather extensive implementation of the first, `substitute()`, which is used by a number of other functions, although it's worth noting that a simpler method in the function `calculateValue()`, which uses the Lingo keyword `value`, works just fine for expressions which are written in a computer-readable form. The trick to this, and all of these examples, is to use recursion extensively. For example, when simplifying an expression, we can simplify each part of it separately, and to do that we can simplify its subsidiary parts, and so on until it's as simple as we can make it.

■ **Exercise 4.1** `solvetriangle(triangle)`
Mostly this is a simple exercise in bookkeeping: there are rather a lot of different combinations of data which need to be dealt with separately. The simplest way is to try applying each of the rules (sine, cosine) in succession until you can't apply any more.

■ **Exercise 4.2** `rotatetofollow(triangle,point)`
The simplest way to do this is to use some of the functions we create later in the book, such as `rotateVector()`. If you're trying to do it without having read Chapter 5 and beyond and you're struggling, then read on and it should become clearer. In a nutshell, though, you need to calculate the angles made by

the lines from the centrum to the triangle vertices, as well as the angle from the centrum to `point`, calculate the difference between the two and then recalculate the positions of the triangle positions using `sin()` and `cos()`.

■ **Exercise 5.1**   Vector drawing
There isn't really an "answer" to this as such, it's just a suggestion for something to try, but you should take a look at the `createA()` function in *chapter 5 (vectors)* and use that as your inspiration. There's very little limit to what you can do—if you get confident, try doing the same with 3D images.

■ **Exercise 5.2**   `calculateTrajectory (oldPosition, newPosition, speed)`
Hopefully this should be self-explanatory. It's something that you should always be doing in any working example (see, for instance, *javelin.dir*)

■ **Exercise 6.1**   `drawDifferentialEquation(function)`
If you find this difficult, then don't be afraid: creating the one in the figure was hard work as you can see from the solution code in Chapter 6. Having said that, most of the complexity of this matches to the similar work done on other graphs, namely calculating an appropriate scale, working out how best to label the axes and so on. The main meat of the function is just these lines:

```
d=calculate2DValue(functionToDraw,pt[1], pt[2])
if d=#infinite then
    p1=0
    p2=yspacing
else if d<>#undefined then
    p=point(1.0,d)
    len=sqrt(1.0+d*d)
    p=p/len
    p1=p[1]*xspacing
    p2=p[2]*yspacing
else
    next repeat
end if
```

Here, we are at a particular point, we draw a line from that point, then start again from the end of that line. The hardest part is creating a reasonable spread of lines, which is solved by the rather cheeky expedient of simply choosing a number of random start points and seeing where they take us.

■ **Exercise 6.2** `secantMethod()`
This is a fairly simple extension of the examples in the chapter, but it's worth looking at the CD-ROM (*chapter 6 (calculus)*), as for once this function is designed to be as fast as possible, which is done by cacheing as many reference values as we can make use of.

■ **Exercise 7.1** `javelin(throwAngle, throwSpeed, time)`
This function can be seen in the *javelin.dir* demo movie, which is crude but effective. The key trick is to calculate the velocity vector at each stage, and rotate the javelin to follow it. Notice that the movie also includes some simple collision detection mechanisms to determine when the javelin reaches the edge of the screen (although it's allowed to go off the top).

■ **Exercise 7.2** `aimCannon(cannonLength, muzzleSpeed, aimPoint)`
This exercise was included as something of a trick, because it's not at all an easy calculation. Let's work through it:

Suppose the cannon has length l and speed v, and we're trying to hit the point with position vector $\mathbf{p}$. The ball leaves the cannon from the point with speed v, so at time t its position is $\left((l+tv)\cos\theta,(l+tv)\sin\theta-\dfrac{gt^2}{2}\right)$. So we are solving

$$(l+tv)\cos = p_1$$

$$(l+tv)\sin\theta-\frac{gt^2}{2} = p_2$$

Now, there are a number of possible approaches to this. It is solveable directly (substituting for $\sin\theta$ in the second equation yields a quartic equation in t, which can be solved algebraically), but it's really easier to use an approximation method to approach the solution iteratively.

We can start by creating a function that tests whether the current aim is high or low (by working out the ball's y position when its x position is p_1). This function should return 1 for high, –1 for low, and 0 for a hit (or close to it). Notice first of all that if we aim the cannon directly at the target point, it will always fall short. If we use this angle as our baseline, then work up in increments until we find a firing angle that is aiming high, we can then use a simple binary approximation method to find the solution.

■ **Exercise 7.3** `fireCannon(massOfBall, massOfCannon, energy)`
This should be a straightforward application of the formulas in the chapter.

■ **Exercise 8.1:** `pointParallelogramCollision(pt, parr, tm)`
The chapter suggests using a skew transformation to turn the parallelogram into a normal rectangle. If you would prefer to solve the problem directly, you can represent it as a collision with four separate walls: you can work out which two walls are potential collision material by finding the dot product of their normals with the particle velocity, and then use the usual methods to determine which of them collide.

■ **Exercise 8.2** Inner collisions
The solutions to these can be found in *collisions.dir*. Generally, inner collisions are rather simpler to deal with than outer ones: for example, a rectangle inside a circle can only collide at its vertices, while a circle inside a rectangle can never collide with a vertex (actually, a circle inside a rectangle collides just like a point inside a smaller rectangle), and a rectangle inside a rectangle can only collide at a vertex if they are axis-aligned.

■ **Exercise 9.1** `checkCollision()`
This is a tricky thing to do in abstract: you may find that without creating a generic collision detection environment like *collisions.dir* you can't really test how well it's working. But the version in the chapter includes quite a lot of detail, so keep trying.

■ **Exercise 9.2** Newton's Cradle
Depending on quite *how* simplified you want this to be, it can be either very easy or extremely difficult (a programmer from Havok once said in conversation that the Newton's cradle is one of the toughest tests on a generic collision detection system). But by simple, we do mean simple here.

■ **Exercise 10.1** `splitPolygon(poly)`
As suggested in the chapter, this is best done recursively: choose three adjacent vertices, check if the third line of their triangle intersects with any others in the shape, if so, split it off.

■ **Exercise 10.2** `smoothNormals(collisionMap)`
This is found in *chapter 10 (object modeling and collisions)*, and can be seen working in *collisionMaps.dir*. Each step, the function checks through all the pixels of the collision map, and for any edge pixel it finds any adjacent pixels and sets the normal to the average of adjacent pixels. After about four iterations you get a very close fit to the surface.

■   **Exercise 11.1**   Checking for a potted ball
The *pool.dir* demo works by calculating another collision, with a virtual circle inside the pocket. If the ball passes between the pocket jaws, it will definitely intersect this circle, so this should be foolproof, although it never seems very elegant. Another method would be to check against a line drawn along the pocket entrance.

■   **Exercise 11.2**   Ball preview.
This is easier to do than you might think: the trick is to perform a regular collision detection, but with an extremely high "velocity." When we've found our first collision, we can calculate its resolution, and draw the result into our image. As mentioned in the chapter, you can access this function in *pool.dir* by selecting the Preview option.

■   **Exercise 12.1**   Worlds in Collision
These functions are implemented in *orbits.dir*. As noted in the chapter, the simulation is only of limited success because of problems of scale. Nevertheless, it works as far as it goes.

■   **Exercise 13.1**   `resolveCushionCollision(obj1, obj2, normal, moment, prop)`
This function is incorporated into *pool.dir* in the version that includes spin. Some notes on how it is achieved are included in the chapter.

■   **Exercise 13.2**   A moving, rotating square and a wall
This is a tricky problem but not insurmountable. Since we don't need to deal with the ends of the wall, the only possible collision is between the vertices of the square and the wall. We can calculate this to a precise degree of accuracy by an approximation method, but really this is a good example of a case where it's easiest just to calculate whether any vertex of the square starts on one side of the wall and ends up on the other. The result will be close enough for any common purpose. Again, check out *collisions.dir*.

■   **Exercise 14.1**   `applyFriction(velocity, topSpin, radius, mass, muK, muS, time)`
Although fairly straightforward, this is something of a drop in the ocean where implementing spin fully in the pool game is concerned, as you can see by looking at *pool.dir*. The real difficulty is dealing with how to calculate the topspin in the first place. As soon as the ball changes direction, it is spinning at a strange angle compared to the direction of travel, and this complicates things quite a bit. Our pool simulation cheats: you might like to think about how to do things more realistically.

■ **Exercise 15.1**   Rockets
This one should be pure book work.

■ **Exercise 16.1**   Springs
The demo *springs.dir* includes a working version of this. You'll find that the versions quite quickly start to behave differently as a result of calculation errors. The hardest thing to get right is the elastic limit, and this movie doesn't quite achieve it: can you do better?

■ **Exercise 17.1**   Drawing a 3D cube and culling the back faces
The way we do this is quite simple: we don't draw any face whose outward normal is pointing away from us (has a positive dot product with the vector from the camera to the face). In a wireframe drawing, we can work on a vertex-by-vertex basis: a vertex is culled if all faces sharing that vertex are facing backward. Then we only draw lines both of whose vertices are visible. You can see this in action in *simple3D.dir*. The next step in this movie would be to create *z*-ordering, that is, to draw objects nearer to the camera in front of those further away: you might want to try to do this.

■ **Exercise 18.1**   Applying relative transforms
These can be found in *chapter 18 (transforms)*. They should be straightforward enough: try incorporating them into the *simple3D* example, or make one of your own.

■ **Exercise 19.1**   3D collisions
The exercise didn't specify which collision to implement, as by now you should be used to the formula. At the very least, you should find spheres and planes reasonably simple.

■ **Exercise 20.1**   Texture maps
An example of this can be found in *textures.dir*. There's a lot of 3D Lingo involved in creating the mesh, but you only really need to look at the lines involving the `textureCoordinates` property.

■ **Exercise 21.1**   2D NURBS
This is implemented in the *splines.dir* demo (along with various other splines). Experiment with it: there's really no better way to understand how the various elements of the NURBS description fit together. However, the implementation is fairly simple if you just follow the equations in the chapter.

■ **Exercise 21.2** `IKapproach(chain, target)`
The trick with this is to work backwards: start by adjusting the most central limb to rotate it toward the target, then adjust the next one out, and so on until you get to the last bone. It really works!

■ **Exercise 22.1** Complete `drawBresenham()`
This can be found in *chapter 22 (optimization)*. It should be a simple extension of the function in the chapter.

■ **Exercise 22.2** Car control
One of the great goals of pseudo-physics is "how simple can this be and still feel complicated?" The aim here is to get the perfect balance between simplicity and complexity. There is a demo driving movie on the Web site, which also uses a collision map.

■ **Exercise 23.1** `box3DTileTopCollision()`
You think this is hard, try it with a non-aligned box.

■ **Exercise 24.1** Maze navigation
The file *mazes.dir* includes functions for creating mazes, and an implementation of A*. Try including this function within it. The recursive backtracker for maze creation is there, so you may be able to adapt it.

■ **Exercise 25.1** Heads or tails
The file *headsOrTails.dir* shows how this can be done. It includes a number of tricks to try to make it even more successful, but really these are no great improvement on the basic method.

■ **Exercise 25.2** Boids
Boid rules are well-documented, so if you have trouble with this, you might want to do some research online. Try Craig Reynolds' own site (*http://www.red3d.com/cwr/boids*) to start with, it's well worth a visit.

■ **Exercise 26.1** Eight queens genetic algorithm
The demo *geneticAlgorithm.dir* shows how this can be done, and includes a system of varying radiation to speed things up a little. It also demonstrates some examples of how you can keep tabs on your program's performance when running this kind of extended search.

Index